Surveys in Economics

VOLUME II

on behalf of the
Royal Economic Society

Edited by
ANDREW J. OSWALD

BLACKWELL
Oxford UK & Cambridge USA

First published 1991

Basil Blackwell Ltd
108 Cowley Road, Oxford, OX4 1JF, UK

Basil Blackwell, Inc.
3 Cambridge Center
Cambridge, Massachusetts 02142, USA

British Library Cataloguing in Publication Data
A CIP catalogue record for this book is available from the British Library.

Library of Congress Cataloging in Publication Data
Surveys in economics/edited by Andrew J. Oswald on behalf of the
Royal Economic Society.
p. cm.
Includes bibliographical references and index.
ISBN 0-631-17972-0 (v. 1): ISBN 0-631-17973-9 (pbk.:
v. 1): ISBN 0-631-17974-7 (v. 2): ISBN
0-631-17975-5 (pbk.: v. 2)
1. Economics. I. Oswald, Andrew J. II. Royal Economic Society
(Great Britain)
HB171.5.S9615 1991
330—dc20 90-19344 CIP

Printed in Great Britain at the University Press, Cambridge

SURVEYS IN ECONOMICS

VOLUME II

CONTENTS

PREFACE

In 1986 the Royal Economic Society decided to commission a set of survey papers in Economics. It was the incoming editor, John Hey, who suggested that it was time to revive this tradition. I was given the task of selecting authors and topics.

The ECONOMIC JOURNAL has published surveys for fifty years, but the last papers appeared in the journal more than a decade ago. Many of the articles – such as Hahn and Matthews on growth in 1964 and Laidler and Parkin on inflation in 1975 – became instant classics. Most defined the reading lists, and moulded the thinking, of generations of students.

Survey articles are valuable. They help to focus debates; they teach; they allow the experienced to point out avenues that the young might miss. None of this means that survey papers could or should play a dominant role in academic research.

Twelve papers seemed a good number. However, a very few of those people invited were unable to accept. The survey series moved rapidly towards a natural equilibrium of ten papers, and there it has remained. I have taken the view throughout that the ECONOMIC JOURNAL should be as able to stop publishing surveys as to start. Although there is no doubt that one could include an article per issue forever, it is not clear (at least to me) that this would be appropriate for a research journal.

I should like to express my gratitude to the eleven economists who contributed papers and to the dozens who acted as referees. We all discovered the difficulties of running consecutive articles. With luck the results have been worthwhile.

Each author was given identical instructions. The aim of the series was to provide surveys that could be read fairly easily by researchers in other sub-disciplines of Economics. As readers will see, the styles of the surveys differ somewhat, and this was to be expected. Subjects are different. Experts are, by and large, best left alone. To those who find article X too polemical, article Y too theoretical or article Z too informal, I apologize. It should be borne in mind that the ECONOMIC JOURNAL has one of the most diverse readerships in the world of economics journals.

In choosing authors, my view was that two criteria had to be met. First, an author should have an international research reputation. Second, he or she should be able to cover both theoretical and empirical aspects of the chosen topic. My hope is that readers will sympathise with these aims and see the group as satisfying them.

A special word of thanks is due to Professor John Black of the University of Exeter. His careful reading helped improve these volumes.

I was delighted when these eleven economists – busy people all – generously consented to write survey papers in their specialist fields.

ANDREW J. OSWALD

I

CONSUMER BEHAVIOUR: THEORY AND EMPIRICAL EVIDENCE – A SURVEY

*Richard Blundell**

INTRODUCTION

There are very few aspects of economic policy that do not require some knowledge of household or individual consumer behaviour. Moreover, the close interplay between theoretical and empirical considerations together with the rapid expansion in the availability of different types of data have continued to make the analysis of consumer behaviour an attractive area for research. For some policy questions the importance of empirical evidence on consumer behaviour is indisputable. Amongst these stand the optimality and impact of tax proposals, the effect of credit constraints, real interest rate changes and uncertainty on savings behaviour and the appropriate choice of cost of living indices. However, the methods of analysis in modern consumer theory and empirical research are applicable to a much wider set of problems. Although I have compiled an extensive, if not exhaustive, bibliography at the end of this survey, the principal aim is to present and evaluate some of the more recent ideas and methods of investigation relating to consumer behaviour rather than to provide a complete literature survey.

Perhaps the most appealing feature of economic research into consumer behaviour is the close relationship between theoretical specification and appropriate estimation technique. This is most apparent when empirical analysis and testing takes place at the individual or micro level. However, even at the macro or aggregate level, given that some notion of consumer optimising behaviour is often assumed to underlie the evolution of the aggregate data, effective assessment of the model specification requires judgement from the theoretical as well as the empirical standpoint. Indeed empirical models can often be unwittingly restrictive once viewed from an appropriate theoretical perspective.

Although far from profound, some illustrations of these points are probably warranted. Empirical demand systems are often used to design and analyse the impact of indirect tax policy. Commonly used specifications of empirical demand systems typically rule out many theoretically plausible types of substitution behaviour and thus prejudge the indirect tax results. Additive linear models (the Stone–Geary for example), still popular in many policy

* This chapter was first published in the ECONOMIC JOURNAL, vol. 98, March 1988. I am grateful to Gordon Anderson, Paul Baker, Vanessa Fry, Costas Meghir, John Micklewright, Panos Pashardes, Ranjan Ray, Richard Smith, Ian Walker and Guglielmo Weber for allowing me to draw on jointly authored material and for their comments on this work. Additional comments on earlier drafts by John Burbidge, John Ham, John Muellbauer and Andrew Oswald have also resulted in significant improvements. However, all remaining errors are mine alone. Finance for this research was provided by the ESRC under project B0225 0004.

based studies, not only rule out complementarity but essentially tie substitution effects directly to income effects allowing little independent role for relative prices or real wages in forecasts of consumer behaviour (see Deaton, 1974*a*). Indeed, models that express commodity demand in terms of prices and total expenditure alone implicitly assume separability between consumption and labour supply decisions and thereby emasculate most optimal tax theory. As a result, welfare improving directions for tax changes are governed almost entirely by the properties underlying the estimated model and not necessarily those underlying the data.

At another level, theoretically consistent dynamic consumption models are often surprisingly simple (see Hall, 1978, for example). However, this simplicity is usually a result of particularly strong underlying assumptions, namely intertemporal separability, perfect credit markets and the separability of consumption and labour market decisions. Very little empirical evidence supports such hypotheses but the specification of theoretically consistent models that relax these assumptions requires considerable ingenuity. For example, theory tells us that, despite its popularity, there may be little to be learnt from simply adding lagged variables to an otherwise static or at least intertemporally separable model. If one is not careful the resulting model is only rationalisable under completely myopic consumer behaviour – an assumption almost as restrictive as the separability and capital market assumptions themselves. This is not to say that only theoretically consistent models should be entertained. Without confronting theoretical restrictions with a more general empirical model, there would be little progress in economic thought. However, unless the implications of a general theoretical process determining the consumer's behaviour are fully understood, estimated models may often unknowingly rule out plausible types of behaviour and empirical specification searches may look in uninformative directions.

It is not the intention of this survey to provide a catalogue of empirical results or to cover all theories of consumer behaviour but rather to point out areas where analysing the interplay between theoretical and empirical considerations has either produced or is likely to produce new insights into consumer behaviour. The main areas which will be considered fall into two broad levels of analysis and are reflected in the two main sections of this survey. The first is the study of disaggregate behaviour. By this I shall mean the disaggregation of consumption into its components. These will include the consumption of specific commodity groups like clothing and alcohol as well as the allocation of time including the supply of labour. The interest here will be on the relative size and sign of substitution effects indicating the degree of separability and commodity grouping that can take place. It will also allow us to assess the impact of rationing in some markets (housing, labour), the implications for tax policy design and the construction of cost of living indices. The temporal aspect of behaviour will largely be ignored in this work. Under certain theoretical restrictions on the consumer's optimising model this is a legitimate approach to take but under more general intertemporal or dynamic behaviour these models will need to be extended. In the second broad area the emphasis will be placed more directly on dynamic and life-cycle behaviour.

There is often little reason to believe that theoretical predictions will hold in aggregate even if they hold at the individual level. In both of these broad areas, therefore, the most persuasive level of analysis must be at the individual consumer or household level. However, reliable longitudinal data sets that follow the *same* consumers over long time periods are rare and some form of aggregation prior to empirical analysis is often inevitable. Precisely how this aggregation should be done and the relationship between micro and macro level analyses is a highly interesting aspect of applied consumer economics in its own right. The clear attraction of individual level data is that they avoid aggregation bias. Such bias can result both because of the complex interactions between individual characteristics and price/income effects and also because of nonlinearities in consumption behaviour due to nonlinear Engel curves, corner solutions, rationing, nonlinear taxation and imperfect credit markets. However, working at some level of aggregation may often be unavoidable and some time will be spent in this survey in the analysis of consistent aggregation.

Despite the progress that has been achieved since the Brown and Deaton (1972) survey, there still remain major areas of reconciliation between different levels of behavioural modelling and between the theoretical models and the data themselves. Two obvious applications stand our here. First is the precise nature of the relationship between the mostly rather static disaggregated analyses of household behaviour (both concerning the demand for commodities and the supply of labour) and the nmore aggregate dynamic models. Second is the ability of the various theoretically based dynamic models to match the data process. There seems no doubt that the major advances that are currently occurring and that will occur in the empirical analysis of consumer behaviour will be predominantly in these two areas. The layout of this survey is chosen to reflect this. However, we shall consider other loosely related aspects of consumer theory and testing that have more distinct bearing on welfare analysis and public policy.

Before setting off on this survey it is fair to say that without the landmark in writings on consumer behaviour provided by the Deaton and Muellbauer (1980*b*) volume this task would be unthinkable. At a more practical level the Deaton and Muellbauer book provides a useful historic point from which to define recent developments in the area in which this survey, albeit at a less technical level, will concentrate.

I. DISAGGREGATED DEMAND ANALYSIS

I. 1. *Separability, Additivity and Preference Restrictions*

The ability to group commodities by type or time period stands as one of the most valuable forms of restrictions on consumer preferences. Precisely what different types of grouping imply for consumer behaviour is an important preliminary before any application of consumer theory. For example, grouping prices 'price aggregation' has somewhat different implications than grouping commodities 'direct separability'. The requirements for a *single* price aggregator or index, something that is often assumed in application, are even stronger. However, without some form of grouping, all relative prices for all goods both within and outside the current period may have an independent effect on the commodity demand under consideration. This very fact suggests that, if consumers optimise at all, they probably will use some form of grouping to enable some simplification of the decision-making process.

The most obvious method of grouping and one which is used extensively in empirical application rests on the hypothesis of two-stage budgeting. This idea was investigated in the important work of Gorman (1958) and still underlies many new innovations in applied consumer theory. Under two-stage budgeting the direct utility function is weakly separable and consumers allocate expenditure first to broad commodity groups and then to detailed within group demands. This enables allocations within groups to be determined solely by the within group relative prices and the allocation of expenditure to that group. If $x_1, \ldots, x_n$ represents all consumption goods (including leisure time or labour supply) and $\mathbf{q}_1, \ldots, \mathbf{q}_k$ represents a smaller number of commodity vectors to which $x_1, \ldots, x_n$ can be uniquely allocated, then if utility is weakly separable across these groups, direct utility may be written

$$U(x_1, \ldots, x_n) = F[U_1(\mathbf{q}_1), \ldots, U_k(\mathbf{q}_k)]. \tag{1}$$

The allocation of expenditure to any x_i in $\mathbf{q}_s$ may then be expressed as

$$p_i x_i = f_i(\mathbf{p}_s, y_s) \quad \text{for} \quad i = 1, \ldots, n \quad \text{and} \quad s = 1, \ldots, k, \tag{2}$$

where f_i is related to the utility function, $\mathbf{p}_s$ is the vector of prices corresponding to $\mathbf{q}_s$ and y_s is the allocation of total expenditure to group s. Of course, underlying this result are concavity and continuity conditions on $U(.)$, $F(.)$, and each $U_s(\mathbf{q}_s)$ as well as the linearity of the budget constraint. These imply that the expenditure equations (2) are linear homogenous in $\mathbf{p}_s$ and y_s and that the Hicksian or compensated price derivatives are symmetric forming a negative semi-definite Slutsky substitution matrix. Once y_s is determined at the first stage, each $\mathbf{q}_s$ can be determined without reference to prices outside this group.

Under *intertemporal* weak separability, once the optimal level of saving is determined for each period, prices outside any period have no independent effect on within period allocations. The variable y_s acts as a sufficient statistic for *all* intra group substitution allowing no further impact of prices outside the group in question. Separability conditions are as vital to the recent temporally separable 'surprise' consumption function of Hall (1978) as they were to Stone (1954) and his colleagues in their Linear Expenditure System. In addition, separability of goods and leisure is a crucial assumption in the 'separate' modelling of consumption and labour supply decisions. Being perhaps the most important of assumptions in applied consumer theory, separability must also stand as one of the most unreasonable in many applications, including those mentioned above.

Certain additional requirements are often placed on consumer behaviour which are rather stronger than we have mentioned so far. One of these is additive separability in which case (1) is replaced by

$$U(x_1, \ldots, x_n) = F[\textstyle\sum_s U_s(\mathbf{q}_s)], \tag{3}$$

where Σ_s refers to the summation of arguments indexed by s. As Deaton (1974*a*) illustrated, this assumption can be quite restrictive. However, it is typically used in intertemporal consumer behaviour where maximisation is expressed over expected lifetime utility conditional on current information and each s refers to a separate time period. Under expected utility maximisation some form of *forward* looking additivity is reasonably plausible although we may well expect $U_s(.)$ to depend on *past* period behaviour. We shall return to this point later in Section II.

A popular further condition to place on preferences is for the top stage allocation to each subgroup expenditure y_s out of total expenditure y to depend on single subgroup price indices $P_s(\mathbf{p}_s)$. In this case the determination of each y_s can be written

$$y_s = f_s[P_1(\mathbf{p}_1), \ldots, P_k(\mathbf{p}_k), y], \tag{4}$$

where each $P_s(\mathbf{p}_s)$ represents the true price index for group s. For example, in the intertemporal allocation problem, each period's consumption expenditure could then be expressed in terms of a single price index for each period. Although this is a common enough assumption it is restrictive. Weak separability (or even additive separability for that matter) is not a sufficient condition for such a price aggregation result. If preferences are homothetic within each group, that is elasticities with respect to total within group expenditure are unity, then weak separability is sufficient. However, if homotheticity is to be relaxed only a very particular set of preferences derived by Gorman (1959) will generate expenditure equations of the form (4).

In the homothetic case we may write each expenditure equation (2) as

$$p_i x_i = f_i(\mathbf{p}_s)\, y_s \tag{5}$$

so that each expenditure share of good i out of group s expenditure y_s

$$s_i^s = f_i(\mathbf{p}_s) \tag{6}$$

is independent of y_s and only depends on within group prices. Group s preferences then have the most simple of forms since although substitution elasticities are not directly restricted they are deemed independent of the level of y_s, guaranteeing a unitary income or expenditure elasticity $(\partial \ln x_i/\partial \ln y_s)$. Using Roy's Identity (see Deaton and Muellbauer, 1980*b*, p. 41), indirect utility for group s in the homothetic case is given by

$$V_s = G_s[y_s/b_s(\mathbf{p}_s)], \tag{7}$$

where G_s is some monotone increasing function and $b_s(\mathbf{p}_s)$ is a general linear homogenous function of prices conveniently expressed as

$$\ln b_s(\mathbf{p}_s) = \Sigma_i f_i(\mathbf{p}_s) \ln p_i. \tag{8}$$

Notice that in this case the 'Stone' price index which weights each $\ln p_i$ by s_i is exact as can be seen by comparing (8) and (6). Replacing U_s by V_s in the weakly separable utility function yields

$$V(\mathbf{p}_1, \ldots, \mathbf{p}_k, y) = G\{G_1[y_1/b_1(\mathbf{p}_1)], \ldots, G_k[y_k/b_k(\mathbf{p}_k)]\} \tag{9}$$

so that the $b_s(\mathbf{p}_s)$ are exactly the appropriate *single* group price indices $P_s(\mathbf{p}_s)$ that uniquely deflate each y_s.

If we wish to generalise (5) to allow linear Engel (expenditure/income) curves with non-zero intercepts so that expenditure on good i may be written

$$p_i x_i = a_i(\mathbf{p}_s) p_i + f_i(\mathbf{p}_s) y_s \tag{10}$$

then indirect utility (6) takes the form

$$V_s = G_s\{[y_s - a_s(\mathbf{p}_s)]/b_s(\mathbf{p}_s)\}, \tag{11}$$

where $a_s(\mathbf{p}_s) = \sum_i p_i a_{si}(\mathbf{p}_s)$. Preferences (11) are known generally as Gorman Polar Form and display quasi-homothetic (linear Engel curve) behaviour. Although restrictive, they do not imply unitary elasticities with respect to total within group expenditure and underly the Linear Expenditure System of Stone (1954) as well as motivating more recent work on consumer behaviour (see, for example, Atkinson and Stern, 1980, Blackorby, Boyce and Russell, 1978, Blundell and Walker, 1982, Browning *et al.*, 1985 and Pollak and Wales, 1978). Notice that if G_s is linear *and* overall utility is *explicitly* additive then V may be written

$$V = \sum_s [y_s - a_s(\mathbf{p}_s)]/b_s(\mathbf{p}_s), \tag{12}$$

in which case only $b_s(\mathbf{p}_s)$ enters the determination of y_s. However, although we are back to a single index result (the $b_s(\mathbf{p}_s)$ indices alone determine y_s) the solution for y_s is not continuous since both V and the budget constraint are linear in y_s. More specifically, all expenditure over and above $a_s(\mathbf{p}_s)$ is placed in the group with the lowest price index $b_s(\mathbf{p}_s)$.

To avoid the problems associated with (12) we may follow Anderson's (1979) application of Gorman's result and allow for single price aggregates and nonlinear Engel curves. If we assume explicit additivity at the top stage and write indirect utility as

$$V_s = G_s[y_s/b_s(\mathbf{p}_s)] + h_s(\mathbf{p}_s), \tag{13}$$

where $h_s(\mathbf{p}_s)$ is a linear homogenous concave function, then, provided $G_s(.)$ is *not* linear, a well-behaved solution can be found under which the determination of y_s depends only on $b_1(\mathbf{p}_s), \ldots, b_k(\mathbf{p}_k)$ and y as required. However, as $G_s(.)$ approaches linearity *all* expenditure over and above $a_s(\mathbf{p}_s)$ is placed in the group with the lowest price index $b_s(\mathbf{p}_s)$. This is exactly the discontinuous solution referred to above. This case must therefore be taken as the exception that proves the rule: a single price aggregator or index for group expenditure is in general difficult to justify.

At a more general level we can see that even for the quasi-homothetic case, under weak separability two price indices $a_s(\mathbf{p}_s)$ and $b_s(\mathbf{p}_s)$ are crucial in the determination of any y_s. For in that case overall utility may be written

$$V = G(G_1\{[y_1 - a_1(\mathbf{p}_1)]/b_1(\mathbf{p}_1)\}, \ldots, G_k\{[y_k - a_k(\mathbf{p}_k)]/b_k(p_k)\}) \tag{14}$$

so that maximising V subject to the constraint $y_1 + y_2 + \ldots + y_k = y$ results in group expenditures of the general form

$$y_s = f_s[a_1(\mathbf{p}_1), b_1(\mathbf{p}_1), \ldots, a_2(\mathbf{p}_2), b_2(\mathbf{p}_2), \ldots, a_k(\mathbf{p}_k), b_k(\mathbf{p}_k), y]. \tag{15}$$

These points will crop up time and again throughout this survey indicating the absolutely crucial role both separability *and* homotheticity (or lack of them) play in applications of consumer theory.

Before moving on to our discussion of functional forms for describing indirect or direct preferences it may be worth briefly deriving the form for the consumer's cost or expenditure functions which correspond to the indirect utility representations described above. As we shall see, the cost function has achieved wide use in recent applied consumer theory taking a special place in welfare measurement. Since it is defined as the minimum expenditure necessary to achieve some given level of utility it has a natural use in measures of compensating variations and equivalence scales.

The cost function corresponding to homothetic preferences described above in (5) has the form

$$C(\mathbf{p}_s, U_s) = b_s(\mathbf{p}_s)\, U_s, \tag{16}$$

where $b_s(\mathbf{p}_s)$ is the linear homogenous concave function of prices described in equation (8). Since the price derivatives of C are the corresponding Hicksian or compensating demands, traditional Marshallian demands (5) can be derived by simply substituting the corresponding indirect utility for U_s in the compensated demand function. Compensated demands are given by

$$C_i(\mathbf{p}_s, U_s) = p_i^{-1} f_i(\mathbf{p}_s)\, b_s(\mathbf{p}_s)\, U_s, \tag{17}$$

where C_i is the ith price derivative of C and Marshallian demands by

$$x_i = p_i^{-1} f_i(\mathbf{p}_s)\, y_s \tag{18}$$

identical to those in equation (5). Of course, inverting (16) will give the corresponding indirect utility function up to some monotonic transformation. The relationship between the cost function and the compensated demand curve has some considerable appeal, not least because the second order price derivatives give the constant utility 'Slutsky' substitution effects.

I. 2. *Some Functional Forms*

Choice of functional form for the representation of consumer preferences must stand as one of the most dominant issues in the literature on the empirical analysis of consumer behaviour. Our ability to assess the importance of preference restrictions described in the previous section will, in general, rely on choosing a functional form that is tractable without being unduly restrictive. For example, testing for additive separability in a model that assumed homothetic preferences may be easy but is probably worthless. The degree of misspecification that is engendered by the homotheticity assumption of unit income elasticities could severely distort the additivity test. However, theoretically consistent models that allow general income and price effects which also nest interesting simplifying specifications are few and far between.

The widespread use of the consumer's cost or indirect utility function as a representation of preferences in empirical analysis has produced a number of attractive specifications. The majority of these are well known and I shall only pick on those that appear particularly convenient. The first is the translog indirect utility function of Christensen *et al.* (1975), which is one of a class of flexible functional forms discussed by Diewert (1974). In this model indirect utility is written as the following second order logarithmic expansion

$$V = \alpha_0 + \sum_j \alpha_j \ln p_j^* + \tfrac{1}{2}\sum_j \sum_i \gamma_{ij} \ln p_j^* \ln p_i^*, \tag{19}$$

where $p_j^* = p_j/y$ and the α_0, α_j and γ_{ij} refer to unknown preference parameters. Using Roy's Identity the expenditure share equations have the form

$$s_j = (\alpha_j + \sum_i \gamma_{ji} \ln p_j^*)/k, \tag{20}$$

where $k = -1 + \sum_i \sum_j \gamma_{ij} \ln p_j^*$. Within this broad group of flexible specifications for expenditure shares should also be placed the Generalised Leontief form of Diewert (1971) in which the $\ln p_j^*$ terms in (20) would be replaced by $(p_j^*)^{\frac{1}{2}}$. Clearly, (20) can be used to investigate the validity of symmetry and homogeneity restrictions. Moreover, when $\gamma_{ij} = 0$ for all i and j, the model describes homothetically additive preferences.

Closely related to these 'flexible functional form' models are the models of Muellbauer (1975, 1976) and Deaton and Muellbauer (1980*a*). In these papers a particularly convenient specification entitled 'Almost Ideal' was developed from a more general class of Price Independent Generalised Linear (PIGL) models. In its various forms we shall be returning to this general class of models at a number of points in this survey. There is no doubt that this specification displays some considerably attractive features. In general the PIGL class has an indirect utility function of the form

$$V = G\{[y^\alpha - a(\mathbf{p})^\alpha]/[b(\mathbf{p})^\alpha - a(\mathbf{p})^\alpha]\}, \tag{21}$$

where $a(\mathbf{p})$ and $b(\mathbf{p})$ are linear homogenous, concave functions of prices. Clearly, when $\alpha = 1$ the indirect utility equation (21) becomes quasi-homothetic and by appropriate choice of $a(\mathbf{p})$ and $b(\mathbf{p})$ can be made to nest the popular Stone–Geary or LES model. However, the share equations corresponding to (21) are highly nonlinear and to avoid this, Deaton and Muellbauer (1980*a*) work with the logarithmic (PIGLOG) case in which $\alpha \to 0$. Choosing $\ln a(\mathbf{p})$ to be of a Translog form and $\ln b(\mathbf{p})$ to $\Pi_j p_j^{\beta_j} + \ln a(\mathbf{p})$ the share model reduces to the Almost Ideal form

$$s_j = \alpha_j + \sum_j \gamma_{ij} \ln p_i + \beta_j \ln [y/a(\mathbf{p})], \tag{22}$$

where the α_j, γ_{ij}, and β_j are all constant unknown parameters. If $a(\mathbf{p})$ in each share equation is approximated by some readily available price index, then (22) is linear in parameters and variables. Homotheticity requires $\beta_j = 0$ for all j whereas homogeneity requires $\sum_j \gamma_{ij} = 0$. Similarly, symmetry implies $\gamma_{ij} = \gamma_{ji}$ for all i not equal j. As we shall mention later these specifications possess some attractive aggregation characteristics, which was clearly the initial motivation of Muellbauer's work. As might be expected, they do restrict preferences to some degree and one might certainly wish to investigate higher order income terms in (22) (see, for example, Gorman, 1981) as well as more general forms for $b(\mathbf{p})$.

In this direction of functional form specification Blundell and Ray (1984) and Blundell and Walker (1986) use a class of preferences similar to (21) but with certain simplifying characteristics. In their model the indirect utility function is written

$$V = G\{[y^{\alpha} - a(\mathbf{p}, \alpha)^{\alpha}]/b(\mathbf{p}, \alpha)^{\alpha}\}, \quad \alpha > 0 \tag{23}$$

in which $a(\mathbf{p}, \alpha)$ and $b(\mathbf{p}, \alpha)$ are linear homogeneous functions which are allowed to depend directly on α. Share equations corresponding to (24) have the same general form as in the PIGL case, quasi-homothetic preferences occurring when $\alpha = 1$. However, by defining $p_i^* = p_i/y$ and expressing

$$a(\mathbf{p}, \alpha) = [\Sigma_{ij}\, \theta_{ij}(p_i^* p_j^*)^{\alpha/2}]^{1/\alpha}, \tag{24}$$

and

$$b(\mathbf{p}, \alpha) = [\Pi_i\, p_i^{f_i(\mathbf{p})\,\alpha}]^{1/\alpha}, \tag{25}$$

where Π_i represents the product over arguments indexed by i, the expenditure share equations take the form

$$s_j = \Sigma_i\, \theta_{ij}(p_i^* p_j^*)^{\alpha/2} + f_j(\mathbf{p})\,[1 - \Sigma_{ij}\, \theta_{ij}(p_i^* p_j^*)^{\alpha/2}] \tag{26}$$

in which case the nonlinearity appears simply through the α in the $(p_i^* p_j^*)^{\alpha/2}$ terms. A simple grid search over $\alpha > 0$ can be used to choose α. When $\alpha = 1$, setting $\theta_{ij} = 0$ for $i \neq j$ and setting all $f_j(\mathbf{p}) = \beta_j$ generates the popular additive LES or Stone–Geary system. The advantage of this latter system is that it easily nests (and can therefore be used to test the Linear Expenditure System. However, if on prior grounds it is felt that LES is not worth entertaining and a PIGLOG system is more likely, then working directly with the PIGL model would seem preferable.

1. 3. *Rationing, Corner Solutions and Zero Expenditures*

In many instances observations will relate to consumers whose behaviour is in some way constrained. It may be, for example, that consumers are rationed with respect to their current level of housing consumption or their current level of labour supply. Alternatively, they may face binding non-negativity constraints (corner solutions) which at current income and prices make it optimal to consume only some commodities. Not all zero expenditures, however, will reflect corner solutions or rationed behaviour. Indeed, in household surveys of limited duration, we may not observe consumption at all! Infrequency of purchase or durability may result in expenditures that reflect stocking-up for consumption in future periods rather than simply for consumption within the given period.

These problems are real enough. It is difficult to believe that all consumers are free to vary consumption and labour supply at will. It is also reasonable to believe that consumption of some items and indeed some labour supplies may well be zero because the current price or wage makes such a corner solution optimal. Moreover, the durability of some goods makes a deviation of recorded expenditure from consumption quite likely. Nevertheless, it is only recently that, following the move to the use of more micro level data, empirical analysis has sought to deal with these issues in any depth.

The theoretical framework for analysing the first two of these issues is well established and hinges on the discussion of virtual prices – the price at which the rationed level would just be chosen. The best single source for this work is Neary and Roberts (1980) although Deaton and Muellbauer (1981) provide a more detailed guide to functional form specification under rationing. However, as empirical models of female labour supply have had to cope with the single corner solution at zero hours, many economic and econometric developments can also be found in that earlier literature (see, for example, Heckman, 1974*b*). Moreover, as constraints are never very far from any empirical analysis of labour supply, models of rationing can also be found in the labour supply literature (see, for example, Ashenfelter and Ham, 1979 and Ham, 1982). Perhaps the most important feature of the Neary and Roberts work is in the study of rationing or binding constraints within a *system* of consumer decisions. What impact will labour market unemployment or rationing in the housing market have on the demand for clothing or services? To answer this we need to analyse how virtual prices or wages, themselves functions of the ration, feed through to affect unrationed consumer decisions.

Needless to say separability is as crucial here as in any other aspect of applied consumer theory. Quite simply, if a good that is rationed is weakly separable from the one under consideration the only impact of rationing will be via the total budget or total expenditure available. This is useful in many respects. Labour market rationing has only an income effect on disaggregated commodity demand if separability between goods and 'leisure' time can be assumed. Under intertemporal separability, rationing in the current period only affects future period consumption decisions via the total amount of wealth allocated to that future period. Again separability is a convenient but invariably strong assumption.

Things get considerably worse, at least for the empirical economist, when more than one non-negativity or other inequality constraint is allowed to bind simultaneously. Again the theoretical issues are not too arduous but finding a suitable empirical specification that relaxes additive separability can be extremely tough and has generally prohibited work in this area. Two notable exceptions to this are the papers by Wales and Woodland (1983) and Lee and Pitt (1986). However, in these studies only non-negativity constraints are considered, which for the translog model used in the Lee and Pitt study provides a particularly convenient simplification. Before discussing these issues in rather more detail it should be pointed out that possibly the main difficulty faced in this work is in the econometric rather than economic specification. For even under preference separability, although rationing of one decision variable may have rather straightforward effects on the systematic part of other decisions, correlation between the stochastic components on the rationed and unrationed equations results in bias if standard least squares estimators are utilised.

Perhaps the neatest way to deal with rationing or binding inequality constraints on consumer behaviour is via the expenditure or cost function. Suppose that good j is rationed at x_j^r, then the cost minimising problem for the consumer may be written as

$$C^r(\mathbf{p}^j, x_j^r, U^r) = \min_{x_j} (\mathbf{p}^j \mathbf{x}^j \mid U \geqslant U^r) - p_j x_j^r, \tag{27}$$

where the superscript j refers to a vector with the jth element excluded. The cost function C^r describes the minimum cost over unconstrained expenditures of achieving U^r at prices $\mathbf{p}^j$ and with the consumption of x_j fixed at x_j^r. The variable x_j^r may represent hours of work in which case the constraint could refer to involuntary unemployment. The system of 'conditional' demand functions for unrationed goods is then simply obtained from the derivatives of (27). In practice, defining p_j^r to be the virtual price at which x_j^r would be freely chosen enables C^r to be derived by replacing p_j in the unconditional cost function by p_j^r, itself a function of all other prices, x_j^r and U^r.

As an illustration, which has been used to assess both rationing and separability, consider the following simple extension to the LES model in which x_j – the good to be rationed or to have a corner solution – is allowed to be non-separable from other goods. The unconditional cost function is written

$$C(\mathbf{p}, U^r) = a(\mathbf{p}) + d(\mathbf{p}^j)\, p_j + b(\mathbf{p})^{1-\theta_j} p_j^{\theta_j}\, U, \tag{28}$$

where
$$a(\mathbf{p}) = \Sigma_r p_r \alpha_r,$$
$$d(\mathbf{p}^j) = \delta_j \Pi_r p_r^{\delta_r} \quad \text{not including } r = j,$$
and
$$b(\mathbf{p}) = \Pi_r p_r^{\beta_r}, \quad \text{also not including } r = j.$$

The unrationed demand equations take the form

$$p_i x_i = p_i \alpha_i + \delta_i \delta_j p_j + (1-\theta_j)\, \beta_i [y - a(\mathbf{p}) - d(\mathbf{p}^j)\, p_j] \quad \text{for all } i \neq j \tag{29}$$

and
$$p_j x_j = (1-\theta_j)\, p_j d(\mathbf{p}^j)\, p_j + \theta_j [y - a(\mathbf{p}) - d(\mathbf{p}^j)\, p_j], \tag{30}$$

which are all but identical to the Linear Expenditure System apart from the 'non-separability' term $\delta_i \delta_j p_j$ in (29).

The convenience of this system is that the reservation price for good j at which x_j^r would just be chosen can be solved explicitly from (30) as

$$p_j^r = \{[\beta_j b^{(1-\theta_j)} U]/[x_j^r - d(\mathbf{p}^j)]\}^{1/(1-\theta_j)}. \tag{31}$$

This enables derivation of the 'matched pair' of rationed and unrationed demand equations. Indeed, the rationed expenditure equations for other goods corresponding to (29) are of the form

$$p_i x_i = p_i \alpha_i + \{\beta_i + k d(\mathbf{p}^j)\, \delta_i / [x_j^r - d(\mathbf{p}^j)]\} [y - a(\mathbf{p}) - p_j x_j^r], \tag{32}$$

where $k = \theta_j/(1-\theta_j)$. These conditional or rationed demand equations show immediately the ways in which rationing on one good may influence other consumption decisions. First, there is the direct income effect $p_j x_j^r$, which is subtracted from (supernumerary) total expenditure. Secondly, there is the effect on the marginal propensity to consume which alters β_i to the extent by which δ_i differs from zero. If $\delta_i = 0$ then separability would prevail and only the income effect would remain. Blundell and Walker (1982) use this 'matched pair' specification (with more general forms for $a(\mathbf{p})$ and $b(\mathbf{p})$) to test the separability of commodity demand decisions from labour supply. In that illustration the separability assumption is rejected whether or not labour supply is considered rationed.

I. 4. *Estimation Issues*

Aggregation. As much of the empirical evidence concerning consumer theory relates to models using aggregate data, it is worth considering the issue of aggregation across consumers. This is tied intimately with the degree of nonlinearity in individual level behaviour. For example, suppose the individual level Engel curve is quadratic in income. Further, suppose the objective of the empirical exercise is to recover parameters describing the time series relationship between mean expenditure and mean income. In this case aggregation bias will depend on the importance of the quadratic term and the sample covariance (over time) between the first and second order moments of income. In general, if movements in the higher order characteristics of the income distribution are related to movements in the mean and if the Engel curve is nonlinear then bias will occur. Of course, even where the aggregation bias is small, knowing how the distribution of expenditures over individuals or households evolves over time may be of considerable interest in its own right.

The importance of linear Engel curves for the micro foundations of aggregate consumer demand relationships was highlighted by Gorman (1953). If we wish to provide an exact micro interpretation of an aggregate relationship between per capita consumers' expenditure and per capita income then individual Engel curves must be linear and parallel. Intercept shifts across individuals are all that is allowed. Given the inherent nonlinearity between expenditures and income (see, Working, 1943, for example) this result of Gorman's provides a fairly pessimistic story for aggregate analysis. The breakthrough in this stalemate came with Muellbauer's (1975) and (1976) papers. Herein lay the reconciliation between the shape of individual Engel curves preferred by the Working study – expenditure shares linear in the logarithm of income or total expenditure – and the popular translog demand systems for modelling substitution behaviour at the aggregate level attributable to Jorgenson and his colleagues (see equation (19) above). Muellbauer's work showed that aggregation was possible within demand systems generated by the PIGL family described by equation (26) above. This could be achieved with the addition of a single additional parameter reflecting the shape of the income distribution. As we noted, the PIGL family of consumer preferences includes the Almost Ideal model (22), which has many similar features to both the Working Engel curves and the translog demand model.

The importance of the aggregation debate cannot be underplayed since, if reasonably general forms for demand patterns can be found that aggregate consistently, then we can recover information about individual level behaviour from aggregate data and expect consistent predictions from aggregate models. These issues were considered by Lau (1982), Jorgenson *et al.* (1982) and Stoker (1984). They showed that for exact aggregation to underpin an aggregate model (where labelling of consumers or households is unimportant) demand equations must be expressed as the sum of terms each one being the product of a function of prices and a function of individual income or expenditure and characteristics. Imposing integrability conditions on these demand equations further restricts the class. Indeed, as Gorman (1981) shows (see also Browning, 1987*b* and Russel, 1983), at most three independent terms are allowed in the sum referred to above. Since one must be total expenditure in order to preserve adding-up and the others must be chosen to preserve homogeneity the form for individual demands is significantly restricted but clearly not as tightly as in the original Gorman (1953) linear class. Although this ties one's hand in choosing suitable aggregate demand functions, certain specifications of both the translog and the Almost Ideal model satisfy these requirements.

Perhaps the most illuminating way of illustrating the relationship between aggregate and micro level studies is to take the Almost Ideal model (22) and make it household specific by adding an '*h*' subscript to denote household '*h*'. A 'household' here refers to the micro level consuming unit and may refer to an individual, a family or some other collection of individuals whose consumption decisions are taken together. Household specific expenditure shares are then given by

$$s_{ih} = \alpha_{ih} + \textstyle\sum_j \gamma_{ijh} \ln p_j + \beta_{ih} \ln (y_h/P), \tag{33}$$

where we have replaced $a(\mathbf{p})$ by the price index P. Equation (33) focuses attention on various important issues in aggregation. Indeed, premultiplying (33) by $y_h/\sum_h y_h$ and summing over h generates the aggregate share equation

$$s_i = \textstyle\sum_h \mu_h \alpha_{ih} + \sum_h \sum_j \mu_h \gamma_{ijh} \ln p_j + \sum_h \mu_h \beta_{ih} \ln (y_h/P), \tag{34}$$

where $\mu_h \equiv y_h/\sum_h y_h$. If θ_{ijh} and β_{ih} are constant across h and if, in addition α_{ih} depends linearly on a vector of characteristics $\mathbf{z}_h$, then (34) becomes

$$s_i = \boldsymbol{\alpha}_i' \mathbf{z}^0 + \textstyle\sum_j \gamma_{ij} \ln p_j + \beta_i \ln \bar{y} + \beta_i \ln y^*, \tag{35}$$

where $\mathbf{z}^0$ is the vector of total expenditure shares out of aggregate total expenditure associated with each of the characteristics, $\ln \bar{y}$ is the log of mean total expenditure and $\ln y^*$ equals $\sum_h \mu_h \ln (y_h/\bar{y})$. Interestingly $\ln y^*$ is an entropy measure of income inequality. In populations where $\mathbf{z}^0$ and $\ln y^*$ are approximately constant over reasonable time intervals, aggregate time series data could be used to recover estimates of θ_{ij} and β_i consistently. Where $\ln y^*$ was constant over time and $\mathbf{z}^0$ varied, the consistency of resulting parameter estimates from aggregate data hinges on the independence or otherwise of the evolution of the mean characteristics with the $\ln p_j$ and $\ln \bar{y}$. As $\mathbf{z}^0$ would normally contain slowly changing characteristics such as the average size of demographic groups it could well be captured by a simple trend. Even so since $\ln \bar{y}$ can also be expected to trend, estimation of β_i may be biased unless trend terms are included. Moreover, the correlation of omitted $\mathbf{z}^0$ factors over time may appear as autocorrelated disturbances or misspecified dynamics (see Stoker, 1986).

In general, census or survey data could be used to construct the $\mathbf{z}^0$ and $\ln y^*$

components, which could then be introduced into aggregate demand systems. Indeed, (35) shows how evidence on income inequality entering through $\ln y^*$ helps pin down the β_i coefficient. However, this relies on the parameters γ_{ijh} and β_{jh} being independent of household characteristics. This seems unlikely, and in the microeconometric study of fuel expenditures by Baker *et al.* (1987), for example, both price and income coefficients are found to vary systematically across households. Moreover, we shall see in the empirical evidence from household data provided later on in this section, the variables that are likely to influence preference parameters are many and cover not only demographic but also tenure, ownership and employment status variables.

Zero Expenditures and Corner Solutions. Household expenditure patterns often differ radically from the simple continuous expenditure share expressions of the model described above. We have seen earlier how rationing and/or corner solutions can lead to the introduction of reservation or virtual prices. In general and for a number of different possible reasons, we may observe households with zero expenditures in any period over which we survey them. Although at the micro level, provided we can identify the cause of the zero expenditure, modelling and estimation can proceed using standard micro econometric procedures (see Blundell and Meghir, 1987*b* for a more detailed analysis), at the aggregate level life is not so easy. Indeed, aggregation across corner solutions poses some interesting econometric problems in itself.

To examine the issues involved we first define the indicator variable

$$I_{th} = \begin{cases} 1 & \text{if individual } h \text{ buys} \\ 0 & \text{otherwise} \end{cases}, \tag{36}$$

which describes whether in period t individual h is observed buying a particular good. In order to allow for a general process determining the buy/non-buy decision, we suppose that the buy decision depends on observable characteristics $\mathbf{z}_{th}$ and unobservables v_{th} and we write the following reduced form latent equation

$$I^*_{th} = \mathbf{z}'_{th}\boldsymbol{\beta} + v_{th}, \tag{37}$$

for which $I_{th} = 1$ if $I^*_{th} > 0$ and $I_{th} = 0$ if $I^*_{th} \leqslant 0$. In this framework, 'latent' demand is given by $x^*_{th} = d_{th}(p_t, y_{th}) + u_{th}$ where $d_{th}(\ )$ can be thought of as f_i/p_i in (2) for some commodity i and each u_{th} represents other random factors influencing demand. Observed demand may then be written as

$$x_{th} = I_{th}\, d_{th}(p_t, y_{th}) + \theta_{th} + e_{th}, \tag{38}$$

where $\theta_{th} = E\{I_{th} . u_{th}\}$ and by definition $e_{th} = I_{th}\, u_{th} - \theta_{th}$. Assuming a joint normal distribution for u_{th} and v_{th} (rather weaker assumptions can be made), the expectational term θ_{th} is proportional to the standard normal density $\phi(\mathbf{z}'_{th}\boldsymbol{\beta})$.

Now suppose that $\mathbf{Z}_t$ represents the per capita values of $\mathbf{z}_{th}$ and suppose these exogenous average measures were available at the aggregate level. Similarly, let $\mathbf{D}_t$ be the per buyer demand functions (i.e. averaged across buyers only) and let it be assumed that each $d_{th}(p_t, y_{th})$ is linear in parameters and not dependent on $\mathbf{z}_{th}$. In this case standard aggregation conditions for a model without corners or rationing would prevail. However, the aggregate relationship corresponding to (38) above satisfies

$$X_t = \mathbf{I}_t . \mathbf{D}_t(.) + \theta_t + e_t, \tag{39}$$

where X_t is per capita demand, $\mathbf{I}_t$ is the proportion of buyers and θ_t can be written proportional to $\phi(\mathbf{Z}_t' \boldsymbol{\beta})$ (see MaCurdy, 1986). Notice that (39) is nonlinear in $\mathbf{Z}_t$ and depends on the per *buyer* variables in $\mathbf{D}_t$ (income, for example). Even assuming both per buyer and per capita variables are available, the aggregate equation is still nonlinear. Indeed, a model of the form

$$X_t = \mathbf{D}_t(.) + w_t, \tag{40}$$

where w_t was assumed to have the same properties as e_t in (39), would display instability and general misspecification in so far as I_t varies over time and in so far as the nonlinear term θ_t was important in (39). Simply including the proportion of buyers as an additional explanatory variable in estimation at the macro level model may well pick up the misspecification underlying (40) but would be unlikely to provide consistent estimates of the parameters in (39).

Although the corner solution problem described above invalidates the usual interpretation of aggregate consumer relationships, estimation at the micro level is also complicated by corner solutions. Essentially, estimation requires the evaluation of the statistical expectation of the unrestricted demands conditional on those at corner solutions. This in turn involves the evaluation of the joint probability of the corner solutions. Since corner solutions are expressed as an inequality constraint this probability will require the evaluation of an integral for each corner. Where the stochastic terms on commodities are correlated, multiple integrals have to be solved. Until the recent work of McFadden (1986) such computations have been virtually intractable and only systems with relatively few corners (Wales and Woodland, 1983 and Lee and Pitt, 1986, for example) have been considered.

In assessing the importance of corner solutions, the level of commodity aggregation is crucial. If, for example, consumption of individual clothing items are under analysis, then multiple corner solutions for any individual household in an expenditure survey seem highly likely. However, at a more aggregate level – the total of clothing for example – zero expenditures are more likely to derive from the infrequency of purchase relative to the period of survey. Purchase infrequency implies that the theoretical concept of consumption differs from its measured counterpart: expenditure. As this discrepancy affects both the dependent variable and the total expenditure variable, Ordinary Least Squares estimates of the share equations are biased.

All surveys on individual or household expenditures cover purchases over a limited period of time. Indeed, the more accurate the measurement in terms of precise diary records the shorter the period over which the survey can be afforded and the more likely the occurrence of reported zero expenditures. Even where the expenditure in question relates to an item or group of items for which actual consumption is positive, infrequency of purchase or the 'durability' of the good may result in a recorded zero expenditure. Deaton and

Irish (1984), Kay *et al.* (1984), Pudney (1987) and Blundell and Meghir (1987) have developed a class of bivariate models for the joint determination of the purchase and expenditure decision. Measurement error in total consumption is critical in the estimation of the parameters of utility consistent demand systems since it is usually assumed that total consumption is measured without error and demand analysis can proceed to examine the way in which consumption on specific commodities is allocated conditional on total consumption. Keen (1986) has shown that an instrumental variable estimator (which will be described in the following discussion of exogeneity) is also sufficient to remove the OLS bias in the infrequency of purchase model. In the more structural infrequency of purchase models, a purchase probability is explicitly introduced. For example, in the Blundell and Meghir (1987*a*) approach this probability is allowed to vary with income and other household characteristics so as to minimise the extent to which 'unobservable' characteristics are left to explain the distribution of purchases.

Exogeneity and Corner Solutions. In general, although many variables in empirical demand analysis are appropriately treated as conditioning variables, there is no reason why they should be assumed exogenous. Any exogeneity assumption can be checked against the data at the outset. However, two difficulties arise. How do we test exogeneity across a system of equations where corner solutions may occur and how should we re-estimate if exogeneity is rejected?

As an example, we consider the exogeneity of total expenditure in a standard Marshallian or y-conditional demand system. For estimation purposes, we shall write the system of y-conditional demands as

$$\mathbf{s}_{th} = \mathbf{d}_t(\mathbf{p}_t, y_{th}) + \mathbf{u}_{th}, \tag{41}$$

where $\mathbf{s}_{th}$ represents a vector of expenditure shares for household h in period t and $\mathbf{u}_{th}$ the corresponding vector of stochastic error terms. If the demand model is estimated from panel data then $\mathbf{d}_{th}(.)$ may include a household or individual fixed effect for each commodity. For aggregate time series we may drop the h subscript. For the purposes of testing the exogeneity assumption we shall add a reduced form equation for y_t

$$y_t = \pi' \mathbf{z}_t + v_t, \tag{42}$$

where $\mathbf{z}_t$ are a vector of observed exogenous (instrumental) variables with π as their unknown constant coefficients and v_t a random error term. The question of focus here relates to the exogeneity of y_t for the estimation of the preference parameters in the model (41). Where $\mathbf{z}_t$ contains prices alone, so that homogeneity is required to generate an exclusion restriction on (41), Attfield (1985) has neatly shown the equivalence of the exogeneity and homogeneity tests. However, using the two-stage budgeting theory described earlier, we may expect to be able to define many other additional instruments in (42) allowing the separate assessment of exogeneity and homogeneity.

Where there are no corner solutions, the procedure for testing (and estimation) is straightforward and follows the analysis of Hausman (1978). Inclusion of the reduced form residual $\hat{v}_t$ in each equation in (41) and estimation of the extended system provides consistent estimates for the demand parameters. In addition, an F-test for the exclusion of the residual in the demand system provides an asymptotically efficient exogeneity test.

Where corner solutions arise, Smith and Blundell (1986) show that little of the standard analysis for exogeneity testing discussed above changes. Consistency of the estimates in the extended system under the alternative remains and the exogeneity test is again asymptotically efficient. The only problem to note, in this limited dependent variable case, is that the form for y_{th} (which depends on either the market or reservation price) switches when any decision variable is rationed or at a corner solution. As Ransom (1987) has shown, the coherency conditions (see Gourieroux *et al.*, 1980) required for estimation are equivalent to the integrability conditions (concavity, symmetry, ...) for utility maximising behaviour. This is a general result for switching models derived from consumer behaviour and extends to the case of many binding non-negativity constraints or corner solutions discussed earlier. Integrability is by no means an innocuous condition since concavity restrictions can severely restrict the flexibility of commonly used 'flexible' demand systems. This point has been highlighted in the recent paper of Diewert and Wales (1987).

Cross-equation restrictions and the Minimum Chi-Square Estimator. Even though each of the above issues – aggregation, corner solutions, purchase infrequency and exogeneity – are important, the principles of estimating demand systems referred to in the earlier survey by Brown and Deaton (1972) are still relevant. Briefly, adding-up across expenditure or expenditure share equations implies a singular variance-covariance matrix for the stochastic terms across equations – the stochastic term on any one share equation cannot be independent of *all* other share equations. However, provided there are *no* cross-equation restrictions single equation estimation remains efficient. Endogeneity of total expenditure and purchase infrequency do not detract from this result. However, since restrictions like Slutsky symmetry are an integral part of empirical demand analysis, estimation under cross-equation restrictions has played a major role in producing parsimonious theoretically consistent demand systems.

Estimation under such cross-equation restrictions usually requires system-wide optimisation and for large samples this can be computationally difficult. The Minimum Chi-Square (MCS) approach introduced into the econometrics literature by Rothenberg (1973) provides a simple and yet relatively under-utilised method of deriving estimates subject to system-wide restrictions. Moreover, these are equivalent to those derived from application of the Full Information Maximum Likelihood approach. The attraction of the MCS method relates to the separate stages of unrestricted and restricted estimation. At the first stage estimates of the parameters of the unrestricted model are recovered which for a standard demand system (the LES or AI system, for example) would involve estimating unrestricted share equations. These estimates together with their covariance matrix summarise all information available in the data concerning preference parameter estimation. In effect they act as sufficient statistics for the purposes of demand system estimation.

Denoting the unrestricted parameters by $\boldsymbol{\theta}$, theoretical restrictions (symmetry, homogeneity, etc.) may usually be expressed as

$$\boldsymbol{\theta} = \mathbf{S}\boldsymbol{\theta}^*. \tag{43}$$

To impose these restrictions the MCS method chooses $\hat{\boldsymbol{\theta}}^*$ so as to minimise the quadratic form

$$m = (\hat{\boldsymbol{\theta}} - \mathbf{S}\boldsymbol{\theta}^*)' \hat{\boldsymbol{\Sigma}}_{\theta}^{-1} (\hat{\boldsymbol{\theta}} - \mathbf{S}\boldsymbol{\theta}^*), \tag{44}$$

where $\hat{\boldsymbol{\Sigma}}_{\theta}$ is the estimated variance-covariance matrix for $\hat{\boldsymbol{\theta}}$. Indeed, consistency of the resulting MCS estimator simply requires that the restrictions are correct and that $\hat{\boldsymbol{\theta}}$ is a consistent estimator. Any positive definite weight matrix can be used to replace $\hat{\boldsymbol{\Sigma}}_{\theta}^{-1}$. However, where the optimal weight matrix is used, the MCS estimator is asymptotically equivalent to the maximum likelihood estimator and the minimised value of m is an optimal chi-squared test of the restrictions (see Ferguson, 1958). Under linear restrictions like (43) the MCS estimator itself is given by

$$\hat{\boldsymbol{\theta}}^* = (\mathbf{S}^{+\prime}\mathbf{S}^+)^{-1}\mathbf{S}^{+\prime}\boldsymbol{\theta}^+, \tag{45}$$

where $\mathbf{S}^+ = \hat{\boldsymbol{\Sigma}}_{\theta}^{-\frac{1}{2}}\mathbf{S}$ and $\boldsymbol{\theta}^+ = \hat{\boldsymbol{\Sigma}}_{\theta}^{-\frac{1}{2}}\hat{\boldsymbol{\theta}}$.

In practice, this method proceeds as follows. First, each unrestricted demand equation is estimated separately. Then the *restricted* estimators are recovered by fitting the restrictions using (44) which, being in the dimension of $\boldsymbol{\theta}$, can be significantly less than the number of observations. The application of the MCS method therefore makes constrained estimation and testing available in very large samples. In general $\mathbf{S}\boldsymbol{\theta}^*$ can be replaced by some $g(\boldsymbol{\theta}^*)$ in (44). To implement constrained maximum likelihood estimation there is no need therefore to exclude observations for computational tractability – all information in the unrestricted model is exploited and summarised by simply defined statistics in the first stage of unrestricted estimation. An application of this technique is provided in the empirical illustration reported below.

I. 5. *Assessing the Evidence*

Rather than providing a comprehensive catalogue of empirical results in the literature, this section will be used to present a summary of some recent empirical results based on micro-data. The idea here is to provide the reader with an example of the power of empirical demand analysis and the attractiveness of working at the individual household level. Given the different levels of aggregation and commodity grouping used in other empirical studies, it should be clear that comparison of estimated parameters (or elasticities for that matter) can be a hazardous activity. Working at the household level reveals a more detailed analysis of the distribution of elasticities by household type and will also have implications for the degree of aggregation bias one might expect. These results, drawn from the Blundell *et al.* (1987) study, adopt the minimum chi-squared principle described in the previous section, to recover estimates of a seven good Almost Ideal model of demand from a pooled cross-section over 15 annual time series covering more than 65,000 non-pensioner households. These data are drawn from the annual UK *Family Expenditure Survey* for the years 1970–84 and provide an ideal basis for the application of the minimum chi-squared method. In one form or another this data base has been the cornerstone of many empirical studies of consumer behaviour including, for example, the papers by Atkinson and Stern (1980), Browning *et al.* (1985), Muellbauer (1977) and Pollak and Wales (1981).

On micro data the wide variation in demographic and other individual characteristics is all too evident. The extent to which price and income parameters vary with these characteristics is clearly important for the aggregation results described earlier in this survey. Estimation results for the price and income variables in the homogeneity and symmetry constrained model are presented in Table 1. Here to account for the likely endogeneity and measurement error due to purchase infrequency discussed in Section 1.4 we have instrumented the total expenditure variable. As already mentioned many individual demographic, locational and labour market characteristics were allowed to enter each share equation and each of these was used as an instrument for the total expenditure variable. In addition instruments included normal disposable income, other prices, interest rates and local unemployment rates. It was found necessary to interact the seasonal dummies (S_1, S_2 and S_3) and young child dummy (C) with the log of total expenditure $\ln y$. These are

Table 1

*Restricted Price and Income Parameter Estimates**

Variable	Food	Alcohol	Fuel	Clothing	Transport	Services	Other
ln *PFOOD*	0·096247	0·012114	−0·013891	−0·004471	−0·040401	−0·015352	−0·034246
	(0·01006)	(0·00687)	(0·00554)	(0·00813)	(0·01120)	(0·00830)	—
ln *PALCL*	0·012114	−0·062385	0·064331	−0·006507	0·041337	−0·005995	−0·042895
	(0·00687)	(0·00898)	(0·00598)	(0·00629)	(0·01067)	(0·00804)	—
ln *PFUEL*	−0·013891	0·064331	0·006570	−0·001917	−0·050553	−0·016588	0·012049
	(0·00554)	(0·00598)	(0·00670)	(0·00534)	(0·00876)	(0·00634)	—
ln *PCLOTH*	−0·004471	−0·006507	−0·001917	0·016439	−0·003078	−0·014020	0·013554
	(0·00813)	(0·00629)	(0·00534)	(0·00948)	(0·01075)	(0·00801)	—
ln *PTRPT*	−0·040401	0·041337	−0·050553	−0·003078	0·055560	0·007129	−0·009994
	(0·01120)	(0·01067)	(0·00876)	(0·01075)	(0·02390)	(0·01323)	—
ln *PSERV*	−0·015352	−0·005995	−0·016588	−0·014020	0·007129	0·017884	0·026943
	(0·00830)	(0·00804)	(0·00634)	(0·00801)	(0·01323)	(0·01338)	—
ln *PFUEL*	−0·013891	0·064331	0·006570	−0·001917	−0·050553	−0·016588	0·012049
	—	—	—	—	—	—	—
*C*ln*y*	0·002523	−0·002844	0·000950	0·002197	−0·004886	0·001003	0·001057
	(0·00033)	(0·00027)	(0·00019)	(0·00036)	(0·00045)	(0·00037)	—
*S1*ln*y*	−0·006934	−0·004172	−0·005013	−0·005053	0·015405	0·010654	−0·004886
	(0·00240)	(0·00198)	(0·00138)	(0·00261)	(0·00330)	(0·00270)	—
*S2*ln*y*	−0·012277	−0·004113	0·004914	−0·007424	0·010277	0·013280	−0·004658
	(0·00240)	(0·00198)	(0·00137)	(0·00260)	(0·00330)	(0·00270)	—
*S3*ln*y*	−0·015690	−0·007975	0·012040	−0·006440	0·005457	0·014733	−0·002126
	(0·00235)	(0·00194)	(0·00135)	(0·00255)	(0·00324)	(0·00264)	—
ln*y*	−0·123882	0·057474	−0·059123	0·028762	0·034726	0·070948	−0·008906
	(0·00204)	(0·00169)	(0·00118)	(0·00221)	(0·00281)	(0·00230)	—

* Source: for Tables 1, 2 and 3: Blundell *et al.* (1987). Other explanatory variables included demographic, tenure, regional and seasonal dummies.

Standard errors in parentheses.

presented along with the price coefficients in Table 1. It is comforting to note that many of the price coefficients are significant despite the large number of other characteristics allowed to influence expenditure shares.

To gauge the importance of working with individual data and to provide an example of the type of price and income elasticities one can expect to elicit from empirical demand systems of this type, Tables 2 (*a*) and 2 (*b*) provide a detailed description of Marshallian price and budget elasticities for households with and without children. It should be noted that our sample excludes all pensioners. In Tables 3 (*a*) and 3 (*b*) a similar analysis is conducted for two of the commodity categories to assess the distribution of elasticities across households with differing income in our sample. These results show that household characteristics have important impacts on consumer behaviour acting both through income and price effects.

Table 2

Price and Income Elasticities

	Commodity Group					
	Food	Alcohol	Fuel	Clothing	Transport	Services
		(*a*) *Households with Children*				
Budget elasticities	0·668	2·014	0·329	1·269	1·212	1·654
Uncompensated price elasticities						
Food	−0·494	−0·006	0·051	−0·005	−0·088	−0·076
Alcohol	−0·541	−1·983	0·865	−0·136	0·668	0·000
Fuel	0·342	−0·653	−0·747	−0·008	−0·534	−0·258
Clothing	−0·242	−0·030	−0·089	−0·852	−0·045	−0·103
Transport	−0·404	0·276	−0·364	−0·023	−0·674	0·066
Services	−0·629	0·020	−0·327	−0·143	0·027	−0·767
Compensated price elasticities						
Food	−0·246	0·032	0·110	0·066	0·021	−0·004
Alcohol	0·210	−1·869	1·043	0·080	0·999	0·218
Fuel	0·464	0·671	−0·718	0·027	−0·480	−0·223
Clothing	0·231	0·042	0·023	−0·716	0·163	0·045
Transport	0·048	0·345	−0·257	0·106	−0·475	0·197
Services	−0·012	0·114	−0·181	0·034	0·298	−0·587
		(*b*) *Households without Children*				
Budget Elasticities	0·613	1·738	0·278	1·301	1·180	1·556
Uncompensated Price Elasticities						
Food	−0·431	0·001	0·057	−0·010	−0·092	−0·081
Alcohol	−0·355	−1·731	0·635	−0·090	0·465	−0·014
Fuel	0·330	0·717	−0·733	−0·017	−0·553	−0·264
Clothing	−0·255	−0·040	−0·098	−0·830	−0·059	−0·121
Transport	−0·333	0·231	−0·308	−0·018	−0·728	0·052
Services	−0·504	0·006	−0·274	−0·115	0·006	−0·813
Compensated Price Elasticities						
Food	−0·235	0·049	0·107	0·048	0·027	−0·003
Alcohol	0·201	−1·596	0·777	0·076	0·801	0·208
Fuel	0·419	0·739	−0·710	0·010	−0·499	−0·228
Clothing	0·161	0·062	0·008	−0·706	0·192	0·045
Transport	0·044	0·323	−0·212	0·095	−0·500	0·203
Services	−0·007	0·127	−0·147	0·034	0·307	−0·614

Table 3
Distribution of Elasticities by Income Group

	Children		No children		All	
Income Percentile	Mean	STD	Mean	STD	Mean	STD
			(a) Uncompensated Own Price Elasticities			
			Food			
Low 5%	−0·51	0·06	−0·48	0·07	−0·49	0·06
6–10%	−0·50	0·07	−0·44	0·10	−0·47	0·07
11–25%	−0·48	0·04	−0·40	0·10	−0·45	0·05
Mid 50%	−0·42	0·04	−0·32	0·09	−0·39	0·04
76–90%	−0·36	0·10	−0·24	0·21	−0·31	0·11
Top 10%	−0·29	0·23	−0·12	0·44	−0·22	0·24
All	−0·40	0·04	−0·29	0·07	−0·36	0·04
			Fuel			
Low 5%	−0·92	0·04	−0·08	0·05	−0·90	2·04
6–10%	−0·90	0·04	−0·83	0·07	−0·87	2·04
11–25%	−0·86	0·03	−0·78	0·06	−0·83	3·03
Mid 50%	−0·77	0·03	−0·68	0·05	−0·74	4·02
76–90%	−0·67	0·08	−0·55	0·11	−0·62	6·07
Top 10%	−0·56	0·14	−0·41	0·19	−0·50	9·12
All	−0·75	0·03	−0·65	0·04	−0·71	5·02
			(b) Income (Budget) Elasticities			
			Food			
Low 5%	0·72	0·05	0·67	0·06	0·69	0·05
6–10%	0·71	0·06	0·64	0·08	0·68	0·05
11–25%	0·69	0·03	0·61	0·08	0·66	0·03
Mid 50%	0·65	0·03	0·56	0·06	0·62	0·08
76–90%	0·61	0·07	0·51	0·14	0·52	0·16
Top 10%	0·56	0·15	0·43	0·28	0·51	0·16
All	0·64	0·03	0·54	0·05	0·60	0·03
			Fuel			
Low 5%	0·62	0·08	0·53	0·04	0·56	0·07
6–10%	0·58	0·08	0·43	0·13	0·52	0·08
11–25%	0·49	0·05	0·35	0·11	0·44	0·06
Mid 50%	0·33	0·04	0·17	0·08	0·28	0·04
76–90%	0·17	0·13	−0·03	0·18	0·09	0·11
Top 10%	−0·01	0·23	−0·24	0·31	−0·11	0·19
All	0·31	0·04	0·13	0·06	0·24	0·04

In terms of the historical development of empirical demand analysis an important consideration is the degree of consistency between household behaviour and integrability conditions – homogeneity, symmetry and concavity. One interesting outcome of the empirical study described above is that homogeneity is acceptable across all goods. This contrasts markedly with results on aggregate data – see, for example, Deaton and Muellbauer (1980*a*). Moreover, both in the Deaton and Muellbauer study and in many that follow – Anderson and Blundell (1983), for example – dynamic misspecification is suggested as the root cause of homogeneity rejections. As was noted earlier in the survey and emphasised by Stoker (1986), the omitted characteristics in aggregate models implied from this study may evolve in a way that is captured by the introduction of dynamic adjustment or trend-like terms.

The symmetry restriction is less coherent with data within the empirical illustration described above. The symmetry test has a Chi-Square value of 79·20 with 15 degrees of freedom. However, further analysis suggests three possible problems with these results. First is the degree of heteroscedasticity underlying the model, second the likely importance of interactions between prices and individual household characteristics and finally the importance of higher order terms in the logarithm of total expenditure along the lines suggested in Gorman (1981). None of these considerations are accounted for in Table 1. Adjusting for heteroscedasticity tends to lower the test statistic referred to above while allowing price coefficients to depend on characteristics may make symmetry more acceptable. Nevertheless, the symmetry and homogeneity constrained parameter estimates reported in Table 1 display well-determined coefficients with plausible values for the elasticities presented in Tables 2 and 3. By looking at the matrix of compensated price elasticities in Table 2 it can be observed that own price effects are large and negative while the cross-effects are generally positive. This shows a close adherence to concavity and taken together with the above results suggests, perhaps surprisingly, that integrability conditions are not too much at odds with observed micro behaviour once individual characteristics are allowed for.

From the discussion in Section I.4, the implications for work on aggregate data are clear. Even ignoring the interaction of the income and price coefficients with individual characteristics, aggregate models that explain demands in terms of price and total expenditure variables exclude many important explanatory factors. These factors – for example, the proportion of total expenditure associated with particular family size or tenure groups – change over time in a way that is probably correlated with real total expenditure and relative price movements making it difficult to identify the separate effects from aggregate data. In turn without the separate identification of these factors, it is difficult to test theoretical hypotheses concerning pure price and income terms. Once it is also acknowledged that the total expenditure, and to some extent price, coefficients in the estimated Almost Ideal model vary systematically with individual characteristics, then the conditions for exact aggregation described in Section I.4 themselves fail.

These results suggest particular care should be taken in interpreting estimated demand elasticities and tests of theoretical restrictions based on them from studies using aggregate data. They also suggest that a comparison of estimates across either different time periods or different countries in which important characteristics (or the income shares going to households with such characteristics) may not be constant and may very likely display coefficient instability. It is quite possible that polynomial time trends or dynamic adjustment terms may correct for these omitted factors and thereby make results more comparable. However, the importance of these issues coupled with intertemporal considerations that will be raised in the next section point to exciting research areas that have yet to be satisfactorily explored. As a result, in writing this survey paper, I have been drawn towards a more detailed discussion of these issues rather than towards a comparison of estimates from other empirical studies. However, a reasonably detailed list of empirical demand studies is to be found in the bibliography.

Turning to dynamic considerations we may note from our discussion of intertemporal separability in Section I.2 that, if intertemporal substitution is possible, then consumers will adjust the total expenditure variable in response to intertemporal price and interest rate changes. In order to assess, therefore, the total effect of price and other variables on consumer behaviour one cannot simply work within the models described in this section. Moreover, if intertemporal separability is not satisfied, then the two-stage budgeting rules for life-cycle expenditure allocations which can be used to justify most of the 'static' models described in this section will be subject to misspecification and may not even recover within period preference parameters consistently. It is to the assessment of these intertemporal issues and the dynamic process of consumer behaviour to which we now turn.

II. THE LIFE-CYCLE MODEL AND DYNAMIC CONSUMER BEHAVIOUR

II. 1. *Overview*

At the aggregate consumption level some form of dynamic behaviour has usually been incorporated in empirical specification. Broadly speaking two types of model have emerged – those that take a more traditional time series view of the dynamic specification leaving theory to play most of its role in the long-run or steady state solution and those that explicitly incorporate forward looking behaviour distinguishing between unanticipated and anticipated effects. Both of these approaches have their drawbacks just as both have led to major developments in our understanding of intertemporal consumer behaviour. The forward looking models are in principle better suited to policy analysis since they can identify the effect of an *unanticipated* temporary or permanent shock which in turn reflects many policy changes. However, the dynamic paths and underlying preferences in the majority of the empirical specifications of these models are highly restrictive. They have tended to ignore adjustment problems, habits and liquidity constraints and have been subjected to the apparently contradictory criticisms of both excess sensitivity to current income changes and excess smoothness of consumption. Moreover, empirical work at the aggregate level generally appeals to the notion of a representative consumer, even though modelling dynamic behaviour places even stricter aggregation conditions than those discussed in Section I.4 since agents must now be comparable across time. Indeed, unless individuals entering the population can be assumed to take on the same expectations and place in the wealth distribution as individuals leaving, estimation will generally result in some degree of aggregation bias.

As with all good empirical research, a synthesis of these two strands of research is producing a new breed of dynamic forward looking models which appear a good deal more satisfactory. Even more encouraging, although not without its own difficulties, is the application to individual panel data where aggregation bias, at least, is removed. It is these recent developments on which I wish to concentrate. However, before turning to the importance of the debate over life-cycle models and dynamics, we briefly return to the models of the previous section to evaluate their place in all this.

Although apparently static, we noted earlier that under intertemporal two-stage budgeting the models of the previous sections can be given a life-cycle consistent interpretation. This will be dealt with in more detail in the next section where the simplest, and to some extent most popular, life-cycle models are considered more critically. Nevertheless, it is correct to say that models in which disaggregated commodity expenditures are explained in terms of within period prices and the total current period expenditure allocation can easily be generated by an intertemporally separable life-cycle model. In this application of a two-stage budgeting, (expected) life-cycle wealth is allocated across periods so as to equalise the discounted marginal utility of wealth while each period's optimal allocation is distributed across goods. This simple idea applies equally well to models of the joint determination of commodity demand and labour supply decisions. However, the intertemporal separability assumption on which they rest is precisely that which rules out the liquidity constraints, habits and explicit dynamics alluded to above.

It is worth, at this stage, stressing the strength of the capital markets assumptions which enable the budget constraint to be written as a single additive lifetime (expected) wealth constraint. Where borrowing is restricted by asset levels or some fixed multiple of current earnings, additional constraints may well bind, thus invalidating the simple perfect capital markets model (see Mariger, 1987*b* and Hayashi, 1985*b*, for example). Moreover, as King (1986) demonstrates, a differential rate between borrowing and lending ensures that marginal utility may not be equalised. These issues seem particularly relevant for interpreting the relationship between macro and micro estimates of intertemporal consumer behaviour since a good deal of the empirical evidence (Hall and Mishkin, 1982, for example) suggests that the importance of capital market imperfections may differ systematically across the population.

The problem for empirical analysis in this life-cycle or dynamic framework is choosing the most appropriate avenues for generalisation that maintain some degree of parsimony. The debates in this area are by no means over and the choice of model will, as ever, be determined by the objective to which the model is to be used. However, whether one is working with a pooled time series of cross-sections, a true household panel or simply with aggregate time series there are clear avenues which must be explored in order to evaluate the restrictiveness of any assumed specification. As this survey is designed specifically to investigate the interplay between theory and testing, our initial discussion in the next section will be concerned with the restrictiveness of the (implicit) theoretical models of consumer behaviour underlying various of the life-cycle specifications.

II. 2. *Empirical Representations of Life-Cycle Models*

Initially we shall assume that consumers have perfect foresight and that utility is separable over time. In each period decisions are made so as to maximise discounted lifetime utility subject to time and asset constraints with perfectly predicted future market wages, prices, transfer income and demographic characteristics.

An attraction of the time separable life-cycle framework is the ease by which the perfect foresight assumption can be relaxed so as to allow uncertainty and replanning. This is not altogether surprising since, as we saw in Section I.2, the separability assumption allows the direct application of two-stage budgeting theory and ensures that life-cycle consistent current demands can be written in terms of a single variable capturing both past decisions and future anticipations. With uncertainty or dynamic replanning care needs to be taken in assessing the exogeneity of any explanatory factors; however, in this case the theoretical model also provides a partition of variables into those that may be assumed exogenous for the purposes of estimating intertemporal preference parameters.

Defining $\mathbf{x}_s$ to be the choice vector in period s, lifetime utility in any period 't' may be written as the following discounted sum of (concave twice differentiable) period by period utility indices $U_s(\mathbf{x}_s)$

$$U_t^* = \Sigma_s \phi^{s-t} U_s(\mathbf{x}_s) \quad \text{for} \quad s = t, \ldots, L, \tag{46}$$

where L is the number of periods in the lifetime of the household decision-maker and ϕ $(= 1/(1+\delta))$ represents the subjective time discount factor (see Ghez and Becker, 1975). Although $\mathbf{x}_s$ can easily include leisure or labour supply components, for ease of illustration it will initially be assumed to include consumption goods alone. Life-cycle utility is then maximised subject to the combination of a within period budget identity

$$\mathbf{p}_s' \mathbf{x}_s = y_s,$$

where y_s is total period s consumption expenditure, and the asset accumulation constraint

$$y_s = \mu_s + r_s A_{s-1} - \Delta A_s,$$

where y_s is the sum of earned and transfer income μ_s, interest income $r_s A_{s-1}$ and asset decumulation $-\Delta A_s$; A_s being the level of household assets at the end of period s, r_s the certain rate of interest earned on A_{s-1} during period s and Δ is the first difference operator. ΔA_s is therefore the change in assets over period $s-1$. In developing this life-cycle framework we have added the crucial perfect capital markets condition. Under this assumption the interest rate r_s is independent of current net worth A_s so that given perfect foresight any amount of future labour or nonlabour income can be discounted into current period income. In this case a sequence of asset levels A_s or savings decisions for $s = 1, \ldots, L$ can be freely chosen so as to maximise life-cycle utility.

To complete this outline of the life-cycle framework it is useful to combine the two budget 'constraints' above to define the following lifetime wealth constraint

$$\begin{aligned} \Sigma_s \mathbf{p}_s' \mathbf{x}_s &= (1+r_t) A_{t-1} + \Sigma_s \mu_s \\ &= W_t, \end{aligned} \tag{47}$$

where each Σ_s refers to summation for $s = t, \ldots, L$ and where for convenience we define all prices, wage rates and transfer incomes to be discounted back to period t. If $\mathbf{x}_s$ contains 'leisure' time as well as goods then y_s can be redefined to represent full income as described in Section I.1. A fuller description of the life-cycle model incorporating labour market considerations is developed in Blundell (1986). For the most part it will be convenient to interpret y_t to be total consumption expenditure. However, this is equivalent to assuming that life-cycle utility (46) is *explicitly* additive in goods and labour supply. The marginal utility of consumption in any period is then completely independent of current period labour supply decisions – except for their effect on life-cycle wealth. Although we shall argue later that explicit additivity assumptions of this kind are excessively restrictive and largely unnecessary, they have been commonly adopted in empirical studies of intertemporal consumption behaviour and serve as a useful starting-point for our discussion.

Under the two-stage budgeting allocation of total consumption expenditure in period t of the life-cycle, y_t is given by

$$y_t = g_t(\mathbf{p}_t, \mathbf{p}_{t+1}, \ldots, \mathbf{p}_L, W_t), \tag{48}$$

where g_t is homogeneous of degree zero in discounted prices $\mathbf{p}_t, \mathbf{p}_{t+1}, \ldots, \mathbf{p}_L$ and wealth W_t. If perfect foresight is relaxed $g_t(.)$ can be replaced by its conditional expectation given information in period t. It is clear from (48) that $g_t(.)$ accounts for the influence of all future expectations concerning economic (and demographic) variables on current period as well as for the influence of past decisions through A_{t-1} in W_t.

The demand models of the previous section which explained commodity demands as a function of within period prices and total expenditure are therefore fully consistent with this life-cycle story. However, if the life-cycle model is valid, we can see from (48) that the price elasticities generated from these demand equations will not describe the full effects of a price change. In general price changes will affect the period allocation of total expenditure through the life-cycle 'consumption function' (48). The second stage allocation then determines within period demands according to

$$\mathbf{x}_t = \mathbf{d}_t(\mathbf{p}_t, y_t), \tag{49}$$

where $\mathbf{d}_t$ is a vector of 'standard' Marshallian demand equations homogeneous of degree zero in the price vector $\mathbf{p}_t$ and the conditioning variable y_t.

Should there be a corner solution or other binding constraint on an element of $\mathbf{x}_t$, the forms of the demand equations for all remaining choice variables will generally change. The effect of a corner in the budget constraint is precisely the same as described in the 'static' models of Section I.3 so long as the total expenditure variable y_t is correctly measured in each of the regimes. Binding constraints on $\mathbf{x}_s$ where $s > t$ will simply alter the form of (48) and will have no direct impact on (49). Indeed, where the emphasis is on estimating life-cycle consistent within period preferences, the precise form for $g_t(.)$ in (48) across regimes is unimportant.

Under certain representations for $U_s(\mathbf{x}_s)$ in (46), the total expenditure equation (48) takes particularly convenient forms. For example, from Section

1.1 we have seen that where within period commodity allocations are homothetic the corresponding indirect utility functions can be written solely in terms of real consumption expenditure $y_s/P(\mathbf{p}_s)$, where $P(\mathbf{p}_s)$ is an appropriate price index. Defining c_s to be $y_s/P(\mathbf{p}_s)$, we may then replace each $U_s(\mathbf{x}_s)$ by the indirect utility measure $V_s(c_s)$. Then, assuming a quadratic form for $V_s(.)$, equation (48) becomes

$$c_t p_t = rW_t, \tag{50}$$

where $p_t = P(\mathbf{p}_t)$ and where we have also assumed a real interest rate equal to the subjective discount rate δ and an infinite horizon. This in turn may be written more familiarly as

$$c_t = r^* W_t^*, \tag{51}$$

where r^* is the real interest rate and W_t^* is real life-cycle wealth as seen or expected in period t. From (50) and (51) we can see that consumption is allocated to 'low cost' periods in such a way as to equalise expenditure. Notice that in deriving this consumption model we have not only restricted the form of within period preferences to be homothetic but have also restricted the form of intertemporal preferences – both through the explicit additivity assumptions (across the life-cycle *and* between consumption and other decisions) and through the choice of monotonic transformation on within period preferences over consumption goods. These together permit the extremely simple description of the life-cycle consumption path described above.

Although (50) and (51) are based on strong underlying preference restrictions they serve as a useful illustration of the predictions of life-cycle theory. Under uncertainty, for example, specific expressions for the movement of consumption behaviour over time can be derived. More precisely in moving from period t to $t+1$, once real interest rates are assumed constant it is only through the discounted income terms μ_{t+1}, μ_{t+2}, etc. in (47) that revisions to wealth can occur. As a result, if we define E_{t+1} and E_t to be the expectation operator conditional on period $t+1$ and period t information respectively, then apart from transitory consumption effects, revisions to real consumption take the form

$$c_{t+1} - c_t = r^* \sum_{s=t}^{\infty} (\mathrm{E}_{t+1} - \mathrm{E}_t)\, \mu_s, \tag{52}$$

where μ now refers to real (discounted) income. For example, if real (undiscounted) income follows a random walk so that $(1+r^*)\,\mu_s = \mu_{s-1} + \epsilon_s$ where ϵ_s is an unpredictable innovation, then the right-hand side of (52) reduces to ϵ_t alone. That is consumption would adjust to take full account of the latest innovation or 'surprise' in real income. An extremely attractive alternative way of expressing (52) is provided by the 'rainy day' saving equation of Campbell (1987) (see also Deaton and Campbell, 1987). If we define s_t to be real saving in period t then we may write

$$s_t = -\sum_{s=t}^{\infty} \mathrm{E}_t(\mu_s - \mu_{s-1}) \tag{52'}$$

explaining saving as the present value of expected declines in discounted real income. Of course, more complicated forms for preferences, real interest rates and the process generating real income may be adopted but the basic idea, developed by Hall (1978), that consumption responds only to unpredictable events underlies all 'surprise' consumption models.

Although extremely convenient for both estimation and interpretation surprise models like (52) rest on extremely strong restrictions both on within and between period preferences. In order to assess these specifications of the time separable life-cycle model and their extensions more formally, it is worth turning to the first order Euler conditions for the intertemporal utility maximising problem (see Heckman and MaCurdy, 1980 or Hansen and Singleton, 1983) in which

$$\partial U_t / \partial x_{it} = \lambda_t p_{it}, \tag{53}$$

and

$$\tau_{t+1} \lambda_{t+1} = \lambda_t \tag{54}$$

for each good $i = 1, \ldots, n$ and all time periods $t = 1, \ldots, L-1$. In (53) and (54) the Lagrange multiplier λ_t represents the marginal utility of wealth in period t and τ_{t+1} is the discount factor $[\phi(1+r_{t+1})]$. In equation (54) the marginal utility of wealth in each period can be seen to provide the link between current and other period decisions. Indeed, apart from the discount factor, each x_{it} is chosen in such a way that marginal utility is kept constant over the life-cycle. Rearranging (53) to express within period demands x_{it} in terms of $\mathbf{p}_t$ and λ_t generates the Frisch or λ-constant demand equations. In this formulation marginal utility λ_t acts as a summary of between period allocations and therefore performs the same function as y_t in (49) above representing the (expected) evolution of future variables. Each Frisch or λ-constant demand may then be written

$$x_{it} = f_{it}(\mathbf{p}_t, \lambda_t), \tag{55}$$

which is homogenous of degree zero in $\mathbf{p}_t$ and λ_t^{-1}.

The general properties of demand equations (55) are described in detail in Browning *et al.* (1985) and provide direct measures of the degree of intertemporal substitution. For example, the price derivatives of (55) conditional on λ_t represent the effect of fully anticipated price changes. An important advantage of using (55) directly is that the Euler equation (54) can be usefully exploited to eliminate λ_t in empirical implementation on time series or panel data. Under certain forms for (55) this will result in a system of first differenced commodity demand and labour supply functions similar to the surprise model above and attributable to the work of MaCurdy (1981*a*).

An equivalent derivation of the λ-constant model is given by Browning *et al.* (1985) using the individual's profit function defined by

$$\pi(\mathbf{p}_t, 1/\lambda_t) = \max_{U_t}[U_t/\lambda_t - C(\mathbf{p}_t, U_t)], \tag{56}$$

where $C(\mathbf{p}_t, U_t)$ is the consumer's expenditure or cost function as defined in Section I.1. The profit function $\pi(\mathbf{p}_t, 1/\lambda_t)$ is linear homogeneous in $\mathbf{p}_t$ and $1/\lambda_t$, decreasing in $\mathbf{p}_t$ and increasing in $1/\lambda_t$. The λ-constant demands are derived from the negative of the price derivatives of π, i.e.

$$x_{it} = -\partial \pi(\mathbf{p}_t, 1/\lambda_t)/\partial p_{it}. \tag{57}$$

Equations (57) are equivalent to demands derived from a rearrangement of (53).

In comparison to the y-conditional models of Section I.2 the λ-constant demands directly measure the parameters of intertemporal substitution and therefore require an explicit choice for the complete description of life-cycle utility (46). That is any system of λ-constant demands rests on the choice of a particular monotonic transformation of within period preferences. For example, if we represent within period preferences by a quasi-homothetic indirect utility with a *logarithmic* monotonic transformation (i.e. $G\{.\}$ is the log transformation and $\alpha = 1$ in (23)), then the marginal utility λ_t is simply given by

$$\lambda_t = 1/[y_t - a_t(\mathbf{p}_t)]. \tag{58}$$

In this case the λ-constant demands take the form

$$x_{it} = a_{it}(\mathbf{p}_t) + [b_{it}(\mathbf{p}_t)/b_t(\mathbf{p}_t)]\,\lambda_t^{-1}. \tag{59}$$

If time series or panel data were available λ_t could be written using (54) in terms of initial period marginal utility λ_0. If $b_{it}(\;)/b_t(\;)$ were constant as in the LES model, λ_0 would enter as a fixed or individual specific effect over the panel.

In most empirical representations of the life-cycle model the consumer is allowed to be uncertain about future prices, wages and other relevant future events. Revisions to life-cycle wealth occur as new information or 'surprises' arise. In this case it is *expected* life-cycle utility that is maximised and the Euler equation (54) is replaced by

$$\mathrm{E}_t(\tau_{t+1}\lambda_{t+1}) = \lambda_t. \tag{60}$$

Hansen and Singleton (1983) use this condition directly to derive an optimal estimator for the time separable model and we will discuss some further details of this approach in Section II.3. Combining (53) or (55) with (60) provides an extremely attractive framework for analysing life-cycle demand systems. For example, if we assume sufficient conditions on preferences so that marginal utility can be written in terms of real consumption alone then we can use (60) to generate the surprise consumption models described earlier.

As an illustration we can examine how (60) could generate the loglinear surprise models popularised by Breeden (1979), Mankiw *et al.* (1985) and Heckman and MaCurdy (1980) among others. We first assume that the distribution of $\tau_{t+1}\lambda_{t+1}$ can be approximated by a lognormal with (conditional) variance σ_t^2, so that $\mathrm{E}_t \ln(\tau_{t+1}\lambda_{t+1}) = \ln \mathrm{E}(\tau_{t+1}\lambda_{t+1}) + \frac{1}{2}\sigma_t^2$. Combining this result with (60) the consequent revision of λ_{t+1} is given by

$$\ln \lambda_{t+1} - \ln(\tau_{t+1}) = \ln \lambda_t + \tfrac{1}{2}\sigma_t^2 + e_{t+1}, \tag{61}$$

where e_{t+1} is a random variable representing all new information. Indeed, from condition (60), e_{t+1} is by definition independent of all information dated t or earlier. In the case where λ_t is a non-stochastic function of the expenditure variable y_t, (61) defines a straightforward dynamic process for y_t and therefore a dynamic process for life-cycle savings and consumption. Where $\ln \lambda$ can be assumed proportional to the log of consumption, (61) reduces to a simple first differenced log consumption model similar to (52) above. These models and the restrictions underlying them will be further discussed in Section II.3. Even though the models impose strong conditions on intertemporal and atemporal preferences, their simplicity and the properties of the innovation error e_{t+1} have made them popular in empirical research.

The underlying dynamics of the intertemporally separable models discussed above are not easy to extend in a theoretically consistent manner while retaining empirical tractability. Anderson and Blundell (1983, 1984), for example, start with the time separable specification of the y-conditional model and generalise that structure by allowing flexible interrelated dynamics. This assumes that the y-conditional model represents steady state behaviour but does not capture disequilibrium short-run responses. These '*ad hoc*' disequilibrium dynamic models clearly act as a useful test of intertemporal separability and can be partially rationalised in a life-cycle framework. However, where intertemporal separability is rejected their use in policy analysis is limited to the extent that they do not identify the separate sources of dynamic adjustment. For this objective some sort of theoretical model of short-run adjustment under uncertainty is required that relaxes the time separability assumption.

Deriving theoretical models that are fully consistent with life-cycle utility maximisation under costs of adjustment or habit persistence, for example, is in principle a straightforward extension of the previous discussion. The remainder of this section will briefly examine some of the rather more popular ways of relaxing the critical separability assumption. To begin with we will consider specifications where (expected) life-cycle utility (46) is replaced by

$$U_t^* = U_t(\mathbf{x}_t, \mathbf{x}_{t-1}) + \mathrm{E}_t[\Sigma_s \phi^{s-t} U_s(\mathbf{x}_s, \mathbf{x}_{s-1})], \tag{62}$$

where the presence of $\mathbf{x}_{t-1}$ may reflect adjustment costs in consumption (Weissenberger, 1983) or habit persistence (Pollak and Wales, 1982; Boyer, 1982; Phlips and Spinnewyn, 1981; Spinnewyn, 1981; and Muellbauer and Pashardes, 1982). The first order conditions are now written

$$\partial V_t/\partial x_{it} = \partial U_t/\partial x_{it} + \mathrm{E}_t\, \partial U_{t+1}/\partial x_{it} = \lambda_t p_{it} \tag{63}$$

with $\mathrm{E}_t(\tau_{t+1}\lambda_{t+1} - \lambda_t) = 0$ as before and retain homogeneity in terms of $1/\lambda_\tau$ and prices p_{it}.

Under certain circumstances the explicitly dynamic form of life-cycle expected utility considered in the model above can be reduced by a suitable transformation of variables into simple forms that correspond to those considered in the time separable case. For example, in the habit persistence model where utility in each period is defined over consumption after removing habitual consumption (see Pollak, 1970), (63) reduces to a system similar to the time separable Marshallian demand model. However, in this case each price term depends on the whole future of expected prices. Nevertheless, this model forms the basis of the useful studies of Spinnewyn (1981) and Muellbauer and Pashardes (1982).

As an alternative to the procedure of breaking time separability by adding in lags to the arguments of direct utility, Browning (1987*a*) has developed a useful class of non-separable models using the profit function representation of preferences. The idea is to extend the λ-constant or Frisch demands described above to include *prices* from other periods. That is we may wish to extend the profit function (56) so that each demand equation becomes

$$\mathbf{x}_t = f_t(\mathbf{p}_{t-1}, \mathbf{p}_t, \mathbf{p}_{t+1}, \lambda_t), \tag{64}$$

where $\mathbf{p}_{t+1}$ and $\mathbf{p}_{t-1}$ refer to appropriately discounted future and past prices. The reason for their inclusion is shown to derive from the form of the consumer's profit function under non-separability. If we write the profit function corresponding to period t preferences as $\pi(\mathbf{p}_{t-1}, \mathbf{p}_t, 1/\lambda_t)$, then the λ-constant demands are given by

$$\mathbf{x}_t = -\partial\pi_t/\partial\mathbf{p}_t - \mathrm{E}_t\,\partial\pi_{t+1}/\partial\mathbf{p}_t \tag{65}$$

analogous to (63) above. Since the Euler equation for λ_t is still valid the Hansen and Singleton approach to estimation can be adopted. The form of the profit function in this case is the mirror image of the habit persistence model with first order dynamics. Indeed, the form of (65) will often allow the elimination of λ_t using the within period budget constraint so that non-separable analogues to the y-conditional models can be recovered. Just as in the time separable model these may, in certain situations, turn out to be more useful in estimation than the corresponding Euler equation form. These issues and others will be raised in more detail in the next two sections where we turn to estimation and empirical evidence.

II. 3. *Preference Restrictions and Estimation in Intertemporally Separable Models*

In order to assess the restrictions underlying any specification of the life-cycle model, it is necessary to define a suitable measure of intertemporal substitution. Following Browning (1985), the elasticity which measures the λ-constant proportionate change in current period expenditure from a uniform change in current period prices can be written

$$\Phi = V_y/y\,.\,V_{yy}, \tag{66}$$

where V_y is the y-derivative of indirect utility. Interestingly, Φ is the inverse of the standard risk aversion measure since it reflects the concavity of the monotonic transformation of within period preferences. Consider, for example, the loglinear transformation of quasi-homothetic preferences (i.e. $G\{.\}$ is the log transformation and $\alpha = 1$ in (23)). The intertemporal elasticity is then given by

$$\Phi = -[y_t - a_t(\mathbf{p}_t)]/y_t. \tag{67}$$

Since this elasticity measure summarises intertemporal substitution behaviour it provides a useful way of evaluating the flexibility underlying particular forms for life-cycle models.

As we saw in Section II.2 there is no real need for the first order conditions underlying the intertemporally separable model to be linear or loglinear.

Indeed, the Euler equation approach laid out by Hansen and Singleton (1983) allows quite general nonlinear forms for marginal utility. However, nonlinear forms will generally require that time varying stochastic terms enter only through innovations in marginal utility. Where measurement error is likely to be serious one may wish to choose a linear differenced specification precisely because it can be seen to relax this restriction. Nevertheless, the linear or log-linear models have a cost in so far as rather tighter restrictions on within period and intertemporal substitution than one would usually like to assume are imposed.

For the estimation of λ-constant or Euler equation models an instrumental variable estimator is suggested directly from the properties of the innovation error $-e_{t+1}$ in (61), for example. As an illustration, consider the case where the demand equations from (53) or the derivatives of the profit function can be expressed with a term linear in $\ln \lambda_t$. This clearly contains the loglinear consumption models referred to above and as also noted above the unobservable marginal utility of wealth in such models can be eliminated by first differencing. The resulting differenced model now contains the innovation error e_{t+1} as part of its disturbance term. The conditional variance term may either be assumed constant or used to assess the importance of risk terms in consumption. Although e_{t+1} will not be independent of variables dated $t+1$ appearing on the right-hand side of the differenced model that are not fully anticipated, it will be independent of variables dated t or earlier. Provided there are no time aggregation problems (see Hall, 1985, for discussion), a simple consistent estimator can therefore be derived using variables dated t or earlier as instruments. In their generalisation of this linear estimator, Hansen and Singleton (1983) exploit the orthogonality condition underlying the Euler condition to derive a general nonlinear instrumental variable estimator.

Empirical applications to individual expenditure or labour supply decisions have generally required the λ-constant demands take the form:

$$g(x_{it}) = \mathbf{d}_i' \mathbf{f}(\mathbf{p}_t) + \gamma_i \ln \lambda_t, \tag{68}$$

where $g(.)$ is a log or linear transformation, $\mathbf{d}_i$ is a vector of constant unknown parameters for the ith equation and $\mathbf{f}(\mathbf{p}_t)$ is a known function of $\mathbf{p}_t$. Using (61) the model may then be written (assuming a constant discount factor) as the following linear differenced specification

$$\Delta g(x_{it}) = \mathbf{d}_i' \Delta \mathbf{f}_t(\mathbf{p}_t) + \gamma_i e_{t+1}. \tag{69}$$

This equation represents a reasonably typical form for empirical versions of the time separable λ-constant equation models under uncertainty. For example, Attfield and Browning (1985) rather neatly exploit the symmetry and homogeneity restrictions on a system of λ-constant demands to derive consistent estimators of the $\mathbf{d}_i$ parameters.

A number of recent papers (Blundell *et al.*, 1985; Browning, 1986; and Nickell, 1986) have noted restrictions imposed on life-cycle and within period preferences from estimating models of the form (68) and (69). Working with the loglinear transformation for $g(.)$, the form of (69) generally requires the utility derivative in (53) be a function of x_{it} alone. That is, U_t must be *explicitly* additive over time and goods. In this case the general form for λ-constant demands takes the form

$$\ln x_{it} = \gamma_i \ln \alpha_i - \gamma_i \ln p_{it} - \gamma_i \ln \lambda_t \tag{70}$$

as in Heckman and MaCurdy (1980). This explicit additivity restriction on atemporal preferences may be generalised but only at the expense of assuming homothetic preferences. That is, relaxing additivity in (70) requires unitary within period full income elasticities. For demand equations linear in x_{it}, Browning *et al.* (1985) use the profit function to derive an alternative class of models. Moreover, their class of models implies neither explicit additivity nor homothetic preferences. It does, however, impose some strong restrictions on within period and intertemporal preferences.

The λ-constant demands corresponding to (68) in the Browning *et al.* class are of the form

$$x_{it} = n_i(\mathbf{p}_t) - k_i \ln p_{it} - k_i - k_i \ln \lambda_t, \tag{71}$$

where $n_i(\mathbf{p}_t)$ is the ith price (or wage) derivative of a general linear homogeneous function of prices $n(\mathbf{p}_t)$ and k_i is some unknown parameter. Since n_i can contain price interactions additivity is relaxed. Within period preferences are quasi-homothetic (see (9)) with necessary costs are given by

$$a(\mathbf{p}_t) = n(\mathbf{p}_t) - \Sigma_i k_i p_{it} \ln [p_{it}/(\Sigma_i k_i p_{it})] - \Sigma_i k_i p_{it} \tag{72}$$

and the price index for supernumerary consumption is given by

$$b(\mathbf{p}_t) = \Sigma_i k_i p_{it}. \tag{73}$$

As $b(\mathbf{p}_t)$ describes the substitution possibilities for richer individuals (those with large supernumerary consumption) the Leontief form for $b(\mathbf{p}_t)$ implies these substitution effects tend to zero as consumption increases. Intertemporal preferences are also restricted through this choice of preferences. To see this consider the corresponding indirect utility function which has exponential form

$$V_t = -\exp\{-[y_t - a(\mathbf{p}_t)]/b(\mathbf{p}_t)\} \tag{74}$$

implying an intertemporal elasticity $\Phi_t = -b_t(\mathbf{p}_t)/y_t$. Although, the intertemporal elasticity Φ in this exponential case is always negative it approaches zero as the income allocation y_t increases. For an arbitrarily rich household therefore this intertemporal elasticity of substitution is zero. This contrasts rather dramatically with the loglinear transformation whose corresponding intertemporal elasticity is given in (67) and which is bounded between zero and -1 approaching -1 as the income allocation y_t rises. The loglinear transformation allows the elasticity to grow away from zero with increasing income whereas the exponential transformation assumes the opposite.

It is useful to contrast these approaches with the alternatives that recover life-cycle consistent within period preferences by substituting out the unobservable marginal utility of wealth across two or more contemporaneous decisions (see Altonji, 1982, 1983) or eliminate it using the within period budget constraint (see Betancourt, 1971; Blundell and Walker, 1986; and MaCurdy, 1983). Where the monotonic transformation of within period preferences is fixed and not estimated as in the log case (59) or the explicitly additive case (70), the parameters estimated from such alternative representations are sufficient to identify all intertemporal substitution elasticities. Moreover, these estimates of within period preferences are invariant to the choice of monotonic transformation. In general one should attempt to work with a specification that breaks the tight structure placed on preferences in the models described above. However, as was noted above as soon as a nonlinear Euler equation is specified estimation requires tighter restrictions on the stochastic components of the model.

In an interesting application, MaCurdy (1983) uses standard Marshallian demands to recover within period preference parameters as in the alternative procedures described above. Given these parameters the remaining intertemporal parameters are estimated from the Euler condition. This seems possibly the most attractive estimation procedure for the time separable model. In the case of the quasi-homothetic model, this would involve estimating the y-conditional model and constructing $[y_t - a_t(\mathbf{p}_t)]/b_t(\mathbf{p}_t)$ for each time period of data available (having chosen a normalisation for the parameters of $b_t(\mathbf{p}_t)$). If we define this variable as real supernumerary outlay (income) y_t^r then, introducing new intertemporal parameters α_t and β, we could define a suitable monotonic transformation of within period preferences as

$$V_t = \alpha_t (y_t^r)^\beta / \beta \quad (\beta < 1) \tag{75}$$

similar to the transformation of within period preferences adopted by MaCurdy (1983). In this case the intertemporal elasticity of substitution Φ equals $(1 - a_t/y_t)/(\beta - 1)$ and marginal utility is given by

$$\lambda_t = \alpha_t (y_t^r)^{\beta - 1} / b_t(\mathbf{p}_t). \tag{76}$$

Using the Euler equation for λ_τ described by (60) we can then identify β and α_t from a first difference model of the form

$$\Delta \ln y_t^r = \rho \Delta \ln \alpha_t - \rho \Delta \ln b_t(\mathbf{p}_t) + \rho \ln \tau_t - e_t, \tag{77}$$

where $\rho = 1/(1-\beta)$. The intertemporal parameters can probably be most effectively recovered using panel data observations given the estimates of $b_t(\cdot)$ and y_t^r. Of course, there is no reason why quasi-homothetic preferences should be adopted and it may be preferred to recover within period preferences from a general nonlinear demand system of the PIGL type.

As one might have inferred from the discussion of equation (61) above, the log differenced model (72) relates directly to the loglinear 'surprise' consumption–savings models. To be able to define y_t over consumption expenditure alone we have already seen that consumption and labour supply have to be assumed explicitly additively separable in the life-cycle utility. Then, setting $a(\mathbf{p})$ to zero and approximating $b(\mathbf{p})$ by the retail price index, y_t^r becomes equal to real consumers' expenditure c_t and (77) may be written

$$\Delta \ln c_t = \rho \Delta \ln \alpha_t + \rho(\ln \tau_t - \Delta \ln b_t) + e_t. \tag{78}$$

Since $\ln \tau_t \simeq r_t - \delta$ the second term on the right-hand side of (78) is equivalent to the real interest term introduced by Muellbauer (1983) and Wickens and

Molana (1984). The intertemporal elasticity Φ is now directly measured by $-\rho$. However, current dated variables in (78) may still be correlated with the error term and as a result instrumental variable estimation is required to recover the intertemporal substitution parameters consistently. Where there are many assets with uncertain returns, an Euler equation of the form (78) will exist for each asset (see Hansen and Singleton, 1983) and $-\rho$ will continue to measure the intertemporal elasticity. However, multiple asset information enables the degree of risk aversion to be separately identified (see Hall, 1985).

Where labour supply is included in estimation (or where explicit additive separability between time and goods is not assumed) rationing in the labour market from one period to the next will be reflected in the determination of savings or consumption behaviour through the price aggregators $a(.)$ and $b(.)$. In periods where constraints occur, unconstrained elements of $\mathbf{x}_t$ will depend on the level of the rationed goods through the virtual price or wage. In this case these prices (and wages) for rationed goods can be replaced in the Euler condition for the unrationed demands by virtual price or wage. This provides a simple way of introducing unemployment or rationing into the savings function as has been suggested by King (1985) among others. Once explicit additivity between goods and leisure in life-cycle utility is relaxed, the level of labour supply or the wage in any period directly affects the marginal utility of consumption in that period. In this case the life-cycle consumption path will not be smoothed independently of labour market decisions and falls in consumption may occur during periods of unemployment or during retirement.

II. 4. *Aggregation, Excess Sensitivity and the Evaluation of Empirical Evidence*

Aggregation. In order to assess the empirical evidence on life-cycle and dynamic behaviour and the debates therein it is worth extending the aggregation issues described in Section I.4 to cover the case of intertemporal models. The work of Stoker (1986) referred to in that section could have a particularly important bearing here because of the dynamic misspecification he observed when estimating aggregate consumption–income models. Similarly, corner solutions rationing and liquidity constraints may well lead to misspecification at the aggregate level. More importantly perhaps for aggregation are the stationarity assumptions that need to be placed on the evolution of the population over time. These assumptions essentially rule out cohort-specific effects since the 'representative consumer' results only hold if new individuals take the place of individuals leaving the sample. Also related to the aggregation issue is the argument by King (1986) for a piecewise nonlinear Euler equation reflecting the nonlinear nature of the interest rate facing individuals as they move from saving to higher levels of borrowing. All of these arguments suggest that analysis at a more micro or at least cohort-based level would be preferable. However, there is no one micro data set that is ideally suited to all aspects of life-cycle modelling and therefore it is worth going through each of these issues in order to assess their likely impact on aggregate estimates of consumption behaviour.

Turning first to aggregation in the simple Euler equation model we work within a linear model since nonlinear models will not generally aggregate except where there are sufficient restrictions placed on the evolution of the mean in relation to the other moments of the distribution (see Section I.4). If utility is exponential and additive across goods (see MaCurdy, 1986, for example), the λ-constant demand for household h corresponding to (70) has the form

$$x_{it,h} = n_{it,h} - k_i \ln p_{it} - k_i \ln \lambda_{t,h}, \tag{79}$$

which is a restrictive form of the Browning *et al.* (1985) model (see equation (71)). Indeed, where prices are constant across individuals in any time period the complete Browning *et al.* (1985) model will aggregate in the manner described below. This is assuming all individual specific characteristics enter linearly in (79). Before aggregation can take place we also require conditions on the stochastic terms entering the following individual level Euler equation

$$\ln \lambda_{t,h} = \ln \tau_t + \ln \lambda_{t+1,h} + e_{t+1,h}. \tag{80}$$

Splitting $e_{t+1,h}$ into its macro component and micro component, u_{t+1} and $\epsilon_{t+1,h}$ respectively, and provided these two components are mutually independent, (79) and (80) can be written

$$X_{it+1} - X_{it} = -k_i \ln \tau_t + N_{it+1} - N_{it} + k_i(\ln P_{it+1} - \ln P_{it}) + u_{t+1}, \tag{81}$$

where X_{it+1} refers to per capita summation of $x_{it+1,h}$ over the population and so on.

In deriving (81) it is implicitly assumed that it is the same individuals in each period over which aggregation occurs. If they are not the same then certain stationarity assumptions are required. Essentially new entrants must take the place (in terms of intertemporal preferences and wealth) of those leaving the population. This precludes cohort-specific effects and suggests that aggregation over individuals by cohort may be more acceptable. However, aggregation of this type (as adopted by Browning *et al.*, 1985) requires accurate cohort level data. This would usually be built up from cross-section surveys in which case it may be better to use the individual survey level data directly to estimate in two steps following the procedure suggested for equation (77). Indeed, we might well expect preferences to change across cohorts and the proportion of the population in any stage of the life-cycle to change over time. In this case it is risky to assume that a linear differenced model of the form (81), even if true at the micro level, will accurately estimate the intertemporal price elasticity (k_i in equation (79)) from aggregate data. Adding in factors to capture the changes in the higher order moments of the characteristics of the population may at least indicate the degree of bias.

Where corner solutions, rationing or piecewise linear marginal rates of return prevail, aggregation problems become quite severe. As an illustration consider first the corner solution case developed for the intertemporal labour supply model by MaCurdy (1985). Following the framework developed for aggregating over corner solutions in Section I.4 we define an indicator variable I_{th} which equals unity if there is an interior solution and zero for a corner solution. Underlying this indicator is the latent variable $I^*_{th} = \mathbf{z}'_{th}\boldsymbol{\beta} + v_{th}$ as in equation (37). Assuming the linear specification (79) is valid for the commodity in question, observed expenditure is now given by

$$x_{th} = I_{th}\, n_{th} - kI_{th} \ln P_t - kI_{th} \ln \lambda_{th}. \tag{82}$$

Corresponding to equation (36) is the aggregate difference equation

$$\Delta X_t = I_t N_t - I_{t-1} N_{t-1} - k(I_t \ln P_t - I_{t-1} \ln P_{t-1}) + k \ln \tau_t + \theta_t - \theta_{t-1} + e_t, \tag{83}$$

where N_t again refers to the per buyer average and where θ_t is again proportional to the normal density evaluated at $\mathbf{Z}'_t\boldsymbol{\beta}$. Clearly there is no longer an aggregate linear difference equation and in particular $\theta_t - \theta_{t-1}$ cannot be written in terms of the difference in $\mathbf{Z}_t$. As a result, interpreting the coefficient on $\ln P_t - \ln P_{t-1}$ in (81) as a measure of intertemporal elasticity in the case where there is rationing or corner solutions is likely to be unreliable.

These illustrations highlight the problems of aggregation in life-cycle models where individuals can be in different regimes of behaviour. Another example of this can arise under liquidity constraints. Indeed, where liquidity constraints act as a binding constraint on behaviour – borrowing constrained to be less than net worth would be a good example – a problem much like the corner solution case occurs and a similar analysis of aggregation bias will prevail. Where there exists a wedge between borrowing and lending rates of interest, King (1986) has developed a useful asymmetric information model. In this model the borrowing rate exceeds the lending rate and borrowers may default but are monitored so as not to exploit the consequences of default. The consumer may either then choose to lend, stay at the kink point determined by the wedge, borrow with no risk of default or borrow with risk. In equilibrium this leads to four regimes of behaviour and in each case a different Euler equation.

Working within the Euler equation (77), those households who are neither at a kink or in risk of default find this wedge alters the discount factor τ_t so as to reflect the appropriate borrowing or lending rate. For those at the kink, on the other hand, the next period consumption level simply equals the next period exogenous expected income plus forecast error. Finally, for those in risk of default – borrowing in excess of net worth – a probability term is incorporated to reflect the chance of default occurring in which case only a basic 'subsistence' consumption level is achieved. These regimes are clearly endogenous just as in the corner solution case and aggregation would again involve summing across regimes much as in (83) above.

The evidence. As in the discussion of disaggregate models in Section I, I have used this survey to evaluate the interplay between theoretical and empirical considerations rather than providing a catalogue of empirical estimates. To date the evidence on intertemporal elasticities is mixed and from our discussion above may simply reveal the underlying nature of the model being estimated rather than the process underlying the data itself. For this reason the studies described below will refer more to *evaluation* rather than estimation of the life-cycle model and will also reflect the bias in this survey towards micro-data-based models. The literature in this area is still in its infancy and has generally focused on the degree to which the simplest of the intertemporally separable models described above can adequately summarise the path of consumers' expenditure. It has largely ignored the issue of time separability and the interaction of goods with labour supply decisions, emphasising instead the importance of liquidity constraints and the implied excess sensitivity of consumption to movements in current disposable income.

These are indeed important issues and perhaps the most impressive recent contributions to this debate are those of Hall and Mishkin (1982), Hayashi (1985), Blinder and Deaton (1985), Deaton (1985), Altonji and Siow (1985), Altonji *et al.* (1986), Muellbauer and Bover (1986), MaCurdy (1986), Mariger (1987*a*, *b*) and Campbell and Deaton (1987). These studies use a variety of data sources both at the aggregate and individual level. There is general agreement that time separable models of the form given by (78) do not provide a complete description of intertemporal behaviour, at least for a significant group of consumers. Why this is so and how robust these results are is, however, more difficult to assess. Broadly speaking liquidity constraints provide an argument for excess sensitivity of consumption to current income innovations while habits or more generally lagged consumption terms lead to further smoothing. Of course, relaxation of the explicit additivity assumption between leisure and goods is sufficient to bring current income terms into these consumption models, even if labour supply is rationed. Nevertheless, the evidence for liquidity constraints in certain groups in the population – the young or unemployed – is reasonably compelling. As are habits for certain types of goods.

As Campbell and Deaton (1987) point out so clearly, the simple time separable life-cycle model is really defined by both the consumption and income process. Statements concerning the properties of the innovation error on such a consumption function relate directly to the income process since as we saw from equation (52) it is innovations to this process which drive the innovations to life-cycle wealth and in turn the marginal utility of wealth which underlies the stochastic Euler equation. If it is income innovations alone – and not liquidity constraints or habits – which drive the first difference of consumption then they should not be predictable from past income (or any other) information. Of course, time aggregation problems can cloud this simple condition, but leaving these aside the force of this point focuses attention on the *joint* process of both consumption and income. It is the study of this joint process that allows the *evaluation* rather than simply the *estimation* of the underlying model.

Although panel data provide possibly the best environment for this analysis, Altonji and Siow (1985) have emphasised the contaminating effects of measurement errors in dynamic panel data models. This is particularly true of the expenditure data from the Michigan PSIO panel used in the panel data studies of household income and consumption reported in the papers of Hall and Mishkin (1982) and Altonji and Siow (1985). Moreover, these data only record weekly expenditures on food derived from an annual average figure and provide little other information on commodity expenditure.

Hall and Mishkin (1982) assume a constant real return on assets and work with a model similar in essence to (51) and (52). They allow for two types of innovation in real income by splitting nondeterministic income into two stochastic components μ_t^L representing fluctuations in lifetime prospects and μ_t^S representing transitory influences. This is a useful distinction since we may expect μ_t^L to follow a random walk while μ_t^S could well be a moving average of past transitory innovations. Under the life-cycle model, the impact of these innovations on the nondeterministic part of consumption should be equivalent to the annuity value of the added wealth implied by a unit amount of unexpected transitory income – the real interest rate under an infinite horizon. If this can be measured accurately then the life-cycle hypothesis can be tested by examining the coefficient of such a variable in the first differenced consumption model since the transitory components enter as one part in the innovation error process. Indeed if we redefine c_t to be real consumption in period t after having removed all deterministic components (i.e. the effect of age, demographics, trend...) then, under a quadratic utility assumption with constant real interest rates, the form for the marginal utility in (60) will be linear in c_t. Moreover from this Euler equation or more directly from (52) the change in c_t is simply given by

$$\Delta c_t = \epsilon_t + \beta_t n_t, \tag{84}$$

where n_t is the transitory income component, β_t is the annuity value described above and Δ is the first difference operator. The stochastic component ϵ_t is simply the innovation in μ_t^L. This approach of splitting the innovation in 'surprise' consumption function into its various separate factors has some considerable attraction for interpreting rational expectations models of this form. However, it should be noted at the outset that the innovation error property in these models that implies independence with past information is valid for expectations taken over time and not across agents. This point, noted by Hayashi (1985*b*), may have important implications for 'Euler equation' models of this type estimated on short panels.

To identify the components on the right-hand side of (84) separately the deterministic path for real income is first estimated so that the sum of the nondeterministic components μ_t^L and μ_t^S can be constructed. Calling this sum μ_t, the innovations ϵ_t and n_t enter the update of μ_t quite simply as

$$\Delta \mu_t = \epsilon_t + n_t - n_{t-1}, \tag{85}$$

where it is assumed $\Delta \mu_t^L = \epsilon_t$ and where $\mu_t^S = n_t$ is assumed serially uncorrelated. This equation can then be used to show that the variance of $\Delta \mu_t$ is the variance of ϵ_t (σ_ϵ^2) plus twice the variance of n_t (σ_n^2) while, from (85), the covariance of $\Delta \mu_t$ and $\Delta \mu_{t-1}$ is simply $-\sigma_n^2$.

Since the consumption measure in the panel data used by Hall and Mishkin refers to food they could not use (84) directly but by defining α to be the marginal propensity of food consumption out of permanent income, they rewrite (84) as

$$\Delta c_t = \alpha \epsilon_t + \alpha \beta n_t, \tag{86}$$

where the assumption of constant β_t over time is also being made. Combining (85) and (86) we can evaluate the contemporaneous covariance of Δc_t and

$\Delta\mu_t$ as $\alpha\sigma_\epsilon^2 + \alpha\beta\sigma_n^2$. Defining this to be C_0 and defining C_1 to be the corresponding covariance of Δc_t and $\Delta\mu_{t+1}$, which from (85) and (86) equals $-\alpha\beta\sigma_n^2$, it is easy to see that

$$\alpha = (C_0 + C_1)/\sigma_\epsilon^2 \tag{87}$$

and

$$\beta = (\alpha\sigma_n^2)^{-1}. \tag{88}$$

The procedure used by Hall and Mishkin to test the underlying model is to evaluate the sample analogues of (87) and (88) in order to estimate α and β. In doing so they allow for measurement error in consumption as well as a more general process for the evolution of transitory income. Indeed, they also allow for advance information about income.

Although the Hall and Mishkin estimates are sensitive to this latter point, the main result is an estimate of the marginal food propensity α at around 0·11 and an estimate of β around 0·29. Since the average propensity for food is approximately 0·19, food is a necessity as expected. However, the value for β is unreasonably high given its annuity value interpretation. The closer β is to unity the more excessively sensitive current consumption is to transitory income innovations. Even though β is larger than expected, the completely liquidity constrained case where consumption equalled current income and β equals unity, is clearly rejected.

In the light of these results they investigate the impact of $\Delta\mu_{t-1}$ on Δc_t, which in the life-cycle model should be zero but would be significant under liquidity constraints or excess sensitivity. They discover a small significant negative coefficient. Rewriting the model to allow a fraction δ of consumption to have β equal to 1, they find a δ of 0·2 and an estimate of β for the remaining consumption equal to 0·174, a much more reasonable value, while α remains precisely estimated at 0·1. The results therefore suggest that around 20% of consumption does not follow the simple life-cycle hypothesis and Hall and Mishkin interpret this as evidence of liquidity constraints. Hayashi (1985*a*) finds similar evidence for liquidity constraints in his study of a Japanese panel of household expenditures.

If liquidity constraints are important, consumption and therefore borrowing will be depressed, which in turn suggests that saving will be too large. Moreover, the relative efficiency loss of income taxation in comparison with a consumption tax is reduced since liquidity constrained individuals behave as if they had a zero intertemporal substitution elasticity. The importance of liquidity constraints and the validity of the life-cycle model are therefore crucial to policy considerations and the Hall and Mishkin results have stimulated a number of further studies. One drawback of their results is that only two extremes of behaviour – either on the life-cycle path or on the current income constrained path – are allowed. Mariger (1987*a*, *b*) has recently developed a rather more attractive model of liquidity constraints in which current income constrained behaviour is only an extreme in a continuum of liquidity constrained positions. Here, as in the King model described earlier, liquidity constraints do not necessarily force consumption to relate directly to the contemporaneous level of disposable income alone.

Panel data on individual households seem by far the most reasonable source for both evaluating and estimating models of dynamic consumer behaviour. Indeed, Hall and Mishkin note 'aggregate data is not really powerful enough to settle the important questions about the behaviour of consumers'. Nevertheless, the shortness of typically available panels and the likely importance of measurement error could weaken the conclusions drawn from such sources. We have seen that issues such as corner solutions and constraints are not overcome in aggregate data; rather they are 'covered up'. However, measurement error, at least in linear models, can be reduced by grouping and it is useful to assess the robustness of the results described above to such error. Altonji and Siow (1985) and Altonji *et al.* (1986) using data drawn from the same source as Hall and Mishkin derive estimates for the factors on the right-hand side of equations like (86) using additional information from other determinants of income – for example, wage rates, employment and other labour market information. Although these are also contaminated with measurement error, the extra information they contain provides a way of estimating parameters like β consistently even though the income process itself suffers from measurement error. With the information used in the Hall and Mishkin study, β cannot be identified when μ_t is measured with error. Since measurement error in the Michigan panel may explain more than 50% of the variance in $D\mu_t$ this is a severe drawback. The Altonji *et al.* studies confirm the rejection of the current income constrained model ($\beta = 1$) but do not find the same evidence of liquidity constraints. This suggests that the importance of the lagged income term found by Hall and Mishkin may not be robust. It may well indicate the short panel bias noted by Hayashi (1985*b*) and referred to above. The fact that Altonji and Siow use a longer time series of the Michigan panel is also supportive of this view.

Rather than estimating β directly, Altonji and Siow estimate the implied discount factor for consumers with infinite horizon. The estimates display considerable variation and range from −0·04 to 1·6 underlining the difficulty of recovering precise estimates after dealing with measurement problems in panel data. These may be compared to the corresponding estimated discount factor in the Hall and Mishkin model of around 0·77.

Focusing on the discount factor and with it the time horizon provides a useful approach for analysing more general dynamic models with liquidity constraints. Mariger (1987*b*), for example, presents a description of a framework in which there is a minimum net worth constraint below which households cannot borrow. This type of 'asymmetric' model is close in spirit to that of King (1986) and suggests that one sensible way of viewing liquidity constraints is through their impact on the 'optimal' time horizon. Using two cross-sections of survey data Mariger finds that only a very small percentage of households face one period horizons which would correspond to the extreme current income liquidity constraint used by Hall and Mishkin (1982) and Hayashi (1985*b*) among others. Instead, many consumers have horizons much less than their remaining lifetime but are able to incur some intertemporal substitution. This could well explain much of the observed variation in discount factors alluded to above and such models are worthy of further analysis.

Whether or not consumption is excessively sensitive to current income innovations, it is useful to ask whether we might expect the resulting consumption series to be smoother or more variable than otherwise. The answer to this question depends critically on the relative smoothness of current compared with permanent income. Campbell and Deaton (1987) in a persuasive study of post-war US aggregate income and consumption patterns not only confirm the excess sensitivity result of Hall and Mishkin but also note that the underlying smoothness of the current income process leads additionally to excess smoothing of consumption. This paper neatly ties together these apparently contradictory criticisms of the simple life-cycle model and sets the scene for a more extensive analysis of the other issues underlying life-cycle models that have been mentioned above.

Rather than providing a complete description of empirical estimates of intertemporal elasticities I will finish this section by summarising the results from the Blundell and Walker (1986) study. In that paper intertemporal elasticities for male and female labour supply as well as consumption are presented. Within period preferences in that study are assumed to be quasi-homothetic of the form described in equation (75) with β equal zero. We can compare these intertemporal elasticities with those under more general assumptions concerning β. These elasticities are presented in Table 4 where the

Table 4
*Some Intertemporal Elasticities**

β	Sample	Elasticities			
		E_{ff}	E_{mm}	E_{qq}	Φ
0	(*a*)	0·191	0·020	−0·171	−0·069
	(*b*)	0·080	0·046	−0·175	−0·130
	(*c*)	0·025	0·024	−0·137	−0·077
0·5	(*a*)	0·618	0·078	−0·496	−0·138
	(*b*)	0·299	0·106	−0·520	−0·160
	(*c*)	0·236	0·082	−0·507	−0·154
0·75	(*a*)	0·808	0·106	−0·659	−0·276
	(*b*)	0·408	0·135	−0·693	−0·520
	(*c*)	0·354	0·110	−0·692	−0·308

* E_{ff} and E_{mm} refer to labour supply elasticities. Source: Blundell (1986).

E_{ff}, E_{mm} and E_{qq} columns are the own female, male and goods λ-constant elasticities. These relate to the standard Marshallian price and income elasticities (e_{ij} and η_i respectively) by $E_{ij} = e_{ij} + \eta_i \eta_j s_j \Phi + \eta_i s_j$ where s_j is the share of good j. Again Φ is the overall λ-constant elasticity defined in Section II.3. The samples (*a*), (*b*) and (*c*) refer to three groups of households from data on families with working women. Group (*a*) are families with two children aged 5 years or older, group (*b*) are families where all children have left home and group (*c*) are the total sample of 1,378 families with working women. These 3 groups were chosen from the 7 presented in the original study since they adequately displayed the range in intertemporal elasticities. Allowing β to rise towards unity increases, as expected, the absolute value of all elasticities but even for group (*c*) the male labour supply elasticities are small and the female elasticities remain below unity. The elasticities for consumption are of the correct sign and lie in a similar range. These estimates also appear of the same order as those reported in Altonji (1983) and Browning *et al.* (1985). The intertemporal elasticity Φ again is of the correct sign and is close to the values suggested in the study by Browning (1985).

The general conclusion from micro-data studies, although far from definitive, must be that the overall intertemporal substitution elasticity is small and probably less than $-0{\cdot}5$. Referring to the commodity-specific λ-constant intertemporal elasticities, that for the labour supply of prime-aged men is small and imprecise, the corresponding elasticities for married women are larger but more various and mirror the pattern of the consumption elasticity. However, given the discussion earlier in this survey we might expect the ranges of these reported elasticities to be somewhat constrained by the underlying preference restrictions.

CONCLUSIONS AND LESSONS

To suggest that this survey has provided or could have provided anything but a glimpse at a rapidly expanding area would be foolish. Moreover, the view taken has been biased towards the perspective of demand analysis – stressing the importance of preference restrictions and questioning the interpretation of models using aggregate data. Much to the annoyance of many I have shied away from providing a catalogue of empirical estimates choosing instead to emphasise the interplay between theory and empirical analysis that can be found in the more exciting recent developments in this field. This was not just for reasons of space but also to underline a belief that much is still to be learned and received results, although useful, could hardly be considered definitive.

The increasing availability of micro or individual level data has forced the student of applied consumer behaviour to consider many new aspects of analysis hitherto overlooked. Rationing, corner solutions, infrequency of purchase and liquidity constraints are among those that have been emphasised in this survey and can be expected to form the motivation for many new publications in the field. Our increased knowledge of individual level behaviour has focused attention once again on the conditions under which simple relationships between aggregate measures can be justified. It is not satisfactory, for example, to assume that all individual consumers are either liquidity constrained or not, rationed in the labour market or not, etc. It is more likely that individuals switch in and out of these different regimes of behaviour and that in any population at any one period no one relationship holds for all consumers. As has been emphasised throughout this survey, aggregate models that ignore these issues do so at their peril. Resulting policy prescriptions for tax reform or fiscal policy, for example, will, in general, be misleading.

Perhaps one of the most attractive areas of current research – certainly one of the most popular – is the further development of intertemporal models. For example, knowledge of intertemporal substitution elasticities is crucial to the debate on the taxation of consumption versus income. In this survey I have tried to put this research in the context of general consumer demand analysis so as to emphasise the importance of preference restrictions underlying many popular empirical models that have been used to bring evidence to bear on this debate. We have seen that many models assume explicit additivity between consumption and labour market decisions implying that the marginal utility of consumption in any period is essentially independent of labour market considerations. Thus apart from an overall wealth effect, periods of retirement or unemployment are assumed to have no impact on the path of consumption. Additivity and separability conditions more generally were shown to be crucially important here. Liquidity constraints have a similar implication for the importance of current (earned) income in consumption decisions and we can expect (or hope for) many new empirical and theoretical results in this area.

Devising methods for cutting through the strong assumptions that underlie many applications of consumer behaviour while maintaining empirical tractability has been a focal point of this survey. We have shown that the evaluation of models is rarely the sole domain of empirical analysis. Understanding the theoretical properties of the model can be equally rewarding. The parameters of interest from a theoretical, and indeed, policy point of view may be overshadowed in absolute size and statistical significance by other determinants of behaviour but may be no less important.

Many aspects of consumer behaviour have been unavoidably omitted in this survey. Notable among these is the importance of durables – especially in intertemporal models where the level of net worth has been shown to play such an important role. Similarly, we have omitted certain new developments in the testing of consumer theory. Perhaps most significant is the work of Varian (1982, 1983) on non-parametric testing. For this reason an extensive bibliography is included, many papers of which are unfortunately not referred to directly in this survey.

Bibliography

Abbott, M. and Ashenfelter, O. (1976). 'Labour supply, commodity demands, and the allocation of time.' *Review of Economic Studies*, vol. 43, pp. 389–411.

Altonji, J. G. (1982). 'The intertemporal substitution model of labour market fluctuations: an empirical analysis.' *Review of Economic Studies*, vol. 49, pp. 783–824.

—— (1983). 'Intertemporal substitution in labour supply: evidence from micro-data.' Columbia University Working Paper. *Journal of Political Economy*, vol. 94 (3.2), pp. S176–S215.

—— Martins, A. P. and Siow, A. (1986). 'Dynamic factor models of consumption, hours and income.' Mimeo, North Western University, November.

—— and Siow, A. (1985). 'Testing the response of consumption to income changes with (noisy) panel data.' IRS Working Paper 186, Princeton University, forthcoming *Quarterly Journal of Economics*.

Amemiya, T. (1973). 'Regression analysis when the dependent variable is a truncated normal.' *Econometrica*, vol. 41, pp. 1193–205.

Anderson, G. J. and Blundell, R. W. (1982). 'Estimation and hypothesis testing in dynamic singular equation systems.' *Econometrica*, vol. 50, pp. 1559–71.

—— and —— (1983). 'Testing restrictions in a flexible dynamic demand system: an application to consumers expenditure in Canada.' *Review of Economic Studies*, vol. 50, pp. 397–410.

Anderson, G. W. and Blundell, R. W. (1984). 'Consumer non-durables in the UK: a dynamic demand system.' ECONOMIC JOURNAL (Conference Papers), pp. 35–44.
—— and —— (1985). 'Empirical approaches to dynamic consumer demand.' McMaster University Economics Discussion Paper 85-16.
—— and Browning, M. (1985). 'Allocating expenditure: demand systems and the consumption function, an integrated approach.' Mimeo, McMaster University, December.
Anderson, R. W. (1979). 'Perfect price aggregation and empirical demand analysis.' *Econometrica*, vol. 47, pp. 1209–30.
Ando, A. and Modigliani, F. (1963). 'The life-cycle hypothesis of saving: aggregate implications and tests.' *American Economic Review*, vol. 53, pp. 55–84.
Ashenfelter, O. and Ham, J. (1979). 'Education, unemployment and earnings.' *Journal of Political Economy*, vol. 87, pp. S99–S166.
Atkinson, A. B. and Stern, N. (1980). 'On the switch from direct to indirect taxation.' *Journal of Public Economics*, vol. 14, pp. 195–224.
——, Gomulka, J. and Stern, N. (1984). 'Household expenditure on tobacco 1970–1980.' London School of Economics ESRC Programme on Taxation, Incentives and the Distribution of Income, Discussion Paper 57.
Attfield, C. L. F. (1985). 'Homogeneity and endogenity in systems of demand equations.' *Journal of Econometrics*, vol. 27, pp. 197–210.
—— and Browning M. J. (1985). 'A differential demand system, rational expectations and the life-cycle hypothesis.' *Econometrica*, vol. 53, pp. 31–48.
Baker, P., Blundell, R. W. and Micklewright, J. W. (1987). 'Modelling energy demand and household welfare using micro data.' UCL Discussion Paper in Economics, 87-14, ECONOMIC JOURNAL.
Barten, A. P. (1964). 'Family composition, prices and expenditure patterns.' In *Colston Papers*, vol. 16. Butterworths.
Bean, C. (1986). 'The estimation of "surprise" models and the "surprise" consumption function.' *Review of Economic Studies*, vol. 53, pp. 497–516.
Benanke, B. S. (1985). 'Adjustment costs, durables and aggregate consumption.' *Journal of Monetary Economics*, vol. 15, pp. 41–68.
Betancourt, R. R. (1971). 'Intertemporal allocation under additive preferences: implications for cross-section data.' *Southern Economic Journal*, vol. 37, pp. 458–68.
Bewley, T. (1977). 'The permanent income hypothesis: a theoretical formulation.' *Journal of Economic Theory*, vol. 16, pp. 252–92.
Blackorby, C., Primont, D. and Russell, R. R. (1978). *Duality, Separability and Functional Structure.* New York: North-Holland.
——, Boyce, R. and Russell, R. R. (1978). 'Estimation of demand systems generated by the Gorman polar form: a generalization of the S-branch utility tree.' *Econometrica*, vol. 46, pp. 345–63.
Blinder, A. S. and Deaton, A. S. (1985). 'The time-series consumption function revisited.' *Brookings Papers on Economic Activity*, vol. 2, pp. 465–521.
Blundell, R. W. (1980). 'Estimating continuous consumer equivalence scales in an expenditure model with labour supply.' *European Economic Review*, vol. 14, pp. 145–57.
—— (1986). 'Econometric approaches to the specification of life-cycle labour supply and commodity demand behaviour.' *Econometric Reviews*, vol. 5, pp. 89–170.
—— and Meghir, C. (1986*a*). 'Selection criteria for a microeconometric model of labour supply.' *Journal of Applied Econometrics*, vol. 1, pp. 55–80.
—— and —— (1987*a*). 'Engel curve estimation with individual data.' In *The Practice of Econometrics: Studies on Demand, Forecasting, Money and Income* (ed. R. D. H. Heijmans and Heins Neudecker). Dordrecht: Martinus Nijhof Publishers.
—— and —— (1987*b*). 'Bivariate alternatives to the Tobit model.' *Journal of Econometrics*, vol. 34, pp. 179–200.
——, Fry, V. and Meghir, C. (1985). 'λ-Constant and alternative empirical models of life-cycle behaviour under uncertainty.' In *Advances in Microeconometrics* (eds. J. J. Laffont *et al.*). Tieto Press.
——, Ham, J. and Meghir, C. (1987). 'Unemployment and female labour supply.' ECONOMIC JOURNAL, vol. 97, pp. 44–64.
——, Pashardes, P. and Weber, G. (1987). 'A household expenditure model for indirect tax analysis.' Institute for Fiscal Studies. (Mimeo.)
——, —— and —— (1988). 'What do we learn about consumer demand patterns from micro data?' Institute for Fiscal Studies Working Paper 88-1a.
—— and Ray, R. (1984). 'Testing for linear Engel curves and additively separable preferences using a new flexible demand system.' ECONOMIC JOURNAL, vol. 94, pp. 800–11.
—— and Smith, R. J. (1984). 'Separability exogeneity and conditional demand models.' University of Manchester, Department of Econometrics. (Mimeo.)
—— and Walker, I. (1982). 'Modelling the joint determination of household labour supplies and commodity demands.' ECONOMIC JOURNAL, vol. 92, pp. 351–64.

—— and —— (1983). 'Limited dependent variables in demand analysis: an application to modelling family labour supply and commodity demand behaviour.' University of Manchester, Discussion Paper in Econometrics ES126.

Blundell, R. W. and Walker, I. (1984). 'A household production specification of demographic variables in demand analysis.' ECONOMIC JOURNAL (Conference Papers), pp. 59–68.

—— and —— (1986). 'A life-cycle consistent empirical model of family labour supply using cross-section data.' *Review of Economic Studies*, vol. 53, pp. 539–58.

Boyer, M. (1983). 'Rational demand and expectations patterns under habit formation.' *Journal of Economic Theory*, vol. 58, pp. 99–122.

Breeden, D. T. (1979). 'An intertemporal asset pricing model with stochastic consumption and investment opportunities.' *Journal of Financial Economics*, vol. 7, pp. 265–96.

Brown, A. and Deaton, A. S. (1972). 'Models of consumer behaviour: survey no. 4 in applied economics.' ECONOMIC JOURNAL, vol. 82, pp. 1145–236.

Brown, T. M. (1952). 'Habit persistence and lags in consumer behaviour.' *Econometrica*, vol. 20, pp. 355–71.

Browning, M. J. (1982). 'A dual approach to the analysis and testing of the life-cycle hypothesis.' University of Bristol. (Mimeo.)

—— (1984). 'A non-parametric test of the life-cycle rational expectations hypothesis.' Department of Economics, McMaster University. (Mimeo.)

—— (1985). 'Which demand elasticities do we know and which do we need to know for policy analysis?' McMaster Economics Discussion Paper 85-13.

—— (1986). 'The costs of using Frisch demand functions that are additive in the marginal utility of expenditure.' *Economics Letters*. (Forthcoming.)

—— (1987*a*). 'A simple non-additive class of intertemporal preferences.' McMaster University, February. (Mimeo.)

—— (1987*b*). 'Individual heterogeneity and perfect aggregation: a study of the Canadian microdata, 1969–82.' McMaster Economics Discussion Paper 87-07.

——, Deaton, A. S. and Irish, M. (1985). 'A profitable approach to labour supply and commodity demands over the life-cycle.' *Econometrica*, vol. 53, pp. 503–44.

Campbell, J. Y. (1987). 'Does saving anticipate declining labour income? An alternative test of the permanent income hypothesis.' *Econometrica*. (Forthcoming.)

—— and Deaton, A. S. (1987). 'Is consumption too smooth?' NBER, January. (Mimeo.)

Cragg, J. G. (1971). 'Some statistical models for limited dependent variables with applications to the demand for durable goods.' *Econometrica*, vol. 39, pp. 829–44.

Christensen, L. R., Jorgenson, D. W. and Lau, L. J. (1975). 'Transcendental logarithmic utility functions.' *American Economic Review*, vol. 65, pp. 367–83.

Davidson, J. E., Hendry, D. F., Srba, F. and Yeo, S. (1978). 'Econometric modelling of the aggregate time series relationship between consumers' expenditure and income in the United Kingdom.' ECONOMIC JOURNAL, vol. 88, pp. 661–92.

Deaton, A. S. (1974*a*). 'Reconsideration of the empirical implications of additive preferences.' ECONOMIC JOURNAL, vol. 84, pp. 338–48.

—— (1974*b*). 'The analysis of consumer demand in the United Kingdom, 1950–70.' *Econometrica*, vol. 42, pp. 341–67.

—— (1977). 'Involuntary saving through unanticipated saving.' *American Economic Review*, vol. 67, pp. 899–910.

—— (1983). 'Demand analysis.' In *Handbook of Econometrics* (eds Z. Griliches and M. Intriligator.) JAI Press.

—— (1985). 'Life-cycle models of consumption: is the evidence consistent with the theory?' Invited paper for the Fifth World Congress of the Econometric Society, Cambridge, Mass. August, NBER Working Paper 1910.

—— (1986). 'Consumers' expenditure.' Paper prepared for 'The New Palgrave'. Woodrow Wilson School, July. (Mimeo.)

—— and Irish, M. (1984). 'Statistical models for zero expenditures in household budgets.' *Journal of Public Economics*, vol. 23, pp. 59–80.

—— and Muellbauer, J. (1980*a*). 'An almost ideal demand system.' *American Economic Review*, vol. 70, pp. 312–26.

—— and —— (1980*b*). *Economics and Consumer Behaviour*. Cambridge: Cambridge University Press.

—— and —— (1981). 'Functional forms for labour supply and commodity demands with and without quantity restriction.' *Econometrica*, vol. 49, pp. 1521–32.

—— and —— (1986). 'On measuring child costs: with applications to poor countries.' *Journal of Political Economy*, vol. 94, pp. 720–44.

Diamond, P. A. and Hausman, J. A. (1984). 'Individual retirement and savings behaviour.' *Journal of Public Economics*, vol. 23, pp. 81–114.

Diewert, W. E. (1971). 'An application of the Shephard duality theorem: a generalised Leontief production function.' *Journal of Political Economics*, vol. 79, pp. 481–507.

Diewert, W. E. (1974). 'Applications of duality theory.' In *Frontiers of Quantitative Economics*, II (eds M. D. Intriligator and J. W. Kendrick). North-Holland.

—— and Wales T. J. (1987). 'Flexible functional forms and global curvature conditions.' *Econometrica*, vol. 55, pp. 43–68.

Duesenberry, J. S. (1949). '*Income, Saving and the Theory of Consumer Behaviour*.' Cambridge, Mass.: Harvard University Press.

Eichenbaum, M., Hansen, L. P. and Singleton, K. J. (1986). 'A time series analysis of representative agent models of consumption and leisure choice under uncertainty.' Graduate School of Industrial Administration, Carnegie-Mellon University. (Mimeo.)

Epstein, L. G. (1975). 'A disaggregate analysis of consumer demand under uncertainty.' *Econometrica*, vol. 43, pp. 877–95.

—— and Yatchew, A. (1985). 'The empirical determination of technology and expectations: a simplified procedure.' *Journal of Econometrics*, vol. 27(2), pp. 235–58.

Farrell, M. J. (1952). 'Irreversible demand functions.' *Econometrica*, vol. 20, pp. 171–86.

Ferguson, T. (1958). 'A method of generating best asymptotically normal estimates with application to the estimation of bacterial densities.' *Annals of Mathematical Statistics*, vol. 29, pp. 1046–61.

Flavin, M. (1981). 'The adjustment of consumption to changing expectations about future income.' *Journal of Political Economy*, vol. 89, pp. 974–1009.

—— (1985). 'Excess sensitivity of consumption to current income: liquidity constraints or myopia?' *Canadian Journal of Economics*, vol. 18, pp. 117–36.

Friedman, M. (1975). *A Theory of the Consumption Function*. Princeton University Press.

Ghez, G. and Becker, G. S. (1975). *The Allocation of Time and Goods over the Life Cycle*. New York: Columbia University Press.

Gorman, W. M. (1953). 'Community preference fields.' *Econometrica*, vol. 21, pp. 63–80.

—— (1959). 'Separable utility and aggregation.' *Econometrica*, vol. 27, pp. 469–81.

—— (1967). 'Tastes, habits and choices.' *International Economic Review*, vol. 8, pp. 218–22.

—— (1968). 'Conditions for additive separability.' *Econometrica*, vol. 36, pp. 605–9.

—— (1976). 'Tricks with utility functions.' In *Essays in Economic Analysis* (eds M. Artis and R. Nobay). Cambridge: Cambridge University Press.

—— (1981). 'Some Engel curves.' In *Essays in the Theory and Measurement of Consumer Behaviour* (ed. A. S. Deaton). Cambridge: Cambridge University Press.

—— and Myles, G. D. (1986). 'Separability and characteristics.' Nuffield College Discussion Papers in Economics, 6, November.

Gourieroux, G., Laffont, J.-J. and Montfort, A. (1980). 'Disequilibrium econometrics in simultaneous equation systems.' *Econometrica*, vol. 48, pp. 75–96.

Hall, R. E. (1978). 'Stochastic implications of the life-cycle permanent income hypothesis: theory and evidence.' *Journal of Political Economy*, vol. 86, pp. 971–88.

—— (1985). 'Real interest and consumption.' NBER Working Paper No. 1694.

—— (1986). 'Consumption.' Paper presented for *Handbook of Modern Business Cycle Theory* (ed. R. J. Barro). NBER, September. (Mimeo.)

—— and Mishkin, F. (1982). 'The sensitivity of consumption to transitory income: estimates from panel data on households.' *Econometrica*, vol. 50, pp. 461–81.

Ham, J. (1982). 'Estimation of a labour supply model with censoring due to unemployment and underemployment.' *Review of Economic Studies*, vol. 49, pp. 335–53.

Hansen, L. P. and Sargent, T. (1981). 'Linear rational expectations models for dynamically interrelated variables.' In *Rational Expectations and Econometric Practice* (eds R. Lucas and T. Sargent). Minneapolis: University of Minnesota Press.

—— and Singleton, K. J. (1982). 'Generalised instrumental variables estimation of non-linear rational expectations models.' *Econometrica*, vol. 50, pp. 1269–86.

—— and —— (1983). 'Stochastic consumption, risk aversion and the temporal behaviour of asset returns.' *Journal of Political Economy*, vol. 91, pp. 249–65.

Hausman, J. A. (1978). 'Specification tests in econometrics.' *Econometrica*, vol. 48, pp. 697–720.

Hayashi, F. (1982). 'The permanent income hypothesis: estimation and testing by instrumental variables.' *Journal of Political Economy*, vol. 90, pp. 895–918.

—— (1985*a*) 'Permanent income hypothesis and consumption durability: analysis based on Japanese panel data.' *Quarterly Journal of Economics*, vol. 90, pp. 895–916.

—— (1985*b*). 'Tests for liquidity constraints: a critical survey.' NBER Working Paper No. 1720.

Heckman, J. J. (1974*a*). 'Life cycle consumption and labour supply: an explanation of the relationship between income and consumption over the life cycle.' *American Economic Review*, vol. 64, pp. 1188–94.

—— (1974*b*). 'The effect of child care programs on women's work effort.' *Journal of Political Economy*, vol. 82, pp. S136–S63.

—— and MaCurdy, T. E. (1980). 'A life cycle model of female labour supply.' *Review of Economic Studies*, vol. 47, pp. 47–74.

Hotz, V. J., Kydland, F. E. and Sedlacek, G. L. (1985). 'Intertemporal preferences and labour supply.' Carnegie-Mellon University. (Mimeo.)

Houthakker, H. S. (1960). 'Additive Preferences.' *Econometrica*, vol. 30, pp. 244–57.

—— and Taylor, L. D. (1970). '*Consumer Demand in the United States 1929–70*. 2nd ed. Cambridge, Mass.: Harvard University Press.

Jorgenson, D. W., Lau, L. J. and Stoker, T. M. (1980). 'Welfare comparisons and exact aggregation.' *American Economic Review*, vol. 70, pp. 268–72.

——, —— and —— (1982). 'The transcendental logarithmic model of aggregate consumer behaviour.' In *Advances in Econometrics* (eds. R. L. Bassman and G. Rhodes). JAI Press, pp. 97–238.

Kay, J. A., Keen, M. J. and Morris, C. N. (1984). 'Estimating consumption from expenditure data.' *Journal of Public Economics*, vol. 23, pp. 169–82.

Keen, M. J. (1986). 'Zero expenditures and the estimation of Engel curves.' *Journal of Applied Econometrics*, vol. 1, no. 3, pp. 277–86.

Kennan, J. (1979). 'The estimation of partial adjustment models with rational expectations.' *Econometrica*, vol. 47, pp. 1141–65.

Killingsworth, M. R. (1983). *Labour Supply*. Cambridge: Cambridge University Press.

King, M. A. (1980). 'An econometric model of tenure choice and demand for housing as a joint decision.' *Journal of Public Economics*, vol. 14(2), pp. 137–60.

—— (1985). 'The economics of saving: a survey of recent contributions.' In *Frontiers in Economics* (eds K. Arrow and S. Houkapohja). Oxford: Basil Blackwell.

—— (1986). 'Capital market "imperfections" and the consumption function.' *Scandinavian Journal of Economics*. Conference Proceedings, pp. 59–84.

Lau, L. J. (1982). 'A note on the fundamental theorem of exact aggregation.' *Economic Letters*, vol. 9, pp. 119–26.

Lewbel, A. (1985). 'A unified approach to incorporating demographic or other effects into demand systems.' *Review of Economic Studies*, vol. 52, pp. 1–18.

Lee, L.-F. and Pitt, M. M. (1986). 'Microeconometric demand systems with binding nonnegativity constraints: the dual approach.' *Econometrica*, vol. 54, pp. 1237–42.

MaCurdy, T. E. (1981 *a*). 'An empirical model of labour supply in a life cycle setting.' *Journal of Political Economy*, vol. 89, pp. 1059–85.

—— (1981 *b*). 'Intertemporal analysis of taxation and work disincentives: an analysis of the Denver income maintenance experiment.' NBER Working Paper 624.

—— (1982). 'Interpreting empirical models of labour supply in an intertemporal framework with uncertainty.' Stanford University. (Mimeo.)

—— (1983). 'A simple scheme for estimating an intertemporal model of labour supply and consumption in the presence of taxes and uncertainty.' *International Economic Review*, vol. 24, pp. 265–89.

—— (1985). 'A framework for relating microeconomic and macroeconomic evidence on intertemporal substitution.' Program in Quantitative Economic Analysis, Discussion Paper 8-22, Chicago.

—— (1986). 'Modelling the time series implications of life-cycle theory.' Stanford University. (Mimeo.)

McFadden, D. (1980). 'Cost, revenue and profit functions.' In *Production Economics: A Dual Approach to Theory and Application* (eds M. Fuss and D. McFadden). Amsterdam: North-Holland.

—— (1986). 'A method of simulated moments for estimation of multinomial probits without numerical integration.' Massachusetts Institute of Technology, Cambridge, Mass. *Econometrica*. (In the Press.)

Mankiw, N. G., Rotemberg, J. J. and Summers, L. H. (1985). 'Intertemporal substitution in macroeconomics.' *Quarterly Journal of Economics*, C(1), no. 399, pp. 225–51.

Mariger, R. P. (1987 *a*). *Consumption Behaviour and the Effects of Government Fiscal Policies*. Harvard University Press.

—— (1987 *b*). 'A life-cycle consumption model with liquidity constraints: theory and empirical results.' *Econometrica*, vol. 55, pp. 533–58.

Meghir, C. (1985 *a*). 'The comparative statics of consumer demand under uncertainty.' UCL Economics Discussion Paper 85-21.

Modigliani, F. and Brumberg, R. (1955). 'Utility analysis and the consumption function: an interpretation of cross-section data.' In *Post Keynesian Economics* (ed. K. K. Kurihara). London: George Allen and Unwin.

Mortensen, D. (1973). 'Generalised costs of adjustment and dynamic factor demand theory.' *Econometrica*, vol. 41, pp. 657–66.

Muellbauer, J. (1974). 'Household composition, Engel curves and welfare comparisons between households.' *European Economic Review*, vol. 5, pp. 103–22.

—— (1975). 'Aggregation, income distribution and consumer demand.' *Review of Economic Studies*, vol. 42, pp. 523–43.

—— (1976). 'Community preferences and the representative consumer.' *Econometrica*, vol. 94, pp. 979–1000.

Muellbauer, J. (1977). 'Testing the Barten model of household composition effects and the cost of children.' ECONOMIC JOURNAL, vol. 87, pp. 460–87.

—— (1983). 'Surprises in the consumption function.' ECONOMIC JOURNAL (Conference papers), pp. 34–50.

—— (1986). 'Habits, rationality and myopia in the life-cycle consumption function.' CEPR Discussion Paper No. 112.

—— and Bover, O. (1986). 'Liquidity constraints and aggregation in the consumption function under uncertainty.' Oxford Institute of Economics and Statistics, Discussion Paper, 7.

—— and Pashardes, P. (1982). 'Tests of dynamic specification and homogeneity in demand systems.' Birkbeck College Discussion Paper, No. 125.

Murphy, A. (1986). 'Intertemporal substitution and consumption.' Maynooth College, Dublin. (Mimeo.)

Neary, J. P. and Roberts, K. W. S. (1980). 'The theory of household behaviour under rationing.' *European Economic Review*, vol. 13, pp. 25–42.

Nickell, S. J. (1986). 'The short-run behaviour of labour supply.' Oxford Institute of Economics and Statistics, Discussion Paper, 4.

Pashardes, P. (1987). 'Myopic and forward looking behaviour in a dynamic demand system.' *International Economic Review*, vol. 27(2), pp. 387–97.

Phlips, L. (1983). *Applied Consumption Analysis*, 2nd ed. Amsterdam: North-Holland.

—— and Spinnewyn, F. (1981). 'Rational and myopic demand system.' In *Advances in Econometrics* (eds R. Bassman and J. Rhodes). JAI Press.

—— and —— (1982). 'Rationality versus myopia in dynamic demand systems.' *Advances in Econometrics*, vol. 1, pp. 3–33, JAI Press.

Pindyck, R. S. and Rotemberg, J. J. (1983). 'Dynamic factor demands under rational expectations.' *Scandinavian Journal of Economics*, vol. 85(2).

Pollak, R. A. (1970). 'Habit formation demand function.' *Journal of Political Economy*, vol. 78, pp. 77–8.

—— (1971). 'Conditional demand functions and the implications of separability.' *Southern Economic Journal*, vol. 37, pp. 423–33.

—— (1972). 'Generalised separability.' *Econometrica*, vol. 40, pp. 431–53.

—— and Wales, T. J. (1969). 'Estimation of the linear expenditure system.' *Econometrica*, vol. 37, pp. 611–28.

—— and —— (1979). 'Welfare comparisons and equivalence scales.' *American Economic Review*. Papers and Proceedings, vol. 69, pp. 216–21.

—— and —— (1981). 'Demographic variables in demand analysis.' *Econometrica*, vol. 49, pp. 1533–52.

Poterba, J. M. and Rotemberg, J. J. (1986). 'Money in the utility function: an empirical implementation.' NBER.

Pudney, S. E. (1981). 'An empirical method of approximating the separable structure of consumer preferences.' *Review of Economic Studies*, vol. 48, pp. 561–78.

—— (1987). 'Frequency of purchase and Engel curve estimation.' London School of Economics. (Mimeo.)

Ransom, M. R. (1987). 'A comment on consumer demand systems with binding non-negativity constraints.' *Journal of Econometrics*, vol. 34, pp. 355–60.

Ray, R. (1983). 'Measuring the costs of children: an alternative approach.' *Journal of Public Economics*, vol. 22, pp. 89–112.

Rothenberg, T. J. (1973). *Efficient Estimation with A Priori Information*. Cowles Foundation Monograph 23. Yale: Yale University Press.

Russell, R. T. (1983). 'On a theorem of Gorman.' *Economics Letters*, vol. 11, pp. 223–4.

Sargan, J. D. (1958). 'The estimation of econometric relationships using instrumental variables.' *Econometrica*, vol. 26, pp. 393–415.

Sargent, T. J. (1978). 'Estimation of dynamic labour demand schedules under rational expectations.' *Journal of Political Economy*, vol. 86, pp. 1009–44.

Smith, R. J. and Blundell, R. W. (1986). 'An exogeneity test for the simultaneous equation Tobit model with an application to labour supply.' *Econometrica*, vol. 54, pp. 679–86.

Spinnewyn, F. (1979). 'The cost of consumption and wealth in a model with habit formation.' *Economics Letters*, vol. 2, pp. 145–8.

—— (1981). 'Rational habit formation.' *European Economic Review*, vol. 15, pp. 91–109.

Stern, N. (1986). 'On the specification of labour supply functions.' In *Unemployment, Search and Labour Supply* (eds R. W. Blundell and I. Walker). Cambridge: Cambridge University Press.

Stoker, T. M. (1984). 'Completeness, distribution restrictions and the form of aggregate functions.' *Econometrica*, vol. 52, pp. 887–908.

—— (1986). 'Simple tests of distributional effects on macroeconomic equations.' *Journal of Political Economy*, vol. 94, pp. 763–95.

Stone, J. R. N. (1954). 'Linear expenditure systems and demand analysis: an application to the pattern of British demand.' ECONOMIC JOURNAL, vol. 64, pp. 511–27.

—— (1964). 'Private saving in Britain, past, present and future.' *Manchester School of Economic and Social*

Studies, vol. 32, pp. 79–112, reprinted in R. Stone, *Mathematics in the Social Sciences and Other Essays*. London: Chapman and Hall, 1966.

Stone, J. R. N. (1966). 'Spending and saving in relation in income and wealth.' *L'Industria*, 4, reprinted in R. Stone, *Mathematical Models of the Economy and Other Essays*. London: Chapman and Hall, 1970.

—— and Rowe, D. A. (1958). 'Dynamic demand functions: some econometric results.' ECONOMIC JOURNAL, vol. 68, pp. 256–70.

—— and —— (1962). 'A post-war expenditure function.' *The Manchester School of Economic and Social Studies*, vol. 30, pp. 187–201.

Tobin, J. (1958). 'Estimation of relationships for limited dependent variables.' *Econometrica*, vol. 26, pp. 24–36.

Varian, H. R. (1982). 'The non-parametric approach to demand analysis.' *Econometrica*, vol. 50, pp. 945–73.

—— (1983). 'Non-parametric tests of consumer behaviour.' *Review of Economic Studies*, vol. 50, pp. 99–110.

Wales, T. J. and Woodland, A. D. (1983). 'Estimation of consumer demand systems with binding non-negativity constraints.' *Journal of Econometrics*, vol. 21, pp. 263–85.

Weissenberger, E. (1983). 'An intertemporal system of dynamic consumer demand functions.' London School of Economics, Centre for Labour Economics, Discussion Paper No. 186.

—— (1984). 'Consumption adjustment costs and rational expectations: an application to UK consumers' data.' London School of Economics, Centre for Labour Economics, Discussion Paper No. 183.

Wickens, M. and Molana, H. (1984). 'Stochastic life-cycle theory with varying interest rates and prices.' ECONOMIC JOURNAL, vol. 94, Supplement, pp. 133–47.

Working, H. (1943). 'Statistical laws of family expenditure.' *Journal of the American Statistical Association*, vol. 38.

2

INDUSTRIAL ECONOMICS: AN OVERVIEW*

Richard Schmalensee†

Two decades ago George Stigler (1968, p. 1) described the boundaries of industrial economics or, as the field is frequently labelled, industrial organisation:

> ... there is no such subject as industrial organization. The courses taught under this heading have for their purpose the understanding of the structure and behaviour of the industries ... of an economy. These courses deal with the size structure of firms (one or many, 'concentrated' or not), the causes ... of this size structure, the effects of concentration on competition, the effects of competition upon prices, investment, innovation, and so on. But this is precisely the content of economic theory – price or resource allocation theory ...

Stigler went on to note that industrial economics deals not only with theory but also with measurement and hypothesis testing and with the analysis of public policies toward business. A fairly accurate capsule description is that industrial economics is the study of the supply side of the economy, particularly those markets in which business firms are sellers.

Industrial economics emerged as a distinct field after the rise of the large modern manufacturing corporation around the turn of the century (Chandler, 1977; Hay and Morris, 1979, ch. 1). For many years it was generally viewed as an intellectually isolated empirical field without much scope for formal theory or non-routine econometrics. But in the last two decades much of the significant work in industrial economics has been theoretical, and much of it has been produced and consumed by non-specialists. The game-theoretic tools now generally used in this research (and regularly sharpened thereby) are described in Section I. The late 1980s seems to have witnessed a shift of interest back to empirical studies, and Section I also provides a brief overview of the methods that have been developed and employed in this work.

Industrial economics is now best defined by three main topical foci, two of which are discussed systematically in what follows. Section II considers determinants of the behaviour, scale, scope, and organisation of *business firms*. Research in this broad area has spilled over into labour economics and corporate finance and has informed the study of the relation between corporate strategies and organisational structures (Caves, 1980).

* This chapter was first published in the Economic Journal, vol. 98, September 1988.

† I am pleased to acknowledge a great debt to my teachers, colleagues, and students at MIT, who have taught me much of what I know about industrial economics. I am especially indebted for helpful comments on an earlier version of this essay to Timothy Bresnahan, Joseph Farrell, Paul Geroski, Donald Hay, Andrew Oswald, Nancy Rose, Julio Rotemberg, Jean Tirole, John Vickers, and two anonymous referees. As usual, creditors cannot be held liable for defects in the final product.

The second focus is *imperfect competition*. When the structural prerequisites of perfect competition are not satisfied, how do market *conduct* and *performance* depend on relatively stable observable variables – that is, on market *structure*, broadly defined? When will rivalry be intense, so that rents are dissipated, and when will it be restrained, so that performance is nearly monopolistic?[1] Work on these core questions is discussed in Sections III and IV. Section III considers choices of price, output, and capacity, while Section IV deals with non-price rivalry: product selection, advertising, and technical change. Models of imperfect competition developed in industrial economics have been imported into the scientific and policy sides of international economics (Krugman, 1986) and, recently, macroeconomics, and have been employed prescriptively to determine business strategies (Porter, 1980).

The third focus is *public policy toward business*. One normative question and two positive questions arise here. The normative question has been central to the field since it began: What policies are optimal? Historically industrial economists have concentrated on antitrust (or competition) policy, regulation, and government enterprise. In recent years they have paid increasing attention to deregulation, liberalisation of entry restrictions, privatisation (Vickers and Yarrow, 1988), and industrial policies aimed at affecting technical progress and international competitiveness (Krugman, 1986; Yarrow, 1985). Length restrictions preclude systematic discussions of all these policy domains. Instead, I discuss policy implications of research findings at several points in Sections II–IV and offer a few general observations in Section V.

Length restrictions also preclude a systematic review of attempts to answer the two related positive questions. The first is the natural complement to normative studies: What are the effects of actual policies? Specific answers of course vary considerably, but it is clear that governments often intervene in markets in ways that do not enhance efficiency. Stimulated in large part by Stigler's (1971) discussion of the discrepancy between economic theory and political practice, industrial economists have addressed a second positive question: What determines actual policies? These scholars have encountered a substantial number of political scientists also using rational actor models to study policy formation.

The topical and methodological breadth of industrial economics, the pace at which it has developed in recent years, and limits on the length of this essay confine me to a broad overview of research on some central topics.[2] Comprehensive expository surveys are provided in Schmalensee and Willig (1989) and Tirole (1988); I have drawn heavily on those works and

[1] It is conventional in industrial economics to use 'rivalry' instead of 'competition' when markets may be only imperfectly competitive.

[2] Two other limitations of this essay should be noted. First, I confine my attention to the English-language literature. Continental European research tends to have a more Austrian flavour and to stress the importance of disequilibrium behaviour and the effects of institutions (de Jong, 1986). Second, because comprehensive bibliographies are available in Schmalensee and Willig (1989) and Tirole (1988), I have felt free to cite an idiosyncratic selection of classic, neglected, recent, illustrative, and atypical studies, along with some surveys, tilting toward recent writings that discuss earlier contributions. My apologies to those whose important works were thereby omitted from this essay's long but seriously incomplete bibliography.

recommend both to the reader who wishes to learn what lies behind the many facades displayed in this essay.

I. TOOLS AND METHODS

This section provides a brief overview of research methods in industrial economics that is designed to complement the substantive discussions that follow. The tools employed in theoretical research, which are considered first, have become more uniform in the last decade, while the methods used in empirical work have become more diverse.

Theory of Strategic Behaviour

Except where monopoly is assumed and the possibility of entry is assumed away, theoretical research in industrial economics today employs the tools of non-co-operative game theory.[3] Modelling typically begins with the specification of the *extensive form* of a game: a description of which players move when, the actions and information available at each move, the probabilities of any random events to be chosen by 'nature', and the functions determining each player's payoff.[4] Some information may be *private*; each firm may know only its own cost function, for instance. Other information may be *common knowledge*; all firms may know the market demand function, for instance, and also know that all other firms have this same information as well.

It is then assumed that observed behaviour will correspond to a *Nash equilibrium* of the specified game, a situation in which each firm's *strategy* (a list of the moves it will make in all possible situations) is a best response to the strategies of its rivals. Nash equilibria can involve *pure strategies* (conditional choices of actions) or *mixed strategies* (conditional choices of probability distributions over actions). Equilibria involving only pure strategies seem generally to have more intuitive appeal.

In game-theoretic terms, the familiar Cournot model is a one-period game in which N firms ($N \geqslant 2$) simultaneously choose output levels of identical products. If Q is total output, and $P(Q)$ is the market inverse demand function, which is assumed to be common knowledge, sellers' payoffs are given by their profit functions:

$$\Pi_i = q_i P(q_i + q_{-i}) - C_i(q_i) \quad i = 1, \ldots, N, \tag{1}$$

where q_i is firm i's output and $q_{-i} = Q - q_i$ is the total output of its rivals. The first-order necessary conditions for each q_i to be a best response to the corresponding q_{-i} are as follows:

$$\partial \Pi_i / \partial q_i = P(Q) + q_i P'(Q) - MC_i(q_i) = 0 \quad i = 1, \ldots, N, \tag{2}$$

[3] For a detailed exposition of game theory, see Friedman (1986). The discussion of game-theoretic work in this essay has been heavily influenced by Fudenberg and Tirole (1987) and Milgrom and Roberts (1987).

[4] The alternative *normal form* or *strategic form* condenses all this and simply gives payoffs as functions of the players' strategies. The extensive form seems to be more convenient and informative in most applications in industrial economics.

where MC_i is firm i's marginal cost, dC_i/dq_i, and $P'(Q) = dP(Q)/dQ$. A Nash equilibrium in pure strategies must be a solution to equation (2).[5]

Perhaps the greatest merit of the game-theoretic approach is that it disciplines theoretical discussion by, in effect, forcing theorists to specify and then abide by the rules of the games they analyse. There is no place in the analysis of the basic Cournot game for discussions of conjectured rival response, for instance; the (unbounded) rationality of all players is common knowledge in this game and most others. Similarly, dynamic adjustment paths can only arise in more complex games that unfold over time. And imperfections or asymmetries in information give rise to different games and thus cannot be handled informally. Since market behaviour often involves making decisions over time or without full information, much recent work has involved games with these features.

Dynamics. While time is most naturally treated as continuous in many situations, continuous-time dynamic games (usually called differential games) are technically more challenging than discrete-time games, and the latter dominate the literature. These can be solved by working backwards from the last period if there is a last period. Infinite-horizon games are often more appealing in principle and, where stationarity can be exploited, simpler to analyse. But they typically have equilibria that do not appear even in the limit of the corresponding finite-horizon games.

The analysis of multi-period games in industrial economics relies heavily on the principle of (*subgame*) *perfection.* Roughly, in a (subgame) perfect Nash equilibrium each player's strategy is a best response to those of its rivals, subject to the constraint that no player's strategy can involve threats that it would not be the player's interest to carry out if his bluff were called. For example, a strategy involving reducing price to zero if any entry occurs contains a threat that is not generally credible (because it generally does not maximise post-entry profits) and is thus ruled out by the perfectness restriction.

In a variety of economic settings the ability to make credible threats can induce other actors to behave 'nicely' to avoid the threatened behaviour. Much attention has accordingly been devoted to devices that firms can use to obtain credibility. These generally involve taking irreversible actions, which would often be undesirable except for their impact on the incentives and behaviour of others, and go under the general heading of *commitment.* If an established monopolist could build a Doomsday Machine (as in the film *Dr. Strangelove*) that would somehow force it to drive market price to zero if entry occurred, and if it could make the existence of that device common knowledge, it could credibly deter entry. The ability to commit often (but not always) gives an advantage to the first player to move in economic games.[6]

[5] Some properties of such equilibria are discussed in Section III. It is worth noting that plausible cost and demand functions exist that do not yield a unique pure-strategy Cournot equilibrium (Novshek, 1985).

[6] In a Bertrand (price-setting) duopoly with differentiated products, for instance, the second mover has an advantage because he can undercut the first mover. Issues of commitment can also arise in the specification of dynamic models. The *open-loop* equilibrium concept, for instance, assumes that players decide once and for all what moves they will make at each date. Open-loop equilibria thus rest on the assumption that players can commit to ignore to their rivals' subsequent moves. (In *closed-loop* equilibria, which are

Much interest in recent years has attached to *repeated games* or *supergames* – in which a relatively simple *constituent* or *stage* game (such as the one-period Cournot or Prisoners' Dilemma games) is played repeatedly by a fixed set of players. Strategies of simply playing Nash equilibrium strategies of the constituent game in each period form a Nash equilibrium of the repeated game. But strategies in the repeated game may involve taking actions conditional on past history, and there are usually many other equilibria when the horizon is infinite. In fact, many of the main results in the supergame literature are variants on the so-called *Folk Theorem*, which says that virtually any set of payoffs can arise in a perfect equilibrium if the horizon is long enough and the discount rate is low enough (Fudenberg and Maskin, 1986).

Information. Players are said to have *incomplete information* if they do not know their opponents' payoff functions and to have *imperfect information* if they do not observe the actions of all players. Most interest has attached to games in which information is incomplete and asymmetric. Each firm in a Cournot setup might know its own costs, for instance, with the probability distribution from which cost function parameters are drawn assumed to be common knowledge.

In multi-period games with incomplete or imperfect information, it is natural to require players to optimise at each move using subjective probabilities that they update according to Bayes rule. This requirement yields *Bayesian–Nash equilibria*. In such equilibria, actions in any period may affect other players' actions in future periods by altering their beliefs. These models thus often exhibit *generalised signalling* (Milgrom and Roberts, 1987): costly actions are taken for the purpose of altering other actors' beliefs. Since all parties are rational, such signalling cannot bias any player's beliefs on average but may nonetheless occur because all players interpret their observations in light of others' incentives to induce bias. Multiple equilibria are the norm in multi-period games of incomplete information, and Folk Theorems indicate that a small amount of incomplete information can produce almost any equilibrium payoffs when the discount rate is low and the horizon is long (Fudenberg and Maskin, 1986).

A particularly interesting class of games of asymmetric information is explored in *agency theory* (Hart and Holmstrom, 1987). In the basic agency problem, one party (the principal) hires another (the agent) to act on his behalf in the first period. The principal can generally observe the consequences of the agent's second-period action, but his information about that action (e.g. the level of managerial effort) or about the relevant environment (e.g. the level of demand) is inferior to that of the agent.[7] The principal's task is to design a compensation scheme based on observables in order to maximise his own utility

---

generally more plausible, players' strategies consist of functions that map histories into actions (or probability distributions) at each date.) Similarly, discrete-time models involve the assumption that players cannot move within periods, so that period length (as measured by the discount factor) often affects the nature of the equilibrium.

[7] If potential agents have hidden knowledge about their differences before the principal makes his hiring decision, the situation is said to involve *adverse selection*: less able potential agents, with poorer alternatives, may try harder to be hired. Information asymmetries that arise after hiring give rise to *moral hazard*: if the agent's effort cannot be directly observed, he may have little or no incentive to work hard.

or wealth, subject to the constraints that he be able to hire an agent and that the agent will then act in his own self-interest, as defined by the compensation scheme.[8]

Approaches to Empirical Research

The early years of industrial economics were marked by the production of a number of book-length industry studies, often relying heavily on information made public during antitrust cases. These comprehensive works remain a rich source of examples of business behaviour, such as the evolution of price leadership in the interwar US cigarette industry (Nicholls, 1951), that seem to involve the exercise of monopoly power. This literature also provides a sense of business reality and a detailed understanding of particular markets not frequently encountered in more formal studies. But relatively few industry studies of this sort have been done in recent years.

Inter-industry studies. In the early 1950s, Joe Bain (1951, 1956) shifted the focus of empirical research in industrial economics away from industry studies by showing the apparent power of statistical analysis of industry-level cross-section data. This approach seemed to promise more rapid and objective development of general relations than the case study approach. Most of the cross-section studies that filled the journals during the 1960s and 1970s used government-supplied data and ran regressions designed to 'explain' differences in industry-average profitability.

Critics of this research strategy have noted serious limitations of available data. Government statistics often ignore foreign competition and regional markets and define industries that do not correspond to economic product markets. Accounting profitability is at best a noisy measure of economic profitability; problems include the accounting treatments of inflation, advertising, and depreciation (Fisher and McGowan, 1983).[9] There is no fully satisfactory way to handle diversified firms that operate in multiple markets. In addition, it is difficult to construct defensible proxies for a number of variables, including expectations and fundamental attributes of products and technologies, that are important in theory. If unobservable variables are correlated with the independent variables used in cross-section regressions, as often appears likely, coefficient estimates will be biased.

A second set of criticisms turns on the difficulty of using cross-section data to identify key structural parameters. Economists usually argue that cross-section

[8] The analysis of agency-theoretic problems is often simplified considerably by invoking the *revelation principle* (Harris and Townsend, 1981). Suppose that possible agents differ according to the value of some parameter, θ, that the principal cannot observe directly and that affects performance. Then the revelation principle says, roughly, that any optimal scheme in which equilibrium compensation depends on θ is generally equivalent to a scheme in which the agent is asked to report his θ to the principal and is given incentives that make it optimal to tell the truth. One can thus limit attention to compensation arrangements of the latter form.

[9] Since oligopoly theory deals with the relation between price and marginal cost, not with the rate of return on investment, it can be argued that the best performance measure would be the *Lerner index*, (price − marginal cost)/price. This argument has led to the use of the so-called price-cost margin, (revenue − labour and materials cost)/revenue, in some studies, but there is no reason to think that marginal cost is accurately measured by unit labour and materials cost. Moreover, rates of return on investment, not price-cost margins, should be equalised by free entry.

studies can reveal differences among long-run equilibria as long as deviations from equilibrium are uncorrelated with independent variables. But in the long run almost all observable industry-level variables are affected by firms' decisions and are thus logically endogenous. While lack of identification is not an absolute bar to inference (Breusch, 1986), its definitive symptom, the existence of more than one plausible structural interpretation of estimated parameters, is frequently encountered in the cross-section literature.

Despite these problems, inter-industry studies have an important role to play. It is difficult to design broad public policies, such as antitrust and tariff policies, without a feel for the main economy-wide relations (structural or otherwise) among affected markets. A number of recent inter-industry studies rely on specially constructed data sets to deal with some of the problems noted above. Comparisons between matched industries in different countries, for instance, hold constant a host of unobservable industry-specific quantities (Pryor, 1972; Baldwin and Gorecki, 1985), while industry-level panel data can reveal the effects of macroeconomic conditions and permit analysis of stability and change (Domowitz *et al.*, 1986). Interview and survey methods can provide information not otherwise available (Scherer *et al.*, 1975; Levin *et al.*, 1987).

A great deal of interest has recently attached to the use of firm-level panel data (Mueller, 1986). While there are significant differences in industry-average profitability, there are often even greater differences within industries (Schmalensee, 1985), and variations in the performance of leading firms over time is often not well explained by changes in the industries in which they participate (Cubbin and Geroski, 1987).

Econometric industry studies. Many industrial economists have reacted to the limitations of the inter-industry approach by studying particular industries. Industry-specific studies cannot describe economy-wide patterns, but, like the earlier case-study literature, such research can provide reliable data points that can inform both theorising and inter-industry research. A number of studies involve comparisons of geographically isolated markets for a single product and thus hold constant unobservable industry-specific variables (Benham, 1972). Such variables are also held constant in before-and-after analyses of the effects of exogenous industry-specific structural changes (Rose, 1987).

In the last decade or so, changes in stock prices over short periods have been employed with increasing frequency in industrial economics (Schwert, 1981).[10] On the widely-accepted assumption that the stock market makes full use of publicly available information, stock price changes over some period, corrected for movements in the market as a whole, give the expected present value of the change in profit associated with firm-specific or industry-specific news of that period.

In recent years many authors have used firm-level panel data to estimate industry-specific structural models designed to reveal directly the intensity –

[10] Some authors have used the ratio of a firm's market value to the estimated replacement cost of its assets – Tobin's q – to measure profitability. This approach does not avoid accounting problems, of course, since replacement cost estimates are always based on accounting data.

and sometimes the pattern – of rivalry. Research of this sort involves particularly heavy investment in data set construction and in developing modelling strategies tailored to available data. Accordingly, a host of techniques for econometric industry analysis have been developed, but most have been employed only once or twice.

Much of this literature has been concerned with estimation of variants of the following quasi-supply relations:

$$P = MC_i(q_i, X_i) + (1 + \lambda_i)\, q_i P'(Q, Z) \quad i = 1, \ldots, N. \tag{3}$$

If the λ_i are all zero, equations (3) are just the Cournot first-order conditions (2) with the addition of exogenous variables X_i and Z that shift firm i's cost and market demand, respectively. The λ_i are *conjectural variations* that are best interpreted as reduced form parameters that summarise the intensity of rivalry that emerges from what may be complex patterns of behaviour. If estimated λ's are all equal to minus one, sellers behave as if perfect competition prevailed; higher values of λ correspond to larger $(P - MC)$ gaps and thus to less intense rivalry (Iwata, 1974).

Marginal cost is usually not treated as directly observable in this work; the X_i usually include input prices. The quasi-supply relations are often estimated with the industry inverse demand relation, $P = P(Q, Z)$, and sometimes also with total cost or input demand functions. Identification of the λ's may rest on the availability of exogenous variables in Z that change the slope of the demand curve (Lau, 1982), or on information about marginal cost or its determinants (Iwata, 1974; Panzar and Rosse, 1987).

Some studies in this literature have test alternative models of conduct, such as competition and collusion (Bresnahan, 1987); others examine differences in conjectural variations over time or among firms (Geroski *et al.*, 1986). Still others develop alternative approaches to the detection of non-competitive behaviour in particular settings (Baker and Bresnahan, 1985; Panzar and Rosse, 1987).

Laboratory experiments. Given the difficulty of obtaining detailed data on an informative set of natural market experiments, a good deal of interest has recently attached to the use of laboratory experiments to test industrial economic hypotheses (Plott, 1982; Smith, 1982). Many variables that are unobservable outside the laboratory (such as beliefs and marginal costs) can be fixed in experimental settings, and the sensitivity of behaviour to environmental and institutional changes can be explored directly.

While the experiments reported in the literature to date have frequently been criticised as artificially simple, they generally do involve actors with financial incentives to optimise and markets of at least the same order of complexity as those studied in theoretical analyses. Developments in computer software and experimental procedures will likely make more 'realistic' experiments possible. Still, laboratory research seems best suited for testing the predictive power and robustness of particular theories; it is less useful for determining the class of real markets for which particular theories are useful.

II. BUSINESS STRUCTURE AND BEHAVIOUR

There are three main points of tension between the textbook model of firm behaviour and organisation and reality. First, it is not obvious that the managers of real firms maximise profits. Second, few long-run average cost curves seem to be either U-shaped or everywhere declining, so that the textbook models of competition and natural monopoly do not explain how the scales of many real firms are determined. Third, the textbook model deals with single-product firms and ignores their internal structures, even though real firms produce multiple products and must decide the scope of their activities and their internal organisations. This section considers research bearing on these three points.

Managerial Behaviour

There have historically been two main criticisms of the traditional assumption that firms maximise profits, properly generalised where appropriate to mean maximisation of shareholders' wealth.[11] While both have force, neither has yet produced a superior alternative assumption.

Behavioural theories. The first criticism begins by noting that many decisions that managers make regularly are much harder than the simplified problems with which theorists struggle. Thus limits to human information processing capabilities – *bounded rationality* – make strict profit maximisation fundamentally implausible. And nobody who observes real firms closely can avoid noticing managerial blunders.[12]

But, while there is evidence that managers often follow simple rules of thumb in lieu of consciously maximising, it has proven difficult to characterise such rules at the level of generality required for a tractable model implying systematic departures from profit-maximisation. Additional difficulties arise because competition acts to weed out rules of thumb that do not at least approximately maximise profit (Nelson and Winter, 1982). This evolutionary process plainly does not work instantly or perfectly in real markets, but it has proved difficult to specify its imperfections in a useful, general way.

Agency relations. The second major critique of profit-maximisation, which has attracted considerably more attention in recent years, begins with the observation that most large corporations are not managed by their owners. Thus managers are likely to have objectives other than maximising owners' wealth. Moreover, many boards of directors are dominated by managers, not owners. And, while owners can and do replace directors and managers whose performance is unsatisfactory, the mechanisms available for this purpose

[11] This is the most natural and common generalisation, but it ignores two problems. When capital markets are incomplete, shareholders will not necessarily vote unanimously for wealth maximisation – or for anything else (Drèze, 1985). And in strategic settings, owners' interests may be best served by managers who do not aim to maximise profit (Vickers, 1985). If the owners of a monopoly want to deter entry, for instance, they might want to hand control of the firm over to irrational managers who would be willing to incur any losses necessary to drive any entrants out of business – as long as these managers can convince all potential entrants of their irrationality and job security.

[12] There is an obvious tension between these observations and the extreme rationality assumed in many game-theoretic models.

(takeovers and proxy fights) are hardly frictionless. Thus managers are likely to have some freedom to pursue their own objectives at owners' expense.

This critique led initially to the development of models in which managers maximised some specific personal objective, such as revenue, employees, growth, or managerial perquisites, subject to a profitability constraint imposed by product and capital markets. It is not clear what is the 'correct' managerial objective, and the determinants of the crucial profitability constraint are typically left unspecified. Related empirical work has produced mixed results (Smirlock and Marshall, 1983).

More recently, the tools of agency theory have been employed to model the implications of asymmetric information when ownership and control are separated (Jensen and Meckling, 1976). The firm is viewed through the lens of agency theory as a set of contracts (some provisions of which may be fixed by law or custom) among input suppliers. These contracts are generally incomplete; they do not fully specify the consequences for all parties of all possible actions in all possible states of nature. Incompleteness may occur because of asymmetric information (e.g. about managerial effort) or because some observable variables (e.g. the riskiness of investments) are too complex to be objectively verified by third parties, so that contract provisions involving them would be unenforceable.

Optimal contract terms are then derived under relatively specific assumptions about information and strategy sets. These contracts are then often compared informally to actual laws, customs, and institutions. Departures from profit maximisation are usually treated as managerial slack or failure to provide effort, not as pursuit of alternative objectives. This research has turned up a number of theoretical phenomena discussed at more length in the next section: actions may be rationally undertaken mainly to affect others' perceptions even when the others are aware of this possibility and are not fooled, for instance. In many situations, optimal contracts cannot induce the behaviour that would occur under full or symmetric information, and systematic departures from profit-maximisation are predicted in a variety of settings. But few of these predictions have been tested empirically, and no tractable, general alternative to the profit-maximisation assumption has yet emerged from this research.

Agency-theoretic work on the firm spills over into finance when it considers the operation of capital markets; it spills over into labour economics when it considers employment arrangements and superior/subordinate relations. The tools of agency theory have also been used to study the design of institutions or mechanisms for regulating natural monopolies or supervising public enterprises under asymmetric information. Many models have been analysed, and prescriptions seem sensitive to details of the assumed information structures. Beyond the result that 'cost plus' regulatory (or other) contracts are rarely optimal, little in the way of operational policy guidance has yet emerged from this work (Joskow and Schmalensee, 1986). Similarly, no terribly strong arguments for privatisation of government-owned natural monopolies have been developed (Vickers and Yarrow, 1988).

Conglomerate Mergers. An interesting set of issues broadly related to the separation of ownership and control has been raised by the wave of *conglomerate mergers* and acquisitions – combinations of firms that are not participants in the same product markets – in the United States in the 1980s. Shareholders of acquired firms seem generally to benefit from the announcement of these events, and acquiring firms' shareholders do not suffer visible losses (Jensen and Ruback, 1983). This favourable *ex ante* verdict from the stock market has been interpreted as implying that mergers on balance enhance efficiency, often by replacing inept management.

But studies of actual post-merger performance paint a rather different picture. Numerous studies in the United Kingdom and the United States have found post-merger declines in productivity, profitability, market share, and even stock prices (Cowling *et al.*, 1980; Ravenscraft and Scherer, 1988). It is unclear why *ex ante* and *ex post* evaluations of mergers point in such different directions, though the latter suggest the possibility that at least some mergers serve managers better than shareholders in the long run.

Scale and Concentration

Most work on the determinants of firms' scales has been motivated by a desire to understand how *seller concentration* is determined.[13] Common measures of seller concentration increase as the number of sellers declines and as their shares become less equal; each thus gives an industry's location on some line between competitive and monopoly structures. Measures of this sort include the four-firm concentration ratio, the share of output accounted for by the four largest sellers, and the Herfindahl–Hirschman H index, the sum of all sellers' squared market shares. These and other plausible concentration measures are highly (but not perfectly) correlated, and they tend to change slowly over time.

It seems clear that firms' scales – and thus market concentration – reflect what Scherer (1980, ch. 1) has termed *basic conditions* of technology and demand as well as business decisions and historical accidents. Concentration is thus endogenous in the long run.

Economies of scale. Rank correlations of manufacturing industries' concentration levels between industrialised nations are very high (Pryor, 1972), suggesting that some important common factor is at work. Technology is the most obvious candidate. Industrial economists have traditionally devoted considerable attention to the hypothesis that the more important are *economies of scale* in any particular industry, the higher will be seller concentration in that industry, all else equal.

Empirically, long-run average cost (LAC) curves seem generally to be L-shaped: at small scales average cost declines with increases in output, but average cost is approximately constant for output rates above some minimum efficient scale (MES). The importance of scale economies is typically measured by the ratio of MES to the total capacity or output of the industry, sometimes

[13] Curry and George (1983) provide a useful survey of the literature on measures and determinants of seller concentration.

augmented by a measure of the steepness of the LAC curve at scales below MES.

Estimates of MES have been obtained by interviewing engineers and executives, by studying the variation of cost or profitability with scale, by seeing what sizes of plants or firms seem to prosper, and by assuming that some fraction (usually half) of an industry's output is produced in efficient plants either in the country of interest or in some larger country (typically the United States). Estimates based on real data inevitably reflect competitive conditions and historical investment patterns, along with the characteristics of best-practice technology that are of primary interest. Answers given in interviews may be speculative when questions go beyond the design decisions with which interviewees are familiar: many people design plants, but few design firms.

Despite these measurement problems, a large number of studies have found significant positive relations between seller concentration and the market share of a MES plant or (in only a few studies) firm. But the leading firms in many US markets are apparently much larger than MES, so that concentration is higher than is strictly required for production efficiency (Scherer, 1980, ch. 4). (In smaller national markets the opposite problem is often encountered, particularly where high tariff barriers are present.) A related finding is that the expected negative relation between market growth and changes in concentration tends to be weak. Similarly, among large industrialised nations, concentration levels do not decline much with increases in the size of the economy (Pryor, 1972). The sizes of leading firms tend to increase with the size of the national market, in part through increases in the extent of multi-plant operations (Scherer *et al.*, 1975).

Learning by doing. Since it was noticed during World War II that the labour required to build particular types of ships and aircraft declined with the cumulative volume of production, similar *learning economies* have been observed in a wide variety of settings. But only a few empirical studies have analysed variations in the importance of learning in particular processes (Lieberman, 1984). Even less work has been done on variations in the extent to which the benefits of one firm's learning spill over to other firms or lower the costs of other products produced by the same firm.

Confining himself to the case, stressed in the business strategy literature, in which learning spillovers are completely absent, Spence (1981) explored the analogy between learning economies and economies of scale. Holding constant the ultimate total cost decline that learning can produce, Spence argued that learning would affect concentration most like economies of scale when learning economies are exhausted at 'moderate' values of cumulative output. If exhaustion occurs at 'low' cumulative output, a new firm needs essentially to incur only a small fixed cost to exploit economies of learning fully. At the other extreme, if full exploitation of learning economies requires 'large' cumulative output, large differences in cumulative production imply only small cost differences. Unfortunately, I know of no empirical studies of the impact of learning economies on market structure.

Other Forces. If LAC curves are indeed approximately flat above MES, apparently 'excessive' concentration is not surprising. Relative sizes of firms that have attained MES might well change because of apparently random innovations in production and marketing, with 'better' firms growing at the expense of their rivals (Demsetz, 1973). Any particular innovation might tend to increase or decrease concentration, depending on whether it was made by a relatively large or relatively small firm. As this reasoning would suggest, US manufacturing industries that experience large increases or decreases in concentration tend to show above-average increases in productivity and below-average increases in price (Gisser, 1984). A variety of stochastic processes that might plausibly summarise this mechanism tend over time to produce skewed firm size distributions with considerable inequality in firm sizes, broadly consistent with the facts in most US and UK industries.[14] Similarly, concentration can be maintained or increased by strategic behaviour aimed at deterring entry or disadvantaging small rivals.

Another process leading to 'excessive' concentration is *horizontal mergers* – combinations of competitors. The importance of this process has been vigorously debated, particularly in the United Kingdom (Curry and George, 1983). On balance, mergers seem to have been important sources of concentration in some EEC nations, but not in the United States, where policy toward horizontal mergers was quite strict from the early 1950s until the Reagan years. Shareholders of rival firms tend to gain from major horizontal mergers, as the frequently-hypothesised relation between concentration and monopolistic behaviour implies, but the size of the gain appears unrelated to the level of concentration (Eckbo, 1985). On the other hand, some horizontal mergers do seem to raise prices (Barton and Sherman, 1984).

Scope and Organisation

When firms produce multiple products, as virtually all real firms do, long-run cost functions cannot be described solely in terms of single-product economies of scale. Indeed in the multi-product context, product-specific average costs are not in general well defined, and the definitions of economies of scale and natural monopoly must be significantly generalised (Baumol *et al.*, 1982). Moreover, it seems clear that the boundaries between firms and markets and the internal organisation of business firms are not determined only by the technology of production; the technology of transaction governance and supervision also matters.

Economies of scope. One of the more useful concepts that emerges from recent work on multi-product cost and production functions is *economies of scope*, which are present when total cost can be reduced by consolidating production of multiple products within a single enterprise. Roughly, economies of scope arise if (but not only if) there are scale economies in the provision of services used to produce more than one output: the same switch can be used for both local and long-distance telephone service, for instance, or the same trucks can be used to

[14] In the US data, which have been most intensively studied in this respect, it appears that the variance in year-to-year firm growth rates declines with firm size, while the mean growth rate declines somewhat with both size and firm age (Evans, 1987).

deliver a wide array of products to grocery stores. One would expect firms to design product lines to exploit important scope economies, just as one would expect generally to observe firms large enough to exploit important economies of scale. But, while a number of authors have estimated multi-product cost functions, serious empirical use of multi-product cost concepts is not common.

Transaction governance. The agency theory view of the firm is complementary to a line of research based on the argument that under competitive conditions, economic activity will be organised so as to economise on production costs plus *transactions costs* (Williamson, 1985). The many forms of transaction governance observed in practice can be thought of as forming a continuum, with classic spot markets and internal governance within firms at the extremes and contracts of varying duration and complexity in between.

Work on transactions costs has concentrated on the identification of transaction attributes that generally affect the comparative performance of alternative governance structures in a world of selfish, boundedly rational actors, asymmetric information, and incomplete contracts. The transaction attribute most stressed in recent work has been *asset specificity*, the extent to which a particular transaction requires tangible or intangible assets that would be of substantially less value if redeployed to alternative transactions. Asset specificity is closely related to the notion of *sunk costs*, costs that could not be recovered if a particular activity were abandoned. The costs of digging a coal mine are sunk, for instance, since they would be lost if the coal business were abandoned. But no asset specificity is involved if a coal mine can easily sell on a spot market to many alternative customers. On the other hand, if an electric generating plant is built at the mouth of a coal mine, asset specificity is important, since the value of both the mine and the plant would decline if the mine had to sell its coal elsewhere and the generating plant had to ship in its coal from other mines.

The general argument is that when asset specificity is important, contractual incompleteness inevitably puts at least one party to the transaction at considerable risk, since the value of his investment would decline substantially if the transaction broke down. Even if *ex ante* many firms compete to dig a coal mine next to some particular power plant, *ex post*, after one firm has dug a mine, there is bilateral monopoly for the remainder of the life of the transaction. High degrees of asset specificity are predicted to lead to complex long-term contracts or internal governance within firms. This and related predictions from this framework are difficult to test because it is not clear, for instance, how asset specificity can be routinely quantified. Still, a fair number of empirical studies have produced supportive results (Joskow, 1987).

Internal organisation. Depending on the technology of supervising employees, individually and in groups, and on a particular firm's market environment(s) and long-run strategy, different internal structures may be optimal. Considerable research, much of it outside the usual boundaries of economics, has been done on the determinants and effects of firms' internal structures (Caves, 1980). This work seems to have shown, among other things, that both the rise of middle management around the turn of the century (Chandler, 1977) and the more recent shift toward organisations based on multiple, relatively independent operating divisions (Williamson, 1985) reflected organisational innovations of considerable value under a fairly broad range of market and strategic conditions.

Vertical relations. Two closely related lines of work have focused on vertical integration decisions and on contractual arrangements between manufacturers and firms providing wholesale and retail distribution services. This work has been motivated in large measure by the traditional hostility of antitrust authorities toward *vertical mergers* – combinations of a buyer and a seller – and toward a set of contractual provisions that are called *vertical restraints* in the United States. These provisions limit a distributor's freedom to compete – for instance by specifying prices to be charged at retail.

Much of the literature on vertical integration employs the agency theory or transactions costs framework and thus focuses on sources of efficiency gains. But vertical integration may also be a response to or source of competitive imperfections. A number of early authors argued that industry-wide vertical integration that eliminated an intermediate product market could make entry more difficult by requiring an entrant to both produce and consume that product. Vertical integration may be profitable but have at best ambiguous welfare effects if it permits a monopoly manufacturer to price discriminate or to avoid downstream substitution away from its output in production, or if it arises as a response to rationing caused by price rigidities (Carlton, 1979). Very little empirical work has been devoted to integration related to market imperfections, however.

Because vertical restraints typically limit retail competition, antitrust authorities have historically viewed them as signs of retailer cartels. But it is now clear that individual manufacturers can sometimes use vertical restraints to compete more effectively. For instance, a manufacturer might want to fix retail markups in order to induce all retailers to compete by providing demand-enhancing services from which all would benefit (Telser, 1960). Alternatively, placing floors on retail prices might allow high-cost 'prestige' stores to stock the product, and thereby to provide a quality signal to buyers, by removing the threat of price competition from low-cost discounters. But when competition is imperfect at manufacturer or retailer levels, the net welfare effect of privately-profitable vertical restraints is often ambiguous (Rey and Tirole, 1986), in part because they change the nature and intensity of rivalry among manufacturers or retailers. The limited empirical work that has been done in this area (primarily case studies) suggests that vertical restraints serve a wide variety of purposes and that they rarely reflect retailer cartels. But generally ambiguous welfare analyses make it hard to make strong policy prescriptions.

III. PRICE, OUTPUT, AND PROFITABILITY

A central problem of industrial economics since its emergence as a distinct field has been to devise techniques for using observable variables (*market structure*, broadly defined) to predict *conduct* in and *performance* of markets that do not meet the strict structural conditions of perfect competition. This section and the next review work on this problem, which is made difficult because, as we saw above in the case of concentration and will discuss further below, market structures are themselves endogenously determined. The focus here is on choices of price, output, and capacity; non-price rivalry is considered in Section IV.

I begin with research on the exercise of *monopoly power* or, equivalently, *market power*. It is useful here and in what follows to distinguish between short-run and long-run market power. Short-run market power is the ability to raise price profitably above marginal cost; it arises whenever firms face downward-sloping demand curves. Long-run market power is the ability to earn persistently supra-normal profits by setting price above average cost. In the textbook tangency equilibrium of Chamberlinian monopolistic competition, for instance, firms have short-run market power but no long-run market power.

Most work on the exercise of market power employs variants of the standard monopoly model. In an industry with more than one firm, sellers' profits depend on the intensity of rivalry and, in the long run, on the entry of new firms. The next two subsections review theoretical work on these dimensions of behaviour. The final two subsections consider related empirical work on market conduct and performance.

The Exercise of Monopoly Power

Price discrimination. A common symptom of monopoly power is *price discrimination*, which can be roughly defined as selling units of related goods at different percentage markups over marginal cost (Phlips, 1983). In order to discriminate profitably, a firm must be able to affect the prices it receives for its output, to sort units potentially demanded according to their optimal prices, and to avoid arbitrage. The first of these conditions is satisfied whenever firms have short-run monopoly power; price discrimination is consistent with free-entry, zero-profit equilibria involving no long-run power. The monopoly models that dominate this literature are thus potentially components of models of discrimination under other market structures.

Following Pigou, it is useful to consider three basic types of price discrimination. A monopolist practising first-degree or perfect discrimination leaves all its customers just indifferent between buying and not buying. Unlike a non-discriminating monopolist, it does not restrict output. Instead, it maximises total surplus, as under competition, and then appropriates it all. It does not follow that real price discrimination is generally efficiency-enhancing, however, since first-degree discrimination is a limiting case found only in texts and journals.

The simplest of Pigou's other two types is third degree discrimination, which involves sorting customers into groups according to their demand elasticities and charging group-specific prices that vary inversely with elasticity. Case studies provide a rich array of sorting mechanisms: discounts for air travellers who reserve far in advance sort tourists from business travellers, for instance, and supermarket coupons are used only by price-sensitive consumers. In these and other cases, transactions costs seem to be the main check on arbitrage.

Since price discrimination makes marginal rates of substitution unequal, an increase in total output is a necessary condition for third-degree discrimination to increase (Marshallian) social welfare (Varian, 1985). Output is unaffected by discrimination if all group demands are linear and all groups make purchases under both uniform and discriminatory pricing; total output is more likely to increase if sales to some groups are profitable only under discrimination. Ambiguous welfare results of this sort make it hard to prescribe general policies toward price discrimination.

The final Pigouvian type, second-degree discrimination, involves *nonlinear pricing*, in which the buyer's average cost per unit depends on the quantity purchased (Maskin and Riley, 1984). The simplest case of non-linear pricing is the so-called two-part tariff: buyers must pay a fixed charge, F, for the right to purchase any amount at a per-unit cost of P. If individual demand curves do not cross, profits are maximised with F positive and P between marginal cost and the ordinary monopoly price (Oi, 1971). Intuitively, it pays a monopoly to reduce P a bit if it can capture some of the increased consumer's surplus by raising F. If there are a finite number of consumer types with non-crossing demand curves, then under general nonlinear pricing regimes, all types but the one with the largest demand have marginal valuations for the good that exceed marginal cost, and all types but the one with the smallest demand enjoy positive consumer's surplus. Under some conditions the optimal nonlinear price schedule can be implemented by allowing buyers to select from a set of two-part tariffs.

Actual pricing decisions and theoretical studies often involve variations on and combinations of the last two Pigouvian themes. An extensive literature has developed on spatial price discrimination. Random variations in price over time or space may profitably sort buyers according to their costs of search. Multi-product monopolies must consider cross-price elasticities and may find it profitable to sell bundles of two or more products or to use nonlinear pricing (Spence, 1980). Finally, one might think that a monopolist selling a durable good could discriminate intertemporally by lowering price over time, thus effecting first-degree discrimination by sweeping out the demand curve. But sophisticated buyers will anticipate price cuts under these conditions and will postpone their purchases until price falls to marginal cost, so that the monopolist would actually be better off if he could commit never to change price (Gul *et al.*, 1986).

A number of authors have studied the problem of pricing to maximise the welfare generated by a natural monopoly that is subject to a break-even constraint. This research, which has had a significant impact on public utility pricing, is closely related to work on optimal commodity taxation. Since price discrimination is generally profit-maximising, profit-constrained welfare maximisation generally involves departures from marginal-cost pricing in the direction of discriminating monopoly pricing. The use of nonlinear pricing is often particularly attractive in this setting, since it can Pareto-dominate linear pricing (Willig, 1978).

Non-price consequences. Spence (1975) showed that a single-product monopoly could choose a sub-optimal or supra-optimal quality level depending on the details of the demand structure. In order to maximise profit, a monopoly considers the effect of quality only on the reservation price of the marginal consumer, who is indifferent between purchasing and not, rather than on the value of the product to the average consumer. For basically the same reason, multi-product monopolies may offer too much or too little variety. If consumers differ in their willingness to pay for increments to quality, a multi-product monopolist will generally increase quality differences above socially optimal levels (under standard assumptions by lowering qualities at the low end of the product line) in order to facilitate price discrimination.

Oligopoly Theory

The Holy Grail of research in oligopoly theory has been the ability to use observable quantities to predict the intensity of rivalry in markets dominated by a small number of sellers. The literature now contains dozens of formal oligopoly models. These have provided insights that can be used to structure the analysis of particular markets, but they have given us a multitude of possibilities rather than the Holy Grail. Indeed, collectively they suggest that the Grail may not exist.

Cournot versus Bertrand. This point is illustrated by two important oligopoly models that were introduced well before the emergence of industrial economics as a distinct field: the one-period Cournot (output-setting) and Bertrand (price-setting) models. When products are homogeneous, the former predicts behaviour intermediate between competition and monopoly with any finite number of sellers, with competition generally emerging in the limit as the number of sellers grows. Multiplying each of equations (2) by q_i, adding, and rearranging, we obtain

$$(P-\overline{MC})/P = H/E, \tag{4}$$

where E is the market price elasticity of demand, $-P/P'(Q)Q$, H is the sum of squared market shares, $\Sigma(q_i/Q)^2$, and $\overline{MC}$ is average marginal cost, $\Sigma q_i MC_i/Q$. If all N firms have the same cost functions, $H = 1/N$, and the gap between price and marginal cost declines smoothly from the monopoly level to zero as N rises.

The Bertrand model, in contrast, predicts essentially competitive outcomes with two or more sellers when products are homogeneous. If all sellers have the same cost function and there are no capacity constraints, no pure strategy equilibrium with prices above marginal cost can exist, since any seller could increase profits by undercutting the lowest price slightly and capturing the entire market. Even when products are differentiated, outcomes tend to be noticeably more competitive when price is the strategic variable than when quantities are chosen. Intuitively, any single seller's demand curve has roughly the slope of the market curve when rivals' quantities are fixed; its demand curve is much flatter when it can steal sales from rivals by undercutting their fixed prices.

Neither of these classic models is fully satisfactory. The mechanics of price determination are unclear in the Cournot model, while the Bertrand model depends on the absence of capacity constraints. A natural way to unify them is by observing that prices are generally more easily adjusted than capacities and considering a two-period game with capacities chosen in the first period and prices chosen in the second. Unfortunately, the equilibria of this game may either be Cournot or substantially more competitive, depending on how excess demand (which is never observed in equilibrium) is assumed to be rationed (Davidson and Deneckere, 1986).

Two-period games of this sort, in which irreversible first-period commitments are made with a view to affecting second-period play, provide a useful approach to modelling a wide variety of situations. By signing contracts binding themselves to matching the lowest price offered by another firm, for instance, or engaging in a variety of related 'facilitating practices', sellers may be able to support collusive outcomes (Salop, 1986). The observation that government policies (such as export subsidies) may serve as valuable commitments to firms in open economies has led to a fundamental reexamination of the case for free trade (Brander and Spencer, 1985; Krugman, 1986).

Fudenberg and Tirole (1984) have shown that the qualitative nature of first-period strategies in two-period games of this sort depends simply on the signs of two second-order partial derivatives of firms' payoff functions. (See also Bulow *et al.*, 1985.) In particular, first-period strategies generally depend critically on whether the second-period game is of the Bertrand or the Cournot type. While in Cournot models a firm's best response to an aggressive increase in its rivals' output is generally to retreat by reducing its own output, in a Bertrand model (with differentiated products) the best response to an aggressive price reduction is usually to counterattack by cutting price.

Supergames and collusion. In an influential paper, Stigler (1964) argued that oligopoly theory should be based on the theory of cartels. Any cartel has two tasks (Scherer, 1980, chs. 5–7). Its first task is to agree on a course of action – a set of firm-specific outputs, for instance. Agreement is likely to be more difficult the more sellers that must be involved and the greater the differences among their costs and products. Stigler and most subsequent authors have placed more stress on the second task; to deter violations of the cartel agreement. When prices are raised to monopoly levels, each seller stands to gain by making undetected price cuts or output increases. Such cheating is less attractive the more quickly it can be detected and the more severe the punishment that can be credibly threatened. Cartel members may facilitate detection by dividing customers among themselves or adopting a number of related practices. Stigler noted that these same two problems must be solved by firms that attempt *tacit collusion*, on which the subsequent literature has concentrated, and try to mimic the explicit or overt collusion of a cartel without a formal agreement.

Because detection and punishment take time, the supergame framework has often been employed to study the stability of collusive agreements, most often with variants of the Cournot model as the stage game. But with full information, collusion cannot emerge as a perfect equilibrium when the number of periods is finite and known in advance. To see why, suppose the stage game is Cournot. In the last period, firms face a one-period Cournot game, and the outcome must be the Cournot solution. Threats to behave otherwise are not credible. But since nothing done in the second-last period can affect what happens in the last period (beliefs are fixed with full information), the firms face a one-period Cournot game at the start of the second-last period as well. By backward induction, rational players will simply repeat their one-period Cournot strategies whenever there is a known, finite last period.

Thus collusive equilibria can only appear when the horizon is infinite. But in this case the Folk Theorem comes into play: in a large class of models *many* collusive perfect equilibria almost always seem to exist, in which average payoffs exceed those in the stage game equilibrium. Suppose, for instance, that the basic Cournot game discussed in Section I is to be played an infinite number of times and that $MC_i(q_i) = M$, a constant for all firms. Then the single-period monopoly output, Q^m, is well-defined. Let q^c be the single-firm Cournot output obtained by solving equations (2). Suppose each firm's strategy is to produce $q^m = Q^m/N$ in period 1 and in every later period in which the previous period's total output has been Q^m, and to produce q^c otherwise. If all other firms play this strategy, firm i could increase its profits in any single period by increasing its output. But in all subsequent periods it would then earn only Cournot, not monopoly profits. (If all other firms will produce q^c, firm i's best response, by definition, is to produce q^c also.) If the discount rate is low enough, the present value of these future losses will exceed the single-period gains from cheating, and the strategies discussed above will form a Nash equilibrium in which the monopoly output is produced in all periods.

Of course, as Stigler stressed, firms may not be able to observe each others' outputs directly. But even if players can only observe market price, which depends on industry output and a random variable, there generally exists a continuum of collusive equilibria supported by *trigger price* strategies for any finite number of sellers (Green and Porter, 1984). These involve producing a low (collusive or monopoly) output unless market price drops below some level, and then (assuming symmetry) producing q^c for some punishment period. (This threat is credible, as above, since if everyone expects everyone else to produce q^c, the best response is to follow suit.) In these equilibria cheating never occurs, but punishments are nonetheless sometimes carried out.

This literature shows clearly that the more damaging the threats that can be credibly made and the smaller the gains from cheating, the greater the scope for profitable collusion (Abreu, 1986). Thus, somewhat paradoxically, the best sustainable collusive outcomes may be more monopolistic when the stage game is Bertrand than when it is Cournot, since the single-period Bertrand equilibrium involves zero profits, and excess capacity that can be used to fight price wars may instead sustain monopoly prices. Collusion may be more effective at business cycle troughs than at peaks if cheating is more profitable when demand is strong (Rotemberg and Saloner, 1986).

The supergame literature raises some serious questions that have not yet been completely answered. In the absence of explicit collusion, how can firms select a single equilibrium from a continuum – particularly if (as in reality) the firms are not identical? What are we to make of the fact that collusive equilibria generally exist for reasonable numbers of firms – is collusion really almost universal? Is it plausible to think that cheating on collusive understandings never occurs? What happens if firms can renegotiate collusive agreements during a punishment period (Farrell and Maskin, 1987)? The supergame literature seems so far mainly to have added to the long list of possible behaviour patterns developed in other branches of oligopoly theory, not to have placed strong restrictions on observable conduct.

Entry and Exclusion

Bain (1956) defined *barriers to entry* as factors that make it possible for established firms in an industry to enjoy supra-normal profits without attracting new entry.[15] Without entry barriers, there can be no long-run market power; collusive behaviour cannot succeed in raising profits in the long run. Thus preventing the entry of new firms is roughly as important in the long run as restraining rivalry among established sellers. Bain listed four sources of entry barriers: economies of scale, cost advantages of established firms, product differentiation advantages of established firms, and absolute capital costs. This list has generated both controversy and research on the possible exploitation of these factors to deter entry or induce exit. Recent work here, as in other areas, has paid particular attention to the implications of asymmetric information.

Scale economies. In the presence of economies of scale, a viable entrant would add a non-negligible amount to total industry output. Bain (1956) argued a monopolist would engage in *limit pricing* to deter entry in this case by setting pre-entry output high enough (generally above the ordinary monopoly level) so that the addition of an entrant's output would force price below cost. But this argument has a serious game-theoretic problem: the implicit threat to maintain output in response to entry is not credible, since the incumbent (quantity-setting) firm would generally do better to reduce production.

Spence (1977) observed that an incumbent's irreversible pre-entry investment in capacity might make threats of this sort credible by lowering its post-entry marginal cost, thus enhancing its incentives to maintain high output. (See also Dixit, 1979.) Similarly, learning economies may induce an established firm to increase its pre-entry output in order to lower its post-entry marginal cost. In a variety of two-period models, an established monopoly over-invests in the first period to deter entry.[16] Pre-entry output generally exceeds the

[15] Stigler (1968) offered an alternative definition: costs that must be borne by an entrant that were not borne by an incumbent. The main difference is that scale economies cannot constitute an entry barrier according to Stigler. The related concept of *mobility barriers*, obstacles to mimicking other firms' strategies, is often useful in industry analysis (Caves and Porter, 1977).

[16] Most models of entry deterrence assume a single established firm. In oligopolies, incentives to over-invest to deter entry are reduced because deterrence is a public good but increased because investment tends

monopoly level, as in limit-pricing, and profit may be much lower unless scale economies are very important (Schmalensee, 1981). The welfare implications of this behaviour are generally ambiguous, since entry tends to be socially excessive in the presence of economies of scale (Mankiw and Whinston, 1986).

The effects of scale economies also depend critically on timing assumptions and on the importance of sunk costs. In the limiting case of a *perfectly contestable* market there are no sunk costs, so that firms can enter or exit an industry costlessly, and entrants can enter, undercut incumbents' prices, and exit before incumbents can react. Under these strong assumptions about costs and differential reaction lags, and with other sources of entry barriers assumed away, potential entrants can enforce essentially competitive outcomes even in natural monopolies (Baumol *et al.*, 1982). More generally, the higher are sunk costs, the greater the risk assumed by entrants, and thus the less attractive is entry. Thus *barriers to exit*, tangible and intangible sunk costs that make exit unattractive even when economic profits are negative, also serve to discourage entry.

In some markets scale economies imply that capacity is most economically added in large lumps, and investment costs are mostly sunk. Under these circumstances entry may be rationally prevented by *pre-emption*, the seizing of a discrete opportunity by an incumbent firm with market power before it can be used by an outsider to enter. The value of a new plant to an incumbent monopolist in a growing market is the difference between the monopoly profit it would enjoy with the plant and its share of the duopoly profit that it would receive if a potential entrant built the plant and entered. The value to an entrant is its share of duopoly profit in the latter case. As long as monopoly profit exceeds total duopoly profit, the plant will be worth more to the incumbent – who will thus have an incentive to build it before the market has grown enough to attract an entrant.

Other Bainian barriers. The effects of incumbents' cost advantages on entry incentives is sensitive to assumptions regarding post-entry rivalry.[17] If the post-entry game would be Bertrand (with simultaneous moves) even a tiny cost advantage of an established monopoly serves to deter entry. But in the Cournot case, entry may be profitable despite higher costs. Indeed, with linear demand and constant costs, it is easy to show that high-cost but profitable entry may lower total surplus in the latter case.

Switching costs may be important sources of product differentiation advantages of established firms in some markets. Switching costs may be objective, as in the case of computer systems, or subjective, deriving from a satisfied customer's rational reluctance to experiment with an untried entrant (Schmalensee, 1982). While it seems clear that these costs can advantage early

---

to raise pre-entry profits if price is above cost. In some models the second effect dominates, and oligopolies facing potential entrants invest more (and deter entry more effectively) than a monopoly would.

[17] Some recent work has treated cost advantages as endogenous, stressing the ability of firms under some conditions to advantage themselves, and possibly induce exit, by actions in input markets that differentially raise rivals' costs (Krattenmaker and Salop, 1986).

entrants, the critical role of expectations in buyers' decisions makes multi-period modelling difficult outside steady states.

Bain's argument that an entrant's need to invest absolutely large sums of money might serve as a barrier to entry has been widely criticised because it seems to rest on capital market imperfections; incumbents also had to invest large sums. Bain might have been groping toward the sunk cost issues discussed above. Or, he might have anticipated the point that even perfectly competitive capital markets may be seriously affected by asymmetric information regarding a potential entrant's prospects.

Information and reputation. Information asymmetries can rationalise a variety of policies to deter entry or induce exit (Roberts, 1987). If its costs are unobservable, an established monopolist may set price below the monopoly level, as in earlier limit-pricing models, in order to signal to potential entrants that its costs are lower than theirs would likely be. On the other hand, if potential entrants know only that their post-entry costs would be similar to those of an incumbent monopolist, the latter may set price *above* the monopoly level in order to signal that its costs are high and the market is thus relatively unattractive (Harrington, 1986). Of course, since rational actors understand opponents' incentives perfectly and probability distributions of cost levels are common knowledge, nobody is fooled on average in equilibrium in either case.

Imperfect information can also provide a rationale for *predatory pricing*, a legal term of art generally taken to mean charging unprofitably low prices in order to eliminate an established rival.[18] Until relatively recently, the following points were taken as a proof that predatory pricing is rarely if ever rational. The predator's losses generally exceed the prey's, since the prey can shut down temporarily, while the predator must make substantial sales to keep price low. Even if the prey is driven into bankruptcy, the predator may need to acquire the prey's assets in order to avoid their being operated by a new rival. But then it will surely be cheaper simply to merge with the prey at the outset than to incur losses driving it from the market.

A number of recent studies have argued that potential entrants might well attach some positive probability (assumed of course to be common knowledge) to the possibility that an established monopoly is irrational – that it will always prey on entrants regardless of the costs. Then a rational established firm facing a finite set of potential entrants will often find it optimal to prey on the first few entrants in order to build (or, more precisely, to avoid destroying) a useful *reputation* for irrationality (Kreps and Wilson, 1982). With incomplete information, predation may also serve to lower the cost to the predator of acquiring the prey (Saloner, 1987). Unfortunately, since unobservable beliefs play a critical role in reputation models, these models place relatively weak restrictions on observed behaviour; they imply the potential rationality of predation under almost any observable conditions.

[18] Most proposed policy rules for evaluating charges of predation employ tests based on market structure and cost-price relations (Joskow and Klevorick, 1979). Such rules lack formal welfare-theoretic rationales and are not well-suited for handling the sort of predation discussed in the next paragraph, though they do serve in practice to dispose of many groundless cases brought by high-cost producers.

Does Market Structure Matter?

Let us now turn to empirical research.[19] Many of the industry case studies discussed in Section I seemed to detect tacitly collusive patterns of behaviour in a variety of concentrated markets. But later, more quantitative studies have produced less clear-cut evidence of market power.

Profitability differences. Oligopoly theory suggests at least the plausibility of the hypothesis that there is a negative relation between seller concentration and the average intensity of rivalry. Bain (1951) argued that this implies that concentration should be positively correlated with industry-average profitability, and he found some support for such a correlation. Literally hundreds of subsequent studies have examined the relation between concentration and profitability in cross-section data.

Through the early 1970s, most such studies found a weak, positive correlation between concentration and industry-average profitability. The weakness of this relation was generally attributed to problems of defining markets and measuring profitability, and these results were generally interpreted as confirming the hypothesis that concentration tends to facilitate collusion and otherwise limit rivalry.

Then Demsetz (1973) provided a plausible and disturbing alternative interpretation. To illustrate his argument, suppose that the single-period Cournot model developed above describes price formation in all markets, regardless of the level of concentration. Since cross-section regressions aim to reveal differences in long-run equilibria, suppose further that all production takes place under constant returns to scale (all firms are above MES) but that costs may differ within individual markets. Then equation (4) implies that for any individual industry

$$\Pi/(PQ) = H/E, \tag{5}$$

where $\Pi/(PQ)$ is the industry's rate of return on sales.[20] For any value of N, H will be larger the greater the variance in firms' costs.

This model thus predicts that in industries in which all firms are roughly equally efficient, concentration and industry-average profitability will be low. In industries in which some firms are noticeably more efficient than others, the more efficient firms will tend to capture large market shares, so that concentration will be high. And more efficient firms will earn rents, so that industry-average profits will also be high. Thus concentration and industry-average profitability will be positively correlated even though there is no collusion anywhere.

This formal model probably overstates the dependence of concentration on idiosyncratic cost differences in light of the high correlations between concentration levels in different nations. But Demsetz's basic argument has received some empirical support. Bain's (1951, p. 320) did note that in his data,

[19] Pakes (1987) and Geroski (1988) provide useful discussions of recent empirical work on the topics considered here.

[20] Generalised versions of this equation appear in Cowling and Waterson (1976) and a number of later studies.

'Smaller firms tended to fare about the same regardless of industry concentration; the dominant firms in general had earnings rates that were positively influenced by concentration,' and other US studies have confirmed this finding. Similarly, at the firm or business unit level, market share is strongly correlated with profitability in samples that include many industries, and the coefficient of concentration is negative or insignificant in profitability regressions including market share (Ravenscraft, 1983). On the other hand profitability is not strongly related to market share in a sizeable fraction of manufacturing industries (Porter, 1979). A variety of attempts to discriminate between the Bain and Demsetz interpretations have produced mixed results – suggesting at least that both mechanisms may be at work in the economy.

The 1970s also saw the publication of a host of industry-level studies in which the concentration-profitability correlation was zero or negative. In US data this correlation weakened dramatically in that decade (Domowitz *et al.*, 1986); UK data seem to yield a monotonic relation between concentration and profitability very reluctantly (Geroski, 1981). Thus not only is it now hard to interpret a significant positive correlation between concentration and profitability, it is hard to find such a correlation in many data sets.[21]

Bain (1956) noted that collusion could not sustain high profits in the long run in the absence of barriers to entry. This calls for an interactive (concentration × barriers) specification, but such specifications have not fared well empirically, perhaps in part because it is difficult to measure barriers to entry reliably. The most robust interactive result of this general sort is that the impact of imports on domestic profitability seems to be higher when domestic concentration is high (Caves, 1985).

A sizeable number of authors have simply added proxies for various sources of entry barriers to regressions of profitability on concentration. In these linear (concentration + barriers) specifications, measures of scale economies or capital requirements of entry tend to be positively related to profitability, as do measures of advertising intensity. (The interpretation of the advertising results is discussed in Section IV.)

In Bain's (1951) data, if one takes average profitability in the unconcentrated subsample to be the competitive rate of return, it follows that monopoly profits in the concentrated subsample average less than 5% of sales.[22] Indeed, even ignoring concentration, observed profitability differences, which are magnified by short-run disequilibria, are generally small relative to those implied by theoretical comparisons between competition and monopoly.[23] For this reason, studies of the total social cost of market power based on observed profitability differences tend to produce tiny deadweight loss estimates.

Industry-specific and behavioural evidence. Inter-industry profitability studies

[21] It is plausible to suppose that high buyer concentration would tend to reduce the effect of seller concentration on profitability. The few empirical tests of this countervailing power hypothesis have produced rather mixed results, however.

[22] The argument underlying this assertion is spelled out in my chapter in Schmalensee and Willig (1989).

[23] On the other hand, it is worth noting that accounting profitability differences among large firms, as well as large firms' market shares, seem to persist for long periods (Mueller, 1986).

suffer from the limitations of accounting data and the inability to measure a host of industry-specific variables. A number of authors have dealt with these problems by examining the correlation between seller concentration and the level of price across markets (often geographically separated) within individual industries. Most find a significant positive relation (Branman *et al.*, 1987), tending to support an association between concentration and restrained rivalry. And there is some evidence that prices, like profits, are raised by tariff protection of concentrated industries. But few price studies attempt to investigate systematically the effects of conditions of entry.

The wave of econometric industry studies that have appeared in recent years generally conclude that firms set price above marginal cost (Cubbin, 1975; Bresnahan, 1987). Estimates of λ_i in equations like (3) always exceed (-1) and seem to be positive more often than negative. The data necessary for these studies are most readily available for concentrated industries, particularly those that have been subjected to antitrust prosecution, many of which sell differentiated products, and many different techniques have been employed in this work. Thus very little has been learned from econometric industry studies about general relations between market conduct and observable elements of market structure. But this work does suggest strongly that short-run market power is exercised in at least some concentrated industries.

The experimental literature mirrors recent theoretical findings: behaviour in laboratory markets seems sensitive to small changes in information and institutional structures (Plott, 1982). In both large-numbers and monopoly situations, the cases that have received the most attention in this literature, performance seems to vary considerably depending on whether prices are posted, negotiated, or called out. A wide variety of outcomes has been observed in broadly similar experimental oligopoly markets. Some practices that have been alleged to facilitate collusion (Salop, 1986) have been observed to have this effect in the laboratory (Grether and Plott, 1984).

Many market settings and hypotheses about strategic behaviour have been investigated experimentally only once or twice; some parts of the theoretical literature have remained untouched by experiments. Like econometric industry studies, laboratory experiments have not yet yielded a set of robust empirical findings that can serve to replace or underlie a general formal theory of imperfect competition. But they do seem generally to support the hypothesis that (exogenous) market structure affects behaviour.

Two additional bits of evidence deserve mention here. Hay and Kelley (1974) found that price-fixing conspiracies, at least those that were detected by US antitrust authorities, tended to occur in concentrated industries. And Hall (1987) has argued that the assumption of short-run monopoly power provides the best explanation for the observation that productivity varies pro-cyclically in many industries.

Rent Dissipation and Rent Sharing

The preceding discussion suggests that short-run market power is not uncommon, but the high profits that would be predicted by long-run market power are rare. It would seem that either the rents produced by pricing above marginal cost are dissipated, perhaps by entry or non-price rivalry, or they are shared by firms' owners with suppliers of other inputs. I deal here with entry and rent sharing and treat non-price rivalry in Section IV.

Entry. If entry is easy, we have known since Chamberlin (and been recently reminded by contestability theory) that prices above marginal cost are consistent with zero economic profits. Official data usually show large numbers of small entrants in most industries, though most obtain tiny market shares, and small new entrants have particularly high failure rates (Dunne *et al.*, 1987).

One might explain away the lack of a robust positive correlation between concentration and profitability by arguing that collusive behaviour tends to attract small inefficient entrants, whose performance depresses industry averages. But the fraction of output produced in inefficiently small plants seems if anything to be negatively related to concentration. On the other hand, the inefficient entry hypothesis is consistent with the finding that tariff protection increases this fraction, particularly in concentrated industries (Baldwin and Gorecki, 1985).

Alternatively, one might argue that monopoly rents are largely dissipated in the process of obtaining market power and deterring the entry of effective rivals. High estimates of the welfare cost of market power are implied by this argument (Cowling and Mueller, 1978), but the theoretical and empirical case for substantial rent dissipation of this sort is somewhat weak (Fudenberg and Tirole, 1987). In particular, little direct evidence of strategic behaviour to deter entry has been detected in industry studies (Lieberman, 1987), though unfortunately few attempts have been made to detect it.

A few studies have examined correlates of measures of the importance of entry. Estimates of the market share of a plant of minimum efficient scale and of the capital cost of such a plant tend to be negatively related to observed entry, as does advertising intensity. Profitability is not generally strongly correlated with subsequent entry, but it is unclear whether this reflects expectations that significant entry would lower profits or the difficulty of measuring profitability.

Labour costs. One might expect managerial behaviour that is not in shareholders' interests to be more prevalent, *ceteris paribus*, when rivalry, and thus market discipline, is weak. And one might expect costs to rise as a consequence of such behaviour, either because managers treat themselves to high salaries, plush offices, and large staffs or because they simply fail to perform the unpleasant task of cost control. There appears to be little empirical support for this view of the world (Smirlock and Marshall, 1983), but measurement problems are obviously severe.

A good deal of work has recently been done on inter-industry wage differences that cannot be explained by differences in worker characteristics

(Krueger and Summers, 1987). Like market concentration, these differences seem stable over time and highly correlated internationally. A number of authors have found that after controlling for worker characteristics, wage rates tend to be high in industries with high profitability (Dickens and Katz, 1987), suggesting that monopoly rents may be largely captured by workers. Rose's (1987) before-and-after study of trucking deregulation in the United States indicates that unionised workers captured over two thirds of the rents produced by regulation. On the other hand, the pattern of wage differences in the Eastern Bloc seems to be highly correlated with that in the West. For this and other reasons, the exact roles of technology, market power, and unobservable worker characteristics in the determination of wage differences remain controversial, though the view that monopoly profits tend to be shared with workers (particularly unionised workers) is coming to be widely held.

IV. NON-PRICE RIVALRY

Despite the picture painted by most microeconomics texts, business managers do not devote all their waking hours to setting price, output, and capacity. Major changes in capacity are infrequent, and prices tend to be rigid, especially in concentrated industries (Carlton, 1986). Important decisions regarding product quality and variety, advertising, and research and development are more frequent in many market settings. These decisions in turn often have important effects on the evolution of market structures.

There is relatively little in the academic empirical literature – or even in the folklore of antitrust – to suggest that non-price rivalry is often much muted by collusive behaviour. Perhaps this is because it is more difficult to monitor rivals' research, advertising, and design activities than their prices and because it takes longer to retaliate along these dimensions than to change prices. At any rate, the literature on non-price rivalry has been more concerned with the social efficiency of noncollusive behaviour than with the possibility of collusion. Little support has been found for the notion that non-price rivalry generally dissipates rents in a socially optimal manner.

Product Selection

Competing sellers rarely choose to offer exactly identical products, since product differentiation generally makes firm demand curves less elastic and thus tends to enhance short-run market power. And product-specific fixed costs (related to design, tooling, and introductory advertising, among other things) imply that production of all possible products is rarely an optimal or equilibrium outcome in any market.

Equilibria and optima. Three types of models dominate the theoretical literature on product selection. In *representative consumer* models (Dixit and Stiglitz, 1977), there is a single buyer who consumes all products on the market and whose utility increases in the number of products available; variety is valued for its own sake. These models are consistent with Chamberlinian large-group monopolistic competition, since a change in any one product's price affects all others symmetrically. They have been used to show that intra-industry international trade, which effectively enlarges markets, can increase welfare by increasing equilibrium variety (Helpman and Krugman, 1985).

The other two types of models involve heterogenous buyers who purchase only one product and products that are described as points in a space with dimensions corresponding to product characteristics. In these models rivalry tends to be *localised* because a change in any product's price mainly affects its nearest neighbours. Thus even in markets with many firms or brands, all sellers may be effectively in small-numbers situations. In models of *horizontal differentiation* (Salop, 1979), buyers would make different choices if all possible products were available free. The analysis of these models generally takes an explicitly spatial form; greater variety gives buyers on average products closer to their ideal points. In contrast, *vertical differentiation* arises if buyers agree on quality comparisons among all possible products but differ in their willingness to pay for increments to quality (Shaked and Sutton, 1983).[24]

Models of all three types indicate that market equilibria rarely involve optimal arrays of products. The optimal (second-best) array would maximise consumer plus producer surplus (conditional on firms' pricing rules). Variety tends to be under-supplied because (without perfect price discrimination) the profit produced by a new product is less than its contribution to total surplus. But variety tends to be over-supplied because (with multiple sellers) the profit earned on a new product generally exceeds its contribution to total industry profit, since the profits earned by rivals' existing products fall. Whether variety is under- or over-supplied on balance depends on the details of the model studied.

Entry deterrence. It has been argued that established firms may find it profitable to bar entry by pre-empting locations in the space of potential products (Schmalensee, 1978). The argument rests on product-specific economies of scale and basically parallels the discussion of pre-emption in Section III: any given product opportunity is more valuable to an established monopolist than to an entrant because entry would increase rivalry and reduce total profits from all products. But without product-specific barriers to exit the game-theoretic problem of the original limit-pricing model reappears: the threat to leave 'nearby' products in place after entry may not be credible (Judd, 1985).

Empirical studies. The marketing literature contains a large set of techniques for estimation of the demand sides of markets with horizontal and/or vertical differentiation (Shocker and Srinivasan, 1979). But these techniques have not been employed by economists. The relevant empirical literature in industrial economics is thin and concentrates on methods of econometric industry analysis when products are differentiated. For instance, Bresnahan (1987) uses a complex econometric model to test conduct hypotheses in a market with

[24] A related literature studies situations in which buyers can verify quality only by use, and sellers have reputations for quality. High quality products will then be priced above cost in equilibrium and yield a flow of excess profits. If not, firms with reputations for high quality will prefer to exploit them by secretly lowering quality (and thus cost) and selling at the same price as high quality products until buyers catch on.

vertical differentiation. Baker and Bresnahan (1985) present a reduced form technique, which avoids the need for structural estimation of demand parameters, for estimating product-specific net demand elasticities that capture the effects of rivals' reactions to price changes. Little work has been done on testing for localised rivalry or distinguishing among alternative forms of differentiation.

Advertising

Advertising has long polarised industrial economists. Some view it as a device for differentiating products, and thus increasing market power, and for building barriers to entry. Others view advertising as a source of consumer information, which thus reduces market power, and as a means of effecting entry by informing consumers of new products. Since advertising ranges from uninformative televised skits about well-known products to newspaper advertisements that provide detailed price and availability information, it would not be a great surprise if both groups were sometimes right.

Theoretical analyses. A number of authors have constructed models of advertising rivalry, treating advertising outlays simply as demand shifters (Friedman, 1983). Such rivalry dissipates profits most effectively when advertising has strong effects on market shares, since then firms' advertising elasticities of demand exceed the corresponding industry elasticity. (Recall the comparison of Bertrand and Cournot models in Section III.) Related models show how economies of scale in advertising interact with those in production to determine the net advantages of size. But to analyse the effects of advertising rivalry on welfare and conditions of entry, one must know exactly how advertising shifts demand.

If advertising alters tastes, for instance, welfare conclusions depend on which set of tastes is used to evaluate advertising-induced output changes (Dixit and Norman, 1978). And, while imperfect information is a potentially important source of market power even when there are no barriers to entry, equilibrium levels of even purely informative advertising are not generally socially optimal (Grossman and Shapiro, 1984). Under some circumstances, equilibrium advertising outlays may provide quality signals to alert consumers, since high-quality producers have the greatest incentive to have buyers sample their wares, but such signalling inevitably involves waste. Overall, the existing theoretical literature indicates that advertising equilibria are generally not welfare optima and that the nature and extent of the differences depend on the details of the model.

If advertising has long-lived effects on demand, it may be rational in a two-period model for an established firm to over-advertise in the first period to deter potential second-period entry. But optimal first-period strategies depend on exactly how advertising is assumed to affect demand and, as in any two-period model, on the type of second-period game assumed.

Evidence. A number of studies have found that advertising/sales ratios in consumer goods industries first rise and then fall as concentration increases (Buxton *et al.*, 1984). While this suggests the possibility that the intensity of advertising rivalry diminishes as concentration reaches high levels, bivariate relations between endogenous variables are inevitably difficult to interpret.

In many cross-section studies, manufacturing industry advertising intensity, typically measured by the advertising/sales ratio, is strongly correlated with accounting profitability.[25] This correlation was initially interpreted as revealing the ability of advertising outlays to differentiate products and create entry barriers. But because advertising is treated as an expense, rather than as an investment, accounting profitability is generally over-stated when advertising has long-lived effects on demand. The over-statement is greater the higher is the advertising/sales ratio and the more slowly advertising effects decay (Demsetz, 1979). Similarly, if (partial) collusion produces high price-cost margins, both optimal advertising spending and profits will generally be high. The existing evidence does not definitively rule out any of these structural interpretations, in part because it is difficult to estimate the rate at which advertising effects decay or to observe exogenous determinants of advertising outlays.

A number of empirical studies suggest that the effects of advertising on market performance depend critically on the nature of the advertising involved and on the roles played by retailers and other information sources (Porter, 1976). In particular, it appears that restrictions on retailer advertising tend to raise prices (Benham, 1972).

Research and Development

It is a commonplace that technical progress, the development and use of new products and processes, is the most important source of increases in consumer welfare in modern economies. Slight reductions in the rate of progress outweigh any plausible estimates of the static welfare costs of monopoly power after only a few years. It is also frequently noted that this subject has received much less study than its importance warrants. But, perhaps because of productivity slowdowns during the 1970s, studies of the sources of technical change have multiplied in the last few years.

Models of technological rivalry. Theoretical work in this area has generally assumed a known, possibly stochastic relation between research and development (R & D) spending and the advance of knowledge. Most studies have considered non-co-operative equilibria in which firms incur R & D costs in the hope of securing a single possible patent.[26] It is sometimes assumed (particularly when firms are asymmetric in some respect) that the firm that spends the most gets the patent. More recent work tends to assume that spending levels instead affect success probabilities; some studies assume that several successive successes are necessary to win the patent.

It has long been accepted that the market system is unlikely to yield the

[25] Comanor and Wilson (1979) survey much of the literature on the arguments discussed in this paragraph. These arguments are also relevant to the positive correlation between profitability and research and development intensity reported in several studies.

[26] There are also interesting recent studies of technology adoption, particularly in the presence of *network externalities* (which imply that the value of a technology to any one user increases with the number of users), and on the strategic uses of patent licensing.

socially optimal rate of technical progress. The traditional view has been that there is generally too little technical progress. Unless patent protection is permanent and patent-holders can practise perfect price discrimination, the private returns to innovation will fall short of the social returns. Monopolies not threatened by entry have particularly weak incentives to innovate, since innovation in effect ends the profit flow produced by their initial monopoly position (Arrow, 1962).

But recent work that explicitly models multi-firm R & D rivalry makes it clear that there can be both too much R & D spending and too much technical progress in equilibrium (Dasgupta and Stiglitz, 1980). Duplication of R & D efforts is a source of social waste, and intense competition for a valuable patent can lead to innovation occurring sooner than would be socially optimal. The efficiency problem here parallels that in the product selection literature; increased R & D spending by a single firm involves an externality because it lowers the expected profits of rivals. A new wrinkle is that because patents are awarded to the first firm to innovate, there is an incentive to adopt excessively risky research strategies, since it does not matter if one loses by a day or a decade. If patent protection is imperfect, so that rivals benefit from each others' R & D, waste is reduced, but so are incentives to invest in research (Spence, 1984).

Market structure is clearly endogenous in the presence of R & D rivalry, since success brings with it some (generally temporary) market power. A number of authors have explored the possibility of pre-emptive patenting to deter entry.[27] In the simplest case, an incumbent monopoly will always outbid a potential entrant for a patent on a new production process that either could use, exactly as a new plant or a new product is more attractive to an established monopoly than to a new entrant (Gilbert and Newbery, 1982). But pre-emption is less likely to be rational if the patent does not yet exist (since the monopoly generally has less to gain from invention), if there is uncertainty in the research process (since a potential entrant may have a positive probability of winning the patent race with even a very small-scale research effort), or if there are multiple patents that can be used to effect entry (Reinganum, 1983). In general, whether R & D rivalry tends to perpetuate concentrated market structures depends on the details of the model studied (Vickers, 1986).

Empirical studies. A number of studies make clear some of the limits of the theoretical literature.[28] Most research is devoted to the development of new products, not new processes, and development (post-invention) spending far outweighs research spending in most industries. In some industries (e.g. chemicals) patents are effective and important instruments for preventing imitation, but they can often be invented around, and in many industries (e.g. electronics) patents are neither effective nor important (Levin *et al.*, 1987). In some cases the time required to copy an innovation is the main source of an

[27] The issues discussed in this paragraph also arise in connection with the acquisition of natural resource deposits.

[28] Surveys of the empirical literature are provided by Kamien and Schwartz (1982) and Stoneman (1983).

innovator's rewards, even though copying is usually cheaper than innovating. It would seem that corporate R & D efforts can only rarely be well described as patent races with a single prize.

Many authors have attempted to test Joseph Schumpeter's assertions that large firms and concentrated industries are disproportionately important sources of technical progress. But, aside from very small firms, which pose particular measurement problems, R & D spending as a percentage of sales does not seem to rise with firm size in most industries (Cohen *et al.*, 1987). Moreover, the largest firms are not disproportionately important producers of major innovations, nor are they quickest in all cases to adopt innovations originating elsewhere. And, adjusting for differences in technological opportunity, increases in seller concentration do not appear to spur R & D effort.

Schumpeter also stressed that R & D rivalry shapes market structures, a theme that runs through the theoretical literature and is broadly consistent with the arguments of Demsetz (1973) discussed above. But this mechanism has received little explicit empirical attention (Temin, 1979).

V. STATUS AND IMPLICATIONS

In this final section I offer a brief overall assessment of the state of industrial economics and discuss some implications for research priorities and policy design.

Status of the Field

Industrial economists have adopted a common theoretical language in recent years and have produced a host of formal models. This work has uncovered a number of general principles, such as the importance of credibility and the consequent value of commitment, that have proved useful in a wide variety of contexts. And our understanding of a number of classic problems, including entry deterrence and cartel stability, has been considerably advanced. But we have also learned two unpleasant features of the game-theoretic approach to the analysis of imperfect competition.

First, even apparently simple multi-period games of incomplete information often have multiple (perfect Bayesian–Nash) equilibria that can be uncovered only by very sophisticated analysis. The assumption that boundedly rational humans can solve the much more complex games they face in real life seems to push the rationality assumption very far indeed. (Chess is soluble in theory, for instance, but not in practice.) But it is not clear how to replace that assumption.[29] Nor is it clear, despite a great deal of effort devoted to refining the equilibrium concepts discussed in Section I, how to deal in general with models possessing multiple perfect Bayesian–Nash equilibria.

Second, the predictions of game-theoretic models seem delicate and are often difficult to test. Important qualitative features of equilibria often depend

[29] Note that learning arguments have very little appeal here, since allowing for the possibility of rational learning requires formulating a new and more complex game. For an interesting alternative (evolutionary) approach to this class of problems, see Axelrod (1984).

critically on whether prices or quantities are choice variables, on whether discrete or continuous time is assumed, on whether moves are sequential or simultaneous, and, perhaps most disturbing of all, on how players with incomplete information are assumed to alter their beliefs in response to events that cannot occur in equilibrium. When information is incomplete, strategies depend on unobservable beliefs, and the often empirically questionable assumption that key parameters and probability distributions are common knowledge is central to the analysis.

I do not mean at all to suggest that the game-theoretic approach should be scrapped. It can not be wrong in principle to spell out explicitly the details of the situation analysed and to derive their implications rigorously. And there is simply no attractive alternative approach available. Still, recent theoretical research has taught us much more about what *might* happen in a variety of market situations than about what *must* happen conditional on observable quantities.

Advances have also been made on the empirical front, particularly in the analysis of individual industries. But, while the empirical research discussed in the preceding sections has uncovered a number of interesting regularities, it has not yet managed substantially to erase the impression that 'anything is possible' left by the theoretical literature. Empirical studies in most areas are still concerned with the existence of hypothesised effects rather than with precise estimation of their magnitudes. Debates still rage, for instance, on whether there is any structural relation at all between market concentration and the intensity of rivalry. Industrial economists can thus speak the same theoretical language and yet disagree sharply as to the empirical relevance of particular theoretical results.

Research Strategies

Most central questions in industrial organisation have by now received considerable game-theoretic attention; the problem is not too little theory but too many different theories. It would appear that research on the theoretical front should be aimed, at least in part, at unification of diverse models and identification of particularly non-robust predictions.

Until game-theoretic analysis either begins to yield robust general predictions or is replaced by a mode of theorising that does so, it seems a fair bet that most major substantive advances in industrial economics will come from empirical research. Only empirical studies can reveal which theoretical models are 'empty boxes' and which have wide domains of applicability. And without the discipline provided by a solid base of facts, theorists cannot be expected to concentrate on deducing the implications of empirically interesting assumptions.

Much of the most valuable and persuasive empirical research in industrial economies employs carefully-constructed data sets. In many cases these are industry-specific; most industrial economists are more confident about the workings of a few well-studied markets than about markets in general. Still other data sets use interviews or surveys to supplement government statistics or contain both time-series and cross-section variation. Since data collection is usually neither intellectually exciting nor highly valued by the economics profession as a whole, progress in industrial organisation may depend critically on the availability of financial support for this important activity.

Policy Design

As I noted at the start of this essay, industrial economists have long been concerned with public policies toward business, and the set of such policies has expanded in recent years. In some domains we are much better able to meet the demand for policy prescriptions than in the past; in others we have mainly learned how little we can confidently assert.

On the positive side, the conceptual and empirical tools available for the analysis of individual markets have been considerably improved.[30] The procedures now used by US antitrust authorities to evaluate proposed mergers, for instance, are radically different from and, on balance, much sounder than those used in earlier decades. The quality of economic analysis in individual antitrust cases and in debates about regulatory policies affecting particular industries has risen sharply.

On the negative side, recent research has cast doubt on many positive and normative relations that were once widely believed to be generally valid. This makes it harder to speak confidently about policies that apply across the economy. In particular, it now seems clear that the level of seller concentration is at best a poor predictor of the intensity of rivalry, so that simple concentration-based rules that once seemed attractive now have little appeal.

Recent theoretical research suggests that market conduct depends in complex ways on a host of factors, and the empirical literature offers few simple, robust structural relations on which general policies can be confidently based. Moreover, formal models of imperfect competition rarely generate unambiguous welfare conclusions. In such models, feasible policy options usually involve movements *toward* but not *to* perfect competition, so that welfare analysis involves second-best comparisons among distorted equilibria. In particular, there is no guarantee that making markets 'more competitive' will generally enhance welfare, particularly if non-price rivalry is intensified.

Even though it is sometimes painful to recognise the limitations of existing knowledge, it can also be quite exciting. Industrial economics today is an intellectually lively field. And the practical importance of understanding the supply side of the economy is certainly not diminishing.

References

Abreu, D. (1986). 'External equilibria of oligopolistic supergames.' *Journal of Economic Theory*, vol. 39, pp, 191–225.

Arrow, K. J. (1962). 'Economic welfare and the allocation of resources for invention.' In *The Rate and Direction of Inventive Activity* (ed. R. R. Nelson). Princeton: Princeton University Press.

Axelrod, R. (1984). *The Evolution of Cooperation.* New York: Basic Books.

[30] These developments have also made industrial economists better able to provide useful strategic advice to business decision-makers, and the academic and commercial markets have generally reacted rationally.

Bain, J. S. (1951). 'Relation of profit rate to industry concentration: American manufacturing, 1936–1940.' *Quarterly Journal of Economics*, vol. 65, pp. 293–324.

—— (1956). *Barriers to New Competition.* Cambridge, Mass.: Harvard University Press.

Baker, J. B. and Bresnahan, T. F. (1985). 'The gains from merger or collusion in product-differentiated industries.' *Journal of Industrial Economics*, vol. 33, pp. 427–44.

Baldwin, J. R. and Gorecki, P. K. (1985). 'The determinants of small plant market share in Canadian manufacturing industries in the 1970's.' *Review of Economics and Statistics*, vol. 67, pp. 156–61.

Barton, D. M. and Sherman, R. (1984). 'The price and profit effects of horizontal merger: a case study.' *Journal of Industrial Economics*, vol. 33, pp. 165–77.

Baumol, W. J., Panzar, J. C., and Willig, R. D. (1982). *Contestable Markets and the Theory of Industry Structure.* New York: Harcourt Brace Jovanovich.

Benham, L. (1972). 'The effects of advertising on the price of eyeglasses.' *Journal of Law and Economics*, vol. 15, pp. 337–52.

Brander, J. A. and Spencer, B. J. (1985). 'Export subsidies and international market share rivalry.' *Journal of International Economics*, vol. 18, pp. 83–100.

Branman, L., Klein, J. D., and Weiss, L. W. (1987). 'The price effects of increased competition in auction markets.' *Review of Economics and Statistics*, vol. 69, pp. 24–32.

Bresnahan, T. F. (1987). 'Competition and collusion in the American automobile industry: the 1955 price war.' *Journal of Industrial Economics*, vol. 35, pp. 457–82.

Breusch, T. S. (1986). 'Hypothesis testing in unidentified models.' *Review of Economic Studies*, vol. 53, pp. 635–51.

Bulow, J., Geanakoplos, J. and Klemperer, P. (1985). 'Multimarket oligopoly: strategic substitutes and complements.' *Journal of Political Economy*, vol. 93, pp. 488–511.

Buxton, A. J., Davies, S. W. and Lyons, B. R. (1984). 'Concentration and advertising in consumer and producer markets.' *Journal of Industrial Economics*, vol. 32, pp. 451–64.

Carlton, D. W. (1979). 'Vertical integration in competitive markets under uncertainty.' *Journal of Industrial Economics*, vol. 27, pp. 189–209.

—— (1986). 'The rigidity of prices.' *American Economic Review*, vol. 76, pp. 637–58.

Caves, R. E. (1980). 'Corporate strategy and structure.' *Journal of Economic Literature*, vol. 28, pp. 64–92.

—— (1985). 'International trade and industrial organization: problems, solved and unsolved.' *European Economic Review*, vol. 28, pp. 377–95.

—— and Porter, M. E. (1977). 'From entry barriers to mobility barriers.' *Quarterly Journal of Economics*, vol. 91, pp. 241–67.

Chandler, A. D. (1977). *The Visible Hand: The Managerial Revolution in American Business.* Cambridge, Mass.: Harvard University Press.

Cohen, W. M., Levin, R. C., and Mowery, D. C. (1987). 'Firm size and R & D intensity: a re-examination.' *Journal of Industrial Economics*, vol. 35, pp. 543–65.

Comanor, W. S. and Wilson, T. A. (1979). 'The effect of advertising on competition: a survey.' *Journal of Economic Literature*, vol. 17, pp. 453–76.

Cowling, K. and Mueller, D. (1978). 'The social costs of monopoly power.' ECONOMIC JOURNAL, vol. 88, pp. 727–48.

—— and Waterson, M. (1976). 'Price-cost margins and market structure.' *Economica*, vol. 43, pp. 267–74.

—— *et al.* (1980). *Mergers and Economic Performance.* Cambridge: Cambridge University Press.

Cubbin, J. (1975). 'Quality change and pricing behaviour in the U.K. car industry.' *Economica*, vol. 42, pp. 45–58.

—— and Geroski, P. A. (1987). 'The convergence of profits in the long run: inter-firm and inter-industry comparisons.' *Journal of Industrial Economics*, vol. 35, pp. 427–42.

Curry, B. and George, K. D. (1983). 'Industrial concentration: a survey.' *Journal of Industrial Economics*, vol. 31, pp. 203–55.

Dasgupta, P. and Stiglitz, J. E. (1980). 'Uncertainty, industrial structure, and the speed of R & D.' *Bell Journal of Economics*, vol. 11, pp. 1–28.

Davidson, C. and Deneckere, R. (1986). 'Long-run competition in capacity, short-run competition in price, and the Cournot model.' *Rand Journal of Economics*, vol. 17, pp. 404–15.

Demsetz, H. (1973). 'Industry structure, market rivalry, and public policy.' *Journal of Law and Economics*, vol. 16, pp. 1–10.

—— (1979). 'Accounting for advertising as a barrier to entry.' *Journal of Business*, vol. 52, pp. 345–60.

Dickens, W. T. and Katz, L. F. (1987). 'Interindustry wage differences and industry characteristics.' In *Unemployment and the Structure of Labour Markets* (ed. K. Lang and J. Leonard). Oxford: Basil Blackwell.

Dixit, A. K. (1979). 'A model of duopoly suggesting a theory of entry barriers.' *Bell Journal of Economics*, vol. 10, pp. 20–32.

—— and Stiglitz, J. E. (1977). 'Monopolistic competition and optimum product diversity.' *American Economic Review*, vol. 67, pp. 297–308.

—— and Norman, V. (1978). 'Advertising and welfare.' *Bell Journal of Economics*, vol. 9, pp. 1–18.

Domowitz, I., Hubbard, R. G., and Petersen, B. C. (1986). 'Business cycles and the relationship between concentration and price-cost margins.' *Rand Journal of Economics*, vol. 17, pp. 1–17.

Drèze, J. H. (1985). 'Uncertainty and the firm in general equilibrium theory.' ECONOMIC JOURNAL (*Supplement*), vol. 95, pp. 1–20.

Dunne, T., Roberts, M. J., and Samuelson, L. (1987). 'Pattern of firm entry and exit in U.S. manufacturing industries.' Mimeographed, Pennsylvania State University.

Eckbo, B. E. (1985). 'Mergers and the market concentration doctrine: evidence from the capital market.' *Journal of Business*, vol. 58, pp. 325–49.

Evans, D. S. (1987). 'The relationship between firm growth, size, and age: estimates for 100 manufacturing industries.' *Journal of Industrial Economics*, vol. 85, pp. 657–74.

Farrell, J. and Maskin, E. (1987). 'Renegotiation in repeated games.' Mimeographed, University of California, Berkeley.

Fisher, F. M. and McGowan, J. J. (1983). 'On the misuse of accounting rates of return to infer monopoly profits.' *American Economic Review*, vol. 73, pp. 82–97.

Friedman, J. W. (1983). 'Advertising and oligopolistic equilibrium.' *Bell Journal of Economics*, vol. 14, pp. 464–73.

—— (1986). *Game Theory with Applications to Economics*. Oxford: Oxford University Press.

Fudenberg, D. and Maskin, E. (1986). 'The Folk theorem in repeated games with discounting and with incomplete information.' *Econometrica*, vol. 54, pp. 533–54.

—— and Tirole, J. (1984). 'The fat-cat effect, the puppy-dog ploy, and the lean and hungry look.' *American Economic Review* (*Papers and Proceedings*), vol. 74, pp. 361–6.

—— and —— (1987). 'Understanding rent dissipation: on the use of game theory in industrial organization.' *American Economic Review* (*Papers and Proceedings*), vol. 77, pp. 176–83.

Geroski, P. A. (1981). 'Specification and testing the profits-concentration relationship: some experiments for the U.K.' *Economica*, vol. 48, pp. 279–88.

—— (1988). 'In pursuit of monopoly power: recent quantitative work in industrial economics.' *Journal of Applied Econometrics*, forthcoming.

——, Ulph, A. and Ulph, D. (1986). 'A model of the crude oil market in which conduct varies over time.' ECONOMIC JOURNAL (*Supplement*), vol. 97, pp. 77–86.

Gilbert, R. J. and Newbery, D. (1982). 'Preemptive patenting and the persistence of monopoly.' *American Economic Review*, vol. 72, pp. 514–26.

Gisser, M. (1984). 'Price leadership and dynamic aspects of oligopoly in U.S. manufacturing.' *Journal of Political Economy*, vol. 92, pp. 1035–48.

Green, E. J. and Porter, R. H. (1984). 'Noncooperative collusion under imperfect price information.' *Econometrica*, vol. 52, pp. 87–100.

Grether, D. M. and Plott, C. R. (1984). 'The effects of market practices in oligopolistic markets: an experimental examination of the Ethyl case.' *Economic Inquiry*, vol. 22, pp. 479–507.

Grossman, G. and Shapiro, C. (1984). 'Informative advertising with differentiated products.' *Review of Economic Studies*, vol. 51, pp. 63–82.

Gul, F., Sonnenschein, H. and Wilson, R. (1986). 'Foundations of dynamic monopoly and the Coase conjecture.' *Journal of Economic Theory*, vol. 39, pp. 155–90.

Hall, R. E. (1987). 'The relation between price and marginal cost in U.S. industry.' Mimeographed, Hoover Institution.

Harrington, J. E., Jr. (1986). 'Limit pricing when the potential entrant is uncertain of its cost function.' *Econometrica*, vol. 54, pp. 429–37.

Harris, M. and Townsend, R. (1981). 'Resource allocation under asymmetric information.' *Econometrica*, vol. 49, pp. 33–64.

Hart, O. and Holmstrom, B. (1987). 'The theory of contracts.' In *Advances in Economic Theory, Fifth World Congress* (ed. T. Bewley). Cambridge: Cambridge University Press.

Hay, D. A. and Morris, D. J. (1979). *Industrial Economics*. Oxford: Oxford University Press.

Hay, G. A., and Kelley, D. (1974). 'An empirical survey of price-fixing conspiracies.' *Journal of Law and Economics*, vol. 17, pp. 13–38.

Helpman, E. and Krugman, P. (1985). *Market Structure and Foreign Trade*. Cambridge, Mass.: MIT Press.

Iwata, G. (1974). 'Measurement of conjectural variations in oligopoly.' *Econometrica*, vol. 42, pp. 947–66.

Jensen, M. C. and Meckling, W. (1976). 'Theory of the firm: managerial behavior, agency costs, and capital structure.' *Journal of Financial Economics*, vol. 3, pp. 305–60.

—— and Ruback, R. (1983). 'The market for corporate control.' *Journal of Financial Economics*, vol. 11, pp. 5–50.

de Jong, H. W. (1986). 'European industrial organization: entrepreneurial economics in an organizational setting.' In *Mainstreams in Industrial Organization*, Book I (ed. H. W. de Jong and W. G. Shepherd). Dordrecht: Kluwer.

Joskow, P. L. (1987). 'Contract duration and relationship-specific investments.' *American Economic Review*, vol. 77, pp. 168–85.

—— and Klevorick, A. K. (1979). 'A framework for analyzing predatory pricing policy.' *Yale Law Journal*, vol. 89, pp. 213–70.

—— and Schmalensee, R. (1986). 'Incentive regulation for electric utilities.' *Yale Journal on Regulation*, vol. 4, pp. 1–49.

Judd, K. L. (1985). 'Credible spatial preemption.' *Rand Journal of Economics*, vol. 16, pp. 153–66.

Kamien, M. and Schwartz, N. (1982). *Market Structure and Innovation*. Cambridge: Cambridge University Press.

Krattenmaker, T. G. and Salop, S. (1986). 'Anticompetitive exclusion: raising rivals' cost to achieve power over price.' *Yale Law Journal*, vol. 96, pp. 209–95.

Kreps, D. M. and Wilson, R. (1982). 'Reputation and imperfect information.' *Journal of Economic Theory*, vol. 27, pp. 253–79.

Krueger, A. B. and Summers, L. H. (1987). 'Reflections on the inter-industry wage structure.' In *Unemployment and the Structure of Labour Markets* (ed. K. Lang and J. Leonard). Oxford: Basil Blackwell.

Krugman, P. R., ed. (1986). *Strategic Trade Policy and the New International Economics*. Cambridge, Mass.: MIT Press.

Lau, L. (1982). 'On identifying the degree of competitiveness from industry price and output data.' *Economics Letters*, vol. 10, pp. 93–9.

Levin, R. C., Klevorick, A. K., Nelson, R. R., and Winter, S. G. (1987). 'Appropriating the returns from industrial R & D.' Mimeographed, Yale University.

Lieberman, M. B. (1984). 'The learning curve and pricing in the chemical processing industries.' *Rand Journal of Economics*, vol. 15, pp. 213–28.

—— (1987). 'Excess capacity as a barrier to entry: an empirical appraisal.' *Journal of Industrial Economics*, vol. 35, pp. 607–27.

Mankiw, N. G. and Whinston, M. D. (1986). 'Free entry and social inefficiency.' *Rand Journal of Economics*, vol. 17, pp. 48–58.

Maskin, E. and Riley, J. 'Monopoly with incomplete information.' *Rand Journal of Economics*, vol. 15, pp. 171–96.

Milgrom, P. and Roberts, J. (1987). 'Informational asymmetries, strategic behavior, and industrial organization.' *American Economic Review (Papers and Proceedings)*, vol. 77, pp. 184–93.

Mueller, D. (1986). *Profits in the Long Run*. Cambridge: Cambridge University Press.

Nelson, R. R. and Winter, S. G. (1982). *An Evolutionary Theory of Economic Change*. Cambridge, Mass.: Harvard University Press.

Nicholls, W. (1951). *Price Policies in the Cigarette Industry*. Nashville: Vanderbilt University Press.

Novshek, W. (1985). 'On the existence of Cournot equilibrium.' *Review of Economic Studies*, vol. 52, pp. 85–98.

Oi, W. Y. (1971). 'A Disneyland dilemma: two-part tariffs for a Mickey-Mouse monopoly.' *Quarterly Journal of Economics*, vol. 85, pp. 77–96.

Pakes, A. (1987). 'Mueller's "Profits in the Long Run".' *Rand Journal of Economics*, vol. 18, pp. 319–32.

Panzar, J. C. and Rosse, J. N. (1987). 'Testing for "monopoly" equilibrium.' *Journal of Industrial Economics*, vol. 35, pp. 443–56.

Phlips, L. (1983). *The Economics of Price Discrimination*. Cambridge: Cambridge University Press.

Plott, C. R. (1982). 'Industrial organization theory and experimental economics.' *Journal of Economic Literature*, vol. 20, pp. 1485–527.

Porter, M. E. (1976). *Interbrand Choice, Strategy, and Bilateral Market Power*. Cambridge, Mass.: Harvard University Press.

—— (1979). 'The structure within industries and companies' performance.' *Review of Economics and Statistics*, vol. 61, pp. 214–27.

—— (1980). *Competitive Strategy*. New York: Free Press.

Pryor, F. L. (1972). 'An international comparison of concentration ratios.' *Review of Economics and Statistics*, vol. 54, pp. 130–40.

Ravenscraft, D. J. (1983). 'Structure-profit relationships at the line of business and industry level.' *Review of Economics and Statistics*, vol. 65, pp. 22–31.

—— and Scherer, F. M. (1988). *Mergers, Sell-Offs, and Economic Efficiency*. Washington: Brookings Institution.

Reinganum, J. (1983). 'Uncertain innovation and the persistence of monopoly.' *American Economic Review*, vol. 73, pp. 741–8.

Rey, P. and Tirole, J. (1986). 'The logic of vertical restraints.' *American Economic Review*, vol. 76, pp. 921–39.

Roberts, D. J. (1987). 'Battles for market share.' In *Advances in Economic Theory, Fifth World Congress* (ed. T. Bewley). Cambridge: Cambridge University Press.

Rose, N. L. (1987). 'Labor rent-sharing and regulation: evidence from the trucking industry.' *Journal of Political Economy*, vol. 95, pp. 1146–78.

Rotemberg, J. J. and Saloner, G. (1986). 'A supergame-theoretic model of business cycles and price wars during booms.' *American Economic Review*, vol. 76, pp. 390–407.

Saloner, G. (1987). 'Predation, mergers, and incomplete information.' *Rand Journal of Economics*, vol. 18, pp. 165–86.

Salop, S. C. (1979). 'Monopolistic competition with outside goods.' *Bell Journal of Economics*, vol. 10, pp. 141–56.

—— (1986). 'Practices that (credibly) facilitate oligopoly coordination.' In *New Developments in the Analysis of Market Structure* (ed. G. F. Mathewson and J. E. Stiglitz). Cambridge, Mass.: MIT Press.

Scherer, F. M. (1980). *Industrial Market Structure and Economic Performance*, 2nd Ed. Chicago: Rand McNally.

——, Beckstein, A., Kaufer, E., and Murphy, R. D. (1975). *The Economics of Multi-Plant Operation.* Cambridge, Mass.: Harvard University Press.

Schmalensee, R. (1978). 'Entry deterrence in the ready-to-eat breakfast cereal industry.' *Bell Journal of Economics*, vol. 9, pp. 305–27.

—— (1981). 'Economies of scale and barriers to entry.' *Journal of Political Economy*, vol. 89, pp. 122–38.

—— (1982). 'Product differentiation advantages of pioneering brands.' *American Economic Review*, vol. 72, pp. 349–65. (*Errata*, vol. 73, p. 250.)

—— (1985). 'Do markets differ much?' *American Economic Review*, vol. 75, pp. 341–51.

—— and Willig, R. D., eds. (1989). *Handbook of Industrial Organization.* Amsterdam: North-Holland.

Schwert, G. W. (1981). 'Using financial data to measure the effects of regulation.' *Journal of Law and Economics*, vol. 24, pp. 121–58.

Shaked, A. and Sutton, J. (1983). 'Natural oligopolies.' *Econometrica*, vol. 51, pp. 1469–83.

Shocker, A. D. and Srinivasan, V. (1979). 'Multiattribute approaches for product concept evaluation and generation: a critical review.' *Journal of Marketing Research*, vol. 16, pp. 159–80.

Smirlock, M. and Marshall, W. (1983). 'Monopoly power and expense-preference behavior: theory and evidence to the contrary.' *Bell Journal of Economics*, vol. 14, pp. 166–78.

Smith, V. L. (1982). 'Microeconomic systems as an experimental science.' *American Economic Review*, vol. 72, pp. 923–55.

Spence, A. M. (1975). 'Monopoly, quality, and welfare.' *Bell Journal of Economics*, vol. 6, pp. 417–29.

—— (1977). 'Entry, capacity, investment, and oligopolistic pricing.' *Bell Journal of Economics*, vol. 8, pp. 532–44.

—— (1980). 'Multi-product quantity-dependent prices and profitability constraints.' *Review of Economic Studies*, vol. 47, pp. 821–42.

—— (1981). 'The learning curve and competition.' *Bell Journal of Economics*, vol. 12, pp. 49–70.

—— (1984). 'Cost reduction, competition, and industry performance.' *Econometrica*, vol. 52, pp. 101–22.

Stigler, G. J. (1964). 'A theory of oligopoly.' *Journal of Political Economy*, vol. 72, pp. 44–61.

—— (1968). *The Organization of Industry.* Homewood: Irwin.

—— (1971). 'The theory of economic regulation.' *Bell Journal of Economics and Management Science*, vol. 2, pp. 3–21.

Stoneman, P. (1983). *The Economic Analysis of Technological Change.* Oxford: Oxford University Press.

Telser, L. G. (1960). 'Why should manufacturers want fair trade?' *Journal of Law and Economics*, vol. 3, pp. 86–105.

Temin, P. (1979). 'Technology, regulation, and market structure in the modern pharmaceutical industry.' *Bell Journal of Economics*, vol. 10, pp. 429–46.

Tirole, J. (1988). *The Theory of Industrial Organisation.* Cambridge, Mass.: MIT Press.

Varian, H. R. (1985). 'Price discrimination and social welfare.' *American Economic Review*, vol. 75, pp. 870–5.

Vickers, J. (1985). 'Delegation and the theory of the firm.' Economic Journal (*Supplement*), vol. 95, pp. 138–47.

—— (1986). 'The evolution of market structure when there is a sequence of innovations.' *Journal of Industrial Economics*, vol. 35, pp. 1–12.

—— and Yarrow, G. (1988). *Privatization: An Economic Analysis.* Cambridge, Mass.: MIT Press.

Williamson, O. E. (1985). *The Economic Institutions of Capitalism.* New York: Free Press.

Willig, R. D. (1978). 'Pareto-superior nonlinear outlay schedules.' *Bell Journal of Economics*, vol. 9, pp. 56–69.

Yarrow, G. (1985). 'Strategic issues in industrial policy.' *Oxford Review of Economic Policy*, vol. 1, pp. 95–109.

3

LABORATORY EXPERIMENTATION IN ECONOMICS: A METHODOLOGICAL OVERVIEW*

Alvin E. Roth

Informal experimentation in economics goes back at least as far as Bernoulli (1738) (in connection with the Petersburg game), and formal reports of laboratory experiments as such have appeared for some time now (see e.g. Allais, 1953; Chamberlin, 1948; Flood, 1958; Friedman, 1963; May, 1954; Sauermann and Selten, 1959; Siegel and Fouraker, 1960; Smith, 1962; Stone, 1958). There are even survey articles on the subject which precede this present one by more than twenty years.[1] Nevertheless, it is probably only in the last ten or fifteen years that laboratory experimentation can be clearly seen to have truly begun its now steady and sustained transformation from an occasional curiosity into a regular means for investigating many kinds of economic phenomena.

Incidentally, when I speak of 'laboratory' experiments, I am not speaking of the location where experiments are conducted, which we will see may be in a casino or an Indian village as well as at a university. Rather I am speaking of experiments in which the economic environment is very fully under the control of the experimenter, who also has relatively unimpeded access to the experimental subjects. This distinguishes laboratory experiments from 'field' experiments, in which relatively few aspects of the environment can be controlled, and in which only limited access to most of the economic agents may be available.[2] It is precisely this control of the environment, and access to the agents (sufficient to observe and measure attributes that are not controlled) that give laboratory experiments their power.

The volume and variety of contemporary experimental work is now sufficiently large that, in a survey of (even) this size, I would be unable to represent it all adequately. Instead, I will aim for the more modest,

* I have enjoyed many helpful discussions about this paper with Jack Ochs and Emilie Roth, both of whom have cheerfully read various preliminary drafts, and suggested many improvements. I have also received useful comments and references to the literature from John Kagel and Graham Loomes, and from John Hey and Andrew Oswald. Any errors of omission, commission, or confusion which have nevertheless made their way into the paper are of course my own responsibility. This work has been partially supported by grants from the National Science Foundation, the Office of Naval Research, and the Alfred P. Sloan Foundation. This chapter was first published in the ECONOMIC JOURNAL, vol. 98, December 1988.

[1] E.g. Cyert and Lave (1965) extolled the promise of controlled experimentation (and excoriated theorists) in a review of experiments bearing on oligopolistic collusion. Friedman (1969) gave a thoughtful review (still well worth reading today) of several experiments, including his own, concerned with oligopolistic competition. Interestingly, his paper appeared in a special 'Symposium on Experimental Economics' that also included reports of experiments by Hogatt (1969), MacCrimmon and Toda (1969), Sherman (1969), Carlson and O'Keefe (1969), and Cummings and Harnett (1969), and which is probably as good an indicator as any that experimentation had by that time already begun to draw sustained attention.

[2] A discussion of field experiments is well beyond the scope of this survey, as they raise some very different methodological issues (cf. Ferber and Hirsch, 1982 or Hausman and Wise, 1985).

methodological goal of illustrating how economists can use the tools they find in the laboratory to make steady, incremental progress on answering questions that would otherwise be intractable.

For this reason my survey will focus on *sets* of experiments which together tell us more than any one of them. By 'more' I do not mean that these sets of experiments permit us to draw *broader* conclusions than might have seemed warranted on the basis of one experiment alone. While this will sometimes be so, it can also be that subsequent experiments serve to define more narrowly the conditions under which some phenomenon initially observed can be expected to occur, or even that subsequent experiments will cause the results of an initial experiment to be entirely reinterpreted. What I want to illustrate is how series of experiments can be constructed to allow us to draw more *reliable* conclusions, both about what we know and about what we know we don't know.

The first four sections of this paper recount several series of experiments, chosen to illustrate both some of the different areas of inquiry to which laboratory experimentation has been applied in economics, and some of the important methodological themes around which debates among experimenters sometimes revolve. Each of the areas I have chosen is sufficiently complex to allow room for experts to differ in their assessment of the nature and causes of some of the principal phenomena encountered. In each of the series of experiments I will describe, initial experiments serve to focus the investigation, and subsequent experiments help to identify potentially critical variables. When we get to the present in each of these series, there is still room for experts to differ, but the room for disagreement has been considerably narrowed, and the nature of remaining disagreements has been clarified. This is, I think, typical of what we can expect of experiments.

Section I concerns several series of experiments investigating two-person bargaining. Among the methodological themes which these experiments will introduce is the importance, and the difficulty, both of creating an experimental environment in which theories being tested give unambiguous predictions, and of controlling or measuring the preferences of experimental subjects.

Section II concerns experiments investigating both the free rider problem and the prisoner's dilemma. The early experiments concerned with each problem concentrated on single decisions, and the later experiments concentrated on repeated decisions, shifting the debate to the role of experience in each case.

Section III concentrates on a controversy that arose over certain kinds of conjectured auction behaviour. While the controversy arose out of differing interpretations of field data, experimental methods proved useful in studying the nature of the phenomenon, and have suggested that the problem can be studied in field data by observing certain qualitative relationships identified in the laboratory.

Section IV concerns experiments involving individual choice behaviour, and focuses on one of many anomalies, from the point of view of expected utility theory, that have been experimentally observed by both economists and psychologists. Even more than the other sections, the experiments discussed here illustrate the extent to which the interpretation of experimental results is influenced by the theoretical predispositions of the investigators.

Section V attempts to tie together some of the methodological themes that arise in the course of the paper, by means of some questions and answers, and Section VI concludes.

Let me close this introduction by apologising to the reader for the fact that I have found it necessary to include a reasonable amount of detail in my description of at least some of the experiments described here. While the details are obviously important in all kinds of work (and good surveys nevertheless manage, mercifully, to leave them out), I think a survey of experiments would be critically incomplete if it failed to at least suggest how very much the details of experimental design are at the heart of how experimental results are interpreted, and sometimes contested. The reader unfamiliar with experimentation may derive what comfort he can from knowing that my experimental colleagues will criticise me for the many crucial details of each experiment (as well as for the many important experiments) that I have omitted.

I. BARGAINING BEHAVIOUR

Theories of bargaining that depend on purely ordinal descriptions of bargainers' preferences tend to predict large sets of outcomes, and for this reason many economists (at least since Edgeworth, 1881) have argued that bargaining is fundamentally indeterminate. In the language of co-operative game theory, the difficulty is associated with the fact that the core corresponds to the entire set of individually rational Pareto optimal outcomes. Similarly, in strategic models (i.e. in the tradition of non-co-operative game theory) the problem is that all of this typically large set of outcomes can be achieved as equilibria of the game. Consequently, theories of bargaining that seek to make stronger predictions have attempted to make use of more detailed information about bargainers' preferences or strategic options.

Since this kind of information is hard to observe in uncontrolled environments, these theories have been notoriously difficult to test with field data. While there have been some attempts to explain observed bargaining outcomes by inferring what the utility functions of the bargainers would have to have been in order to be consistent with the prediction of some particular theory (i.e. with the prediction that could have been made had these utility functions been observable), such exercises cannot serve to provide any sort of direct test of the theory itself. Similarly, the detailed procedural information required to specify a strategic model of bargaining is mostly unobservable in field environments. Consequently, for tests of such theories it is natural to look to the kind of controlled environment and relatively unlimited access to the bargainers that can be obtained in the laboratory.

Although there has been an increasing convergence between the theoretical literature concerned with strategic and co-operative models of bargaining (see e.g. Sutton, 1986), the bargaining environments for which their predictions can be most clearly derived are rather different. Section I.1 will therefore be concerned with experimental tests of co-operative models, and section I.2 will take up a more recent experimental literature concerned with strategic models.

I.1 *Experimental Tests of Axiomatic Models.*[3]

Perhaps the best known family of game-theoretic models of bargaining arises from the work of John Nash (1950). Because of the way he specified his assumptions, these models are referred to as 'axiomatic', and many specific models other than the one originally proposed by Nash have entered the literature (see Roth, 1979).

Nash considered the 'pure bargaining problem' in which two bargainers must agree on one alternative from a set A of feasible alternatives over which they have different preferences. If they fail to reach agreement, some fixed disagreement alternative δ results. Nash modelled such a problem by a pair (S,d), where S is a subset of the plane, and d a point in S. The set S represents the feasible expected utility payoffs to the bargainers, i.e. each point $x = (x_1,x_2)$ in S corresponds to the expected utility payoffs to players 1 and 2, respectively, from some alternative α in A, and $d = (d_1,d_2)$ corresponds to the utility payoffs to the players from the disagreement alternative δ. That is, the theory of bargaining he proposed, and the other theories that have followed in this tradition, take as their data the set (S,d), and thus represent the feasible outcomes (solely) in terms of the expected utility functions of the bargainers. So such theories predict that the outcome of bargaining will be determined by the preferences of the bargainers over the set of feasible alternatives, together with their willingness to tolerate risk.

Because of the difficulty of attempting to capture the information contained in bargainers' expected utility functions, there were sometimes claims in the experimental literature that such a theory was essentially untestable.[4] To get around the difficulty, the earliest experiments[5] designed to test Nash's theory assumed, for the purpose of making predictions about the outcome, that the utility of each bargainer was equal to his monetary payoff. That is, they assumed that the preferences of all bargainers were identical and risk neutral.

Important aspects of the predictions of the theory obtained in this way were inconsistent with the experimental evidence. This disconfirming evidence, however, was almost uniformly discounted by game theorists, who felt that the results simply reflected the failure to measure the relevant parameters. Nash's theory, after all, is a theory that predicts that the preferences and risk aversion of the bargainers exercise a decisive influence on the outcome of bargaining (and, furthermore, that these are the only personal attributes that can influence

[3] Some of the descriptive material in this section is adapted from the generally more detailed presentation in Roth (1987a).

[4] For example, Morley and Stephenson (1977) state 'these theories... do not have any obvious behavioral implications' (p. 86).

[5] Which are reviewed in Roth and Malouf (1979).

the outcome when bargainers are adequately informed). If the predictions made by Nash's theory *under the assumption* that bargainers had identical risk neutral preferences were disconfirmed, this merely cast doubt on the assumption. The theory itself had yet to be tested.[6]

It was therefore clear that, in order to provide a test of the theory that would withstand the scrutiny of theorists, an experiment would have to either measure or control for the expected utility of the bargainers.

A class of games that control for the bargainers' utilities was introduced in the experiment of Roth and Malouf (1979). In these *binary lottery games*, each agent i can eventually win only one of two monetary prizes, a large prize λ_i or a small prize σ_i (with $\lambda_i > \sigma_i$). The players bargain over the distribution of 'lottery tickets' that determine the probability of receiving the large prize: e.g. an agent i who receives 40% of the lottery tickets has a 40% chance of receiving λ_i and a 60% chance of receiving σ_i. Players who do not reach agreement in the allotted time each receive σ_i. Since the information about preferences conveyed by an expected utility function is meaningfully represented only up to the arbitrary choice of origin and scale (and since Nash's theory of bargaining is explicitly constructed to be independent of such choices), there is no loss of generality in normalising each agent's utility so that $u_i(\lambda_i) = 1$ and $u_i(\sigma_i) = 0$. The utility of agent i for any agreement is then precisely equal to his probability of receiving the amount λ_i, i.e. equal to the percentage of lottery tickets he has received. Thus in a binary lottery game, the pair (S,d) which determines the prediction of Nash's theory is precisely equal to the set of feasible divisions of the lottery tickets.[7]

Note that the set of feasible utility payoffs to the players of a binary lottery game is insensitive to the magnitudes of λ_i and σ_i for each agent i. Furthermore, the bargainers have what the game theory literature calls 'complete' information whether or not they know the value of one another's prizes, since knowing a bargainer's probability of winning his prize is equivalent to knowing his utility. Thus a theory of bargaining under conditions of complete information, that depends only on the utility payoffs to the bargainers, predicts that the outcome of the game will depend neither on the size of the prizes, nor on whether the bargainers know the monetary value of one another's prizes.

The experiment of Roth and Malouf (1979) was designed in part to test this prediction, and determine whether or not changes in the size of the prizes, and whether the bargainers knew one anothers' prizes, influenced the outcome. All

[6] Of course it is commonplace in interpreting field data in economics that one is often obliged to accept or reject joint hypotheses, which cannot be separated from one another. Much of the power of experimental methods comes from the fact that they often allow us to test such hypotheses separately.

[7] Note that no assumptions have been made here about the behaviour of the experimental subjects themselves in binary lottery games. (That is, the subjects might not be utility maximisers (see Section IV), or they might have preferences over distributions of payoffs to both players, rather than over their own monetary payoffs (see Sections I.2 and I.3). What binary lottery games do allow us to know is the utility of utility maximisers who are concerned with their own payoffs. Since this is the kind of data required by Nash's theory, experiments using binary lottery games allow us to use the theory to make precise predictions. It is this which was missing from earlier experiments, and from efforts to analyse bargaining data by inferring *ex post* what the utility of the bargainers might have been.

games were played by bargainers seated at separated computer terminals, who could send text messages to each other, but who were prevented from identifying themselves to one another, or from otherwise determining with whom they were bargaining. Each bargainer played games with different prizes against different opponents in one of two information conditions. In the 'full information' condition, each bargainer knew both his own prize and his counterpart's; while bargainers in the 'partial information' condition each knew only their own prize value. (In each of these games, under both information conditions, the prediction of Nash's theory is that the bargainers would each receive 50% of the lottery tickets.)

The results were that, in the partial information condition, and also in those games of the full information condition in which the two bargainers had equal prizes, observed agreements clustered very tightly around the 'equal probability' agreement that gives each bargainer 50% of the lottery tickets. In the full information condition, in those games in which the bargainers' prizes were unequal, agreements tended to cluster around two 'focal points': the equal probability agreement, and the 'equal expected value' agreement that gives each bargainer the same expected value. The mean agreement in these games fell approximately half way between the equal-probability and equal expected value agreements. That is, in these games the bargainer with the lower prize tended to receive a higher share of the lottery tickets. Thus, contrary to the prediction of the theory, the monetary values of the bargainers' prizes were clearly observed to influence the agreements reached when the bargainers knew each other's prizes.

Subsequent experiments (Roth *et al.*, 1981; Roth and Malouf, 1982; Roth and Murnighan, 1982; Roth and Schoumaker, 1983) were conducted to verify that these results were not artefacts of the particular experimental procedures, and to explore further the unpredicted effects of information in bargaining that the data from Roth and Malouf (1979) so clearly revealed. Because I have recently discussed most of these experiments in Roth (1987*a*), I will not describe them again here. But for the purposes of this paper, three further points are worth making.

The first is that the appearance from the results of Roth and Malouf (1979) that Nash's theory was a good point predictor of agreements in the partial information condition did not survive examination of a wider class of games. The robust feature of those results, rather, was that when players did not know one another's monetary value for agreements, there was a tendency to reach agreements that gave each bargainer an equal share of the commodity being divided, whether this was lottery tickets or some more usual medium (see Roth and Malouf, 1982).

The second point is methodological. All these experiments make critical use of the control that laboratory environments allow. For example, in Roth and Murnighan (1982), one of the eight cells of the experiment involved a binary lottery game, with prizes $\lambda_1 = \$20$, $\lambda_2 = \$5$, and $\sigma_1 = \sigma_2 = 0$, in which both players were aware that the \$5 player knew the size of both players' prizes and the \$20 player knew only his own prizes. Another cell of the experiment involved different players playing the same game, again with the \$5 player knowing both players' prizes and the \$20 player knowing only his own, except in this cell each player was uninformed about what the other player knew. (In both cells, players were free to make any statements they wished about what their prizes were, and about what they knew.) This experimental manipulation, which did not alter what the bargainers knew about each other's prizes, but only what they knew about what the *other* knew, was observed to have a significant effect on the frequency of disagreement. (The highest frequency of disagreement in the experiment, 33%, was observed in the second of the two cells described above, in contrast, for example, to a 19% frequency of disagreement in the first of those cells.) It is hard even to imagine any field data that might allow the effect of this kind of information difference to be observed. But, in view of the importance of notions such as 'common knowledge' in contemporary game theory, differences of precisely this kind are increasingly encountered in the theoretical literature.[8] Laboratory experiments give us what has at least so far proved to be the only direct way to investigate them.

Note finally that the regularities among these unpredicted effects of information make it unlikely that they can be attributed primarily to mistaken or irrational behaviour on the parts of the bargainers. For example, in the four cells of the above experiment in which the bargainers do not know what information their counterpart has, the tradeoffs between the higher payoffs demanded by the \$5 player when he knows both prizes and the correspondingly increased frequency of disagreements is what would be expected at equilibrium, in that the increase in the number of disagreements almost exactly offsets the increased share obtained by the \$5 player when agreements are reached.

These experiments involved variables which the theories in question predict will not influence the outcome of bargaining. They revealed ways in which the theories systematically fail to be descriptive of observed behaviour. As such, the experimental results demonstrate serious shortcomings of the theories. However, in order to evaluate a theory fully, we also need to test the predictions it makes about those variables it predicts *are* important. For theories based on bargainers' expected utilities, risk posture is such a variable.

The predictions of these theories concerning the risk posture of the bargainers were developed in a way that lent itself to experimental test in Roth (1979), Kihlstrom *et al.* (1981), and Roth and Rothblum (1982). A broad class of apparently quite different models, including all the standard axiomatic models, yield a common prediction regarding risk aversion. Loosely speaking, they all predict that risk aversion is disadvantageous in bargaining, except when the bargaining concerns potential agreements that have a positive probability of yielding an outcome worse than disagreement.

Three closely related experimental studies exploring the predicted effects of risk aversion on the outcome of bargaining are reported in Murnighan *et al.*

[8] For example, just such distinctions are made in the theoretical literature on reputations, such as that growing out of Selten's (1978) famous example of the 'chain store paradox'. See for instance the papers by Kreps and Wilson (1982) and Milgrom and Roberts (1982), or the general review by Wilson (1985).

(1988). Whereas binary lottery games were employed in the earlier experiments precisely in order to control out the individual variation due to differences in risk posture, these studies employed *ternary* lottery games having three possible payoffs for each bargainer i. These are large and small prizes λ_i and σ_i obtained by lottery when agreement is reached, and a disagreement prize δ_i obtained when no agreement is reached in the allotted time. (In the binary lottery games, $\sigma_i = \delta_i$.)

The bargainers' risk postures were first measured by having them make a set of risky choices. (Note that, in contrast to the experiments just discussed, the strategy in this experiment was to measure preferences rather than to control them.) Statistically significant differences in risk aversion were found among the population of participants, even on the relatively modest range of prizes available in these studies (in which typical choices involved choosing between receiving \$5 for certain or participating in a lottery with prizes of $\lambda_i = \$16$ and $\sigma_i = \$4$).

Those bargainers with relatively high risk aversion bargained against those with relatively low risk aversion in pairs of games such that the disagreement prizes were larger than the small prizes in one game and smaller in the other. The prediction of game theoretic models such as Nash's is that agreements reached in the first game should be more favourable to the more risk averse of the two bargainers than agreements reached in the second game.

Let me be precise. The theory actually makes a stronger prediction, but only the weaker form is confirmed by the experiments, and the reasons for this illuminate not only the design and analysis of these experiments, but of many experiments designed to test economic theories. When the prizes of both bargainers are all equal (i.e. $\lambda_1 = \lambda_2 = \lambda$, $\sigma_1 = \sigma_2 = \sigma$, and $\delta_1 = \delta_2 = \delta$) the theories in question predict that the more risk averse player will get more than 50% of the lottery tickets when $\delta > \sigma$, and less than 50% of the lottery tickets when $\delta < \sigma$. Thus the prediction is not only that the more risk averse player should do better in the first game than he does in the second, but that he should do better than the less risk averse player in the first game, and worse in the second.

Now, as had already been established by the earlier experiments, these axiomatic theories fail to predict the effects of the bargainers' information about one anothers' prizes. Among the earlier observations was the very high concentration of (50%, 50%) agreements in games with equal prizes or in which bargainers know only their own prizes, and a shift in the direction of equal expected values in games with unequal prizes known to both bargainers. The strongest form of the predictions about risk aversion concern games in which the bargainers have equal prizes, and so the first experiment of Murnighan *et al.* (1988) used such a symmetric game. However, a test of the predictions requires data from pairs of agreements between the same subjects, and it was quickly observed that a high percentage of pairs reached (50%, 50%) agreements in the game with $\delta < \sigma$, and ended in disagreement in the game with $\delta > \sigma$. Although there was a weak effect of risk aversion in the predicted direction, it was not significant. One way to read this, of course, is as a rejection of the prediction, but in view of the relatively small scale of the prizes it was thought that any effect of risk aversion might simply be overpowered by the 'focal point' effect already observed in connection with the equal probability agreement. So it was decided to run a subsequent experiment in which the prizes were unequal, in order to give any effect of risk aversion a wider range on which to be observed.[9] But, as had already been noted, this meant that the player with the smaller prize could be expected to receive the higher percentage of lottery tickets, irrespective of the relative risk aversion of the two bargainers. Consequently only the weaker form of the risk aversion prediction could be tested on such a game, and it is this prediction that was ultimately confirmed by the data. That is, the results of these experiments support the predictions of the game theoretic models that more risk averse bargainers do better when the disagreement prize is high than when it is low. But these results also suggest that, in the (relatively modest) range of payoffs studied here, the effects due to risk aversion may be much smaller than some of the effects due to changes in information observed in previous experiments. How much this has to do with the size of the payoffs remains to be determined.[10]

So one lesson that can be drawn from all this is that it is possible to design experiments to investigate the qualitative predictions of theories that may already be known not to be good point predictors. Because of the relative complexity of economic phenomena compared to the relative simplicity of economic theories intended to account for them, this is frequently the problem facing economic experimenters, one they have in common with econometricians studying field data.

The results also illustrate a frequent and perplexing problem in interpreting experimental work: how should one assess the 'size' (or relative importance) of effects observed in the laboratory, particularly when these may be sensitive

[9] That is, it was thought that the high concentration of agreements around a 'focal point' such as (50%, 50%) might reflect forces at work which made it unprofitable for bargainers to try to achieve small deviations from equal division, but that, once the bargaining had shifted away from such a compelling focal point (into a region in which previous experiments had shown agreements would have greater variance), the influence of risk aversion on the precise terms of agreement might be greater.

[10] When prizes are small, the relatively small effect of risk aversion observed here suggests that it may not be critical to always control for unobserved effects of risk aversion by employing binary lottery games in an experimental design, particularly when risk aversion is not a primary cause of concern for the phenomenon being investigated. Roth and Malouf (1982) report experiments similar to those of Roth and Malouf (1979), but in which players are paid in money rather than in lottery tickets, and observe that the qualitative effects of information are very similar. Harrison and McCabe (1988), Radner and Schotter (1987), and Cox *et al.* (1985*a*) also observe only small differences between certain observations made with and without binary lottery games. (Cox *et al.* take the position that, if one is confident that all experimental observations conform to some theoretical prediction stated in terms of expected utility functions, then the risk posture of bargainers can be estimated from experimental results without any need to directly measure or control for differences in subjects' risk posture. In the context of an auction experiment they further argue that, in this way, the results of binary lottery games can be used to detect violations of expected utility theory (on which see Section IV), by using observed results to estimate what agents' utilities would have to have been to make these results conform to the theoretical prediction, and comparing these estimated utilities to the risk neutrality that utility maximisers exhibit on binary lottery games.) Baiman and Lewis (1988) report in passing a direct test to see if subjects are indifferent between equivalent compound and simple binary lotteries (as utility maximisers would be), and based on somewhat ambiguous evidence they tentatively conclude that the binary lottery procedure does induce risk neutral behaviour in their subjects. (Their paper also contains an exceptionally clear exposition of their methodological concerns.)

to the size of the payoffs to the subjects. Since it has so far proved far easier to observe the unpredicted effects of information than the predicted effects of risk aversion on the outcome of bargaining, can we conclude that the former are more important than the latter? I do not think that the available evidence justifies this conclusion. The problem is that there is reason to believe that risk aversion is a phenomenon many of whose consequences are easiest to observe when decisions involve very large gambles. While in principle this presents no obstacle to experimental investigation (just conduct experiments with very large prizes), in practice, experimental budgets always make it likely that payoffs in the laboratory will be smaller than those in some situations to which economic theories are naturally applied. Not being able to compare the significance of these unpredicted and predicted effects means that, on the evidence so far available, we cannot deliver a conclusive verdict on the overall health of theories of bargaining such as Nash's.

In looking over this whole series of experiments, two other phenomena stand out. First, there was a non-negligible frequency of disagreements. Second, there was a clear 'deadline effect'. (In all the experiments discussed above, there was a fixed time limit, typically from 9 to 12 minutes, by which time any agreements must be concluded. Three minutes before the deadline, a clock came on the screen.) Across all experiments, which varied considerably in the terms and distribution of agreements, the data reveal that a high proportion of agreements were reached in the very final seconds before the deadline (see Roth *et al.*, 1988). The methodological point I want to make about these two regularities is that the experiments reported above, which were designed to permit the effects of particular manipulations to be observed, do not cast much direct light on either of these phenomena, other than to indicate that they are easy to observe.[11] Convincing evidence that particular variables are of importance in producing deadline effects, for example, must come from experiments in which the concentration of agreements near the deadline can be shown to respond to changes in those variables.

In closing, I should remark that while I have emphasised in this section the way theoretical predictions can be tested experimentally, experimental results also suggest theoretical directions. The clearest and most often replicated result discussed above is that information about the underlying commodities influences the outcome of bargaining in a way precluded by theories stated only in terms of bargainers' utilities. This suggests we should examine bargaining theories in which information about commodities can play a role, and there have been a number of recent attempts in this direction, as well as renewed interest in earlier theories that can be reinterpreted in light of the evidence. (See Roth (1979) for some of these earlier theories which allow comparisons between bargainers. For one of the most recent, see Roemer (1988).) These theories too yield testable predictions, and experiments have begun to help distinguish among them (see e.g. Roth and Malouf, 1982).

[11] Some other experiments cast some light on factors that may contribute to disagreements. Malouf and Roth (1981) look at variations in the set of feasible outcomes, and Coursey (1982) compares single play bargaining under loose time constraints with repeated bargaining under tight time constraints.

I.2 *Experimental Tests of Strategic Models*

Recently a good deal of attention has been given to models of bargaining in which two bargainers, 1 and 2, alternate making offers over how to divide some amount k (of money). Time is divided into periods, and in even numbered periods t (starting at an initial period $t = 0$) player 1 may propose to player 2 any division $(x, k-x)$. If player 2 accepts this proposal the game ends and player 1 receives a utility of $(\delta_1)^t x$ and 2 receives a utility $(\delta_2)^t(k-x)$, where δ_i is a number between 0 and 1 reflecting player i's cost of delay. (That is, a payoff of y dollars to player i at period t gives him the same utility as a payoff of $\delta_i y$ dollars one period earlier, at period $t-1$.) If player 2 does not accept the offer, and if t is not the final period of the game, then the game proceeds to period $t+1$, and the roles of the two players are reversed. If an offer made in the last period of the game is refused, then the game ends with each player receiving 0. A game with a maximum number of periods T will be called a T-period game.[12]

A *subgame perfect equilibrium* can be computed by working backward from the last period. An offer made in period T is an ultimatum, and so at such an equilibrium player i (who will receive 0 if he rejects the offer) will accept any non-negative offer. So at a subgame perfect equilibrium, player j, who gets to make the proposal in period T, will receive 100% (if payoffs are continuously divisible) of the amount k to be divided, if the game continues to period T. Consequently at period $T-1$ player j will refuse any offer of less than $(\delta_j)k$ but accept any offer of more, so that at equilibrium player i receives the share $k-(\delta_j)k$ if the game goes to period $T-1$, and so forth. Working back to period 0, we can compute the equilibrium division: i.e. the amount that the theory predicts player 1 should offer to player 2 at period 0, and player 2 should accept. (When payoffs are continuous this equilibrium division is unique.)

Recent experimental studies of this kind of bargaining have reported markedly different results. Their authors have drawn quite different conclusions about the predictive value of perfect equilibrium models of bargaining, and about the role that experience, limited foresight, or bargainers' beliefs about fairness might play in explaining their observations. (Questions of fairness arise because in some of these experiments many observed agreements give both bargainers 50% of the available money.) In reviewing these experiments here, my aim is to show how, even in the earliest stages of a programme of experimental research, when there is room for substantial disagreement about what is being observed, early experiments suggest later ones, subsequent experimental results suggest reinterpretations of earlier ones, and the process of experimentation offers the prospect of steadily (if somewhat slowly) narrowing the areas of potential disagreement.

[12] Much of the recent theoretical work using this kind of model follows the treatment by Rubinstein (1982) of the infinite horizon case. An exploration of various aspects of the finite horizon case is given by Stahl (1972). This literature considers the cost of delay in more general form than only the discounting discussed here. An experiment motivated by this literature which considers a fixed cost per period of bargaining is Rapoport *et al.* (1988). An experiment with a similar cost structure, motivated by earlier theoretical attempts to deal with costs of delay, is Contini (1968).

In each of the following experiments, the predictions tested involved only the ordinal utilities of the bargainers, not their risk posture. Following standard practice in the experimental literature when only ordinal utilities are of concern, the utility of the bargainers was assumed to be measured by the amount of money they receive.

Guth *et al.* (1982) examined one-period ('ultimatum') bargaining games. Player 1 could propose dividing a fixed sum of k Deutsche Marks any way he chose, by filling out a form saying 'I demand DM $\underline{x}$'. Player 2 could either accept, in which case player 1 received x and player 2 got $k-x$, or he could reject, in which case each player received 0 for that game.

The perfect equilibrium prediction for such games is that player 1 will ask for and get (essentially) 100% of k. However the average demand that players 1 were observed to make was for under 70%, both for players playing the game for the first time and for those repeating the game a week later. About 20% of offers were rejected. The authors conclude that '...subjects often rely on what they consider a fair or justified result. Furthermore, the ultimatum aspect cannot be completely exploited since subjects do not hesitate to punish if their opponent asks for "too much".'

Binmore *et al.* (1985) write: 'The work of Guth *et al.* seems to preclude a predictive role for game theory insofar as bargaining behaviour is concerned. Our purpose in this note is to report briefly on an experiment that shows that this conclusion is unwarranted...'.[13] Their experiment studied a 2-period bargaining game, in which player 1 makes a proposal of the form $(x, 100-x)$ to divide 100 pence. If player 2 accepts, this is the result. Otherwise 2 makes a proposal $(x', 25-x')$ to divide 25 pence. If player 1 accepts, this is the result, otherwise each player receives 0. Thus in this game $\delta_1 = \delta_2 = 0{\cdot}25$, and (since proposals are constrained to be an integer number of pence) at any subgame perfect equilibrium player 1 makes an opening demand in the range 74–6 pence, and player 2 accepts any opening demand of 74 pence or less. Subjects played a single game, after which player 2 was invited to play the game again, as player 1. In fact there was no player 2 in this second game, so only the opening demand was observed.

The modal first demand in the first game was 50 pence, and 15% of the first offers were rejected. In the second game (in which only first demands were observed), there was a mode around a first demand near 75 pence. There was thus a clear shift between the two distributions of first demands, in the direction of the equilibrium demand. The authors conclude 'Our suspicion is that the one-stage ultimatum game is a rather special case, from which it is dangerous to draw general conclusions. In the ultimatum game, the first player might be dissuaded from making an opening demand at, or close to, the "optimum" level, because his opponent would then incur a negligible cost in making an

[13] They add: 'This does not mean that our results are inconsistent with those of Guth *et al.* Under similar conditions, we obtain similar results. Moreover our full results would seem to refute the more obvious rationalizations of the behavior observed by Guth *et al.* as "optimising with complex motivations". Instead, our results indicate that this behaviour is not stable in the sense that it can be easily displaced by simple optimizing behavior, once small changes are made in the playing conditions.'

"irrational" rejection. In the two-stage game, these considerations are postponed to the second stage, and so their impact is attenuated.'

Guth and Tietz (1987) responded with an experiment examining two two-stage games with discount factors of 0·9 and 0·1 respectively. So the subgame perfect equilibrium predictions (in percentage terms) for the two cases are (10 %, 90 %) and (90 %, 10 %) respectively. They say 'Our hypothesis is that the consistency of experimental observations and game theoretic predictions observed by Binmore *et al.* as well as by Fouraker and Siegel is solely due to the moderate relation of equilibrium payoffs which makes the game theoretic solution socially more acceptable.' Subjects played one of the two games twice, each with a randomly chosen other bargainer. Subjects who played the first game as player 1 played the second game as player 2. One difference from the sequential bargaining games discussed above was that disagreement automatically resulted if player 2 rejected an offer from player 1 but made a counterproposal that would give him less than player 1 had offered him.[14]

In the first game, the average first demand in games with a discount factor of 0·1 was 76 %, and in the second game 67 %. For games with a discount factor of 0·9, the average first demand in the first game was 70 %, and in the second game 59 %. (Recall that when the discount factor is 0·9, the equilibrium first demand is only 10 %.) The authors conclude 'Our main result is that contrary to Binmore, Shaked and Sutton "gamesmenship" is clearly rejected, i.e., the game theoretic solution has nearly no predictive power.'

Neelin *et al.* (1988) also responded to Binmore *et al.* (1985). They reported two experiments involving 2-period, 3-period, and 5-period bargaining games. Neelin *et al.* observe that the data for all their (2, 3, and 5 period) games are near the perfect equilibrium prediction for 2 period games. They conclude '...the strong regularity of the behaviour we observed is one of the most noteworthy aspects of our results and lends power to our rejection of both the Stahl/Rubinstein theory and the equal-split model'.[15]

Following most of this exchange, Ochs and Roth (1989) noted that the prior analyses had focused on the accuracy of the perfect equilibrium as a point predictor, i.e. on whether the observed outcomes were distributed around the perfect equilibrium division or around some other division of the available money. Their experiment was designed to test the predictive accuracy of some of the *qualitative* predictions of the perfect equilibrium in sequential bargaining, and was designed to detect whether changes in the parameters of the game influence the observed outcomes in the predicted direction, even in the case that there might be a systematic error in the point predictions (recall the discussion of risk aversion in Section I.1). To this end the experiment was

[14] Note that this rule makes the games more like ultimatum games, since some demands of player 1 (e.g. demands of less than 90 % in games with discount factor of 0·1) can only be rejected at the cost of disagreement.

[15] In a reply, Binmore *et al.* (1988*a*) decline to attribute the same significance to these results, and conjecture that the various differences described among these experiments may be due to the various differences in experimental procedures employed, which, they suggest, may make the theoretical model more appropriate for their experiment than for some of the others. (A related view is expressed by Harrison and McCabe (1988).)

implemented in a way that allowed the discount factors of the two bargainers to be varied independently.[16] In order to compare games like those considered in the earlier experiments, the experimental design allowed comparisons between different combinations of discount factors for games of fixed length, as well as between games of different length for given discount factors. The eight cells of the experiment compare two and three period games using all four combinations of discount factors (δ_1, δ_2), with δ_i equal to 0·4 or 0·6.

Overall, although the data reveal some striking regularities, the perfect equilibrium predictions do poorly both as point predictions and in predicting qualitative differences between cells, such as mean first period offers. (The authors write '...we can just barely reject the null hypothesis that, as a predictor of the direction of differences in pairwise comparisons of means, the theory does no better than coin flipping'.) While parts of the data appear to be consistent with similar observations made in the earlier experiments, larger experimental designs allow more comparisons to be made, so that observations which, piecewise, appear contradictory, emerge as part of a larger picture.[17] Perhaps the most interesting part of this picture, for our present purposes, concerns what happens when first period offers are rejected, both in this experiment and, as it turns out, in the previous experiments.

Briefly, approximately 15% of first offers met with rejection (including those in games with experienced subjects who had played ten games against different opponents), and of these well over half were followed by counter-proposals in which player 2 demanded *less* cash than he had been offered. That is, a significant number of players 2 were rejecting small shares of the relatively large gains available in the first period in favour of large shares of the much smaller gains available in the second period. Since, after player 1 has made a proposal, player 2 is faced with an individual choice problem, we can conclude by revealed preference that these player 2's utility is *not* measured by their monetary payoff, but must include some non-monetary component. When the data of the previous experiments were reanalysed with this in mind, it turned out that this pattern of rejections and counter-proposals was strikingly similar in all of these experiments.[18]

[16] Each of the earlier experiments was designed to correspond to the case that the players have equal discount factors, i.e. $\delta_1 = \delta_2 = \delta$, with the costliness of delay implemented by making the amount of money being divided in period $t+1$ equal to δ times the amount available at period t. Since half the cells of the experimental design of Ochs and Roth require different discount rates for the two bargainers, the discounting could not be implemented in this way. Instead, in each period, the commodity to be divided consisted of 100 'chips'. In period 1 of each game, each chip was worth \$0.30 to each bargainer. In period 2, each chip was worth δ_1(\$0.30) to player 1 and δ_2(\$0.30) to player 2, and in period 3 of the three period games each chip was worth $(\delta_1)^2$ (\$0.30) and $(\delta_2)^2$ (\$0.30) respectively. That is, the rate at which subjects were paid for each of the 100 chips that they might receive depended on their discount rate and the period in which agreement was reached.

[17] In this regard, the paper notes '...if we had looked only at Cell 1 our conclusions might have been similar to those of Binmore *et al.*, since the data for that cell looks as if after one or two periods of experience, the players settle down to perfect equilibrium proposals... And if we had looked only at Cells 1 and 5, our conclusions might have been similar to those of Neelin *et al.*, since in those two cells both the two and three period games yield observations near the two period predictions... And if we had looked only at cells 5 and 6, we might have concluded, like Guth and Teitz, that the phenomena observed here was closely related to the relatively extreme equilibrium predictions in those cells.'

[18] When the necessary data from these earlier experiments were not contained in published accounts, they

Ochs and Roth (1989) go on to argue that this and other patterns in the data can plausibly be explained if the unobserved and uncontrolled components of utility in these experiments have to do with subjects' perceptions of 'fairness', which involve comparing their share of the available wealth to that of the other bargainer. They note that in most cases agents propose divisions that give them more than half of the proceeds, and say '...we do not conclude that players "try to be fair". It is enough to suppose that they try to estimate the utilities of the player they are bargaining with, and... at least some agents incorporate distributional considerations in their utility functions.' That is, if agents' preferences are such that they will refuse 'insultingly low' offers, then this must be taken into account in making offers.

Note that uncontrolled elements in the bargainers' utility in these experiments suggests that none of them can be easily interpreted as tests of perfect equilibrium *per se*, since to compute a perfect equilibrium we need to know the preferences of the players (and so do they).[19] But the uniformity with which 'disadvantageous counter-proposals' have appeared in the experiments to date, in contrast to their otherwise quite varied results, suggests that bargaining may be an activity that systematically gives bargainers motivations distinct from simple income maximisation. One natural direction in which to continue this (still young) series of experiments is to attempt to observe directly or manipulate these so far uncontrolled motivating factors.

I.3 *Bargaining as a Complex 'Social' Phenomenon*

To the extent that these other motivations may reflect some element of bargainers' perceptions of 'fairness', this may help explain why the results of these various experiments may have been more sensitive than might have been expected to details of the experimental environment. Studies of fairness (based on survey questions) suggest that peoples' ideas about what is 'fair' may be both clear and very labile, subject to dramatic change in response to how the issue is presented. (This is particularly clear in the study reported by Yaari and Bar-Hillel (1984). See also the related work of Kahneman *et al.* (1986*a*; *b*) and of Bazerman (1985) and Farber and Bazerman (1986).[20]) So variations in experimental procedures may have had unanticipated effects.

---

were readily available from the working papers circulated by the authors. That this is a good experimental practice cannot be over-emphasised, since the easy availability of data permits just these sorts of comparisons.

[19] However, Ochs and Roth (1989) do report consistency across subgames, which could be interpreted as indirect evidence supporting the subgame perfectness hypothesis with respect to the unobserved preferences.

[20] In the psychology literature, some ideas concerned with beliefs about fairness have been explored under the name of 'equity theory'. The interpretation of various experimental results in this literature is that the outcome of various kinds of interactions can best be understood as reflecting the common beliefs among the participants about what constitutes a fair outcome. I think that one of the contributions of the experimental bargaining results is that they reveal that subjects may possess multiple, different notions of fairness, and employ them selectively, for strategic purposes. Thus, for example, the agreements reported in the binary lottery games of Roth and Murnighan (1982) had modes at both the equal probability and the equal expected value agreements, and the transcripts of the bargaining reveal that notions of 'fairness' were employed by both bargainers in arguing for their claims. But the bargainer who saw the equal expected value agreement as 'fair' was invariably the one with the smaller ($5) prize, while the player with the larger ($20) prize was the champion of the fairness of equal division of the lottery tickets.

Just such effects were revealed in a rather different bargaining environment in experiments conducted by Hoffman and Spitzer (1982; 1985). In one of the experiments in their 1982 paper pairs of subjects were asked to agree on how to divide up to $14, in face to face negotiations. However, if no agreement was reached one of them (the 'controller', chosen just before negotiations began by the toss of a coin) could simply choose an outcome that would give him up to $12 and the other bargainer nothing. When bargainers negotiated with each other twice under these conditions, twelve out of twelve agreed to split the proceeds equally, so that the controller settled for a smaller cash payoff than he could have obtained unilaterally. In their 1985 paper, Hoffman and Spitzer report that in similar experiments in which the position of 'controller' was allocated to the winner of a simple game, and in which the instructions to the participants gave the controller 'moral authority' to claim his prize unilaterally, the frequency of equal splits was reduced.[21]

Now, we should hesitate to draw too close a parallel between these differences in outcomes caused by differences in experimental environments and those that may have occurred in other experiments, because there is reason to believe that face to face negotiations for relatively small prizes may be a rather special situation. In particular, face to face interactions call into play all of the social training we are endowed with, and may make it unusually difficult to control preferences. (Ask yourself if you would agree to be very rude to the next stranger you meet at a party if I offer to pay you $5.) There is now a small body of comparable experiments that make it possible to begin to assess how results of face to face negotiations may differ from results obtained in more anonymous laboratory negotiations. Such comparisons will allow us to assess some of the potential sensitivity of reported results to experimental procedures.

First, it seems that the frequency of disagreement is sharply less in face to face negotiations than in anonymous negotiations concerning comparable prizes. Aside from the general results of the experiments cited above to this effect (which involve comparisons which must be treated cautiously, since they involve other differences than whether bargaining was face to face), a reduced frequency of disagreement in face to face bargaining is reported by Radner and Schotter (1987), who report a 'within experiment' comparison involving just this variable.[22] Regarding the frequency of equal divisions when one of the bargainers has an 'outside option' worth more than half the total proceeds, Binmore *et al.* (1988*b*) report an experiment roughly parallel to that of Hoffman and Spitzer (1982) but involving anonymous negotiations, and find a preponderance of proposals that give the player with the outside option as much as he could have got unilaterally. And in another pair of closely parallel experiments Roth and Malouf (1982) report fewer equal splits in anonymous

[21] For some related results which look at other variations in experimental procedures, see Harrison and McKee (1985). For a subsequent experiment on a somewhat more complicated environment (related to the one explored by Plott (1983)), see Harrison *et al.* (1987).

[22] Radner and Schotter's experiment concerns the efficiency of bargaining between a buyer and seller neither of whom know the other's reservation price. For some related experiments concerning bargaining with incomplete information, see Hogatt *et al.* (1978) and Forsythe *et al.* (1987).

bargaining than are observed by Nydegger and Owen (1975) in face to face bargaining. Again, 'between experiment' comparisons have to be treated with caution. But they give us a strong indication that the difference between face to face and anonymous interaction that has been reliably reported in multi-person negotiations (see e.g. Murnighan, 1985) is also liable to account for significant differences among experiments of the kinds considered here.

As I have indicated, my own suspicion is that these differences in results are due to the fact that bargainers' incentives in the more social, face to face environment may correspond less closely to their monetary payoffs than when bargaining is anonymous. However, this is not the only possible explanation. Face to face bargaining also allows many more channels of communication (e.g. tone of voice and facial expression) than does anonymous bargaining, in which subjects may be restricted to written messages, and perhaps the differences are due to this. The difference between these two hypotheses could be important, for example in judging the claim that some of the face to face evidence should be seen as supporting policy implications of the Coase Theorem (Coase, 1960), which rest on the presumed efficiency of bargaining.[23]

In conclusion, the evidence to date suggests that bargaining is a complex social phenomenon, so that special care must be taken in designing and interpreting bargaining experiments. In addition to refining theories of bargaining stated in terms of abstract preferences, the evidence suggests that it will be worth investigating what (non-monetary) motivations may be engendered by bargaining itself. The extent to which such non-monetary motivations would remain important if the bargaining concerned much larger payoffs is of course also an open question, but I see no obvious reason to jump to the conclusion that some of the very consistent patterns of behaviour discussed in this section would disappear as the stakes become large, particularly when they become large for both bargainers. Also, there is evidence that the 'social' aspects of bargaining involve more than just the incentives of the players, but also their expectations and their ability to co-ordinate with one another.[24] Finally, this conclusion need not be 'bad news' for the prospect of developing more descriptive theories of bargaining: the very regularity of the behaviour, and the fact that bargainers often appear to be able

[23] If the absence of disagreement is due to the lack of control of subjects' incentives, we might suspect it would diminish as the monetary consequences become larger. But if it is due to having many channels of communication, then we might investigate whether similarly effective channels might be available to bargainers in situations of the sort to which the Coase Theorem is typically thought to apply. Thus the experimental results suggest some different directions to investigate the efficiency assumption of the Coase Theorem than those which have surfaced from other considerations (see e.g. Farrell, 1987).

[24] Roth *et al.* (1981) show that strategically equivalent games can produce different results, and argue that this may be due to the existence of social conventions which contribute to determining the credibility of different bargaining positions, and which (thus) help bargainers co-ordinate their expectations. (Roth and Schoumaker (1983) report an experiment which manipulates the expectations of the bargainers, and provides some indirect support for this view.) To the extent that bargaining involves elements of co-ordination, a better understanding of the problems of pure co-ordination will likely be of help in developing theories of bargaining. In this regard I have been glad to notice a number of recent experiments concerned with co-ordination, such as Cooper *et al.* (1990), Ochs (1990), and Van Huyck *et al.* (1990).

to anticipate it and turn it to strategic use, suggest that theorists should also be able to do so.

II. FREE RIDERS, AND PERPLEXED PRISONERS

This section is in part a story of a dog that didn't bark, at least not initially, or at least not as loudly as might have been expected. It concerns two closely related problems, both of which have captured the imaginations of theorists and experimenters. Both the free rider problem and the prisoner's dilemma concern the potential difficulties in achieving gains from co-operation when those gains must be allocated in a fixed way. For both problems, there were theoretical formulations predicting that virtually none of such potential gains could be achieved, and different opinions about how real this predicted predicament was. Early experiments concerned with both problems did not observe the phenomenon, at least not in its severest form, and later experiments did, at least to a degree.

Curiously, the experimental literatures concerned with the two problems seldom refer to each other. Although my discussion of both literatures will be necessarily brief, I hope that some of the parallels between them will become apparent.

II.1 *The Free Rider Problem*

The free rider problem in the provision of public goods was noted in connection with the debate among nineteenth century economists about whether taxation for public goods should be related to the benefit each agent derived from those goods. The nature of a public good is that once it has been created everyone may use it, and so if each individual is to be taxed in proportion to the profit he derives from the public good, there will be an incentive for individuals to claim that these profits are small, since small contributors will derive the same benefit from the good as if they had been large contributors. The potential for under-contribution to a public good is particularly clear when contributions are voluntary. (American listeners to National Public Radio will immediately recognise the problem.)

The first clear formulation of the free rider problem is generally attributed to an essay written at the end of the last century by the Swedish economist Knut Wicksell, who also anticipated the direction of much subsequent theoretical research by suggesting that the mechanism by which public projects were decided upon would be important. (He suggested that a way to deal with the problem would be to require that proposals for public projects be considered together with proposals to raise the necessary revenue, and that the whole package should be subject to [close to] unanimous approval.) For references and an introduction to much of the subsequent theory focusing on the role of the decision mechanism, see Green and Laffont (1979).

Because it is readily apparent that some more-or-less public goods are in fact produced even though they depend on voluntary contributions, the focus of debate shifted both to assessing how serious the free rider problem might be, and what circumstances or mechanisms might ameliorate it. So at the same time as a good deal of theoretical progress was being made in 'solving' the free rider problem (e.g. Groves and Ledyard, 1977), scepticism was being voiced about the importance of the problem and the quality of the empirical evidence in support of it (e.g. Johansen, 1977). Since it is difficult to collect field data to determine, for example, how close to the optimum amount of some public good is being supplied, this problem presented a natural opportunity for laboratory experiments. In addition, since some of the mechanisms proposed for solving or ameliorating the free rider problem had no counterpart in existing institutions, some of the questions that presented themselves could not be addressed except by experimentation.

The experiment of Bohm (1972) was sponsored by the Swedish Radio-TV broadcasting company. A sample of adult residents of Stockholm was invited to come to the broadcasting company for an interview, and asked to state how much (of their interview fee) it would be worth to them to see a half-hour programme by two well known comedians. They were told they would see the programme only if the sum of the amounts stated (by their group and others) exceeded the cost of showing it. The experimental variable consisted of five different rules for how they would in fact be charged on the basis of their stated amounts, ranging from the full amount, to some percentage of that amount, to a lottery related to the amount, to a small fixed fee, to nothing.

The responses of the different groups of subjects given these different instructions were found not to vary significantly. Bohm argues that the first payment mechanism (everyone pays their stated amount) gives no incentive to overstate willingness to pay, and the last (no actual payment required) gives no incentive to understate willingness to pay, so the similarity of the responses under the two conditions suggests there may not in fact be much of a practical problem in estimating people's demands for a public good.[25] In short, these results suggest that free riding may not be a big problem.

Several other experiments employed what I will loosely call the same general design, of presenting subjects with some public good whose value to them was unknown to the experimenter, and comparing the results of different methods of eliciting their willingness to pay. Sweeney (1973) considered the willingness of subjects to power an electric light by pedalling an exercise bicycle (free 'riding' indeed), and found that this responded to whether they perceived themselves as being in a small or large group (a perception he manipulated by controlling the brightness of the light with a rheostat). The public good was whether they would all receive credit for participating in the experiment, which depended on how brightly the light remained lit. Scherr and Babb (1975) compare voluntary contributions with those elicited in pricing schemes proposed for public goods by Clarke (1971) and by Loehman and Whinston (1972), and found no significant differences in the amount of public goods (in

[25] However he notes that a sixth group of subjects who were asked in a purely hypothetical way how much such a programme would be worth to them gave significantly different responses from the other five groups. He says (p. 125) '...this result may be seen as still another reason to doubt the usefulness of responses to hypothetical questions...'

this case concert tickets and books donated to the library) provided under the three schemes. In general, the experiments using this design support the proposition that at least some public good can be supplied even by voluntary contribution. But it is much more difficult to interpret how much (if any) free riding is being observed, since the true value of the public good to each subject is unknown.

In order not to miss the opportunity to tell a colourful story (in the midst of so many dry recitals), let me describe one more experiment of this general type, which was conducted by Schneider and Pommerehne (1981) at the University of Zurich, and which would be unlikely, I think, to have been permitted at an American university.[26] The subjects for their experiment were a group of economics students preparing for their comprehensive examinations. Without knowing that they were the object of an experiment, these students were approached by a confederate of the experimenters posing as the representative of a publishing company. She informed them that their professor (who, I surmise, would write the comprehensive exam) was writing a book on the subject of the exam which would not be available until after the exam. However, the publishing company was interested in getting feedback on the book, and for this purpose might be willing to make specimen copies available, *before* the exam. (The authors remark that the students 'had a strong incentive to try to obtain the book beforehand'.) The students were then told they could submit written bids of how much they were willing to pay to get an advance copy, with copies going to the ten highest bidders from both this group and two others from which bids had already been solicited. After these bids were collected the two highest bidders were told that they were among the ten winners. The remaining students were then told that there was another way in which they could obtain the book before the exam: if together with the two other groups they could raise SFr.4,200, they would each get a copy. Again, written bids for the now public good were collected, and the heart of the analysis is the comparison of the two bids.[27] The authors note that the second bids were less than the first, but not by much.[28] They conclude (p. 702) that 'there is only modest evidence for free riding as compared with the importance attributed to it in the literature'.

A different kind of experimental design, in which the public good is an

[26] Experiments with human subjects in the United States are now regulated by State and Federal laws which require that universities maintain review boards to determine in advance that experiments do not violate certain guidelines. These laws were passed in response to some hair-raising abuses, with notable contributions from both psychologists and biomedical researchers.

[27] However, the experiment did not end here. The students were told that they had failed to reach the required sum, so only the two original high bidders would get the book, although the offer would remain (p. 696) 'open for a few days should the students still want to try to bring the money together'. The (now surely desperate?) students were then presented with a third scheme, in which they were told essentially that any bids they submitted would be sufficient. These bids provided a third comparison, and while they were significantly less than the previous two bids, they were significantly greater than the minimum bid required to be included among those who would (supposedly) receive the books before the exam. (Unfortunately we do not learn how the students did on the exam, or if their bids were good predictors of their grades...)

[28] There are some complexities in the data, since 10 students bid zero in the first auction, but contributed positive amounts when the book was offered as a public good. The authors consider the possibility that this was a result of coalition formation in the auction.

artificial one, makes it possible to employ an experimental strategy of trying to control each subject's value for the good, rather than trying to measure it. The idea is that if the experimenter assigns to each agent a payment depending on the quantity of the public good, then so long as the public good is not one which itself induces strong preferences among the agents, their preferences can be equated with their monetary payoffs.[29] In this way the payments of the agents for the public good and the amount of public good provided under a given decision mechanism can be compared not only with the amounts under another decision mechanism, but also with *a priori* notions about the optimal amount, such as the Lindhal equilibrium.

Smith (1979*a,b*; 1980) reports three such experiments.[30] In the first, he compared a version of a mechanism proposed by Groves and Ledyard (1977), designed to eliminate incentives to free ride by disentangling the price each agent pays from the price he states, with a procedure in which each agent pays his stated willingness to pay. Both procedures were implemented in an iterative manner which allowed agents to revise their statements in light of those of the others. Smith observed that, under some settings of the experimental parameters determining agents' demands, the Groves-Ledyard mechanism resulted in decisions at the Lindhal equilibrium while the other mechanism exhibited substantial free riding, sometimes to the point that no public good was produced. A third iterative mechanism was then investigated, which Smith (1979*a*) called the Auction mechanism, and which incorporates the features suggested by Wicksell, in that the quantity of the public good and the amount to be contributed by each agent must be unanimously agreed to before the agreement is effective. (In the absence of agreement, no public good is produced.) The theoretical properties of this mechanism are somewhat unclear since it has many Nash equilibria. However, under this mechanism too, Lindhal prices and quantities were observed to be good predictors for the market parameters considered.

In the light of these results, Smith suggests that the results of Bohm's (1971) experiment might be reinterpreted, since the mechanism he considered to have the most probability of producing free riding (everyone pays their stated amount) resembled the auction mechanism in the sense that if too much free riding took place, no public good would be produced. That is, Smith suggests that the similarity of the bids in all of Bohm's procedures may merely reflect that the situation he considered (inadvertently) gave subjects good incentives *not* to free ride, because of the fear that no public good would be provided. In this spirit, Smith (1979*b*) reports an experiment designed to determine which aspects of the auction mechanism may have contributed to its apparent success. He compares the auction mechanism, in which agents propose both a

[29] However, Palfrey and Rosenthal (1987) speculate that in a number of these experiments the monetary payoffs cannot simply be taken as equivalent to the utility of the agents, because there may be an unobserved 'altruistic' component to agents' preferences. They go on to study the effect that this could have in a strategic situation in which being able to estimate how much others will contribute is important.

[30] Another interesting experiment using this general design is that of Ferejohn *et al.* (1979). They examined a public goods provision mechanism abstracted from one used by station managers in the (American) Public Broadcasting Service to decide on what shows to purchase collectively.

contribution and a quantity of the public good, with a 'Free Rider Mechanism' in which each agent simply states his contribution and the quantity of the public good is whatever the summed contributions will buy. (A mechanism intermediate between the two was also considered.) All mechanisms were implemented with a unanimity rule that gave agents a chance to examine (and accept or reject) the outcome before it was implemented. Although the Auction mechanism provided an amount of the public good nearer to the Lindahl quantity than the other mechanisms when it reached agreement, its frequency of agreement was sufficiently less than that of the other two mechanisms to make the overall quantity of public good similar under all mechanisms. Smith concludes by noting that under none of the mechanisms was a very strong free rider effect observed, and conjectures that this may be due to the rule of unanimous approval.

While the variable of primary concern in these experiments was the decision mechanism, in the design of an experiment of this complexity it is clear that many essentially arbitrary choices have to be made, and are held constant over the course of the experiment. Smith (1980) reports a subsequent examination of the Auction mechanism with different functions assigning subjects' values to the public good (and allowing for income effects). In these markets, a substantial amount of free riding was observed. So these results suggest it may be fruitful to study the way decision mechanisms interact with demand parameters for public goods.

Of course, different theoretical dispositions suggest different regularities in the data. For example Smith (1980) reports in connection with his experiment that (p. 597) 'On average subjects contribute approximately one-half their endowments to the public good and retain one-half for private use.' Marwell and Ames (1981), drawing primarily on a series of their own studies that also use a controlled, artificial public good, suggest that this may be an important kind of regularity. They noted that previous studies examined fairly small groups (mostly of fewer than ten individuals), and conducted a study in which both small and large groups could be examined. In a series of studies in which subjects were mostly high school students, subjects were told that they were part of a group, and that each member of the group had an endowment of tokens to invest in either a public or private good. The public good had the higher return, but its proceeds were distributed equally to all group members. Over a number of conditions, Marwell and Ames report that on average the percentage of resources invested in the public good was surprisingly regular, in the range of 40 to 60%, with some indication of a decrease when the stakes were raised.[31] Among the few exceptions they noted was that a group of first semester economics graduate students only invested 20% in the public good, leading them to suggest that economists may be different from everyone else (and hence the title of their paper).[32]

[31] One feature of the procedures in this study which differed from the studies so far discussed is that subjects knew they would be required to explain their decisions to the experimenter (cf p. 297).

[32] However, they attribute this to selection rather than training, noting that few of the economics graduate students 'could specifically identify the theory on which this study was based'. In view of the fact that there were other obvious differences between the subject pools (e.g. graduate students versus high school students),

The remaining experiments I will discuss differ from these previous ones in that they investigate how some of these mechanisms behave when they are used repeatedly, instead of just once. Thus each of these experiments, by Kim and Walker (1984), Isaac *et al.* (1985) and Banks *et al.* (1988) give subjects the chance to gain some experience with how the mechanisms work.

Isaac *et al.* seek to show that the free rider problem is alive and well, by examining a mechanism already suspected of being favourable to free riding and letting repetition have what effect it would. The mechanism chosen was that of direct contribution: each agent stated his contribution, and the amount of public good the summed contributions would buy was produced. (There was no requirement that the allocation be unanimously approved.) After all agents were informed of how much public good had been produced, and had computed their payoff for that period, the process was repeated, with the same individuals and the same demand parameters. The results from a number of trials involving groups of ten subjects were that positive levels of the public good were produced in initial periods, but by around the fifth period these levels declined to near zero. The authors write '...our results unambiguously demonstrate the existence of the under-provision of public goods and related "free riding" phenomenon and thereby discredit the claims of those who assert as a general proposition that the phenomenon does not or cannot exist'. (They also note in reply to Marwell and Ames [who are sociologists] that their experiment included a group of undergraduate sociology students as well as groups of undergraduate economics students, and no differences were found.)

Kim and Walker (1984) report a similarly motivated experiment with similar results, using a much larger (simulated) group size. In their experiment subjects were instructed that they were part of a group of 100, and given a payoff table indicating how much each would be paid as a function of the total contributions made that day to a 'common fund'. (For example, if the fund received $100 [e.g. from $1 per person], each person would be paid $2.) Each day each subject phoned in his contribution, and had his earnings for the day delivered to him that evening.[33] The results of the experiment, like that of Isaac *et al.*, were that positive initial contributions sharply diminished in succeeding days, so that substantial free riding was observed.

That results from repeated trials may differ from those in a single trial was confirmed by Banks *et al.* (1988), who examined both the direct contribution mechanism and Smith's auction mechanism, both with and without the rule of unanimous consent. Although they observed that the auction mechanisms outperformed the direct contribution mechanisms as producers of the public good, they found that the unanimity rule *decreased* efficiency in the repeated

I suspect that the authors do not take this result as seriously as some of the other they report. However, the point that different subject pools may behave differently is always a matter of potential concern, and one which can be addressed empirically. See sections III and V on this point.

[33] Since in fact there were only 5 subjects, payoffs were based on calculating the total contributions to the fund as if each subject represented 20, with some modifications designed to conceal from the subjects how few of them there were.

setting. They note that (p. 319) 'This result is directly counter to expectations formed from data and conjectures found in the literature.' They also found that efficiency decreased over time, suggesting that more free riding occurs with increased experience with these mechanisms. They conclude 'A more reliable process must be found before we proceed with an application at the practical/political level of analysis.'

In summary, the experiments discussed here began with studies of one-shot decisions about various kinds of public goods, in which different decision mechanisms were compared. These experiments often reported little or no free riding. These were followed by experiments in which the public good was artificial, and therefore more easily controllable. These experiments began to detect some degree of free riding, and differences among mechanisms and environments. The most recent experiments introduced repetition, and reported results at odds with the experiments preceding them. Since the theoretical properties of these mechanisms under repeated play are not well understood, it would be premature to attribute these results confidently merely to increased experience with the mechanisms.[34] So the experimental results suggest a further theoretical agenda, as well as a continued experimental examination of other mechanisms. In the course of these experiments, the debate has thus shifted from whether free riding occurs, to how much and under what conditions it occurs, to what mechanisms and environments may be most vulnerable and most invulnerable to its effects. At this stage there still remains a considerable gap between the experimental results and the various related questions about the free rider problem in natural environments. (But, as we will see in Section III.1 in connection with a different problem, such gaps between experimental and field data need not remain unbridgeable.)

II.2 *The Prisoner's Dilemma*

The now famous story which gives the prisoner's dilemma its name was apparently first told by A. W. Tucker (1950).[35] He referred to a game we can represent by the following matrix, with $b > a > c > d$.

	confess	not confess
confess	(c, c)	(b, d)
not confess	(d, b)	(a, a)

The 'dilemma', of course is that it is a dominant strategy for each prisoner to confess, since $c > d$ and $b > a$, but that both of them would be better off if neither confessed, since $a > c$. So the only equilibrium of this game is the dominant strategy equilibrium at which both prisoners confess and each receives the (non Pareto optimal) payoff of c.

The observation that equilibria could be inefficient did not strike game-theorists as odd (always assuming, of course, that the situation facing the

[34] But see Isaac *et al.* (1984) who observe some related results in a design that helps separate experience from repetition among a fixed group.

[35] See Straffin (1980) who arranged for Tucker's 1950 note to be published, and recounts a bit of its history.

players, and their preferences over the outcomes, are accurately modelled by the above matrix), rather it served to emphasise the usefulness of being able to write binding contracts. However, to many social scientists this conclusion seemed to represent an error in analysis, their feeling being that when players properly understood the game, they would choose to co-operate with one another and not confess.

A related observation, however, struck (even) game theorists as symptomatic of problems with the notion of equilibrium. If a prisoner's dilemma game is repeated finitely many times, say 100, and if the payoffs to the players are the sum of their payoffs in each game, then it can be seen by backwards induction starting from the last period that no equilibrium of the game yields co-operation at *any* period.[36] Not only did this seem contrary to intuition, it was also disturbing to note that the equilibrium prediction was unchanged no matter how many times the game was repeated. So even as the number of repetitions increases, the finitely repeated game does not approach the infinitely repeated game (or the game played in continuous time) in which co-operation is an equilibrium behaviour. For these reasons the finitely repeated game received special note in the game theory literature.

The prisoner's dilemma has motivated literally hundreds of experiments, and so I will not even attempt to review them individually. (Representative examples from economics and psychology are Lave (1962) and Rapoport and Chammah (1965).) Typical experiments concerning the one-period game reported a level of co-operation which responded readily to various kinds of experimental manipulation but which was bounded well away from either zero or 100 per cent. A number of experiments were conducted to isolate various factors[37] contributing to the level of co-operation.

However, many experiments which were analysed as one-period games were in fact conducted on various kinds of repeated games, using rules that made it difficult to determine precisely what the equilibria were. In a paper about designing prisoner's dilemma experiments Roth and Murnighan (1978) wrote

> It is often contended in the literature that if subjects are not informed of the number of periods to be played, the resulting game yields the same equilibria as the infinite game, since no period is known to be the last. However, this is a considerable oversimplification. Since it is apparent that the game must eventually terminate, subjects must form subjective probabilities greater than zero that a given period might be the last. Although such probabilities have neither been observed nor controlled by experimenters, we shall see that they play a critical role in determining the nature of equilibrium outcomes.

The papers goes on to derive the conditions for equilibrium in the repeated game with a fixed probability p of continuing after each play: co-operation can

[36] The argument is that any strategy which calls for co-operation on the last period is dominated, and so we can reduce the problem to the 99-period game, and so on. Note that unremitting non-co-operation remains an equilibrium strategy in the repeated game even though it is no longer a dominant strategy.

[37] From payoffs and number of trials to personality differences: see e.g. Lave (1965) and Terhune (1968).

be achieved at equilibrium only if the probability of continuing is sufficiently large.[38]

A pilot experiment was then conducted, in large part to show that the design was feasible.[39] The payoff matrix was chosen so that co-operation was consistent with equilibrium if and only if $p \geqslant \frac{1}{3}$, and subjects played three games, with probabilities of continuing of 0·1, 0·5, and 0·9. (Half the players played in that order, half the players in the opposite order.) The results of the experiment were that significantly more co-operative choices were made in the two higher probability conditions (in which these are equilibrium choices) than in the low probability condition. However, even in the high probability condition, only 36% of first period choices were co-operative. So the results remain equivocal.

Similarly equivocal results seem to be typical. A recent experiment, whose results help crystallise a lot of what I think has (in retrospect) been observed piecemeal in previous experiments, is reported by Selten and Stoecker (1986). In their experiment, subjects played 25 'supergames', each of which was a (ten-period) repeated prisoner's dilemma.[40] So this experiment looked at repeated play of the *repeated* game, and thus gave subjects the opportunity to gain experience with the ten-period game.

By far the most common pattern of observed play was initial periods of mutual co-operation (at least 4), followed by an initial defection, followed by non-co-operation in the remaining periods. After about round 16 almost all of the plays exhibit this pattern in each round. (A round is a play of the supergame, i.e. round 22 is the 22nd repetition of the ten-period repeated game.) Even more common is the pattern of 'end-effect play', which the authors define to be at least 4 consecutive rounds of mutual co-operation (not necessarily starting from period 1), with no further co-operation following the first defection. (Notice that this pattern includes the previous one.)

The most striking result concerns the progress in the observed (and 'intended') period of first defection. Having learned to co-operate, players start to defect earlier and earlier in subsequent supergames – i.e. the co-operation starts to unravel from the end.[41]

The paper then develops a learning theory model in which each player is

[38] Co-operation can be achieved by some equilibrium if and only if $p \geqslant (b-a)/(b-c)$, and it can be achieved 'easily', i.e. by the 'tit for tat' strategy of first co-operating and then doing whatever the other player did in the previous period, if and only if $p \geqslant (b-a)/(a-d)$ also.

[39] Subjects played against a programmed strategy (without knowing what it was). In fact the programmed opponent always played the 'tit for tat' strategy. And the players' incentives were only loosely controlled. Note that, since the equilibrium calculations depend on expected values, it would have been necessary to control for expected utility, not just ordinal utility, in order to do a proper job of controlling the equilibrium predictions. The experimental tools for doing that (via binary lottery games, as discussed in Section I.1) were not introduced until Roth and Malouf (1979).

[40] The payoffs were $b = 1{\cdot}45$ German marks, $a = 0{\cdot}6$, $c = 0{\cdot}1$, and $d = 0{\cdot}5$. The choices were phrased as setting a high price (co-operation) or a low price. (For early discussions of the prisoner's dilemma as a model for co-operation among oligopolists, see Shubik (1955). An early experiment on collusion among several oligopolists that refers to the prisoner's dilemma as such a model is Dolbear, Lave, Bowman, Lieberman, Prescott, Rueter, and Sherman (1968). [I have always suspected that so many authors may indicate a predisposition to collusion...])

[41] The authors caution, however (p. 54), 'Even if it is very clear from the data that there is a tendency of the end-effect to shift to earlier periods, it is not clear whether in a much longer sequence of supergames this trend would continue until finally cooperation is completely eliminated.'

represented by the period in which he intends to defect, and updates this, via three probabilities, depending on whether he defects first, simultaneously, or last. Steady state probability distributions are computed for various parameter configurations: it appears that in the typical stable distribution, co-operation either breaks down very early or very late. Monte-Carlo simulations based on parameters estimated for each subject based on the first 20 rounds are then made for the pairings in the last 5 rounds. Like the observed behaviour, these predictions have co-operation unravelling from round 20 to round 25.

I think it is fair to summarise these observations as follows: in the initial rounds players learned to co-operate (and consequently exhibited more periods of mutual co-operation starting from the very beginning and breaking down only near the end). In the later rounds, players learned about the dangers of not defecting first, and co-operation began to unravel. There is a sense in which this observed behaviour mirrors the game-theoretic observation that the equilibrium recommendation is not a good one, but that all other patterns of play are unstable.

These observations are consistent with many earlier observations of finitely repeated games in which co-operation is observed for some periods, but breaks down near the end. A number of new theories have been motivated by such experimental observations. For example Kreps *et al.* (1982) propose a model in which players may entertain certain slight doubts about the nature of their opponent, and observe that at equilibrium there will be co-operation until near the end.[42]

In summary, as in the case of experiments concerned with the free rider problem, interest over the course of many experiments has shifted from the one-time game to the repeated game. The theory for the repeated case is further developed for the prisoner's dilemma than for the free rider problem, and the contemporary discussion proceeds on both theoretical and experimental lines.

III.3 *Experiments versus Simulations: A Methodological Digression*

Let me digress to note that one still encounters in some quarters a distressing tendency to confuse computer simulations, and the kinds of investigations one can do with them, with experiments involving the observation of real people in controlled environments. Selten and Stoecker's use of both technologies makes the distinction clear. Computer simulations are useful for creating and exploring theoretical models, while experiments are useful for observing behaviour.

Perhaps the distinction can be made most clearly by considering an interesting set of computer simulations that have an unusually experimental flavour, and are reported in Axelrod (1980*a*, *b*; 1984). These have their origin in a pair of computer 'tournaments'. In the first of these, the author invited

[42] Other theoretical attempts have been directed at changing the notion of equilibrium entirely (see e.g. Rosenthal, 1980), or at studying closely related problems, see e.g. Selten's (1978) chain store paradox and the papers by Kreps and Wilson (1982) and Milgrom and Roberts (1982). An experimental study motivated in turn by this literature is reported in Camerer and Weigelt (1988).

fourteen scholars in several disciplines who had written on the prisoner's dilemma to submit short computer programs encoding a strategy to play the repeated game. Each of the programs played each of the others, as well as a copy of itself and a program which generated random choices, in a 200 play repeated prisoner's dilemma. The strategy with the highest cumulative score was 'tit for tat', which starts with co-operation and then echoes the other program's previous move. It and all of the other highest scoring rules were 'nice' in the sense that they never defected first.[43] Some programs got into sequences of alternating moves with 'tit for tat', with one program defecting on the odd numbered moves and co-operating on the even number moves and tit for tat doing the opposite, which for the parameters used in the tournament was not nearly as profitable as steady co-operation.[44] This is a pattern you might expect humans would be able to avoid, although it is easy to see how short computer programs could fall into it.

Axelrod (1980*b*) presented a second round of the tournament, with new entries, in which the game was repeated with a fixed probability of continuation after each round (with $p = 0{\cdot}99$, so that now co-operation is an equilibrium strategy), as discussed above in connection with Roth and Murnighan (1978). Again, 'tit for tat' was the winner. Some simulations of different possible tournaments were presented to show that there are some senses in which this result is robust, but other results were reported to show that this is not an entirely simple matter: (p. 402) '...had only the entries which actually ranked in the top half been present, then TIT FOR TAT would have come in fourth after the ones which actually came in 25th, 16th, and 8th'.

These computer tournaments thus suggest that behaviour will eventually converge to co-operation. This conclusion is at odds with experimental results such as Selten and Stoecker's. I suspect that the difference in results has a great deal to do with the difference between computer simulations and actual experiments. While the computer simulations which produce this result were conducted with an element of experimental flavour that is missing from conventional computer simulations (in that tournament entries were solicited from others),[45] experiments with human subjects introduce a certain amount of open-ended complexity in the form of human behaviour that is absent from a tournament in which individuals are represented by short (or even moderately long) computer programs.

III. THE WINNER'S CURSE, AND OTHER AUCTION PHENOMENA

III.1 *The Winner's Curse*

My topic in this section is in some ways the reverse of the one in section II.1. Instead of discussing a theoretical prediction that seemed difficult to investigate

[43] It turns out that there were two 'kingmakers', i.e. two programs which largely determined how the other programs did.

[44] Of course the results are also sensitive to the payoff matrix, which in this tournament had payoffs of $b = 5$, $a = 3$, $c = 1$, and $d = 0$, so that this kind of alternation gives up a half point each period in comparison to steady co-operation.

[45] One virtue of this, which it shares with experimental work, is to open up the process to ideas that might not have occurred to a single investigator designing a conventional computer simulation.

with field data and initially proved difficult to detect experimentally, this section discusses an *un*predicted effect that was initially postulated on the basis of field data, whose existence was debated, and which proved to be easy to observe in the laboratory. Of course, questions remain about how the experimental evidence applies to assessing the importance of this phenomenon in field data. Experience and motivation, the usual suspects, play a role here too. But in this case some ingenious comparisons between experimental and field data have been suggested which I think have promise of furthering this part of the debate.

The story begins with a 1971 article by Capen, Clapp, and Campbell, three petroleum engineers employed by the Atlantic Richfield Company. They claimed that returns on oil leases won by competitive bidding yield unexpectedly low rates of return, 'year after year', and that this has to do with the fact that the winning bidder is typically the one with the highest estimate of the value of the recoverable oil, and that the highest estimate is often an overestimate.

The important feature of this kind of auction is that all the bidders are trying to estimate a common value, in this case the value of the oil in a given tract. So even if all bidders have unbiased estimates of the true value, one bidder's estimate would convey valuable information to other bidders: the expected true value given a single estimate is higher than the expected true value given the information that the estimate is the highest of n, where n is the number of bidders. The hypothesis behind the 'winner's curse' is that winning bidders must frequently have the highest estimate but fail to take this into account.

Now, the idea that bidders persistently make mistakes flies in the face of standard notions of equilibrium, and so this thesis was greeted with scepticism by many economic theorists, particularly as the details of equilibrium behaviour in auctions became increasingly well understood (in which regard see particularly Wilson (1977) and Milgrom and Weber (1982)). It seemed likely to many that a simpler explanation of why oil company engineers might urge others to lower their bids could be found in cartel theory rather than bidding theory.

Nevertheless, evidence from field data drawn from common value auctions of other kinds was increasingly cited in support of the thesis that this 'winner's curse' might frequently account for low or negative returns to the winners. But such field data as is available is sufficiently complex and incomplete so as to allow many interpretations. The profitability of an oil field, for example, cannot be known for years after the drilling rights auction, and so the auction price is only one of many determinants of the rate of return. So the debate continued much as before. (For some of the flavour of the argument, see Cox and Isaac (1984), Brown (1986) and Cox and Isaac (1986).)

Laboratory experiments provide an opportunity to investigate at least the basic questions associated with whether the winner's curse is a robust phenomenon, and to what features in the auction environment it might respond. As we will see, they also reveal patterns in the data, associated with the presence or absence of a winner's curse, that suggest directions in which the field data can be further investigated.

Bazerman and Samuelson (1983) reported an experiment designed to see not merely if the winner's curse could be observed in the laboratory, but to explore how it might be related to the bidders' uncertainty about the value of the object being auctioned. The basic idea of their experiment was the following: subjects were asked to estimate the number of coins in a jar that in fact contained 800 pennies. (To motivate the subjects to be accurate in this part of the task, a small prize was given for the closest estimate.) Subjects were then asked to bid for the jar, with the understanding that the highest bidder would pay the amount of his bid and receive in return the value of the coins in the jar.[46] Subjects were also asked to write down their 90% confidence interval around their estimated value, and to bid on other similar objects (e.g. a jar of nickels), also worth $8.

The main results were that a clear winner's curse was observed in the data, with average winning bids around $10, which is two dollars more than the value of the objects being auctioned. This is in contrast to the average estimated value, which at around $5 underestimates the number of coins in the jar. So auctions were mostly being won by bidders with high estimates, and these were overestimates often enough to make the average winning bid higher than the true value. Analysis of various factors contributing to the level of bids suggested that when the reported valuations were more uncertain, a winner's curse would start to appear among smaller numbers of bidders. (The amount that the highest value estimate must be discounted is greater when it is the highest of 20 than when it is the highest of 4, so it is unsurprising that the winner's curse should be more readily observable among larger numbers of bidders.)

While the results show that the winner's curse is not hard to observe, the subjects in this experiment had no prior experience, and so the results could be attributed to the mistakes of novice bidders. Also, there was a wide range of bidding behaviour, so the results could potentially be attributed to the mistakes of just a few bidders. (Bazerman and Samuelson report that the average winning bid is sensitive to (p. 629) 'a handful of grossly inflated bids'.) One might suppose that in the natural economic environments in which questions about the winner's curse arose, bidders would have some opportunity to learn from their mistakes, and those who did not might be driven from the market by their losses. It is therefore still a reasonable question whether the phenomenon observed in this experiment could occur in environments in which experience could be gained, and in which bankruptcy could occur.

The experiment of Kagel and Levin (1986) was designed to address these issues, and also to control (rather than simply to measure) the uncertainty surrounding the value of the object being auctioned. Their experiment involved auctions in which a value x_0 was chosen from a known uniform distribution, and each bidder was given a private information signal x_i drawn from a uniform distribution on $[x_0-\epsilon, x_0+\epsilon]$, for known ϵ (which was one of the experimental variables, varying from $12 to $30).[47] If the high bid is b, the

[46] Not the coins themselves (to control for 'penny aversion').

[47] Thus private signals are 'positively affiliated' in the sense of Milgrom and Weber (1982).

high bidder earns $x_0 - b$ and everyone else earns 0. Subjects were given an initial cash endowment, and the opportunity to bid in a series of auctions. Subjects whose losses exhausted their initial endowments were declared bankrupt, and were no longer allowed to bid. In addition, after each auction, the subjects were all given feedback about the results. In some of the auctions not only was the winning bid announced, but all bids were posted next to the signal that had been received by that bidder, and the true value x_0 was announced. Thus bidders not only had an opportunity to learn from their own experience, but also from the experience of others. In particular, all bidders had an opportunity to observe the actual earnings of the high bidder. In addition, all subjects in this experiment had had some prior experience in experimental auctions.[48]

The main results for this part of the experiment are that bids were observed to be below the (risk neutral) Nash equilibrium bids. Profits were generally positive for groups of 3 or 4 bidders (at around 65 % of the equilibrium profits) and negative for groups of 6 or 7 bidders.[49] Overall, the data are consistent with the conclusion that the winner's curse diminishes with experience, but that changes in the environment (particularly in the number of bidders) require some readjustment during which profits are lower than they are after some additional experience has been accumulated.

Although a winner's curse was clearly observed in this experiment, there is still room to question the relevance of the findings for the kinds of field data which motivated the initial questions. After all, the results do suggest that the phenomenon might eventually disappear as bidders become more experienced. One might suppose that professional bidders for, say, oil companies would have far more experience than can be obtained in a series of laboratory auctions. This may be so, but it should be noted that the argument can also be made the other way: in this experiment, bidders received immediate feedback on the true value of the object and the profit made by the winning bidder. The field data on, say, drilling rights in the Gulf of Mexico, come from bids most of which were made before good information on the value of oil fields ultimately became available. And in many cases, only the winning bidder knows this information in any detail, so, unlike in the experimental environment, it might be that the only bidders to have experience with the winner's curse are its victims. Under this point of view, the bidders in the experimental environment might be thought to have more relevant experience than do bidders in natural environments.

Another line of attack concerns the subject pool itself: maybe the students who were the subjects in this experiment have not been selected for the kind of judgement that successful bidders may possess. Dyer *et al.* (1988) address this question in a subsequent experiment, in which the behaviour of student

[48] For a similar experiment with previously inexperienced subjects, see Kagel *et al.* (1988), who report similar results.

[49] It is a little difficult separating group size from experience and selection in these results, since although group size was one of the design variables, some of the small groups are the result of bankruptcies by overbidders in early periods.

subjects was compared with that of construction industry executives, and found to be qualitatively similar.[50]

Of course, there are always going to be differences between laboratory and field environments that make judgements such as these largely matters of taste. However, the second part of the experiment reported by Kagel and Levin (1986) suggests a way to make a direct connection between the experimental and field data. That part of the experiment concerned the effect of introducing public information.

To understand what is at issue here, first note that the equilibrium prediction is that as public information about the value of the object being auctioned is increased, winning bids will rise. The reason is that, at equilibrium, agents must discount their private information about the value, in order to avoid the winner's curse. The more uncertainty there is about the value, the more they must discount their private information. So *in a market at equilibrium*, additional public information, which reduces uncertainty about the true value, will cause agents to discount their private information less, and should on average cause winning bids to *rise*. However, the winner's curse occurs when winning bidders overestimate the true value. To the extent that increased public information reduces the uncertainty about the value, it should help bidders with high private signals to correct their overestimates. So, *in a market in which the winner's curse is present*, additional public information should on average cause winning bids to *fall*.

Kagel and Levin's experimental results are that in auctions with small numbers of bidders and positive profits, introducing public information (e.g. by announcing the lowest signal value publicly) does cause the winning bids to rise, but in auctions with large numbers of bidders and negative profits the public information causes winning bids to fall.

So, when the effect of public information can be observed, this suggests a test of field data for whether the winner's curse is present. In fact, some data about the effects of information is available for oil auctions from the work of Mead *et al.* (1983; 1984), who compare differential rates of return between *wildcat* and *drainage* tracts. A wildcat tract is one for which no positive drilling data are available, while a drainage tract is one in which hydrocarbons have been located on an adjacent tract. The neighbour(s) of a drainage tract are the companies who lease the adjacent tract(s). They have some private information unavailable to other bidders. There is also a public component to this information. Kagel and Levin argue that (p. 915)

> If the information available on drainage leases were purely public, it should, according to Nash equilibrium bidding theory, raise average seller's revenues, hence reducing bidder's profits... If the information were purely private, under Nash equilibrium bidding theory it would increase

[50] The authors remark 'We believe that the executives have learned a set of situation specific rules of thumb which permit them to avoid the winner's curse in the field but which could not be applied in the lab.' (It is of course also possible that the bidding environment encountered in the field is not well represented by the one created for the experiment. For example, in a field study of machine tool auctions, Graham and Marshall (1984; 1987) found that collusion among bidders was pervasive.)

> the rate of return for insiders (neighbors) relative to outsiders (nonneighbors) *and* reduce the average rate of return for nonneighbors... If the added information on drainage leases contains both public and private information elements, rates of return for neighbors should be greater than for nonneighbors, but with nonneighbor returns definitely less than in the absence of the additional information (both the public and private information components push in this direction for nonneighbors).
>
> What Mead *et al.* found were high rates of return on drainage compared to wildcat leases for *both* neighbors (88·6% higher) *and* nonneighbors (56·2% higher). Further, nonneighbors won 43·2 percent of all drainage leases. While the higher rate of return for neighbors compared with nonneighbors can be explained by the presence of insider information (the explanation Mead *et al.* offer, 1983, 1984), the substantially higher rates of return for nonneighbors remains puzzling within the context of Nash equilibrium bidding theory. However, the higher rate of return for *both* neighbors and nonneighbors on drainage leases is perfectly consistent with our experimental findings, given the existence of a winner's curse in bidding on wildcat leases. According to this explanation, the additional information available from neighbor tracts served to correct for the overly optimistic estimate of lease value recorded in the average winning bid on wildcat tracts, thereby raising average profits for both neighbors and nonneighbors alike. In this respect the OCS lease data parallel our experimental results with public information in the presence of a winner's curse.

While this argument may go somewhat beyond the available mathematical theory, and while Kagel and Levin are careful to note that there are alternative explanations for why both non-neighbours and neighbours do better on drainage leases, the experimental results establish a qualitative relationship among the data that are associated with the presence of the winner's curse, and this relationship opens new avenues for the investigation of field data.[51]

III.2 *Some Other Auction Results*

There is quite a large and distinguished experimental literature concerned with different auction rules in various economic environments. One of the striking and by now well known results from that literature is that in certain kinds of markets it is possible to observe trades converge to competitive equilibrium, in repeated markets with relatively few traders, often in relatively few periods, as traders gain experience, through repetition, with the parameters of the market. This is particularly so in repeated *double auction* markets, in which both buyers and sellers are free to make and revise bids and offers. For surveys of these results, see Plott (1982) or Smith (1982). (For an account of how some of the earlier conclusions fare in the light of subsequent experiments, in the kind of process that is the subject of this survey, see section 3 of my earlier survey, Roth (1987*b*).)

[51] For a new analysis of the field data, see Hendricks *et al.* (1987).

Before going on, note how these results, like the results of the experiments discussed at greater length here, change the ground of debate, even while not ending it. While there remains room to debate what dimensions of the experimental environment foster competitive outcomes, that competitive outcomes can be observed can be reliably demonstrated even in class. So whether markets are competitive is a question about real markets, not only about those with infinitely many agents. And in evaluating theories of competition, therefore, the experimental results point us in the direction of theories like that of Ostroy (1980), which do not depend on large numbers of agents.

Two recent papers which offer some interesting comparisons with those in Section III.1 are those by Kagel, Harstad and Levin (1987), and Kagel, Levin and Harstad (1987).

Kagel, Levin and Harstad (1987) study *second-price* common value auctions. In a second price auction, the high bidder wins but the price he pays is the second highest bid. Vickery (1961) noted that it is a dominant strategy in such auctions to bid one's true willingness to pay (and such auctions are sometimes called 'Vickery auctions'). Thus in contrast to the first price auctions considered earlier (in which the price is equal to the highest bid, and in which there is a strategic incentive to underbid), second price auctions disentangle the issue of evaluating how much an object is worth from strategic questions about how much to bid. Nevertheless, the authors report similar behaviour as was observed by Kagel and Levin (1986): positive profits were earned in small groups of bidders, and negative profits in larger groups. Thus these results support the hypothesis that the winner's curse derives primarily from errors in judgement about the value of the object.

Kagel, Harstad and Levin (1987) study a number of issues concerned with *private value* auctions, in which each agent knows with certainty the value to him of the object being auctioned, but has only probabilistic information about the value of the object to other agents. So in private value auctions there is no problem of evaluating how much the object is worth; the problem of choosing a bid is all strategic. Nevertheless, the authors observed that in the second price auctions, bidders had a persistent tendency to bid somewhat above their true values, and that the bids did not exhibit any tendency to converge to the true values over time. (Recall that it is a dominant strategy to bid true values in such an auction.) Because the winning bidder does not pay his bid, but only the amount of the next highest bid, this tendency to overbid had only a small effect on the (positive) expected payoffs to the bidders.[52] The authors conjecture that the overbidding is due to 'the illusion that it improves the probability of winning with no real cost to the bidder...'.

A striking feature of this result is that it is just the opposite of some previously reported results about second price auctions, which had concluded that bids tended to be *below* true values. However, upon inquiry Kagel *et al.* learned that (p. 1286).

[52] The authors report that the probability of losing money based on the observed amount of overbidding averaged only 0·06.

> ...in these earlier private value auction experiments subjects were *not permitted* to bid in excess of their private values. (emphasis in original)

They go on to remark (p. 1298)

> This persistent excess of market price above the dominant strategy price stands in marked contrast to reports of second price sealed bid auctions with independent private values (Coppinger, Smith and Titus, 1980; Cox, Roberson and Smith, 1982). Results from those experiments show average market price consistently below the dominant strategy price... The key institutional feature responsible for these different outcomes is, we believe, that those earlier second-price auction experiments did not permit bidding in excess of private valuations.[53]

Notice what this illustrates about the power of experimental methods. As economists, we have become accustomed to the fact that, because field data are noisy and incomplete, apparently similar data sets may yield different conclusions. With experimental data, however, since the collection of the data is fully under the control of the researchers, we can hope to be able to identify the causes of such differences. In this case, by inquiring of the authors, Kagel *et al.* were able to learn that an inadvertently unreported procedure of the earlier experiments had been that bids in excess of a bidder's private value were not allowed. Once this point had been clarified, the differences between the two data sets also became rather clear.

Kagel, Harstad and Levin (1987) also consider the effect of information on bids in first price private value auctions. Here, there is a closer correspondence between the equilibrium predictions and the observed outcomes than there was in the case of common value auctions discussed earlier. This adds some weight to the conclusion of Kagel and Levin (1986) that the contrary information effects they observed for common value auctions were due to the presence of the winner's curse.

III.3 *Some Methodological Remarks*

One topic I should mention in passing concerns the recurring methodological theme that it is difficult to control subjects' preferences. An aspect of this problem is raised in a penetrating critique by Harrison (1987), who reanalyses the conclusions reached by Cox *et al.* (1982), and Cox *et al.* (1983*a*, *b*; 1985*b*; 1988) in a series of experiments concerned with first-price private value auctions. In those experiments, subjects' ordinal preferences were taken to be equivalent to their monetary payoffs, and the authors estimated the expected

[53] The 'we believe' is due to the fact that the values here are not *independent*, but rather affiliated. However, they note (footnote 22), 'It is unlikely that positive affiliation is responsible for these differences. We have conducted one second-price experiment with independent private values which showed average market prices in excess of the predicted dominant strategy price. Further, recently published nondiscriminatory, multiple unit sealed bid auctions with independent private values, where the dominant strategy is to bid one's value, show a substantial (and persistent) percentage of all bids in excess of private values (Cox, Smith, and Walker, 1985 [*b*]).' And in a subsequent experiment, Kagel and Levin (1988) replicate the overbidding in second price single object auctions with independent private values, as part of a very interesting experiment designed to investigate the qualitative differences predicted to hold for first, second, and *third* price auctions.

utilities of the bidders, under the assumption that the experimental data represent a Nash equilibrium. Their analysis of the bid data under this assumption led them to reject the hypothesis that all the bidders have identical and risk neutral preferences. However, they observed that the bidding data conform well to the equilibrium hypothesis once different risk aversion parameters have been estimated for each bidder.

Harrison concludes that the control of the bidders' ordinal preferences via their monetary payoffs in these experiments was insufficient to reach this conclusion. His point is that it is not the total payoff to the bidders that is relevant, but the difference in payoffs that bidders get corresponding to different bids they might make. Harrison's key observation is that when one examines the expected payoffs to the bidders, the bids which appear to be significantly different from the risk neutral equilibrium bids differ only by pennies in expected payoff.[54]

The methodological thrust of Harrison's argument is that the whole point of paying subjects in experiments is to gain control of their incentives, i.e. to create an environment in which their incentives are known. But if the observed bids frequently differ from the equilibrium bid by only pennies of expected income, other (uncontrolled) incentives that the bidders might have may be stronger than the effective monetary incentive. Harrison concludes that 'It is the purpose of an experimental design to make the monetary payoffs salient enough to be used as a surrogate for subjects' utilities. If we cannot conclude that this is the case for observed deviations from predicted behavior, then we are unable to reject the theory generating those predictions.'

I think that there is an even more general point involved here, which is that the difficulty of indirectly inferring an unobserved or uncontrolled variable is as great in experimental data as in other kinds of data. A similar critique of quite a different kind of experiment is made by Brown and Rosenthal (1990), who reanalyse the data which led O'Neill (1987) to conclude that his experimental subjects had played the minimax mixed strategy in a zero-sum game. Brown and Rosenthal conclude that this is not the case, by disaggregating the data by pairs of players. The part of their analysis that is germane here is that they note that near equilibrium the payoff to the players is very 'flat' as a function of the strategies, and consequently the observation that the average payoff was near the equilibrium payoff cannot be interpreted as strong evidence that the strategies were near the equilibrium strategies.[55]

I think that these critiques show that the issue of control in experimental design is a subtle one, in that a degree of control sufficient to support some conclusions may be insufficient to support others. Since many economic phenomena are predicted to happen on the margin, where agents may be more

[54] Deviations in expected payoffs from the equilibrium payoff will differ less than the deviation of the bids from the predicted bid, since the former is the latter times the probability that the bid will be the winning bid. So, particularly for low bids, which have low probability of winning, substantial changes in the bid can have very small consequences for the payoff.

[55] They say (p. 7) 'As it turns out, the structure of O'Neill's game is such that a wide range of non-minimax behaviour can also lead to a winning percentage for the row player that is close to [the equilibrium value of] ·400.'

or less indifferent between a number of choices, the issues raised here will need to be of concern to a wide range of experimenters, both in choosing experimental designs and in interpreting experimental results.[56]

IV. PREFERENCE REVERSALS AND OTHER INDIVIDUAL CHOICES

Almost simultaneously with the rise of expected utility theory to pride of place among economists' models of individual choice behaviour, early experiments began to establish that there are at least some situations in which a substantial percentage of experimental subjects can be observed to exhibit systematic patterns of choice that violate predictions of the theory. The best known of these is due to Allais (1953), who observed that certain kinds of risky choices could not be squared with utility theory. Around the same time, May (1954) observed that intransitive choices could be systematically elicited over multi-dimensional alternatives that did not even involve risk.

These observations did not materially impede the adoption of utility maximisation as the primary vehicle for modelling individuals in economic theory. To the extent that utility theory is in part viewed as a prescriptive theory of rational choice, this is unsurprising, since it is unclear how experimental evidence of this kind can, or should, be incorporated into a theory of 'ideally rational' behaviour. But even when utility theory is viewed as a descriptive theory of actual choice behaviour, this is not too surprising, since the nature of the regular violations of the theory were still unclear, no powerful alternative theories had been proposed, and there was ample room to question the importance of the reported violations for students of economic phenomena.

In the intervening years, the nature of these and many other reliable 'anomalies' in choice behaviour have started to be much more thoroughly explored in experiments by both psychologists and economists, and in the last few years these have prompted the proposal of several interesting alternative theories of choice. There still remains ample room to question the importance of these anomalies for economics, but of necessity these questions must now be more pointed and specific, and hence seem more likely to be answerable.

IV.1 *Preference Reversals*

The anomaly I will consider in detail here is the discovery that it is possible to construct pairs of lotteries with the property that many people, when asked at what price they would be willing to sell (or buy) the lotteries, put a higher price

[56] Note the relationship to other phenomena we have discussed, such as the observation of 'disadvantageous counter-offers' by Ochs and Roth (1988) (see Section I.1), or the observation of Kagel, Harstad, and Levin (1987) of overbidding in second price private value auctions (see Section III.2). In both cases, actions that would be 'irrational' if expected monetary income could be equated with utility result in only small expected monetary losses, and so in neither case can the observations be regarded as strong evidence of irrational behaviour. They may simply be evidence that small monetary differences may be insufficient to override non-monetary elements in subjects' utility, or that negative feedback that occurs with only small probability may be insufficient to correct misconceptions. Similarly, in a set of experiments designed to investigate how subjects shop for low prices when search is costly, Hey (1982; 1987) concluded that they employed non-optimal 'rules of thumb' that, because of the flatness of the payoff function, performed almost as well as optimal search.

on one, but when asked to choose which they would prefer to participate in, choose the other.

Investigation of this phenomenon, called 'preference reversal', had its roots in a paper by Slovic and Lichtenstein (1968) that considered how different ways of assessing lotteries were differently influenced by the lotteries' prizes and probabilities. On the set of (hypothetical) lotteries they examined, how much subjects were willing to pay to play a given lottery was correlated more highly with the amount of the potential loss than with any other dimension, while the stated 'attractiveness' of the lottery correlated most highly with the probability of winning. They argued that this difference was evidence that subjects considered different kinds of information when asked to choose between lotteries than when asked to price them. They conjectured that being asked to bid (an amount of money) for the right to participate in a lottery caused subjects to concentrate on the monetary values of the prizes, in a way that choosing between lotteries did not.

This motivated their 1971 study (Lichtenstein and Slovic, 1971), in which preference reversals were first reported. In that paper they wrote (p. 47)

> The notion that the information describing a gamble is processed differently for bids than for choices suggested that it might be possible to construct a pair of gambles such that S[ubjects] would choose one of them but bid more for the other. For example, consider the pair consisting of Bet *P* (0·99 to win \$4 and 0·01 to lose \$1) and Bet \$ (0·33 to win \$16 and 0·67 to lose \$2). Bet *P* has a much better probability of winning but Bet \$ offers more to win. If choices tend to be determined by probabilities, while bids are most influenced by payoffs, one might expect that S[ubject]s would choose Bet *P* over Bet \$, but bid more for Bet \$.

To test this conjecture, three experiments were performed. In the first, subjects were presented with matched pairs of *P* and \$ bets with positive expected values, and asked to pick the bet they would prefer. Later, subjects were presented with the bets singly, and asked to name the minimum price for which they would be willing to sell each bet rather than play it. Subjects were told that all lotteries were hypothetical, and would not actually be played or sold.

The results were that, while subjects preferred the *P* bets to the \$ bets only about half the time, they put a higher price on the \$ bet far more often. In fact, 73% of the subjects were observed to always make the predicted reversal: (p. 48) 'for every pair in which the *P* bet was chosen, the \$ bet later received a higher bid'. In contrast the unpredicted reversal (choosing the \$ bet but putting a higher price on the *P* bet) was much less frequent, and only 17% of the subjects ever made this kind of reversal.

The second experiment was much like the first except that, instead of being asked at what price they would be willing to sell each bet, subjects were asked at what price they would be willing to *buy* it. The prices thus elicited were lower than the corresponding selling prices in the first experiment, and this decrease in price was substantially more pronounced for the \$ bets than for the *P* bets.

This decreased the number of predicted reversals, and increased the number of unpredicted reversals.

In the third experiment, which was intended (p. 51) '...to maximize motivation and minimize indifference and carelessness', transactions were actually carried out. All outcomes were stated in 'points' which would be converted into cash at the end of the experiment. (However subjects were not informed of the rates at which they would be paid.) The data again yielded a high proportion of predicted reversals, and a low proportion of unpredicted reversals.

One feature of this third experiment worth mentioning is that care was taken to motivate the subjects to reveal their 'true' selling prices for each lottery. The technique employed was proposed for this purpose by Becker *et al.* (1964). Each subject was told that the selling price he named would be compared with a price to be determined randomly, by spinning a roulette wheel. If the randomly determined price (the offer price) was higher than the named selling price, then the experimenter would buy the lottery from the subject *for the randomly determined offer price* (not for the named selling price), and otherwise the subject would keep the lottery. It is not hard to see that the dominant strategy for a utility maximiser faced with such a mechanism is to state his true selling price, i.e. the price that makes him indifferent between selling the lottery or keeping it.[57]

Based on these three experiments, the authors concluded that the preference reversal effect is robust, that it is inconsistent with not only utility theory but with 'every existing theory of decision making', and that it gives strong support to the view that subjects process information differently in making choices and in stating prices. They favour the view that subjects employ what has come to be called an 'anchoring and adjustment' heuristic in stating prices, in which they first 'anchor' on the amount of money to be won, and then 'adjust' their price to reflect that a win is not certain. In this view, preference reversals arise because subjects fail to adjust sufficiently. (For an account of other decision heuristics considered in the psychology literature, see Kahneman *et al.* (1982).)

A similar experiment by Lindman (1971) found qualitatively similar results over a set of hypothetical lotteries that included some with negative expected values. Shortly thereafter, Lichtenstein and Slovic (1973) sought to replicate the basic results using potentially significant amounts of money, and a different subject pool. (In the previous studies, subjects had been college students.) In the new experiment, subjects were volunteer participants in a Las Vegas casino. Lichtenstein and Slovic describe the environment as follows (p. 17):

[57] The argument, which Lichtenstein and Slovic presented to their subjects, is the same as the now familiar argument of Vickery (1961), that it is a dominant strategy to bid your true value in a second-price auction. The basic idea seems to have been independently developed a number of times: Smith (1979*a*, footnote 1) recounts how he heard this kind of procedure described by Jacob Marschak in 1953. Interestingly, Becker *et al.* (1964) report that they used this technique to estimate the utility functions of two experimental subjects repeatedly. They concluded that their subjects' responses were not consistent with utility maximisation, although their behaviour became more consistent with repeated exposure to the problem.

> The game was located in the balcony of the Four Queens Casino... The game was operated by a professional dealer... The S[ubject]s were volunteers who understood that the game was part of a research project. Only 1 *S*[ubject] could play the game at a time. Anyone could play the game, and the player could stop playing at any time (the dealer politely discouraged those who wanted to play for just a few minutes; a single complete game took 1–4 hr.)... At the start of the game, *S* was asked to choose the value of his chips. Each chip could represent 5¢, 10¢, 25¢, $1, or $5, and the value chosen remained unchanged throughout the game. The player was asked to buy 250 chips; if, during the game, more chips were needed, the dealer sold him more. At the end of the game (or whenever the player quit), the player's chips were exchanged for money.

In the choice part of the experiment, each subject was faced with four bets at a time, all with the same absolute expected value, two positive and two negative. Subjects were instructed to choose one of the positive and one of the negative expected value bets, and these were played with the aid of a roulette wheel. In the pricing part of the experiment, subjects were presented with the lotteries, one at a time, and told to state a price such that either 'I will pay the dealer _ chips to get rid of this bet' or 'The dealer must pay me _ chips to buy this bet'. The Becker *et al.* procedure was used to determine transaction prices, with the dealer's offer being determined by the roulette wheel, so it was a dominant strategy for utility maximisers to state their true reservation price. Again, predicted reversals were frequent and unpredicted reversals rare.[58] The authors conclude that (p. 20) 'The widespread belief that decision makers can behave optimally when it is worthwhile for them to do so gains no support from this study. The source of the observed information-processing bias appears to be cognitive, not motivational.'

These results, which all appeared in the psychology literature, were viewed with suspicion by many economists. This is well expressed in the report of a subsequent experiment by Grether and Plott (1979), who were concerned that the earlier experiments (and also Slovic, 1975) either did not use real payoffs, or did not control for income effects. (That is, in the course of choosing between real lotteries the subjects become richer, which might change their preferences sufficiently to produce the reported reversals.) They also expressed concerns related to the fact that most of the experimental subjects were psychology undergraduates ('... one would be hesitant to generalize from such very special populations') and that the experimenters were psychologists ('Subjects nearly

[58] For the pairs of negative expected value bets, the prediction is (since subjects are predicted to focus in the pricing task on the size of the potential loss) that they will be willing to pay more to avoid playing the $ bet, with its large potential loss, than they are to avoid playing the *P* bet. The 'predicted reversal' thus occurs when the bets are priced in this way, but the $ bet is chosen over the *P* bet. For these bets also, the predicted reversals outnumbered the unpredicted reversals. The authors note that, by including negative expected value bets in the design, they are able to rule out one alternative hypothesis for the results in the positive expected value case, namely that subjects price the $ bets in such a way as to increase the likelihood that they will retain them (either out of a strategic impulse to state high selling prices, or out of a preference for playing out gambles). Such a strategy for negative expected value gambles would involve stating a less negative price, and this would have diminished the number of predicted reversals.

always speculate about the purposes of experiments and psychologists have the reputation for deceiving subjects'). They therefore proposed experiments to address these questions, designed, in their words, '...to discredit the psychologists' works as applied to economics'.

They employed the same gambles as in the third experiment of Lichtenstein and Slovic (1971), using subjects recruited from economics and political science classes. In the first experiment, subjects were divided into two groups. Subjects in the first group were paid a flat rate of $7 for participating, and made only hypothetical choices, while subjects in the second group were told they had a credit of $7, with their final payment being the sum of the initial $7 and any gains or losses they might get from the lotteries. They were told that, at the end of the experiment, *one* of their decisions would be chosen at random to be actually played. (The authors remark that this procedure, rather than one in which all lotteries are played, should reduce any income effect.) Finally, the design of the experiment counterbalanced the two tasks, so that subjects first chose between lottery pairs, then priced lotteries, then chose between the remaining lottery pairs. Prices were elicited as selling prices using the Becker *et al.* second price auction procedure. (In a second experiment, all mention of 'selling' was suppressed, in case this should be a reason why subjects might overstate their reservation prices.)

The chief result was that preference reversals persisted. There were observable differences between the data from hypothetical and from real lotteries, with a *higher* percentage of reversals arising from the real lotteries. The propensity to reverse was the same for lottery choices made before the pricing task as for those made after it. As before, prices for $ bets were generally higher than those for *P* bets, and higher than their expected values, so the data remain consistent with the hypothesis that pricing decisions are reached by 'anchoring' and (insufficient) 'adjustment'.

These results did not settle the matter. Two subsequent studies, by Pommerehne *et al.* (1982) and Reilly (1982) were motivated by concern that the experiment of Grether and Plott had not been effective in giving the subjects substantial motivation, because the amounts involved were not large. Pommerehne *et al.* conducted an experiment with higher payoffs, and reported a frequency of reversals that is still substantial, but lower than that observed by Grether and Plott.[59] Reilly's experiment provides a within experiment comparison that supports the conclusion that increased payoffs do reduce the rate of reversals. But in his experiment also, substantial percentages of reversals were observed. Thus this series of experiments supports the notion that preference reversals are not simply an artefact of certain narrow experimental procedures.[60]

[59] In their reply, Grether and Plott (1982) note that Pommerehne *et al.* did not replicate the earlier experiment, so that it is premature to attribute the lower rate of reversals to the higher payoffs, since the experiments differed in other ways as well.

[60] In a comment on these experiments, Slovic and Lichtenstein (1983) urge economists to view such reversals not as an isolated phenomenon, but as part of a family of choice anomalies that may arise from information processing considerations.

Reilly's results suggest that the rate of reversals does decrease as financial motivation increases (at least for some range of payoffs, since Grether and Plott report the reverse effect in moving from hypothetical lotteries to small payoffs), so it is reasonable to ask whether the rate of reversals might decline to insignificance if the subjects were sufficiently well motivated. This kind of question remains after many experimental studies in economics. However, the following experiment of Berg *et al.* (1985), shows that such questions can sometimes be addressed by means other than simple extrapolation.

Briefly, their experiment was designed to assess the effect of making subjects pay for every preference reversal they stated, by running them around a 'money pump'. Using a pricing task in which subjects were required to state for each lottery a price at which they would be willing either to buy or sell it, they extracted a fine from subjects who stated preference reversals in a first set of choices by first selling them the high price lottery (the $ bet) for the indicated price, then trading it for the low price lottery (the preferred *P* bet) and then buying back that lottery at its (lower) price. (Note that at this point these transactions were not voluntary: subjects had been told that they would be obliged to honour their stated preferences and prices, for either buying or selling.) Comparing those conditions of their experiment that do not extract this fine with those that do, they found no significant differences in the *number* of reversals, but a significant decrease in the dollar *value* of the reversals (i.e. the difference in prices between the two bets). As subjects gained more experience, the dollar value of the reversals declined, but reversals did not disappear. Thus the evidence suggests that subjects tried to eliminate reversals but were unable to do so fully.

This lends some indirect support, I think, to the view among psychologists that this phenomenon may reflect a 'cognitive illusion' in the pricing task, similar in some ways to familiar optical illusions. By analogy, consider an experiment where the paired comparison task is to estimate the length of two horizontal lines each of which is 'framed' with sideways 'V's (facing either out or in) to make them look longer or shorter. The 'pricing' part of the experiment is to look at lots of horizontal lines, framed one way or the other, in random order, and estimate their length in inches. Even after you know that outward 'V's make the lines look longer, it might remain hard to estimate them in inches, and increasing your motivation would not be expected to solve the problem.

IV.2 *Alternative Theoretical Directions*

But this is not the only way to view the evidence, and here the different theoretical points of view of psychology and economics suggest different directions in which it might be fruitful to proceed. Loosely speaking, much of the work by psychologists on this and related subjects has been motivated by the point of view that people make choices in a manner analogous to interrogating a data base, and that how questions are asked therefore makes a difference in what answers will be obtained. In contrast, economists (who are generally interested in choice behaviour at a somewhat different level of detail, and are therefore typically more willing to sacrifice some accuracy for some generality) have viewed choice behaviour as reflecting underlying, already existing, and reasonably stable preferences. The assumptions about such preferences embodied in standard expected utility theory are of course not the only ones imaginable, and one way of seeking to capture the kinds of behaviour discussed here is by relaxing such assumptions, while preserving the idea that at some useful level of approximation agents do indeed have preferences. A number of such theories have now been proposed (for a good introductory survey see Machina (1987)).

Loomes and Sugden (1983) discuss how preference reversals are consistent with a theory of choice, called 'regret theory', they earlier proposed in a 1982 paper, in which choices between risky alternatives reflect not only some underlying 'choiceless' utility, but also comparisons ('regret' or 'rejoicing') with what might have been. These comparisons depend on the subsequent realisation of the underlying random events. Different comparisons are involved in choosing between two bets than are involved in choosing between each of them and a selling price, and the previous experiments allowed subjects to make some of these comparisons. That is, a subject might choose the *P* bet over the $ bet in part because of the regret he would feel if he chose the $ bet and the random device (e.g. roulette wheel) subsequently produced a number that meant a loss in the $ bet but would have meant a win in the *P* bet. But the same subject, with appropriately specified regret function, might still set a higher price on the $ bet, because the pricing task involves different comparisons between the random outcome of each lottery and the selling price.

Now, one of the nice things about experiments is that they can help to distinguish between alternative hypotheses. Consider the kinds of experiments we might contemplate to distinguish between the competing hypotheses that preference reversals arise from information processing or regret-theoretic causes. Since the predictions derived from regret theory appear to be sensitive to whether lotteries share comparable random events (so that the 'might have beens' can be compared), this suggests that choices between lotteries in which these comparisons cannot be made might yield different results. Similarly, since the regret theory hypothesis is stated in terms of the same kinds of comparisons both for the choice between lotteries and for the setting of a price, it suggests that reversals are only one of a species of intransitivities. Since neither of these effects is obviously predicted by the information-processing hypothesis as it has so far been presented, appropriate experimental results will help to distinguish between these competing hypotheses, and to suggest refinements and elaborations of each.[61]

Notice I am not predicting that we will soon see some 'critical experiment' that will cause one of these hypotheses to fall by the wayside. Even in the laboratory, things are rarely so simple, since terse theories about complex phenomena permit a variety of interpretations and elaborations. Indeed, one

[61] In this connection, see Loomes *et al.* (1988*a*).

of the main uses of experiments is to prompt the refinement of the theories used to explain them. And of course, experimental results intended to distinguish between two such hypotheses as these may yield ambiguous results, particularly if the phenomenon turns out to be due to some third cause.

Just such a third hypothesis to account for preference reversals has been suggested independently by Holt (1986) and Karni and Safra (1987). This is that individuals may possess preferences that violate the 'independence' assumption of expected utility theory, but not necessarily the transitivity assumption. (Following Machina (1982) a number of choice theories without independence have been proposed.) Independence is the assumption that says an outcome A is weakly preferred to B if and only if a lottery between A and C is weakly preferred to a lottery with the same probabilities between B and C, for any lottery C. It is this assumption that makes the utility of a lottery a linear function of the probabilities, so that compound lotteries may be decomposed in the standard way. And it is this which implies that the price a utility maximiser will state in the Becker *et al.* elicitation procedure can be interpreted as his reservation price: i.e. it implies he is indifferent between a lottery A and a selling price p if and only if p is the price that maximises the utility of the compound lottery between A and prices greater than p that he faces after stating a price.[62] To emphasise that preference reversals may be compatible with transitive preferences over lotteries, Karni and Safra (1987) couch their discussion in terms of such a family of generalisations of utility theory proposed by Quiggan (1982) and Yaari (1987).

Holt further notes that the procedure of paying subjects for only one of their decisions, randomly chosen after all decisions are made, which was employed by Grether and Plott (1979) to control for income effects, only can be interpreted as having that effect if the independence assumption is satisfied. That is, the assumption is that the optimal choice in each decision evaluated separately is also the optimal choice when each decision is evaluated as part of the compound lottery consisting of the whole experiment, but without independence this may not be the case. And Karni and Safra note that the direct elicitation of preferences may present difficulties if preferences do not satisfy independence. So there is ample room for further experiments exploring these hypotheses.[63]

It should be emphasised that the Becker *et al.* elicitation procedure allows us to predict what prices *utility maximisers* would state. That non-utility-maximisers may have incentives to respond differently is in no way a criticism of the experimental designs which incorporate this procedure. On the contrary, the virtue of those experimental designs is that they allow us to test predictions made in terms of utility theory, by permitting unambiguous predictions about what utility maximisers would do. In the absence of such a design, we would be unable to conclude that the observed phenomenon constituted a violation

[62] As noted above, the argument for the Becker *et al.* procedure is the same as that for second-price auctions, and so violations of independence have the same implications there: see Karni and Safra (1985).

[63] An initial experiment in this direction is that of Loomes *et al.* (1988*b*).

of the theory.[64] This is a point worth repeating: one of the major virtues of laboratory experiments well designed to test theoretical predictions is that they allow us to make observations in theoretically unambiguous circumstances. To appreciate the power of this, see if you can think of any *field* observations that might possibly allow us to observe preference reversals.

IV.3 *Market Behaviour*

The very difficulty of making such observations in the field raises again the question of what is the importance of such phenomena for economics. I think it is fair to say that quite a broad range of opinions have been expressed on this point, with some economists taking the view that choice anomalies have not yet been shown to occur in typical economic environments such as markets.

To give a brief account of how that discussion has begun to be pursued by experimental means, it will be helpful to consider not only preference reversals, but the related phenomenon that stated buying prices have been observed to be substantially below (i.e. more than can be accounted for by income effects) stated selling prices in a number of studies of hypothetical choice (recall experiment 2 of Lichtenstein and Slovic 1971). Knetsch and Sinden (1984) review these results from hypothetical choice experiments and report an experiment showing this disparity between buying and selling prices persists for real transactions.

In a reply to Knetsch and Sinden, Coursey *et al.* (1987) propose to test what I will call the *market hypothesis*, which is that agents in a market environment will behave like utility maximisers, i.e. experimental subjects in a market will receive feedback and experience of a kind that will extinguish such anomalies as the buying and selling price disparity.[65] The market environment in their experiment is a second price auction, so that it will be a dominant strategy for utility maximisers to state their true reservation prices.[66] (Buying and selling auctions were conducted separately: what is being bought and sold is the right not to taste, a 'bitter... non toxic... very unpleasant' substance called SOA.) In addition, the auction result would only be considered final if it was unanimously agreed to: otherwise another trial would be conducted to determine which (four out of eight) subjects would taste the SOA. The authors report that, although initial trials yielded the familiar disparity between buying and selling prices, and while the auction results continued to show some continued disparity, this diminished over auction periods, and by the final period the remaining gap between the two prices was no longer statistically significant. (Most of the movement came in subjects' declining prices for

[64] Note the parallel to the use of binary lottery games discussed in Section I.1.

[65] A similarly motivated experiment concerned with anomalies in the perception of probabilities is reported in Camerer (1987).

[66] Kagel and Levin (1988) note that Coursey *et al.* rely on the second-price auction results reported by Coppinger *et al.* (1980) and Cox *et al.* (1982) in interpreting their own results. As these now seem to be erroneous (recall the discussion in section III.2), Kagel and Levin suggest that the results of Coursey *et al.* may also require reinterpretation. In particular, while the observed overbidding is in general small, Kagel and Levin observe that this may be consequential in an experiment in which bids are taken to equal the true reservation prices, and they note that the direction of the anomalous behaviour in second price auctions is such that it could provide an alternative explanation for Coursey *et al.*'s results.

agreeing to taste the SOA.) They conclude that '...the divergence obtained in early trials of the experiment...may result mainly from lack of a market experience'.[67]

In their rejoinder, Knetsch and Sinden (1987) decline to attribute the same significance to the diminution of the buying and selling price disparity in the above experiment. Apart from critiquing aspects of the experiment (they are not persuaded that tastes of SOA are a typical economic commodity), they also cite some stylised facts about market behaviour that they think may reflect choice anomalies similar to this price disparity. Knetsch *et al.* (1987) present some evidence in support of this view, from a market experiment in which half the subjects have been endowed with a small consumer good (e.g. mugs, pens). In these experiments subjects who wished to buy or sell a good (with their own money) were free to do so, and the authors report that substantially fewer trades were transacted than would be expected in the absence of an endowment effect.[68]

Another experiment, concerned with both preference reversals and buying and selling price disparities in a market setting, is reported by Knez and Smith (1987). They propose to test a version of what I will call the *strong market hypothesis*, which is that markets equilibrate as if agents were utility maximisers even if the agents do not themselves behave as if they were utility maximisers. They state this point of view as follows (p. 132):

> The efficiency and social significance of markets does not depend on the validity of any particular theory of individual demand...the empirical validity or falsity of efficient markets theory is a proposition that is entirely distinct from the empirical validity or falsity of theories of individual demand in markets.

Knez and Smith observed several repeated markets in which subjects were first asked to state hypothetical preferences and buying or selling prices for a *P* bet and a $ bet with expected values of $3·85, and were then allowed to trade. Trading was conducted in two separate double auction markets, first a market for *P* bets, then for $ bets. In each market each buyer was given an endowment of $5·50, and was allowed to buy no more than a single lottery. Each seller was given an endowment of one lottery (and was also paid $1·65). After both markets had been conducted, buyers and sellers were again asked to state hypothetical preferences and reservation prices, and all initial endowments were replenished. The whole process was repeated several times, with each subject remaining always a buyer or always a seller.

Although Knez and Smith observe numerous and persistent price disparities and preference reversals in the hypothetical responses (p. 142, 'It seems clear that there is a hard core of 35 to 38% reversals that continue to be exhibited

[67] In a related experiment, Brookshire and Coursey (1987) go on to compare different methods of eliciting values for public goods and report a similar decrease in price discrepancies elicited from a repeated market-like elicitation procedure as compared to data elicited in a hypothetical survey.

[68] Interestingly, Marshall *et al.* (1986) report that individuals exhibit a much smaller buying/selling price disparity when they are asked to act as an agent for someone else than when they are acting on their own behalf.

by the reported preferences and values...') they argue that very few of the prices at which lotteries change hands are inconsistent with utility theory, in the sense that they do not lie outside the interval of possible payoffs of the lotteries. In fact, most transactions occur sufficiently close to the expected value to be consistent with plausible risk preference or risk aversion. On the basis of this evidence they conclude (p. 152) 'The results of this study call into question the interpretation, reliability, and robustness of preference reversal phenomena in the joint context of repetitive responses and market trading.'

It should be clear by now why it is unlikely that this conclusion will meet with universal acceptance. Rather it provides another piece of the continuing debate among experimenters interested in these issues. Since their experiment is too recent to have drawn a reply as of this writing, let me play the Devil's advocate. For example, one might speculate that the moderate trading prices observed by Knez and Smith have more to do with the specific market parameters they have chosen than with general properties of markets. Since preference reversals seem to be associated with the overpricing of the \$ bets (which in this case had a prize of \$16), anomalous trades might be easier to observe in a market in which buyers had cash endowments larger than \$5·50, and in which \$ bets were in shorter supply (e.g. by having fewer sellers than buyers). Or, since preference reversals involve choices between *P* and \$ bets, it might be easier to observe them in some market in which both lotteries could be traded simultaneously. My object here is not to try to design or to guess the outcome of the 'next' experiment, but to re-emphasise that experiments provide a method for continuing the argument, in a way that can steadily narrow the grounds for potential disagreement.

IV.4 *Other Phenomena*

I have concentrated on preference reversals here because they have been the subject of a long series of experimental investigations, from different points of view, which serve well to illustrate some ways in which experimental investigations may proceed. There are other individual choice phenomena with equal (and equally contested) claims to importance. For a discussion of some of these, see Kahneman and Tversky (1979; 1984), or Thaler (1987) (who particularly concentrates on what in his view is the importance of these phenomena for economics). These other choice phenomena offer other possibilities to design experiments by which various generalisations of expected utility theory may be tested. In this regard see e.g. Camerer (1988), Loomes (1988), Loomes and Sugden (1987), or Battalio *et al.* (1988) (who succinctly summarise the present state of theoretical affairs by stating: '...none of the rival formulations considered consistently organises choices, indicating that we have a long way to go before having a complete descriptive model of choice under uncertainty'). In fact, even laboratory animals have been observed to exhibit some choice behaviours of this kind (see Battalio *et al.*, 1985, Kagel, 1987), so experiments on these matters need not be confined to humans.

Before leaving the subject of individual choice behaviour, I will mention one more experiment, which differs from those so far discussed in the scale of rewards that were offered. Binswanger (1980) reports the results of an experiment carried out among village farmers in areas of India, where 'The average physical wealth of the households...is very low by international standards.' Villagers from a sample with substantial variations in wealth were repeatedly given the opportunity to choose among a set of gambles which could be ranked in order of riskiness. ('To overcome moral problems confronting low income people involved in gambling, the gambling was limited so that the worst possible outcome was a zero gain.') First relatively small gambles were offered, with the prizes eventually increasing to levels 'commensurate with monthly wage rates or small agricultural investments'. Subjects considered their choices for several days.

The chief results were that, at very low payoff levels, there was a wide distribution of observed levels of risk aversion, but at higher payoff levels there was much less variance, with most responses concentrated in an 'intermediate to moderate' level of risk aversion. Furthermore, subjects' risk aversion at these high payoff levels did not appear to be significantly influenced by their wealth.[69] Binswanger also observed that these results obtained from actual gambles varied in important ways from the answers initially obtained from hypothetical questions about high stakes gambles. The hypothetical results showed both many more severely risk averse choices, and more risk neutral or risk preferring choices, than did the comparable data from actual choices.

In summary, in the series of experiments reported here the focus of debate was initially on whether certain kinds of anomalous choice behaviour were artefacts of the experimental procedure, and in particular whether they would persist in non-hypothetical choice situations. In the case of preference reversals, the phenomenon survived both the change from hypothetical to real choices, and increases in the payoff level. (However, questions about the reliability of hypothetical choices are not always resolved in this way, as is shown by the results of Binswanger.) The debate has now shifted to the underlying causes of the phenomena, and whether market environments will moderate the observed effects. Some of the various theories which have been advanced as possible explanations of certain kinds of choice behaviour not only suggest new experiments, but new directions for pursuing traditional kinds of economic theory (see e.g. Crawford, 1988). It is clear that the degree of success such theories achieve in organising and explaining phenomena in domains other than individual choice behaviour itself will be important. At the same time, the question of whether individual choices in market and other economic environments are systematically different from what can be observed in various unstructured environments (either because certain kinds of choices do not arise in markets, or because markets provide a certain kind of feedback) will undoubtedly require proponents of different points of view to sharpen their hypotheses about market phenomena.

[69] In Binswanger (1981) and Quizon *et al.* (1984), this is interpreted as reflecting utility functions defined in terms of changes in wealth, rather than in terms of net wealth (cf. Markowitz, 1952; Kahneman and Tversky, 1979), or else as reflecting some deviation from expected utility maximisation such as those involving failures of the independence assumption.

V. SOME COMMON METHODOLOGICAL QUESTIONS

I will try to organise briefly some of the methodological themes encountered in this survey into a set of commonly asked questions, together with my answers and evasions (which may not always reflect a consensus among experimenters).

Are experiments involving hypothetical choices reliable? This question is one of the fault lines dividing some economists and psychologists. There are examples which allow one to answer in either direction. For example, preference reversals were initially identified from data on hypothetical choices, and proved to be robust to better motivated choices. On the other hand, the study of Binswanger (1980) showed that large differences in responses will sometimes be observed.[70] Of course, Binswanger also observed important differences between gambles for small stakes and for large stakes, and so the question is really related to questions about the effects of the scale of payoffs.[71] As Thaler (1987) notes (p. 120), 'Asking purely hypothetical questions is inexpensive, fast, and convenient.' Since many experiments have binding budget constraints, this is not a frivolous point. Personally, I am most comfortable with responses to hypothetical choices when they are presented together with some evidence that the answers are not too dissimilar from those obtained from actual choices. To the extent that the size of actual payoffs may be critical for some phenomena, I am prepared to entertain experimental designs in which some parts of the design use hypothetical choices, while other parts use the money thus saved to make a comparison with more substantial monetary payoffs than would otherwise have been possible.

Do college students behave like real people? The answer to this one must be clear to all the college professors among my readers: you can never be sure. But for most purposes there is little evidence that they do not, since results initially obtained with college students seem to be robust more often than not (e.g. Lichtenstein and Slovic's casino gamblers, or Dyer *et al.*'s construction executives). That is not to say that special groups of subjects, such as commodities traders or meteorologists, might not have some properties not found among college students, or in the general population. I certainly do not want to discourage anyone from conducting experiments with different subject populations. In my own opinion, there has been a shortage of carefully controlled cross cultural experiments, which might reveal unanticipated (or anticipated) differences or similarities in various kinds of economic behaviour among subjects in different societies.

Do economic experiments have to be done in computer controlled laboratories? No. Certainly not. Many are, because such a laboratory facilitates many kinds of control (e.g. always presenting subjects with certain information in the same way, or keeping them anonymous), and record

[70] There are several studies that have made explicit comparisons between hypothetical and real choices, and they typically report some differences, but often not qualitatively important ones (cf. Battalio *et al.*, 1988; Grether and Plott, 1979; Jamal and Sunder, 1988; Marshall *et al.*, 1986).

[71] See also Kroll *et al.* (1988) in this regard. They report an experiment in which subjects' behaviour (regarding the diversification of investments) changed significantly in response to an increase in payoffs by a factor of ten.

keeping (e.g. recording the time of each transaction). However, many of the experiments discussed here were conducted without such a laboratory, and most of the rest could have been. If you are planning to do a lot of experiments, however, the investment in time and energy to establish such a laboratory may be worth it. But no one should let the start up costs of a computerised lab be a deterrent to conducting experiments, and for many purposes it will be most sensible at least to begin experimental work with simpler arrangements.

Is it possible to 'lie' with experiments? Yes, of course it is. I suppose we will know that economic experimentation has really come of age when we start to have outright fraud to contend with, of the kind that sometimes afflicts other areas of science, in which researchers desperate to establish priority or show progress on their grant proposals, or simply to 'prove' a treasured theory fabricate data out of whole cloth.[72] In the meantime, I think what this question most often means is 'If I believe theory *A* and you believe theory *B*, cannot I do an experiment whose results will seem to support *A* while you do one whose results seem to support *B*?' Here too, I think the answer must be, in a limited way, yes. The reason is that the designer of an experiment may have to make many particular decisions, and choose the level of many parameters that may affect the phenomena under study. If there is reason to believe that the resulting observations depend in important ways on some of these choices, variations may be incorporated into the experimental design, or into subsequent experiments, to see if this is the case. But there are often too many essentially arbitrary choices for this approach to be applied to all but a few of them. (It is for this reason that the strongest conclusions from an experimental study come from *within experiment* comparisons, which report the effect of the change of a single variable, while holding all others constant.)

I think the major pitfall to be aware of here is that, since decisions made in the design of the experiment cannot be regarded as random samples from the space of possible design choices, there is room for an experimenter's prior beliefs about the likely outcome of the experiment to influence the outcome, through these design decisions.[73] Sometimes this is explicit, deliberate, and desirable, as when the experimenter wishes to demonstrate that some phenomenon is possible, rather than general. The danger is of inadvertently reading experimental evidence as supporting an overly general conclusion based on observations made in special cases. Sometimes this will be unavoidable, when the relevant variables simply have not yet been identified. However, it may be possible to address some aspects of this problem, since experiments are often preceded by pilot studies, designed to determine inexpensively and quickly if a full scale experiment will yield useful data. Final design decisions may be made on the basis of these pilot studies, which therefore may include parameters and design choices not included in the experiment. I think that reporting such pilot experiments in a little more detail than is presently customary in the

[72] If space allowed, I would report a series of computerised cross cultural experiments involving large numbers of identical triplets, one raised in a market economy, one in a command economy, and one by wolves.

[73] The same could of course be said for econometrics.

experimental literature may be a good practice, particularly in so far as it may sometimes help to alert other investigators to alternative hypotheses for the results presented.[74] (However, I should note in this regard that experimenters would often like to report more detail than the guardians of scarce journal space allow.) In the meantime, I think that experimentation is well served by sceptical readers, and particularly by experimenters with different theoretical predispositions.

VI. CONCLUDING REMARKS

This essay has focused on experimental methods, and how experiments can be used to further an investigation, and often a debate.[75] Lest this emphasis on debate leave the reader with the mistaken impression that we never get anywhere with all this, let me recall a few of the things clearly learned from experiments: The outcome of bargaining can be systematically effected by information other than that which goes into determining bargainers' expected utility; the winner's curse is a real phenomenon; competitive equilibria can be observed in small repeated markets; reliable violations of expected utility theory can be observed in well motivated individual choice behaviour.

Each of these is now a well established, often reproduced experimental result, but was once a matter capable of generating considerable controversy, at least in some circles. I think the results I have just stated are no longer themselves grounds for much controversy, although their significance may still leave room for debate. But experiments give us directions to further this debate too, and to continue to narrow the grounds for disagreement. This is so even in areas in which some of the experimental results remain equivocal: for example, the regularities observed in repeated play of the prisoner's dilemma have prompted new kinds of theoretical models, just as the results on public information and the winner's curse suggest new kinds of analyses of field data.

What I have tried to make clear is that experimentation is more than the sum of the facts that have so far been established. Like econometrics, and like deductive theory, it is a method of investigation. For this reason, I have concentrated in this survey on methodological themes, broadly construed, by which I mean not merely how experiments are conducted, but how it is decided *what* experiments to conduct, and how results are interpreted, and sometimes challenged. In doing so, I hope I have presented a clearer picture of the experimental endeavour, and how it complements more traditional kinds of economic research, both theoretical and empirical.

[74] For an example, see Conlisk (1987), who makes something of the same point in the context of individual choice behaviour.

[75] There are uses of experiments I have not even touched on here, such as for stimulating particular target markets (see Plott, 1987 or section 4 of Roth, 1987*b*) or for constructing compelling classroom demonstrations. I do not mean to slight them, I just did not have enough room to speak about them here. Similarly, I have not concentrated specifically on the development of experimental methodology as such (e.g. the development of further procedures for implementing binary lottery games (recall Section I.1, and cf. Berg *et al.*, 1986), which is an as yet small part of the literature that will grow in importance as experiments concentrate on phenomena that are increasingly difficult to measure or control.

References

Allais, Maurice (1953). 'Le comportement de l'homme rationnel devant le risque: critique des postulats et axiomes de l'école americane.' *Econometrica*, vol. 21, pp. 503–46.

Axelrod, Robert (1980*a*). 'Effective choice in the iterated prisoner's dilemma.' *Journal of Conflict Resolution*, vol. 24, pp. 3–25.

—— (1980*b*). 'More effective choice in the prisoner's dilemma.' *Journal of Conflict Resolution*, vol. 24, pp. 379–403.

—— (1984). *The Evolution of Cooperation*, New York: Basic Books.

Baiman, Stanley and Lewis, Barry L. (1988). 'An experiment testing the behavioral equivalence of strategically equivalent employment contracts.' *Journal of Accounting Research*, forthcoming.

Banks, Jeffrey S., Plott, Charles R. and Porter, David P. (1988). 'An experimental analysis of unanimity in public goods provision mechanisms.' *Review of Economic Studies*, vol. 55, pp. 301–22.

Battalio, Raymond C., Kagel, John H. and Komain Jiranyakul (1988). 'Testing between alternative models of choice under uncertainty: some initial results.' Mimeo.

—— —— and McDonald, Don N. (1985). 'Animals' choices over uncertain outcomes: some initial experimental results.' *American Economic Review*, vol. 75, pp. 597–613.

Bazerman, Max H. (1985). 'Norms of distributive justice in interest arbitration.' *Industrial and Labor Relations*, vol, 38, pp. 558–70.

—— and Samuelson, William F. (1983). 'I won the auction but don't want the prize.' *Journal of Conflict Resolution*, vol. 27, pp. 618–34.

Becker, Gordon M., DeGroot, Morris M., and Marschak Jacob (1964). 'Measuring utility by a single-response sequential method.' *Behavioral Science*, vol. 9, pp. 226–32.

Berg, Joyce E., Daley, L. A., Dickhaut, John W. and O'Brien, John R. (1986). 'Controlling preferences for lotteries on units of experimental exchange.' *Quarterly Journal of Economics*, pp. 281–306.

—— Dickhaut, John W. and O'Brien, John R. (1985). 'Preference reversal and arbitrage.' In V. Smith, ed., *Research in Experimental Economics*, vol. 3, pp. 31–72. Greenwich: JAI Press.

Bernoulli, Daniel (1738). 'Specimen theoriae novae de mensura sortis.' *Commentarii Academiae Scientiarum Imperialis Petropolitanae*, vol. 5, pp. 175–92. (English translation in *Econometrica*, vol. 22, 1954, pp. 23–36.)

Binmore, Ken, Shaked, Avner and Sutton, John (1985). 'Testing noncooperative bargaining theory: a preliminary study.' *American Economic Review*, vol. 75, pp. 1178–80.

—— —— and —— (1988*a*). 'Testing noncooperative bargaining theory: a reply.' *American Economic Review*, forthcoming.

—— —— and —— (1988*b*). 'An outside option experiment.' Mimeo, London School of Economics.

Binswanger, Hans P. (1980). 'Attitudes toward risk: experimental measurement in rural India.' *American Journal of Agricultural Economics*, vol. 62, pp. 395–407.

—— (1981). 'Attitudes toward risk: theoretical implications of an experiment in rural India.' Economic Journal, vol. 91, pp. 867–90.

Bohm, Peter (1972). 'Estimating demand for public goods: an experiment.' *European Economic Review*, vol. 3, pp. 111–30.

Brookshire, David S. and Coursey, Don L. (1987). 'Measuring the value of a public good: an empirical comparison of elicitation procedures.' *American Economic Review*, vol. 77, pp. 554–66.

Brown, James N. and Rosenthal, Robert W. (1990). 'Testing the minimax hypothesis: a re-examination of O'Neill's game experiment.' *Econometrica*, 58, pp. 1065–1081.

Brown, Keith C. (1986). 'In search of the winner's curse: comment.' *Economic Inquiry*, vol. 24, pp. 513–15.

Camerer, Colin F. (1987). 'Do biases in probability judgment matter in markets? Experimental evidence.' *American Economic Review*, vol. 77, pp. 981–97.

—— (1988). 'An experimental test of several generalized utility theories.' *Journal of Risk and Uncertainty*, forthcoming.

—— and Weigelt Keith (1988). 'Experimental tests of a sequential equilibrium reputation model.' *Econometrica*, vol. 56, pp. 1–36.

Capen, E. C., Clapp, R. V. and Campbell, W. M. (1971). 'Competitive bidding in high-risk situations.' *Journal of Petroleum Technology*, vol. 23, pp. 641–53.

Carlson, John A. and O'Keefe, Terrence B. (1969). 'Buffer stocks and reaction coefficients: an experiment with decision making under risk.' *Review of Economic Studies*, vol. 36, pp. 467–84.

Chamberlin, Edward H. (1984). 'An experimental imperfect market.' *Journal of Political Economy*, vol. 56 (2), pp. 95–108.

Clarke, Edward H. (1971). 'Multipart pricing of public goods.' *Public Choice*, vol. 11, pp. 17–33.

Coase, A. (1960) 'The problem of social cost.' *Journal of Law and Economics*, vol. 1, pp. 1–44.

Conlisk, John (1987). 'Verifying the betweenness axiom with questionnaire evidence, or not: take your pick.' *Economics Letters*, vol. 25, pp. 319–22.

Contini, Bruno (1968). 'The value of time in bargaining negotiations: some experimental evidence.' *American Economic Review*, vol. 58, pp. 374–93.

Cooper, Russell, DeJong, Douglas V., Forsythe, Robert and Ross, Thomas W. (1990). 'Selection criteria in coordination games: some experimental results.' *American Economic Review*, 80, pp. 218–233.

Coppinger, Vicki M., Smith, Vernon L. and Titus, Jon A. (1980). 'Incentives and behavior in English, Dutch and sealed-bid auctions.' *Economic Inquiry*, vol. 18, pp. 1–22.

Coursey, Don L. (1982). 'Bilateral bargaining, Pareto optimality, and the empirical frequency of impasse.' *Journal of Economic Behavior and Organization*, vol. 3, pp. 243–59.

—— Hovis, John L. and Schulze, William D. (1987). 'The disparity between willingness to accept and willingness to pay measures of value.' *Quarterly Journal of Economic*, vol. 102, pp. 679–90.

Cox, James C. and Isaac, R. Mark (1984). 'In search of the winner's curse.' *Economic Inquiry*, vol. 22, pp. 579–92.

—— and —— (1986). 'In search of the winner's curse: reply.' *Economic Inquiry*, vol. 24, pp. 517–20.

—— Roberson, Bruce and Smith, Vernon L. (1982). 'Theory and behavior of single object auctions.' (In V. L. Smith, ed.), *Research in Experimental Economics*, Volume 2, Greenwich: JAI Press, pp. 1–43.

—— Smith, Vernon L. and Walker, James M. (1983*a*). 'Tests of a heterogeneous bidders theory of first price auctions.' *Economics Letters*, vol. 12, pp. 207–12.

—— —— and —— (1983*b*). 'A test that discriminates between two models of the Dutch-first auction non-isomorphism.' *Journal of Economic Behavior and Organization*, vol. 4, pp. 205–19.

—— —— and —— (1985*a*). 'Experimental development of sealed-bid auction theory; calibrating controls for risk aversion.' *American Economic Review Papers and Proceedings*, vol. 75, pp. 160–5.

—— —— and —— (1985*b*). 'Expected revenue in discriminative and uniform price sealed-bid auctions.' (in V. L. Smith, ed.), *Research in Experimental Economics*, Volume 3, Greenwich, JAI Press, pp. 183–232.

—— —— and —— (1988). 'Theory and individual behavior of first-price auctions.' *Journal of Risk and Uncertainty*, vol. 1, pp. 61–99.

Crawford, Vincent P. (1988). 'Equilibrium without independence.' *Journal of Economic Theory*, forthcoming.

Cummings, L. L. and Harnett, D. L. (1969). 'Bargaining behaviour in a symmetric bargaining triad: the impact of risk-taking propensity, information, communication and terminal bid.' *Review of Economic Studies*, vol. 36, pp. 485–501.

Cyert, Richard M. and Lave, Lester B. (1965). 'Collusion, conflit et science economique.' *Economie Appliquee*, vol. 18, pp. 385–406.

Dolbear, F. T., Lave, L. B., Bowman, G., Lieberman, A., Prescott, E., Rueter, F. and Sherman, R. (1968). 'Collusion in oligopoly: an experiment on the effect of numbers and information.' *Quarterly Journal of Economics*, vol. 82, pp. 240–59.

Dyer, Douglas, Kagel, John H. and Levin, Dan (1988). 'A comparison of naive and experienced bidders in common value offer auctions: a laboratory analysis.' ECONOMIC JOURNAL, forthcoming.

Edgeworth, F. Y. (1881). *Mathematical Psychics*, London: Kegan Paul.

Farber, Henry S. and Bazerman Max H. (1986). 'The general basis of arbitrator behavior: an empirical analysis of conventional and final offer arbitration.' *Econometrica*, vol. 54, pp. 1503–28.

Farrell, Joseph (1987). 'Information and the Coase theorem.' *Journal of Economic Perspectives*, vol. 1, pp. 113–29.

Ferber, Robert, and Hirsch, Werner Z. (1982). *Social Experimentation and Economic Policy*, (Cambridge Surveys of Economic Literature), Cambridge: Cambridge University Press.

Ferejohn, John, Forsythe, Robert and Noll, Roger (1979). 'An experimental analysis of decision making procedures for discrete public goods: a case study of a problem in institutional design.' In (V. L. Smith, ed.), *Research in Experimental Economics*: Volume 1, Greenwich: JAI Press, pp. 1–58.

Flood, Merrill M. (1958). 'Some experimental games.' *Management Science*, vol. 5, pp. 5–26.

Forsythe, Robert, Kennan, John and Sopher, Barry (1987). 'An experimental analysis of bargaining and strikes with one sided private information.' Working paper no. 87–4, Department of Economics, University of Iowa.

Friedman, James W. (1963). 'Individual behaviour in oligopolistic markets: an experimental study.' *Yale Economic Essays*, vol. 3, pp. 359–417.

—— (1969). 'On experimental research in oligopoly.' *Review of Economic Studies*, vol. 36, pp. 399–415.

Graham, Daniel A. and Marshall, Robert C. (1984). 'Bidder coalitions at auctions.' Duke University Department of Economics, mimeo.

—— and —— (1987). 'Collusive bidder behavior at single object second price and English auctions.' *Journal of Political Economy*, vol. 95, pp. 1217–37.

Green, Jerry R. and Laffont, Jean-Jacques (1979). *Incentives in Public Decision-Making*, Amsterdam: North-Holland.

Grether, David M. and Plott, Charles R. (1979). 'Economic theory of choice and the preference reversal phenomenon.' *American Economic Review*, vol. 69, pp. 623–38.

—— and —— (1982). 'Economic theory of choice and the preference reversal phenomenon: reply.' *American Economic Review*, vol. 72, p. 575.

Groves, Theodore and Ledyard, John (1977). 'Optimal allocation of public goods: a solution to the "free rider" problem.' *Econometrica*, vol. 45, pp. 783–809.

Guth, Werner, Schmittberger, R. and Schwarz, B. (1982). 'An experimental analysis of ultimatum bargaining.' *Journal of Economic Behavior and Organization*, vol. 3, pp. 367–88.

—— and Tietz, Rienhard (1987). 'Ultimatum bargaining for a shrinking cake – An experimental analysis.' mimeo.

Harrison, Glenn W. (1987). 'Theory and misbehavior of first-price auctions.' *American Economic Review*, forthcoming.

—— and McCabe, Kevin A. (1988). 'Testing bargaining theory in experiments.' Mimeo, University of Western Ontario.

—— and McKee, Michael (1985). 'Experimental evaluation of the Coase theorem.' *Journal of Law and Economics*, vol. 28, pp. 653–70.

—— Hoffman, Elizabeth, Rutstrom, E. E. and Spitzer, Matthew L. (1987). 'Coasian solutions to the externality problem in experimental markets.' ECONOMIC JOURNAL, vol. 97, pp. 388–402.

Hausman, Jerry A., and Wise, David A. (eds.) (1985). *Social Experimentation*, National Bureau of Economic Research.

Hendricks, Kenneth, Porter, Robert H. and Boudreau, Bryan (1987). 'Information, returns, and bidding behavior in OCS auctions: 1954–1969.' *Journal of Industrial Economics*, vol. 35, pp. 517–42.

Hey, John D. (1982). 'Search for rules for search.' *Journal of Economic Behavior and Organization*, vol. 3, pp. 65–81.

—— (1987). 'Still searching.' *Journal of Economic Behavior and Organization*, vol. 8, pp. 137–44.

Hoffman, E. and Spitzer, M. L. (1982). 'The Coase theorem: some experimental tests.' *Journal of Law and Economics*, vol. 25, pp. 73–98.

—— and —— (1985). 'Entitlements, rights, and fairness: an experimental examination of subjects' concepts of distributive justice.' *Journal of Legal Studies*, vol. 14 no. 2, pp. 259–97.

Hoggatt, Austin C. (1969). 'Response of paid student subjects to differential behavior of robots in bifurcated duopoly games.' *Review of Economic Studies*, vol. 36, pp. 417–32.

—— Selten, Reinhard, Crockett, David, Gill, Shlomo and Moore, Jeff (1978). 'Bargaining experiments with incomplete information.' In (H. Sauermann, ed.), *Bargaining Behavior*, Tubingen: J. C. B. Mohr.

Holt, Charles A. (1986). 'Preference reversals and the independence axiom.' *American Economic Review*, vol. 76, pp. 508–15.

Isaac, R. Mark, McCue, Kenneth F. and Plott, Charles R. (1985). 'Public goods provision in an experimental environment.' *Journal of Public Economics*, vol. 26, pp. 51–74.

—— Walker, James M. and Thomas, Susan H. (1984). 'Divergent evidence on free riding: an experimental examination of possible explanations.' *Public Choice*, vol. 43, pp. 113–49.

Jamal, Karim and Sunder, Shyam (1988). 'Money vs. gaming: effects of salient monetary payments in double oral auctions.' Working Paper, University of Minnesota.

Johansen, Lief (1977). 'The theory of public goods: misplaced emphasis?' *Journal of Public Economics*, vol. 7, pp. 147–52.

Kagel, John H. (1987). 'Economics according to the rats (and pigeons too): what have we learned and what can we hope to learn?' in (A. E. Roth, ed.), *Laboratory Experimentation in Economics: Six Points of View*, Cambridge: Cambridge University Press, pp. 155–92.

—— Harstad, Ronald M. and Levin Dan (1987). 'Information impact and allocation rules in auctions with affiliated Private Values: A Laboratory Study.' *Econometrica*, 55, pp. 1275–1304.

—— and Levin Dan (1986). 'The winner's curse and public information in common value auctions.' *American Economic Review*, vol. 76, pp. 894–920.

—— and —— (1988), 'Independent private value auctions: bidder behavior in first, second and third-price auctions with varying numbers of bidders.' Mimeo.

—— —— Battalio, Raymond C. and Meyer, Donald J. (1988). 'First-price common value auctions: bidder behavior and the "winner's curse"', *Economic Inquiry*, forthcoming.

—— —— and Harstad, Ronald M. (1987). 'Judgment, evaluation and information processing in second-price common value auctions.' Mimeo.

Kahneman, Daniel, Knetsch, Jack L. and Thaler, Richard H. (1986*a*). 'Fairness and the assumptions of economics.' *Journal of Business*, vol. 59, no. 4 pt 2, pp. S285–S300.

—— —— and —— (1986*b*). 'Fairness as a constraint on profit seeking: entitlements in the market.' *American Economic Review*, vol. 76, pp. 728–41.

—— Slovic, Paul and Tversky, Amos ed. (1982). *Judgment under Uncertainty: Heuristics and Biases*. Cambridge, Cambridge University Press.

—— and Tversky, Amos (1979). 'Prospect theory: an analysis of decision under risk.' *Econometrica*, vol. 47, pp. 263–91.

—— and —— (1984). 'Choices, values, and frames.' *American Psychologist*, vol. 39, pp. 341–50.

Karni, Edi, and Safra, Zvi (1985). 'Vickrey auctions in the theory of expected utility with rank dependent probability.' *Economics Letters*, vol. 20, pp. 15–8.

—— and —— (1987). '"Preference reversal" and the observability of preferences by experimental methods.' *Econometrica*, vol. 55, pp. 675–85.

Kihlstrom, Richard, Roth, Alvin E. and Schmeidler, David (1981). 'Risk aversion and solutions to Nash's bargaining problem.' In *Game Theory and Mathematical Economics* (ed. O. Moeschlin and D. Pallaschke). Amsterdam: North-Holland, pp. 65–71.

Kim, Oliver and Walker, Mark (1984). 'The free rider problem: experimental evidence.' *Public Choice*, vol. 43, pp. 3–24.

Knetsch, Jack L. and Sinden, J. A. (1984). 'Willingness to pay and compensation demanded: experimental evidence of an unexpected disparity in measures of value.' *Quarterly Journal of Economics*, 99, pp. 507–21.

—— and —— (1987). 'The persistence of evaluation disparities.' *Quarterly Journal of Economics*, vol. 102, pp. 691–5.

—— Thaler, Richard and Kahneman, Daniel (1987). 'Experimental tests of the endowment effect and the Coase theorem.' Mimeo.

Knez Marc and Smith, Vernon L. (1987). 'Hypothetical valuations and preference reversals in the context of asset trading.' In *Laboratory Experimentation in Economics: Six Points of View* (ed. A. E. Roth.) Cambridge: Cambridge University Press, pp. 131–54.

Kreps, David M. and Wilson, Robert B. (1982). 'Reputation and imperfect information.' *Journal of Economic Theory*, vol. 27, pp. 253–79.

—— Milgrom, Paul, Roberts, John and Wilson, Robert (1982). 'Rational cooperation in the finitely repeated prisoners' dilemma.' *Journal of Economic Theory*, vol. 27, pp. 245–52.

Kroll, Yoram, Levy, Haim and Rapoport, Amnon (1988). 'Experimental tests of the separation theorem and the capital asset pricing model.' *American Economic Review*, vol. 78, pp. 500–19.

Lave, Lester B. (1962). 'An empirical approach to the prisoners' dilemma game,' *Quarterly Journal of Economics*, vol. 76, pp. 424–36.

—— (1965). 'Factors affecting co-operation in the prisoner's dilemma.' *Behavioral Science*, vol. 10, pp. 26–38.

Lichtenstein, Sarah and Slovic, Paul (1971). 'Reversal of preferences between bids and choices in gambling decisions.' *Journal of Experimental Psychology*, vol. 89, pp. 46–55.

—— and —— (1973). 'Response-induced reversals of preference in gambling: an extended replication in Las Vegas.' *Journal of Experimental Psychology*, vol. 101, pp. 16–20.

Lindman, Harold R. (1971). 'Inconsistent preferences among gambles.' *Journal of Experimental Psychology*, vol. 89, pp. 390–7.

Loehman, Edna and Andrew Whinston (1972). 'A new theory of pricing and decision-making for public investment.' *The Bell Journal of Economics and Management Science*, vol. 2, pp. 606–25.

Loomes, Graham (1988). 'When actions speak louder than prospects.' *American Economic Review*, vol. 78, pp. 463–70.

—— Starmer, Chris and Sugden, Robert (1988*a*). 'Preference reversal: information-processing effect or rational non-transitive choice?' Mimeo, presented at the Royal Economic Society Conference, March.

—— —— and —— (1988*b*). 'Observing violations of transitivity by experimental methods.' Mimeo, presented at the Foundations of Utility and Risk IV Conference, Budapest, June.

—— and Sugden, Robert (1982). 'Regret theory: an alternative theory of rational choice under uncertainty.' ECONOMIC JOURNAL, vol. 92, pp. 805–24.

—— and —— (1983). 'A rationale for preference reversal.' *American Economic Review*, vol. 73, pp. 428–32.

—— and —— (1987). 'Testing for regret and disappointment in choice under uncertainty.' ECONOMIC JOURNAL, Conference Papers, vol. 97, pp. 118–29.

MacCrimmon, K. R. and Toda, M. (1969). 'The experimental determination of indifference curves.' *Review of Economic Studies*, vol. 36, pp. 433–51.

Machina, Mark J. (1982). '"Expected utility" analysis without the independence axiom.' *Econometrica*, vol. 50, pp. 277–323.

—— (1987). 'Choice under uncertainty: problems solved and unsolved.' *Economic Perspectives*, vol. 1, pp. 121–54.

Malouf, Michael W. K. and Roth, Alvin E. (1981). 'Disagreement in bargaining: an experimental study.' *Journal of Conflict Resolution*, vol. 25, pp. 329–48.

Markowitz, Harry (1952). 'The utility of wealth.' *Journal of Political Economy*, vol. 60, pp. 151–8.

Marshall, James D., Knetsch, Jack L. and Sinden, J. A. (1986). 'Agents' evaluations and the disparity in measures of economic loss.' *Journal of Economic Behavior and Organization*, vol. 7, pp. 115–27.

Marwell, Gerald and Ames, Ruth E. (1981). 'Economists free ride, Does anyone else? Experiments on the provision of public goods, IV.' *Journal of Public Economics*, vol. 15, pp. 295–310.

May, Kenneth O. (1954). 'Intransitivity, utility, and the aggregation of preference patterns.' *Econometrica*, vol. 22, pp. 1–13.

Mead, Walter J., Moseidjord, Asbjorn and Sorensen, Philip E. (1983). 'The rate of return earned by leases under cash bonus bidding in OCS oil and gas leases.' *Energy Journal*, vol. 4, pp. 37–52.

—— —— and —— (1984). 'Competitive bidding under asymmetrical information: behavior and performance in Gulf of Mexico drainage lease sales, 1959–1969.' *Review of Economics and Statistics*, vol. 66, pp. 505–8.

Milgrom, Paul R. and Roberts, John (1982). 'Predation, reputation, and entry deterrence.' *Journal of Economic Theory*, vol. 27, pp. 280–312.

Milgrom, Paul R. and Weber, Robert J. (1982). 'A theory of auctions and competitive bidding.' *Econometrica*, vol. 50, pp. 1089–122.

Morley, I. and Stephenson, G. (1977). *The Social Psychology of Bargaining*, London: Allen and Unwin.

Murnighan, J. Keith (1985). 'Coalitions in decision-making groups: organizational analogs.' *Organizational Behavior and Human Decision Processes*, vol. 35, pp. 1–26.

—— Roth, Alvin E. and Schoumaker, Francoise (1988). 'Risk aversion in bargaining: an experimental study.' *Journal of Risk and Uncertainty*, vol. 1, pp. 101–24.

Nash, John (1950). 'The bargaining problem.' *Econometrica*, vol. 28, pp. 155–62.

Neelin, Janet, Sonnenschein, Hugo and Spiegel, Matthew (1988). 'A further test of noncooperative bargaining theory.' *American Economic Review*, forthcoming.

Nydegger, Rudy V. and Owen, Guillermo (1975). 'Two person bargaining: an experimental test of the Nash axioms.' *International Journal of Game Theory*, vol. 3, pp. 239–349.

Ochs, Jack (1990). 'The coordination problem in decentralized markets: an experiment.' *Quarterly Journal of Economics*, May 1990, pp. 545–559.

—— and Roth, Alvin E. (1989). 'An experimental study of sequential bargaining.' *American Economic Review*, 79, pp. 355–384.

O'Neill, Barry (1987). 'Nonmetric test of the minimax theory of two-person zerosum games.' *Proceedings of the National Academy of Sciences*, vol. 84, pp. 2106–9.

Ostroy, Joseph M. (1980). 'The no-surplus condition as a characterization of perfectly competitive equilibrium.' *Journal of Economic Theory*, vol. 22, pp. 65–91.

Palfrey, Thomas R. and Rosenthal, Howard (1987). 'Private incentives in social dilemmas: the effects of incomplete information and altruism.' Social Science Working Paper 659, California Institute of Technology.

Plott, Charles R. (1982). 'Industrial organization theory and experimental economics.' *Journal of Economic Literature*, vol. 20, pp. 1485–527.

—— (1983). 'Externalities and corrective policies in experimental markets.' ECONOMIC JOURNAL, vol. 93, pp. 106–27.

—— (1987). 'Dimensions of parallelism: some policy applications of experimental methods.' In (A. E. Roth, ed.) *Laboratory Experimentation in Economics: Six Points of View*, Cambridge: Cambridge University Press, pp. 193–219.

Pommerehne, Werner W., Schneider, Friedrich and Zweifel, Peter (1982). 'Economic theory of choice and the preference reversal phenomenon: a reexamination.' *American Economic Review*, vol. 72, pp. 569–74.

Quizon, Jaime B., Binswanger, Hans P. and Machina, Mark J. (1984). 'Attitudes toward risk: further remarks.' ECONOMIC JOURNAL, vol. 94, pp. 144–8.

Quiggan, J. (1982). 'A theory of anticipated utility.' *Journal of Economic Behavior and Organization*, vol. 3, pp. 225–43.

Radner, Roy and Schotter, Andrew (1987). 'The sealed bid mechanism: an experimental study.' Research report no. 87-41, Department of Economics, NYU.

Rapoport, Anatol and Chammah, Albert M. (1965). *Prisoner's Dilemma: A Study in Conflict and Cooperation*, Ann Arbor: University of Michigan Press.

Rapoport, Amnon, Weg, Eythan and Felsenthal, Dan S. (1988). 'Effects of fixed costs in two-person sequential bargaining.' Mimeo, Department of Psychology, University of North Carolina.

Reilly, Robert J. (1982). 'Preference reversal: further evidence and some suggested modifications in experimental design.' *American Economic Review*, vol. 72, pp. 576–84.

Roemer, John E. (1988). 'Axiomatic bargaining theory on economic environments.' *Journal of Economic Theory*, forthcoming.

Rosenthal, Robert (1980). 'New equilibria for noncooperative two-person games.' *Journal of Mathematical Sociology*, vol. 7, pp. 15–26.

Roth, Alvin E. (1979). *Axiomatic Models of Bargaining*, Lecture Notes in Economics and Mathematical Systems no. 170, Springer Verlag.

—— (1987*a*). 'Bargaining phenomena and bargaining theory.' In (A. E. Roth, ed.) *Laboratory Experimentation in Economics: Six Points of View*. Cambridge: Cambridge University Press, pp. 14–41.

—— (1987*b*). 'Laboratory experimentation in economics.' In (Truman Bewley, ed.) *Advances in Economic Theory, Fifth World Congress*. Cambridge: Cambridge University Press, pp. 269–99. (Preprinted in *Economics and Philosophy*, vol. 2, 1986, pp. 245–73.)

—— and Malouf, Michael W. K. (1979). 'Game-theoretic models and the role of information in bargaining'. *Psychological Review*, vol. 86, pp. 574–94.

—— and —— (1982). 'Scale changes and shared information in bargaining: an experimental study,' *Mathematical Social Sciences*, vol. 3, pp. 157–77.

—— —— and Murnighan, J. Keith (1981). 'Sociological versus strategic factors in bargaining.' *Journal of Economic Behavior and Organization*, vol. 2, pp. 153–77.

—— and Murnighan, J. Keith (1978). 'Equilibrium behavior and repeated play of the prisoner's dilemma.' *Journal of Mathematical Psychology*, vol. 17, pp. 189–98.

—— and—— (1982). 'The role of information in bargaining: an experimental study.' *Econometrica*, 50, pp. 1123–42.

—— —— and Schoumaker, Francoise (1988). 'The deadline effect in bargaining: some experimental evidence.' *American Economic Review*, forthcoming.

—— and Rothblum, Uriel G. (1982). 'Risk aversion and Nash's solution for bargaining games with risky outcomes.' *Econometrica*, vol. 50, pp. 639–47.

—— and Schoumaker, Francoise (1983). 'Expectations and reputations in bargaining: an experimental study.' *American Economic Review*, vol. 73, pp. 362–72.

Rubinstein, Ariel (1982). 'Perfect equilibrium in a bargaining model,' *Econometrica*, vol. 50, pp. 97–109.

Sauermann, Heinz and Selten, Reinhard (1959). 'Ein Oligolpolexperiment.' *Zeitschrift fur die Gesamte Staatswissenschaft*, vol. 115, pp. 427–71.

Scherr, Bruce A. and Babb, Emerson M. (1975). 'Pricing public goods: an experiment with two proposed pricing systems.' *Public Choice*, vol. 23, pp. 35–48.

Schneider, Friedrich and Pommerehne, Werner W. (1981). 'Free riding and collective action: an experiment in public microeconomics.' *Quarterly Journal of Economics*, vol. 116, pp. 689–704.

Selten, Reinhard (1978). 'The chain-store paradox.' *Theory and Decision*, vol. 9, pp. 127–59.

—— and Stoecker, Rolf (1986). 'End behavior in sequences of finite prisoner's dilemma supergames: a learning theory approach.' *Journal of Economic Behavior and Organization*, vol. 7, pp. 47–70.

Sherman, Roger (1969). 'Risk attitude and cost variability in a capacity choice experiment.' *Review of Economic Studies*, vol. 36, pp. 453–66.

Shubik, Martin (1955). *Strategy and Market Structure*, New York: Wiley.

Siegel, Sidney and Fouraker, Lawrence E. (1960). *Bargaining and Group Decision Making: Experiments in Bilateral Monopoly*, New York: McGraw-Hill.

Slovic, Paul (1975). 'Choice between equally valued alternatives.' *Journal of Experimental Psychology: Human Perception and Performance*, vol. 1, pp. 280–7.

—— and Lichtenstein, Sarah (1968). 'Relative importance of probabilities and payoffs in risk taking.' *Journal of Experimental Psychology Monograph Supplement*, vol. 78, no. 3 (Part 2), pp. 1–18.

—— and —— (1983). 'Preference reversals: a broader perspective.' *American Economic Review*, vol. 73, pp. 596–605.

Smith, Vernon L. (1962). 'An experimental study of competitive market behavior.' *Journal of Political Economy*, vol. 70, pp. 111–37.

—— (1979*a*). 'Incentive compatible experimental processes for the provision of public goods.' In (V. L. Smith, ed.). *Research in Experimental Economics*, vol. 1. Greenwich: JAI Press, pp. 59–168.

—— (1979*b*). 'An experimental comparison of three public good decision mechanisms.' *Scandinavian Journal of Economics*, vol. 81, pp. 198–215.

—— (1980). 'Experiments with a decentralized mechanism for public good decisions.' *American Economic Review*, vol. 70, pp. 584–99.

—— (1982). 'Microeconomic systems as an experimental science.' *American Economic Review*, vol. 72, pp. 923–55.

Stahl, Ingolf (1972). *Bargaining Theory*. Economic Research Institute, Stockholm.

Stone, Jeremy J. (1958). 'An experiment in bargaining games.' *Econometrica*, vol. 26, pp. 286–97.

Straffin, Philip D., Jr. (1980). 'The prisoner's dilemma.' *UMAP Journal*, vol. 1, pp. 102–3.

Sutton, John (1986). 'Non-cooperative bargaining theory: An introduction.' *Review of Economic Studies*, vol. 53, pp. 709–24.

Sweeney, John W., Jr. (1973). 'An experimental investigation of the free-rider problem.' *Social Science Research*, vol. 2, pp. 277–92.

Terhune, K. W. (1968). 'Motives, situations, and interpersonal conflict within prisoner's dilemma.' *Journal of Personality and Social Psychology Monograph Supplement*, vol. 8, pp. 1–24.

Thaler, Richard (1980). 'Toward a positive theory of consumer choice.' *Journal of Economic Behavior and Organization*, vol. 1, pp. 39–60.

—— (1987). 'The psychology of choice and the assumptions of economics.' In (A. E. Roth, ed.) *Laboratory Experimentation in Economics: Six Points of View*. Cambridge: Cambridge University Press, pp. 99–130.

Tucker, A. W. (1950). 'A two-person dilemma.' Mimeo, Stanford University. Published under the heading 'On jargon: the prisoner's dilemma.' *UMAP Journal*, vol. 1, 1980, p. 101.

Van Huyck, John B., Battalio, Raymond C. and Beil, Richard O. (1990). 'Tacit coordination games, strategic uncertainty, and coordination failure.' *American Economic Review*, 80, 234–248.

Vickrey, W. (1961). 'Counterspeculation, auctions, and competitive sealed tenders.' *Journal of Finance*, vol. 16, pp. 8–27.

Wilson, Robert (1977). 'A bidding model of perfect competition.' *Review of Economic Studies*, vol. 4, pp. 511–8.

—— (1985). 'Reputations in games and markets.' In (A. E. Roth, ed.) *Game-Theoretic Models of Bargaining*. Cambridge: Cambridge University Press, pp. 27–62.

Yaari, Menahem E. (1987). 'The dual theory of choice under risk.' *Econometrica*, vol. 55, pp. 95–115.

—— and Bar-Hillel, M. (1984). 'On dividing justly.' *Social Choice and Welfare*, vol. 1, pp. 1–24.

4

THE ECONOMICS OF DEVELOPMENT: A SURVEY*

Nicholas Stern

I. THE SUBJECT

Our definition of the subject will be the use of economic analysis to understand the economies of poor or developing countries. This includes, in particular, how standards of living in the population are determined, and how they change over time, and further how policy can or should be used in the influence of these processes. The definition contains, in principle, much or most of analytical methods in economics in so far as they can be put to use in the examination of the issues of interest. This is as it should be but it poses a problem for a survey in a journal. A comprehensive treatment is infeasible so we shall follow a different route. The survey will focus on what I take to be the major themes and approaches which characterise the productive aspects of the subject. There is, therefore, no pretence at being exhaustive. The purpose is rather to highlight some of the advances. Many of these have been of real substance.

There are a number of possible purposes for a survey and it is important to be clear at the outset for whom it is intended, what it is, and what it is not. This survey is addressed to economists and students of economics who know the tools of their trade but not necessarily how they have been applied to, and fashioned for, the analysis of the economics of developing countries. It is a description of the ways in which problems can be productively formulated and approached, in terms of examples chosen for their intrinsic importance and interest. The vastness of the subject means that we have to be highly selective. It does not seek to provide a summary evaluation of the current view of the 'appropriate' response to immediate policy questions. It is not a history of thought, nor a research manifesto nor an attempt to adjudicate or settle the major debates. Where they arise naturally from the major purpose some judgements on these subjects will be offered, but they do not themselves constitute the primary intent of this survey.

There are three lines of enquiry, or sets of questions, which have, I suggest, been distinctive of the most fruitful work in development economics. They will be used to organise this survey. The first set of questions (Section III) concerns what we may call the grand issues of the subject. These include: the objectives

* This chapter was first published in the Economic Journal, vol. 99, September 1989. The contributions of Robin Burgess, Peter Lanjouw and Stephen Ludlow of the Suntory Toyota International Centre for Economics and Related Disciplines at the London School of Economics to this survey have been most valuable. I am greatly indebted to them and to the Centre for their support. Helpful comments were provided by Ehtisham Ahmad, Sudhir Anand, David Bevan, David Coady, Jean Drèze, Dennis de Tray, Christopher Heady, Gordon Hughes, Athar Hussain, James Gordon, Mervyn King, Deepak Lal, David Newbery, Massimo Ricottelli, Christopher Scott, Amartya Sen, Max Steuer and Pan Yotopoulos, and graduate students at the People's University of China, Beijing and the London School of Economics. Special thanks are due to Tony Atkinson, Angus Deaton and Michael Lipton. The editor of the series, Andrew Oswald, provided helpful advice as did three referees, for which I am most grateful. The errors are mine.

of economic policy, or what constitutes development; the role of the state and the merits of planning and of markets; the determinants of growth and distribution; policies towards industrialisation and international trade; and the effects of population growth. These questions have, of course, long been part of economics in general. But it is a distinguishing feature of development economics that they have always been central and many of the major economic contributions to their understanding have come from research on development. One can, of course, have too much of the grand issues, especially when their size is taken as an excuse for a lack of rigour, but it is to the credit of the subject that it has not lost sight of the big questions.

The second set (Section IV) concerns the development of techniques and tools for the analysis of problems of policy, principally planning models, cost–benefit analysis, and methods for the examination of tax and price reform. Such issues, if narrowly defined simply as problem-solving techniques, are in some respects less deep and exciting than the former class but, on the other hand, they allow for greater clarity of analysis and for results which are more explicit. Many of the most important contributions to these basic analytical methods in economics have come from development economics. From a broader perspective they may be seen as part of a central and difficult area of economics – the theory of policy in imperfect economies.

The third group of questions (Section V) is more heterogeneous but the common feature is the tightly focused microeconomic study of a phenomenon, market or location where the details of institutions, geography, health or culture play a crucial role. The studies assembled under this heading do not together reflect a single theme but illustrate an approach to intellectual enquiry which has found some of its most notable examples in development economics. However, in order not to overdo the heterogeneity I have chosen the examples predominantly from an area where the approach has been particularly productively applied, the analysis of rural markets. Some of the studies included in this third group are theoretical but the majority are applied and nearly all of these involve the collection of primary data, an enterprise which is sadly rare in the rest of economics. Whilst it is often the grand issues which catch the economics headlines it is these tightly focused studies which usually involve the harder work, analysis and scholarship and which in many respects form the bedrock of the discipline.

Notwithstanding the length of the agenda already described the subject is so large that there are many important omissions. Many of the omissions could be, and have been, the subject of recent surveys and they will not be entirely neglected since the reader will be guided (Section VI.2) to some of these. A measure of the size of the subject is that a recent bibliography (Gemmell, 1987) of surveys in development economics from 1970–86 contained over 60 entries and this does not include around 1,700 pages and 33 surveys in the *Handbook of Development Economics* edited by Chenery and Srinivasan (vol. I, 1988 and vol. II, 1989). In the next section we describe briefly some aspects of the historical experience of the growth of developing countries and some empirical studies of that experience. Concluding remarks are provided in Section VI.

Notwithstanding our division of the survey into the 'big picture', the 'problem-solving techniques', and the 'detailed picture' much of the richness and difficulty of the subject lies in the integration of all three. Thus, for example, when one studies the functioning of markets in a single village, the economic status of a particular group, or the development of certain businesses, one is also testing and developing the broad ideas of how poor economies function, or mis-function, and which policies are likely to be desirable and effective. It is this type of blend of analytical approaches that provides much of the challenge and distinctive flavour of the economics of development in the past and features in the research agenda included in Section VI.

In the recent past there has been a curious outbreak of assessments of development economics (Bhagwati, 1988*b*; Chakravarty, 1987; Hill, 1986; Hirschman, 1981; Lal, 1983; Lewis, 1984; Sen, 1983*b*; for example). Such a flurry might make one suspicious that all is not well and some (e.g. Hill, Hirschman and Lal) have been somewhat negative or even caustic. This survey will be optimistic in terms of what can be achieved by the serious application of analytical methods. This is not to deny that some or many influential contributions have been superficial or misguided. But attacks on the subject have usually been based on a very narrow view of what it entails, for example, that it is concerned largely with the propagation of the virtues, or necessity, of rigid and pervasive government control over the economy. Indeed Lal and Hirschman do make clear that they are attacking only a particular part of the subject which insists on a special kind of theory and which often supports 'dirigisme'. This part they have labelled 'development economics'. Whilst it may be noted that this is not the title of our survey, the use of a narrow definition of a subject to mount an attack, when the title 'development economics' gives the impression of a rather broad area, is a ploy which leaves me somewhat uneasy. We shall use, interchangeably, 'development economics', 'the economics of developing countries', 'the economics of less developed countries', 'the economics of development', and 'the economics of poor countries'.

II. SOME ASPECTS OF DEVELOPMENT EXPERIENCE

A distinctive feature of development economics from its early days has been the attempt to learn about the problems of development and the processes of growth by comparing the situations and growth experiences of different countries. We review in this section some of the main contributions to these comparative studies and at the same time present some basic background. In more recent years the main source of information for this type of work has been the data base assembled by the World Bank and published annually in the World Development Reports (WDR) since 1978 (see also the World Bank *World Tables* 1976, 1980, 1983, 1987). Cross-country statistical comparisons are fraught with problems since there will be different standards of data availability, collection and care, different coverage and conventions, different activities and practices associated with geography, climate, political system and so on, in addition to all the usual problems of different prices in aggregating economic variables (Kravis *et al.* 1978, Usher, 1980). Nevertheless the UN statistical conventions for national accounts (usually termed SNA, see United Nations, 1968) have been helpful in bringing procedures closer together and used with caution these cross-country data sets are a valuable resource which can yield constructive lessons. The third and fourth editions of the *World Tables* (1983, 1987) are now available on magnetic tape (World Bank, 1984, 1988*a*).

Whilst the World Bank *World Tables* have been the major data source for large-scale cross-country studies their dominant position is likely to be eroded by the recent work of Summers and Heston (1988), the latest product of a long-standing programme known as the International Comparison Project (ICP), based at the University of Pennsylvania. They have published, and simultaneously made available on diskettes, a set of international comparisons of 121 market and 9 centrally planned economies (which they call the Penn World Table, Mark 4) extending their earlier work with Kravis, for example Kravis *et al.*, 1978. For the 121 market economies there are annual data, from as early as 1950, on 17 variables which include population and exchange rates, real product and price level estimates for four different national income concepts and for the major subaggregates, consumption, investment and government. Their main concern is with the production of comparable accounts which use similar sets of prices thus overcoming one of the substantial worries over comparisons using SNA methods and data. Whilst many other difficulties remain (e.g. the requirements for heating in Nigeria and Nepal are very different) the use of common prices or purchasing power parity yields important insights. In their words 'these new insights arise because purchasing power parities (PPPs) replace the exchange rate as the means of converting GDP and its components to a common currency.' (Kravis *et al.* 1978, p. 4). Their work, and their making the data readily available, constitute a major public good and an important statistical event.

The differences in national incomes and rankings across countries when we change from the World Bank to the Summers–Heston data can be large, particularly at the bottom end. Generally speaking the estimates of income for the very poor countries are raised substantially whereas for the richer countries the alterations are minor. But within the very poor countries the effects of the change can be very different. For example, taking a comparable group of 114 countries (the two sets of countries do not coincide exactly) from both sources, Bangladesh shows a real 1985 GDP *per capita* in Summers and Heston (1988) of $647 and is ranked 86 out of the 114, whereas in the World Bank *World Development Report* (1987) it is, at $150, less poor than only Ethiopia. Ethiopia moves up from $110 (World Bank) to $310 (Summers–Heston) although only one place, whereas Zaire drops six places (to bottom) since its estimate increases only from $170 to $210 (and thus has an income *per capita* 68% of the next poorest country in Summers–Heston, Ethiopia). Such changes are remarkable and indicate how cautious one has to be in making cross-country comparisons. The changes reflect the different price levels ruling in the different countries. Thus prices of the main items of national income in Bangladesh, for example, must be particularly low relative to other countries. And notice that some commodity prices can be volatile. For a general discussion of some lessons from their data see Summers and Heston (1988).

We shall focus here on the more quantitative aspects of cross-country comparisons and on large samples of countries. We include demographic, educational, nutritional, and medical indicators as well as the usual economic variables. The unit of observation is the country. This unit may have only limited economic rationale. Thus it may be more interesting, for example, to compare Singapore and Hong Kong with Guangzhou (Canton) and Bombay rather than with China and India. Given the very wide disparities within countries we can learn little about the individual or household distribution of income at this level. Different units for comparison will appear at a number of points below.

In making comparisons across countries, whether more formal by using econometric models or less formal by using tables and examples, we face some basic problems of modelling and method. We usually wish to associate differences in outcomes with differences in policies or circumstances. In order to do this we have to assume broad similarity in the underlying processes so that the differences we isolate in outcomes may reasonably be associated with the causes indicated. This is a standard problem in cross-section econometrics where we have, for example, samples of households or firms. But one is perhaps less uncomfortable with the assumption that General Motors, Toyota and Renault share similar functions when we are trying to estimate a relationship between employment and output in the motor industry, than we would be with the corresponding assumption when we are trying to estimate the effect of the rate of growth of labour on the rate of growth of output using data from, *inter alia*, China, Brazil, Indonesia, India, Pakistan and Bangladesh. One can try to divide samples appropriately, to include the relevant measurable explanatory variables, and to avoid taking the models too literally, but nevertheless one has to treat the results from cross-country regressions with a great degree of circumspection. Whilst there are no doubt many common underlying processes, the idea that there are common parameters in a basic model and that Brazil and China are different drawings from a similar underlying (conditional) distribution is hard to swallow. It is better to treat these cross-country regressions as simple data descriptions, although as such they can be suggestive. From this perspective we should not, therefore, argue that the relationships derived from a cross-section are necessarily relevant for the progress of a single country over time. The state of a richer country now is not a description of where a poorer country will be in the future just as India now is not in the same position as, say, the United Kingdom, in previous centuries. Knowledge, the influence of other countries and a host of other factors will all play a role in invalidating the analogy.

There is a different kind of analysis of growth experience which can be particularly illuminating. This concerns the careful, analytical and detailed study of the growth of a particular country or small group of countries. This approach is more time-consuming than cross-country regressions but can yield deeper insights – it forms a major part of the discipline of economic history. We cannot review economic history as well as the economics of development but shall simply draw attention to attempts to apply this kind of method by economists. Notable examples include Little *et al.* (1970), Bhagwati (1978), Bhagwati and Desai (1970), Krueger (1978), Bevan *et al.* (1988 and forthcoming), Harberger (1984). It should also be recorded that major practitioners of cross-country regression analysis have also been involved in this kind of work, see, for example, Chenery *et al.* (1986). The two approaches have some complementarity.

Our discussion is divided into three subsections. We begin Section II. 1, by showing the great diversity in the circumstances, attainments and difficulties across the world's countries. This teaches us a number of lessons, in particular, that simple dichotomies such as North and South, developed and under-developed, and so on, can be extremely misleading. In Section II. 2 we present simple data on growth experience and link them to some of the ideas and issues to be discussed in Section III and in Section II. 3 we describe briefly some of the more formal econometric analyses of cross-country information.

II. 1. *Diversity of Current Position*

In Table 1 we present some basic socioeconomic and demographic indicators from the most recent, 1988, World Development Report (World Bank, 1981–8). The WDR uses six categories or sub-groups of countries: low-income, lower middle-income, upper middle-income, high-income oil exporters, industrial market economies and non-reporting non-members (not presented here). Within the categories countries are ranked by per capita income (see column 4 of Table 1). It is immediately clear that even in this one dimension there is enormous diversity and, further, that countries are spread fairly evenly over the spectrum. In terms of GNP/*capita* in 1986 dollars we have eight countries between $100 and $200, thirteen between $200 and $300, nine between $300 and $400,... seven between $800 and $1,000,..., nine between $2,000 and $3,000, and so on. There is no obvious clustering into groups in this dimension. Furthermore the 'upper middle-income' countries overlap in terms of GNP/*capita* with the industrial market economies – Trinidad and Tobago, for example, having a higher GNP/*capita* than Spain and Ireland, and Hong Kong and Singapore being close to New Zealand, Italy and the United Kingdom. A simple split into rich and poor or North and South is hopelessly invalid as a description of this distribution. And it should be noted that a similar conclusion applies if we use the Summers–Heston data (see Table 1, column 10).

GNP *per capita* is, of course, an aggregate and in addition to all its attendant problems of measurement conceals the distribution of income. Further, GNP *per capita* says nothing about quality of life, aspects of which are reflected to some extent in some of the other indicators in Table 1. Indeed it is interesting how the structure of the World Development Report's Basic Indicators (Table

Table 1
Basic Indicators

	Pop.	Pop. Growth	IMor.	GNP PC	LEB	CSPC	GDS	ODA	PEDU	RGDP
Low-income economies										
1 Ethiopia	43·5	2·4	155	120	46	1,704	3	11·5	36	310
2 Bhutan	1·3	2·0	139	150	45	2,477	—	19·3	25	—
3 Burkino Faso	8·1	2·5	140	150	47	2,003	−7	19·3	32	377
4 Nepal	17·0	2·6	130	150	47	1,997	9	11·7	79	526
5 Bangladesh	103·2	2·6	121	160	50	1,804	2	9·5	60	647
6 Malawi	7·4	3·2	153	160	45	2,415	7	17·5	62	387
7 Zaire	31·7	3·1	100	160	52	2,151	13	8·0	98	210
8 Mali	7·6	2·3	144	180	47	1,810	4	22·7	23	355
9 Burma	38·0	2·0	64	200	59	2,508	12	5·1	102	557
10 Mozambique	14·2	2·7	120	210	48	1,617	−1	9·8	84	528
11 Madagascar	10·6	3·3	130	230	53	2,452	10	12·7	121	497
12 Uganda	15·2	3·1	105	230	48	2,483	11	5·7	—	347
13 Burundi	4·8	2·7	114	240	48	2,233	9	15·7	53	345
14 Tanzania	23·0	3·5	108	250	53	2,316	2	15·2	72	355
15 Togo	3·1	3·4	96	250	53	2,221	13	18·5	95	489
16 Niger	6·6	3·0	135	260	44	2,276	7	15·2	28	429
17 Benin	4·2	3·2	117	270	50	2,248	0	10·0	65	525
18 Somalia	5·5	2·9	134	280	47	2,074	−5	27·8	25	348
19 Central African Rep.	2·7	2·5	134	290	50	2,059	2	14·8	73	434
20 India	781·4	2·2	86	290	57	2,126	21	0·9	92	750
21 Rwanda	6·2	3·3	116	290	48	1,935	9	11·5	64	341
22 China	1,054·0	1·2	34	300	69	2,620	36	0·4	124	2,444
23 Kenya	21·2	4·1	74	300	57	2,214	26	6·9	94	598
24 Zambia	6·9	3·5	82	300	53	2,126	13	31·2	103	548
25 Sierra Leone	3·8	2·4	154	310	41	1,784	8	7·0	—	443
26 Sudan	22·6	2·8	108	320	49	2,168	4	12·8	49	540
27 Haiti	6·1	1·8	119	330	54	1,784	6	8·2	78	631
28 Pakistan	99·2	3·1	111	350	52	2,180	7	2·9	47	1,153
29 Lesotho	1·6	2·7	102	370	55	2,299	−78	16·1	115	771
30 Ghana	13·2	3·5	89	390	54	1,785	8	6·6	66	349
31 Sri Lanka	16·1	1·5	29	400	70	2,485	13	8·9	103	1,539
32 Mauritania	1·8	2·6	127	420	47	2,071	15	23·9	—	550
33 Senegal	6·8	2·9	130	420	47	2,418	6	16·0	55	754

34 Afghanistan	—	—	—	—	—	2,179	—	—	—	—
35 Chad	5·1	2·3	134	—	45	1,733	—	—	38	—
36 Guinea	6·3	2·4	148	—	42	1,731	13	—	30	452
37 Kampuchea, Dem.	—	—	—	—	—	2,171	—	—	—	—
38 Lao PDR	3·7	2·0	146	—	50	2,317	—	—	91	—
39 Viet Nam	63·3	2·6	47	—	65	2,281	—	—	100	—
Lower middle-income economies										
40 Liberia	2·3	3·3	87	460	54	2,373	18	9·6	—	491
41 Yemen, PDR	2·2	3·1	142	470	50	2,255	—	5·7	66	—
42 Indonesia	166·4	2·2	87	490	57	2,476	24	1·0	118	1,255
43 Yemen, Arab Rep.	8·2	2·5	152	550	46	2,266	−15	4·7	67	978
44 Philippines	57·3	2·5	46	560	63	2,260	19	3·2	106	1,361
45 Morocco	22·5	2·5	85	590	60	2,729	13	2·4	81	1,221
46 Bolivia	6·6	2·7	113	600	53	2,171	5	7·2	91	1,089
47 Zimbabwe	8·7	3·7	74	620	58	2,144	20	4·2	131	948
48 Nigeria	103·1	3·3	104	640	51	2,139	10	0·1	92	581
49 Dominican Republic	6·6	2·4	67	710	66	2,530	12	2·1	124	1,753
50 Papua New Guinea	3·4	2·1	64	720	52	2,145	15	10·9	64	1,374
51 Côte d'Ivoire	10·7	4·2	96	730	52	2,308	22	2·1	78	920
52 Honduras	4·5	3·6	72	740	64	2,224	13	8·5	102	911
53 Egypt. Arab Rep.	49·7	2·7	88	760	61	3,275	9	4·1	85	1,188
54 Nicaragua	3·4	3·4	65	790	61	2,464	−2	5·6	101	1,989
55 Thailand	52·6	2·0	41	810	64	2,399	25	1·2	97	1,900
56 El Salvador	4·9	1·2	61	820	61	2,155	7	9·2	70	1,198
57 Botswana	1·1	3·5	69	840	59	2,159	26	10·4	104	1,762
58 Jamaica	2·4	1·5	19	840	73	2,578	19	8·5	106	1,725
59 Cameroon	10·5	3·2	96	910	56	2,080	28	2·1	107	1,095
60 Guatemala	8·2	2·9	61	930	61	2,345	9	1·9	76	1,608
61 Congo, People's Rep.	2·0	3·3	75	990	58	2,511	30	5·9	—	1,338
62 Paraguay	3·8	3·2	43	1,000	67	2,873	7	1·9	101	1,996
63 Peru	19·8	2·3	90	1,090	60	2,120	18	1·1	122	2,114
64 Turkey	51·5	2·5	79	1,110	65	3,218	22	0·6	116	2,533
65 Tunisia	7·3	2·3	74	1,140	63	2,796	17	2·3	118	2,050
66 Ecuador	9·6	2·9	64	1,160	66	2,005	20	1·4	114	2,387
67 Mauritius	1·0	1·0	35	1,200	66	2,717	25	4·2	106	1,869
68 Colombia	29·0	1·9	47	1,230	65	2,588	20	0·2	117	2,599
69 Chile	12·2	1·7	20	1,320	71	2,544	18	0·0	109	3,486
70 Costa Rica	2·6	2·4	18	1,480	74	2,807	24	4·9	101	2,650
71 Jordan	3·6	3·7	46	1,540	65	2,968	−9	12·0	99	2,113
72 Syrian Arab Rep.	10·8	3·5	50	1,570	64	3,235	14	4·9	108	2,900
73 Lebanon	—	—	—	—	—	3,046	—	—	—	—

Table 1 (*cont.*)

	Pop.	Pop. Growth	IMor.	GNP PC	LEB	CSPC	GDS	ODA	PEDU	RGDP
Upper middle-income economies										
74 Brazil	138·4	2·2	65	1,810	65	2,657	24	0·1	104	3,282
75 Malaysia	16·1	2·7	27	1,830	69	2,601	32	0·8	99	3,415
76 South Africa	32·3	2·2	74	1,850	61	2,926	30	—	—	3,885
77 Mexico	80·2	2·2	48	1,860	68	3,126	27	0·2	115	3,985
78 Uruguay	3·0	0·4	28	1,900	71	2,791	13	0·4	110	3,462
79 Hungary	10·6	−0·1	19	2,020	71	3,544	25	—	98	5,765
80 Poland	37·5	0·9	18	2,070	72	3,224	30	—	101	4,913
81 Portugal	10·2	0·5	18	2,250	73	3,122	20	0·5	112	3,729
82 Yugoslavia	23·3	0·7	27	2,300	71	3,499	40	0·0	96	5,063
83 Panama	2·2	2·2	24	2,330	72	2,423	21	1·0	105	2,912
84 Argentina	31·0	1·6	33	2,350	70	3,216	11	0·1	108	3,486
85 Korea, Rep. of	41·5	1·4	25	2,370	69	2,806	35	0·0	96	3,056
86 Algeria	22·4	3·1	77	2,590	62	2,799	31	0·3	94	2,142
87 Venezuela	17·8	2·9	37	2,920	70	2,485	21	0·0	108	3,548
88 Gabon	1·0	4·4	105	3,080	52	2,448	19	2·7	123	3,103
89 Greece	10·0	0·5	12	3,680	76	3,637	14	0·0	106	4,464
90 Oman	1·3	4·7	103	4,980	54	—	—	1·3	89	7,792
91 Trinidad and Tobago	1·2	1·5	21	5,360	70	2,915	18	0·4	95	6,884
92 Israel	4·3	1·7	12	6,210	75	3,019	11	6·8	99	6,270
93 Hong Kong	5·4	1·2	8	6,910	76	2,692	27	0·0	105	9,093
94 Singapore	2·6	1·1	9	7,410	73	2,696	40	0·2	115	9,834
95 Iran, Islamic Rep.	45·6	2·8	109	—	59	3,115	—	—	112	3,922
96 Iraq	16·5	3·6	71	—	63	2,891	—	—	100	2,813
97 Romania	22·9	0·5	26	—	71	3,413	—	—	98	4,273
High-income oil exporters										
98 Saudi Arabia	12·0	4·1	64	6,950	63	3,057	18	0·0	69	5,971
99 Kuwait	1·8	4·4	19	13,890	73	3,102	—	0·0	101	14,868
100 United Arab Emirates	1·4	5·6	33	14,680	69	3,652	—	0·2	99	12,404
101 Libya	3·9	3·9	85	—	61	3,585	—	—	127	—

Industrial market economies										
102 Spain	38·7	0·6	11	4,860	76	3,303	23	0·0	104	6,437
103 Ireland	3·6	0·8	9	5,070	74	3,736	23		100	5,205
104 New Zealand	3·3	0·9	11	7,460	74	3,393	24		106	8,000
105 Italy	57·2	0·3	10	8,550	77	3,493	23		98	7,425
106 United Kingdom	56·7	0·1	9	8,870	75	3,148	18		101	8,665
107 Belgium	9·9	0·0	10	9,230	75	3,679	20		95	9,717
108 Austria	7·6	0·0	10	9,990	74	3,140	25		99	8,929
109 Netherlands	14·6	0·5	8	10,020	77	3,348	25		95	9,092
110 France	55·4	0·5	8	10,720	77	3,358	20		114	9,918
111 Australia	16·0	1·4	10	11,920	78	3,302	21		106	8,850
112 Germany, Fed. Rep.	60·9	−0·2	9	12,080	75	3,519	24		96	10,708
113 Finland	4·9	0·5	6	12,160	75	2,961	24		104	9,232
114 Denmark	5·1	0·0	8	12,600	75	3,489	22		98	10,884
115 Japan	121·5	0·7	6	12,840	78	2,695	32		102	9,447
116 Sweden	8·4	0·1	6	13,160	77	3,007	21		98	9,904
117 Canada	25·6	1·1	8	14,120	76	3,443	22		105	12,196
118 Norway	4·2	0·3	9	15,400	77	3,171	26		97	12,623
119 United States	241·6	1·0	10	17,480	75	3,682	15		101	12,532
120 Switzerland	6·5	0·3	7	17,680	77	3,406	27		—	10,640

Key: Pop., Population (millions) mid-1986. Pop. growth, Average annual growth of population (percent) 1980–86. IMor., Infant mortality (per 1,000 live births before 1 year of age) 1986. GNP PC, GNP per capita (dollars) 1986. LEB, Life expectancy at birth (years) 1986. CSPC, Daily calorie supply per capita 1985. GDS, Gross domestic savings 1986 as a % of GDP. ODA, Net disbursements of Official Development Assistance: receipts as a percentage of GNP 1986. PEDU, Percentage of primary age group enrolled in education (male plus female; some of the non-primary age group are enrolled in primary education). RGDP, Real GDP per capita (dollars) 1985, in 1980 international prices except for Centrally Planned Economies which are Real GNP per capita in 1980 International Prices (underlined).

Note (*i*): Low-income economies are countries with GNP per capita of less than 460 U.S. dollars in 1986. Lower middle-income economies are countries with GNP per capita of less than 1,810 U.S. dollars in 1986. Upper middle-income economies are countries with GNP per capita of less than 7,410 U.S. dollars in 1986, except for some high-income oil exporters and industrial market economies.

Note (*ii*) Figures underlined are for years other than specified (except RGDP). '—' signifies missing values. Source for RGDP is Summers and Heston (1988).
Source: World Bank, *World Development Report* (1988) except where specified.

1 in the WDRs) has changed since 1978 as a result, one presumes, of shifting emphasis in the profession. For example, energy consumption, highly topical in the 1970s, was included in the early tables but dropped in 1980 when adult literacy and life expectancy were added. The index of food availability *per capita* (as Sen, 1981, argued, a poor indicator of the probability of famine) was dropped in 1983. There are now 33 Tables of World Development Indicators (WDR, 1988) compared to 18 in 1978. This reflects the growing availability of data (which has expanded partly in response to the World Bank's own initiatives) but the statistical newcomers (which include data relating to income distribution and women in development) are themselves significant as indicators of changing concerns.

Most of the indicators also show considerable variation across countries with often only a weak relationship with GNP *per capita* (in parentheses in the following). Infant mortality rates in China ($300) and Sri Lanka ($400), for example, are less than a quarter of those in Yemen PDR ($470) and Yemen Arab Republic ($550), one-third of those in Gabon ($3,080) and Oman ($4,980), and half those of Jordan ($1,540) and Brazil ($1,810). Life expectancy follows a broadly similar pattern to infant mortality (although there are some important differences) and again is only weakly related to GNP *per capita*. Daily calorie supply *per capita* has a slightly stronger relationship with income but again the relationship is far from monotonic with those for Venezuala ($2,920) and Gabon ($3,080) being close to Malawi ($160) and Bhutan ($150). Calorie supply *per capita* is again an aggregate, of course, and has problems of measurement.

II.2. *The Growth Experience*

Some aspects of the process of growth over the two decades 1965–86 are presented in Table 2. The growth rates also show a great diversity over this period with some countries achieving sustained and rapid growth of income *per capita* and other countries in decline. Growth of over 4% a year in income *per capita* over two decades was achieved for example, by China, Indonesia, Thailand, Botswana, Brazil, Malaysia and South Korea. Growth at 4% doubles income *per capita* in 18 years so that the increase in affluence in these countries has been remarkable. Sri Lanka, Pakistan, Egypt, Turkey, Colombia, Philippines, Mexico, Algeria, Hungary and Yugoslavia, for example, all showed growth rates in income *per capita* above 2·4%, notwithstanding population growth rates well above 2% per annum in a number of cases. Zaire, Madagascar, Uganda, Niger, Zambia, and Ghana, on the other hand, had rapid declines with growth rates of −1·7% or lower. Uganda's income *per capita*, for example, declined at a rate of 2·6% for the 21 years 1965–86 representing a fall of a factor of 1·7, or an income *per capita* in 1986 only 60% of the level in 1965. All the examples of rapid decline are in Africa, south of the Sahara, whereas rapid growth has been seen by several major countries in various different parts of Asia and Latin America, and also in Egypt.

The importance of savings and industrialisation in the growth process was emphasised by early writers (for example, Rosenstein-Rodan, 1943; Singer,

1952; Nurkse, 1953; Lewis, 1954, 1955). Sen (1983*a*) has argued that countries with more rapid growth in incomes have indeed been those with higher savings rates and more rapid industrialisation. He did this by inspecting data such as those displayed in Tables 1 and 2 and pointing to those countries which had grown most rapidly and those which had grown least rapidly. Prominent amongst the former for the low income countries were China and Sri Lanka with relatively high savings rates and for the latter a number of African countries with relatively low savings rates (and similarly for industrialisation). Arguing in this way Sen suggests that the emphasis of the early writers may not have been misplaced.

Unfortunately drawing conclusions about issues such as savings and growth is more difficult than might appear from these simple examples, and it is instructive to spend a moment seeing why. There are (at least) two major problems. First, a few examples may be misleading. A simple correlation of growth rates of GNP *per capita* (averaged over 1965–86) against savings rates (1986) for the 105 countries permitted by Tables 1 and 2 shows a significant correlation coefficient for all countries of +0·24. But the correlation coefficient for the 31 low-income countries is −0·26 and for the 32 lower-middle and middle-income countries is +0·11 both of which are insignificant at the 5% level. The high (and significant) positive correlations come from the upper-middle-income countries (20 observations) with a coefficient of +0·64 and the industrial market economies (19 observations) with +0·54. Hence savings ratios are positively correlated with growth rates for richer countries but not for poorer. Second, one cannot think in terms of a single direction of causation going from savings rates to growth rates. We know from life-cycle ideas of individual or household saving (see, e.g. Modigliani, 1970 and Farrell, 1970 for early discussions and Gersovitz, 1988 for recent references) that growth rates influence savings rates. How important this relationship actually is will depend on the country at hand (it may not have been relevant for China, for example) but it cannot be dismissed. Third, if on the other hand investment rates are used in place of savings rates we find significant positive correlations for all groups of countries. This last observation is broadly confirmed using the Summers–Heston data. In addition to the problems mentioned one must also recognise that savings are subject to substantial measurement error as well as being difficult to define (they require a concept of income and are generally measured as a residual with respect to that income). Our purpose here is not to provide a serious investigation into the relation between saving and growth but simply to show that such an investigation using cross-country data would be problematic and that a few apparently suggestive examples are not enough.

There are examples of rapid growth, as Sen (1983*b*) emphasises, amongst many different types of economy, including economies which have been tightly controlled with a large public sector (such as China) and those where public and private decisions have been closely integrated (such as South Korea). Thus the broad picture does not, by itself, allow one to proclaim either the success or failure of planning with any general degree of confidence or truth (and see Section III below for further discussion).

Table 2

Growth Rates 1965–1986

	GNP PC	GNP PCG	GDP 1965	GDP 1986	GDPG 65–80	GDPG 80–86	Dist. of GDP (%) 1965 and 1986							
							AGR		IND		MANU		SERV	
Low-income economies														
1 Ethiopia	120	0·0	1,180	4,960	2·7	0·8	58	48	14	15	7	10	28	36
2 Bhutan	150	—	—	210	—	—	—	—	—	—	—	—	—	—
3 Burkino Faso	150	1·3	260	930	3·5	2·5	53	45	20	22	—	—	27	33
4 Nepal	150	1·9	730	2,200	2·4	3·5	65	—	11	—	3	—	23	—
5 Bangladesh	160	0·4	4,380	15,460	2·4	3·7	53	47	11	14	5	8	36	39
6 Malawi	160	1·5	220	1,100	6·1	2·4	50	37	13	18	—	12	37	45
7 Zaire	160	−2·2	3,140	6,020	1·4	1·0	21	29	26	36	16	—	53	35
8 Mali	180	1·1	—	1,650	4·1	0·4	—	50	—	13	—	7	—	37
9 Burma	200	2·3	1,600	8,180	3·9	4·9	35	48	13	13	9	10	52	39
10 Mozambique	210	—	—	4,300	—	−9·0	—	35	—	12	—	—	—	53
11 Madagascar	230	−1·7	670	2,670	1·6	−0·1	31	43	16	16	11	—	53	41
12 Uganda	230	−2·6	1,100	3,310	0·8	0·7	52	76	13	6	8	5	35	18
13 Burundi	240	1·8	150	1,090	3·6	2·3	—	58	—	17	—	10	—	25
14 Tanzania	250	−0·3	790	4,020	3·7	0·9	46	59	14	10	8	6	40	31
15 Togo	250	0·2	190	980	4·5	−1·1	45	32	21	20	10	7	34	48
16 Niger	260	−2·2	670	2,080	0·3	−2·6	68	46	3	16	2	4	29	39
17 Benin	270	0·2	220	1,320	2·3	3·6	59	49	8	13	—	4	33	37
18 Somalia	280	−0·3	220	2,320	2·5	4·9	71	58	6	9	3	6	24	34
19 Central African Rep.	290	−0·6	140	900	2·6	1·1	46	41	16	12	4	4	38	47
20 India	290	1·8	46,260	203,790	3·7	4·9	47	32	22	29	15	19	31	39
21 Rwanda	290	1·5	150	1,850	5·0	1·8	75	40	7	23	2	16	18	37
22 China	300	5·1	65,590	271,880	6·4	10·5	39	31	38	46	30	34	23	23
23 Kenya	300	1·9	920	5,960	6·4	3·4	35	30	18	20	11	12	47	50
24 Zambia	300	−1·7	1,060	1,660	1·8	−0·1	14	11	54	48	6	20	32	41
25 Sierra Leone	310	0·2	320	1,180	2·6	0·4	34	45	28	22	6	4	38	33
26 Sudan	320	−0·2	1,330	7,470	3·8	0·3	54	35	9	15	4	7	37	50
27 Haiti	330	0·6	350	2,150	2·9	−0·7	—	—	—	—	—	—	—	—
28 Pakistan	350	2·4	5,450	30,080	5·1	6·7	40	24	20	28	14	17	40	47
29 Lesotho	370	5·6	50	230	6·6	0·9	65	21	5	27	1	13	30	52
30 Ghana	390	−1·7	2,050	5,720	1·4	0·7	44	45	19	17	10	12	38	39
31 Sri Lanka	400	2·9	1,770	5,880	4·0	4·9	28	26	21	27	17	15	51	47

32 Mauritania	420	−0·3	160	750	2·0	1·0	32	34	36	24	4	—	32	42
33 Senegal	420	−0·6	810	3,740	2·1	3·2	25	22	18	27	14	17	56	51
34 Afghanistan	—	—	600	—	2·9	—	—	—	—	—	—	—	—	—
35 Chad	—	—	290	—	0·1	—	42	—	15	—	12	—	43	—
36 Guinea	—	—	520	1,980	3·8	0·9	—	40	—	22	—	2	—	38
37 Kampuchea, Dem.	—	—	—	—	—	—	—	—	—	—	—	—	—	—
38 Lao PDR	—	—	—	—	—	—	—	—	—	—	—	—	—	—
39 Viet Nam	—	—	—	—	—	—	—	—	—	—	—	—	—	—
Lower middle-income economies														
40 Liberia	460	−1·4	270	990	3·3	−1·3	27	37	40	28	3	5	34	35
41 Yemen, PDR	470	—	—	930	—	1·7	—	—	—	—	—	—	—	—
42 Indonesia	490	4·6	3,830	75,230	7·9	3·4	56	26	13	32	8	14	31	42
43 Yemen, Arab Rep.	550	4·7	—	4,760	—	4·3	—	34	—	16	—	7	—	50
44 Philippines	560	1·9	6,010	30,540	5·9	−1·0	26	26	28	32	20	25	46	42
45 Morocco	590	1·9	2,950	14,760	5·4	3·3	23	21	28	30	16	17	49	49
46 Bolivia	600	−0·4	710	4,180	4·5	−3·0	23	24	31	23	15	13	46	52
47 Zimbabwe	620	1·2	960	4,940	4·4	2·6	18	11	35	46	20	30	47	43
48 Nigeria	640	1·9	4,190	49,110	8·0	−3·2	53	41	19	29	7	8	29	30
49 Dominican Republic	710	2·5	890	5,280	7·3	1·1	23	17	22	30	16	16	55	53
50 Papua New Guinea	720	0·5	340	2,530	4·1	1·8	42	34	18	26	—	9	41	40
51 Côte d'Ivoire	730	1·2	760	7,320	6·8	−0·3	47	36	19	24	11	16	33	40
52 Honduras	740	0·3	460	2,960	4·2	0·6	40	27	19	25	12	14	41	48
53 Egypt. Arab Rep.	760	3·1	4,550	40,850	6·7	4·7	29	20	27	29	—	—	45	51
54 Nicaragua	790	−2·2	570	2,900	2·6	0·2	25	23	24	33	18	27	51	44
55 Thailand	810	4·0	4,050	41,780	7·4	4·8	35	17	23	30	14	21	42	53
56 El Salvador	820	−0·3	800	3,980	4·3	−1·0	29	20	22	21	18	15	49	59
57 Botswana	840	8·8	50	1,150	14·3	11·9	34	4	19	58	12	6	47	38
58 Jamaica	840	−1·4	970	2,430	1·3	0·0	10	6	37	40	17	22	53	54
59 Cameroon	910	3·9	750	11,280	5·1	8·2	32	22	17	35	10	—	50	43
60 Guatemala	930	1·4	1,330	7,470	5·9	−1·2	—	—	—	—	—	—	—	—
61 Congo, People's Rep.	990	3·6	200	2,000	5·9	5·1	19	8	19	54	—	6	62	38
62 Paraguay	1,000	3·6	440	3,590	6·9	1·1	37	27	19	26	16	16	45	47
63 Peru	1,090	0·1	5,020	25,370	3·9	−0·4	18	11	30	38	17	20	53	51
64 Turkey	1,110	2·7	7,660	52,620	6·3	4·9	34	18	25	36	16	25	41	46
65 Tunisia	1,140	3·8	880	7,790	6·6	3·7	22	16	24	33	9	15	54	52
66 Ecuador	1,160	3·5	1,150	11,510	8·7	1·8	27	14	22	42	18	19	50	45
67 Mauritius	1,200	3·0	190	1,160	5·3	4·4	16	15	23	32	14	23	61	53
68 Colombia	1,230	2·8	5,570	29,660	5·7	2·4	30	20	25	25	18	18	46	56
69 Chile	1,320	−0·2	5,940	16,820	1·9	0·0	9	—	40	—	24	—	52	—
70 Costa Rica	1,480	1·6	590	4,260	6·2	1·3	24	21	23	29	—	—	53	50

Table 2 (*cont.*)

	GNP PC	GNP PCG	GDP 1965	GDP 1986	GDPG 65–80	GDPG 80–86	Dist. of GDP (%) 1965 + 1980 AGR		IND		MANU		SERV	
71 Jordan	1,540	5·5	—	4,000	—	5·1	—	8	—	28	—	14	—	63
72 Syrian Arab Rep.	1,570	3·7	1,470	17,400	8·7	1·5	29	22	22	21	—	—	49	58
73 Lebanon	—	—	1,150	—	−1·2	—	12	—	21	—	—	—	67	—
Upper middle-income economies														
74 Brazil	1,810	4·3	19,450	206,750	9·0	2·7	19	11	33	39	26	28	48	50
75 Malaysia	1,830	4·3	3,130	27,580	7·4	4·8	28	—	25	—	9	—	47	—
76 South Africa	1,850	0·4	10,540	56,370	4·0	0·8	10	6	42	46	23	22	48	49
77 Mexico	1,860	2·6	20,160	127,140	6·5	0·4	14	9	31	39	21	26	54	52
78 Uruguay	1,900	1·4	930	5,320	2·4	−2·6	15	12	32	33	—	—	53	56
79 Hungary	2,020	3·9	—	23,660	5·6	1·6	—	17	—	41	—	—	—	43
80 Poland	2,070	—	—	73,770	—	1·5	—	—	—	—	—	—	—	—
81 Portugal	2,250	3·2	—	27,480	5·5	1·4	—	10	—	40	—	—	—	51
82 Yugoslavia	2,300	3·9	11,190	61,640	6·0	1·2	23	12	42	42	—	—	35	46
83 Panama	2,330	2·4	660	5,120	5·5	2·6	18	9	19	18	12	8	63	73
84 Argentina	2,350	0·2	16,500	69,820	3·4	−0·8	17	13	42	44	33	31	42	44
85 Korea, Rep. of	2,370	6·7	3,000	98,150	9·5	8·2	38	12	25	42	18	30	37	45
86 Algeria	2,590	3·5	3,170	60,760	7·5	4·4	15	12	34	44	11	13	51	44
87 Venezuela	2,920	0·4	8,290	49,980	5·2	−0·9	7	9	41	37	—	23	52	54
88 Gabon	3,080	1·9	220	3,190	9·5	1·5	26	10	34	35	—	—	40	55
89 Greece	3,680	3·3	5,270	35,210	5·6	1·5	24	17	26	29	16	18	49	54
90 Oman	4,980	5·0	60	7,320	12·5	5·7	61	—	23	—	0	—	16	—
91 Trinidad and Tobago	5,360	1·6	690	4,830	5·1	−6·3	8	5	48	35	—	8	44	59
92 Israel	6,210	2·6	3,590	29,460	6·8	2·0	—	—	—	—	—	—	—	—
93 Hong Kong	6,910	6·2	2,150	32,250	8·5	6·0	2	0	40	29	24	21	58	71
94 Singapore	7,410	7·6	970	17,350	10·4	5·3	3	1	24	38	15	27	73	62
95 Iran, Islamic Rep.	—	—	6,170	—	6·2	—	26	—	36	—	12	—	38	—
96 Iraq	—	—	2,430	—	—	—	18	—	46	—	8	—	36	—
97 Romania	—	—	—	—	—	—	—	—	—	—	—	—	—	—

High-income oil exporters														
98 Saudi Arabia	6,950	4·0	2,300	78,480	10·9	−3·4	8	4	60	50	9	9	31	46
99 Kuwait	13,890	−0·6	2,100	22,310	3·1	−0·9	0	—	73	—	3	—	27	—
100 United Arab Emirates	14,680	—	—	25,280	—	−3·8	—	—	—	—	—	—	—	—
101 Libya	—	—	1,500	—	4·2	—	5	—	63	—	3	—	33	—
Industrial market economies														
102 Spain	4,860	2·9	23,320	229,100	5·2	1·8	15	6	36	37	—	27	49	56
103 Ireland	5,070	1·7	2,340	21,910	5·1	0·7	—	14	—	45	—	—	—	41
104 New Zealand	7,460	1·5	5,640	26,630	3·1	2·6	—	11	—	33	—	—	—	56
105 Italy	8,550	2·6	72,150	599,920	3·9	1·3	11	5	41	39	23	22	48	56
106 United Kingdom	8,870	1·7	88,520	468,290	2·2	2·3	3	2	46	43	34	26	51	55
107 Belgium	9,230	2·7	16,600	112,180	3·9	0·9	5	2	41	33	31	23	53	64
108 Austria	9,990	3·3	9,480	93,830	4·3	1·8	9	3	46	38	33	28	45	59
109 Netherlands	10,020	1·9	19,890	175,330	3·7	1·0	—	4	—	34	—	18	—	62
110 France	10,720	2·8	99,660	724,200	4·4	1·3	8	4	39	34	28	—	53	63
111 Australia	11,920	1·7	24,050	184,940	4·0	3·1	9	5	39	34	26	17	51	62
112 Germany, Fed. Rep.	12,080	2·5	114,790	891,990	3·3	1·5	4	2	53	40	40	32	43	58
113 Finland	12,160	3·2	7,540	62,370	4·1	2·7	16	8	37	37	23	25	47	55
114 Denmark	12,600	1·9	8,940	68,820	2·7	2·8	8	6	36	28	23	20	55	66
115 Japan	12,840	4·3	91,110	1,955,650	6·3	3·7	9	3	43	41	32	30	48	56
116 Sweden	13,160	1·6	19,610	114,470	2·8	2·0	6	3	40	35	28	24	53	62
117 Canada	14,120	2·6	45,940	323,790	4·4	2·9	6	3	40	36	27	—	53	61
118 Norway	15,400	3·4	7,080	69,780	4·4	3·5	8	4	33	41	21	14	59	56
119 United States	17,480	1·6	701,670	4,185,490	2·8	3·1	3	2	38	31	28	20	59	67
120 Switzerland	17,680	1·4	13,920	135,050	2·0	1·5	—	—	—	—	—	—	—	—

Key: GNP PC, GNP *per capita* (dollars 1986). GNP PCG, GNP *per capita* (average annual growth rate (%) 1965–86). GDP 1965, GDP (mn dollars) 1965. GDP 1986, GDP (mn dollars) 1986. GDPG 65–80, GDP average annual growth rate (%) 1965–80. GDPG 80–86, GDP average annual growth rate (%) 1980–86. AGR 65, Distribution of GDP (%), Agriculture 1965. AGR 86, Distribution of GDP (%), Agriculture 1986. IND 65, Distribution of GDP (%), Industry 1965. IND 86, Distribution of GDP (%), Industry 1986. MANU 65, Distribution of GDP (%), Manufacturing 1965. MANU 86, Distribution of GDP (%), Manufacturing 1986. SERV 65, Distribution of GDP (%), Services, etc. 1965. SERV 86, Distribution of GDP (%), Services, etc. 1986.

Note (*i*): Figures underlined are for years other than specified. '—' signifies missing values. *Source*: see Table 1.

Note (*ii*): Low-income economies are countries with GNP per capita of less than 460 U.S. dollars in 1986. Lower middle-income economies are countries with GNP per capita of less than 1,810 U.S. dollars in 1986. Upper middle-income economies are countries with GNP per capita of less than 7,410 U.S. dollars in 1986, except for some high-income oil exporters and industrial market economies.

Shifts in the structure of industry in the growth process are also illustrated in Table 2. Generally we see a shift out of agriculture over time. Notice that the share of services is high in all countries and is generally rising over time reaching two-thirds of GDP in the richest countries. Excluding China and India the share of industry in GDP is higher for richer countries, but it is already strikingly high for both China and India. The investigation of the process of structural change was a central concern of the work to be described in the next sub-section and plays a key role in some of the models of growth discussed in Section III. 2.

II. 3. *Cross-Country Statistical Analyses*

The early contributors to cross-country statistical analysis were Clark (1940) and Kuznets (1961, 1971). Chenery and his collaborators (Chenery and Syrquin, 1975; Chenery, 1979; Chenery *et al.* 1986) and Adelman and Morris (1973, and Morris and Adelman, 1988) have been leading figures in this area in the 1970s and 1980s. Kuznets pointed to a number of characteristics of the growth process for developed nations. Prominent are high rates of growth of *per capita* output and high rates of increase in total factor productivity, especially labour productivity, as well as a rapid structural transformation of the economy. The work of Chenery and his colleagues constituted 'an attempt to interpret the interaction of the principal factors that cause the structural changes reflected in Kuznets' cross-country and time-series patterns' (Chenery *et al.*, 1986, p. 2).

Chenery's earlier work (Chenery and Syrquin, 1975, Chenery, 1979) was largely based on cross-section analysis which leaned heavily on cross-country regressions 'explaining' dependent variables such as exports and production of manufactures in terms of 'explanatory variables' such as *per capita* GNP, population and foreign resource inflow. Many of these cross-country regressions generate similar difficulties of interpretation to those indicated in the preceding sub-section.

The methods of analysis were considerably broadened in the work described in the 1986 Chenery *et al.* volume. There were (i) detailed studies (some in book form) of Colombia, Israel, Japan, Korea, Mexico, Norway, Taiwan, Turkey and Yugoslavia, which together represent a broad spectrum of economies and strategies; (ii) sources of growth studies for 39 economies of the type developed by Solow (1957) (and described below in Section III. 2); (iii) disequilibrium cross-section models estimated on 34 economies; and (iv) a computable general equilibrium model based on Korea. They found (p. 358) 'that economies which pursued export-led growth – as opposed to a strategy of import substitution – grew faster, industrialised sooner, had higher rates of total factor productivity growth, and tended to achieve the input-output structure of an advanced economy faster'. But they add (p. 358): 'It appears that an economy must develop a certain industrial base and set of technical skills before it can pursue manufactured exports'. This may involve high capital flows to certain sectors with import substitution in the early stages and low total factor productivity growth; and it is clear from this statement that the development of human capital would also be central. The early stages have often been accompanied by strong and non-uniform protection (see, for example, Wade, 1985, and Section III below for further discussion of such issues).

A longer-term cross-section study dealing with the period 1850–1980 and building on lines suggested by Kuznets (1971) and Lewis (1978) is provided in Reynolds (1983). He indicates a number of conclusions, notably the following. First, intensive growth 'before 1940 was intermittent, invariably export led, with moderate population growth' (p. 975) whereas since 1950 'population has grown considerably faster, *per capita* income in most countries has also grown faster, there are cases of non-export led growth...'. Second, the '"top tier" of third-world countries now have not only a much higher *per capita* income than in 1950 but also more effective economic institutions and a more diversified pattern of production'. Third, the faster growth of some countries is not easily explained. His hypothesis (p. 976) is that the single most important explanatory variable is 'political organisation and the administrative competence of government'. Morris and Adelman (1988) also caution against the argument that the lessons of comparative growth experience point unambiguously to the superiority of certain strategies.

III. THE GRAND ISSUES

The grand issues have always been prominent in the economics of development and this, we have suggested, has constituted one of its main strengths. It can bring dangers too in that the magnitude of the issues tempts one into less than rigorous analysis, selective or inappropriate use of evidence and strident assertion in the place of argument. Nevertheless a number of the controversies have generated productive debate and we shall try to give some of the flavour of the more important. Given the divergence of the views, the difficulty of the problems and their intertwining with political persuasion, one cannot expect settled answers or a consensus.

We begin in Section III.1 with what is, in many respects, the most basic of questions, the role of the state. In III.2 we examine possible processes of growth and change using fairly aggregated models. Understanding these processes is central to the economics of development and whilst there are major limitations on the insights available from simple growth models, they have made a substantial contribution. Policies toward industrialisation and trade, discussed in Section III.3, have been subject to continued controversy, with that surrounding trade being particularly fierce, and the balance of views has been radically shifted, in part by experience. The relations between richer and poorer countries, particularly concerning aid, trade and debt, are examined in III.4. Recently, we have seen 'structural adjustment' and 'stabilisation' as prominent problems (Section III.5). The economic effects of population change, discussed in III.6, have been a central issue for two hundred years or more (Malthus, 1798). We conclude this section by considering the possible objectives for development and strategies for achieving them. From one perspective one should start with objectives as a determining element in topic selection. In this case it is instructive to put objectives at the end, since having seen the major debates we may ask whether their focus should be broadened or readjusted in the light of objectives.

III. 1. *Markets and Government*

There is one answer to the question of the appropriate role of government which asserts that the only role for the state should be to establish and preserve law and order and the defence of the realm. To go any or much further, it is claimed, would constitute an unacceptable interference with freedom and liberty. This version of the argument for the 'minimalist state' (e.g. Nozick, 1974) is often primarily based on views of individual rights and responsibilities and of justifiable, or unjustifiable, methods of transfer and in this sense is concerned with procedures and opportunities rather than consequences or end-states in terms of, for example, the production and allocation of goods.

A view of markets as processes has also been part of the Austrian School which has shown a revival in the last twenty years (see Kirzner, pp. 145–51, Austrian School of Economics, in *The New Palgrave*, 1987). The central idea is that decentralised markets with individual decision-making provide incentives for learning, discovery and innovation. Thus the argument goes beyond the ethical justification of markets as processes of exchange in that, ethical or not, they are crucial to economic advancement. This Austrian School shares some similarity of spirit with standard ideas of the combination of individual maximisation and markets leading to economic efficiency but its emphasis on the unknown is not easily captured by the standard extension of the competitive model to contingent goods and insurance markets.

Much of the discussion of markets and governments has been and continues to be dominated by the idea of 'market failure'. The progress of theory, as we shall argue briefly below, has given us much clearer insights into what constitutes market failure than was available to the early and influential writers (e.g. Nurkse, 1953; Rosenstein-Rodan, 1943; Scitovsky, 1954; Hirschman, 1958) who pointed to market failure as a reason for comprehensive planning. At the same time a much keener appreciation has developed, from experience and theory, of the problems of government intervention which are now set, as 'government failure', alongside market failure. Much of the theory of government failure is based on ideas of the way in which governments actually function and the incentives they create for individuals inside and outside the government.

The ideas involved clearly encompass a very large part of economics and we cannot hope to do them justice here. We shall summarise a number of the main issues in two tables which list problems of the market (Table 3) and problems of state intervention (Table 4) and discuss only briefly some of the theory and ideas. The list of problems of the market is based on the scrutiny of the assumptions of the two standard theorems that describe, first, the circumstances under which a competitive equilibrium is Pareto efficient (notably one assumes all markets exist and are competitive and there are no externalities) and, second, circumstances under which a given Pareto efficient allocation can be achieved as a market equilibrium (additionally one assumes convexity of

Table 3

Reasons for Market Failure

(i)	Markets may be monopolised or oligopolistic.
(ii)	There may be externalities.
(iii)	There may be increasing returns to scale.
(iv)	Some markets, particularly insurance and futures markets, cannot be perfect and, indeed, may not exist.
(v)	Markets may adjust slowly or imprecisely because information may move slowly or marketing institutions may be inflexible.
(vi)	Individuals or enterprises may adjust slowly.
(vii)	Individuals or enterprises may be badly informed about products, prices, their production possibilities, and so on.
(viii)	Individuals may not act so as to maximise anything, either implicitly or explicitly.
(ix)	Government taxation is unavoidable and will not, or cannot, take a form which allows efficiency.

Table 4

Some Problems of State Intervention

(i)	Individuals may know more about their own preferences and circumstances than the government.
(ii)	Government planning may increase risk by pointing everyone in the same direction – governments may make bigger mistakes than markets.
(iii)	Government planning may be more rigid and inflexible than private decision-making since complex decision-making machinery may be involved in government.
(iv)	Governments may be incapable of administering detailed plans.
(v)	Government controls may prevent private sector individual initiative if there are many bureaucratic obstacles.
(vi)	Organisations and individuals require incentives to work, innovate, control costs and allocate efficiently and the discipline and rewards of the market cannot easily be replicated within public enterprises and organisations.
(vii)	Different levels and parts of government may be poorly co-ordinated in the absence of the equilibrating signals provided by the market, particularly where groups or regions with different interests are involved.
(viii)	Markets place constraints on what can be achieved by government, for example, resale of commodities on black markets and activities in the informal sector can disrupt rationing or other non-linear pricing or taxation schemes. This is the general problem of 'incentive compatibility'.
(ix)	Controls create resource-using activities to influence those controls through lobbying and corruption – often called rent-seeking or directly unproductive activities in the literature.
(x)	Planning may be manipulated by privileged and powerful groups which act in their own interests and, further, planning creates groups with a vested interest in planning, for example bureaucrats or industrialists who obtain protected positions.
(xi)	Governments may be dominated by narrow interest groups interested in their own welfare and sometimes actively hostile to large sections of the population. Planning may intensify their power.

production and preferences, i.e. diminishing marginal rates of transformation and substitution, and the availability of lump-sum transfers to raise revenue and redistribute income). This is a view of the issues which is clearly based on outcomes as end-states in contrast to a view of 'markets as processes' embodied in Nozick (1974) or the Austrian perspective discussed above. Our emphasis on these tables is based in part on the greater facility with which the issues embodied in them can be analysed theoretically and empirically, as compared with, for example, the Austrian approach, which is more difficult to formulate, make precise and test.

The issue of market versus government even within the narrow 'end-state' perspective should not, however, be seen as one of simply listing the problems, studying and thinking over Tables 3 and 4 or the like, and then voting one way or the other (legend has it that Winston Churchill used to take decisions by listing the arguments for and against and seeing which list was longer – the numerate reader will notice that Table 4 is longer than Table 3). All governments intervene and many of the reasons, such as raising revenue for law and order or defence, are virtually inescapable. How should it intervene? One question which arises immediately for those who wish to discuss or comment on policy is therefore that of the best, or optimal, way to intervene given certain objectives, concerned notably with efficiency and equity, and constraints on action. But this is not the whole or even necessarily the major part of the question. We have to be concerned with what will work administratively and with the political economy of any action and its environment. The term 'political economy' can be somewhat nebulous but here we mean how any suggested policy is likely to be received, manipulated, obstructed or supported by various different groups. The predictive, or positive, requirements of the analyses of optimality and of political economy, i.e. the consequences of actions for different sections of the population, are clearly very close. We return briefly to the question of policy design in Section IV.

We turn to a brief discussion of Table 3. Some of the points, for example (iii)–(viii), may pose problems for the establishment or maintenance of equilibrium and most of them can prevent efficiency of equilibrium if one is established. The points should be familiar or self-explanatory, except possibly (iv) and (ix). On (iv) we can point to the problems of moral hazard and adverse selection in insurance markets or to bankruptcy and the possibility of default in capital and future markets. Some evidence that the problems are real for developing countries is discussed in Section V. On (ix) we simply recognise that any tax which is not lump-sum generates inefficiency – desirable lump-sum taxes (e.g. those related to ability to pay) cease to be lump-sum when their basis is recognised. For example if income is the basis then taxation is not lump-sum as the tax payment is affected by work input with corresponding disincentives to work. Hence where redistribution is a concern taxation implies inefficiency and the standard efficiency theorems cannot provide justification for the unfettered competitive market.

A typical response to a market failure is the proposal of a tax or bargaining mechanism to deal with it. One must be wary, however, since if several failures occur simultaneously it can be misleading to analyse them one by one. A prominent and important example of a market failure concerns externalities. Standard solutions, in principle, include Pigovian taxes/subsidies, where, for example, a polluter is taxed according to the marginal damage caused, and the allocation of rights together with bargaining, à la Coase, where an individual provides compensation if he damages another. Such 'solutions' it can be argued operate rather badly in developing countries. Thus the reaction to market failure is often the suggestion of state intervention.

This leads us to consider the problems described in Table 4. Again this table should be largely self-explanatory except possibly for items (viii) and (ix). The problem of incentive compatibility is important for both planning and the market and indeed can be regarded as the central question in linking the two. It underlies problem (ix) in Table 3 as well as (viii) in Table 4. A planning proposal or tax that is inconsistent or incompatible with opportunities and incentives open to individuals (in markets or otherwise) will be frustrated (see, for example, Dasgupta, 1980, for a simple introduction to these issues which have been prominent in formal economic theory for at least 20 years). Rent-seeking and directly unproductive activities ((ix) in Table 4) refer to the actions of individuals to lobby, bribe or threaten in favour of their receipt of state generated privileges. Such activities are difficult to quantify but they are of substantial importance.

In considering Tables 3 and 4 one has to look carefully at the economy and political system under consideration. Not all political systems are corrupt and not all governments are incompetent; competent governments may or may not be manipulated by special interest groups. Indeed as we saw at the end of Section II, Reynolds' (1983) review of comparative growth concluded that differences amongst governments in these respects was a key element in explaining comparative growth rates. Similarly markets and entrepreneurship appear to function rather better in some environments, situations and cultures than others whether or not governments are prepared to let them flourish. Thus we should be wary of taking a universal view on the balance of considerations embodied in Tables 3 and 4.

We now comment briefly on the historical literature on markets and government in relation to these ideas. Writers on development have ranged dramatically in their views of market failures and correspondingly in their views on government policy. On traditional rural agriculture, for example, we have Schultz (1964) at one end of a spectrum, who argued that traditional agriculture is efficient given the existing constraints on knowledge and assets and, at the other, Myrdal (1968) who, referring to agriculture, argued (p. 912) 'Few people calculate in terms of costs and returns, and if they do, their economic behaviour is not primarily determined by such calculations.' He concluded that direct government actions were necessary and that attempts to operate through markets would not work. The evidence used by both Schultz and Myrdal is highly debatable (see Section IV) and much of Myrdal's logic is dubious as is evidenced both by the quote (the 'as if' interpretation of maximisation is overlooked) and the conclusion, which does not follow from the observation even if the former were acceptable.

The experience of the Second World War in the United Kingdom is emphasised by Little (1982) as being particularly influential in shaping the early debates on planning. There were shared goals and a clear requirement to act quickly and precisely. The changes needed in the allocation of resources, particularly labour, were enormous and great reductions in consumption were required. It was argued that these adjustments could not have been achieved quickly enough using the price and wage mechanisms. The problems identified appear to be (v), (vi) and (vii) of Table 3, (see Weitzman, 1977, for an interesting theoretical discussion of the circumstances under which rationing might be preferred to the price mechanism). Little classifies the view that responses are too slow or too small to make the price system work well as *structuralist*. This view has been most closely associated with Latin American writers (see e.g. Olivera, 1964, and, amongst others, Balogh, 1961).

The early discussion was also much influenced by three theoretical arguments proposed by Rosenstein-Rodan, Scitovsky and Hirschman, of which the most interesting, in my judgement, was that of Rosenstein-Rodan. Rosenstein-Rodan's (1943) arguments for a 'big push' (he was thinking particularly of South and Southeast Europe) seem to be a combination of Keynesian notions of effective demand and Smithian ideas of the size of the market. He assumed unemployed labour and argued that a single shoe factory may not be profitable because at current incomes demand for its output would be insufficient. But if many investments for consumer goods took place simultaneously they could all be profitable, since the income increase could be sufficient to provide a large enough market for all the outputs. He appears, implicitly, to have assumed a closed economy in that if international trade is possible the argument has much less force since there is a very large world market for shoes. The theory was not very clearly articulated but its strong Keynesian element would point to problems (iv) and (v) in Table 3 and the emphasis on the size of the market would indicate increasing returns (problem (iii)). In this last respect Rosenstein-Rodan built on the work of Young (1928). Some further development of the approach was offered by Nurkse (1953), but successful formalisation of these ideas was limited for many years. However, recently the work of Basu (1984) and an important pair of papers by Murphy *et al.* (1988*a*, *b*) has shown how they can be made rigorous and be developed. Murphy *et al.* (1988*a*) show in particular the importance of income distribution and the size of population in generating demand sufficiently large to make manufacturing viable. In (1988*b*) they show how a big push can move an imperfectly competitive economy with multiple equilibria from a 'bad' one to a 'better' one. Shared infrastructure, as well as the creation of demand, can also generate benefits which flow from one investing firm to another.

Scitovsky (1954) distinguished between technological externalities (this is the standard, and our, use of the term) and 'pecuniary' externalities. By the latter he meant, for example, that an investment by one firm could bring down the price of an input to another firm so making an investment profitable for the second firm (notice that international trade is again ignored) thus creating additional demand. The use of the term 'pecuniary externality' seems, however, to be a recipe for confusion since the major part of relationships between agents in market economies operates through prices. It would be better avoided. One can think of the problem as agents being unable to forecast future equilibrium prices (problems (iv)–(vii) could be involved here). Scitovsky took this as an argument for co-ordinated investment planning. Rosenstein-Rodan and Scitovsky were seen as proponents of *balanced growth*, i.e. investments taking place on many fronts simultaneously.

Hirschman's (1958) analysis was similar to Scitovsky's in his concern with the inter-relation of investment decisions. He argued that the great shortage in developing countries was entrepreneurial decision-making. The government should attempt to stimulate decisions and the best way to do this was to make demands for inputs explicit by making an investment which required inputs which could be, but were not yet, locally made. He called this a *backward linkage*. Thus the government should deliberately create imbalances to stimulate investment. This strategy was called *unbalanced growth*. The argument is somewhat mysterious and seems to have defied effective formalisation or serious empirical analysis but seems nevertheless to have been influential or at least prominent. The arguments are close to Scitovsky's (again problems (iv)–(vii) appear to be involved) but the conclusions are very different.

One could continue the list much further. For example, Myint (1985) emphasised the lack of markets in backward sectors (problem (iv)). Chenery (1958) pointed to the combination of increasing returns, (iii), and the inability to forecast, (vii), as requiring the co-ordination of investment decisions. Griffin (1979) stressed monopolistic practices, (i), in credit markets and so on. Leibenstein (1978) developed the concept of X-inefficiency as being inside the production possibility frontier, i.e. essentially non-maximising behaviour (viii). For further references the reader may consult Arndt (1985, 1988) and the excellent discussion in Little (1982, ch. 3).

Many of the problems of state intervention have long been recognised. Distinguished members of my own institution, the London School of Economics, von Hayek (1967, 1986) and Bauer (1971, 1984), in particular, have been consistent, clear, and insistent in their emphasis on its vicissitudes (as listed, for example, in Table 4). The investigation of many of these problems is not amenable to the same kind of theorising as that of the problems of market failure. There has, however, been a literature on the 'political economy' of state intervention with von Hayek and Bauer as leading figures.

A productive development has been the attempt to model some of the processes described in the 'political economy' of government action. Buchanan has been a notable, early and consistent contributor (see Buchanan, 1986, for a review and references) using the idea of 'public choice' as being determined by the interaction of different interest groups. A related theme has been the notion of 'directly unproductive' or 'rent-seeking' activities (see Rowley *et al.* 1988). This has come to be seen as an important part of a literature on political economy which has a strong bent against government intervention. Given the subjects of the discussion 'solid' data for formal testing of hypotheses are not easily acquired, although telling examples can be offered. An area where systematic evidence of avoidance of state controls is becoming increasingly available concerns informal labour markets (see Mazumdar, 1987; Peattie, 1987; Cole and Sanders, 1985). Voluntary labour market movements were often assumed to be from the informal to the formal sectors. However Fields (1988) presents evidence of significant movements in the opposite direction.

The balance of opinion in the 1940s and 1950s appears to have been in favour of substantial state intervention, particularly in the investment process. The leading example for the discussion was India (China was little discussed as information was very scarce and Western economists were not involved). Disenchantment with planning increased from the early 1960s through the 1970s and 1980s. This formed a central part of what Little (1982) describes as the 'neoclassical resurgence'. This shift of the balance of views was based on the apparently heavy hand of planning in countries such as India and the rapid advance of countries which, it was argued, followed more laissez-faire policies. The outstanding growth performance of the so-called 'four dragons', South Korea, Taiwan, Hong Kong and Singapore was particularly influential. It was argued that the achievements of countries which both encouraged response to prices and which made an effort to 'get prices right' belied the arguments of the structuralists who had emphasised the sluggishness of economic reactions and the ineffectiveness of a decentralised price system. The stultifying effect of large-scale planning was, it was suggested, exemplified by India. Particularly prominent in the early days of the neoclassical resurgence in the 1960s was the work of Little *et al.* (1970). Concern with the deficiencies of planning generally came with a criticism of the price distortions, associated particularly with protectionist and import substitution policies, which had usually accompanied planning. The literature on effective protection, domestic resource cost and shadow prices was important here, for example, Balassa (1971), Bruno (1972), Corden (1971), Dasgupta *et al.* (1972), Krueger (1972), Little and Mirrlees (1974).

The association between planning and protection was strong for India, for example, but protection-cum-import substitution on the one hand and planning on the other are distinct both in logic and often historical example, and one should not reject or approve of them both in the same breath. The two important examples of South Korea and Brazil illustrate the point. South Korea has grown quickly with an outward orientation but with substantial government intervention in the investment process (Jacobs, 1985; Wade, 1985; Bahl *et al.* 1986; Kim and Yun, 1988), and following a period of import substitution. Brazil has also grown quickly (whilst not showing the extraordinary rapidity of South Korea) with a strong emphasis on import substitution through protection but much less planning (Taylor, 1980; Leff, 1982). The hugely important case of China is not easy to place in these stories since it too has shown rapid growth through a number of different planning regimes. But it has never been an example of a free-trading country with minimalist government (see Riskin, 1987; Perkins, 1988).

The apparent swing in the profession from the whole-hearted espousal of extensive government intervention to its rubbishing seems to be an example of unbalanced intellectual growth, although perhaps development economics is no more subject to this kind of fluctuation than other parts of the subject. There are problems and virtues of both state intervention and the free market. The problem should not be viewed as one of a simple choice. There is no doubt, however, that whether one sees a very large or very small role for the market depends on how one judges the seriousness of the problems with markets and planning which we have been describing. In my judgement the problems of the market are particularly severe (relative to those of state intervention) in the areas of health, infrastructure (roads, communications, power, water and so on), education, and social security. Those of planning appear most strongly when the government gets heavily involved in production activities outside the infrastructure. Even in those areas where one might argue the balance of the argument is clear, however, we still have crucial questions of pricing, regulation and taxation. Thus the problem is the design of workable and incentive-compatible policies which take account of the political processes of the country at hand. Unfortunately space forbids us from pursuing these basic and fascinating questions much further although we return briefly to some aspects in Section V.

III. 2. *The Process of Growth and Change*

The study of the process of economic growth is clearly central to the economics of development. This requires from theory an examination of simple economic dynamics and from empirical analysis a study of the economic history of single countries over time and the comparison of cross-sections of countries at different stages of development. We begin with the theory. We focus in this sub-section on highly aggregated models. Some more disaggregated approaches will appear in Sections IV and V.

Simple growth theory still forms a part of many postgraduate options in the economics of development, although it is remarkable that this basic element of the grammar of economic dynamics has gone missing from the more central courses in economics. It was Harrod (1939) who made the first important contribution to aggregate growth theory and the Harrod–Domar equation is the natural point of departure. We take a closed economy. Equilibrium in the output market requires (planned) investment to be equal to (planned) saving so that we have

$$I = sY, \tag{1}$$

where I is investment, Y income and s the savings rate. I is equal to $\dot{K}$ (or dK/dt) where K is the capital stock, so that (1) gives us, on dividing by K, the Harrod–Domar equation

$$g = s/v, \tag{2}$$

where $g \equiv \dot{K}/K$, the growth rate of the capital stock and v is K/Y the capital–output ratio. *Ex post* one can treat (1) as an identity so that (2) will generally describe the growth of capital, although Harrod was particularly concerned with the *ex ante* or equilibrium analysis. If v is constant then output also grows at g. The Harrod–Domar analysis leads to a concentration on savings rates and capital–output ratios as determinants of the growth rate and these are still amongst the first aspects that are examined in any proposed or actual growth path (see, for example, the World Bank's 1985 report on China's development options, World Bank, 1985). The experience of a number of developing countries, particularly India, has been of a substantial increase in s but only a very small increase in g. It follows that v has risen and this can lead one to look for reasons as to how and why this increase in v may have occurred.

These aggregate growth models were extended by many authors in the 1950s and 1960s with Solow's articles of 1956 and 1957 playing a leading role in the way in which economists have seen the questions of growth. The former used an aggregate production function and demonstrated that in this model the long-run growth rate, s/v, will come into equality with the natural growth rate of the labour force n by adjustment of the capital–output ratio v. Increasing the savings rate will increase the growth rate in the short run, but not in the long run, since v rises to bring it back to n. A higher s will lead to a higher long-run output per head (where we ignore problems of 'over-saving' connected with s being permanently above the 'golden-rule' level).

In these models long-run growth of output per head is possible only if there is technical progress which, if it is labour-augmenting (i.e. acts on output in an analogous manner to an expansion of labour input) at rate a, allows long-run growth with $s/v = a+n$ and output per head growing at rate a. Solow's 1957 paper showed how technical progress could be decomposed into contributions from factors and from the growth of total factor productivity. Where for example $Y = F(K, L, t)$, we have, on differentiating with respect to t,

$$\dot{Y}/Y = \alpha \dot{K}/K + \beta \dot{L}/L + F_t/Y, \tag{3}$$

where $\alpha = KF_K/Y$ and $\beta = LF_L/Y$, the competitive shares of capital and labour respectively (subscripts here denote partial derivatives). The first two terms give the 'contribution' to output growth of higher factor inputs and the last term, or residual, the growth in 'total factor productivity'. This equation gave rise to a number of studies in growth accounting where technical progress and capital accumulation in different countries where compared (an early and major exponent was Denison, 1967). Such calculations should not be taken too literally since the model and the competitive factor pricing assumptions are generally unbelievable at this level of aggregation but, as we shall see below, they can be suggestive and are a useful method for the assembly of data.

These models have been elaborated in many ways and have provided a basic organising framework for thinking about growth processes. Many authors have, however, shared an unease about the description of accumulation and technical progress underlying the aggregate production function. Its immediate implications include that technical progress is divorced from capital accumulation, higher savings do not increase the long-run growth rate and there is no learning. Salter (1960) first proposed a partial response to the first of these issues by developing vintage models where the state of the art is embodied in capital equipment at the time of investment. This introduces the important ideas of economic obsolescence but still leaves the progress of the state of the art as exogenous.

Arrow (1962) provided a genuinely seminal piece where he showed the economic implications of learning by doing. In a vintage model with fixed coefficients the productivity of labour working on new machines is related to G the total of past investment as G^{μ} (i.e. a 1% increase in total past investment implies a μ% increase in labour productivity on new machines). His model can produce steady-state growth with no exogenous technical progress at the rate $n/(1-\mu)$. This is rather similar to the rate of steady growth in an ordinary neoclassical model with increasing returns (consider $Y = AK^{\alpha} L^{\beta}$ with $\alpha+\beta > 1$

and $\dot{Y}/Y = \dot{K}/K = g$ and we find $g = \beta n/(1-\alpha) > n$). A crucial difference, however, is that Arrow's model permits a competitive equilibrium (since the technical progress which acts like increasing returns arises as an externality) whereas the ordinary neoclassical model with increasing returns does not.

This particular feature, where the benefits of investment in terms of technical progress act like an externality has characterised the recent upsurge of interest in growth and technical progress associated with Romer (1986), Lucas (1988) and Scott (1989). Romer (1986) considers a model where investment by a firm is only in the stock of knowledge but where firms can gain some benefit from the knowledge acquired through the investment of others. There are increasing returns from the overall stock of knowledge via this externality but not from the point of view of an individual firm. This type of model has been assembled and contrasted with Solow-type models in Lucas (1988). Romer and Lucas share a curious predilection for viewing aggregate saving in the economy as arising from a single consumer (with an infinite horizon) optimising his or her intertemporal consumption plan. I must plead guilty, Stern (1972), to developing optimal growth models myself but this was in a planning context whereas Romer and Lucas in their use of cross-country evidence appear to suggest that it is a useful way to model actual aggregate savings. Given the disparate nature of the economies of developing countries (including strong differences between sectors and fragmented capital markets) this representation of savings being determined as if by a single maximiser is hard to take seriously (and it does not have the virtue of simplicity). Nevertheless the focus on endogenous growth in productivity is most valuable and the work constitutes an important advance. Further in subsequent papers (e.g. 1987, 1988) Romer has investigated models where firms do capture privately the benefits of technological advance and show increasing returns. Equilibrium can no longer be perfectly competitive. Scott (1989) in a very substantial piece of work provides a careful review of growth theory and evidence and proposes a model where undertaking investment itself creates and reveals further opportunities.

Some insights, such as externalities of knowledge and experience, generating a social rate of return higher than the private were available from earlier work (e.g. Arrow, 1962). And the models generally retain the competitive assumption in contrast to Schumpeter's emphasis on monopoly profit as the key to major innovatory advance. However, the increased emphasis on the process of learning and on human capital (see also Uzawa, 1965) and the rejection of the mysterious and exogenous 'residual' technical progress are to be wholly welcomed.

At the same time as the aggregate models were being developed in the mid-1950s Lewis set out his classic model of dualistic development. This was perhaps the single most influential article in the history of the economics of development and raised a number of crucial issues in a clear and systematic way. Many of these have been central to subsequent discussion and they include (*a*) the determinants of saving and its influence on growth (*b*) the appropriate choice of capital intensity in investment (*c*) the inter-relationships between growth and income distribution in the process of change and (*d*) the importance of labour allocation in economic development. He pioneered the view of development as a transformation from traditional forms of production and economic organisation to an advanced capitalist economy. He was concerned with the classical questions of the 18th- and 19th-century economists – the analytical description of the processes of distribution, accumulation and growth. He also made classical assumptions, particularly (i) an unlimited supply of labour at a fixed wage, (ii) accumulation of fixed capital only in the advanced sector, (iii) savings only out of profits.

In its simplest form with one good (or fixed prices) and no technical progress the factor proportions in the advanced sector are determined by the profit-maximising hiring of labour at a given wage – the advanced sector capital–output ratio is determined by this hiring choice. The given savings rate s_p out of profits leads to aggregate savings and investment at $s_p P$, where P is profits. Then output, capital and labour in the advanced sector all grow at a rate of $s_p P/K$, so that the rate of growth is $s_p r$ where r is the rate of profit. With no technical progress, profit maximisation and a constant returns production function of capital and labour in the advanced sector, a fixed w fixes r. The process of growth may be seen as simply an absorption of labour by the advanced sector at a constant proportional rate with the savings rate for the whole economy increasing over time, as the share of profits rises along with the increasing share of the advanced sector in total income (and constant profit share in the advanced sector). The story needs eventual modification as the labour pool from the traditional sector runs out.

In this way Lewis answered his question (1954, p. 155).

> The central problem in the theory of economic development is to understand the process by which a community which was previously saving and investing 4 or 5 per cent of its national income or less, converts itself to an economy where voluntary saving is running at about 12 to 15 per cent of national income or more. This is the central problem because the central fact of economic development is rapid capital accumulation (including knowledge and skills with capital). We cannot explain any 'industrial' revolution (as the economic historians pretend to do) until we can explain why saving increased relatively to national income.

The model provides simple basic prototypes for a number of important theories, including those of migration (see Section V) and choice of technique (Section IV), and carries important implications for economic inequality, on which we shall comment below. It was very fruitful and Lewis put it to use in his paper to comment on a number of questions. For example, the fixity of the wage as the given supply price of labour implies that workers (on e.g. sugar plantations) do not get any gain from technical progress whereas in a tighter labour market the price of labour would be bid up.

The model came under brief attack by Jorgensen (1961) who produced an alternative neoclassical model with profit maximisation in both sectors and a competitive labour market. However Marglin (1966) showed that some of the contrasting results which Jorgensen claimed for his model and which, he argued, better fitted historical data for Japan were a consequence of his use of the Cobb–Douglas production function and Dixit (1973) showed that others were an artefact of the comparison between long-run results in the Jorgenson model with short-run results in the Lewis model. The Lewis model justifiably retains its influential place in the development literature.

As with all models, however, it is useful for some problems and issues but misleading or unhelpful for others. This applies particularly in this case to its treatment of the traditional sector. Lewis did not identify the traditional sector solely with agriculture (capitalist agriculture was included in the advanced sector) but peasant agriculture was obviously considered a dominant element in the traditional sector and backward. This was an assumption shared by a number of classical writers (for example, Marx) and many of the contemporary writers of the 1950s. Agriculture should not be seen as static and its change has been a major factor in the long-run processes of economic development – for interesting discussions which shift the focus back to agriculture see Mellor (1976) and Lipton (1977).

We comment briefly now on three empirical aspects of the process of growth. The first concerns agriculture, the second the measurement of technical progress and the third inequality. The late 1960s and early 1970s saw a particularly sharp change in agricultural conditions in some parts of the world with the so-called Green Revolution. As Lipton and Longhurst (1989) show, the influence of the Green Revolution is highly regionalised, with some areas, particularly Africa, hardly touched. It is heavily concentrated on wheat and rice.

This 'revolution' involved an intensification of irrigation, increased use of chemical fertilisers and improved varieties of seed which showed greater responsiveness to water and fertilisers. Whilst agriculture is rarely static it is the Green Revolution which has been the agricultural change which has been most prominent in discussions of development economics. A valuable historical perspective on the process of agricultural change has, however, been provided by Boserup (1965) and (1981) who offers an interesting thesis of agricultural change as a response to population growth with, for example, population pressure bringing a switch from very land intensive techniques such as hunting and gathering to those of shifting cultivation and then of fixed cultivation. Viewed in this light we can see the intensification of irrigation, perhaps the most important element of the Green Revolution, as part of a longer-term trend in the intensification of agriculture. The Boserup story is supported by Lal's (1988) account of Indian economic history.

The experience of the Green Revolution has been the subject of lively controversy and has provided many lessons both on the way in which rural economies may function and also on government policy. There is no doubt that the responses of individual farmers to the new opportunities was far from sluggish and that governments played a crucial role in assisting in the provision of these new opportunities. It is a clear example of the potential effectiveness of the joint operation of public policy and private response. The evidence suggests that, provided appropriate rural institutions exist (Prahladachar,

1983), neither tenure nor farm size has been an important source of differential rates of growth of agricultural productivity in the medium-term, (see, for example, Ruttan, 1977, and Glaeser, 1987), although, some have argued, in the early days of the Green Revolution it was the larger farmers who reacted first (see, for example, Griffin, 1979, or Pearse, 1980). The technical progress is land-augmenting (for example, increased irrigation may facilitate double cropping) and as land is often very unequally distributed one might therefore expect to see a worsening of the income distribution. There is some evidence that this may have occurred (again, see Ruttan, 1977 and Glaeser, 1987). Further as Lipton and Longhurst (1989) argue, the rural poor are mainly to be found amongst the landless and for them it is the price at which they can sell their labour which matters and on which the Green Revolution may have had only a small effect. The poorest may therefore be left behind in this form of agricultural growth.

The source of productivity change at the aggregate level has been the subject of detailed empirical analysis following the growth accounting techniques originated by Solow (1957) and described above. A useful summary of this and other empirical research on the process of development is provided in Chenery (1983). For the period 1960–73 most developed countries show more than half the growth rate as explained by growth in total factor productivity (TFP). However, for middle-income developing countries the contribution of TFP was less than a quarter of the growth rate. The outliers in this study, with growth rates averaging over 10%, were Japan, Israel, Spain, Hong Kong, Taiwan and South Korea with roughly half of the growth associated with increased TFP and half with greater factor inputs.

These studies have been extended (see Robinson, 1971 and Feder, 1982) to cross-country regressions of growth rates in output on growth rates of factor inputs where further explanatory variables are included intending to capture 'structural change' or 'disequilibrium' phenomena (a literal interpretation of the simple Solow calculations requires equilibrium in output and factor markets). When these changes are made fits are substantially improved and with the attribution of some growth to the sectoral reallocation of factors (20–30% for developing countries) considerably less growth is attributed to capital accumulation (note that it is presumably the reallocation of labour out of agriculture that is playing a key role since it is not obvious that capital productivity is less high in agriculture than elsewhere). The structural variables contributed little to the explanation of growth in advanced countries.

Whilst these results can only be suggestive, for the reasons given, they do seem to indicate that in the process of growth of less advanced countries, structural change and capital accumulation are rather more important than for more advanced countries. In this sense the simple Lewis model may not be too misleading as a broad-brush initial picture.

Our last empirical example on the overall process of growth concerns its relationship with inequality. The debate was started by Kuznets (1955) who, measuring inequality by shares of various quintiles, and comparing India, Ceylon, Puerto Rico, United Kingdom and the United States found that inequality was greater in the poorer countries. He confirmed the finding in a 1963 study with a larger sample of countries and postulated a relationship between inequality and development (as measured by *per capita* GDP) as an inverted U, i.e. inequality increases in the early stages of development but then later falls. The idea, again stimulated by dualistic notions, is that a poor society dominated by a traditional sector will be fairly equal as will a society dominated by a modern sector. In the transition however the between-group inequality will initially grow (as people become involved in the richer sector) and later decline. Superimposed on this between-group process, one could imagine increasing within-group inequality if the growing sector has more unequal distribution than the declining one.

Kuznets' inverted U hypothesis appeared to be given some support by Adelman and Morris (1973), who studied a sample of 43 countries in the late 1960s and early 1970s, Paukert (1973) with a sample of 56 countries and Chenery and Syrquin (1975), Ahluwalia (1974, 1976*a*, *b*) and Lydall (1979). Lecaillon *et al.* (1984) surveyed the existing literature and argued that the Kuznets' hypothesis is supported by the behaviour of the shares of the top 5% (highest in middle-income countries) but not for other aspects of the distribution (the share of the bottom 20% appears generally to be around 5–6% for most income groups of countries). There are major problems however, if the argument rides on the share of the top 5% since it is often here that the data are at their worst and it would not fit well with the dualistic theoretical tale, which is not predominantly about the richest 5%.

The most recent substantial contribution is a careful study by Anand and Kanbur (1989*a*, *b*) who throw considerable doubt on the empirical status of the inverted U. They look closely at two issues. The first concerns the measure of inequality and its functional relationship with 'explanatory' variables and the second the choice of data set. They show that the results are very sensitive to these two aspects and that one can get U relationships, inverted U relationships or very little relationship at all by making different choices. The selection of data set is particularly important as many of the earlier studies mixed data sets some of which had income defined on an individual basis, some on a household basis, some for urban areas only, some based only on earnings, and so on. When data sets and variables were defined in a consistent manner the inverted U relationship for their sample disappeared. In common with a number of earlier writers (particularly Ahluwalia) they used the cross-country sample assembled by Jain (1975). Given the sensitivity exposed by the Anand–Kanbur study and that longitudinal studies, in so far as they have been possible, have not shown any general relationship between inequality and development, we must conclude that at this stage the evidence in favour of the inverted U hypothesis (or any other general relationship between inequality and development) is not convincing.

We have seen that a central role in the explanation of growth has been allocated in various models to accumulation, technical change, human capital and population. It is interesting that the most prominent economic models have not brought trade to the centre stage. Indeed some (e.g. Kravis, 1970) have suggested directly that trade is the handmaiden (or accompaniment) to growth rather than the 'engine' which drives it.

III.3. *Trade and Industrialisation*

The theory of comparative advantage, described clearly by Ricardo in 1817, has been a fundamental underpinning of economists' arguments for the gains from trade for nearly 200 years. As a normative theory it argues that, in the absence of trade, there will be some goods whose opportunity costs on world markets will be lower than those from obtaining them at home, and that the country should therefore import such goods. Correspondingly it should export those goods in which it has a comparative advantage. This crucial idea underlies, and one could argue has dominated, much of the argument about the role of trade in development strategies. It is so simple, robust and basic that it has, and will, continue as one of the most important and enduring insights of economics.

Our discussion of trade policies will be divided between this sub-section and the next. Here we focus on the trade strategy for a particular country – its theoretical foundation, the validity of empirical assumptions and the historical experience. In the next sub-section we examine trade as one aspect of the relationship between richer and poorer countries. A major part of this section examines the arguments concerning whether a country should adopt inward or outward looking policies, following the debate from the 1950s to the present. We begin, however, by drawing attention to the substantial advances in the theory of international trade which have radically altered the standard story which essentially saw international trade as a particular example of the ordinary theory of competitive general equilibrium (see Dixit and Norman, 1980 for an elegant presentation).

The recent advances have concerned the increasing recognition of the role of intra-industry trade, increasing returns to scale and monopolistic competition (e.g. Helpman and Krugman, 1985; Krugman, 1986) on the one hand and uncertainty and insurance on the other (see below). The traditional arguments associated with the benefits of unfettered trade become less clear as issues of strategic behaviour (absent in competitive models) become central. Pro-trade arguments have now shifted towards trade as allowing the benefits of increasing returns. We find that calculations of the gains from trade can appear much larger (see, for example, Harris and Case, 1984), than they did from more traditional models.

Another line of theoretical argument which may appear to cloud the case for free trade concerns uncertainty. If one sector of the economy is subject to particular risk then involvement in that activity may be overly discouraged unless it is protected. Newbery and Stiglitz (1984) construct an example where autarky is Pareto superior to free trade and Eaton and Grossman (1985) provide numerical simulations in a more general model which suggest that some protection is usually optimal. Dixit in a series of papers (1987, 1989*a*, *b*) has complained that this particular comparison is unwarrantedly tilted in favour of government intervention and against the market by the exclusion of insurance markets (on the grounds of the problems of adverse selection or moral hazard). If insurance markets are incorporated, but where explicit account is taken of the two problems, he shows that a free-trade market equilibrium is (informationally constrained) Pareto efficient.

The advance of theory has not overthrown the case for free trade but it has now become a matter of balanced judgement based on an understanding of the different types of theoretical arguments, historical experience and political circumstances rather than an overwhelming case founded on the clear message of comparative advantage. As Krugman (1987) puts it: 'Its status has shifted from optimum to reasonable rule of thumb. There is still a case for free trade as a good policy, and as a useful target in the practical world of politics, but it can never again be asserted as the policy that economic theory tells us is always right.' For further discussion see Bliss (1985, 1987), Dixit (1983), Krugman (1986) and Srinivasan (1987*a*).

The 1950s saw a great emphasis on import substitution as a means to industrialisation and growth. This was strongly influenced by the thesis of Singer and Prebisch (Singer, 1950; United Nations, 1949) who argued that the terms of trade facing developing countries for their traditional exports were deteriorating (i.e. the world prices of their exports – primary commodities – were declining relative to those for their imports-manufactures) so that as time progressed they would have to export more and more primary products to buy a given quantity of manufactures. Thus, it was suggested it was necessary both to industrialise and to control the increasingly expensive imports. They claimed that an attempt to sell more primary products abroad by devaluing and lowering their price would be unsuccessful because foreign elasticities of demand were low. Foreign exchange for imports could not be easily controlled using prices, it was suggested, because domestic demands were inflexible. This, in brief, was their case for an import substitution policy with physical controls on imports. The controls would allow local industries to learn to establish themselves at a competitive scale (the infant industry argument) without foreign competition and would also conserve foreign exchange. The argument was particularly influential in Latin America where Prebisch was working in the Economic Commission for Latin America (ECLA) and is clearly of the type Little (1982) labels as 'structuralist' with its emphasis on weak price responses requiring direct controls of imports. The Singer–Prebisch ideas led to a literature on North–South modelling which variously includes the possibility of differences across countries in endowments, market structure (e.g. with a Lewis labour market in developing countries) and technology – see, for example, McIntosh (1986) for a discussion and some references.

Nurkse (1961) based his case for balanced growth in large part on his view that the trade engine of growth, which he saw as a 'basic inducement' to 19th-century growth, was not available to developing countries. He argued that the prospects for primary exports from developing countries were poor (low income elasticities of demand, increasing use of synthetics and protection of markets by developed countries) as well as those for the export of manufactures (problems of increasing returns, learning and again protection). Thus he suggested a balanced programme of 'linked progress' in agriculture and manufacturing. Kravis (1970) looked carefully at the evidence for both the 19th century and for the 1950s and 1960s for developing countries and raised considerable doubts about the Nurkse story both concerning the role of trade in 19th-century growth and the development of exports from developing countries.

There are a number of questions one should ask directly about the recommendation for import substitution behind protective barriers.

(i) Is it true that the long-run trend of the terms of trade was against the developing countries? Spraos (1980) found that from 1900–70 there was no evidence of a trend. More recently it has been argued (see ODI, 1988; Sapsford, 1985) that the period 1870–1930 saw a long-period decline, followed by a sharp rise around the Second World War and then a substantial decline over the last 30 years (all this excludes oil). A detailed study has been provided by Grilli and Yang (1988) and we reproduce two graphs (see Fig. 1) from that study, one for the relative price of food and one for non-food agricultural commodities. It can be seen that much depends on the choice of period in both cases. Evidence of a long-term downward trend would appear to be stronger for the non-food agricultural commodities, particularly since the 1950s. The last 15 years have also seen a major decline in food prices.

(ii) Is it true that the responsiveness of imports and exports to relative price changes are weak? On the export side one should distinguish between a particular country and developing countries as a group. A recent study of aggregate demand (price and income) and supply elasticities has been provided by Bond (1987), who also provides a survey of other estimates. The conclusions are that 'income elasticities for developing countries' commodity exports fall in the range of 0·3–3·5. A further conclusion is that the demand for agricultural products is income inelastic... A further broad conclusion is that the demand for commodity exports is not very sensitive to short-run price changes' (p. 221). Longer-run price elasticities were found to be higher. The basic tenets of the early writers (Prebisch *et al.*) do not receive clear-cut support but they are not completely without foundation. And it is striking that the rapid advances of the exports of many developing countries are more in manufactures than primary products (see next sub-section). For further evidence on price elasticities see Lipton (1987).

(iii) If it is true that local industries have to be encouraged before they can grow then are import controls the best way? Note that one can subsidise directly, and that import controls cannot help directly in the promotion of non-traded goods. Further they are generally inferior to tariffs because they do not provide direct revenue to the government. Tariffs themselves, since they raise prices for both producers and consumers, may be seen as a form of production subsidy on a good financed by a consumption tax on the same good. Is this an appropriate way to finance the production subsidy?

(iv) If an industry can survive only if it is subsidised or protected then is that industry worthwhile? The resources it uses may be employed more valuably elsewhere.

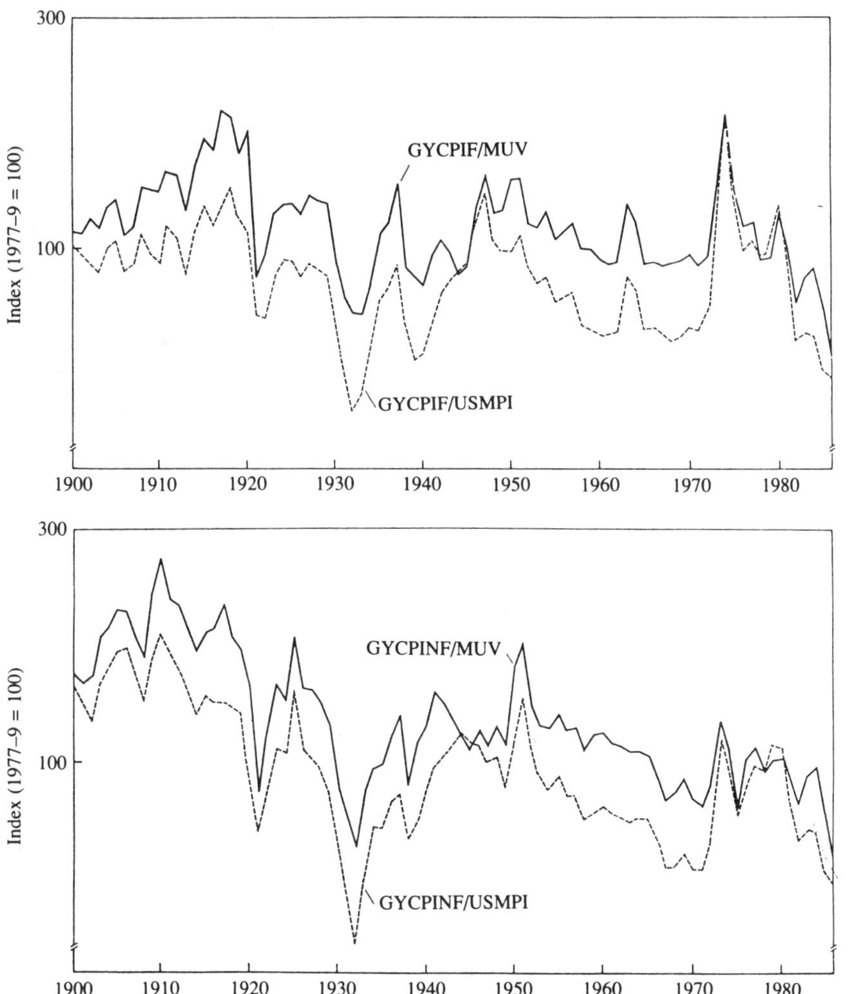

Fig. 1. Indexes of relative prices of (*a*) food commodities, 1900–86; (*b*) non-food agricultural commodities, 1900–86. *Key*: GYCPIF, Grilli–Yang Commodity Price Index for Food; MUV, Manufacturing Unit Values; USMPI, United States Manufacturing Price Index; GYCPINF, Grilli-Yang Commodity Price Index for Non-food. *Source*: Grilli and Yang (1988).

There were some economists putting these questions in the 1950s but they do not seem to have been taken very seriously – at least they do not seem to have dislodged the predominant view. As experience grew, however, the questions were put more forcefully and were investigated more carefully. In response to these investigations and to the experience of both the more planned and less trade oriented countries on the one hand, and the less planned and more trade oriented on the other, views started to change (although as remarked above in Section III.1 we must not equate more planning with less trade orientation).

The export pessimism of the 1950s was embodied in the so-called 'two-gap' model (see e.g. Chenery and Bruno, 1962). The two gaps are associated with demand and supply for foreign exchange (import demand may exceed exports plus net foreign transfers) and demand and supply for output (the excess of planned investment over domestic savings may exceed net foreign transfers). It was argued that investment might be restrained not simply by the availability of savings plus foreign aid but additionally, and perhaps more severely, by the availability of foreign exchange (necessary for crucial parts of the investment) since there was an upper limit on the foreign exchange available from exports.

The whole model and approach came under fire for its assumptions of fixed coefficients and fixed export potential and its ignoring of relative prices. If there is excess demand for foreign exchange, so the counter-argument can go, then the relative price of foreign exchange can change (and will if permitted to do so) and export potential and import demands will respond to prices. Similarly equilibrium in output and labour markets can be restored by the adjustment of the appropriate relative prices. The issue becomes an empirical one concerning the old questions of how well markets and individuals adjust to price incentives and the experience of some of the fast-growing export-oriented countries was cited as counter evidence to the 'structuralist' assumptions of poor price responses. For techniques for measuring the price distortions with import substitution (and planning) policies see Section IV.

By the mid 1980s the suggested positive influence of export promotion (or absence of discrimination against exports) on growth had become a dominant theme of the World Bank. Much of the *World Development Report* of 1987 was devoted to supporting this view. In that report, 41 developing countries were classified into four groups according to their trade orientation (strongly outward-oriented, moderately outward-oriented, moderately inward-oriented and strongly inward-oriented) and it was suggested that there was a strong positive relationship between outward orientation and the growth rate (over the period 1963–85). Unfortunately enthusiasm for the viewpoint being espoused led to a somewhat unquestioning view of evidence (to put it charitably) and if the only three strongly outward-oriented countries, South Korea, Singapore and Hong Kong, are removed from the sample the evidence is much less clear-cut. According to various indicators such as growth of real GDP *per capita*, savings, and inflation, the moderately outward- and moderately inward-oriented countries showed comparable performance (see World Bank 1987, fig. 5.2). A somewhat more careful assembly of the arguments for the superiority of more open trade policies is contained in Lal and Rajapatirana (1987) and it does seem, that, on average, the performance of the strongly inward-oriented countries is weaker than the rest. Even then there are important exceptions within this group, such as Pakistan where growth has been relatively rapid (see Section II).

As we noted in Section II, two recent, extensive and careful studies of comparative growth experience (Chenery *et al.*, 1986; Morris and Adelman, 1988) have cautioned that there is no single formula or gospel which for trade (as with planning) necessarily leads to, or is required for, rapid growth. We do seem able to say, however, that cutting oneself off from or greatly restricting trading opportunities is generally associated with slower growth.

III.4. *Relations between Rich and Poor Countries: Aid, Trade and Debt*

There are three related issues which have dominated discussion of relations between richer and poorer countries, aid, trade and debt. We consider them in turn. Flows from richer to poorer countries can take many forms and which of them should be described as aid is not clear-cut. Following the broad thrusts of three recent surveys Cassen (1986), Riddell (1987) and Mosley (1987), we shall concentrate on official development assistance, i.e. aid from governments and multilateral agencies and not military aid or aid from individuals and charities. In the 1960s aid occupied a central position in the economic literature and in political discussion, the Pearson (1969) report on aid was, for example, a major event at the time, but it appears to have moved to the wings of both stages. The quantity of aid has been small relative to the UN criterion of 0·7% of GNP for official aid. In 1986 of 18 OECD countries only France (0·82%), Netherlands (1·20%), Denmark (1·30%), Norway (1·43%) and Sweden (1·06%) (*World Development Report*, 1988) had proportions exceeding 0·6%. The largest proportions were achieved by Saudi Arabia (4·29%) and Kuwait (2·90%) although the largest donors were United States ($9,395m.), Japan ($5,761m.) and France ($4,876m.). During the period 1980–6 14 out of the 18 OECD countries (Table 21, *World Development Report*, 1988) have increased official development assistance as a percentage of GNP. In the longer period (1965–86) a similar pattern emerges with 14 out of 18 raising aid as a percentage of GNP. Note however that the percentages for the United States and for the United Kingdom have fallen over both periods.

For the low income countries as a group, aid receipts were 2·4% of GNP in 1986 (see Table 22, *World Development Report* 1988). For China and India they were only 0·6% whereas, on average, for other low-income countries they were 9%. For individual countries aid can be very important, over 20% of GNP for Mali, Somalia, Zambia and Mauritania, and above 10% for most African countries. For larger countries the percentage tends to be much smaller and amongst these only Bangladesh at 9·5% approaches 10% (China 0·4%, India 0·9%, Pakistan 2·9%). A figure of 10% or more of GNP is, however, of great importance to a developing country – compare for example with investment, government expenditure or imports each of which may typically be 20% or so of GNP.

The case for aid depends on both establishing or agreeing its moral basis on the assumption that it is beneficial, and also on showing that it is, or can be, beneficial according to appropriate criteria (see Stern, 1974). Riddell (1987) has provided a helpful review of the moral basis of aid. After discussing the contributions of modern theorists of ethics, notably Nozick (1974) and Rawls (1973), he (Riddell, p. 42) follows Miller (1979) in pointing to three strands of justice 'to each according to his rights, to each according to his deserts and to each according to his needs'. We are not forced to regard any of these three strands as universally dominant and, indeed, an attempt to found a theory of justice on one of them alone, he suggests, will fail. Riddell (1987, p. 42) concludes 'The moral obligation to provide aid is based on the obligation to help or the obligation to correct previous injustices.'

In the 1960s and 1970s there was much discussion of whether aid should be bilateral or multilateral, tied or untied to purchases from donor countries, what conditionalities in terms of policies or projects should be attached and so on (Bhagwati, 1970, Clifford, 1966, Singer, 1965, Seers and Streeten, 1972). Recently such discussion of tying has been less vigorous. Tied aid remains common, although the proportion which is untied appears to have risen – the development assistance committee (DAC) of the OECD records the average of total (OECD) overseas development assistance (ODA) classified as *untied* for 1973 being 34%, while for 1982–3 it was 56% (see Cassen, 1986, p. 286). However, conditionalities on policies to be pursued by recipients are increasingly popular amongst both multilateral and national agencies. Governments such as the United Kingdom's appear to be linking their own aid to the conditionalities applied by the World Bank in their packages which often involve tight control of public expenditure and liberalisation of trade policies.

As we have argued, a crucial and central question is whether aid is effective or beneficial. This raises considerable empirical difficulties since we must decide on criteria of effectiveness which can be implemented and be able to characterise the consequences of aid. When the effects of aid may permeate the whole economy this last step is very problematic. From the right, Bauer (1971, 1984) for example, attacked aid as often being wasted on unproductive prestige projects. He went further and argued that it encouraged governments to spend time, resources and energy chasing aid, thus promoting a supplicant and unentrepreneurial mentality and sapping financial discipline. It was also criticised from less right-wing positions, by for example, Griffin and Enos (1970) who argued that it lowered savings rates, and by Hayter (1971), who suggested it played an imperialistic role. Unfortunately all these attacks were weak on empirical analysis, either offering only a few examples (e.g. Bauer and Hayter) or employing flawed analytical techniques (e.g. Griffin and Enos, 1970; see commentaries by Papanek, 1972, 1973; Mosley, 1980; Stewart, 1971).

Recently, Mosley *et al.* (1987) have made another attempt to isolate the effects of aid on growth using cross-country data. They recognise the problems of simultaneous causation (aid may go to those countries with the weakest growth performance) and attempt to employ standard simultaneous equation techniques of econometrics (two and three stage least squares). However, the procedures for excluding and including variables in their three equations (for growth, aid and mortality) leave one a little uneasy as to whether identification is securely based. And they do not allow for the endogeneity of savings (see Section II above). Thus their inability to identify an effect of aid on growth probably says more about the problems of doing cross-country regression analysis than it does on the effectiveness of aid.

Cassen (1986), Riddell (1987) and Mosley (1987), for example have looked at historical evidence of particular experiences in attempts to examine the effects of aid more directly and have concluded that aid can be and often is, beneficial. That, of course, leaves us with the question of how the probability that it is beneficial can be increased. Each of the authors cited offer some advice with management and monitoring playing a prominent role. It is clear both that guarantees of productive performance are unlikely to be available and that the moral case for aid does not require the probability of beneficial use to be 100%.

The flow of aid from charities and non-governmental bodies is much smaller than that from official bodies but such aid can often be extremely productive. Agencies such as Oxfam would appear to have a very good record in pioneering innovative projects which involve initiative and training and, particularly, helping weaker groups in direct action to help themselves. Their *Field Directors' Handbook* (1985), an assimilation of project experience of over 40 years or so, contains a wealth of practical and productive common sense concerning the selection, guidance and monitoring of projects.

Whilst the most flexible aid from the point of view of the recipient country is untied foreign exchange, aid is frequently in kind. Amongst aid-in-kind, food aid has come under particular scrutiny and often criticism. It is sometimes held that food aid can be damaging in that it depresses food prices and dampens incentives for agricultural activity (see e.g. Lappé and Collins, 1980; Eade and Jackson, 1982). It is plausible that disincentive effects do exist and that these may reduce the social value of food aid. But it would be absurd to conclude that food aid should be eliminated altogether. Indeed, if it were really true that a little extra and costless food caused harm then it would also be true that destruction of a little food by the developing country would be beneficial. Put this way round the argument is highly implausible and the evidence in favour of the proposition that extra food is damaging is very weak (for a discussion of the issues see, for example, Maxwell and Singer, 1979 and Jennings *et al.* 1987). Nevertheless one would generally presume that untied cash aid is superior to food aid.

Our second aspect of relations between developed and developing countries concerns trade. In the preceding section we commented on trade policies of developing countries. We focus here on the policies of developed countries and of multilateral agencies. To set the background we give a (very) brief review of trade and trade policies in relation to growth. The 1950s and 1960s saw rapid growth in output for both developing and developed countries and trade grew even more rapidly. In the 1970s growth in both output and trade was much slower although that for trade remained faster than for output. From 1953–63, 1963–73 and 1973–83 the growth rates for world output and trade were (Bhagwati, 1988*a*, pp. 3–4): 4·3 and 6·1%; 5·1 and 8·9% and 2·5 and 2·8% in the respective decades. This corresponded to substantial reductions (Bhagwati, 1988*a*, p. 4) in tariff levels through the various GATT rounds from Geneva (1947) to Tokyo (1973–9) (the Uruguay round is now in session). Total world exports are dominated by industrialised countries, with 71% in 1960, but by 1980 this had dropped to 66% (Bhagwati, 1988*a*, p. 4) indicating that the growth for other countries was even more rapid. Developing countries have participated in both the growth in income and in trade over the last 40 years.

From the mid-1960s to 1980 the performance of the middle-income countries was superior in both output and export growth to the low-income countries but this changed in the 1980s (see Table 5). This change was very heavily

Table 5
Growth Rates of Income and Exports for Developing Countries

	1963–73	1973–80	1980–86
Real GDP	6·5	5·4	3·6
Low-income countries	5·5	4·6	7·4
Middle-income countries	7·0	5·7	2·0
Exports	4·9	4·7	4·4
Low-income countries	2·0	4·7	5·4
Middle-income countries	5·3	4·8	4·2
Exports of manufactures	11·6	13·8	8·4
Low-income countries	2·4	8·2	8·4
Middle-income countries	14·9	14·8	8·4

Source: World Bank, *World Development Report*, 1988.

influenced by the acceleration in the growth of the Chinese economy following the reforms which began in 1979. Notice that exports of manufactured goods by developing countries have grown much more rapidly than their exports as a whole and whilst this was primarily, in the 1960s and early 1970s, from the middle-income countries, the low income countries have been participating much more strongly in recent years.

The liberalisations in trade of the 1950s and 1960s were jolted by oil crises and recessions in the 1970s and there was a considerable rise in non-tariff barriers such as Voluntary Export Restraints (VER) in industries such as steel, automobiles, footwear, motorcycles, machine tools, and consumer electronics. VERs had their impact most strongly amongst industrialised countries but given the increased role of manufactured exports developing countries are vulnerable here too.

It has been estimated (Tumlir, 1985) that 30–50% of total world trade moves under quantitative restraint. The VERs are attractive to those lobbying for protection since they may circumvent GATT rules and can be very specific in terms of products or industries. A disadvantage from the point of view of the importing countries is that some element of the rent created by the quantitative restriction is transferred overseas. Krishna (1988) for example, has shown how the predicted effects of VERs on prices and on profits of both domestic and foreign producers depend critically on both the structure of the model of the equilibrium in the game and on whether the imported goods are complementary inputs into domestic production or substitutes for domestically produced goods (the profit-raising effects for both foreign and domestic producer being higher in the latter case). The sharp dependence of consequences on the particularity of the assumptions, and similarly also the calculations of optimal policy, in these oligopolistic models has been emphasised by a number of authors. Bhagwati (1988*a*), for example, suggests that these newer models may therefore be weak vehicles for supporting policies of trade intervention.

Bangladesh has been trying to expand its textile and clothing industry and between 1978 and 1985 the number of operational companies grew from 12 to

450. It would appear that textiles and clothing as a labour intensive industry is one where Bangladesh, with a low price of labour, has a real comparative advantage. Bangladesh is one of the poorest countries in the world. Here is an industry in which Bangladesh has shown her ability to produce and compete and one might think that the many developed countries who are aid givers might also have encouraged her textile trade. Yet in mid-1987 Bangladesh had reached the ceiling on MFA quotas in a number of important categories. A major and promising initiative in a poor country has been substantially curtailed (see *World Development Report*, 1987, for further discussion).

A quantitative analysis of the effects of the MFA on developing countries has been provided by Trela and Whalley (1988) using a computable general equilibrium framework. As ever (see Section IV) a vast number of functional relationships and parameters have to be specified and the results are no doubt sensitive to the specifications. In this case when the issue concerns gains and losses to several different countries some variety of assumptions of the kind they make are unavoidable if quantitative results are to be obtained. Using 1986 data they find global losses from the MFA (comparing the world with it and without it) are $17 billion with the gain to developing countries from its removal being $11 billion. They find that the small countries with advantageous positions in existing quotas (Hong Kong, South Korea, Taiwan) would also benefit since they would expand their share of the market (and the share of developed countries producers would decline). The developed countries gain too since consumers get cheaper clothing – Trela and Whalley put this figure for overall gains to developed countries at $6 billion of which $3 billion is for the United States.

As a very poor country Bangladesh has only small imports and little in the way of retaliatory threats. It is only the largest developing countries such as Brazil, China and Indonesia that have such power. Where it exists, however, this power can be used effectively. For example China successfully resisted harsh quotas in recent MFA negotiations by threatening to reduce grain imports from the United States and thus mobilising the United States farm lobby to its assistance (see Bhagwati, 1988*a*). The examples point both to the vulnerability of small developing countries and the negotiating potential of larger countries or groups.

Where aid played a prominent role in the discussion of relations between rich and poor countries in the 1960s this was displaced from centre stage in the 1980s by debt, and this is the third aspect in our discussion of relations between developed and developing countries. The past 15 years have seen a very big increase in debt for some countries (see the annual *World Debt Tables* from 1975 and the *World Development Reports* from 1978). Amongst the low-income countries the big debtors in terms of debt to GNP ratios are in Africa, for example, Mauritania 210·0%, Zambia 240·5% (figures are for 1986 from WDR 1988, Table 18). However, many of the middle-income Latin American countries are in similar circumstances (Nicaragua 198·2%, Chile 120·1%). In absolute terms the biggest debtors are Brazil and Mexico with debts of $97,164m. and $91,062m., although the debt to GNP ratios are only 37·6 and 76·1% respectively.

Whilst the size of debt and its rate of growth might cause concern it is not immediately obvious that a large debt is a problem since if a country has assets against its liabilities and income to service the debt it may nevertheless be in a strong position. More worrying therefore is that debt–service ratios (defined as debt–service payments as a proportion of exports) are now very high in a number of countries. Amongst the low-income countries, for Somalia (62·1 %), Burma (55·4 %) and Pakistan (27·2 %) (WDR, 1988, Table 18) the ratios are particularly high. However, many middle-income and upper middle-income countries are also in difficult positions – Indonesia (33·1 %), Costa Rica (28·9 %), while in the upper middle-income, Argentina (64·1 %), Algeria (54·8 %) and Mexico (51·5 %) stand out.

The above figures are associated with considerable doubt as to countries' ability or willingness to amortise their debts, the so-called debt crisis. Given that the debt crisis threatens the international financial system and welfare in both developed and developing countries there has, in recent years, been a debate on what measures constitute an appropriate response. To understand this debate and the nature of the measures proposed it is necessary to examine the evolution of the relationship between creditor and debtor nations. Prior to 1982 lending to developing countries was generally based on laissez-faire principles with repayment expected in full, the huge amounts lent during the 1970s indicating the willingness of banks in developed countries to lend to developing economies. A combination of high interest rates, a large budget deficit, rising imports and capital flight in Mexico in 1982 changed all this (Dornbusch, 1986; Krugman, 1988).

The problem debtors were identified by their inability to borrow on a voluntary basis in the international capital markets. However, rather than accepting default, creditors were expected to engage both in rescheduling debt as well as in concerted involuntary lending (Krugman, 1988). Growing awareness that many problem debtors were unlikely to honour their debts and that the debt was artificially overvalued led to proposals for debt reduction and debt forgiveness. One such approach recommends the voluntary implementation by creditors of a variety of market-based schemes – debt buy-backs, securitisation, debt-equity swaps. The most radical proposal concerns the possibility of debt forgiveness whereby creditors offer a once-for-all reduction in the future obligations of countries. Such schemes could be given a more equitable cast if they involved more favourable treatment of poorer countries – notice that the largest debtors are, on balance, those who were more profligate and those who were able to borrow rather than the poorest (Buiter and Srinivasan, 1987). There are also efficiency arguments in favour of partial debt forgiveness (as opposed to short-term inaction) since this may raise developed countries' welfare by leading to a larger expected value of payments (Krugman, 1988, forthcoming; Sachs, 1988*a*; Fischer, 1987). It is important to remember that historically defaults have been real possibilities, for example Latin America in the 1930s (see e.g. Dornbusch, 1986). For a general review see Cardoso and Dornbusch (1989).

Recently a theoretical literature motivated by the debt crisis has emerged which focuses on bargaining. Given the confrontational nature of the situation, the central question is whether and by what mechanism, debt contracts can be enforced. Eaton and Gersovitz (1981) and Eaton *et al.* (1986) created models where the creditors have no legal rights whatsoever and borrowing is thus entirely dependent on a country's 'reputation for repayment'. In this situation the ability of the creditor to threaten cut-off from world capital markets and other penalties can be invoked whenever countries do not pay. Bulow and Rogoff (1989*a*) point out that in the case of sovereign debt, the fact that creditors' legal rights to debtors' assets are limited and voluntary lending is not forthcoming implies that reputation may be of little importance. They (1989*b*) use a Rubinstein (1982) bargaining model to show that, when the cut-off is based on lenders' rights, borrowers can bargain with their creditor and costly penalties are not invoked because a deal can always be made to share the benefits of forbearance (see also Fernandez and Rosenthal, 1988).

III.5. *Structural Adjustment and Stabilisation*

Stabilisation programmes refer to attempts to correct balance of payments deficits and excess demand by changing the real exchange rate, liberalising trade and tightening fiscal policy. They are usually precipitated by excess demand and are particularly associated with the International Monetary Fund in its task of helping to resolve short-run balance of payments problems. The World Bank with its longer-term perspective has been increasingly involved in structural adjustment programmes which share the concern for internal and external balance but go further in seeking to liberalise internal markets and to reduce the role of the state, with the intention of making the economies function more effectively and, *inter alia*, reducing the occurrence of crises in the future. The short- and long-term perspectives of the IMF and World Bank are now much less clearly demarcated with their joint concern (and occasionally joint involvement) with these programmes and we shall discuss structural adjustment and stabilisation programmes together.

Crises which precipitate stabilisation programmes have occurred, particularly in Latin America, fairly frequently since the Second World War (Dornbusch, 1986; Taylor, 1988). Whilst excess demand has been a common thread, precipitating factors have included rapid changes in external conditions such as adverse movements in terms-of-trade and rising world interest rates with high levels of debt. 'Orthodox' packages of expenditure cutting, tax raising, and devaluation were tried for example in Argentina in 1951, 1967, 1977–81, and 1985. The austerity measures often result in great political difficulties, and in many cases they are abandoned early on (for example, Mexico 1971, 1977, and usually in Argentina) – see Ahamed (1986), WDR (1988), Buiter (1988), Taylor (1988), Edwards (1988) and Cornia and Stewart (1987). The frequency of occurrence of these crises and programmes and the repeated failure of attempts at a solution have turned something which is, from one point of view, ordinary macroeconomic management into a major issue in development economics.

Failure to execute the programmes is obviously an occupational hazard when one attempts to administer austerity to a fragile and conflictual political system. A government representative of particular groups may attempt to place the burden of austerity on others. Their strong reaction may lead to the abandonment of the programme. Some have suggested that the secrecy of the discussions and the involvement only of the executive and not the legislative or democratic processes (Sachs, 1988*b*) have exacerbated the problems (see also Avramovic, 1988). There is no doubt that precipitate adjustment can cause real problems of unemployment, and for government programmes concerning, for example, health and nutrition (see Edwards, 1988; Cornia *et al.*, 1987).

The failure of many 'orthodox' programmes both in narrow macroeconomic terms (Edwards, 1988; Sachs, 1988*b*), together with their implications for living standards (Cornia *et al.*, 1987), have led to various fresh approaches. Most of these consist of adding measures to the orthodox adjustment process. In the *World Bank Annual Report* 1988 the endorsement of 'hybrid' loans, comprising a package of sectoral reforms as well as one or more investment components, recognises the need for specific measures to encourage sustained growth as opposed to isolated macroeconomic engineering which tends to produce unsustainable changes. Some authors argue that for countries where investment for growth is unlikely to be consistent with the meeting of liabilities and maintaining adequate consumption (e.g. parts of sub-Saharan Africa), debt forgiveness may represent the most efficient way of restoring macroeconomic equilibrium (Sachs, 1988*b*; Edwards, 1988) and, further that this practice may in fact increase future compliance with conditionality (Sachs, 1988*a*). Avramovic (1988) points to the need for target countries to submit their own adjustment programmes and to engage in open and regular debate with the agencies on the progress of adjustment. He also suggests that the decision to lend and the conditions attached should be based on assessment of the debt servicing capacity and financial management of the debtors as opposed to a willingness to accept conditionality. Cornia *et al.* (1987) have argued for gradualism with more expansionary macroeconomic policy accompanied by policies intended to preserve employment, improve social sector efficiency and protect entitlements of vulnerable groups. This plethora of new propositions contains some with a 'sensible' and 'reasonable' feel to them. However, only time will tell whether they can counteract the existing severe constraints on the effectiveness and sustainability of stabilisation and adjustment programmes.

As well as generating suggestions for different strategies recent research has also produced interesting collections of theoretical and empirical studies. For examples see the volumes edited by Neary and van Wijnbergen (1986), Edwards and Ahamed (1986) and Sachs (1988*b*). There is a real modelling problem here for (at least) two reasons. First, the constraints on what will work are to a large extent political and not easily captured formally. Second, and relatedly, the acceptability of any programme will depend not only on who bears the burden of austerity but on how it is structured over the short and medium term. Our models are not well formulated to capture these intertemporal problems. The macro models are primarily short run and in the medium-term models (usually CGEs) the process of adjustment is usually absent.

III.6. *Population Change and Economic Development*

Discussions of population in development economics have focused mainly on the economic consequences of population growth (see, for example, Birdsall, 1988; Kelley, 1988; World Bank Development Report, 1984). The topic has been seen as a major issue at least since 1798 with the publication of *An Essay on the Principle of Population* by Malthus where it was asserted (1798, p. 14) that 'Population, when unchecked, increases in a geometrical ratio. Subsistence increases only in an arithmetical ratio.' Hence, he argued, eventually food production will not keep pace with population growth and the resultant falling *per capita* products would lead to widespread starvation and misery, which would act to check the population growth.

Though this trend failed to appear in Europe, with which Malthus was concerned, the concept was pursued with reference to rapid population growth in less developed countries. And one need not invoke the finiteness of resources or the Malthus geometric–arithmetic argument to indicate potential problems. In the long-run steady state of a one-sector growth model (with $s/v = n$) a rise in the rate of population growth, n, will with constant s lead to a lower capital–output ratio, v, and thus lower output per head (the so-called capital shallowing effect). Further a higher population growth might lead to greater dependency ratios and thus a lower savings rate and diversion of investment resources towards health and education. These savings–investment–growth considerations were emphasised in the influential work by Coale and Hoover (1958). The climate of opinion in the early 1970s was distinctly alarmist with McNamara (1973) the President of the World Bank, comparing the threat of population growth with that of nuclear war and the spreading of 'rampant population growth' as 'the greatest single obstacle'. The view was shared by many, see, for example, the 1971 (US) National Academy of Sciences report (and Forrester, 1971; Club of Rome, 1972). Population control programmes were seen as having high priority.

The balance of views on population has become less pessimistic during the 1980s, with correspondingly less strident claims as to the primacy for policy of population control programmes. The new National Academy of Sciences (1986) report recognises that some population effects can be positive, although it judges them on balance to constitute a hindrance to raising living standards. It further notes that problems sometimes associated with population growth may be in fact be due mainly to other causes, and that a consequence of population growth has often been the exacerbation of other fundamental problems. Adverse effects appear to have been most prominent in environments where arable land and water are particularly scarce or difficult to acquire and where property rights to land and natural resources are poorly defined (see Kelley, 1988).

The positive effects of population growth have been particularly strongly emphasised by Simon – his book *The Ultimate Resource* published in 1981 being an important event in the debate. There are indeed many adjustments which can be made in response to, or which are generated by population growth, which may appear like increasing returns or technical progress. High population densities may act to decrease per unit costs and increase the efficiency of transportation, irrigation, extension services, markets and communications (Boserup, 1981; Pingali and Binswanger, 1987; Hayami and Ruttan, 1987; Glover and Simon, 1975). Boserup (1965, 1981), as we indicated earlier (Section III.2) has argued, over the long term, that increasing population densities induce a shift to more productive labour and land intensive farming technologies. Farmer generated technologies may then be supplemented by the adoption of exogenous science-based technologies (e.g. fertilisers, new seed varieties, and so on). There is substantial empirical justification for these types of response (Hayami and Ruttan, 1987; Pingali and Binswanger, 1987). Whether these all add up to increasing returns to population alone, however, is a moot point.

What is clear is that population, via its size and composition, is likely to have a major influence on many problems – resource depletion (Slade, 1987; MacKellar and Vining, 1987), education (Schultz, 1987), employment (Bloom and Freeman, 1987; Montgomery, 1987), food (Srinivasan, 1987*b*), economic inequality (Lam, 1987), urbanisation (Henderson, 1987) and social security (King, 1987). But given that population is only one element in many of the problems associated with economic development attempting to control population growth without confronting the other causes of such problems may lead to disappointing results. For reviews of the effects of population growth see Birdsall (1988), Johnson and Lee (1987), Keyfitz (1982) and the WDR (1984), as well as Kelley (1988) and the National Academy of Sciences (1986).

An assessment of the effects of population growth is distinct from the design of effective policies to reduce population growth. It is generally argued that if preferences of individuals or families and opportunities open to them are such that they are not ready and willing to reduce the number of births then the availability of family planning programmes is unlikely to be successful. Urban China since 1979 seems the strongest example to the contrary, but there were powers of coercion in China which other countries may not be willing or able to use. Mothers' schooling and employment and access to child schooling and health facilities appear to be important factors in reducing the desired number of births (see Birdsall, 1988; Boulier, 1985; Mauldin and Lapham, 1985).

III.7. *Objectives and Strategies*

We have so far been reviewing the debates on theory, experience and strategies largely from the point of view of growth in aggregate income *per capita*. Income may be seen as an indicator of status or power and as such may have some significance in its own right but it has its greatest interest as a summary indicator of standard of living. This last concept is inherently individualistic and given any community we may enquire as to the standards of living enjoyed by its individual members. The distribution of income is thus a central concern and has always been a major topic in development economics as has the closely related issue of the incidence and severity of poverty. Standard of living is a concept (discussed below) which requires careful consideration and is not easily defined but it should be clear that more is involved than income. Poverty would then be defined in terms of an indicator or indicators of standard of living falling below a given level or levels, although how such levels should be defined in turn raises difficult questions (see, for example Sen, 1983*a*). A growing explicit focus on other objectives, and on indicators of these objectives, has been a significant feature of development economics over the last two decades or so. There are also additional objectives which cannot easily be subsumed under 'standard of living'. The greater emphasis on objectives other than growth has brought an active debate on the relation between strategies for growth in aggregate income and strategies to achieve these wider objectives (see Drèze and Sen, forthcoming).

The interest in individual or household income is largely as a means to ends. Commentators may differ over relevant ends but most would include health and education, in addition to any ends associated with consumption. Certain positive and negative freedoms – say freedom to vote for the former and from discrimination for the latter – would also be included (being a healthy, well-educated slave may be unattractive), but we shall not concentrate on these here. Sen (see, for example 1987, 1988) has linked some of these objectives to standard of living in arguing that the concept should concern primarily 'capabilities'. 'Capabilities' refer to what a person can do or be or, more precisely, to the set of 'functionings' which a person has the freedom to achieve. But whether or not one argues via capabilities numerical indicators of interest might be life expectancy, infant mortality, nutrition, morbidity and literacy and we would be interested in how these differ across countries and for particular sub-groups, and eventually, in principle, for individuals and households in the population.

Whilst the question of measurement of rights, freedom and discrimination has been less prominent in the economic literature than that of standard of living, there has been considerable concern with gender issues including, for example, differential life expectancy and literacy for males and females and intra-household discrimination (see, for example, Folbre, 1986; Sen, 1984 and Section VI.2).

The recognition that the scope of objectives is wider than aggregate income raises the question of whether the strategies for raising aggregate income would be consistent with the achievement of other objectives. It would be unjust to the earlier writers on development to assert that their emphasis on income was associated with blind ignorance of, or lack of concern for, poverty, inequality, health and education. As Bhagwati (1988*b*) has recently stressed, their focus on income was based in part on the idea that greater income would bring with it less poverty and superior health and education. This indirect route is contrasted with the direct route of targeted transfers and provisions (Drèze and Sen, forthcoming). A growing realisation of the negative distributional and other consequences of some growth experiences led to the greater advocacy of the more direct routes, and in particular the so-called 'basic needs' approach which became popular from the mid-1970s (Streeten, 1984; Stewart, 1985). It was suggested that government strategies should be organised around and assessed by the provision of needs held to be basic. These included nutrition, education, health, shelter, and water and sanitation at minimum levels. Whether or not one counsels a 'direct route' however, the basic needs ideas have real problems. What needs are basic and, more worryingly, what levels are held to be essential minima? What if these levels are infeasible, how should we measure and trade-off different levels of attainment? Who decides which needs are basic and the appropriate level? In what sense are they basic if people who can afford to attain them do not choose to do so? How should these choices influence our evaluation of policies? Is the targeting and attempted delivery of basic needs a productive way of organising limited government resources, administrative and otherwise? How are basic needs related to standard of living? A number of these questions have indeed been raised by some of those who favour this approach (see, for example, Streeten, 1984), but they are not easy to answer in a satisfactory way and one is left with a certain scepticism about the approach (see also Lipton, 1988). These problems are shared with any attempt to stipulate 'minimum' levels be they in terms of 'adequate' housing, food, capabilities and so on, or in terms of poverty lines.

Direct policies can, it seems, be effective if properly designed and research has provided considerable guidance on the value of different methods of intervention. Caldwell (1986), for example, notes that poor countries that had achieved low mortality with low *per capita* GNP shared certain characteristics. These included a strong and sustained commitment to public programmes in health, education and nutrition. Even in countries that have achieved rapid growth, the attainment of rapidly improving indicators of standard of living (other than *per capita* income) seems to have been dependent in large part on public intervention (Drèze and Sen, forthcoming; Bhagwati, 1988*b*). Lipton (1988) in a review based on a series of his World Bank working papers on poverty has emphasised however, the real difficulties, or at least the lack of success in reaching the poorest of the poor or the group he calls the ultra poor. He argues that extreme poverty alters behaviour in fundamental ways and that programmes have to take this into account if the ultra poor are to be reached.

IV. TECHNIQUES FOR THE ANALYSIS AND REFORM OF POLICY

Governments of developing countries have been concerned to influence the allocation of resources, the pattern of growth and the distribution of income. Most developing countries have a Ministry of Finance, a Ministry of Industry and/or Commerce and a Ministry or Commission for Planning whose roles involve in overlapping ways tax, quantity and pricing policies. Correspondingly a major concern in development economics has been the analysis, creation and enhancement of techniques which can be used to guide the government in its policy process. Much of the focus of planning commissions has been on the allocation of investment, a major topic in the development literature and the main issue in the early work on planning. The early plans were, and mostly still are, based on linear models and input–output information and are discussed in Section IV.1. More recently policy analyses (although to a lesser extent planning models) have used nonlinear general equilibrium techniques (IV.2). The analysis of social opportunity costs, or shadow prices, in the allocation of investment has been an important topic for economies where price distortions are thought to be serious and this provides the subject matter for Section IV.3. The approach to policy problems based on the idea of social opportunity cost, i.e. cost–benefit analysis, was originally developed for the appraisal of investments but the concept is obviously basic and has a much broader application. Some are considered in Section IV.4 where the reform and design of tax and price policies are discussed briefly. These issues are becoming increasingly important as many countries attempt to increase the role of market allocation and decentralisation of decisions. They find themselves facing difficult microeconomic problems concerning what it means to 'get prices right' and how to do it, as well as the difficulties with raising sufficient revenue for macroeconomic balance. In the issues and models of the last three sub-sections the problems of integrating the market and planning are absolutely central.

IV.1. *Linear Models*

Early planning models were initially concerned with feasibility or consistency of different sectoral targets and were based on the input–output methods developed by Leontief (1941), Stone (1970), Stone and Stone (1977) and Chenery (1956). They were soon extended in a number of directions. Early examples of the use of input–output and linear programming techniques in the analysis of choice in development planning are Chenery and Clark (1959), Chenery and Bruno (1962), Chenery and Strout (1966), Sandee (1960) (see also Chenery, 1965, for reviews). Capital requirements and growth were introduced at an early stage and dynamic input–output models are now employed in many planning commissions. Clark (1975) surveys the applications of such models in various countries, both developing and developed. A valuable recent example was produced for the Indian 6th Five Year Plan, 1980–5, which also provided a most welcome advance in the publication of the input–output tables (including those for domestic and foreign flows) and models used (see Government of India, 1981; Gupta, 1988).

The problems of assuming linearity in investment planning models were recognised early, and interestingly it was the introduction of economies of scale that was first regarded as of special importance, in marked contrast to the constant or diminishing returns embodied in the later CGE models. In the 1960s in India the appropriate timing and size of lumpy investments in a growing economy were studied by Manne and Weisskopf (1970). Chenery (1956), emphasised the need for explicit co-ordination, within and across sectors, of investments which show economies of scale, and the inadequacies of the market in this respect.

Social Accounting Matrices, or SAMs, extend the analysis of intersectoral flows in the production accounts to government, financial and personal sectors.

Thus they, for example, trace the flows of income to different sorts of factors in each industry, track the flow of funds between personal, business and government sectors, and so on. The detail of particular flows provided will depend on the problem at hand. They are useful, for example, in forcing consistency in different parts of the national accounts, linking them to household survey data, and understanding the structure of the economy in relation to income distribution and savings. The SAMs generally also provide the basic starting point against which the nonlinear CGEs (see below) are calibrated or validated. An introduction to SAMs is provided in Pyatt and Round (1985), particularly the chapter by King.

IV.2. *Computable General Equilibrium Models*

Concern with some of the problems of linear optimisation models coincided with the availability in the early 1970s (Scarf and Hansen, 1973) of the computational techniques and computer power to solve detailed numerical general equilibrium models. The advantages of these models lie in the endogeneity of prices and incomes and in the incorporation of substitutability in consumption and production. Agents are assumed to optimise and their supplies and demands are balanced through the market. In addition to the fixed-point algorithms proposed by Scarf, general equilibrium solutions (supply equal to demand in each market) can be computed by standard techniques for solving simultaneous equations systems.

The problems of the approach do not now lie in the computation of solutions but in information and interpretation. The number of parameters involved in specifying the behaviour of agents can become enormous. A Slutsky matrix for a consumer involves $n(n-1)/2$ entries or, say, with 20 goods, 190 parameters. We need one such matrix for each consumer. Production functions involve a similar number of parameters and we require at least one for each industry. One quickly becomes involved in models with tens of thousands of parameters which we are supposed to specify before we can begin to compute solutions. More fundamentally we know that the functional forms used may exert a strong influence on the results (see Atkinson, 1977; Atkinson and Stiglitz, 1976; Deaton, 1979, 1981; Deaton and Stern, 1986) irrespective of which parameters are chosen; understandably but worryingly, the functional forms generally utilised are very restrictive. It is clear that we cannot know the functional forms and parameters with any degree of confidence and in practice much guesswork and inventing of numbers is involved. The complications of the models also strain our ability to interpret since it is often hard to understand what has driven the answers in models of such detail. One reaction to this is to build much smaller models which we can understand in order to guide intuition for the more complicated.

The complexity of the individual models is associated with the rather narrow class of models which are estimated. They are generally perfectly competitive models with constant elasticity of substitution demand functions (or close relations such as the Linear Expenditure System) and similarly CES production functions. A second class of CGEs has been studied by grafting onto this basic framework certain 'structuralist' features such as restrictions on factor mobility or rigid prices and simple forms of rationing, e.g. Chenery *et al.* (1986). De Janvry and Sadoulet (1987) provide a helpful evaluation of agriculturally focused CGEs and on SAM-based CGE models see the recent special issue of the *Journal of Policy Modelling* (for example, de Melo, 1988; Pyatt, 1988). Taylor (1979, 1983) and others have been concerned to develop 'macro-structuralist' models which blend the essentially Walrasian CGEs with Keynesian concerns for aggregates such as saving, investment, imports and exports and government expenditure and revenue. It is hard to believe, however, that the very special structures assumed for the sectoral markets in these models really add reliably to the basic macro picture.

The strength of CGEs, in general, lies in their ability to examine directly changes which are likely to have ramifications throughout the economy. Effects on demands for and prices of different factors as a result of a tax reform might be a case in point. Their weakness lies in the vast number of specific numerical assumptions required. This can lead to them, in practice, falling between two stools. They do not allow the detail of linear input–output analysis (say with a 110 × 110 table) – it may be partly for this reason that dynamic input–output seems more popular within Planning Commissions than CGEs. And they do not allow the flexibility of assumptions and clarity of results of two- or three-sector models that one might use, for example, to study the possible effects of devaluations. As with many approaches in economics, provided they are used where one can exploit their strengths they may constitute a helpful tool. If they are used as an incomprehensible black box constructed from narrowly stereotyped or weak components and casually invented parameters they can be worse than useless.

IV.3. *Cost–Benefit Analysis*

As we saw in Section III.1 the 1960s saw a disenchantment with comprehensive planning and import substitution. It was argued that these had led to unsatisfactory investment programmes in both public and private sectors. The large distortions in relative prices had the result that many of the activities which were profitable at domestic market prices showed a poor return at world prices (see, for example, Little *et al.*, 1970). World prices, it was suggested, gave the relative social opportunity costs for traded goods. These arguments both generated a number of attempts to measure the distortions involved in domestic prices (based in part on their difference from world prices) and led to propositions for shadow price systems which would correctly measure social opportunity costs. Attempts in this direction included effective rates of protection (see, for example, Corden, 1971), domestic resource cost (see, for example, Bruno, 1967) and systems of accounting prices (see, for example, Little and Mirrlees, 1974; Dasgupta *et al.*, 1972).

The *effective rate of protection* (ERP) for an industry is defined as the difference between the value added calculated at domestic prices and the value added at world prices, this difference being expressed as a percentage of the value added at world prices. It is intended to indicate the extent to which protective measures have raised the returns to factors working in that industry (taking into account effects on input as well as output prices) and thus to act as a measure of resource pull into that industry. As such it is clearly a positive rather than a normative measure and one can ask how far it does successfully measure resource pull. There are some theoretical problems as a positive measure since it is possible that raising effective protection lowers factor use in that industry. This cannot happen if we have fixed coefficients for intermediate inputs (see Dixit and Norman, 1980, ch. 5), and this result provides some justification for the use of ERP as a positive directional indicator of resource pull from protection.

Many have been tempted to see the ERP as providing strong normative lessons as well as being a positive measure. For example it is often argued that tariffs on industries with a higher ERP should be reduced. This is poor theory, as Ramaswami and Srinivasan (1968) pointed out. We have to ask why tariffs are there in the first place. If there is no good reason for them then they should simply be abolished. Where there are good reasons then these arguments should be incorporated into the analysis – but these reasons or arguments play no part in the ERP. It should be emphasised here that one cannot correctly appeal to the various theorems which attempt to show that moves towards uniform proportional rates for tariffs are welfare improving (Bruno, 1972; Hatta, 1986; Corden, 1974, 1984). These theorems apply only under the strong and implausible assumptions which imply that uniform tariffs are optimal. For the simple case of indirect taxes on final goods we can show that uniform proportionate taxes are optimal only where we make very special assumptions on preferences. For the one consumer economy (generally assumed by the authors quoted) we must have all compensated cross-price elasticities with leisure equal (Deaton, 1979; Stern, 1987) or with many consumers we generally need to assume *inter alia*, parallel linear Engel curves plus a uniform lump-sum transfer. Where tariffs impinge also on production and thus disturb production efficiency the establishment of a result that movement towards uniformity is an improvement would involve conditions which are even more stringent.

The notion of the ERP has, however, been important in the empirical discussion and has served a number of useful purposes. It reminds us that the nominal tariff may be an unsatisfactory indicator of protection when input prices are also affected. It provides an (apparently) simple statistic which policy makers may be able to understand and which may indicate to them what the consequences of their policies might be (it is hard without such summary statistics to understand a complex tariff system). And it focuses the question of which sectors and projects we should be supporting, and which should be shut down, in a rather sharp way.

The *domestic resource cost* (DRC) is similar in spirit to the ERP but is in a number of respects more satisfactory. It has been used in Israel since the late 1950s and is also known as the Bruno method after Michael Bruno who described it in Bruno (1967). For each sector we calculate (as described below) the net domestic resource cost per unit of net foreign exchange earning or saving. One then selects for expansion those sectors which earn a dollar at lowest cost of domestic resources. Notice that this concept applies to both exportables and importables. The DRC is clearly superior to the ERP as a normative indicator in that it takes careful account of the role of non-traded inputs whereas the typical ERP calculation ignores the effects of protection on non-traded good prices. In doing this we assume in calculating the DRC that extra quantities of non-tradeables will actually be produced if more are required (as opposed to being diverted from other uses).

The DRC is close in spirit and in method to the techniques of cost-benefit analysis we shall be describing. It has, however, a number of defects as a cost-benefit rule in that (i) it is not properly intertemporal, (ii) it ignores factor market distortions and (iii) it does not produce a decision criterion for non-traded goods. Once these defects are corrected it becomes virtually identical to the standard cost-benefit techniques now in use. For further discussion of the relationships between ERP, DRC and cost-benefit analysis see, for example, Bruno (1972), Krueger (1972) or Little and Mirrlees (1974, pp. 362–6).

Systematic methods of cost–benefit analysis were developed in the late 1960s and early 1970s to provide techniques for project evaluation which could be used across the economy. These would allow the selection of investment programmes to take place at the project level, utilising all the appropriate information on production possibilities and problems at that level rather than in a centralised planning commission where information would be both scanty and aggregated and where planners might have little or no knowledge of the local conditions. To put it this way makes cost-benefit analysis and centralised planning appear to be competitive options as planning tools. But as we shall see they are best seen as complements (see, for example, Little, 1982, p. 130). The techniques suggested by various development agencies, see, for example, Little and Mirrlees (1969) and (1974) for the OECD, Dasgupta *et al.* (1972) for UNIDO, Squire and van der Tak (1975) for the World Bank and the UK Government ODA (1988) are all similar in spirit and for specificity we concentrate on the best known of these, Little and Mirrlees (1974), the first version of which appeared as Little and Mirrlees (1969).

There are three central ingredients.

(i) Relative world prices should be equal to relative shadow prices for traded goods.
(ii) For non-traded goods the shadow price is the marginal cost of production evaluated at shadow prices.
(iii) We should take careful account of how the project changes incomes (including those for future generations) and weight the increments in incomes which accrue to different groups in different ways.

We examine the arguments in favour of these three elements and how they can be put into practice. The arguments for using world prices take a number of forms but are essentially similar. The idea is that the world prices represent the net benefits on the margin associated with an adjustment of production or consumption of a traded good. If, for example, a good is traded at fixed prices then the net effect of an expansion in production is not to change prices and welfare of households directly but simply to save on imports or to increase exports. All that matters therefore is the foreign-exchange earnings or savings. These foreign exchange earnings may have a different value from that given by the official exchange rate but the *relative* values of traded goods are given by the relative world prices.

The first of the ingredients tells us that many of the prices to be used in cost–benefit analysis may be found *without* working out the consequences of a project in a detailed model. This is a very valuable result since it tells us that these shadow prices will be appropriate for many different models and in this respect we save difficult and dubious modelling work. Examination of the underlying theory in detail (see, for example, Drèze and Stern, 1987) shows us that the result is indeed robust. There are, however, problems. First, we must decide which goods will be or should be traded and whether they will be imported or exported, if traded. Second, the level of trade may affect world prices (particularly for a big country like China). Third, world prices for some goods may be volatile and difficult to forecast. Fourth, there may be some varieties of a good which are traded and some which are not. This makes classification and the calculation of prices difficult.

The first of these problems with the argument for using world prices is the most basic from the conceptual point of view. It reminds us forcefully that the shadow prices which should be used depend on the policies which are chosen by the government. For example, if the government places a quota on the imports of certain goods it means that extra supplies must come domestically and the goods should be classified as non-traded. On the other hand the policy analysts working on project appraisal and on trade policy may discuss the appropriate trade policy, and after seeing the effect on project selection of the quota it is possible that the quota may be removed. Hence the appropriate classification will depend on the influence of the policy analysts (see, for example, Sen, 1972). Further, classifications may change over time. For example, for a country with a small but growing domestic industry, the good could be an importable in the first few years, then a non-tradeable, then an exportable. The importance of the classifications is underlined in the often large difference between import (c.i.f.) and export (f.o.b.) prices.

It is this first ingredient above, concerning world prices for traded goods, which has received the most attention and which is often held to be the central message. But a system of cost–benefit analysis must also deal carefully with non-traded goods and with factors and it is important not to forget about the other two ingredients. The second rule is much less robust in that it involves the assumption either that more of a non-traded good actually is produced (rather than diverted from elsewhere) or that there is some optimality in that the social opportunity cost from producing an extra unit is the same as the cost associated with diversion from other uses. Where the economy is large there are likely to be many non-traded goods and much of the practical simplicity of these cost–benefit methods is lost.

The last criteria bring in explicitly value judgements concerning the distribution of income. Government interest (and that of international institutions) in looking beyond aggregate income is embodied in explicit concerns for the alleviation of poverty. It is reasonable to infer that such values should be taken into account in the appraisal of projects which will in general directly or indirectly raise or lower incomes of a number of different households in the economy. A natural way to bring these considerations into the analysis is to use welfare weights to attach higher value to increments in income to those who are worse off. These procedures come in most directly through the shadow wage and the evaluation of profit and other incomes generated by a project (for further discussion, see Little and Mirrlees, 1974, ch. 14). These weights, and their value relative to government income in particular, should, in principle, also take into account problems of profitability. If there are great difficulties in raising public revenue then one can employ a high weight on public revenue which would then, via, for example a higher shadow wage, militate against acceptance of projects which would make losses and in favour of projects likely to run surpluses. See, for example, the discussion of Chenery (1965) and Sen (1968), which emphasised that a higher premium on investible surplus would lead to more capital intensive techniques being chosen.

Given that the notion of social opportunity cost is basic to economic analysis and that shadow prices are its embodiment it is natural to ask why shadow prices are used relatively little. One possible reason is that their calculation and application can involve a great deal of work and involve methods which some might find difficult to understand. A second is that decision-makers or funding bodies may be suspicious that underneath the results which are presented to them may be buried assumptions that they cannot trace, but which deliberately bias the decision in favour of the result desired by some interest group. Whilst they might like their 'bias' out in the open it is not obvious that avoiding cost–benefit analysis allows them to do this, since without an analysis of social opportunity costs and benefits it is hard to tell what is biased and what is not. Third, some might argue that departing from market prices raises problems of accountability and profitability. The former may be a serious issue but the latter, as we have seen, should in principle form part of the analysis in so far as revenue raising is a problem. In my judgement it is the first problem of the amount of work and the last of accountability which are the most serious. It may not be necessary, however, to do very detailed calculations of social opportunity cost to weed out bad projects and great social savings from the use of cost–benefit analysis may be available from a fairly speedy analytical assessment. Generally it is much better to have the economic analysis of economic and social choices conducted by those who understand the notion of opportunity cost than those who do not.

IV.4. *Taxes and Prices*

Governments, however benevolent, could not be sufficiently well informed to calculate what every agent should optimally do and could not successfully command every agent to do what they calculate. They should not try. This means that many decisions should and will be taken by individuals acting in markets. Thus the government will have to decide what activities to undertake itself and how to raise revenue for those activities, to examine what influence it should exert on incentives and to consider the distribution of welfare. The basic problems of public finance – expenditure, revenue, incentives, distribution – are therefore central to any economy with markets. We cannot appeal to the basic theorems of welfare economics for a direct answer to these problems – as we saw in Section III. 1 the desirable lump-sum taxes are not incentive-compatible (when people recognise their basis they cease to be lump-sum). We must therefore ask which of the many possible distorting systems of pricing and taxation should be chosen. The design of such systems must take account of their administrative feasibility, problems of manipulation and evasion, and political acceptability, together with an assessment of how far any proposal squares with the basic considerations of revenue, incentives and distribution.

The pressures of these problems are felt by governments throughout the world. Over the last 10 years, for example, China has been grappling with the problems of introducing a price and tax system into an economy where previously market incentives and taxation played a minor role. Providing incentives to firms via the profit motive simultaneously loses public revenue and control over expenditure – these problems appear to have figured centrally in her current difficulties with inflation. Designing and implementing taxes raise real conceptual and practical difficulties. Many countries have, however, built up tax systems and revenue over time by gradual, and often *ad hoc*, modifications to existing systems. Further pressures for revenue, together with the unwieldy system resulting from the accretion of measures, has led many to consider substantial reform, see, for example, Ahmad and Stern (forthcoming and 1989), Gillis (1985), Goode (1984).

There are a number of ways of approaching the problem of integrating theoretical desirability (the revenue, incentive, distribution questions) with considerations of administration and of politics but they cannot proceed without an understanding of the theory of tax design or of what is theoretically desirable. Some of this theory has recently been reviewed in Newbery and Stern (1987) and Ahmad and Stern (1989) where the balance between direct and indirect taxation and the conditions under which indirect taxes should be uniform are examined (some were described briefly in Section IV. 3). Uniformity has administrative advantages and leaves less scope for special pleading for favourable tax treatment on behalf of lobbyists. Generally the greater the power of the income tax the less force is there in the redistributive arguments for indirect taxes. Clearly in many developing countries the personal income tax is very weak so that redistributional considerations for indirect taxes cannot be ignored. Some compromise between what is desirable from the point of view of equity and efficiency on the one hand and administrative feasibility on the other will therefore be involved and such a compromise cannot be intelligently struck without a serious study of both aspects. It is interesting that questions of political acceptability might point to some differentiation on income distribution grounds whereas problems of political manipulation might point the other way if one is concerned about special pleading by interest groups.

In examining what is administratively feasible one may look for 'tax handles' – see Tanzi (1987), Musgrave (1987), Goode (1984). Tariffs and corporation tax provide sources of revenue which for many countries are easier to tap than some alternatives (Tanzi, 1987). Theory tells us that in indirect taxation we should move away from tariffs and towards taxation of final goods (Dixit and Norman, 1980; Newbery and Stern, 1987) but in the short run many countries will have to rely on tariffs for revenue. This reliance may pose fundamental problems for a country in 'structural adjustment' where the desire to liberalise its trade policy may run counter to its need for revenue. The temptation to insist that *only* certain tax handles are available or to place excessive reliance on just one or two is sometimes overwhelming. Marketing boards, particularly in West Africa, have levied very high (implicit) tax rates, and tariffs have often been pushed to the point where one suspects that revenue is lost in addition to the distortions generated, see Bauer (1963). Increasingly, however, the potential for broad-based internal indirect taxation is being recognised with the spread of the value added tax (Tanzi, 1987; Tait, 1988).

The problem of tax analysis may be approached using the technique of tax reform as well as tax design. An analysis of tax reform compares a proposed system with the existing system and looks at the costs and benefits of the change. One looks at revenue changes, who gains and loses and what happens to the structure of production. The techniques for analysis of marginal reform have been developed by Guesnerie (1977), Ahmad and Stern (1984, 1987) and in Newbery and Stern (1987). The use of household survey data for examining gainers and losers from non-marginal reform is now standard; see, for example, King (1983) and Atkinson *et al.* (1980). Informational requirements for the analysis of both design and reform can be substantial and one must take care since, as we have noted, assumptions on functional forms can have a major influence on outcomes (Atkinson, 1977; Deaton, 1979, 1981; Deaton and Stern; 1986). The analysis of tax reform in a distorted economy requires us, in principle, to integrate social opportunity costs (shadow prices) into the analysis. These problems are examined in Drèze and Stern (1987).

The methods for the analysis of marginal reform which invoke shadow prices are based on the simple idea that the increase in a policy instrument (e.g. tax, price or income transfer) is beneficial if the social value of the direct impact on households exceeds the cost at shadow prices of the extra demands generated. For example, an increase in transfers to widows provides a direct benefit to them from which the shadow cost of the extra demands must be subtracted to arrive at the net benefit. The shadow prices incorporate the full costs of the general equilibrium repercussions. Alternatively one can calculate the marginal (general equilibrium) impact on different income groups and on revenue directly (without invoking shadow prices). One then seeks to identify those reforms which raise revenue at minimum social cost – see Braverman *et. al.* (1987), Newbery and Stern (1987), Drèze and Stern (1987 and 1988) and Ahmad and Stern (forthcoming) for examples and discussion.

Our focus for this discussion has been on taxation but the discussion includes public-sector pricing also – one can regard differences between price and marginal cost in a public-sector firm as a form of taxation. Here the same considerations of revenue, distribution and incentives apply. As problems of revenue raising have become increasingly severe it is now more widely appreciated that the public-sector pricing rule of price equal to marginal cost (see, for example, Newbery and Stern, 1987; Katz, 1987; Jimenez, 1987) is not tenable in a revenue constrained economy (and which economy is not?).

V. MARKETS, VILLAGES AND HOUSEHOLDS

The studies described in this section are heterogenous but have common threads in their approach. They are essentially microeconomic, tightly focused on particular questions, take careful account of the major institutions associated with the issues under study and generally involve the collection of primary data. Such features can, of course, be found amongst micro studies for developed countries. The number and quality of such works for developing countries, however, constitute a major corpus of knowledge which lies at the heart of the subject of development economics. Such micro studies are not generally concerned with narrow or minor issues but with understanding how particular processes operate at a micro level and thus with developing our insights into theories of how the economy works and how policies might be effective. We shall present just a few examples at a little length, rather than a broader selection more briefly, in order to bring out the kind of attention to detail that is necessary. The examples are chosen for their inherent interest, their importance as topics, for their quality as pieces of analysis and as vehicles to introduce some wider areas of research. They are intended as demonstrations of what can be done rather than a survey of what has been done on the issues covered.

The studies will mostly be applied but we shall begin with a group of theoretical studies described below. The focus of the empirical studies discussed here includes (i) the close examination of the economy of a particular locality, principally a village, (ii) the investigation of a particular issue such as nutrition or price stabilisation, (iii) the exploitation of a data resource such as household income and budget surveys. They have been positive rather than normative in the first instance, the initial task being to understand how a particular microeconomy works, but have often been motivated by and led to important policy questions.

V.1. *Theory*

The four theoretical examples we shall present here concern attempts to understand particular phenomena. The first of these is the very rapid growth of urban populations in developing countries. Notwithstanding apparently high rates of urban unemployment, in many countries migrants have been moving to towns in large numbers to seek jobs. The second concerns a related issue, namely the possibility that employers may choose not to lower wages even though they observe excess supply of labour, because lower wages via lower consumption and poorer nutrition might lower the productivity of labour. Third, theorists have been concerned to understand the prevalence of sharecropping as a form of land and labour contract when other forms of contract such as fixed land rents or wage rates may be available and, *prima facie*, more attractive in some important respects. The fourth concerns the allocation of risk in markets, particularly policy concerning the stabilisation of prices. Each of the investigations has led to ideas which contributed (respectively) to theoretical developments in the related areas of labour market search, wage rigidity, corporate structure and the allocation of risks in markets for developed countries.

V.1.1. *Migration*

The study of migration has for long been an important area of research in development economics (see Williamson, 1988). We focus here on one model of particular influence, that of Todaro (1969) (and developed by Harris and Todaro, 1970). Suppose that the urban wage is c and the rural wage is m. Let the total employment in urban areas be E and the number in the urban areas seeking jobs be S. The number of urban unemployed is therefore $U = S - E$. Work in the rural areas at wage m is guaranteed for those who want it. The central hypothesis in the model is that a worker will leave the rural area to seek work in the town if the expected wage in the town, pc, exceeds the wage in the country, m, where p is the perceived probability of finding employment. The theory yields an equilibrium level of unemployment which is given by

$$\left.\begin{aligned} pc &= m \\ p &= \frac{E}{E+U} \end{aligned}\right\} \quad \text{so that} \quad U = \left(\frac{c}{m} - 1\right)E, \tag{4}$$

since it is assumed that the perceived probability of finding employment is given by the number of jobs divided by the total number of job seekers S.

If we assume c and m are fixed and examine the effect on the equilibrium of a change in E we find

$$\frac{dU}{dE} = \left(\frac{c}{m} - 1\right); \quad \frac{dS}{dE} = \frac{c}{m}. \tag{5}$$

Hence in this model an increase in urban employment *increases* urban unemployment. The model itself is rather unsatisfactory in important respects but the explicit treatment of the probability of finding a job was an important advance and has led to fruitful theoretical and empirical research. From the empirical point of view the model generates unemployment rates which are implausibly high – if c/m is 2 the unemployment rate is 50%. From the theoretical point of view the model leaves its driving force, the disparity of c and m and the fixity of c, unexplained. Squire (1981) has argued that minimum wage legislation does not generally provide adequate grounds for assuming c is fixed. Stiglitz (1974) considers labour turnover costs as a possible reason for maintaining wages above the supply price of labour and Calvo (1978) examines monopolistic behaviour by unions. One can also consider the efficiency wage ideas described in the next subsection as a possible explanation of wage rigidity.

The model (with or without fixed wages) can be modified in a number of ways to introduce risk aversion, intertemporal aspects (you may have to wait for a job), priority hiring (so that some applicants have a better chance of finding a job than others), more than one urban sector (for example, a traditional urban sector which allows some further job seeking, see for example, Fields, 1975), different support schemes (e.g. from relatives) whilst a job is being sought, travel costs, and so on (Fields, 1988). Many of these modifications will reduce the level of unemployment as predicted by the model.

The model led to many applied studies most of which confirmed that the relative wages and the perceived probability of finding a job were indeed important determinants of a decision to move (see Sabot, 1982, Yap, 1977, or Todaro, 1976, for surveys). Some of the findings are not so easily understood in the Todaro framework. For example Connell (1975) finds that villages with more inequality tend to produce more migrants. The urban unemployed are often educated and migrants of long-standing (e.g. Bertrand and Squire, 1980). And Stark and his collaborators have developed rather interesting theories based on migration as a portfolio decision of households, i.e. it is seen as part of the collection of risks, agricultural and otherwise, carried by the household (see, for example, Stark, 1988, and others in the Discussion Paper Series, Harvard University, Migration and Development Program).

It must be remembered that the Todaro model is simply an example of research in an area that has been going on for several decades. Whilst work on Todaro-like models is now less active there is no doubt that it has exerted an important and productive influence on research on the operation of labour markets in developing countries. That topic is itself an area of substantial research of which migration is just a part. This wider research contains many further examples of the interesting application of theoretical ideas. These concern, for example, the organisation of family enterprise (Chayanov, 1966; Barnum and Squire, 1979; Sen, 1975; Singh *et al.* 1986) and risk and information (Binswanger and Rosenzweig, 1986) as well as the theories of efficiency wages and share tenancy discussed below. See Rosenzweig (1988) for a useful survey.

V.1.2. *The relation between consumption and productivity*

The idea that there is a link between consumption and job performance and that this link may influence wages and the allocation of labour goes back to Leibenstein (1957). It was set out rigorously by Mirrlees (1976) and Stiglitz (1976) and developed by Bliss and Stern (1978*a*, *b*), who also examined empirical evidence on the assumptions and predictions of the theory (Dasgupta and Ray, 1987, have recently returned to some of these ideas). We present the simplest version here. Suppose that there is a relation $h(\ )$ between productivity, tasks performed per day, and consumption of the form illustrated in Fig. 2. Suppose also that the wage (w) is the only source of consumption.

The employer minimises labour cost wl, where l is days hired, subject to

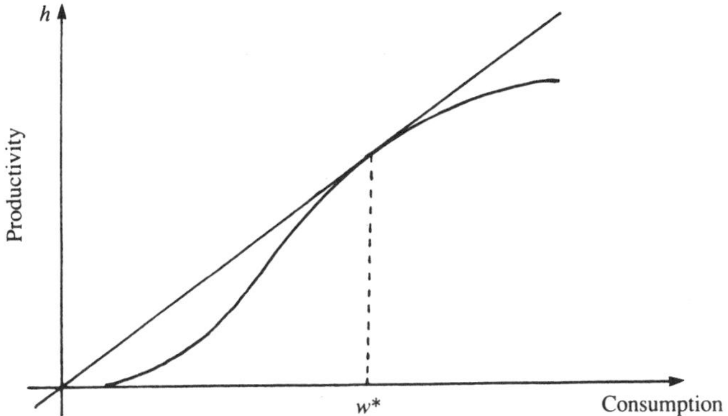

Fig. 2. Relationship between productivity and consumption.

$lh(w) > \bar{H}$ and $w > \bar{w}$, where $\bar{w}$ is the minimum daily wage at which labour is available and $\bar{H}$ is the required number of tasks. This involves minimising w/h or maximising h/w (tasks per rupee) and leads to the choice of w^* (which we suppose is bigger than $\bar{w}$). We call w^* the 'efficiency wage'. Hence employers will voluntarily pay a wage higher than the minimum at which labour is available because the extra productivity offsets the higher cost of the wage. Thus we can have unemployment with no tendency for the wage to fall and we have one explanation of downward wage rigidity. This type of effect has subsequently been adapted to explain wage rigidity in some macroeconomic models for developed countries (see, for example, Weiss, 1980; Shapiro and Stiglitz, 1984). Where workers differ in endowments it is clear that in a general equilibrium framework the wage, level of employment and who gets employed will depend on the distribution of endowments (those with greater endowments are potentially cheaper to employ, see Bliss and Stern, 1978*a*).

The theoretical results are interesting and there is little doubt that many members of the workforce in poor countries have a level of nutrition which may seriously detract from their productivity. The evidence in favour of the view that the theory provides an important explanation of wages is, however, somewhat limited. The most important aspect of this is the prevalence of short-period contracts, often daily, for physical labour in many developing countries. This short period implies that the producer would be unable to reap the benefits of building up the nutritional status of employees. Where labour contracts are longer term such as plantations, the armed forces, or slavery, there is some evidence that employers may try to use their labour force efficiently from the nutritional point of view (see, for example Bliss and Stern, 1978*b*). Strauss (1986) also reviews the empirical evidence and reaches similar conclusions, that the rigorous evidence in support of the theory as an explanation of wages is limited. He also attempts to identify the contribution of consumption to productivity using household survey data for Sierra Leone. He tries to take into account in his econometric analysis the simultaneous influence of output/income on calories, as well as the central relation in question. Bliss and Stern (1978*b*) expressed scepticism that separate identification of the two relationships would be believable. One can always include or exclude 'exogenous' variables to get apparent identification in the two basic equations but the 'identifying' restrictions and labelling of equations remains somewhat dubious. Whilst the theory may not be powerful as an explanation of wages, this should not divert us from the task of analysing the causes and consequences of poor nutrition (see below V.2.2.) and their relationships with productivity – issues of considerable importance.

V.1.3. *Sharecropping*

Sharecropping is an arrangement whereby the tenant taking on land pays to the landlord a fraction r of output (r is often $\frac{1}{2}$). If output depends on labour l and land h, through $F(l, h)$, then if the opportunity cost of labour is w the tenant, if he is free to choose l, will set the level so that $(1-r)\,\partial F/\partial l = w$. This Marshall indicated in his *Principles of Economics* (8th edition, 1920) was inefficient as efficiency would require $\partial F/\partial l = w$. He also pointed out that the landlord will try to insist that the tenant work harder to increase the rent (rF) that the landlord receives (Chapter X, 8th edition).

This point was taken up again by Cheung (1969) who formulated a model of a landlord offering contracts to tenants involving a particular amount of land, a particular level of labour input and a rental share. For the tenant to accept the contract it must offer him at least as good a return to his labour as could be achieved by selling it at w. If the landlord has total land M and offers M/n to each tenant then the landlord's problem may be written:

$$\underset{r,n,l}{\text{Maximise}}\; nrF\left(l, \frac{M}{n}\right) \quad \text{subject to} \quad (1-r)\,F \geqslant wl.$$

It is easy to see that the solution involves $\partial F/\partial l = w$ and that the rent per tenant (rF) will be $(M/n)\,\partial F/\partial h$, so that payments to land are also equal to the marginal product. This is the standard efficient allocation of land and labour. This outcome is unsurprising as a solution given the formulation of the model – the tenant essentially works as a labourer for the landlord at wage w – Marshall saw this point clearly and explained it carefully. Cheung argued that the description of share tenancy involving detailed responsibilities was supported by data from China in the early 20th century.

The puzzle as to why sharecropping should exist if it is inefficient was replaced by the problem of explaining which amongst different forms of equally efficient contracts – sharecropping, land rent, or wage labour – for farming the land might be selected. Theorists then argued that sharecropping may be adopted in preference to other forms of land contract because it allows the sharing of risk. Here we think of inputs being incurred in advance of output, which is uncertain. Notice that if the landowner hires the labourer at a fixed wage then the landowner bears the risk and if the tenant pays a fixed rent he bears the risk. But the risk-sharing achieved by sharecropping could, in principle, also be replicated by competitive markets with fixed wages for labour and rent for land, provided we have constant returns to scale and indifference by agents as to whether they work as labourers, share tenants or fixed-rent tenants. A 50–50 sharecropping contract can be replicated for a share tenant by taking on half the land under fixed-rent tenancy and applying half his labour (thus incurring the risk for this part of his activity), and, in addition, working for wage labour for a non-stochastic wage for the other half of his time. The assumptions, however, for this replication are rather strong (including the certainty of being able to find work at the given wage) and it is reasonable to suppose that the risk-sharing features of sharecropping play an important role in its popularity as a form of contract.

It also provides some economy of supervision as a labour contract, relative to hiring at a fixed wage. Where labour is paid a fixed wage, there is no further incentive to work in a way which increases output and the employer may have to supervise carefully. With sharecropping the worker does take 50% (say) of the output and thus has an incentive to increase it. Note the link between supervision and uncertainty problems since if there were no uncertainty the input could be inferred directly from the output so that shirking on a labour contract could be easily monitored. Payment by commission is, indeed, a common form of incentive in developed countries too.

Important contributions in this area have come from Stiglitz (1974), Newbery (1977), Hallagan (1978), Braverman and Stiglitz (1982), and for an interesting bargaining theoretic approach see Bell and Zusman (1976). Empirical work on hypotheses arising here has also been extensive, see particularly Bell (1977), Bliss and Stern (1982 and discussion in Section V.2.1 below), Shaban (1987). Bell (1977) and Shaban (1987) found some evidence of lower output on tenanted land in cases where the tenant both farms some land of his own and leases in, although Bliss and Stern (1982) did not. For a discussion of inter-linking between land, labour and credit markets see Bell (1988).

V.1.4. *Price stabilisation*

The equilibrium analysis of risk in markets where consumers or producers act to maximise expected utility or profits and where markets allow for some speculation or insurance has seen important application in development economics to the problems of price stabilisation. Most studies of commodity-price stabilisation focus on producers or exporting countries and examine schemes involving buffer stocks, for example, for smoothing prices or incomes – see, for example, Newbery and Stiglitz (1981). Pure stabilisation schemes are distinguished from those in which producing nations act collusively in order to raise average price. They analyse in some detail the general equilibrium allocation of risks and the effect of policy and suggest that the 'optimal buffer stock is very small; indeed sufficiently small that it is not obvious that the amount of stabilisation presently being provided [through the market] is significantly below the optimal level' (p. 444). Two markets which would be potentially useful in reducing the costs of risks would be the futures and credit markets. It is argued that futures markets may actually be superior to price stabilisation via buffer stocks. The authors appear more optimistic with respect to this market (as opposed to the credit market) given the problems of imperfect information, adverse selection, and moral hazard which present major obstacles to credit market improvement.

Food prices, however, affect consumers as well and fluctuations can involve questions of survival. Here the possibilities of holding stocks, borrowing or lending, and the correlation between food prices and income become crucial. We can ask how markets allocate the risks in these contexts and whether the role of speculation is stabilising or destabilising. One should ask whether storage is best carried out publicly or privately and if the latter whether it should be subsidised. For contributions see Newbery (1988), Berck and Cechetti (1985), Ravallion (1988), Bigman (1982, 1985), Turnovsky *et al.* (1980). Newbery (1988), for example, concludes that ration shops and food entitlements may be more cost-effective in protecting consumers than price stabilisation policies.

Ravallion (1987) has applied some of the theoretical ideas of the literature on price uncertainty in his investigation of markets and famines in Bangladesh. He concludes (p. 19) that 'Over-reaction to new information on future scarcity during the famine de-stabilised rice markets. Thus it can be argued that excess mortality in Bangladesh during 1984 was, in no small measure, the effect of a speculative crisis.' The government did attempt to stabilise prices but its response lacked credibility. The markets, he suggests, were informationally inefficient and were not well integrated spatially. We seem to have in this case an example of the failure of both the market and of attempted government intervention.

V.2. *Applied Studies*

We provide three groups of examples of the type of closely focused applied micro study which illustrates development economics at its most productive. Whilst they are micro studies the motivations and theories underlying them concern major issues of policy and of understanding of the functioning of the economy.

We begin with a collection of village studies oriented to understanding the processes of allocation, income distribution, and response to change in poor rural economies. Nutrition, its determinants and policy responses, is examined in V.2.2. We present work on the use of survey data for the estimation of price and income responses, which are crucial ingredients for price and tax analysis and for the analysis of income inequality, in Section V.2.3.

V.2.1. *Village studies*

There has been strong disagreement amongst development economists over the efficiency of the functioning of village economies. At one extreme some, as we saw in III.1, such as Schultz (1964), have asserted that competitive markets and maximising behaviour imply efficient use of assets, whereas others, such as Myrdal (1968) have claimed that rural behaviour is not determined implicitly or explicitly by costs and returns.

The theories and descriptions of the processes of growth which we discussed in III.2 were based on notions of the operation of the rural or traditional sector and how it might respond to change. Different views of that operation will lead to different policies. The perception of the way the village economy functions and how it adapts thus will be crucial in designing and judging policy to improve allocation and assist change. There have been many studies of village economies and peasant behaviour throughout the developing world and it is not possible to do justice to the richness and variety here. We shall instead point to a few studies spread over different decades from different parts of India, a country which has provided some of the most prominent examples.

Our purpose here is not to survey village studies in general or what they have to say on a particular subject. The Village Studies Programme at Sussex University has generated a number of such, e.g. Connell (1975) on labour utilisation and Schofield (1975) on nutrition. And Lipton's (1983*a–d*) series of papers on poverty makes valuable use both of extensive village studies data and of other household surveys. Rather we attempt to demonstrate by example what is involved in a village study and what can be achieved. No village is typical and it is not the purpose of a village study to find and scrutinise such a village. It should be seen as a method of seeing how well theories explain particular phenomena 'on the ground' and of finding and generating further phenomena and hypotheses.

In the early and middle 1950s fascinating village research was under way in several parts of India. Bailey was from 1952 to 1954 working in the village of Bisipara in Orissa in Western India (see Bailey, 1957), Epstein in 1955 and 1956 was studying two villages, Wangala and Dalena, in Karnataka in South India (see Epstein, 1962), and Hopper (1965) used data from 1954 on the village of Senapur in Uttar Pradesh in North India. We discuss their contributions briefly to try to give a flavour of the range and interest of the different questions that can arise. A key feature of all four of them is the strong response (although subject to various institutional constraints, such as caste) to market opportunities and of three of them is the way in which the economy of the village has adapted to changing circumstances including the growth of the economy outside the village.

Bailey described the transition of Bisipara from a purely self-sufficient village economy concentrating solely on the cultivation of paddy to one with links to the modern world, involved in trade and several non-agricultural pursuits. He identified two major trends: first, the decline of the joint family, where siblings cultivate an estate together, and its replacement by the division of land and household wealth between sons on the death of their father; and second, the expansion of employment and earning opportunities outside paddy farming. The first implies a reduction in the size of average land-holdings per household and if risk is not spread through the joint family there is a reduced ability to meet what Bailey calls 'contingent expenditure', unforeseen expenses through illness, death of an ox, etc. This may lead to land sales (after all other sources of wealth in the household have been exhausted) and further vulnerability. The second trend describes the gradual reduction in dependence on agriculture.

Households which took advantage of other earning opportunities could invest their surplus income in land, offsetting the effects of division. Some especially lucrative alternatives were reserved for lower caste households because of pollution boundaries (particularly distilling), and the reservation of government jobs for certain castes. There were still further differences across the two groups which were involved in distilling with one group (Ganjans) being rather more entrepreneurial, more closely connected with the outside world, having a bigger trading network and being less involved in village politics and questions of status.

In the course of the discussion Bailey described the working of various markets in Bisipara. The casual labour market was active as paddy cultivation has periods of high labour demand at various points in the season. It was impossible for most cultivating households to provide the labour themselves. The wage rate, however, was set by the village council (which seemed fairly powerful) and did not move to mitigate excess demand or supply at different points of the year. The market for land sales was fairly active but, whilst sharecropping did occur it was not prevalent. The availability and cost of credit depended on the circumstances of the households. Overall we have a fascinating combination of institutions and the market described with real economic insight by a social anthropologist long before the development of the more formal economic theories that we would now use to describe some aspects of what he found.

Epstein (1962) studied Wangala and Dalena in Karnataka in South India in 1955–6. She returned for a later study (Epstein, 1973) but the former is more detailed and is our focus here. The two villages were almost identical in all aspects of their economic and social life until the 1930s when a large-scale irrigation project brought Wangala into a canal network while Dalena remained with only unirrigated land. Wangala was able to preserve its way of life, its institutions and its economic organisation virtually intact, despite the fact that the irrigation made available by the canal allowed the villagers to intensify their traditional cultivation, to move into paddy and to grow sugar, a lucrative cash crop. Dalena village, on the other hand, did not benefit from the increased availability of irrigation in the surrounding region due to its somewhat more elevated location. Its villagers were compelled to alter their way of life dramatically in order to obtain economic benefits from the irrigation project. The villagers actively sought to purchase land outside their village, they obtained positions in the Public Works Department, they were involved in the transportation of sugarcane to the mill in Mandya, and they acquired jobs in the mill and other places in that town. They recognised the opportunities offered by establishing themselves as a service centre in the region and on the whole they quickly integrated themselves into a much wider economic sphere than did the villagers of Wangala.

In both villages the land market was relatively inactive after an initial spate of purchases and sales following the completion of the irrigation project. Like Bailey's village, a decline in the incidence of joint families was observed.

Hopper (1965) used data for 1954 on Senapur in Uttar Pradesh in a very particular way. He fitted Cobb–Douglas production functions for four different crops where the inputs were land, bullock time, labour time and amount of irrigation water. For each crop, he compared the value of the marginal product of a given input (at geometric means) and found that they were close. He also compared the value marginal product of an input with its price and again found similarity. Thus, he concluded, traditional agriculture was efficient and 'the problem of agricultural development is the problem of introducing new resources, skills and techniques in agriculture. Little progress can be expected from efforts which merely tinker with the traditional production functions, or seek to reallocate traditional resources' (p. 624). There are some methodological difficulties with his work concerning both the measurement of output (see Bliss and Stern, 1982, pp. 81–2) and the estimation techniques (see Nowshirvani, 1967). Further, the conclusion that poor peasants show no risk aversion (in that they maximise expected profit) is hard to believe – see Lipton (1968). The study was very influential both in generating further such work and in its influence on Schultz (1964) and others who leaned heavily on the example as support for the notion that efficient markets and maximising behaviour well-portrayed peasant agriculture.

Later examples from the 1970s included the work of Bliss and Stern (1982) who studied the Uttar Pradesh village of Palanpur in 1974–5 and Binswanger and others who worked on data collected since May 1975 from villages in South India by ICRISAT (International Crops Research Institute for the Semi-Arid Tropics). Bliss and Stern returned to a village which had been studied in the late 1950s and early 1960s. They were concerned particularly with the functioning of markets including share tenancy, farmers' input decisions and the adaptation to the agricultural change associated with the 'Green Revolution' which affected Northern India in the late 1960s and early 1970s. Their broad findings were:

(i) Markets in Palanpur were generally active with prices and farmers responding to market pressures. An exception was the absence of a market for the services of bullocks.

(ii) The land market operated largely in the form of share tenancy, which seemed to function quite well in Palanpur. Output per acre was not lower on share tenanted land. Tenancy appeared important in bringing land to factors where the latter (e.g. bullocks and some people) could not easily be hired.

(iii) Productivity per acre seemed independent of farm size whereas in other studies, see e.g. Sen (1975) for references, it appears to have decreased with farm size.

(iv) Uncertainty seemed very important in understanding farmers' decisions – marginal productivities of factors appeared to be 2 or 3 times their cost and the ratio seemed fairly similar for different inputs. Note the contrast with the Hopper results.

(v) Substantial agricultural change has taken place in Palanpur – a rapid expansion of irrigation, a use of high-yielding varieties of seed, use of fertiliser and so on. Techniques varied greatly across farmers with some farmers applying high levels of fertilisers and water and others following the newer methods in a rather desultory way. The changes in agricultural practice were not confined to the larger farmers.

ICRISAT data have been and continue to be collected from a randomly selected panel of 240 households at intervals of 20–40 days since May 1975. They represent one of the best and most comprehensive LDC household data sets. The data have been used to study the functioning of informal and formal credit markets in rural South India (Bhende, 1983; Binswanger *et al.*, 1985; Binswanger and Rosenzweig, 1986) as well as other matters (e.g. Shaban, 1987, on sharecropping). The authors have linked the data and close knowledge of the local conditions to modern theories of credit, including information costs, collateral, risk, moral hazard and so on (see e.g. Stiglitz and Weiss, 1981; Braverman and Guasch, 1986).

In some of the ICRISAT villages informal credit markets are dominant and local information is used intensively. Larger farmers can obtain substantial loans on reasonably good terms whereas those with poorer credit 'ratings' can borrow only amounts which are closely tied with outputs. The landless could borrow only small sums unless bound into a long-term labour contract. In other villages where institutional credit had largely displaced informal markets, it was found that difficulties in enforcing repayment in the former system resulted in a 'culture of non-payment' which contrasted strongly with low rates of default in the informal system. Institutional credit was provided mainly for loans for production and this practice meant that the poor and assetless were excluded. They consequently became the main recipients of credit in the informal market. Binswanger *et al.* (1985) showed that this shift in the composition of borrowers had significant effects on the nature of the informal market. Loans were smaller, for shorter periods and at higher interest rates reflecting greater risk and a shift towards consumption loans. Credit rationing was an important reality for landless farmers under both systems. Whilst the modern theories of credit with their emphasis on credit rating, risk assessment, information and so on give quite powerful explanations of what is found in the data, these have to be augmented by an understanding of the, often political and corrupt, processes of institutional credit.

These studies are different in their location and focus but they share a number of important features. The first is the careful collection of micro data together with close observation of the way in which the societies and economies, particularly their markets, function. Second, they examine the central ideas and theories of economic development in terms of their ability to explain what happens in a particular locality. Third, and turning to results, they all show the importance of markets in allocating resources. But these do not always follow the simple model of perfect competition under certainty. Uncertainty and problems of information, for example, play crucial roles in the markets for land (sharecropping), input decisions, and in credit markets. Fourth, agents and institutions in the peasant economy can and do respond quickly and radically to changing economic and agricultural conditions and opportunities. Fifth, although they can be flexible, the local structures and customs exert an important influence on economic activity (village councils, caste, the operation of formal and informal credit institutions and so on). Generally economic analysis can take us a very long way in understanding peasant societies, although it cannot proceed without looking very closely at the society and institutions of which the economy forms part.

V.2.2. *Nutrition*

'Malnutrition is largely a reflection of poverty: people do not have enough income for food... The most efficient policies are those that raise the income of the poor' (World Development Report, 1981, p. 59). According to this prominent viewpoint income growth is seen as the major mechanism for improving nutrition. Of course, growth in aggregate income may not reach vulnerable groups and there is abundant empirical evidence to suggest that this is often a real problem (see Fields, 1980; Lipton, 1988). Even if income growth does reach the household there are reasons why this may not result in substantial improvements in nutritional status. First, increases in income may have only weak effects on purchases of nutritive food characteristics. Behrman and Deolalikar (1987), for example, have argued that the income elasticity of demand for calories in an ICRISAT sample was close to zero. They suggested that extra income led to a move towards more attractive expensive foods with a higher price per nutrient. Others, however, for example Strauss (1982) and Pitt (1983) have found much larger income elasticities for Sierra Leone and Bangladesh respectively. Second, there may be environmental or educational constraints to the achievement of nutritional capability. To conclude from these studies that income is irrelevant would, however, be misleading. Historical, regional and cross-country studies (e.g. Caldwell, 1986; Drèze and Sen, forthcoming) suggest a positive correlation between income and nutritional status, for a wide range of nutritional indicators ranging from calorie intake to anthropometric measures.

The recognition of the role of income cautions us against the mistake of seeing the availability of food in a country or region as the key issue in the study of malnutrition. Sen (1981) has demonstrated clearly, in his analysis of famine, that aggregate availability of food does not ensure that individuals are in a position to exercise command over food (Sen introduces the notion of 'entitlement failure'). The victims of famine are generally those whose incomes (or other ways of acquisition) are insufficient to buy food.

An appreciation of the limitations of both the income and availability approaches has led to interesting recent research on the multiple origins of malnutrition. Thomas *et al.* (1988) surveyed a wide range of empirical studies which generally suggested that parental education has a positive effect on the height of children. Behrman and Deolalikar (1988) present evidence which indicates that households in which women have more schooling tend to be substantially better nourished. There is growing awareness that poor sanitation and water supply can act as limiting constraints on the achievement of nutritional goals. Austin and Zeitlin (1981) survey some of the literature and come to the conclusion that direct nutrition interventions require, for their effectiveness, the simultaneous provision of facilities for the removal of faeces *and* for the supply of clean water (see also Osmani, 1987). Castaneda (1984) and Mata and Rosero (1988) provide evidence supporting this view for Chile and Costa Rica respectively. Note that the influence of these different factors can imply a positive effect of income on nutrition even if it does not lead to the purchase of extra nutrients since extra income may be used to buy better education or environment.

The multiple origins of malnutrition raise important questions for policy intervention. Raising the income of vulnerable groups will be part of the story and this is likely to be linked to the growth of the economy as a whole. But the growth of the economy as a whole on a scale likely to provide significant alleviation of malnutrition can take a very long time. Public intervention can be effective in protecting the incomes of vulnerable groups and this is a key element in the prevention of malnutrition. Several recent studies (e.g. Drèze and Sen, forthcoming, Pinstrup-Andersen, forthcoming) suggest that nutritional well-being may also be enhanced by the provision of sanitation, water supply, education and health services. For reasons of externalities, public goods, quality information and increasing returns, the market may not be an especially good vehicle for providing such services and they may be more efficiently and equitably supplied through the public sector.

V.2.3. *The use of national household survey data*

Sample survey data from households has been collected in developing countries for many years with the National Sample Survey in India, for example, going back to the 1940s. They have been used in the compilation of national income accounts, generating price indices, forecasting demands for planning, examining the incidence of poverty, generally measuring living standards and so on. These uses have indeed been valuable but our description here will focus on just two examples (i) the analysis of income distribution, and (ii) their use in pricing and taxation policy and particularly in the estimation of the price elasticities and distributional effects required for the evaluation of these policies. Whilst each of these areas has seen some activity by those working on developed countries there are important respects in which those working on data for developing countries have been leading the way. Within the two topics we have indicated we shall give a few examples to illustrate the kind of research ideas and methods that have been applied.

On income distribution we consider briefly work on household survey data by Anand (1983) and Anand and Harris (1986). In the former Anand provides a careful analysis of the sources of inequality in Malaysia paying particularly close attention to the definition of income and the treatment of household composition. He shows that racial disparities measured in terms of relative mean incomes of the major racial groups in Malaysia are sensitive to the income unit used (household or individual). He argues further that in Malaysia the objective of reducing racial disparities is more effectively advanced by a policy of poverty relief as opposed to a special policy of 'correcting racial imbalances'.

Anand and Harris (1986) were interested in identifying good indicators of the standard of living within a given household data set (for Sri Lanka). Large fluctuations in the income of a household within a year, or from year to year, may make measured household income in a survey a poor indicator of its standard of living. However, they show that if households are ranked by their food expenditure then many of the anomalies associated with ranking by income disappear. They attribute the relative stability (and hence usefulness) of this welfare measure to the following: (*a*) food is given high priority and is not substantially changed in response to short-run income fluctuations; (*b*) food expenditure is monotonically related to long-term income; and (*c*) food expenditure is subject to less measurement error than other items in the household budget.

The increase in the use of survey data in the analysis of tax policy has arisen for a number of reasons including the development of the theory of price and tax reform (see e.g. Newbery and Stern, 1987), increased data availability (for example through the World Bank Living Standards Measurement Study), developments in econometric methodology, and advances in computing. We cannot provide an extended treatment but illustrate briefly with some recent examples from the work of Deaton. Deaton (see his 1989 paper for a summary) focuses on two important questions in the analysis of price reform. The first is the relation between income and the consumption (or production) of a good whose price is under consideration and the second is the measurement of price elasticities. For the first of these the standard method is to simply estimate an Engel curve with a given functional form. However, Atkinson (1977), Deaton (1981) and Atkinson *et al.* (1980) and others have argued that the functional form in tax analysis can itself exert an important influence on the results. Instead Deaton (1989) shows how, using non-parametric methods, the estimated relation between production/consumption and income can be as flexible as we please.

Deaton's second problem concerns the estimation of price elasticities from survey data. Generally it has been suggested that it is only possible to do this by imposing special functional forms which allow the calculation of price elasticities from income elasticities. The difficulty with most developed country surveys is that whilst we can estimate income elasticities directly from the survey since we have income variation in the data, we do not have the price variation which would allow the estimation of price elasticities. In developing countries however, regional price variation does exist and provided care is taken to distinguish price from quality variation then direct estimation of price elasticities can be carried out. Deaton provides ingenious methods for doing this (see Deaton, 1988).

VI. CONCLUSIONS

The study of development economics has come a long way since the 1940s. We have had more than 40 years of experience which has been much more carefully documented and analysed than the periods prior to the Second World War. That experience has shown great diversity of policy and circumstance both across country and over time which has presented opportunities for, and difficulties in, deriving lessons from it. There have also been many conceptual and technical advances in economic theory and econometrics which have been productively applied to the increasing quantity and quality of data which have become available. Much has been learned, many early views have been modified, and a great deal more remains to be understood. We begin our concluding comments with a brief assessment (Section VI. 1) of what has been done, comment on some omissions (Section VI. 2), and then turn to a research agenda (Section VI. 3).

VI. 1. *An Assessment*

We have presented the achievements of development economics in terms of first, the concern for the grand issues of development strategy and the process of growth, second, the formulation and analysis of policy techniques and third, the specially focused micro study. These formed the subject matter of Sections III, IV and V of this survey. For all of these, but particularly Section III, we require a background knowledge of the recent evolution of developing countries and work on the assembly and scrutiny of this experience was reviewed briefly in Section II.

The grand issues which we presented were (i) the role of the state (ii) the process of growth and change (iii) the influence of industrialisation and trade (iv) the relations between developed and developing countries (v) structural adjustment and stabilisation (vi) population and the economy (vii) the objectives of development and strategies for achieving them. Each of the issues involved a voluminous literature and a summary assessment must inevitably be somewhat cavalier.

The ability of governments to plan comprehensively and effectively is now viewed with much greater scepticism than in the years following the Second World War. Thus many would now place equal or greater emphasis on government failure relative to market failure in the balance of the argument than was previously the case with the earlier writers, who concentrated heavily on market failure. The scepticism is born of experience but one must be careful not to be too sweeping. We have learned much about what governments can do effectively as well as where they are likely to perform badly. Whereas it is possible that they may be damaging to efficiency and growth if they try to exert detailed and universal control of production decisions, governments can be effective with direct action to raise standards of education, health and life expectancy, and in improving infrastructure such as water supply, roads, power. There is much to be learned about how to organise such action but we already know enough to realise that really substantial achievements are possible and to be able to begin to indicate the kinds of policies which will work and those which will not. Further we should not assume that all government involvement in the production process is doomed to fail. The South Korean example suggests that the careful integration of state intervention with private-sector initiative can produce most impressive results.

The study of growth and change suggests that many of the early ideas of development theorists such as Lewis have been fruitful in the sense that attention was focused on crucial issues such as industrialisation and saving. Industrialisation has been a major characteristic of growth, and savings rates have risen substantially, indeed far beyond the levels envisaged by the early writers. However, the early emphasis on industrialisation did not necessarily lead to sensible policies concerning, for example, trade and agriculture. And the increase in savings has not been fully understood either in terms of causation or effects.

The simple models beg many important questions. Some countries with high savings and investment rates have not experienced the short- and medium-term rise in growth rates that might have been expected. Thus we still have much to understand not only about the determinants of savings and investment but also why investment is so much more productive in some countries than in others. Whilst we can, of course, offer a number of ideas it is an area where further theoretical and empirical investigation should be concentrated. To put it another way we are re-emphasising that the understanding of why some countries grow more quickly than others is central to economic development. A second area where the early models were perhaps pessimistic, or at best left out major issues, concerns agriculture. The importance of agriculture to most developing countries remains, and will remain, large and we have seen that it can be dynamic as well as pose severe problems. Government policies have not always been helpful towards agriculture including, for example, over-valued exchange rates shifting relative prices against agriculture, heavy government taxation through marketing boards, neglect of rural infrastructure such as water, power and roads, and so on.

On industrialisation and trade we have seen that industrialisation does indeed play an important and major part in development although one should never lose sight of the substantial and growing role of services in all countries. We have also seen that countries which try to isolate themselves from world trade may damage their growth prospects and that in some circumstances rapid growth is associated with expanding involvement in trade. Nevertheless one must recognise that some countries have grown quickly under quite protectionist regimes and further that export expansions have sometimes followed protection or selective promotion of the exporting industries whilst these became established.

The relations between developed and less-developed countries in the long term are likely to turn on trade. Aid has been limited, with most developed countries giving rather little, at least in relation to UN targets in terms of proportions of GNP, and the prospects for sudden upsurges in generosity seem remote. It is of major importance as a source of funds to only a few, generally smaller, developing countries. In the case of debt, whilst some of the short-term problems are severe, in the longer term the problems may be managed more effectively once countries and banks digest the lessons from their mistakes of the 1970s. Trade restrictions, on the other hand, are likely to occupy centre-stage in the international economy indefinitely. The progress in dismantling tariff barriers since the Second World War may have played a major role in the rapid growth of the international economy but new and often sophisticated restraints on trade have emerged. The threat of protectionism is always present and will be a continuing problem to the expansion of developing countries.

Stabilisation and structural adjustment programmes have been precipitated by balance of payments crises with depressing frequency and have often been associated with the IMF and World Bank. The programmes generally have major austerity elements and the political and economic difficulties of who bears the costs and how they are spread over time have often appeared insurmountable, with the effect that programmes are often abandoned. Research and policy design are increasingly concentrated on how programmes can be formulated so that damage to longer-term growth programmes in the process of shorter-term adjustment is limited and so that the more vulnerable elements in the community can be protected.

The research on population reviewed here concentrated on the economic effects of an expanding population with changing composition. The Malthusian alarm of the late 1960s and early 1970s which was associated with the view that population control was the first priority has, to some extent, dissipated and a less pessimistic view prevails. However, expanding population can and has exacerbated existing problems. For example, pressure on land has greatly increased and longer life expectancy, in itself a major success, will make support for the old more difficult. Family planning programmes can themselves have only limited success until circumstances are such that families desire fewer births.

The debate on the objectives of development has seen refreshing advance over the last two or three decades. This is not simply in terms of concern with income distribution – this aspect of development was central from the beginning. We now see a much greater concentration on issues such as health and life expectancy, education and gender, and the study of policies to further these objectives.

The study of methods for planning, for cost–benefit analysis and for pricing and taxation provides an important example of areas where development economics has led the way in theoretical and technical understanding in economics. The early planning models and their development towards, for example, social accounting matrices, have provided valuable tools for assembling information and understanding how an economy works. Computable general equilibrium models have been developed largely in the context of policy analysis for developing countries and can provide useful insights provided they are used sensibly. The theory and practice of cost–benefit analysis has shown how the crucial idea of social opportunity cost can be developed systematically for distorted economies and applied constructively. Applications of this approach are not confined simply to the evaluation of investment projects but can be used over a wide range of policy questions including tax and price reform. Experience and methods for analysing this last issue, where taxation faces many difficulties and constraints, have progressed strongly in recent years.

Finally, we have the detailed micro studies which we have suggested provide in many ways the foundation of the subject. The study of economic development has seen many fine examples of the combination of close and detailed study of particular phenomena with the best practice in theory and statistical technique. The examples of contributions included here were village studies, nutrition, inequality, and household behaviour, but there are many more. These do not usually provide dramatic advances which up-end the subject but their gradual accumulation provides much of the real substance of development economics.

VI.2. *Omissions*

Given the very wide scope of the subject, which we defined as economic analysis applied to poor and developing countries, we have had to be very selective and inevitably there are major omissions. The main reasons for omissions have been the strategy followed here of choosing examples of important contributions, rather than attempting a comprehensive survey, together with my own lack of acquaintance with a number of the subjects or in the detail required for a coherent treatment. In this brief sub-section we offer one or two references of the survey type, recent where possible, designed to help the reader into the literature.

On natural resources and the environment one might begin with Kneese and Sweeney (1988) and Tisdell (1988). Gender appeared briefly in our discussion of nutrition in Section V and there is a large literature – see, for example, Harriss (1986) and Boserup (1970). Marxist analysis of development constitutes a perspective which has been essentially untouched here, see Baran (1957), Bowles (1985), Roemer (1982), Bardhan (1988) for an introduction. Transnational corporations and their effects on developing countries have been a substantial area of research – see Helleiner (1988) for a survey. Finally, whilst we have discussed population and nutrition to some extent, human capital in the form of education, skill formation and acquisition, and health more generally have been major omissions – see Schultz (1988) for a survey of education, and Behrman and Deolalikar (1988) for a survey of health and nutrition.

VI.3. *A Research Agenda*

A research agenda is, and should be, a personal view. It would be very worrying and dangerous if everyone were pursuing the same issues. The following topics therefore represent an individual judgement of priorities and possibilities rather than an attempt to provide a balanced programme for the subject. Many of the topics follow in a direct way from our assessment of what has been achieved.

We begin with some questions arising from the discussion of the grand issues. We still have a great deal to understand about why some countries grow faster than others. Savings rates have been raised in many countries but the productivity of investment shows enormous variation. We would like to know much more about the role of infrastructure, human capital, technical progress, effective management and constructive government in this variation. How can the productivity of investment be raised and what determines investment?

The theoretical and empirical analysis of the process of reform of government policies is a challenging issue. Many governments have decided to, or have been under pressure to, use markets more effectively, or generally reduce the role of the state in production activities. China has been an example of outstanding importance here. The consequences of changing policies and the relations between different policies in that change are often, however, only hazily understood and many are not considered at all. For example, if social security and public service functions are organised through the commune or firm then dismantling the commune or allowing some firms to decline in response to market forces can have wide-ranging implications outside those of simply raising productivity. Public finance, both in terms of raising revenue and controlling expenditure, becomes more important when resources are not commanded and investment is left for firms to decide. Generally then, the understanding and structuring of the process of policy change, particularly in respect to the greater use of markets, is a high priority.

Trade policy has become an increasingly important area for study with, on the one hand, the generation of theories which include oligopolistic competition, increasing returns and intra-industry trade and, on the other, the ever-growing importance of developing countries in international trade and the exhortation by many international institutions and economists to continue the process. Protectionism by richer countries is likely to be a continuing threat to further advancement so that the careful study of the consequences of different trade policies by developed and developing countries will be an ever-present issue.

In the study of both growth and trade we should like to know more about how the government and private sector can work together more effectively. There is a great deal of experience and the careful assembly of that empirical knowledge can be very productive. There are two approaches to this and other aspects of policy which should form important strands in this research. The first is what one might call the detailed historical analysis of the economics of growth, i.e. a historical perspective but with an emphasis on the identification and economic analysis of the central reasons for the economic outcomes, good or bad. The second is the positive analysis of governments in order to find out why they chose the economic policies they did. In this way we may illuminate the constraints and pressures on government and might, for example, be able to point to simple and robust policies which might combine appropriately economic desirability and administrative feasibility with political stability and resistance to manipulation.

The surge of interest in objectives other than consumption or income is likely to continue and this is a promising development. We know enough to say that governments can exert a positive influence in areas such as health, education, nutrition, and social security but we have much to learn about how that influence can be productively operated. We want to know about what will, and what will not, work in different circumstances and why. The interrelation between policies for growth, distribution of income and the protection and raising of living standards in the broadest sense represents a challenging research agenda. It has always been a major theme but is becoming very active.

In this the analysis of policies for income support for the most vulnerable groups will be central.

The newer approaches to industrial economics which stress strategic relations between firms, and between firms and government, could provide a valuable impetus to a comparatively neglected area in the economics of development. Many advances in economic theory and econometrics in recent years have made their mark on work on developing countries including those concerning risk, information, bargaining, taxation, consumer behaviour, survey analysis, labour economics and so on. The effect of the new industrial organisation theories, however, appears to be less substantial other than in issues involving international trade. But markets in developing countries are no less subject to strategic behaviour, oligopoly and so on than those in developed countries and there would appear to be an important area for further research. As we have indicated the efficiency of use of capital equipment is a central issue and it is one, for example, on which the newer theories might throw light.

All this discussion of what governments can and cannot, or should or should not, do is predicated on judgements about government revenues or resource mobilisation. Those who suggest that governments should do less or little often have as part of their argument the difficulties and costs of raising resources. Those who argue that governments should do a great deal more have an obligation to show how the resources can be raised without excessive damage. Thus the study of tax reform and the pricing of goods and services in the public sector must remain a priority. Techniques of analysis have advanced considerably but further empirical study should remain high on the agenda, particularly concerning the combination of administrative feasibility and economic advantage.

Finally the detailed microstudies should continue to add to the fund of experience on which our judgement of the working of poor economies is based. This will in part be driven by some of the large questions which we have been describing. For example, the more precise identification of the weak in individual communities will provide us with guidance on which schemes of support might reach them. And the detailed study of support schemes which have been attempted in practice can tell us how policies might go wrong and how they might be improved. In industry the close study of firms and their relation with government could guide us on how different policy initiatives can stimulate the private sector. These studies should not however necessarily be led by immediate policy concerns. It is the curiosity of the individual researcher who is intrigued to test a theory on the ground or to find out how a particular market or economy functions which has provided us with many of our most valuable insights in the past.

References

There has been no attempt to be exhaustive. We have tried to give references that will take the reader into a literature which has been treated only summarily in the text rather than identify all the important contributions.

Adelman, I. and Morris, C. (1973). *Economic Growth and Social Equity in Developing Countries*. Stanford: Stanford University Press.

Ahluwalia, M. (1974). 'Dimensions of the problem.' In *Redistribution with Growth* (ed. H. Chenery *et al.*), New York: Oxford University Press.

—— (1976*a*). 'Income distribution and development: some stylized facts.' *American Economic Review*, vol. 66 (2), pp. 128–35.

—— (1976*b*). 'Inequality, poverty, and development.' *Journal of Development Economics*, vol. 3 (4), pp. 307–42.

Ahamed, L. (1986). 'Stabilisation policies in developing countries.' *World Bank Research Observer*, vol. 1, pp. 79–110.

Ahmad, E. and Stern, N. H. (1984). 'The theory of tax reform and Indian indirect taxes.' *Journal of Public Economics*, vol. 25 (3), pp. 259–98.

—— and —— (1987). 'Alternative sources of government revenue: illustrations from India and Pakistan.' Discussion Paper No. 2, Development Economics Research Program, London School of Economics, London.

—— and —— (1989). 'Taxation for developing countries.' In Chenery and Srinivasan (1989).

—— and —— (forthcoming). *The Theory and Practice of Tax Reform in Developing Countries.*

Anand, S. (1983). *Inequality and Poverty in Malaysia: Measurement and Decomposition.* Oxford: Oxford University Press. A World Bank Research Publication.

—— and Harris, C. J. (1986). 'Food and standard of living: an analysis based on Sri Lankan data.' Paper presented at the Conference on Food Strategies held at WIDER, Helsinki, 21–25 July, 1986; to be published in Drèze and Sen (forthcoming).

—— and Kanbur, S. M. R. (1989*a*). 'The Kuznets process and the inequality-development relationship.' *Journal of Development Economics* (forthcoming).

—— and —— (1989*b*). 'Inequality and development: a critique.' *Journal of Development Economics* (forthcoming).

Arndt, H. W. (1985). 'The origins of structuralism.' *World Development*, vol. 13 (2), pp. 151–60.

—— (1988). '"Market failure" and underdevelopment.' *World Development*, vol. 16 (2) pp. 219–29.

Arrow, K. J. (1962). 'The economic implications of learning by doing.' *Review of Economic Studies*, vol. 29, pp. 155–73.

Atkinson, A. B. (1977). 'Optimal taxation and the direct versus indirect tax controversy.' *Canadian Journal of Economics*, vol. 10 (4), pp. 590–606.

——, Stern, N. H. and Gomulka, J. (1980). 'On the switch from direct to indirect taxation.' *Journal of Public Economics*, vol. 14 (2), pp. 195–224.

—— and Stiglitz, J. E. (1976). 'Design of tax structure: direct versus indirect taxation.' *Journal of Public Economics*, vol. 6, pp. 55–67.

Austin, J. E. and Zeitlin, M. F. (eds) (1981). *Nutrition Interventions in Developing Countries.* Cambridge, Mass.: Oelgesschlager, Gunn and Hain.

Avramovic, D. (1988). 'Conditionality: facts, theory and policy – contribution to the reconstruction of the international financial system.' World Institute of Development Research Working Paper No. 37.

Bahl, R., Kim, C. K. and Park, C. K. (1986). *Public Finances During the Korean Modernization Process.* Cambridge, Mass.: Harvard University Press.

Bailey, F. G. (1957). *Caste and the Economic Frontier.* Manchester: Manchester University Press.

Balassa, B. (1971). *The Structure of Protection in Developing Countries.* Baltimore: Johns Hopkins University Press.

Balogh, T. (1961). 'Economic policy and the price system.' *Economic Bulletin of Latin America*, vol. 6 (1).

Baran, P. (1957). *The Political Economy of Growth.* New York: Monthly Review Press.

Bardhan, P. (1988). 'Alternative approaches to development economics: an evaluation.' In Chenery and Srinivasan (1988).

Barnum, H. N. and Squire, L. (1979). 'An econometric application of the theory of the farm-household.' *Journal of Development Economics*, vol. 6, pp. 79–102.

Basu, K. (1984). *The Less Developed Economy: A Critique of Contemporary Theory.* Oxford: Basil Blackwell.

Bauer, P. T. (1963). *West African Trade: a Study of Competition, Oligopoly and Monopoly in a Changing Economy.* London: Routledge and Kegan Paul.

—— (1971). *Dissent on Development: Studies and Debates in Development Economics.* London: Weidenfeld and Nicolson.

—— (1984). *Reality and Rhetoric.* London: Weidenfeld.

Behrman, J. R. and Deolalikar, A. B. (1987). 'Will developing country nutrition improve with income? A case study for rural South India.' *Journal of Political Economy*, vol. 95 (3), pp. 492–507.

—— and —— (1988). 'Health and nutrition.' In Chenery and Srinivisan (1988).

Bell, C. (1977). 'Alternative theories of sharecropping: some tests using evidence from North-East India.' *Journal of Development Studies*, vol. 13 (4), pp. 893–920.

—— (1988). 'Credit markets and interlinked transactions.' In Chenery and Srinivasan (1988).

—— and Zusman, P. (1976). 'A bargaining theoretic approach to cropsharing contracts.' *American Economic Review*, vol. 66, pp. 578–88.

Berck, P. and Cechetti, S. G. (1985). 'Portfolio diversification, futures markets, and uncertain consumption prices.' *American Journal of Agricultural Economics*, vol. 67 (3), pp. 497–507.

Bertrand, J. and Squire, L. (1980). 'The relevance of the dual economy models: a case study of Thailand.' *Oxford Economic Papers*, vol. 32 (3), pp. 480–511.

Bevan, D. L., Collier, P. and Gunning, J. W. (1988). 'The political economy of poverty, equity, and growth in Nigeria and Indonesia.' Mimeo, World Bank.

——, —— and —— (forthcoming). *Controlled Open Economies*. Oxford: Oxford University Press.

Bhagwati, J. (1970). 'The tying of aid.' In *Foreign Aid* (ed. J. Bhagwati and R. S. Eckaus). Penguin Modern Economic Readings.

—— (1978). *Foreign Trade Regimes and Economic Development: Anatomy and Consequences of Exchange Control Regimes*. Cambridge, Mass.: Ballinger.

—— (1988*a*). *Protectionism*. Cambridge, Mass: MIT Press.

—— (1988*b*). 'Poverty and public policy.' *World Development*, vol. 16 (5), pp. 539–55.

— and Desai, P. (1970). *India – Planning for Industrialization*. London: Oxford University Press.

Bhende, M. J. (1983). 'Credit markets in the semi-arid tropics of rural South India.' Economics Program Progress Report 56, ICRISAT, Andra Pradesh, India.

Bigman, D. (1982). *Coping with Hunger: Toward a System of Security and Price Stabilisation*. Cambridge, Mass: Balinger.

—— (1985). *Food Policies and Food Security under Instability*. Lexington.

Binswanger, H., Balaramaiah, Bashkar Rao, V., Bhende, M. J. and Kashirsagar, K. V. (1985). 'Credit markets in rural South India: theoretical issues and empirical analysis.' Agriculture and Rural Development Department Discussion Paper. Washington: World Bank.

—— and Rosenzweig, M. R. (1986). 'Credit markets, wealth and endowments in rural South India.' Paper presented at the 8th International Economic Association World Congress, New Delhi, India, 1–5 December.

Birdsall, N. (1988). 'Economic approaches to population growth.' In Chenery and Srinivisan (1988).

Bliss, C. J. (1985). 'Taxation, cost–benefit analysis and effective protection.' In Newbery and Stern (1987).

—— (1987). 'The new trade theory and economic policy.' *Oxford Review of Economic Policy*, vol. 3 (1), pp. 20–36.

—— and Stern, N. H. (1978*a, b*). 'Productivity, wages and nutrition: Part I, the theory' and 'Part II, some observations.' *Journal of Development Economics*, vol. 5 (4), pp. 331–62 and pp. 363–98.

—— and —— (1982). *Palanpur: the Economy of an Indian Village*. Oxford: Clarendon Press.

Bloom, D. E. and Freeman, R. B. (1987). 'Population growth, labour supply, and employment in developing countries.' In Johnson and Lee (1987).

Bond, M. E. (1987). 'An econometric study of primary product exports from developing country regions to the world.' *IMF Staff Papers*, vol. 34 (2), pp. 191–227.

Boserup, E. (1965). *The Conditions of Agricultural Growth. The Economics of Agrarian Change Under Population Pressure*. London: Allen and Unwin.

—— (1970). *Woman's Role in Economic Development*. New York: St Martins Press.

—— (1981). *Population Growth and Technological Change: A Study in Long-Term Trends*. Chicago: University of Chicago Press.

Boulier, B. L. (1985). 'Family planning programs and contraceptive availability: their effects on contraceptive use and fertility.' In *The Effect of Family Planning Programs on Fertility in the Developing World* (ed. N. Birdsall). World Bank Staff Working Paper No. 677, Washington, D.C.

Bowles, S. (1985). 'The production process in a competitive economy: Walrasian, Neo-Hobbesian, and Marxian models.' *American Economic Review*, vol. 75 (1), pp. 16–36.

Braverman, A. and Guasch, J. L. (1986). 'Rural credit markets and institutions in developing countries: lessons for policy analysis from practice and modern theory.' *World Development*, vol. 14 (10/11), pp. 1253–67.

——, Hammer, J. S. and Gron, A. (1987). 'Multimarket analysis of agricultural price policies in an operational context: the case of Cyprus'. *World Bank Economic Review*, vol. 1 (2), pp. 337–56.

——, and Stiglitz, J. E. (1982). 'Share cropping and the interlinking of agrarian markets.' *American Economic Review*, vol. 72 (4), pp. 695–715.

Bruno, M. (1967). 'The optimal selection of export-promoting and import-substituting projects.' In *Planning the External Sector: Techniques, Problems and Policies. Report on the First Interregional Seminar on Development Planning*. New York: United Nations.

—— (1972). 'Domestic resource costs and effective protection: clarification and synthesis.' *Journal of Political Economy*, vol. 80, pp. 16–33.

Buchanan, J. M. (1986). *Liberty, Market and the State: Political Economy in the 1980's*. Brighton; Wheatsheaf.

Buiter, W. H. (1988). 'Some thoughts on the role of fiscal policy in stabilization and structural adjustment in developing countries.' National Bureau of Economic Research Working Paper No. 2603.

—— and Srinivasan, T. N. (1987). 'Rewarding the profligate and punishing the prudent and poor: some recent proposals for debt relief.' *World Development*, vol. 15 (3), pp. 411–7.

Bulow, J. and Rogoff, K. (1989*a*). 'Sovereign debt: is to forgive to forget?' *American Economic Review*, vol. 79 (1), pp. 43–50.

—— and —— (1989*b*). 'A constant recontracting model of sovereign debt.' *Journal of Political Economy*, vol. 97 (1), pp. 155–78.

Caldwell, J. C. (1986). 'Routes to low mortality in developing countries.' *Population and Development Review*, vol. 12 (2), pp. 171–220.

Calvo, G. A. (1978). 'Urban development and wage determination in LDC's: trade unions in the Harris–Todaro model.' *International Economic Review*, vol. 19, pp. 65–81.

Cardoso, E. and Dornbusch, R. (1989). 'Foreign private capital flows.' In Chenery and Srinivasan (1988).

Cassen, R. H. (1986). *Does Aid Work?* Clarendon Press: Oxford.

Castaneda, T. (1984). 'Contexto Socioeconomico y Causas del Descenso de la Mortalida Infantil en Chile.' Documento de Trabajo No. 28, Centro de Estudios Publicos, Santiago, Chile.

Chakravarty, S. (1987). 'The state of development economics.' *The Manchester School of Economics and Social Studies*. vol. 66 (2), pp. 125–43.

Chayanov, A. K. (1925). *The Theory of the Peasant Economy*. Homewood, Ill.: Irwin Press.

Chenery, H. B. (1956). 'Inter-regional and international input output analysis.' In *The Structural Interdependence of the Economy* (ed. T. Barna). New York: John Wiley and Sons.

—— (1958). 'Development policies and programmes.' *Economic Bulletin for Latin America*, vol. 3 (1).

—— (1965). 'Comparative advantage and development policy' in American Economic Association and Royal Economic Society. *Surveys of Economic Theory: Growth and Development*. London: Macmillan.

—— (1979). *Structural Change and Development Policy*. New York: Oxford University Press.

—— (1983). 'Interaction between theory and observation in development.' *World Development*, vol. 11 (10), pp. 853–61.

—— and Bruno, M. (1962). 'Development alternatives in an open economy.' *Economic Journal*, vol. 72 (285), pp. 79–103.

—— and Clark, P. G. (1959). *Interindustry Economics*. New York: John Wiley and Sons.

——, Robinson, S. and Syrquin, M. (1986). *Industrialisation and Growth: A Comparative Study*. Washington: World Bank.

—— and Srinivasan, T. N. (eds) (1988 and 1989). *Handbook of Development Economics*, Vols I and II. North Holland: Elsevier Science Publishers.

—— and Strout, A. (1966). 'Foreign assistance and economic development.' *American Economic Review*, vol. 56, pp. 679–733.

—— and Syrquin, M. (1975). *Patterns of Development, 1950–1970*. London: Oxford University Press.

Cheung, S. N. S. (1969). *The Theory of Share Tenancy*. Chicago: University of Chicago Press.

Clark, C. (1940). *The Conditions of Economic Progress*. London: Macmillan.

Clark, P. B. (1975). 'Intersectoral consistency and macroeconomic planning.', In C. R. Blitzer, P. B. Clark and L. Taylor, *Economy-Wide Models and Development Planning*. Oxford: Oxford University Press.

Clifford, J. (1966). 'The tying of aid and the problem of local costs.' *Journal of Development Studies*, vol. 2, pp. 153–73.

Club of Rome (1972). *The Limits to Growth*. New York: Universe Books.

Coale, A. J. and Hoover, E. M. (1958). *Population Growth and Economic Development in Low-Income Countries*. Princeton: Princeton University Press.

Cole, W. and Sanders, R. (1985). 'Internal migration and urban employment in the third world.' *American Economic Review*, June.

Connell, J. (1975). *Labour Utilization: An Annotated Bibliography of Village Studies*. Village Studies Programme at IDS: University of Sussex.

Corden, M. (1971). *The Theory of Protection*. Oxford: Clarendon Press.

—— (1974). *Trade Policy and Economic Welfare*. Oxford: Clarendon Press.

—— (1984). 'The normative theory of international trade.' In *The Handbook of International Economics* (ed. R. W. Jones and P. Kenen). North Holland: Elsevier Science Publishers.

Cornia, G. and Stewart, F. (1987). 'Country experience with adjustment.' In Cornia *et al.* (1987).

——, Jolly, R. and Stewart, F. (eds) (1987). *Adjustment with a Human Face*. Oxford: Clarendon.

Dasgupta, P. S. (1980). 'Decentralization and rights.' *Economica*, vol. 47, pp. 107–24.

——, Marglin, S. and Sen, A. K. (1972). *Guidelines for Project Evaluation*. New York: United Nations.

—— and Ray, D. (1987). 'Inequality as a determinant of malnutrition and unemployment: theory.' ECONOMIC JOURNAL, vol. 97 (385), pp. 117–83.

De Janvry, A. and Sadoulet, E. (1987). 'Agricultural price policy in general equilibrium frameworks: a comparative analysis.' Department of Agricultural and Resource Economics Working Paper No. 342. University of California, Berkeley.

De Melo, J. (1988). 'SAM based models: an introduction.' *Journal of Policy Modelling*, vol. 10 (3), pp. 321–6.

Deaton, A. (1979). 'Optimally uniform commodity taxes.' *Economics Letters*, vol. 2 (4), pp. 357–61.

—— (1981). 'Optimal taxes and the structure of preferences.' *Econometrica*, vol. 49, pp. 1245–60.

—— (1988). 'Quality, quantity and spatial variation in price.' *American Economic Review*, vol. 78 (3), pp. 418–31.

—— (1989). 'Rice prices and income distribution in Thailand: a non-parametric analysis.' ECONOMIC JOURNAL, vol. 99 (35), pp. 1–35.

—— and Muellbauer, J. (1980). 'An Almost Ideal Demand System', *American Economic Reveiw*, vol. 70 (3), pp. 312–26.
—— and Stern, N. (1986). 'Optimally uniform commodity taxes, taste differences, and lump-sum grants.' *Economics Letters*, vol. 20, pp. 263–6.
Denison, E. F. (1967). *Why Growth Rates Differ: Post-War Experience in Nine Western Countries.* Washington: Brookings Institution.
Dixit, A. K. (1973). 'Models of dual economies.' In *Models of Economic Growth* (ed. J. A. Mirrlees and N. H. Stern). London: Macmillan.
—— (1983). 'International trade policy for oligopolistic industries.' ECONOMIC JOURNAL, vol. 94 (Conference Papers), pp. 1–16.
—— (1987). 'Trade and insurance with moral hazard.' *Journal of International Economics*, vol. 23, pp. 201–20.
—— (1989*a*). 'Trade and insurance with adverse selection.' *Review of Economic Studies*, April.
—— (1989*b*). 'Trade and insurance with imperfectly observed outcomes.' *Quarterly Journal of Economics*, February.
—— and Norman, V. (1980). *The Theory of International Trade.* Cambridge: Cambridge University Press.
Dornbusch, R. (1986). *Dollars, Debts and Deficits.* Leuven: Leuven University Press.
Drèze, J. P. and Sen, A. K. (forthcoming). *Hunger and Public Action*, Oxford: Oxford University Press.
—— and Stern, N. H. (1987). 'The theory of cost–benefit analysis.' In *Handbook of Public Economics* (ed. A. Auerbach and M. Feldstein, 1987). North Holland: Elsevier Science Publishers, B.V.
Eade, D. and Jackson, T. (1982). *Against the Grain.* Oxford: OXFAM.
Eaton, J. and Gersovitz, M. (1981). 'Debt with potential repudiation: theoretical and empirical analysis.' *Review of Economic Studies*, vol. 48.
——, —— and Stiglitz, J. (1986). 'The pure theory of country risk.' *European Economic Review*, vol. 30, pp. 481–513.
—— and Grossman, G. (1985). 'Tariffs as insurance: optimal commercial policy when domestic markets are incomplete.' *Canadian Journal of Economics*, vol. 18 (2), pp. 258–72.
Edwards, S. (1988). 'Structural adjustment policies in highly indebted countries.' National Bureau of Economic Research Working Paper No. 2502.
—— and Ahamed, L. (eds) (1986). *Economic Adjustment and Exchange Rates in Developing Countries.* Chicago: University of Chicago Press.
Epstein, T. S. (1962). *Economic Development and Social Change in South India.* Manchester: Manchester University Press.
—— (1973). *South India: Yesterday, Today and Tomorrow.* London: Macmillan.
Farrell, M. J. (1970). 'The magnitude of 'rate-of-growth' effects on aggregate savings.' ECONOMIC JOURNAL, vol. 80, pp. 873–94.
Feder. G. (1982). *On Exports and Economic Growth.* Washington: World Bank.
Fernandez, R. and Rosenthal, R. W. (1988). 'Sovereign-debt renegotiations: a strategic analysis.' Department of Economics, Boston University.
Fields, G. S. (1975). 'Rural–urban migration, urban unemployment and underemployment, and job search activity in LDCs.' *Journal of Development Economics*, vol. 2 (2), pp. 165–87.
—— (1980). *Poverty, Inequality and Development.* Cambridge: Cambridge University Press.
—— (1988). 'Labor market modelling and the urban informal sector: theory and evidence.' Paper presented at the seminar on 'The informal sector revisited,' held at the Development Centre of the OECD, Paris, 7–9 September.
Fischer, S. (1987). 'Resolving the international debt crisis.' National Bureau of Economic Research Working Paper No. 2373.
Folbre, N. (1986). 'Hearts and Spades: paradigms of household economics.' *World Development*, vol. 14 (2).
Forrester, J. W. (1971). *World Dynamics*, Cambridge, Mass.: Wright-Allen.
Gemmell, N. (1987). *Surveys in Development Economics.* Oxford: Basil Blackwell.
Gersovitz, M. (1988). 'Saving and development.' In Chenery and Srinivasan (1988).
Gillis, M. (1985). 'Micro and macroeconomics of tax reform: Indonesia.' *Journal of Development Economics*, vol. 19, pp. 221–54.
Glaeser, B. (ed.) (1987). *The Green Revolution Revisited: A Critique and Alternatives.* London: Allen and Unwin.
Glover, D. and Simon, J. L. (1975). 'The effect of population density on infrastructure: the case of roadbuilding.' *Economic Development and Cultural Change*, vol. 23 (3), pp. 453–68.
Goode, R. (1984). *Government Finance in Developing Countries.* Washington D.C.: The Brookings Institution.
Government of India (1981). *A Technical Note on the Sixth Plan of India (1980–85)*, Government of India Planning Commission.
Griffin, K. (1979). *The Political Economy of Agrarian Change: An Essay on the Green Revolution*, London: Macmillan.
—— and Enos, J. L. (1970). 'Foreign assistance: objectives and consequences.' *Economic Development and Cultural Change*, April, pp. 313–37.
Grilli, E. R. and Yang, M. C. (1988). 'Primary commodity prices, manufactured goods prices, and the terms

of trade of developing countries: what the long-run shows.' *World Bank Economic Review*, vol. 2 (1), pp. 1–48.

Guesnerie, R. (1977). 'On the direction of tax reform.' *Journal of Public Economics*, vol. 7, pp. 179–202.

Gupta, S. P. (1988). *Planning and Development in India: A Critique*, New Delhi: Allied Publishers Pvt. Ltd.

Harberger, A. C. (1984). *World Economic Growth*, San Francisco, Calif.: ICS Press, Institute for Contemporary Studies.

Hallagen, W. (1978). 'Self selection by contractual choice and the theory of sharecropping.' *Bell Journal of Economics*, vol. 9 (2), pp. 344–55.

Harris, J. R. and Todaro, M. (1970). 'Migration, unemployment and development: a two-sector analysis.' *American Economic Review*, vol. 60, pp. 126–42.

Harris, R. and Case, D. (1984). *Trade, Industrial Policy and Canadian Manufacturing*, Toronto, Ontario: Economic Council.

Harriss, B. (1986). 'The intrafamily distribution of hunger in South Asia.' Paper presented at the Conference on Food Strategies held at WIDER, Helsinki, 21–25 July; to be published in Drèze, J. P. and Sen, A. K. (eds) *The Political Economy of Hunger* (forthcoming), Oxford University Press.

Harrod, R. F. (1939). 'An essay in dynamic theory.' ECONOMIC JOURNAL, vol. 49, pp. 14–33.

Hatta, T. (1986). 'Welfare effects of changing commodity tax rates toward uniformity.' *Journal of Public Economics*, vol. 29 (1), pp. 99–112.

Hayami, Y. and Ruttan, V. W. (1987). 'Population growth and agricultural productivity.' In Johnson and Lee (1987).

Hayter, T. (1971). *Aid as Imperialism*. Harmondsworth: Penguin.

Helleiner, B. (1988). 'Transnational corporations, direct foreign investment, and economic development.' In Chenery and Srinivasan (1988).

Helpman, E. and Krugman, P. R. (1985). *Market Structure and Foreign Trade: Increasing Returns, Imperfect Competition and the International Economy*, Brighton: Wheatsheaf.

Henderson, J. (1987). 'Industrialization and urbanization: international experience.' In Johnson and Lee (1987).

Hill, P. (1986). *Development Economics on Trial: The Anthropological Case for a Prosecution*. Cambridge: Cambridge University Press.

Hirschman, A. O. (1958). *The Strategy of Economic Development*. New Haven, Connecticut: Yale University Press.

—— (1981). *Essays in Trespassing: Economics to Politics and Beyond*, Cambridge: Cambridge University Press.

Hopper, W. D. (1965). 'Allocation efficiency in "traditional Indian agriculture".' *Journal of Farm Economics*, vol. 47, pp. 611–24.

Jain, S. (1975). *Size Distribution of Income: A Compilation of Data*, Washington D.C.: World Bank.

Jacobs, N. (1985). *The Korean Road to Modernization and Development*, Urbana and Chicago: University of Illinois Press.

Jennings, A., Singer, H. and Wood, J. (1987). *Food Aid: the Challenge and the Opportunity*, Oxford: Oxford University Press.

Jimenez, E. (1987). 'The public subsidization of education and health in developing countries: a review of equity and efficiency.' *World Bank Research Observer*, vol. 1 (1), pp. 111–30.

Johnson, D. G. and Lee, R. D. (eds) (1987). *Population Growth and Economic Development: Issues and Evidence*, Madison: University of Wisconsin Press.

Jorgensen, D. W. (1961). 'The development of a dual economy.' ECONOMIC JOURNAL, vol. 71 (282), pp. 309–34.

Katz, M. (1987). 'Pricing publicly supplied goods and services.' In Newbery and Stern (1987).

Kelley, A. C. (1988). 'Economic consequences of population change in the third world.' *Journal of Economic Literature*, vol. 26 (4), pp. 685–728.

Keyfitz, N. (1982). *Population Change and Social Policy*, Lanham, MD: University Press of America.

Kim, W. S. and Yun, K. Y. (1988). 'Fiscal policy and development in Korea.' *World Development*, vol. 16 (1), pp. 65–83.

King, E. M. (1987). 'The effect of family size on family welfare: what do we know?' In Johnson and Lee (1987).

King, M. (1983). 'Welfare analysis of tax reforms using household data.' *Journal of Public Economics* vol. 21 (2), pp. 183–214.

Kneese, A. V. and Sweeney, J. L. (eds.) (1988). *Handbook of Natural Resource and Energy Economics*, Amsterdam: North Holland.

Kravis, I. B. (1970). 'Trade as a handmaiden of growth: similarities between nineteenth and twentieth centuries.' ECONOMIC JOURNAL, vol. 80 (320), pp. 850–72.

Kravis, I. B., Heston, A. W. and Summers, R. (1978). 'Real GDP per capita for more than one hundred countries.' ECONOMIC JOURNAL, vol. 88, pp. 215–42.

Krishna, K. (1988). 'What do voluntary export restraints do?' National Bureau of Economic Research. Working Paper Series, No. 2612.

Krueger, A. O. (1972). 'Evaluating restrictionist trade regimes: theory and measurement.' *Journal of Political Economy*, vol. 80, pp. 48–62.

—— (1978). *Liberalization Attempts and Consequences*. New York: National Bureau of Economic Research.

Krugman, P. R. (1986). *Strategic Trade Policy and the New International Economics*, Cambridge, Mass: MIT Press.

—— (1987). 'Is free trade passé?' *The Journal of Economic Perspectives*, vol. 1 (2), pp. 131–44.

—— (1988). 'Market-based debt-reduction schemes.' National Bureau of Economic Research. Working Paper Series No. 2587.

—— (forthcoming). 'Financing vs. forgiving a debt overhang.' *Journal of Development Economics*.

Kuznets, S. (1955). 'Economic growth and income inequality.' *American Economic Review*, vol. 65 (1), pp. 1–29.

—— (1961). 'Quantitative aspects of the economic growth of nations: IV. Long-term trends in capital formation proportions.' *Economic Development and Cultural Change*, vol. 9, pp. 1–124.

—— (1963). 'Quantitative aspects of economic growth of nations: VIII. Distribution of income by size.' *Economic Development and Cultural Change*, vol. 11 (2), pp. 1–80.

—— (1971). *Economic Growth of Nations: Total Output and Production Structure*. Cambridge, Mass: Harvard University Press.

Lal, D. (1983). *The Poverty of 'Development Economics.'* Institute of Economic Affairs. London: Hobart.

—— (1988). *The Hindu Equilibrium*, Vols 1 and 2. Oxford: Clarendon, (1988, 1989).

—— and Rajapatirana, S. (1987). 'Foreign trade regimes and economic growth in developing countries.' *World Bank Research Observer*, vol. 2 (2), pp. 189–218.

Lam, D. (1987). 'Distribution issues in the relationship between population growth and economic development.' In Johnson and Lee (1987).

Lappé, F. M. and Collins, J. (1980). *Food First*, Great Britain: Souvenir Press.

Lecaillon, J. *et al.* (eds) (1984). *Income Distribution and Economic Development: An Analytical Survey*. Geneva: International Labour Office.

Leff, N. (1982). *Underdevelopment and Development in Brazil*. London: Allen and Unwin.

Leibenstein, H. (1957). *Economic Backwardness and Economic Growth*. New York: John Wiley and Son.

—— (1978). *General X-efficiency Theory and Economic Development*, New York: University Press.

Leontief, W. (1941). *The Structure of the American Economy 1919–1929*. Cambridge: Harvard University Press.

Lewis, W. A. (1954). 'Economic development with unlimited supplies of labour.' *Manchester School*, vol. 22, pp. 139–91.

—— (1955). *The Theory of Economic Growth*. Homewood, Ill.: Irwin.

—— (1978). *Growth and Fluctuations, 1870–1913*. London: Allen and Unwin.

—— (1984). 'The state of development theory.' *American Economic Review*, vol. 74 (1), pp. 1–10.

Lipton, M. (1968). 'The theory of the optimizing peasant.' *Journal of Development Studies*, vol. 4 (3), pp. 327–51.

—— (1977). *Why Poor People Stay Poor: Urban Bias and World Development*. London: Temple-Smith, and Harvard University Press.

—— (1983*a*). 'Poverty, undernutrition and hunger.' *World Bank Staff Working Paper* No. 597, Washington D.C.

—— (1983*b*). 'Labor and poverty.' *World Bank Staff Working Paper* No. 616, Washington D.C.

—— (1983*c*). 'Demography and poverty.' *World Bank Staff Working Paper* No. 623, Washington D.C.

—— (1983*d*). 'Land assets and rural poverty.' *World Bank Staff Working Paper* No. 744, Washington D.C.

—— (1987). 'Limits of price policy for agriculture: which way for the World Bank?' *Development Policy Review*, June.

—— (1988). 'The poor and the poorest: some interim findings.' *World Bank Discussion Paper* No. 25, Washington D.C.

—— and Longhurst, R. (1989). *New Seeds and Poor People*. London: Hutchinson, and Johns Hopkins University Press.

Little, I. M. D. (1982). *Economic Development*. New York: Basic Books.

—— and Mirrlees, J. A. (1969). *Manual of Industrial Project Analysis in Developing Countries: Social Cost Benefit Analysis*. Paris: OECD.

—— and —— (1974). *Project Appraisal and Planning for Developing Countries*. London: Heinemann.

——, Scitovsky, T. and Scott, M. (1970). *Industry and Trade in some Developing Countries*. New York: Oxford University Press.

Lucas, R. E. (1988). 'On the mechanics of economic development.' *Journal of Monetary Economics*, vol. 22, pp. 3–42.

Lydall, H. (1979). *A Theory of Income Distribution*. Oxford: Clarendon Press.

MacKellar, F. L. and Vining, D. R. (1987). 'Natural resource scarcity: a global survey.' In Johnson and Lee (1987).

Malthus, T. R. (1798). *An Essay on the Principle of Population*, London: J. Johnson.

Manne, A. S. and Weisskopf, T. E. (1970). 'A dynamic multi-sectoral model for India, 1967–75.' In *Applications of Input–Output Analysis* (ed. A. Carter and A. Brody). Amsterdam: North Holland.

Marglin, S. (1966). 'Comment on Jorgenson.' In *Theory and Design of Economic Development* (ed. I. Adeleman and E. Thornbecke). Baltimore: Johns Hopkins Press.

Marshall, A. (1890). *Principles of Economics*, 8th edition, 1920. London: Macmillan.

Mata, L. and Rosero, L. (1988). 'National health and social development in Costa Rica: a study of intersectoral action.' Technical Paper No. 13. Pan American Health Organisation, Washington.

Mauldin, W. P. and Lapham, R. J. (1985). 'Measuring family planning effort in developing countries: 1972 and 1982.' In *The Effect of Family Planning Programs on Fertility in the Developing World* (ed. N. Birdsall). World Bank Staff Working Paper No. 677, Washington D.C.

Maxwell, S. and Singer, H. W. (1979). 'Food aid to developing countries: a survey.' *World Development*, vol. 7 (3), pp. 225–46.

Mazumdar, D. (1987). *Rural and Urban Labor Markets in Developing Countries: Analysis and Policy Implications.* World Bank, August.

McIntosh, J. (1986). 'North South trade: export led growth with abundant labour.' *Journal of Development Economics*, vol. 24 (1), pp. 141–52.

McNamara, R. S. (1973). *One Hundred Countries, Two Billion People: The Dimensions of Development.* New York: Praeger Press.

Mellor, J. (1976). *The New Economics of Growth: a Strategy for India and The Developing World.* London: Cornell University Press.

Miller, D. (1979). *Social Justice*, Oxford: Clarendon.

Mirrlees, J. (1976). 'A pure theory of under-developed economies.' In *Agriculture in Development Theory* (ed. L. Reynolds). New Haven: Yale University Press.

Modigliani, F. (1970). 'The life cycle hypothesis of saving and intercountry differences in the saving ratio.' In *Induction, Growth and Trade* (ed. W. A. Eltis, M. F. G. Scott and J. N. Wolfe). Oxford: Oxford University Press.

Montgomery, M. R. (1987). 'The impacts of urban population growth on urban labour markets and the costs of urban service delivery: a review.' In Johnson and Lee (1987).

Morris, C. and Adelman, I. (1988). *Comparative Patterns of Economic Development 1850–1914.* Maryland: The Johns Hopkins University Press.

Mosley, P. (1980). 'Aid, savings and growth revisited.' *Oxford Bulletin of Economics and Statistics*, vol. 42 (2).

—— (1987). *Overseas Aid: Its Defense and Reform.* Brighton: Wheatsheaf.

——, Hudson, J. and Horrell, S. (1987). 'Aid, the public sector and the market in less developed countries.' Economic Journal, vol. 97, pp. 616–41.

Murphy, K. M., Shleifer, A. and Vishny, R. (1988*a*). 'Income distribution, market size, and industrialisation.' National Bureau of Economic Research Working Paper No. 2709 (forthcoming *Quarterly Journal of Economics*).

——, —— and —— (1988*b*). 'Industrialisation and the big push.' National Bureau of Economic Research Working Paper No. 2708 (forthcoming *Journal of Political Economy*).

Musgrave, R. A. (1987). 'Tax reform in developing countries.' In Newbery and Stern (1987).

Myint, H. (1985). 'Organizational dualism and economic development.' *Asian Development Review*, vol. 3 (1), pp. 24–43.

Myrdal, G. (1968). *Asian Drama.* Clinton, Mass.: 20th Century Fund.

National Academy of Sciences (1971). *Rapid Population Growth: Consequences and Policy Implications*, 2 vols. Baltimore: John Hopkins University Press.

—— (1986). *Population Growth and Economic Development: Policy Questions.* Working Group on Population Growth and Economic Development, Committee on Population, Commission on Behavioural and Social Sciences and Education. Washington, DC: National Academy Press.

Neary, J. and van Wijnbergen, S. (1986). *Natural Resources and Macroeconomy.* Cambridge: MIT Press.

Newbery, D. M. G. (1977). 'Risk-sharing, share-cropping and uncertain labour markets.' *Review of Economics Studies*, vol. 56 (3), pp. 585–94.

—— (1988). 'The theory of food price stabilisation.' University of Cambridge Economic Theory Discussion Paper No. 133.

—— and Stern, N. H. (eds) (1987). *The Theory of Taxation for Developing Countries.* Oxford University Press: World Bank Research Publication.

—— and Stiglitz, J. (1981). *The Theory of Commodity Price Stabilisation: a Study in the Economics of Risk*, Oxford: Clarendon.

—— and —— (1984). 'Pareto inferior trade.' *Review of Economic Studies*, vol. 51 (1), pp. 1–12.

New Palgrave (1987). (edited by J. Eatwell, M. Milgate and P. Newman). *The New Palgrave A Dictionary of Economics.* London: Macmillan.

Nozick, R. (1974). *Anarchy, State and Utopia.* New York: Basic Books.

Nowshirvani, V. F. (1967). 'Allocation efficiency in traditional Indian agriculture: a comment.' *Journal of Farm Economics*, vol. 49 (1), pp. 218–21.

Nurkse, R. (1953). *Problems of Capital Formation in Underdeveloped Countries.* Oxford: Blackwell.

—— (1961). *Patterns of Trade and Development.* The Wicksell Lectures. Oxford: Basil Blackwell.

Olivera, J. H. G. (1964). 'On structural inflation and Latin American structuralism.' *Oxford Economic Papers*, vol. 16 (3), pp. 321–33.

Osmani, S. R. (1987). 'Nutrition and the economics of food: implications of some recent controversies.' Working Paper No. 16, WIDER, Helsinki to be published in Drèze and Sen (eds) *The Political Economy of Hunger* (forthcoming) Oxford University Press.

Overseas Development Administration (1988). *Appraisal of Projects in Developing Countries: A Guide for Economists*, 3rd edition. London: HMSO.

Overseas Development Institute (1988). 'Commodity prices: investing in decline.' Briefing Paper, March.

OXFAM (1985). *Field Directors' Handbook: Guidelines and Information for Assessing Projects*. Oxford: Oxfam.

Pananek, G. F. (1972). 'The effect of aid and other resource transfers on savings and growth in less developed countries.' Economic Journal, vol. 82, pp. 934–50.

—— (1973). 'Aid, foreign private investment, saving and growth in less developed countries.' *Journal of Political Economy*, no. 81.

Paukert, F. (1973). 'Income distributions at different levels of development: a survey of evidence.' *International Labour Review*, vol. 108 (2–3), pp. 97–125.

Pearse, A. (1980). *Seeds of Plenty, Seeds of Want: Social and Economic Implications of the Green Revolution*. Oxford: Clarendon Press.

Pearson, L. B. (Chairman) (1969). *Partners in Development*. Report of the Commission on International Development. New York: Praeger.

Peattie, L. (1987). 'An idea in good currency and how it grew: the informal sector.' *World Development*, vol. 15 (7), pp. 851–60.

Perkins, D. H, (1988). 'Reforming China's economic system.' *Journal of Economic Literature*, vol. 26 (2), pp. 601–45.

Pingali, P. L. and Binswanger, H. P. (1987): 'Population density and agricultural intensification.' In Johnson and Lee (1987).

Pinstrup-Andersen, P. (ed.) (forthcoming). *The Political Economy of Food and Nutrition*.

Pitt, M. M. (1983). 'Food preferences and nutrition in rural Bangladesh.' *Review of Economics and Statistics*, vol. 65, pp. 105–14.

Prahladachar, M. (1983). 'Income distribution effects of the green revolution in India: a review of empirical evidence.' *World Development*, vol. 11 (11), pp. 927–44.

Pyatt, F. G. (1988). 'A SAM approach to modelling.' *Journal of Policy Modelling*, vol. 10 (3), pp. 327–52.

—— and Round, J. (1985). *Social Accounting Matrices: A Basis for Planning*, Washington D.C.: The World Bank.

Ramaswami, V. K. and Srinivasan, T. N. (1968). 'Optimal subsidies and taxes when some factors are traded.' *Journal of Political Economy*, vol. 76, pp. 569–82.

Ravallion, M. (1987). *Markets and Famines*. Oxford: Oxford University Press.

—— (1988). 'Expected poverty under risk-induced welfare variability.' Economic Journal, vol. 98, pp. 1171–82.

Rawls, J. (1973). *A Theory of Justice*. Oxford: Oxford University Press.

Reynolds, J. (1983). 'The spread of economic growth to the third world: 1850–1980.' *Journal of Economic Literature*, vol. 21, pp. 941–80.

Riddell, R. C. (1987). *Foreign Aid Reconsidered*. Baltimore: Johns Hopkins University Press.

Riskin, C. (1987). *China's Political Economy: The Quest for Development since 1949*. Oxford: Oxford University Press.

Robinson, S. (1971). 'Sources of growth in less developed countries: a cross-section study.' *Quarterly Journal of Economics*, vol. 85, pp. 391–408.

Roemer, J. (1982). *A General Theory of Exploitation and Class*. Cambridge, Mass.: Harvard University Press.

Romer, P. M. (1986). 'Increasing returns and long-run growth.' *Journal of Political Economy*, vol. 94, pp. 1002–37.

—— (1987). 'Growth based on increasing returns due to specialisation.' *American Economic Review* (Papers and Proceedings), vol. 77, pp. 56–62.

—— (1988). 'Endogenous technical change.' Working Paper University of Chicago and University of Rochester (May).

Rosenstein-Rodan, P. (1943). 'Problems of industrialisation in Eastern and Southeastern Europe.' Economic Journal, vol. 53, pp. 202–12.

Rosenzweig, M. R. (1988). 'Labour markets in low income countries.' In Chenery and Srinivasan (1988).

Rowley, R. K., Tollison, R. D. and Tullock, G. (eds) (1988). *The Political Economy of Rent Seeking*. Boston: Kluwer Academic.

Rubenstein, A. (1982). 'Perfect equilibrium in a bargaining model.' *Econometrica*, vol. 50, pp. 97–109.

Ruttan, V. (1977). 'The Green Revolution: some generalizations.' *International Development Review*, vol. 19, pp. 19–23.

Sabot, R. H. (1982). *Migration and the Labour Market in Developing Countries*. Boulder, Colorado: Westview Press.

Sachs, J. (1987). 'Trade and exchange rate policies in growth-oriented adjustment programs.' In *Growth-Oriented Adjustment Programs* (ed. V. Corbo, M. Goldstein and M. Khan). Washington D.C.: IMF and World Bank.

—— (1988*a*) '*Conditionality, debt relief and the developing country debt crisis*'. National Bureau of Economic Research, Working Paper No 2644.

—— (1988*b*). (ed.). *Foreign Debt and Economic Performance: The Summary Volume.* National Bureau of Economic Research. Chicago: University of Chicago Press.

Salter, W. E. G. (1960). *Productivity and Technical Change*, London: Cambridge University Press.

Sandee, J. (1960). *A Demonstration Planning Model for India.* Bombay: Asia Publishing House.

Sapsford, D. (1985). 'The statistical debate on the net barter terms of trade between primary commodities and manufactures.' ECONOMIC JOURNAL, vol. 95, pp. 781–9.

Scarf, H. and Hansen, T. (1973). *The Computation of Economic Equilibria.* New Haven: Yale University Press.

Schofield, S. (1975). *Village Nutrition Studies: An Annotated Bibliography.* Village Studies Programme, IDS: University of Sussex.

Schultz, T. W. (1964). *Transforming Traditional Agriculture.* New Haven: Yale University Press.

—— (1987). 'School expenditures and enrollments, 1960–1980: the effects of income, prices, and population.' In Johnson and Lee (1987).

—— (1988). 'Education investments and returns'. In Chenery and Srinivasan (1988 and 1989).

Scitovsky, T. (1954). 'Two concepts of external economies.' *Journal of Political Economy*, vol. 52 (2), pp. 143–51.

Scott, M. FG. (1989). *A New View of Economic Growth*, Oxford: Oxford University Press.

Seers, D. and Streeten, P. P. (1972). 'Overseas development policies.' In *The Labour Government's Economic Record: 1964–1970.* (ed. W. Beckerman). Gerald Duckworth.

Sen, A. K. (1968). *Choice of Techniques*, 3rd edition. Oxford: Basil Blackwell.

—— (1972). 'Control areas and accounting prices: an approach to economic evaluation.' ECONOMIC JOURNAL, vol. 82, pp. 112–24.

—— (1975). *Employment, Technology and Development.* Oxford: Oxford University Press.

—— (1981). *Poverty and Famines.* Oxford: Oxford University Press.

—— (1983*a*). 'Poor, relatively speaking.' *Oxford Economic Papers*, vol. 35 (1), pp. 153–

—— (1983*b*). 'Development: which way now?' ECONOMIC JOURNAL, vol. 93, pp. 745–62.

—— (1984). *Resources, Values and Development.* Oxford, Oxford University Press.

—— (1987). *The Standard of Living.* Cambridge: Cambridge University Press.

—— (1988). 'Capability and well-being.' Paper presented at a conference on the Quality of Life held at WIDER, Helsinki, July.

Shaban, R. (1987). 'Testing between competing models of sharecropping.' *Journal of Political Economy*, vol. 95 (5), pp. 893–920.

Shapiro, C. and Stiglitz, J. E. (1984). 'Equilibrium unemployment as a worker discipline device.' *American Economic Review*, vol. 34, pp. 433–44.

Simon, J. L. (1981). *The Ultimate Resource.* Princeton: Princeton University Press.

Singer, H. W. (1950). 'The distribution of gains between investing and borrowing countries.' *American Economic Review*, vol. 40 (2), pp. 473–86.

—— (1952). 'The mechanisms of economic development.' In *The Economics of Underdevelopment* (ed. A. N. Agarwala and A. P. Singh). London: Oxford University Press.

—— (1965). 'External aid: for plans or projects?' ECONOMIC JOURNAL, vol. 75 (229); also in *Foreign Aid* (ed. J. Bhagwati and R. S. Eckaus), London: Penguin.

Singh, I. J., Squire, L. and Strauss, J. (1986). *Agricultural Household Models: Extensions and Applications.* Baltimore: Johns Hopkins University Press.

Slade, M. E. (1987). 'Natural resources: population growth and well-being.' In Johnson and Lee (1987).

Solow, R. (1956). 'A contribution to the theory of economic growth.' *Quarterly Journal of Economics*, vol. 70, pp. 65–94.

—— (1957). 'Technical change and the aggregate production function.' *The Review of Economics and Statistics*, vol. 39 (3), pp. 312–20.

Spraos, J. (1980). 'The statistical debate on the net barter terms of trade between primary commodities and manufactures.' ECONOMIC JOURNAL, vol. 90 (357), pp. 107–28.

Squire, L. (1981). *Employment Policies in Developing Countries: A Survey of Issues and Evidence.* London: Oxford University Press.

—— and Van der Tak, H. G. (1975). *Economic Analysis of Projects.* World Bank: Johns Hopkins University Press.

Srinivasan, T. N. (1987*a*). 'Structural change, economic interdependence and world development.' In *Economic Independence* (ed. J. Dunning and M. Usui). London: Macmillan.

—— (1987*b*). 'Population and food.' In Johnson and Lee (1987).

Stark, O. (1988). 'Migrants and markets.' Migration and Development Program Discussion Paper No. 37. Harvard University.

Stern, N. H. (1972). 'Optimum development in a dual economy.' *Review of Economic Studies*, vol.
118, pp. 171–84.
—— (1974). 'Professor Bauer on development: a review article.' *Journal of Development Economics*, vol.
pp. 191–212.
—— (1987). 'Uniformity versus selectivity in tax structure: lessons from theory and policy.' *Development Economics Research Program ST/ICERD Discussion Paper* No. 9, London School of Economics, London.
Stewart, F. (1971). Comment on Griffin (1970). *Oxford Bulletin of Economics and Statistics*.
—— (1985). *Planning to Meet Basic Needs*. London: Macmillan.
Stiglitz, J. E. (1974). 'Incentives and risk-sharing in sharecropping.' *Review of Economic Studies*, vol. 61 (2), pp. 219–56.
—— (1976). 'The efficiency wage hypothesis, surplus labour and the distribution of income in L.D.C.s.' *Oxford Economic Papers*, vol. 28 (2), pp. 185–207.
—— and Weiss, A. (1981). 'Credit rationing in markets with imperfect information.' *American Economic Review*, vol. 71 (3), pp. 393–410.
Stone, J. R. (1970). *Mathematical Models of the Economy and Other Essays*. London: Chapman and Hall.
—— and Stone, G. (1977). *National Income and Expenditure*, 10th edition. London: Bowes and Bowes.
Strauss, J. (1982). 'Determinants of food consumption in rural Sierra Leone: application of the quadratic expenditure system to the consumption leisure component of a household-firm model.' *Journal of Development Economics*, vol. 11, pp. 327–53.
—— (1986). 'Does nutrition raise farm productivity?' *Journal of Political Economy*, vol. 94 (21), pp. 297–320.
Streeten, P. (1984). 'Basic needs: some unsettled questions.' *World Development*, vol. 12 (9), pp. 973–9.
Summers, R. and Heston, A. (1988). 'A new set of international comparisons of real product and price levels estimates for 130 countries, 1950–1985.' *Review of Income and Wealth*, pp. 1–25.
Tait, A. (1988). *Value Added Tax: International Practise and Problems*. Washington, D.C.: International Monetary Fund.
Tanzi, V. (1987). 'Quantitative characteristics of the tax systems of developing countries.' In Newbery and Stern (1987).
Taylor, L. (1979). *Macro-Models for Developing Countries*. New York: McGraw-Hill.
—— (1980). *Models of Growth and Distribution in Brazil*. New York: Oxford University Press. (A World Bank Research Publication.)
—— (1983). *Structuralist Macroeconomics: Applicable Models for the Third World*. New York: Basic Books.
—— (1988). *Varieties of Stabilisation Experience: Towards Sensible Macroeconomics in the Third World*. Oxford: Clarendon Press.
Thomas, D.., Strauss, J. and Henriques, M. (1988). 'How does mother's education affect child height?' Discussion Paper 89. Development Economics Research Centre, University of Warwick.
Tisdell, C. (1988). 'Sustainable development: differing perspectives of ecologists and economists, and relevance to LDC's.' *World Development*, vol. 16 (3).
Todaro, M. P. (1969). 'A model of labour migration and urban unemployment in less developed countries.' *American Economic Review*, vol. 59 (1), pp. 138–48.
—— (1976). *Internal Migration in Developing Countries: A Review of Theory, Evidence, Methodology and Research Priorities*. Geneva: International Labour Office.
Trela, I. and Whalley, J. (1988). 'Do developing countries lose from the MFA?' National Bureau of Economic Research, Working Paper Series No. 2618.
Tumlir, J. (1985). 'Protectionism trade policy in democratic societies.' American Enterprise Institute for Public Policy Research, Washington, D.C.
Turnovsky, S. J., Shalit, H. and Schmitz, A. (1980). 'Consumer's surplus, price instability, and consumer welfare.' *Econometrica*, vol. 48 (1), pp. 135–52.
United Nations, Department of Economic Affairs (1949). *Relative Prices of Exports and Imports of Under-developed Countries*. New York: United Nations.
United Nations (1968), *A System of National Accounts*. Series F, No. 2, Rev: 3. New York: United Nations.
Usher, D. (1980). *The Measurement of Economic Growth*. Oxford: Blackwell.
Uzawa, H. (1965). 'Optimum technical change in an aggregative model of economic growth.' *International Economic Review*, vol. 6, pp. 18–31.
von Hayek, F. A. (1967). *Studies in Philosophy, Politics and Economics*. London: Routledge and Kegan Paul.
—— (1986). *The Road to Serfdom*. London: Ark Paperbacks. (Originally published: London: Routledge and Kegan Paul, 1944.)
Wade, R. (1985). 'The role of Government in overcoming market failure: Taiwan, South Korea, and Japan.' In *Explaining the Success of East Asian Industrialization* (ed. Helen Hughes). Cambridge: Cambridge University Press.
Weiss, A. (1980). 'Jobs, queues and layoffs in labour markets with flexible wages.' *Journal of Political Economy*, vol. 88 (3), pp. 526–38.
Weitzman, M. (1977). 'Is the price system or rationing more effective in getting a commodity to those who need it most?' *Bell Journal of Economics*, vol. 8 (2), pp. 517–25.

3). 'Migration and urbanisation.' In Chenery and Srinivasan (1988).

Vorld Debt Tables. Washington, D.C.: International Bank for Reconstruction and

ables. Baltimore: Johns Hopkins University Press.

ables, 2nd edition. Baltimore: Johns Hopkins University Press.

Tables, 3rd edition. Baltimore: Johns Hopkins University Press.

orld Tables, The Third Edition. Comparative Analysis and Data Division Economic rojections Department.

Long-Term Development Issues and Options. Baltimore: Johns Hopkins University Press.

Tables, 4th edition. Baltimore: Johns Hopkins University Press.

World Development Reports. World Bank: Oxford University Press.

—— (198 *World Tables, The Fourth Edition*. Socio-Economic Data Division International Economics Department.

—— (1988*b*). *The World Bank Annual Report*. Washington: World Bank.

Yap, L. Y. L. (1977). 'The attraction of the cities: a review of migration literature.' *Journal of Development Economics*, vol. 4 (3), pp. 239–64.

Young, A. (1928). 'Increasing returns and economic progress.' ECONOMIC JOURNAL, vol. 38, pp. 527–42.

5

A SURVEY OF SOME RECENT ECONOMETRIC METHODS*

A. R. Pagan and M. R. Wickens

There is an understandable reluctance by the applied worker to make the effort to master and to keep abreast of current developments in econometric methods, since the pace and diversity of these developments is intimidating. It is often easier, especially in the short term, to make do with familiar techniques. If questioned, there is always the defence that the data are too poor, or the model is too preliminary, to justify the use of more sophisticated or rigorous methods. It may come as a (possibly unwelcome) surprise, therefore, to learn that many of the new results which we describe in this paper are designed for such situations. In part these results exploit the increasing accessibility of cheap and powerful computing facilities which are helping to make the latest econometric methods more readily available to applied workers. The problem of how to do applied econometrics and what econometric methods to choose remains.

In this paper we provide a survey of some of the most recent developments in econometrics which in our view have been, or are likely to be in the future, of particular value in applied economics to those who wish to use best practice techniques. No attempt has been made to write a comprehensive survey as this would be too large an undertaking. Nor have we always provided a detailed account of an issue, particularly where a recent survey of the material is available. But where an idea is likely to be unfamiliar or to be technically difficult to follow we have provided a more extensive treatment. Although the main emphasis is on time series, the discussion in Sections II–IV on estimation, inference and evaluation has general applicability. It might be felt that a logical ordering of the material would be from model formulation through estimation to evaluation. This has not been followed here, however, partly because we believe that applied work rarely proceeds in such a structured way, and partly because it is convenient to introduce estimation methods at an early stage in order to make use of results in later sections. The order of topics in this paper may not reflect, therefore, the sequence that might be followed in an econometric application.

The paper is set out as follows. In Section I we discuss various issues associated with the data that arise prior to modelling, notably prefiltering and integrated series. Estimation is discussed in Section II where we focus on four estimators: maximum likelihood, GMM, M-estimators and non-parametric estimation. Inference, especially with integrated series, is covered in Section

* This chapter was first published in the ECONOMIC JOURNAL, vol. 99, December 1989. The first author's research was supported by Grant No. SES-8719520 from the National Science Foundation, and the second by a grant from the ESRC. We would like to thank Tom Cooley, Angus Deaton, Frank Diebold, Ron Gallant, David Hendry, Grayham Mizon, Hashem Pesaran, Peter Phillips, Baldev Raj, Peter Robinson and Ken Wallis for their comments on an earlier version.

III. Various methodological issues connected with model evaluation are discussed in Section IV. In Section V we consider some problems associated with the formulation of relationships, including dynamic specification, cointegration and conditional expectations. A few brief conclusions are offered in Section VI.

Some abbreviations are used throughout the paper. By a white noise process e_t we will mean one that has a zero mean and is serially uncorrelated. The expressions 'independently and identically distributed' and 'normally and independently distributed' will be abbreviated to i.i.d. and n.i.d. respectively. Furthermore, in discussing asymptotic theory we will frequently ignore a variable and, using the notation established by Mann and Wald (1943), designate it as $o_p(1)$. Finally, the sample size will sometimes be T and sometimes N. For situations which are specifically applicable to time series T is used (with counter t) whereas in discussion meant to be applied both to time series and cross section data it is N (with counter i).

I. ISSUES IN DATA ANALYSIS

I.1. *The Sources of Data*

Economic data come in many forms and from many sources. Early econometricians were frequently both producers and consumers of data; increasingly the institutionalisation of the data gathering process has caused these roles to become distinct. Inevitably one can find instances where this specialisation is disastrous rather than efficient, and Griliches' (1986) comments are a salutary warning in that direction, but it is unlikely that this trend will ever be reversed. Econometrics has replaced 'economic statistics' and it is hard to go back.

Once it is accepted that primary data construction is rarely under an investigator's control, there is a secondary issue of whether what we are given is capable of addressing important policy questions. In a provocative article Lalonde (1986) concluded that experimental data were crucial to an accurate assessment of the impact of manpower training on earnings; when only non-experimental data were analysed a wide variety of estimates was produced, making any inferences 'fragile', to use Leamer's (1983) description. Heckman and Hotz (1987) re-examined this study, concluding that the non-experimental data yielded much sturdier inferences once care was taken to control for effects such as selectivity of the sample. Despite this conclusion it is unlikely that this debate is over, and the issue will be raised again if the cost of generating experimental data continues to decline.

Even if one accepts the need to use official data there has been debate over what transformations need to be applied to them prior to econometric work. Sims (1974) and Wallis (1974) demonstrated that the use of seasonally adjusted data could seriously distort estimated dynamic relationships and recommended that unadjusted data be used in applied work, but the lesson seems to have been ignored in most U.S. research, probably owing to the tendency of data bases such as CITIBASE to provide only adjusted data. Provision of raw data can have other advantages too. Ghysels and Karangwa (1988) have pointed out that many nominal variables are seasonally adjusted before conversion to real terms, and that better estimates could generally be obtained by reversing the process.

Perhaps the issue that has attracted most attention is the perception that questions are sometimes posed that appear to demand 'de-trended' economic data. The following are examples: Are business cycles symmetric? Are wages pro- or contra-cyclical? Can equilibrium models generate business cycles? One response to this issue is to demand that models should account for both trend and cycle. Accounting for growth by economic factors, however, has not been very successful and as a result recourse to exogenous forcing factors such as technical progress is common. Failure to specify correctly a growth component can easily lead to model rejection and this may retard progress in understanding cyclical behaviour.

Data analysts commonly attempt to eliminate the trend without recourse to a formal model. A standard approach is to construct the trend component as $y_t^* = \sum_{j=-s}^{s} w_j y_{t-j}$, observing that in the frequency domain the spectral densities of y_t^* and y_t at frequency λ are related by $f_{y^*y^*}(\lambda) = (\sum_{j=-s}^{s} w_j e^{i\lambda}) f_{yy}(\lambda) = A(\lambda) f_{yy}(\lambda)$. Trend adjustment is then viewed as eliminating the zero frequency whilst preserving all the others; in spectral terms w_j should be selected so that $A(0) = 0$ and $A(\lambda \neq 0) = 1$. No *linear* filter is capable of doing this, implying that trend estimates are always contaminated to some degree. Perhaps the most popular filters have been first differencing $(A_D = 2 - 2\cos\lambda)$ and the Hodrick–Prescott (1980) filter $(A_{HP} = 6400(1-\cos\lambda)^2/[1+6400(1-\cos\lambda)^2])$. King and Rebelo (1988) discuss the form of w_j for the latter and derive the spectral representation. For values of λ greater than $(\pi/10)$, $A_{HP}(\lambda) > 0{\cdot}93$ while for $\lambda \simeq (\pi/2)$, $A_{HP}(\lambda) = A_D(\lambda)$. It is not surprising therefore that different transformations can lead to big differences in the resultant series and hence produce de-trended data of dubious value. The appropriate way to de-trend data remains an open question and comparisons of popular linear filters with the non-linear ones used in programs such as X-11 and X-13 are overdue, as is the identification of what type of component models underlie various filters. In the statistics literature the latter question has a long history, see Cleveland and Tiao (1976), and economists showed early interest in it, e.g. Grether and Nerlove (1970), but it seems to have disappeared until recently – Harvey and Todd (1983).

I.2. *The Nature of Data*

I.2.1. *Integration in data*

The particular characteristics of the data will have an important influence on the specification of the econometric model, on the choice of estimator, on the properties of the estimates and on inference. A recent development has been the growing awareness of the fact that economic data are rarely stationary, and that the particular type of non-stationarity observed has profound effects upon statistical inference. In many instances estimators that are traditionally taken to be normally distributed (in large samples) no longer are if variables that are 'integrated' appear in a model. In this section our attention is devoted to the question of determining whether or not a variable is integrated. Later, in Section III.2, we shall examine the implications of the presence of integrated variables for econometric modelling generally. The wide interest in this area and the newness of many of the results has led us to give a fairly detailed treatment of the issues.

Engle and Granger (1987) provide the following definition of integrability: a series with no deterministic component which has a stationary, invertible, Autoregressive Moving Average (ARMA) representation after differencing d times, is said to be integrated of order d and is denoted I(d). Most economic time series are either I(0) or I(1), i.e. stationary in levels or in first differences. An I(d) variable has d unit roots because it can be written

$$(1-\mathrm{L})^d A(\mathrm{L})\, x_t = B(\mathrm{L})\, e_t, \tag{1}$$

where L is the lag operator $\mathrm{L}^s x_t = x_{t-s}$, $A(\mathrm{L})$ and $B(\mathrm{L})$ are invertible polynomials in L (i.e. $A(\mathrm{L}) = 0$ and $B(\mathrm{L}) = 0$ have roots which lie outside the unit circle) and e_t is a white noise process with variance σ^2. Thus $A^*(\mathrm{L}) = (1-\mathrm{L})^d A(\mathrm{L})$ has d unit roots. Simple, but prominent, examples of (1) in economics are the 'random walk' $\Delta x_t = e_t$ and the random walk with drift $\Delta x_t = \mu + e_t$. Most asset prices are thought to be random walks and there is evidence that a large number of macroeconomic series including GDP and many of its components have a unit root. The most widely quoted results on this are those of Nelson and Plosser (1982), although this evidence is sometimes disputed with studies arguing that a better description of, say, real GDP is that it has cyclical fluctuations about a deterministic trend. In that case, $A(\mathrm{L})\, x_t = \alpha + \beta t + e_t$ where $A(\mathrm{L})$ is invertible, see for example Cochrane (1988).

Engle and Granger (1987) describe a number of the characteristics possessed by integrated varibles. Perhaps the most striking is that their moments can be expressed as polynomial functions of time for a fixed starting value x_0. To illustrate, the random walk x_t can be written as $x_t = x_0 + \sum_1^t e_i$ with $\mathrm{E}(e_t^2) = \sigma^2$ and if x_0 is fixed then var $(x_t) = t\sigma^2$. This is in contrast to I(0) variables which have moments that do not grow with time. Another way to express the difference between integrated and non-integrated variables is in terms of the persistence of the effects of random shocks. Whereas the effect on the level of a stationary variable of a serially independent shock diminishes as time elapses, on an integrated variable the effect persists indefinitely. Much has been made of this distinction in real business cycle theory since, if GDP has a unit root, then deviations from equilibrium will not be temporary as stated in traditional business cycle theory but rather will be permanent. To see this, consider the following representation of an I(1) variable x_t:

$$(1-\mathrm{L})\, x_t = \mu + C(\mathrm{L})\, e_t = \mu + u_t = \mu + \sum_0^\infty c_i\, e_{t-i}, \tag{2}$$

where $C(\mathrm{L})$ is assumed to be invertible. Beveridge and Nelson (1981) express such an integrated series as the unobserved components model

$$x_t = z_t + \xi_t, \tag{3}$$

$$z_t = \mu + z_{t-1} + C(1)\, e_t, \tag{4}$$

$$-\xi_t = F(\mathrm{L})\, e_t, \tag{5}$$

where z_t is the permanent component or stochastic trend (i.e. a random walk with drift), ξ_t is a cyclical or temporary component and $F(\mathrm{L})$ is invertible with coefficients, $f_i = \sum_{i+1}^{\infty} c_s$ $(i = 0, 1, \ldots)$. A serially independent shock e_t will affect x_t both through z_t and ξ_t. As a result of the former the effect will be permanent. If x_t is I(0) then it does not need to be differenced as in (2) and there will be no z_{t-1} term in (4). In fact there is now no need to introduce z_t or (4) at all. Notice that the fraction of the shock which becomes permanent is a function of $C(1)$. This has led to a literature focusing upon the 'magnitude' of permanent shocks, for example Deaton (1987). No consensus has emerged on a suitable measure of persistence since some modellers have argued that the restriction in (3)–(5) that a shock affects both transitory and permanent components is too strong and they would prefer to enforce a zero correlation between z_t and ξ_t. This 'unobserved components' approach to the decomposition of economic time series has a long history in econometrics, see Nerlove (1967), and modern manifestations of it are Harvey and Todd (1983) and Watson (1986). Stock and Watson (1988) have written an excellent survey of this literature and given some applications, while Nelson (1988) has questioned its general suitability over assuming a simple unit root together with lagged dynamics.

There remains the problem of how to estimate $C(1)$. One solution is to truncate the infinite lag and estimate a finite order ARMA model for Δx_t (Campbell and Mankiw, 1987), but this may be a poor estimate. Instead Cochrane (1988) observed that $C(1)^2$ is proportional to the spectral density of Δx_t at the zero frequency and this connection provides a convenient estimator. Quite different results are obtained when both procedures are applied to GDP; partly this is due to the fact that Cochrane's estimator effectively fits a very high order ARMA process and does not drop 'insignificant' terms. Other problems derive from a flat likelihood over part of the parameter space. A recent attempt to reconcile the viewpoints is that of Christiano and Eichenbaum (1989).

The first practical solution to the problem of testing whether or not a variable is integrated was provided by Dickey (1976), Dickey and Fuller (1979, 1981) and Fuller (1976). To illustrate we examine the problem of testing for the existence of a single unit root, i.e. $d = 1$. Consider the AR(1) model

$$x_t = \alpha x_{t-1} + u_t, \tag{6}$$

where x_0 is fixed and x_t has a unit root if $\alpha = 1$. There are two natural ways to check if $\alpha = 1$. One is to compare $\hat{\alpha}$ to unity; the other is to examine whether the ordinary t-statistic that the coefficient of x_{t-1} in the regression of Δx_t against x_{t-1} is zero. In the discussion that follows we will concentrate upon the first option, although the literature always provides significance tables for both versions. Considering therefore the OLS estimator $\hat{\alpha}$, it can be written as

$$\hat{\alpha} - \alpha = T^{-1} \textstyle\sum_2^T x_{t-1} u_t / T^{-1} \sum_2^T x_{t-1}^2 = m_{xx}^{-1} m_{x-1u}, \tag{7}$$

where $m_{ab} = T^{-1} \sum a_t b_t$ is the sample mean of the process $(a_t b_t)$. When x_t and

u_t are I(0) random variables it is generally the case that these sample means converge to their expectations and a central limit theorem applies to m_{xu}, i.e. $T^{\frac{1}{2}}m_{xu}$ and hence $T^{\frac{1}{2}}(\hat{\alpha}-\alpha)$ are asymptotically normal. When the x_t process is I(1), however, things are different. Now it is $T^{-1}m_{xx}$ and unnormalised m_{xu} which converge, but to random variables. As a consequence, asymptotically, $T(\hat{\alpha}-1)$ is the ratio of two random variables. Its asymptotic distribution is not normal but is the 'non-standard' Dickey–Fuller distribution. This has been tabulated by Monte Carlo methods, see Fuller (1976, Table 8.5.1) and also Evans and Savin (1981, 1984). Compared with the normal distribution it is skewed strongly to the left making the normal a very poor approximation. Another interesting feature is that $\hat{\alpha}$ is said to be 'super-consistent', converging in probability to α faster if $\alpha = 1$ than if $|\alpha| < 1$; in fact at the rate T^{-1} instead of $T^{-\frac{1}{2}}$.

One way to test the hypothesis $H_0: \alpha = 1$ against the alternative of I(0) is to use the test statistic $T(\hat{\alpha}-1)$ and look up the lower tail of the tabulated distribution. Although the idea is simple, putting it into practice is much more complex. First, there is the feature that the original work in this area took u_t to be i.i.d., whereas it is much more likely that it will be autocorrelated, and this will affect the asymptotic theory. Second, it turns out that the conclusions over the asymptotic distribution of tests also depends upon two other factors: whether an intercept term or trend term is included in the regression and whether the series actually has drift. The reason why it matters whether extra terms might be included in (6), and what they are, is easily appreciated. Suppose there is an intercept. Then

$$\hat{\alpha}-\alpha = (m_{xx}-m_x^2)^{-1}(m_{xu}-m_x m_u), \tag{7'}$$

where m_x and m_u are the sample means of x_t and u_t respectively. If x_t is I(1), m_x can be shown to converge to a random variable asymptotically, implying that the ratio of random variables forming $T(\hat{\alpha}-\alpha)$ is different in (7) from (7′). This means that the distribution of $T(\hat{\alpha}-1)$ is also different and new tables of critical values need to be consulted; Fuller's Table 8.5.1 therefore covers cases where both an intercept and trend term are included, since it is felt that investigators may wish to add such regressors to safeguard against a pure trend effect being mistaken for a unit root (especially in the absence of an intercept). Having made this qualification it will now be assumed that there are no regressors like an intercept or trend in (6).

This leaves two issues; the possibility that u_t is correlated has been handled by one of two approaches: either we can introduce parametric approximations to the process generating the disturbance term, or we can use 'non-parametric' procedures which take account of the serial correlation but do not explicitly specify how it is generated. An example of the former is the augmented Dickey–Fuller test or ADF test; tests of the second type have been proposed in a series of papers by Phillips and his co-authors. The ADF test is carried out by the OLS estimation of

$$\Delta x_t = \mu-(1-\alpha)\, x_{t-1}+\sum_1^n \theta_i \Delta x_{t-i}+e_t. \tag{8}$$

After (8) is estimated, $T(\hat{\alpha}-1)$ is checked to see if it is significantly different from zero. The same tables as before are used. Comparing (8) and (2) one sees that the role of the second from last term is to 'soak up' the serial correlation $\sum_{i=1}^{\infty} c_i e_{t-i}$. Said and Dickey (1984) showed that setting $n = kT^{\frac{1}{4}}$ would provide an appropriate test for a unit root. Unfortunately, k is not determined. Schwert (1987) suggests the rules of thumb $n = \text{int}\,[4(T/100)^{\frac{1}{4}}]$ or $n = \text{int}\,[12(T/100)^{\frac{1}{4}}]$, where int [.] indicates the integer value of the argument in brackets. One way to make the outcome less sensitive to choice of n is to consider the smallest and largest values of $T(\hat{\alpha}-1)$ as n is varied. Leamer's (1983) extreme bounds analysis would provide that information very cheaply.

Phillips (1987) proceeds by determining analytically the limits of $T^{-1}m_{xx}$ and m_{xu} when the errors e_t are I(0) but are correlated, and he finds that $T(\hat{\alpha}-1)$ would have the Dickey–Fuller distribution once a simple correction is made. Specifically, when the Δx_t is covariance stationary, he forms $Z_{\hat{\alpha}} = T(\hat{\alpha}-1)-0{\cdot}5(\omega^2-s^2)/(T^{-1}m_{xx})$, where ω^2 is (2π) times the spectral density of Δx_t at the origin, while s^2 is the variance of Δx_t. A similar correction can be made to $t_{\hat{\alpha}}$. In both instances the correction terms are proportional to the difference between s^2 and ω^2. When the disturbance term in (2) is serially independent this difference is zero and so Phillips's test statistics reduce to the $T(\hat{\alpha}-1)$ and the DF tests respectively.[1] Phillips and Perron (1986) have extended these non-parametric tests to the case where a drift term is included in the model; a different correction term is involved.

Turning finally to what happens when x_t has a non-zero drift, there are important implications for the asymptotic distributions of the estimators and test statistics derived from regressions *with no time trend in them*. West (1988) has shown that for the model

$$y_t = \alpha x_t + \beta' \mathbf{z}_t + u_t, \tag{9}$$

where x_t is a single I(1) variable with $E(\Delta x_t) = \mu \neq 0$, $\mathbf{z}_t$ is a vector of observable I(0) variables and u_t is I(0), the OLS estimators of $\hat{\boldsymbol{\beta}}$ and $\hat{\alpha}$ possess the property that $T^{\frac{3}{2}}(\hat{\alpha}-\alpha)$ and $T^{\frac{1}{2}}(\hat{\boldsymbol{\beta}}-\boldsymbol{\beta})$ have limiting normal distributions. With one proviso this allows inference to proceed in the usual way using standard computer output. If u_t is serially correlated, the covariance matrix for $\hat{\alpha}$ and $\hat{\boldsymbol{\beta}}$ differ from the usual one in that the residual variance is ω^2, defined above, and not σ^2. In the special case where $x_t = y_{t-1}$ and $z_t = 1$ we have the AR(1) model with an intercept and serially correlated errors. And if instead

$$\mathbf{z}_t = (\Delta y_{t-1}, \Delta y_{t-2}, \ldots, \Delta x_t, \Delta x_{t-1}, \ldots)$$

we have the set-up for the ADF test, equation (8). This implies that, if x_t has a drift term, then, apart from the correction for the residual variance, the usual t-test for $\alpha = 1$ can be used. Durlauf and Phillips (1988) have obtained a similar result to West – see also Park and Phillips (1988). They have shown that when $z_t = 1$ in the above regression model $T^{\frac{3}{2}}(\hat{\beta}-\beta)$ has a limiting $N(0, 12\omega^2/\mu^2)$ density. Our qualification that the regression model used for testing if $\alpha = 1$ does not contain a trend is critical to the asymptotic theory. The reason is that the act of including a trend term in the regression means that x_{t-1}

[1] Phillips actually allows the Δx_t to have some non-stationarity in the sense that the variance of e_t could change over time, although it cannot grow indefinitely. The formulation given here assumes Δx_t is covariance stationary.

has been 'de-trended', that is the drift term has been effectively set to zero and one is back to testing for a unit root with no drift.[2] In that case it is the Dickey–Fuller tables that would need to be consulted. On a practical level it is not clear how much importance to attach to the phenomenon just described. Hylleberg and Mizon (1989) have noted in simulation studies that μ has to be quite large for one to be confident that the trend induced by μ will dominate the effects of the integrated part.

Other approaches to checking for a unit root can be mentioned. The ADF test attempts to correct for the impact of serial correlation in u_t upon the distribution of the OLS estimator of α. Under the alternative that $|\alpha| < 1$ and u_t is an MA(q) with innovation variance $\sigma^2{}_e$ *the instrumental variable estimator* $\tilde{\alpha} = (\sum y_{t-q-1} y_{t-1})^{-1} \sum y_{t-q-1} y_t$, which has y_{t-q-1} $(q > 0)$ as an instrument for y_{t-1}, is consistent. Under the null that $\alpha = 1$, y_{t-q-1} is perfectly correlated with y_{t-1} asymptotically, and this reasoning suggests that a test based upon $T^{\frac{1}{2}}(\tilde{\alpha}-1)$ could be useful. Hall (1989) advocates such an approach, and he finds that the performance tends to be better than the ADF and Z statistics. He shows that $T^{\frac{1}{2}}(\tilde{\alpha}-1)$ has the Dickey–Fuller distribution, while the 't-statistic' from the regression needs to be adjusted by the factor $\sigma_e \sigma_u^{-1}$ where $Eu_t{}^2 = \sigma_u^2$ before reference is made to Fuller's tables for critical values. Park (1988*b*) advocates a variable addition test; he regresses x_t against a trending variable ψ_t not determining x_t (and is hence 'spurious') and uses $T^{-1}t_{\psi}^2$ as the basis of a test. If x_t is I(0), $T^{-1}t_{\psi}^2$ is degenerate as the numerator would be $\chi^2(1)$ asymptotically, but if it is I(1), $T^{-1}t_{\psi}^2$ has a non-standard limiting distribution tabulated in Park *et al.* (1988). Extensions to allow for the addition of a number of variables is straightforward. Perhaps the main issue is where the spurious variables ψ_t come from. One possibility is to employ time trends, but these would have to be of higher order than those naturally occurring in the data. Another is to generate ψ_t as random walk using random numbers on a computer.

Other tests have focused on some of the implications associated with a unit root, rather than on $\hat{\alpha}$ itself. For example, Ouliaris *et al.* (1988) have extended these results to the case of a general polynomial trend or cycle, and derived a bounds test for a unit root based on $\rho^2 = \omega^2/s^2$, the logic being that an I(0) process which has been differenced will have $\omega^2 = 0$. In carrying out these tests it is important to follow the correct sequence in order that the appropriate asymptotic distribution is used. Thus the test for a unit root should be performed before a test for a linear trend. Many other tests for unit roots exist and Diebold and Nerlove (1988) give a comprehensive survey, but at this stage the ADF and Z statistics have the attention of most applied researchers.

Graphical methods can sometimes be more informative than hypothesis tests. Usually, however, it is difficult to tell by simply looking at a plot of a series whether it has, for example, a unit root with drift or is stationary about a non-stochastic trend. Cochrane (1988) set forth a graphical procedure to distinguish between unit root and trend stationary series which is based on long differences. It is also remarkably simple to compute, involving the plot of an

[2] Note that if $\Delta x_t = \mu + e_t$ then $x_t = x_0 + \mu t + \Sigma_1^t e$: i.e. $x_t = \mu t + x_{1t}$ where x_{1t} is a random wall without drift.

estimate of $\phi_k = k^{-1}[\text{var}(\Delta_k x_t)/\text{var}(\Delta_1 x_t)]$, where $\Delta_k x_t = x_t - x_{t-k}$, against $k = 1, 2, \ldots$. The behaviour of the plot of ϕ_k against k, the variance-time plot in the terminology of Diebold and Nerlove (1988), can potentially identify the type of process we are faced with. If x_t is I(1) then $\lim_{k\to\infty} \phi_k$ is a non-zero constant, while if x_t is I(0) ϕ_k converges to zero. Finally, if x_t is generated by a stationary stochastic process about a linear trend, ϕ_k grows, eventually converging on a positively sloped straight line. On the assumption that a unit root is present, Cochrane uses the asymptotic distribution of $\hat{\phi}_k$ to construct standard errors which can be used to form bands around the plot. It is interesting to observe that $\omega^2 = f_x(0)$, the spectral density of x_t at zero frequency, and since ϕ_∞ is proportional to ω^2, it is easily estimated by spectral methods. Although the approach is attractive, common sense indicates that it will be hard to distinguish between (say) an $\alpha = 0{\cdot}98$ and one of unity without very large samples. Nevertheless, in a Monte Carlo study, Lo and MacKinlay (1988) found that the test had power at least as good as that of Dickey–Fuller for detecting a unit root.

There are a number of practical difficulties with all of these tests, foremost of which is that heavy use is being made of the super-consistency of $\hat{\alpha}$. When $\alpha < 1$ it is well known that the OLS estimator of α is inconsistent if the errors u_t are autocorrelated. Therefore, for 'too small' a sample size, it might be expected that $\hat{\alpha}$ could be contaminated by the serial correlation in u_t, even if $\alpha = 1$. Because the DF/Z class of tests is based on $T(\hat{\alpha}-1)$, any 'small sample bias' is greatly magnified. For example if $T = 1000$ even an $\hat{\alpha} = 0{\cdot}98$ will give the test statistic $T(\hat{\alpha}-1)$ a value of -20. To some extent the correction for serial correlation compensates for this effect, although the adjustment is not large enough. Schwert (1987) has shown that the 'small sample' bias in $\hat{\alpha}$ could be quite large if the disturbance is an MA with negative first order serial correlation. To see why, note that the ARMA(1,1) process $x_t = \alpha x_{t-1} + e_t - \theta e_{t-1}$ can be rewritten as an AR process with the partial autocorrelation function obtained from $(1-\alpha L)(1-\theta L)^{-1} \cong 1 + (\alpha - \theta) L + \ldots$. Thus if $\theta > 0$ the estimate of α based on an AR(1) model may be biased downwards. Schwert's simulation shows that both the ADF and Phillips Z tests suffer from this problem even if $T = 1000$, although the ADF seems less sensitive. Since the outcome is to bias towards rejection, if one accepts this should not be an issue. A sensible strategy is always to look at the magnitude of $\hat{\alpha}$ as well as any test statistic; in many instances an $\hat{\alpha}$ equal to $0{\cdot}98$ would have to be regarded as effectively unity. It is noticeable that some researchers are using the tables in Schwert's paper as a guard against the bias problem, e.g. Hoffman and Rasche (1989).

The tests can also be sensitive to the omission of other variables from the equation; in particular shifts in the mean of a series might be interpreted as a unit root. Perron (1989) made this argument about GNP. When he put in shift variables for the Depression and oil price shocks there was no longer any evidence of a unit root. Perhaps this is not surprising as the unit root makes any shocks persistent and dummy variables just do the same thing. Christiano (1988) re-examines Perron's work finding that, if it is assumed that the break point is determined from the same data set, and an allowance made for the pre-test bias on critical values, there is no longer evidence of a shift in post-war GDP.

One might ask what it is that enables the OLS estimator of α to be consistent in the presence of serial correlation when $\alpha = 1$. The answer is the assumption that the variance of u_t is a constant, since this means that the 'signal' x_{t-1} eventually dominates the 'noise'. Put another way, eventually all we would see in a series is its past value, and the change in x_t would become progressively smaller if expressed as a ratio to x_{t-1}. If x_t is the logarithm of a variable X_t, Δx_t is the growth rate of X_t and a constant variance is plausible. But if x_t is a 'levels' variable this is a dubious description of actual data and has given rise to a literature in which the variance of u_t is allowed to grow over time. Wooldridge and White (1988) considered what happens in (6) if u_t was the sum of i.d. $(0, t^p)$ random variables. The distribution of $\hat{\alpha}$ was again non-standard but not of the Dickey–Fuller form. Hansen (1988) looked at the OLS estimator of α in (9) when u_t was the product of an I(1) and an I(0) process and x_t was I(1), establishing that $T^{\frac{1}{2}}(\hat{\alpha}-\alpha)$ had a limiting distribution, although it was not normal. Nevertheless, he managed to find a test statistic for $\alpha = \alpha_0$ that could be treated as a standard normal deviate. Because conclusions about the presence of integration are sensitive to the specification of the variance, and as there is the suspicion that some series could well exhibit non-constant variance after differencing, much more research is needed before one could be confident in reaching conclusions from any of the tests.

I.2.2. *Fractional integration in data*

Although it is widely accepted that economic time series are highly correlated there is more dissent over whether it is as extreme as implied by integrated processes. 'Long memory', or strong correlation between observations far apart in a sample, may come about in other ways. This has led to other characterisations of the data, the most prominent of which is the class of fractional difference models introduced into econometrics by Granger and Joyeux (1980). This model has $(1-L)^d x_t = e_t$, where e_t is i.i.d. $(0, \sigma^2)$, and d can be other than an integer. It is natural to call x_t a fractionally integrated process. Using the binomial theorem for $(1-L)^d$, x_t can be given an infinite autoregressive form $C(L)\, x_t = e_t$, $c_j = \Gamma(j-d)/\Gamma(-d)\,\Gamma(j+1)$, where $\Gamma(.)$ is the gamma function. When $|d| < 0{\cdot}5$ technically the series is covariance stationary but the autocovariances of the x_t decline at rate j^{2d-1}, rather than geometrically as for a stationary and invertible finite order ARMA process. Due to this slow decline shocks can be very 'persistent', even though they eventually die out.

These processes are salutory reminders that the alternative to an integrated process is not always a stationary member of the ARMA class. Distinguishing between a value of d that is unity and one that is close to that value may be very difficult with small sample sizes. If this is so, strong conclusions about the ultimate effects of shocks upon a macroeconomic variable could not realistically be drawn. It is not surprising then that a literature has grown up which attempts to determine whether $d = 1$ or $d \neq 1$. A number of different approaches have been taken. Haubrich and Lo (1988) write $(1-L)^d x_t = (1-L)(1-L)^{d-1}x_t = (1-L)^{d-1}z_t$, and seek to determine if z_t has long memory. For this they use a modified version of the Hurst–Mandlebrot scaled range statistic $R = s^{-1}[\max_{1 \leq k \leq T} \sum_{t=1}^{k}(z_t - \bar{z}) - \min_{1 \leq k \leq T} \sum_{t=1}^{k}(z_t - \bar{z})]$, $\bar{z}$ being the sample mean of z_t and s an estimate of the spectral density of z_t at the origin under the maintained hypothesis. It is the last qualification which is troublesome. As there is no reason to think that z_t could not have 'short memory', the divisor is an attempt to make the test statistic robust to such a possibility. But if too much of the correlation in z_t is captured in s the test will have power only equal to its size, as the distribution of R will be invariant to *any* dependence in z_t. This comes out of their simulations of a $d = \frac{1}{3}$ alternative. For estimation of the spectral density with 1 lag the test rejected the maintained ($d = 0$) model 58·7% of the time, but if 8 lags were used the percentage of rejections was a paltry 2·3% (close to the size of 2·5%).

Rather than test $d = 1$ indirectly from the residual autocorrelation, an alternative strategy is to estimate d directly. Using the fact that the spectral density of z_t, $f_z(\lambda)$, is $[1-\exp(-i\lambda)]^{-2d} f_e(\lambda) = [4\sin^2(\lambda/2)]^{-d} f_e(\lambda)$, it follows that $\log f_z(\lambda) = \log f_e(\lambda) - d\log[4\sin^2(\lambda/2)]$. This led Geweke and Porter-Hudak (1983) to propose estimating d by regressing the periodogram at frequencies $\lambda_j = 2\pi j/T, j = k_1, \ldots, K$, against a constant and $\log[4\sin^2(\lambda_j/2)]$. Kunsch (1986) shows that frequencies around the origin need to be excluded to get a consistent estimator, and how k_1 should vary with N. This strategy requires K to expand with the sample size, for example $K = N^{\frac{1}{2}}$, and that makes convergence of the estimator slow. Obviously one is also maintaining that the density of e_t is constant over the frequencies used as it is being absorbed into the constant term, and this may be inaccurate. One way to obviate the slow convergence problem is to attempt to estimate d by maximum likelihood and Sowell (1987) sets out how to do this. Again one is making assumptions about e_t, and any test that d was unity would need to be careful of the short term memory problem that concerned Haubrich and Lo. An interesting line of work that does not seem to have been followed here is to construct a Lagrange Multiplier test of $d = 1$. As it is computationally quite demanding to maximise the likelihood of z_t for non-integer d, a preliminary test to determine if it is worth doing is appealing.

II. ESTIMATION

A great deal of econometrics concentrates upon getting an estimate of an unknown $(p \times 1)$ vector of parameters $\boldsymbol{\theta}$ from a set of data $y_1, \ldots, y_N, x_1, \ldots, x_N$. This parameter may arise in many different ways. Sometimes it is the conditional moment of one variable y with respect to another x evaluated at a particular value $x = \tilde{x}$. In other cases it is the partial derivative of y with respect to x evaluated either at a point $\tilde{x}$ or globally if the partial derivative does not depend upon x (as would occur if the relation between y and x is linear). The problem of estimating a parameter can arise therefore in many ways. Apart from Bayesian estimation which is not discussed here, econometrics has used four main methods for extracting information about this parameter from a given set of data: maximum likelihood, method of moments, M-estimation and non-parametric analysis. While the first has a long history in econometrics, the others are relatively new, but they are attracting much attention and once their potential is better understood they are likely to be in common use in applied work.

II.1. *Maximum Likelihood*

Maximum likelihood begins by defining a conditional density, $f_i(\boldsymbol{\theta})$, for y_i ($i = 1, \ldots, N$) given x_i, thereby nominating x_i as a 'causal' or exogenous variable, and estimating the parameters of interest $\boldsymbol{\theta}$ by maximising $L = \sum \log f_i(\boldsymbol{\theta})$ with respect to $\boldsymbol{\theta}$ to give the MLE $\hat{\boldsymbol{\theta}}$. Implicit in this method is the supposition that the parameters of interest can be related to the parameters of the density f_i. Despite the fact that Full Information Maximum Likelihood was the preferred estimator of the Cowles Commission, its use in time series modelling has been minimal, although it may undergo a renaissance as a result of current work on the estimation of co-integrating vectors by Johansen (1988) and Phillips (1988) which we discuss later. In the analysis of data on individuals, however, until recently it has reigned supreme. Data that have been censored or which come strictly in qualitative form have been handled most easily from the maximum likelihood perspective.

Much of the appeal of the method derives from the fact that, when the specified density is correct, $\hat{\boldsymbol{\theta}}$ has the property that it is consistent and $N^{\frac{1}{2}}(\hat{\boldsymbol{\theta}} - \boldsymbol{\theta}_0)$ is asymptotically normally distributed with zero mean and covariance matrix $\mathbf{g}_{\theta\theta}^{-1} = -[\text{plim}_{N\to\infty} N^{-1}(\partial^2 L/\partial\boldsymbol{\theta}\,\partial\boldsymbol{\theta}')]^{-1}$, which is the asymptotic version of Fisher's information matrix. The MLE sometimes possesses a degree of robustness to mis-specification of the density. For example, the OLS estimator is MLE when the errors in a regression model are normally distributed, but it remains a consistent estimator under a much wider class of densities for the errors. Technically, if $\text{E}[N^{-1}\sum \log f_i(\boldsymbol{\theta})]$ is maximised at $\boldsymbol{\theta} = \boldsymbol{\theta}_0$, where E(.) is the expectation with respect to the true density, the MLE estimator will be a consistent estimator of $\boldsymbol{\theta}_0$, even though the variance of its limiting distribution is no longer $\mathbf{g}_{\theta\theta}^{-1}$, being instead $\mathbf{g}_{\theta\theta}^{-1}\,\text{E}[(\partial L/\partial\boldsymbol{\theta})\,(\partial L/\partial\boldsymbol{\theta})']\,\mathbf{g}_{\theta\theta}^{-1}$. The theory of such pseudo maximum likelihood estimators is set out in Gourieroux *et al.* (1984).

Maximum likelihood is also an attractive option in handling some complex time series problems as a consequence of the property that the joint density is the product of the conditional and the marginal densities. Suppose $\mathbf{F}_{i-1}$ consists of $\{x_1, \ldots, x_i, y_0, \ldots, y_{i-1}\}$. Then the joint density $f(y_i, \mathbf{F}_{i-1})$ factors as the product $f(y_i | \mathbf{F}_{i-1}) f(\mathbf{F}_{i-1})$ and it follows from repeated application of this rule that the log likelihood will be $\sum_{i=1}^{N} \log f(y_i | \mathbf{F}_{i-1}) + \log f(y_0, x_0)$. Provided the conditional density $f(y_i | \mathbf{F}_{i-1})$ can be determined, the log likelihood is therefore easy to construct. Fortunately, for models that can be cast into a state space form, the Kalman filter produces the conditional density. Recognition of this fact by Schweppe (1965) led to a host of applications in econometrics: Rosenberg (1973) for varying coefficient regression models, Pagan (1975) and Engle and

Watson (1981) for unobserved component models and Harvey and Pierse (1984) for missing data.

The decomposition described above is useful in other applications. Consider the regression model

$$y_i = \mathbf{x}_i' \boldsymbol{\beta} + u_i, \tag{10}$$

and assume that, conditional upon $\mathbf{F}_{i-1}$, the u_i are $N(0, \sigma_i^2)$ with σ_i^2 a function of $\mathbf{F}_{i-1}$. Due to this dependence of the variance upon past information, the u_i cannot be independently distributed. Nevertheless, the log likelihood is easy to write down since $f(y_i|\mathbf{F}_{i-1})$ is $N(\mathbf{x}_i'\boldsymbol{\beta}, \sigma_i^2)$. Engle's (1982) Autoregressive Conditional Heteroskedasticity (ARCH) model sets $\sigma_i^2 = \alpha_0 + \sum_{j=1}^r \alpha_j u_{i-j}^2$, which carries the implication that the *unconditional* density of y_i is non-normal with fat tails. What is interesting here is that, although the joint density is actually unknown, the log likelihood can be constructed solely from the conditional densities (the last term $\log f(y_0, x_0)$ is dominated asymptotically by the sum and is omitted). Other types of dependence of σ_i^2 upon $\mathbf{F}_{i-1}$ can be allowed for, and the conditional density may be non-normal, for example Student's t. Engle and Bollerslev (1986) review many of the options.

Another application that has attracted applied workers is Hamilton's (1987) unobserved states model. Hamilton allows the conditional mean and variance of a process to depend upon different states S_t, for example high volatility and low volatility, or different monetary regimes. These states are taken to be generated by a simple Markov process and the likelihood of the data is maximised with respect to the unknown parameters of the conditional moments and the transition probabilities. Essentially this allows for what appears to be 'structural change' in the data, although the series is still covariance stationary as the model switches are determined by the Markov process. A key factor in obtaining the likelihood is the recursive decomposition above. Applications of the idea have been made to output, interest rates and foreign exchange rates – see Hamilton (1989) for a survey.

II.2. *Method of Moments Estimation*

Method of moments estimation may be thought of as a generalisation of the instrumental variable estimator which has a long history of use in econometrics. It begins with a set of first order or orthogonality conditions $E[\mathbf{g}(y_i, \mathbf{x}_i, \boldsymbol{\theta})] = \mathbf{0}$ and proceeds to a point estimate of $\boldsymbol{\theta}$ by choosing $\hat{\boldsymbol{\theta}}$ to minimise $[\sum \mathbf{g}_i(\boldsymbol{\theta})]'\mathbf{W}^{-1}[\sum \mathbf{g}_i(\boldsymbol{\theta})]$, where $\mathbf{W}$ is some weighting matrix used whenever the $\dim(\mathbf{g}_i)$ exceeds $\dim(\boldsymbol{\theta})$. Hansen (1982) showed that the best choice of $\mathbf{W}$ was the covariance matrix of $\sum \mathbf{g}_i$, which results in his generalised method of moments estimator (GMM). The GMM framework can subsume the MLE in most situations since the MLE of $\boldsymbol{\theta}$ also solves a set of equations $\sum \mathbf{d}_i(\hat{\boldsymbol{\theta}}_{\text{MLE}}) = \mathbf{0}$, where $\mathbf{d}_i(\boldsymbol{\theta}) = \partial \log f_i / \partial \boldsymbol{\theta}$ is the vector of scores. As the dimension of $\mathbf{d}_i$ is the same as that of $\boldsymbol{\theta}$ the GMM and MLE will be identical when $\mathbf{g}_i = \mathbf{d}_i$ and $\mathbf{W}$ is set to any positive definite matrix. Under a range of conditions the GMM estimator $\hat{\boldsymbol{\theta}}$ is a consistent estimator of $\boldsymbol{\theta}_0$ and $N^{\frac{1}{2}}(\hat{\boldsymbol{\theta}} - \boldsymbol{\theta}_0)$ is asymptotically normally distributed with mean zero and covariance matrix $(\text{plim}_{N\to\infty} N^{-1}\mathbf{G}'\mathbf{W}^{-1}\mathbf{G})^{-1}$, where $\mathbf{G}' = \sum (\partial \mathbf{g}_i / \partial \boldsymbol{\theta})$. A precursor of the GMM approach is the Generalised Instrumental Variable Estimator (GIVE) of Sargan (1958). Suppose we write (10) in matrix form as $\mathbf{y} = \mathbf{X\beta}+\mathbf{u}$ and associate a set of orthogonality relations $E(\mathbf{Z}'\mathbf{u})$ with it, where $\mathbf{Z}$ is an $(N\times r)$ matrix of 'instruments'. Sargan minimised $(\mathbf{y}-\mathbf{X\beta})'\mathbf{Z}(\mathbf{Z}'\mathbf{Z})^{-1}\mathbf{Z}'(\mathbf{y}-\mathbf{X\beta})$ with respect to $\mathbf{\beta}$, whereas the GMM philosophy would propose the minimisation of $(\mathbf{y}-\mathbf{X\beta})'\mathbf{Z}(\mathbf{Z\Omega Z}')^{-1}\mathbf{Z}'(\mathbf{y}-\mathbf{X\beta})$, where $\mathbf{\Omega}$ is the covariance matrix of $\mathbf{u}$; both use $\mathbf{W} = \mathrm{cov}\,(\mathbf{Z}'\mathbf{u})$ as the weighting matrix in the quadratic form $\mathbf{u}'\mathbf{ZW}^{-1}\mathbf{Z}'\mathbf{u}$. The two coincide under Sargan's assumption that $\mathbf{\Omega} = \sigma^2\mathbf{I}_N$. Effectively, the optimal way in which instruments should be combined depends upon the nature of the correlation in the errors u_i. Cumby *et al.* (1983) formulate the GMM estimator in this way. Perhaps the most difficult issue is in computing the optimal choice of $\mathbf{W}$, particularly when the $\mathbf{g}_i(\mathbf{\theta})$ are serially correlated. Eichenbaum *et al.* (1988, Appendix B) discuss some options; other ways of computing the covariance matrix are presented in Newey and West (1987) and Andrews (1988*b*).

The GMM estimator has been deservedly popular in macro-econometric and financial research where it provides a unifying framework for the estimation of a very diverse set of models. Thus in the area of rational expectations there is an underlying set of relationships stipulated by the theory which can be used to form GMM estimators. For example, an expectations-augmented Phillips curve of the form $w_i = \beta x_i + \gamma p_i^e + u_i$, where w_i, x_i, p_i^e and u_i are the change in wages, 'demand', the change in expected prices and an error term respectively, can be converted to estimable form by setting $p_i = E(p_i\,|\,z_i)+\epsilon_i$ and identifying p_i^e as $E(p_i\,|\,z_i)$. Rationality then provides the set of orthogonality relations $E[z_i(w_i-\beta x_i-\gamma p_i)] = 0$.

An extension of the GMM framework that is important occurs when the orthogonality conditions can be written as $E[\mathbf{g}(y_i, \mathbf{x}_i, \mathbf{\alpha}, \mathbf{\beta})] = \mathbf{0}$, and some root-$N$ consistent estimator $\tilde{\mathbf{\alpha}}$ replaces $\mathbf{\alpha}$ in these before they are solved for $\mathbf{\beta}$. These 'two-stage' or sequential estimators of $\mathbf{\beta}$ are very common in expectations research, Pagan (1984*a*, 1986), Pesaran (1987), but also appear in many other areas of econometrics. An early example is Two Stage Least Squares where, in Johnston's (1984, pp. 472–82) notation, the orthogonality conditions are $E[(\mathbf{\Pi}_1\mathbf{X})'(\mathbf{y}-\mathbf{Y}_1\mathbf{\beta}-\mathbf{X}_1\mathbf{\gamma})] = 0$, and $\mathbf{\Pi}$ is replaced by $\tilde{\mathbf{\Pi}}$, the OLS estimator of the reduced form coefficients. Newey (1984) has given very general formulae for the covariance matrix of $N^{\frac{1}{2}}(\hat{\mathbf{\beta}}_{\mathrm{SGMM}}-\mathbf{\beta})$, where the 'S' indicates a sequential estimator.

The GMM orientation has the advantage that it can also subsume other approaches, for example the 'estimator generating equation' methodology employed by Hendry (1976) in his unification of simultaneous equation estimators; and the 'calibration' ideas often occurring in real business cycle models. Lee and Ingram (1988) and Singleton (1988) deal with the latter while Christiano and Eichenbaum (1988) provide an application. These authors argue that those who employ calibration are implicitly choosing $\mathbf{\theta}$ by using the condition that $\hat{\mathbf{m}}-\mathbf{m}(\mathbf{\theta})$ should be close to zero, where $\hat{\mathbf{m}}$ and $\mathbf{m}(\mathbf{\theta})$ are the sample and model-generated moments of certain endogenous variables. For a linear model $\mathbf{m}(\mathbf{\theta})$ can generally be given an analytic expression. For nonlinear models Lee and Ingram suggest that it be found by simulating the model for many replications and then taking an average of the moments at each replication. They argue that, as the number of replications grow, an estimator formed in this way would have the same properties as that formed by using the true $\mathbf{m}(\boldsymbol{\theta})$ in the orthogonality relations.

II.3. *M-Estimators*

Maximum Likelihood estimation aims to maximise a particular function of the data namely $\Sigma \log f_i(\boldsymbol{\theta})$. A motivation for doing this is that, under a correct specification for the conditional density, $\boldsymbol{\theta}$ maximises $\lim_{N\to\infty} N^{-1}\mathrm{E}[\Sigma \log f_i(\boldsymbol{\theta})]$ and $N^{-1}\Sigma \log f_i(\boldsymbol{\theta})$ is the sample analogue of the population expectation. This connection has prompted reference to the 'analog principle of estimation', which has been given a very elegant treatment by Manski (1988). Looked at in this light one might wonder if there are other functions of the data and $\boldsymbol{\theta}_0$ which have this property. This idea is central to the principle of M-estimation (the M being for 'maximum likelihood type') which was set out in Huber (1964). It involves selecting a function $\boldsymbol{\rho}(\boldsymbol{\theta}, y_i, \mathbf{x}_i)$ such that $\mathrm{E}[\Sigma\, \boldsymbol{\rho}(\boldsymbol{\theta}, y_i, \mathbf{x}_i)]$ is minimised at $\boldsymbol{\theta} = \boldsymbol{\theta}_0$ and then minimising $\Sigma\, \boldsymbol{\rho}(\boldsymbol{\theta}, y_i, \mathbf{x}_i)$ with respect to $\boldsymbol{\theta}$. This estimator is consistent for $\boldsymbol{\theta}_0$ and $N^{\frac{1}{2}}(\hat{\boldsymbol{\theta}} - \boldsymbol{\theta}_0)$ is asymptotically normal with covariance matrix $[\mathrm{E}(\boldsymbol{\rho}_{\theta\theta})]^{-1}\mathrm{E}(\boldsymbol{\rho}_\theta \boldsymbol{\rho}_\theta')\,[\mathrm{E}(\boldsymbol{\rho}_{\theta\theta})]^{-1}$ if observations are i.i.d. and $\boldsymbol{\rho}$ is differentiable with first and second derivatives $\boldsymbol{\rho}_\theta$ and $\boldsymbol{\rho}_{\theta\theta}$ respectively. In most instances the M-estimator can be regarded as solving a set of first order conditions. Certainly, when $\boldsymbol{\rho}(.)$ is differentiable with respect to $\boldsymbol{\theta}$, the first order conditions $\Sigma\, \boldsymbol{\rho}_\theta(\hat{\boldsymbol{\theta}}) = \mathbf{o}$ can be used to define the M-estimator of $\boldsymbol{\theta}$.

Within the regression context there has been only a moderate use of M-estimators. If $y_i = \mu + u_i$, where u_i is i.i.d. $(0, \sigma^2)$, setting $\rho(\boldsymbol{\theta}) = |y_i - \mu|$ and minimising gives the sample median; this exploits the fact that the derivative of $|z|$ with respect to z is sgn (z) $(z \neq 0)$. This example underscores the point that the efficiency of an estimator of $\boldsymbol{\beta}$ in (10) depends upon the distribution of the errors u_i; in this case the sample mean is the MLE when the errors are normal but the median is the MLE when they are Laplace distributed. An extension of this idea is that of a *quantile* estimator, Koenker and Bassett (1978). An α-quantile estimator of $\boldsymbol{\theta}$ is an M-estimator with $\rho(z) = |\alpha - 1(z < 0)|\,|z|$, where $1(.)$ is the indicator function and $z = y_i - \mu$ when the location parameter $\theta = \mu$ is to be estimated ($\alpha = \frac{1}{2}$ produces the median). When these ideas are extended to regression, z is replaced by $(y_i - \mathbf{x}_i'\boldsymbol{\beta})$, giving the Least Absolute Deviations (LAD) estimator analysed in Ruppert and Carroll (1980) and the α-quantile regression estimator of Koenker and Bassett (1978). Sometimes z is set to $s^{-1}(y_i - \mathbf{x}_i'\boldsymbol{\beta})$, where s is a scaling factor, a possible choice for which is an estimator of σ. Other choices of $\rho(.)$ have been $|\alpha - 1(z < 0)|\,z^2$, $0 < \alpha < 1$, which yields the asymmetric least squares estimator studied by Newey and Powell (1987), and $\rho(.) = z/(1 + sz^2)$ which Potscher and Prucha (1986) advocate after considering the form of the scores for $\boldsymbol{\beta}$ when the u_i are distributed as Student's t.

Although not much favoured in the regression set-up, these estimators have appealed to those working with data that have been censored. This occurs in the multitude of variations of the Tobit model surveyed in Amemiya (1985, ch. 10). In the regression model the accuracy of the distributional assumption is crucial only for the question of how efficient the estimator is, but when data are censored the same error carries with it the virtual certainty of inconsistency in the MLE, making estimators that are robust to such mis-specification a very attractive option. Estimators possessing this property have therefore proved popular in the literature concerned with estimating the determinants of the duration of unemployment, strikes, etc. Common choices are the LAD and α-quantile estimators for Tobit models, (Powell, 1984, 1986), which select $\rho(z)$ as defined above but with $z = y_i - \max(0, \mathbf{x}_i'\boldsymbol{\beta})$, e.g. see Horowitz and Neumann (1987). It seems likely that, whenever the MLE is sensitive in its first moment to distributional mis-specification, M-estimators will be attractive. The key question is to determine what the most useful $\rho(.)$ functions are. To date very little research has been carried out on this question outside the regression context.

II.4. *Non-Parametric Estimation*

This is closely related to the GMM estimator but has the distinctive feature that it employs approximations to an unknown function which improve as the sample size grows. To illustrate its usefulness, consider an issue frequently arising in applied work, namely, the estimation of the moments of y conditional upon $\mathbf{x} = \tilde{\mathbf{x}}$. The following are three examples of this. First, it might be important to know how an output varies with a particular level of a factor. Second, in discrete choice models, where y_i is a binary variable taking the value zero or unity, the probability of making a particular choice, given $\mathbf{x}_i$, is the conditional expectation: $\Pr\{y_i = 1 \mid \mathbf{x}_i\} = (1)\Pr\{y_i = 1 \mid \mathbf{x}_i\} + (0)\Pr\{y_i = 0 \mid \mathbf{x}_i\} = E(y_i \mid \mathbf{x}_i)$. Finally, in many studies of commodity or financial prices interest centres on their volatility, and that can be thought of as a conditional variance, with the conditioning set being the information available to agents for prediction purposes (see Pagan and Ullah, 1988).

For all the cases above denote the unknown conditional expectation by $\theta = m(\tilde{\mathbf{x}})$. Recognising that the conditional expectation is a function of $\mathbf{x}$, one solution would be to seek a function of $\mathbf{x}$ that would be close to $m(\mathbf{x})$ for all values of $\mathbf{x}$, i.e. to approximate the unknown conditional expectation *globally*. Production function estimation was one of the first areas in which suitable approximations to $m(\mathbf{x})$ were sought, and this literature progressed from the Cobb-Douglas function to the C.E.S., V.E.S., generalised Leontief, quadratic, transcendental logarithmic, and flexible functional forms – see Lau (1986) for a comprehensive survey. These approximations have the common characteristic that their quality is invariant to the sample size. Such a feature seems undesirable, and has led to a 'non-parametric' literature where it has been eliminated.

Within econometrics the earliest work aimed at improving the approximation was by Gallant (1981), who suggested that the function $m(\mathbf{x})$ be replaced by a linear combination of variables $\mathbf{z}_i$ that included a low order polynomial in $\mathbf{x}$ and the trigonometric terms $\cos(jx)$, $\sin(jx)$, $j = 1, 2, \ldots, L$ (for a scalar x). The use of trigonometric terms, which produces the Flexible Fourier Form, was desirable because the accuracy of the approximation of $m(\mathbf{x}_i)$ by $\mathbf{z}_i'\boldsymbol{\gamma}$ could be described in a very precise way which was critical when establishing that the estimators had desirable properties. The conditional mean estimator $\hat{m}(\tilde{\mathbf{x}})$ is obtained by regressing y_i against the $\mathbf{z}_i$ and then using the estimated $\boldsymbol{\gamma}$ to form $\hat{\boldsymbol{\theta}} = \tilde{\mathbf{z}}_i'\hat{\boldsymbol{\gamma}}$. A useful way of thinking about what is occurring here is to observe that, if $m(\mathbf{x})$ could be parameterised, the ideal GMM estimator of $\boldsymbol{\theta}$ would be obtained from the orthogonality condition $\mathrm{E}m(\mathbf{x}_i)[y_i - m(\mathbf{x}_i)] = 0$. Since $m(\mathbf{x}_i)$ is unknown it is replaced by $\mathbf{z}_i'\boldsymbol{\gamma}$ such that $\lim_{N\to\infty} \mathrm{E}[\boldsymbol{\gamma}'\mathbf{z}_i(y_i - \mathbf{z}_i'\boldsymbol{\gamma})] = 0$ which will be satisfied if $\lim_{N\to\infty} \mathrm{E}[\mathbf{z}_i(y_i - \mathbf{z}_i'\boldsymbol{\gamma})] = \mathbf{0}$. The GMM estimator for the last orthogonality condition is just the OLS estimator $\hat{\boldsymbol{\gamma}}$ described above and $\hat{m} = \tilde{\mathbf{z}}'\hat{\boldsymbol{\gamma}}$. For this method to work the approximation must improve as $N \to \infty$ and this entails expanding the number of parameters to be estimated. Andrews (1988*a*) has established conditions on the rate at which the number of trigonometric terms (L) must tend to infinity with N to ensure consistency of the estimator as well as asymptotic normality. Applications of this approach to estimation can be found in Gallant (1982), Gallant and Golub (1984), Vinod and Ullah (1986), and Pagan and Hong (1990). A similar approximation scheme would be the method of spline approximation in which $m(\mathbf{x}_i)$ is replaced by a combination of low order polynomials in $\mathbf{x}_i$. In econometrics the main use of splines has been for measuring structural change (Poirier, 1975), and demand analysis, (Engle *et al.*, 1986).

Viewing the series expansion approach, sometimes called 'sieve' estimation in the statistics literature, as a GMM estimator in which the orthogonality conditions only hold asymptotically, leads us to ask if there are other first order conditions for which this is true. The affirmative answer provides an alternative generally referred to as *kernel* estimation, but the approximation is *local* rather than global. In this technique, a kernel function $K[(\mathbf{x} - \tilde{\mathbf{x}})/h]$ is defined, with the properties that it is non-negative, integrates to unity, is symmetric and $\lim_{\psi\to\infty} K(\psi) = 0$. For example, the standard normal density $K(\psi) = (2\pi)^{-\frac{1}{2}} \exp(-\frac{1}{2}\psi^2)$ satisfies these requirements. The quantity h is a window width parameter that declines to zero as a function of N, for example $h = cN^{-\frac{1}{5}}$, with the rate of decrease being determined so as to get desirable properties for the estimator of the conditional moments. It is hard to be more precise about this choice as much depends upon what properties it is felt the estimator should possess. Silverman (1986) and Ullah (1988*a*) discuss the principles involved for density estimation and regression models, while Hall and Horowitz (1988) look at the censored regression situation.

Consider the estimator of $\hat{m}$ given by the solution of the first order conditions $\sum K[(\mathbf{x}_i - \tilde{\mathbf{x}})/h](y_i - \hat{\theta}) = 0$. This gives the estimator $\hat{\theta} = \sum K_i y_i / \sum K_i$ proposed by Nadaraya (1964) and Watson (1964) for the conditional mean. As might be expected from the form of this estimator it can be thought of in the GMM framework by observing that $\lim_{N\to\infty} \mathrm{E}[\sum K_i(y_i - \theta_0)] = 0$. Thus the kernel technique produces a *local* approximation, centred upon $\tilde{\mathbf{x}}$, by computing a weighted average of the y_i corresponding to all those $\mathbf{x}_i$ that are close to the value $\tilde{\mathbf{x}}$, and giving low weights (small K_i) to observations that have $\mathbf{x}_i$ far from

$\tilde{\mathbf{x}}$. Since the weights tend to zero, as the sample size grows, for all $\mathbf{x}_i$ not equal to $\tilde{\mathbf{x}}$, asymptotically one is effectively computing a simple average of the y_i that correspond to $\mathbf{x}_i = \tilde{\mathbf{x}}$. As would be expected this should be a good estimator of the unknown conditional expectation provided the number of observations on $\mathbf{x}_i$ that bunch around $\tilde{\mathbf{x}}$ increase with the sample size. A formal proof of the consistency of the estimator is given in Bierens (1987). Notice that one could generalise the kernel estimator by solving $\sum w_i(y_i - \hat{\theta}) = 0$ where w_i are any set of weights that behave like the kernel weights. An enormous variety of weights has been proposed, and these are discussed in Silverman (1986). Once one has the formula for the conditional moment, derivatives of the conditional moment with respect to any of its arguments can be obtained by differentiation. Hence, marginal products etc. can be estimated at particular factor levels. Ullah (1988*b*) surveys this literature. Powell *et al.* (1989) propose methods to estimate the average derivatives rather than the derivative at a point, and these methods involve forming weighted averages of kernel estimators.

Estimating conditional moments may also be important as part of an estimation strategy. For example, if some of the $\mathbf{x}_i$ in (1) were endogenous in a non-linear system of simultaneous equations that has $\mathbf{z}_i$ as predetermined variables, it is desirable to be able to form the conditional expectation $E(\mathbf{x}_i | \mathbf{z}_i)$ to serve as instruments for $\mathbf{x}_i$ in estimating $\boldsymbol{\beta}$ – see Newey (1988*b*) and Rilstone (1988). For that particular application there are other ways of using the data to form $E(\mathbf{x}_i | \mathbf{z}_i)$, such as the residual based prediction of Brown and Mariano (1984). Another example is the case where (10) is

$$y_i^* = \mathbf{x}_i' \boldsymbol{\beta} + u_i^*, \tag{11}$$

with the u_i' being normally and independently distributed but only an indicator, y_i, of the latent variable is observed. Examples are $y_i = 1(y_i^* > 0)$ (the Probit model) and $y_i = 1(y_i^* > 0) y_i^*$ (the Tobit model). If the error density of the u_i is not normal one might instead consider minimising $\sum_{i=1}^{N} [y_i - E(y_i | \mathbf{x}_i' \boldsymbol{\beta})]^2$, as this mimics least squares. Ichimura (1987) developed this idea, proving the consistency and asymptotic normality of the estimator with $E(y_i | \mathbf{x}_i' \boldsymbol{\beta})$ replaced by its kernel estimator, provided the window width defining the kernel estimator of $E(y_i | \mathbf{x}_i' \boldsymbol{\beta})$ was suitably restricted. Other ways have been broached to get the unknown conditional mean non-parametrically for use in a pseudo-least squares type estimator, notably Horowitz's (1986) idea of exploiting the Kaplan–Meier (1958) estimator of the distribution function of censored data. Recently Horowitz (1988) has shown that by smoothing the Kaplan–Meier estimator with a kernel, the resulting 'least squares' estimator of $\boldsymbol{\beta}$ is consistent and asymptotically normal.

A different econometric problem that has been attacked by non-parametric procedures involves the estimation of a vector $\boldsymbol{\beta}$ in the linear model (10) where the density of the u_i, $f(u_i)$, is unknown. 'Unknown' could be given a number of interpretations. One possibility is that the mean of u_i is known to be zero but the variance might depend upon $\mathbf{x}_i$, i.e. the regression model has heteroskedastic errors. If the density was normal the optimal estimator of $\boldsymbol{\beta}$ would be the Generalised Least Squares (GLS) estimator $(\sum \mathbf{x}_i \mathbf{x}_i' \sigma_i^{-2})^{-1} (\sum \mathbf{x}_i y_i \sigma_i^{-2})$, and this depends upon the unknown conditional variance. Robinson (1987) showed that replacing σ_i^2 by a non-parametric estimate would give an operational estimator of $\boldsymbol{\beta}$ which was asymptotically as efficient as GLS.

Another interpretation would be that the density of the u_i is invariant to i but its format is unknown. Conditional upon the $\mathbf{x}_i$, the density of y_i is $f(u_i)$, and the log likelihood will be

$$L = \sum \log f(y_i - \mathbf{x}_i' \boldsymbol{\beta}). \tag{12}$$

There have been a number of approaches to estimating $\boldsymbol{\beta}$ efficiently, generally termed semi-parametric in the sense that no assumption is made about the precise form of $f(u)$ when estimating $\boldsymbol{\beta}$. Gallant and Nychka (1987) suggested that $f(u)$ be replaced by $\phi(u)\,P(u)$, where $\phi(u)$ is the density of an $\mathrm{N}(0, \sigma^2)$ random variable while $P(u) = 1 + \alpha_1 u + \alpha_2 u^2 + \ldots + \alpha_r u^r$ is a polynomial in u. They then maximise the approximate log likelihood

$$L^* = \sum \log \phi(y_i - \mathbf{x}_i' \boldsymbol{\beta}) + \sum \log P(y_i - \mathbf{x}_i' \boldsymbol{\beta}) \tag{13}$$

with respect to $\boldsymbol{\beta}$. As the approximation improves, that is as $r \to \infty$, it might be expected that the estimator of $\boldsymbol{\beta}$ obtained by maximising L^* converges to that which maximises L. This idea is an application of the standard approach to density approximation in which the unknown density is replaced by the product of a normal density and a polynomial, Spanos (1986, p. 204). Perhaps the major difficulty with this method of estimation is numerical. Gallant and Tauchen (1989) and Gallant *et al.* (1990) report success in maximising (13), but until more computational experience is achieved it is not clear exactly how useful this method is.

Rather than focus upon approximating the likelihood, an alternative is to attempt to solve the first order conditions that come from the scores. Differentiating (12) with respect to $\boldsymbol{\beta}$ yields

$$\mathbf{d}_\beta = -\sum \mathbf{x}_i f(u_i)\,[\partial f(u_i)/\partial u_i] = -\sum \mathbf{x}_i \eta_i, \tag{14}$$

which is a function of $\boldsymbol{\beta}$ through u_i. It is possible to solve the first order conditions $\mathbf{d}_\beta(\hat{\boldsymbol{\beta}}) = 0$ provided the density and its derivative can be estimated. The density of u_i at point $\tilde{u}$ can be estimated consistently by $(Nh)^{-1} \sum K[(u_i - \tilde{u})/h]$ and its derivative by $(Nh)^{-1} \sum \partial K_i / \partial u_i$. Stone (1975) followed this strategy, replacing the u_i with residuals $\hat{u}_i = y_i - \mathbf{x}_i' \hat{\boldsymbol{\beta}}$, where $\hat{\boldsymbol{\beta}}$ is a consistent estimator of $\boldsymbol{\beta}$. One possible initial estimator is the OLS estimator of $\boldsymbol{\beta}$. In fact, Stone and, later, Manski (1984), instead of optimising (14), found the estimator of $\boldsymbol{\beta}$ which solved the first order conditions when linearised around the estimator $\hat{\boldsymbol{\beta}}$. This is the equivalent of the two-step efficient MLE set out in Rothenberg and Leenders (1964). Manski (1984) reports some Monte Carlo studies of this estimator, but we know of no applied study that has yet adopted it.

Continuing with the theme of solving the first order conditions, another suggestion has been to approximate them with a polynomial in u, because the unknown term $\eta_i = f(u_i)^{-1}[\partial f(u_i)/\partial u_i]$ is a function of u. In some instances it is known that η is an odd function of u, for example if the density of u_i is symmetric, and this allows one to restrict the polynomial to odd terms since the

$E(\mathbf{x}_i u_i^j) = 0, j = 1, 3, 5, \ldots$. In other instances all powers of u would need to be employed. Whatever method is used, the score can be thought of as a linear combination of terms involving $\mathbf{x}_i u_i^k$, each of which has zero expectation. This suggests that there is a connection between an estimator solving these first order conditions and GMM estimation. Newey (1988*e*) shows that the GMM estimator based upon the moment conditions $E(\mathbf{x}_i u_i^k) = 0$, $k = 1, \ldots, r$ converges to the MLE of $\boldsymbol{\beta}$ that maximises (1) as $r \to \infty$, although in his proof the speed at which r can tend to infinity needs to be very slow. Notice that when $r = 1$ the estimator of $\boldsymbol{\beta}$ will be OLS, so that the optimal estimator essentially exploits information in higher order moments in order to improve the efficiency of estimation.

Many of the ideas detailed above for the semi-parametric estimation of β carry over to situations where the model features censored or discrete data. For example the log likelihood corresponding to a censored regression model (2) with censoring point of zero is

$$\sum_{i=1}^{N} [(1-y_i)\log F(-\mathbf{x}_i'\boldsymbol{\beta}) + y_i \log f(y_i - \mathbf{x}_i'\boldsymbol{\beta})], \tag{15}$$

where F and f are the distribution and density functions of u_i respectively. To maximise (15) with respect to $\boldsymbol{\beta}$ when F is unknown one could proceed to approximate it as the distribution function of a normal modified by polynomials in u, Gallant and Nychka (1987), or fit spline polynomials in u as in Duncan (1986). Alternatively, an estimator of F, given $\boldsymbol{\beta}$, might be found from the Kaplan–Meier (1958) estimator of the density of a censored random variable, smoothed with a series approximation like the Fourier as in Fernandez (1986), or a kernel, and then used in place of the unknown F in (15). Smoothing is an essential part of the operation in order to make certain that the log likelihood is differentiable in $\boldsymbol{\beta}$. As the Kaplan–Meier estimator of F is the MLE, given that $\boldsymbol{\beta}$ is known, one can interpret this as an experiment in concentrating F out of the log likelihood, leaving it solely a function of $\boldsymbol{\beta}$. A similar literature exists for discrete choice models in which y_i has only a binary form. In those models the log likelihood is (15) with the second term replaced by $y_i \log [1 - F(-\mathbf{x}_i'\boldsymbol{\beta})]$, and again the issue is how to approximate or estimate F. Cosslett (1983) gives a way of computing F for discrete data which is summarised in Amemiya (1985). Unfortunately, all of these estimators have the disadvantage that only consistency has been established, which reduces their appeal a good deal in comparison to the LAD, quantile and pseudo-least squares estimators mentioned earlier, as the latter have a well-developed asymptotic distribution theory associated with them.

Recently, Klein and Spady (1988) have shown how to estimate an F_i for use in (15), when the data y_i come from a discrete choice rather than censored regression model, that will result in a fully efficient estimator of $\boldsymbol{\beta}$. Efficiency here is defined as attaining the 'semi-parametric efficiency bound', which is a generalisation to non-parametric problems of the classical Cramer-Rao bound. Semi-parametric bounds have been worked out for discrete choice models, Coslett (1987), censored regression models, Chamberlain (1986), and for parameters estimated from moment restrictions, Chamberlain (1987). Newey (1988*a*) has a superb exposition of these results and how they relate to the statistics literature. A knowledge of the bounds is crucial to an assessment of how good any proposed estimator is, since it is not always the case that an estimator attaining the bound has been found. Newey (1988*c*) for example exploits the form of the bound to suggest efficient estimators of the Tobit model under various restrictions upon the unknown density.

It is clear from this discussion that strictly non-parametric estimation is not another estimation principle. It is either a member of the class of M or GMM estimators; the Gallant approach where $\rho(.) = \log f(u)$ represents the former, while approximating the score corresponds to the latter. Membership is realised only asymptotically since neither $\log f(u)$ nor the score is utilised but, rather, approximations which are asymptotically equivalent to them. For this reason the orientation is sufficiently distinctive to warrant treating it as a separate estimation principle.

Although the estimation is like all GMM or MLE problems, in that a function is maximised or a set of first order conditions is solved, care must be taken to ensure that the approximations really do overcome the lack of knowledge they are designed to counteract. With that done these techniques should be helpful in a range of applied work, although it is important to realise that the utility of the procedures can vary greatly according to the circumstances. For estimating $\boldsymbol{\beta}$ above, the score approximation methods have been shown to have the same asymptotic properties as if $f(u_i)$ were known, but it is unlikely that a conditional expectation involving a large number of variables can be successfully estimated. An appreciation of the limits of their usefulness can be gained from a perusal of theoretical work which shows that the rate of convergence of the estimator of the conditional moment to its true value is like $(Nh^q)^{\frac{1}{2}}$, where q is the number of conditioning variables, rather than $N^{\frac{1}{2}}$ as with most parametric models. Hence this can be very slow if q is large. In some circumstances it is possible to attain convergence rates of $N^{\frac{1}{2}}$ for a subset of the estimated parameters. For instance, suppose that the conditional expectation is known to be linear in some variables $\mathbf{x}_i$ but non-linear of unknown form in another set $\mathbf{w}_i$. Then the coefficients of $\mathbf{x}_i(\boldsymbol{\beta})$ can be estimated by a 'two-stage' regression, a point demonstrated by Stock (1985), Robinson (1988*a*), and Andrews (1988*a*). This situation occurs a lot in econometrics. For example, in the traditional selectivity model there is a linear part representing the effects of characteristics $\mathbf{x}_i$ (say) upon wages, and a non-linear part that captures the impact of sample selection upon the error term, where the determinants of selectivity depend upon $\mathbf{w}_i$. Powell (1987) has applied the Stock–Robinson estimator to this situation in order to get an estimator of the coefficients of $\mathbf{x}_i$ that is robust to distributional mis-specification in the equation defining the process of selection. In this way the estimated coefficients $\boldsymbol{\beta}$ are more robust than those obtained by the standard Heckman two-step procedure. Newey (1988*d*) provides two-step methods akin to Heckman's that are asymptotically robust to distributional mis-specification.

The use of non-parametric (NP) methods in econometrics in both time series and elsewhere is in its infancy, but it seems likely that researchers will increasingly import the ideas underlying NP methods in an attempt to *improve* upon parametric methods. Such an extensive role for NP methods is one that we believe holds more broadly, and it is unlikely that the NP approach will ever supplant traditional parametric methods. An important element in this belief is the suspicion that, for NP estimators to work exactly as predicted by asymptotic theory, sample sizes far removed from those customarily available for economic investigation may be required. Silverman (1986) observes that to estimate the true value of a six-variate normal density at the origin accurately would require one million observations, and this is only estimating a central tendency! Another factor is that the window width, or its close cousin the number of terms in a series approximation, must always be selected, and this introduces an element of arbitrariness into the estimation process.

At the extensive margin, however, we believe that the NP orientation can be, and has been, beneficial for econometric modelling. A number of facts can be cited in support of this proposition. First, NP methods can disclose features of the data, 'stylised facts', that are not immediately apparent from the raw data. For example, Gallant *et al.* (1990) have noted from their study of non-parametric densities that the marginal densities of many financial series are not only thicker in the tails than the normal but more heavily peaked around zero. Deaton (1989) examines the relation between rice prices and income distribution among Thai farmers with a large data set. He emphasises that NP methods are a very efficient way of examining large data sets, and, being amenable to graphical treatment, may be superior to traditional methods such as cross-tabulations. Second, application of NP estimators may point to the need for a more flexible parametric specification than has traditionally been employed before. Based upon a study of the conditional variances of equity and interest rate yields, Pagan and Hong (1990) conclude that the ARCH model frequently applied in this area does not deliver a rich enough class of non-linearities. Another example in this vein is the relationship between strike duration and cyclical effects explored by Kennan (1985). Estimation of the conditional mean reveals that the function is not monotonically declining as would be asserted by traditional parametric duration models emphasising the Weibull distribution.

Third, NP estimators always provide a benchmark that can be used for specification tests of parametric models. Newey and Powell (1987) used the asymmetric least squares estimator to test for heteroskedasticity and symmetry in the errors, while Koenker and Bassett (1982) argued for a comparison of different quantile estimators as an indicator of heteroskedasticity. One could also compare the NP and parametric estimators via a Hausman (1978) test, or perhaps the score test version of this mentioned in Ruud (1984) (Pagan and Vella (1989) use many of the NP estimators discussed above in this way).

Finally, sometimes the NP literature can provide measures of how important it might be to diverge from a specific parametric estimator. For example, if one looks at the difference between the OLS and MLE first order conditions (equation (14)) for estimating $\boldsymbol{\beta}$ in (1) it is clear that for the MLE to be superior to OLS it is necessary that η_i be a non-linear function of u_i. If it is linear, the case when errors are Gaussian, the scores will be $\sum \mathbf{x}_i u_i$, and setting these to zero yields the OLS estimator of $\boldsymbol{\beta}$. Moreover, using the fact that the information matrix for $\boldsymbol{\beta}$ will be $\mathrm{E}(\eta_i^2)\,[\mathrm{E}(\sum \mathbf{x}_i \mathbf{x}_i')]^{-1}$, the ratio of the asymptotic variance of the OLS estimator to that of the optimal estimator is $\mathrm{E}(\eta_i^2)\,\sigma^2$. Construction of this ratio would allow one to assess the potential efficiency gains available from applying the optimal estimator, while some perspective on how serious any departures from normality in the errors are may be gleaned from observing the extent of departures from linearity of any graph relating η_i to u_i. Both of these things can be done since the residuals after OLS estimation provide an estimate of u_i, while kernel or series-based NP estimation techniques can provide η_i for a variety of values of u.

III. INFERENCE

III.1. *General Issues*

Researchers frequently want to know how reliable any point estimate obtained from the data is, or, put another way, whether it is possible to summarise the information contained in the data by a single estimate. There are a number of aspects to this question. On a philosophical level there is the division between the way the question is posed by the frequentist and the Bayesian statistician. The frequentist begins with the idea that the set of data observed may be unrepresentative of the postulated density, and if a more representative set of data had been drawn the parameter estimate computed by GMM or MLE would be quite different. He tends therefore to summarise the uncertainty about a point estimate by inferring what its distribution would look like over all possible states of the world consistent with the postulated density for the data. Consequently, the derivation of a sampling distribution for the chosen estimator is central to this paradigm, and an estimate of the parameter is regarded as unreliable if the dispersion of the sampling distribution is too large. For a frequentist therefore it is imperative that the shape of the sampling distribution be derived either by analytical or numerical means.

A Bayesian ignores other states of the world and concentrates solely upon the data to hand. He observes that, for certain values of the parameter, it is unlikely that the given set of data could be consistent with the presumed density and the favoured parameter value. For example, if one assumed that y_i was normal with mean μ and variance unity, the observation of a mean of 200 for the data on y_i would hardly be consistent with a value of μ equalling zero, but very probable if μ was 199. Hence the objective is to put some credence upon values of the parameters that would be consistent with the observed data.

These are obviously quite different perspectives and Bayesians often complain, for example Poirier (1988), that frequentists tend to slip into language suggesting that they are deriving information about the uncertainty to be attached to the parameter estimate solely from the observed data, rather than by reference to hypothetical data sets that could have occurred. In some instances it emerges that acting in this way would be legitimate, e.g. when there is an uninformative prior on the parameters of the classical regression model and the errors are normally distributed. But the conditions for this equivalence are strict. With informative prior information on the parameters the p-values of a frequentist can be misleading indicators of the fractiles of a posterior distribution – Berger and Selke (1987). Moreover, even when there is no prior information, differences can arise if the data are distributed normally but the sampling density of the estimator is not asymptotically normal. Prominent examples of this are when the coefficients being estimated are either a unit root in an autoregression or attached to regressors following an integrated process without drift, see Sims (1988).

Which approach is to be preferred seems very much a question of individual taste and perhaps the estimation context. When the data being analysed are drawn from a sample survey, for example, it seems important not to condition upon the data in hand as a Bayesian does. However, for time series data it is not so clear, since it is hard to make sense of an idea that other outcomes for GDP, investment etc. would have been possible. Much depends upon how one interprets the error term u_i in (10). A lot of modern macroeconomics thinks of u_i as 'shocks' that impinge upon the system, and under this interpretation the frequency approach makes a lot of sense. But if one takes the viewpoint that u_i is only what is left over after specifying the main determinants of y_i, a view implicit in much British econometrics as described in Spanos (1986), then the frequentist interpretation is much harder to sustain, because the u_i do not index alternative states of the world but just represent ignorance about all the factors influencing y_i. Thus the validity of a 'physical' identification for u_i is important for how one should interpret any parameter estimate found from data. One solution to this dilemma is to follow the original lead provided by Haavelmo (1944). As he emphasised, the probability model and its attendant concept of 'alternative states' was not to be taken literally, but rather used in much the same way as economists use abstract models for reasoning about the world. With this viewpoint what is important is how often one would be misled when making decisions about how the 'real world' works.

There are some dissenting opinions about whether either of the stances above adequately captures the information that applied workers seek. Common to both approaches was the idea of extracting a *distribution*; a sampling distribution for frequentists or a posterior for Bayesians. Some however see the *point* estimate as the only information that should be conveyed; the question being not what parameter values are compatible with alternative states or the current data, but rather how *sensitive* the point estimate is to variations in the specification of the model. Leamer (1983) has been a vigorous promoter of this idea. His extreme bounds analysis (EBA) computes point estimates of the $\boldsymbol{\beta}$ that would be obtained under all linear combinations of the regressors $\mathbf{x}_i$. He distinguishes between sampling uncertainty, essentially the issue discussed earlier, and specification uncertainty; EBA is meant to shed light on the latter. That this contrast is too stark is apparent from the fact that, as the list of regressors is varied from a minimal to a maximal set, the difference between the minimum and maximum values of $\hat{\boldsymbol{\beta}}$ obtained by applying OLS to (10) can be expressed exactly in terms of the value of the 'F-statistic' for the hypothesis that the coefficients of the regressors common to both sets are zero (see Pagan, 1987, p. 11). Consequently, tabulation of the extreme bounds is very close to doing traditional interval estimation in statistics. There is, however, no resolution to the debates canvassed above. Each researcher must decide what orientation he is most comfortable with. Even when this metaphysical issue is settled, practical questions always remain about the distribution of $\hat{\boldsymbol{\theta}}$, and these need to be addressed prior to any interpretation.

III.2. *Non-Standard Distributional Situations*

In most situations the estimation principles discussed in section II.1 provide estimators of $\boldsymbol{\theta}$ that are *asymptotically* normal in the sense that $T^{\frac{1}{2}}(\hat{\boldsymbol{\theta}}-\boldsymbol{\theta})$ has a limiting normal distribution, thereby making the dispersion of this density sufficient to describe the uncertainty regarding $\boldsymbol{\theta}$. Exceptions to this statement have arisen, notably in the analysis of economic time series, and the results which have emerged demand the attention of any applied researcher. When testing for integration it was seen that $T^{\frac{1}{2}}(\hat{\boldsymbol{\theta}}-\boldsymbol{\theta})$ need not be asymptotically normal. A deeper investigation of this issue is therefore called for. We shall focus on the simple case where there is one I(1) variable x_t and one I(0) variable z_t, leaving until later the complexities of the multivariate case.

$$y_t = x_t\beta + z_t\gamma + u_t. \tag{16}$$

In (16), the error term is I(0) and $x_t = x_{t-1}+\mu+v_t = \mu t + x_{1t}$, with $x_{1t} = x_{1t-1}+v_t$ being a drift-less or pure I(1) process. The correlation of z_t with u_t is zero but that of v_t and u_t need not be. Later it will be shown that the decomposition of an econometric equation into I(1) and I(0) variables is a natural one, and that interest frequently centres on the coefficient β.

To appreciate the problems caused by I(1) regressors it is necessary to know something about the behaviour of sample moments under different patterns of evolution for data. Denote the sample mean of the process $a_t b_t$ by m_{ab}, i.e. $m_{ab} = T^{-1}\sum_{t=1}^{T} a_t b_t$. Table 1 collects some facts about various sample moments important in establishing the limiting properties of the OLS estimators of β and γ. In this table RV means random variable, NRV means a normally distributed random variable and c is a generic constant. Sims *et al.* (1986) and

Table 1

Behaviour of Sample Moments Under Different Evolutionary Patterns to Data

x_t has no drift ($\mu = 0$)	x_t has drift ($\mu \neq 0$)
$T^{-1}m_{xx} \to$ RV	$T^{-2}m_{xx} \to c$
$m_{xz} \to$ RV	$T^{-1}m_{xz} \to c$
$m_{zz} \to c$	$m_{zz} \to c$
$m_{xu} \to$ RV	$T^{-\frac{1}{2}}m_{xu} \to$ NRV
$m_{zu} \to 0$	$m_{zu} \to 0$
$T^{\frac{1}{2}}m_{zu} \to$ NRV	$T^{\frac{1}{2}}m_{zu} \to$ NRV

Table 2

Asymptotic Distribution for the OLS Estimators of β and γ in (16): x_t and z_t Single Variables

	x_t has no drift ($\mu = 0$)	x_t has drift ($\mu \neq 0$)
	$T(\hat{\beta}-\beta)$ is NSRV	$T^{\frac{3}{2}}(\hat{\beta}-\beta)$ is NRV
	$T^{\frac{1}{2}}(\hat{\gamma}-\gamma)$ is NRV	$T^{\frac{1}{2}}(\hat{\gamma}-\gamma)$ is NRV

Park and Phillips (1988, 1989) provide the basic input for the following discussion.

Table 1 points to the fact that there is a considerable variety in what happens asymptotically to sample moments, and that the situation when regressors are I(0) is very special. For a detailed understanding of the differences one should consult one of the references above, but it is helpful to note that an I(1) with drift has a second moment that grows like T^2 (because $x_t^2 \cong \mu^2 t^2$),[3] a pure I(1) process has a second moment that grows like T, and an I(0) has a constant second moment. Roughly, when it comes to asymptotic behaviour, an I(1) with drift dominates a pure I(1) which in turn dominates an I(0). Combine this with the fact that the product of an I(1) and I(0) series is I(1) and some understanding of Table 1's differences should emerge.

Table 2 gives what can be called the 'standard results' on the limiting behaviour of $\hat{\beta}$ and $\hat{\gamma}$; some important caveats are given later. In this table NSRV means a random variable with a non-standard asymptotic distribution. Perhaps the most important point about Table 2 is that the estimated parameters of I(0) variables have the same limiting distribution whether or not there are I(1) variables in the equation. To see why note that the normal equations for γ can be written as

$$m_{zz}(\hat{\gamma}-\gamma)+m_{zx}(\hat{\beta}-\beta) = m_{zu}. \tag{17}$$

After multiplying both sides by $T^{\frac{1}{2}}$, and using column 1 of Table 1 (i.e. assume $\mu = 0$), the term $T^{-\frac{1}{2}}m_{zx}\,T(\hat{\beta}-\beta)$ clearly tends to zero whenever $T(\hat{\beta}-\beta)$ is a random variable. This leaves $T^{\frac{1}{2}}(\hat{\gamma}-\gamma) = m_{zz}^{-1}\,T^{\frac{1}{2}}m_{zu}+o_p(1)$, which from Table 1 is asymptotically normally distributed. The remainder of the results in Table 2 can be established by proceeding in the same way.

The moral of Table 2 is that one cannot normally use the t-statistics associated with the OLS estimator of the coefficients of I(1) regressors. This makes life hard for an applied worker as the exact form of the non-standard density depends upon many factors, and must generally be found by computer simulation. If x_t were y_{t-1} we could consult the Dickey–Fuller distribution, and as rough rule of thumb assume that the true critical value lies between the normal and DF. In Section V.4.1 some other estimators of β that do have normal densities asymptotically will be outlined.

Some caveats are in order. First, suppose x_t was *strictly exogenous*. Then we could condition on $(x_t)_{t=1}^{T}$ and the randomness in $m_{xx}^{-\frac{1}{2}}(\hat{\beta}-\beta)$ comes only from

[3] See footnote 2.

u_t. It is simple to establish that this random variable is asymptotically normal and its parameters do not depend upon x_t. Accordingly, the unconditional density of $m_{xx}^{-\frac{1}{2}}(\hat{\beta}-\beta)$ is normal and the standard t-statistic can be used. Such a felicitious outcome does not extend to our second qualification: *the results in Table 2 for drift apply only when there is a single $I(1)$ regressor*. To see why, let ξ_t be another I(1) regressor with drift μ_1, so that the equation to be estimated is

$$y_t = x_t\beta + \xi_t\delta + z_t\gamma + u_t, \tag{18}$$

or

$$y_t = (\mu\beta + \mu_1\delta)\,t + \beta x_{1t} + \delta\xi_{1t} + u_t, \tag{19}$$

where ξ_{1t} is the pure I(1) part of ξ_t. Obviously, only a linear combination of β and δ can be identified by the trend, and it is this which is asymptotically normal. The parameters β and δ are really attached to pure I(1) variables and the first column of Table 2 applies. Note that the cross product matrix formed from x_t and ξ_t would be asymptotically singular due to the dominance of the deterministic trend term, and it would be necessary to de-trend the data to get x_{1t} and ξ_{1t} before estimation. Park and Phillips analyse this problem and solutions to it.

Third, all the estimators of coefficients of I(1) variables always exhibit super-consistency, that is convergence to the true values at a rate faster than $T^{-\frac{1}{2}}$. What is interesting about this feature is that v_t, the innovations in x_t, can be correlated with u_t, implying that x_t could be an endogenous variable. Kramer (1984) pointed this out for the case where x_t had drift. Finally, care must be taken in consulting Table 2 if a *trend term is in the equation*. The presence of such a term means that x_t has been de-trended and it is now a pure I(1) variable, so it is the first rather than second column that is appropriate.

III.3. *Small Sample Issues*

Sometimes the sample size, N, is too small for users to be comfortable with the application of asymptotic theory, and the distribution of $\hat{\boldsymbol{\theta}}$ for finite N may depart substantially from that for very large N. For example, if u_i in (11) is not normal, neither will the OLS estimator of β be normal in finite samples, even though the central limit theorem would ensure that it is in large samples. Another example arises in testing parameter restrictions in a system of demand equations; it has been found that the statistics used for this purpose do not have the distribution predicted by asymptotic theory when the number of parameters ia large relative to the number of observations – Laitinen (1978).

Analytical responses to this difficulty have been made by, for example, Phillips (1983) and Phillips and Park (1988), but progress has been very slow. By far the most popular solution amongst applied workers has been to resort to numerical methods using a technique that has been dubbed the 'bootstrap' (Effron, 1982). The idea behind this computer-intensive procedure is simple. Suppose we wanted to determine $\Pr(c_1 \leqslant \hat{\beta}_{\text{OLS}} \leqslant c_2)$ in (1) where c_1 and c_2 are specified constants. The probability arises from the fact that different $\hat{\beta}$'s are obtained for each realisation of the u_i's. If the density of u_i was known, we could generate R sets of numbers $(u_i^{(r)}, i = 1, \ldots, N; r = 1, \ldots, R)$ each of which would yield an estimator of β, namely $\hat{\beta}^{(r)}$. Then a natural estimator of $\Pr(c_1 \leqslant \hat{\beta}_{\text{OLS}} \leqslant c_2)$ is $R^{-1}\sum_{r=1}^{R} 1[c_1 \leqslant \hat{\beta}^{(r)} \leqslant c_2]$. This estimate is very simple to compute in any package that enables users to perform Monte Carlo experiments, e.g. GAUSS.

Unfortunately, the simplicity of this concept is undermined by the fact that the density of the u_i is not known and must be estimated. The residuals from an OLS regression of y_i against u_i can be used to construct an empirical distribution function and random numbers $u_i^{(r)}$ can be found from it. Alternatively, non-parametric methods may be used to estimate the density of the errors from these residuals and then the $u_i^{(r)}$ are simulated from this density (this variant is sometimes referred to as the 'smoothed bootstrap', Silverman (1986, pp. 144–5)). However, bootstrap-type methods can suffer from their use of residuals rather than errors, as this introduces additional elements of variability. If β is badly estimated or the sample size is such that only a few observations are made from the tail of the density, the empirical and true densities could depart substantially from each other. Furthermore, there are instances where the quality of the approximation may depend upon the values of the unknown parameters. This would occur, for example, if x_i involved lagged values of y_i. A theoretical analysis of the statistical properties of the bootstrap is given by Hall (1988). Despite these difficulties the bootstrap has become increasingly popular in applied work. Testing the restrictions of demand systems in this framework has been carried out by Bewley and Theil (1987) and Raj and Taylor (1989). Perhaps the greatest use of the bootstrap will not be to models such as (10), but for the interpretation of estimators which are analytically intractable in finite samples. An example is Manski's (1975) 'maximum score' estimator, which was studied in this way by Manski and Thompson (1986).

IV. EVALUATION

IV.1. *Testing Principles*

All models are accompanied by a set of conventions that are used to get a parameter estimate. It seems obvious that one would want to check for any potential violation of these conventions, leading to the query of how investigators have chosen to evaluate their models. Early work on model evaluation was almost exclusively concerned with the regression model, and diagnostic tests were performed on the residuals for the presence of serial correlation, heteroskedasticity and non-normality. The literature on the construction of diagnostic tests is large, with a variety of testing principles and definitions of optimality, e.g. uniformly most powerful tests, unbiased tests, locally most powerful invariant tests, point optimal tests etc. being used to derive these tests. Although in theory these tests were capable of general application, most of them had characteristics that were particularly appropriate for traditional regression models – continuously distributed dependent variables and fixed regressors. Unfortunately, econometricians increasingly began to adopt models characterised by a conjunction of lagged dependent variables and serial correlation, simultaneous equations, censored dependent variables etc. and this trend emphasised the need for a much more general testing framework. For a recent survey of mis-specification tests see Godfrey (1988).

Durbin (1970) made a major contribution in this direction at a high level of generality. He began with the log likelihood $L(\boldsymbol{\alpha}, \boldsymbol{\beta})$, distinguishing between parameters $\boldsymbol{\beta}$ representing the maintained model parameters and another set $\boldsymbol{\alpha}$ that were intended to summarise potential mis-specification in the model. The latter take the value $\boldsymbol{\alpha}_0$ when the maintained model is correct. Maximising $L(\boldsymbol{\alpha}_0, \boldsymbol{\beta})$ with respect to $\boldsymbol{\beta}$ gives an estimator $\hat{\boldsymbol{\beta}}$, and maximising $L(\hat{\boldsymbol{\beta}}, \boldsymbol{\alpha})$ with respect to $\boldsymbol{\alpha}$ gives an estimator $\tilde{\boldsymbol{\alpha}}$ of $\boldsymbol{\alpha}$. Durbin studied the properties of $\tilde{\boldsymbol{\alpha}}$ for the purpose of testing $\boldsymbol{\alpha} = \boldsymbol{\alpha}_0$. Noting that $\tilde{\boldsymbol{\alpha}}$ solves $\mathbf{d}_\alpha(\hat{\boldsymbol{\beta}}, \tilde{\boldsymbol{\alpha}}) = 0$, where $\mathbf{d}_\alpha(.)$ is the score for $\boldsymbol{\alpha}$, a mean value expansion gives

$$\mathbf{d}_\alpha(\tilde{\boldsymbol{\alpha}}, \hat{\boldsymbol{\beta}}) = 0 = \mathbf{d}_\alpha(\boldsymbol{\alpha}_0, \hat{\boldsymbol{\beta}}) + \mathbf{H}_{\alpha\alpha}(\boldsymbol{\alpha}^*, \hat{\boldsymbol{\beta}})(\tilde{\boldsymbol{\alpha}} - \boldsymbol{\alpha}_0), \tag{20}$$

where $\mathbf{H}_{\alpha\alpha} = \partial^2 L / \partial\boldsymbol{\alpha}\,\partial\boldsymbol{\alpha}'$ and $\boldsymbol{\alpha}^*$ lies between $\tilde{\alpha}$ and α_0. Under the maintained hypothesis $\tilde{\boldsymbol{\alpha}}$ will tend in probability to $\boldsymbol{\alpha}_0$. It is clear from (20) that Durbin's test for whether $\boldsymbol{\alpha}$ equals $\boldsymbol{\alpha}_0$ based on $\tilde{\boldsymbol{\alpha}} - \boldsymbol{\alpha}_0$ is really one for whether $\mathbf{d}_\alpha(\boldsymbol{\alpha}_0, \hat{\boldsymbol{\beta}})$ is zero, since in large samples $\mathbf{H}_{\alpha\alpha}$ is non-singular. Consequently, rather than follow Durbin's approach one might instead look at $\mathbf{d}_\alpha(\boldsymbol{\alpha}_0, \hat{\boldsymbol{\beta}})$, the scores evaluated at the MLE's of $\boldsymbol{\beta}$ and $\boldsymbol{\alpha}$ under the null hypothesis. But this is just the Lagrange Multiplier or score test for $\boldsymbol{\alpha} = \boldsymbol{\alpha}_0$.

The LM test was applied to the testing of many over-identifying restrictions in both regression and other models during the 1970s and it yielded a wide variety of test statistics. Sometimes these had been in use before, for example the LM test for heteroskedasticity developed in Godfrey (1978) and Breusch and Pagan (1979). Previous users of these tests had not located them in a more general framework; the advantage of doing so is that it is then much easier to see how to extend the same idea beyond the regression context.

The problem with the LM approach is that it too is not general enough because of its requirements that the maintained model be estimated by MLE and that the likelihood of a suitable alternative model be identified. Given the range of estimation principles outlined in Section I the first of these is a significant limitation. But the second requirement can be equally bothersome. Consider for example the Tobit model (11). To get an estimator of $\boldsymbol{\beta}$ investigators assumed that the errors u_i^* were normally distributed. Because the MLE of $\boldsymbol{\beta}$ is inconsistent if the normality assumption is incorrect, it is crucial that this assumption be tested. If testing is to be by the LM principle an alternative likelihood is needed. But this is not an easy task because there will rarely be an obvious alternative density for u_i^*. One solution is to opt for a very general class of densities. Thus Bera *et al.* (1984) followed Jarque and Bera (1980) in the regression case and made u_i^* a member of the Pearson family, checking if the parameter values of that family which induce normality were compatible with the data. Only after considerable mathematical manipulation did this enable them to construct an LM test.

The two factors identified above – complexity of derivation and the limited range of estimators for which it is appropriate – made it desirable to replace the LM testing principle with something else. Newey (1985*a*) and Tauchen (1985) did just this. They argued that it was profitable to think of failures in the model as involving a set of conditional moment restrictions. For example, in testing whether or not the conditional mean in the regression model (10) is correctly specified, it is natural to introduce another variable z_i and to see if it is correlated with the errors u_i. This gives the conditional moment restriction $E[z_i(y_i - \mathbf{x}_i'\boldsymbol{\beta})] = 0$. Similarly, a test that the error variance does not depend upon some variables z_i, i.e. a test for heteroskedasticity, could be formulated as $E\{z_i[(y_i - \mathbf{x}_i'\boldsymbol{\beta})^2 - \sigma^2]\} = 0$. For the Tobit model in (11) above a natural test for normality would be that the errors u_i^* be symmetrically distributed, implying that $E(y_i^* - \mathbf{x}_i'\boldsymbol{\beta})^3 = 0$. Although y_i^* is unobserved, y_i is observed and the law of iterated expectations can be used to write this restriction as $E[E(y_i^* - \mathbf{x}_i'\boldsymbol{\beta})^3 | y_i] = 0$. Under the null hypothesis of normality, and using the formulae for the moments of the truncated normal distribution, $E[(y_i^* - \mathbf{x}_i'\boldsymbol{\beta})^3 | y_i]$ can be expressed in terms of y_i, $\mathbf{x}_i$, $\boldsymbol{\beta}$ and σ^2. Of course normality implies that *all* odd moments are zero and also that restrictions exist between even moments. Hence there are a number of conditional moments that might be exploited to set up a test. The use of the restrictions on the third and fourth moments gives the LM test statistic derived by Bera *et al.*, see Pagan and Vella (1989).

Diagnostic tests may therefore be gainfully conceived of as imposing a restriction of the form $E_{H_0}[m_i(\boldsymbol{\theta})] = 0$, where $m_i(\boldsymbol{\theta})$ is the conditional moment restriction, for example $z_i(y_i - \mathbf{x}_i'\boldsymbol{\beta})$, and the dependence upon the data has been suppressed, followed by a test for how close this expectation is to zero based on the sample analogue $\hat{\tau} = N^{-1}\sum m_i(\hat{\boldsymbol{\theta}})$. The estimate $\hat{\boldsymbol{\theta}}$ can be any root-N consistent estimator of $\boldsymbol{\theta}$ under the null hypothesis. This approach is attractive not least because it subsumes the LM testing principle. To see this let $m_i(\boldsymbol{\theta})$ be the score for α where $\boldsymbol{\theta} = (\alpha, \beta)$. Under the maintained hypothesis of no mis-specification the score has zero expectation so that $E_{H_0}[m_i(\boldsymbol{\theta})] = 0$, while $\hat{\tau} = N^{-1}\sum m_i(\alpha_0, \hat{\beta})$ provides the basis of the score test. Another general class of widely used diagnostic tests, due to Hausman (1978), can also be formulated in this framework. Hausman's idea was to take two different estimators of $\boldsymbol{\theta}$, $\hat{\boldsymbol{\theta}}$ and $\tilde{\boldsymbol{\theta}}$, both being consistent under the null but having different probability limits under the alternative, and to make the difference $(\tilde{\boldsymbol{\theta}} - \hat{\boldsymbol{\theta}})$ an index of the failure of any conventions. Ruud (1984) pointed out that, if $\sum m_i(\hat{\boldsymbol{\theta}}) = 0$ defines $\hat{\boldsymbol{\theta}}$, then $N^{-\frac{1}{2}}\sum m_i(\tilde{\boldsymbol{\theta}}) = (\text{plim}_{N\to\infty} N^{-1}\sum \partial m_i/\partial\boldsymbol{\theta})\, N^{\frac{1}{2}}(\tilde{\boldsymbol{\theta}} - \hat{\boldsymbol{\theta}}) + o_p(1)$, and this relation will generally mean that $N^{\frac{1}{2}}(\hat{\boldsymbol{\theta}} - \tilde{\boldsymbol{\theta}})$ and $N^{-\frac{1}{2}}\sum m_i(\tilde{\boldsymbol{\theta}})$ are equivalent tests, i.e. testing if $E[m_i(\boldsymbol{\theta})] = 0$ with $\hat{\tau} = N^{-1}\sum m_i(\tilde{\boldsymbol{\theta}})$ is equivalent to a Hausman test.

An important issue is how to attach a variance to $\hat{\tau}$ in order to be able to test whether the conditional moment is zero. More precisely, the variance of the asymptotic distribution of $N^{\frac{1}{2}}\hat{\tau}$ under the null hypothesis is sought. A standard way to do this is to linearise $\hat{\tau}$ around $\boldsymbol{\theta}_0$, the true value of $\boldsymbol{\theta}$, to get (see Goldberger, 1964, p. 124),

$$N^{\frac{1}{2}}\hat{\tau} = N^{-\frac{1}{2}}\sum \mathbf{m}_i(\boldsymbol{\theta}_0) + \{N^{-1}\sum [\partial \mathbf{m}_i(\boldsymbol{\theta})/\partial\boldsymbol{\theta}]\} N^{\frac{1}{2}}(\hat{\boldsymbol{\theta}}-\boldsymbol{\theta}_0) + o_p(1)$$
$$= N^{-\frac{1}{2}}\sum \mathbf{m}_i(\boldsymbol{\theta}_0) + \mathbf{B}N^{\frac{1}{2}}(\hat{\boldsymbol{\theta}}-\boldsymbol{\theta}_0). \tag{21}$$

Most estimators of $\boldsymbol{\theta}$ discussed in Section II solve a set of first order conditions $\sum \mathbf{g}_i(\hat{\boldsymbol{\theta}}) = 0$ and have the property that the distribution of $N^{\frac{1}{2}}(\hat{\boldsymbol{\theta}}-\boldsymbol{\theta}_0)$ is like that of $\mathbf{A}N^{-\frac{1}{2}}\sum \mathbf{g}_i(\boldsymbol{\theta}_0)$. For the MLE $\mathbf{A} = \mathbf{g}_{\theta\theta}^{-1}$ and $\sum \mathbf{g}_i(\boldsymbol{\theta})$ will be the scores for $\boldsymbol{\theta}$. For the GMM estimator $\mathbf{A} = \text{plim}_{N\to\infty} - N^{-1}(\mathbf{G}'\mathbf{W}^{-1}\mathbf{G})^{-1}\mathbf{G}'\mathbf{W}^{-1}$ and $\sum \mathbf{g}_i(\boldsymbol{\theta})$ is the vector of first order conditions. M-estimators have $\mathbf{A} = -\text{E}(\boldsymbol{\rho}_{\theta\theta})$ and $\mathbf{g}_i = \boldsymbol{\rho}_\theta(i)$ if $\rho(.)$ is differentiable. If $\rho(.)$ is not differentiable $\mathbf{A} = -[\partial^2\text{E}(\boldsymbol{\rho})/\partial\boldsymbol{\theta}\,\partial\boldsymbol{\theta}']$ but $\mathbf{g}_i$ needs to be established separately in each case. When $\rho = |y_i - \beta|$, g_i would be sgn $(y_i - \beta)$.

Inserting this general formula for $N^{\frac{1}{2}}(\hat{\boldsymbol{\theta}}-\boldsymbol{\theta}_0)$ into (21) above gives

$$N^{\frac{1}{2}}\hat{\tau} = N^{-\frac{1}{2}}\sum \mathbf{m}_i(\boldsymbol{\theta}_0) + \mathbf{BA}N^{-\frac{1}{2}}\sum \mathbf{g}_i(\boldsymbol{\theta}_0), \tag{22}$$

and the distribution of the right hand side depends upon the nature of the data and the definition of $\mathbf{g}_i(\boldsymbol{\theta})$. Since $N^{-\frac{1}{2}}\sum \mathbf{m}_i(\boldsymbol{\theta}_0)$ and $N^{-\frac{1}{2}}\sum \mathbf{g}_i(\boldsymbol{\theta}_0)$ will generally have a joint limiting distribution with covariance matrix $\mathbf{V}$, it follows that $N^{\frac{1}{2}}\hat{\tau}$ will be normal with covariance matrix $\mathbf{V}_{\hat{\tau}} = [\mathbf{I}\ \mathbf{BA}]\,\mathbf{V}[\mathbf{I}\ \mathbf{BA}]'$. Evaluation of $\mathbf{V}_{\hat{\tau}}$ may be carried out in a number of ways. When both $\mathbf{m}_i(\boldsymbol{\theta}_0)$ and $\mathbf{g}_i(\boldsymbol{\theta}_0)$ are independent, identically distributed processes (or, more generally, are martingale differences), $\mathbf{V}_{\hat{\tau}}$ may be estimated by looking at the outer products of the two vectors. For example the covariance $\mathbf{V}_{mg}$ would be estimated by $N^{-1}\sum \mathbf{m}_i(\hat{\boldsymbol{\theta}})\,\mathbf{g}_i(\hat{\boldsymbol{\theta}})'$. If they are dependent processes modifications are needed to reflect the non-zero correlations between each vector and its past history.

As $\mathbf{A}$ and $\mathbf{V}$ will vary with the estimator employed for $\boldsymbol{\theta}$, and the way in which these might be estimated will be dependent upon the nature of the data, general expressions tend to be rather messy, e.g. see Newey (1985*a*) for the case when data is independent and Newey (1985*b*) when it follows a stationary process; in both instances the estimator of $\boldsymbol{\theta}$ is GMM. In programs with a matrix language it is fairly easy to compute $\mathbf{V}_{\hat{\tau}}$ and no problems should be posed for most applied researchers. Happily, in one context it has proved possible to implement the test with a standard package for estimating systems of seemingly unrelated equations. This is when the data is independent and $\hat{\boldsymbol{\theta}}$ is the MLE under the null. For that situation the test that $\text{E}_{\text{H}_0}[\mathbf{m}_i(\boldsymbol{\theta})] = 0$ reduces to an F-test for the hypothesis that the intercepts in the systems regression of $\mathbf{m}_i(\hat{\boldsymbol{\theta}})$ against unity and the scores for $\boldsymbol{\theta}$, $\mathbf{d}_i(\hat{\boldsymbol{\theta}})$, are jointly zero. If a joint test of the restrictions is not desired this test can be performed with a regression package. The proof of this result is found in Tauchen (1985) and Newey (1985*a*), while a simplified account is available in Pagan and Vella (1989). It is based upon the observation that the requirements for $\hat{\boldsymbol{\theta}}$ to be an MLE are that $\mathbf{g}_i$ be the scores $\mathbf{d}_i$ and $\text{E}[\partial\mathbf{m}_i(\boldsymbol{\theta})/\partial\boldsymbol{\theta}] = -\text{E}[\mathbf{m}_i(\boldsymbol{\theta}_0)\,\mathbf{d}_i(\boldsymbol{\theta}_0)']$. The last result is Beran's (1977) generalised information equality, and it is found by differentiating $\text{E}[\mathbf{m}_i(\boldsymbol{\theta})] = 0$ with respect to $\boldsymbol{\theta}$. Using the outer product form for all covariances, for example, and replacing $\text{E}(\mathbf{m}_i\mathbf{d}_i')$ by $N^{-1}\sum \hat{\mathbf{m}}_i\hat{\mathbf{d}}_i'$ provides a regression interpretation.

In describing model evaluation our preference has been to emphasise a very general approach to diagnostic tests rather than simply to list those that are available, as was done in Pagan (1984*a*). Nevertheless, it may help to work through an example. With $m_i = z_i(y_i - \mathbf{x}_i'\boldsymbol{\beta})$, the test is based on the sample covariance of a potentially omitted variable z_i with the OLS residuals $\hat{u}_i = y_i - \mathbf{x}_i'\hat{\boldsymbol{\beta}}$. It is an easy matter to show that the t-statistic on the intercept in the regression of $z_i\hat{u}_i$ against unity and $\hat{\sigma}^{-1}\mathbf{x}_i u_i$ (the scores for $\boldsymbol{\beta}$) is asymptotically the same as the heteroskedastic consistent t-statistic (White, 1980) for the coefficient of z_i in the regression of $\hat{u}_i$ against z_i and $\mathbf{x}_i$. When there is no heteroskedasticity in the disturbances u_i this is the standard 'variable addition' test for specification error in the conditional mean (Pagan, 1984*b*).

IV.2. *Robustness and Power Considerations for Testing Principles*

Although simple to apply the method adopted to estimate the variance of $\hat{\tau}$ in the preceding sub-section is not without its problems. Taylor (1987), Kennan and Neumann (1988), and Chesher and Spady (1988) have all observed that outer products may yield poor estimators of expectations in some circumstances. For example, when constructing score tests in non-linear models with normally distributed errors, there are better ways to get an estimate of the variance of $\hat{\tau}$. One procedure that seems to work well is the 'double-length regression' of Davidson and MacKinnon (1983). There is another potential problem with the use of outer products. Wooldridge (1987) and Robinson (1988*b*) note that, replacing either $\partial\mathbf{m}_i(\boldsymbol{\theta})/\partial\boldsymbol{\theta}$ by $N^{-1}\Sigma\,[\mathbf{m}_i(\hat{\boldsymbol{\theta}})\,\mathbf{d}_i(\hat{\boldsymbol{\theta}})']$ or $\mathbf{A}$ by $N^{-1}\Sigma\,\mathbf{g}_i(\hat{\boldsymbol{\theta}})\,\mathbf{g}_i(\hat{\boldsymbol{\theta}})'$ (in the MLE case), presumes that the model is correctly specified. If it is assumed that there are *no* mistakes in the specification of the maintained model this seems reasonable, but it is not uncommon for investigators to be interested in only a sub-set of the conventional assumptions, and a test that is robust to departures from the other conventions is to be preferred. For example, in testing for specification errors in the conditional mean of a regression it is clearly desirable to make the test robust to any possible heteroskedasticity. Consequently it can be a very poor strategy to estimate derivatives by outer products of score and moment vectors, as these will be bad estimators if some of the conventions are violated. Robust tests will require that any estimators of $\mathbf{B}$ and $\mathbf{V}$ in $\mathbf{V}_{\hat{\tau}}$ be consistent in the presence of mis-specifications other than the one(s) under investigation. Wooldridge (1987) has forcefully argued the case for such robustness. Although this stricture may involve computations that are considerably more complex, the ready availability of good matrix manipulation packages for PC's suggests that it is an appropriate time to divorce ourselves from the straitjacket imposed by the need to force problems into the regression set-up. At the very least, if one wishes to use the regression approach it needs to be borne in mind that the cost of this convenience may be an incorrect conclusion. Users need therefore to make a careful assessment of whether or not they wish to pay this price.

Issues of robustness intermingle with those of power when it is realised that testing principles frequently involve the specification of a density function for the data, and deviations from this assumption can cause tests to lose power even if the size of the test is unaffected. For example, testing if (10) can be augmented by $\mathbf{z}_i$ can be done by assuming that the errors are normal. The LM test is then based on $N^{-1}\sum \mathbf{z}_i(y_i - \mathbf{x}_i' \hat{\boldsymbol{\beta}}_{\text{OLS}})$. If the errors are not normal the size of the test is not affected, but it is no longer true that the LM test has the same format. If one thinks of (10) as augmented by $\mathbf{z}_i' \boldsymbol{\gamma}$, non-parametric estimation theory points to the best test as being based on the efficient score for $\boldsymbol{\gamma}$ from (14), namely $-\sum \mathbf{z}_i f(u_i)\,[\partial f(u_i)/\partial u_i]$, which involves the covariance between $\mathbf{z}_i$ and a *non-linear function* of the residuals. One can apply the theory mentioned in discussing non-parametric estimation to derive a whole range of tests for omitted variables, heteroskedasticity etc. that are fully efficient in the presence of distributional mis-specification, see Bickel (1978).

All of the above development has the dual characteristics of utilising asymptotic theory to establish the distribution of $N^{\frac{1}{2}}\hat{\tau}$ and ignoring the question of what would be a good choice of estimator for $\boldsymbol{\theta}$. Turning to the latter consideration first, consider testing for first order serial correlation in the regression model. The conditional moment restriction is $\mathrm{E}(u_i u_{i-1}) = 0$ or $\mathrm{E}(y_i - \mathbf{x}_i' \boldsymbol{\beta})(y_{i-1} - \mathbf{x}_{i-1}' \boldsymbol{\beta}) = 0$. What estimate of $\boldsymbol{\beta}$ should be employed in the test based on $\hat{\tau} = N^{-1}\sum (y_i - \mathbf{x}_i' \hat{\boldsymbol{\beta}})(y_{i-1} - \mathbf{x}_{i-1}' \hat{\boldsymbol{\beta}})$? One possibility is to use the OLS estimator of $\boldsymbol{\beta}$ obtained by regressing y_i against $\mathbf{x}_i$; $\hat{\tau}$ is then the first order autocovariance of the regression residuals. This test is equivalent to the Durbin–Watson statistic or Durbin's (1970) h-statistic, depending upon whether $\mathbf{x}_i$ has y_{i-1} in it or not. As the formulation of the conditional moment restriction is independent of how one computes its variance, the *form* of $\hat{\tau}$ is the same irrespective of the composition of $\mathbf{x}_i$. It is in the variance of $\hat{\tau}$ that the situations differ, since in (21) $\mathbf{B}$ is null when $\mathbf{x}_i$ is exogenous. The OLS estimator of $\boldsymbol{\beta}$ is the most efficient estimator of that parameter when there is normality and no serial correlation in the disturbances u_i, a property that extends to 'local alternatives', that is cases where the serial correlation can be taken as 'close' to zero. But if the actual degree of serial correlation is quite high an estimator of $\boldsymbol{\beta}$ which incorporates that knowledge might yield a test statistic with superior power.

This argument provides a rationale for the class of point-optimal tests investigated extensively by King (1988), Bhargava (1986) and Dastoor and Fisher (1988). These tests select an estimator of $\boldsymbol{\beta}$ that would be appropriate under a specific alternative. Suppose, for example, that the alternative is that the serial correlation coefficient is a given value λ. Then the error term in the regression of $(y_i - \lambda y_{i-1})$ against $(\mathbf{x}_i - \lambda \mathbf{x}_{i-1})$ is white noise and $\tilde{\boldsymbol{\beta}}$, the estimator of β from this regression, could be used in place of $\hat{\boldsymbol{\beta}}$ in forming $\hat{\tau}$. King (1985) constructs a test for serial correlation based on particular values of λ such as 0·5 and 0·75, while the value $\lambda = 1$ gives the Berenblut and Webb (1973) test for serial correlation. Other applications of this framework have been to testing for heteroskedasticity, (Evans and King, 1985) and unit roots, (Bhagava, 1986). It should be emphasised that the case for choosing a different estimator of $\boldsymbol{\theta}$ rests on small samples. Newey (1985*a*) gives a detailed discussion of the optimal choice of $\hat{\boldsymbol{\theta}}$ from an asymptotic perspective and, as might be expected, it comes down to either the MLE or the GMM estimator (under the null hypothesis).

Nevertheless, from comparisons made by King (1985) involving data taken to be representative of economic data, there would seem to be a small sample power improvement to be had by selecting $\hat{\boldsymbol{\theta}}$ to reflect the alternative hypothesis.

IV.3. *Small Sample Issues*

Turning to the question of the small sample properties of the asymptotic distribution of $N^{\frac{1}{2}}\hat{\tau}$, Gregory and Veall (1985) point out that the decision to truncate the expansion after the linear term in (21) could be erroneous. From the viewpoint of asymptotic theory this does not matter, as the next term is a quadratic in $(\hat{\boldsymbol{\theta}}-\boldsymbol{\theta}_0)$ and is multiplied by $N^{-\frac{1}{2}}$, so it converges to zero as $N\rightarrow\infty$ provided $\hat{\boldsymbol{\theta}}-\boldsymbol{\theta}_0$ is root-N consistent. But this argument is only valid in the limit. For any finite N this term is non-zero and has the potential to exceed the linear term in numerical value. To see why suppose θ is a scalar. The next term in the expansion of (20) is then $(\frac{1}{2})\,[\sum\partial^2 m_i(\theta_0)/\partial\theta^2]\,(\hat{\theta}-\theta_0)^2$, and this could be large if the second derivative is large. Gregory and Veall point out that for certain types of restrictions this second derivative can easily dominate the linear term. Suppose, for example, that $\partial^2 m_i(\theta)/\partial\theta^2$ involves $1/(1-\theta)$ and that θ is close to unity. The second derivative of m_i could therefore be very large, making the second term in the expansion large as well, giving it the potential of dominating for any finite N. The key to overcoming this problem was explored theoretically by Phillips and Park (1988), and involves choosing a parametrisation of the restrictions that does not exhibit derivatives close to zero in regions of the parameter space likely to contain the true value. For model evaluation exercises this does not seem to be a major issue, but for the situation Gregory and Veall were interested in, namely the testing of rational expectations restrictions, there was a lot of freedom in the parametrisation and so their warning is one that every researcher must take seriously. Exactly how one formulates a restriction can also affect the numerical value of some test statistics. Breusch and Schmidt (1988) and LaFontaine and White (1986) demonstrated that the value of a Wald test is not invariant to the parametrisation of the restriction. Nelson and Savin (1988*a*) and Dagenais and Dufour (1986) observed a similar thing about the LM test when the Hessian rather than the information matrix was used as the variance of the scores. The cause of this invariance is easily found. In the Wald test of $\phi(\theta)=0$, for scalar θ the numerator of the test involves $\phi(\theta)^2$ and the denominator $(\partial\phi/\partial\theta)^2$, and any change in the restriction will invariably cause a change in its derivative of a different magnitude, thereby altering the numerical value of the test statistic.

A similar problem occurs under the alternative hypothesis. Nelson and Savin (1988*b*) have pointed out that it is possible for the information matrix to become singular in some parts of the parameter space, which makes the 'variance' of $\hat{\tau}$ very large at that point and the test statistic very small. It is possible, therefore, for a given sample size, that the power function of $\hat{\tau}$ is not monotonic if regions of the parameter space are entered where there is a near lack of identifiability. Paradoxically, it is possible for the test to be very weak if there are gross departures from the null in the direction of the region in which there is an identifiability problem. Although this is a valid point, it is not as yet clear what practical importance it has. Phillips (1988*d*) provides a theoretical analysis of the phenomenon.

The other question of finding small sample distributions for $\hat{\tau}$ is more serious. There are very few instances in which analytic determination is feasible and resort has been increasingly made to computationally intensive methods of deriving the critical values of the test statistic. Harris (1985) has provided corrections to the asymptotic critical values of LM tests by using Edgeworth expansions to improve the estimators of moments and then utilising these within the characteristic equation. Phillips and Park (1988) have found corrections for the Wald test in a similar way. This involved extensive differentiation and solution of polynomials. Honda (1988) implemented Harris' correction for the LM test for heteroskedasticity in a linear regression model containing fixed regressors, while Chesher and Spady (1988) followed the same route as Phillips and Park when looking at White's (1982) information matrix test of the linear model. As shown by Hall (1987), the latter incorporates tests for both heteroskedasticity and normality. Chesher and Spady found the requisite derivatives by using a package that performed symbolic differentiation; the length of the expressions would suggest that, unless this is done, substantial errors are likely to be made in any derivation. All of these approximations were for tests in which the variance of $\hat{\tau}$ was computed without recourse to the 'outer product' simplifications noted earlier. To date no corrections for the more popular variant of $\mathbf{V}_{\hat{\tau}}$ are available. Honda (1988) tried to use the same corrections but this did not work very well.

Given the need for symbolic differentiation other machine intensive methods of evaluating the critical values might be explored. In some instances $\hat{\tau}$ may be expressed as a ratio of quadratic forms in normal variables and the numerical algorithms flowing from Inmof's (1961) work can be exploited to get the *p*-values associated with any given value of $\hat{\tau}$. Tests for serial correlation and heteroskedasticity in the linear regression model have this structure – see Durbin and Watson (1971), Breusch and Pagan (1979) – as do the point optimal tests surveyed in King (1988). These are however special cases. Sometimes simulation methods can be a relatively cheap way to obtain *p*-values, and Breusch and Pagan (1979) recommended this for certain tests of heteroskedasticity. In this method many sets of artificial data are generated under the null hypothesis and the number of times the computed value of $\hat{\tau}$ exceeds the value determined from the data is recorded. Expressing this number as a fraction of the total number of artificial data sets gives a consistent estimator of the *p*-value. If the density of the data is known, artificial data can be generated from random numbers on a computer, or, if not, they can be generated by the 'bootstrap' method.

IV.4. *Non-Nested Model Comparisons*

Most of our discussion of model evaluation has been concerned implicitly with nested hypotheses. The three standard inferential procedures, namely, the LM, LR and Wald tests together with the conditional moment principle all involve testing restrictions on the parameter space. Even mis-specification tests (diagnostic statistics) are generally derivative from a well defined and more general alternative hypothesis, though here there is usually no necessary implication that a significant test statistic should lead to the adoption of this alternative. Sometimes, however, model evaluation involves non-nested hypotheses. Here rival models are compared which are not special cases of the other. Unlike nested tests, for non-nested tests there is no natural classification of the hypotheses into null and alternative; the status can be reversed and both could be rejected. There are several surveys of non-nested testing, for example, McAleer and Pesaran (1986), MacKinnon (1983) and Godfrey (1984).

Although nested and non-nested hypothesis tests appear to involve different principles, in fact both can be derived as special cases of the encompassing principle, see Hendry and Richard (1983), Mizon (1984) and Mizon and Richard (1986). One model (M_0) is said to encompass another (M_1) if it can account for, or explain, the results obtained by the other model, and is written $M_0 \in M_1$. If M_1 is nested within M_0 then it is trivial that M_0 encompasses M_1. However, it is also possible in this case for M_1 to encompass M_0 if some allowance is made for the relative dimensions of each model. In that situation it is said to be parsimoniously encompassing.

The principle of parametric encompassing can be explained as follows. Consider a sample of N observations which are thought to be generated by one of two models $M_0(\boldsymbol{\alpha})$ and $M_1(\boldsymbol{\beta})$ where $\boldsymbol{\alpha}$ and $\boldsymbol{\beta}$ are the parameters of these models. Suppose we want to compare the two models. Our first problem is to select some criterion upon which to base a comparison. One possibility is to compare the value of $\boldsymbol{\beta}$ predicted on the assumption that M_0 is correct with a good estimator of it if M_1 should be correct. Let $\boldsymbol{\beta}(\boldsymbol{\alpha})$ be the predicted value of $\boldsymbol{\beta}$ for given $\boldsymbol{\alpha}$, while $\hat{\boldsymbol{\alpha}}$ and $\hat{\boldsymbol{\beta}}$ denote estimators of $\boldsymbol{\alpha}$ and $\boldsymbol{\beta}$ that are consistent within the context of their respective models, i.e. $\text{plim}_{M_0}\hat{\boldsymbol{\alpha}} = \boldsymbol{\alpha}$ and $\text{plim}_{M_1}\hat{\boldsymbol{\beta}} = \boldsymbol{\beta}$. On the 'null hypothesis' that M_1 is the correct model we have $H_0: \theta = \beta - \beta(\alpha) = 0$, and a consistent estimator of θ is given by $\theta = \beta - \beta(\hat{\alpha})$. A Wald test of this hypothesis is called a Wald encompassing test (WET). Typically it will be distributed asymptotically as a χ^2_k where $\dim(\boldsymbol{\beta}) = k$.

To illustrate the ideas involved in the WET, consider the problem of the choice of regressors where the two rival models are

$$M_0: \mathbf{y} = \mathbf{X}\boldsymbol{\phi} + \mathbf{e} \quad \mathbf{e} \text{ is NID}(\mathbf{0}, \sigma_0^2 \mathbf{I}_N)$$

$$M_1: \mathbf{y} = \mathbf{Z}\boldsymbol{\delta} + \mathbf{u} \quad \mathbf{u} \text{ is NID}(\mathbf{0}, \sigma_1^2 \mathbf{I}_N).$$

For simplicity, assume that $\mathbf{X}$ and $\mathbf{Z}$ are $N \times h$ and $N \times k$, fixed and have no variables in common. One way to implement the encompassing principle is to identify $\boldsymbol{\beta}$ with $\boldsymbol{\delta}$ and $\boldsymbol{\alpha}$ with $\boldsymbol{\phi}$ and perform a WET on $\boldsymbol{\delta}$. For this we need $\hat{\boldsymbol{\beta}} = \hat{\boldsymbol{\delta}} = (\mathbf{Z}'\mathbf{Z})^{-1}\mathbf{Z}'\mathbf{y}$, $\hat{\boldsymbol{\alpha}} = \hat{\boldsymbol{\phi}} = (\mathbf{X}'\mathbf{X})^{-1}\mathbf{X}'\mathbf{y}$, $\boldsymbol{\beta}(\boldsymbol{\alpha}) = \text{plim}\,(\mathbf{Z}'\mathbf{Z})^{-1}\mathbf{Z}'(\mathbf{X}\boldsymbol{\phi} + \mathbf{e})$, $\boldsymbol{\beta}(\hat{\boldsymbol{\alpha}}) = (\mathbf{Z}'\mathbf{Z})^{-1}\mathbf{Z}'\hat{\boldsymbol{\phi}}$. Thus $\hat{\boldsymbol{\theta}} = \hat{\boldsymbol{\beta}} - \boldsymbol{\beta}(\hat{\boldsymbol{\alpha}}) = (\mathbf{Z}'\mathbf{Z})^{-1}\mathbf{Z}'(\mathbf{y} - \mathbf{X}\hat{\boldsymbol{\phi}})$ which is the estimate of $\boldsymbol{\gamma}$ in the model

$$M_2: \mathbf{y} = \mathbf{X}\boldsymbol{\xi} + \mathbf{Z}\boldsymbol{\gamma} + \mathbf{v}.$$

The F test for $\boldsymbol{\gamma} = \mathbf{0}$ is therefore identical to this WET.

The WET above was based on comparing different estimates of $\boldsymbol{\delta}$. Instead we might choose as $\boldsymbol{\beta}$ the residual variance of M_1; $\hat{\boldsymbol{\beta}}(\hat{\boldsymbol{\alpha}})$ will be the predicted value of that, $\hat{\sigma}^2_{10}$, and is to be compared to an estimate of it from M_1 alone, $\hat{\sigma}^2_1$. The null hypothesis is then $H_0: \theta = \hat{\sigma}^2_1 - \hat{\sigma}^2_{10}$. Because there is only a single variance the resulting WET is distributed asymptotically as a χ^2_1, and not a χ^2_k as before. Moreover the reduction in dimensionality makes it conceivable that the test will be more powerful than that based on the F test above. For further discussion see Mizon (1984). This test is asymptotically equivalent to the non-nested tests of Cox (1961, 1962), the N^2-test of Pesaran (1974), the J-test of Davidson and MacKinnon (1981) and the JA-test of Fisher and McAleer (1981). Of these the most frequently used in applied work seems to be the J-test, which tests if $\boldsymbol{\gamma}$ in M_2 is zero when $\mathbf{Z}$ is replaced by the predictions of model M_1. If $\boldsymbol{\gamma}$ in M_2 is zero it means that model M_1 has no extra information in it for predicting model M_0. There are many other possible criteria that could be employed in the design of an encompassing test. For example one could choose the log likelihood; the Cox and Pesaran tests are closely related to this idea.

The encompassing principle has been applied in several other contexts in which well defined conventional tests exist. For example, Hendry and Richard (1987) describe an encompassing test of linear versus log linear models. There are also forecast, or prediction, encompassing tests; encompassing tests for the choice of regressors in dynamic models; and Bayesian encompassing tests, (see Hendry and Richard, 1987).

Outside the context of a linear model an encompassing test may not be easy to perform. Applied workers have tended to choose between models using some criterion such as minimum residual variance or one of the information criteria such as that due to Akaike or Schwartz. Chow (1983) has a survey of these. A promising recent development in this framework is Horowitz and McAleer (1988), who base a selection test upon the difference in the log likelihoods of the two models. Such a strategy has long been informally used in econometrics, but Horowitz and McAleer manage to bound the probability of getting a prescribed deviation from zero of the criterion when one of the models is correct. Simple small sample corrections are also provided, which effectively make an allowance for the number of parameters in each model, and simulations indicated that the power of the test was very competitive with traditional non-nested tests when choosing between a linear and log linear model.

V. THE FORMULATION OF RELATIONSHIPS

Much of the current research agenda of econometric model building may be traced back to the earliest work in the subject. The necessity of formulating a model which contains *a priori* restrictions derived from economic theory in order to be able to interpret the statistical evidence was recognised by Koopmans (1947, 1949), while Koopmans (1937) and Haavelmo (1944) had previously urged the use of probability theory to provide a statistical framework for the analysis of these models. In Sections III and IV we discussed the interpretation of statistical evidence and in this section we consider the problem of how to specify a model. We focus on three, essentially time series, issues: exogeneity, the dynamic specification of econometric models and modelling conditional moments. In the last few years a large literature has been generated on the last two topics and a number of new results have emerged which have had a profound effect on dynamic econometric modelling.

V.1. *Exogeneity*

One of the first decisions that must be taken in building an econometric model is which variables to treat as endogenous, for which equations may be required, and which exogenous. The concept of exogeneity was recognised in the work of the Cowles Commission as one of great importance for the specification of systems of equations. Recent research has helped to clarify the issues and has been surveyed by Geweke (1984).

Exogeneity and its distinction from predeterminedness was stated precisely by Engle *et al.* (1983). The joint density of the complete sample can always be written

$$f(\mathbf{z}_1, \ldots, \mathbf{z}_T; \boldsymbol{\theta}) = \prod_2^T f(\mathbf{z}_t \mid \mathbf{z}_{t-1}^*; \boldsymbol{\theta}) f(\mathbf{z}_1),$$

where $\mathbf{z} = (\mathbf{y}, \mathbf{x})$, $\mathbf{z}_{t-1}^* = (\mathbf{z}_1, \ldots, \mathbf{z}_{t-1})$. Further,

$$f(\mathbf{z}_t \mid \mathbf{z}_{t-1}^*; \boldsymbol{\theta}) = f(y_t \mid \mathbf{x}_t, \mathbf{z}_{t-1}^*; \theta_1) f(x_t \mid \mathbf{z}_{t-1}^*; \theta_2).$$

If θ_2 does not depend on θ_1 then x_t is said to be *weakly exogenous*. With an additional assumption

$$f(x_t \mid \mathbf{z}_{t-1}^*; \theta_2) = f(x_t \mid x_1, \ldots, x_{t-1}; \theta_2),$$

i.e. x_t does not depend on past values of y_t, x_t is said to be *strongly exogenous*. Assuming normality it may be noted that weak exogeneity implies $\mathrm{E}\{[y_t - \mathrm{E}(y_t \mid \mathbf{z}_{t-1}^*; \theta_1)][x_t - \mathrm{E}(x_t \mid \mathbf{z}_{t-1}^*; \theta_2)]\} = 0$ and hence the disturbance term of the structural equation(s) of y_t is uncorrelated with the disturbance of the x_t equation(s). In this instance weak exogeneity and x_t being predetermined are equivalent restrictions. There is nothing to be gained in terms of efficiency by estimating the equations for y_t and x_t jointly even though there are exclusion restrictions on the variables explaining x_t. For these purposes, therefore, strong exogeneity is unnecessarily restrictive.

Statistical dependence does not imply causality; therefore causality cannot be inferred from correlations unless it is explicitly included in the premisses. Nevertheless, there have been attempts to define causality in terms of the joint distribution of the data, or rather to provide criteria which imply the absence of causality. 'Granger non-causality' is in effect equivalent to strong exogeneity; if x_t is strongly exogenous for y_t then y_t does not 'Granger cause' x_t, or if x_t is weakly exogenous and y_t does not 'Granger cause' x_t then x_t is strongly exogenous, see Engle *et al.* (1983). Sims (1972) provided an alternative definition of causality arguing that if $x_t, x_{t+1}, \ldots$ are not significant in explaining y_t in the presence of lagged values of y_t and x_t then x_t does not cause y_t. The danger with this criterion is that such a correlation could exist if expectations of future x_t affect y_t and if $x_t, x_{t+1}, \ldots$ are correlated with the information set on which expectations are based. Clarifying though these ideas are, they do not provide a very convincing argument in favour of a correlation based concept of causality. Nor do they seem to add anything useful to the more valuable idea of exogeneity.

V.2. *Dynamic Specification*

Although there is a large literature on dynamic specification, our present task is made easier by the existence of several surveys – an outstanding early treatment is Griliches (1967) and a more recent one is Hendry *et al.* (1984). We shall not, therefore, go over the entire ground again here but concentrate instead on the most recent developments.

Early research on dynamics was largely concerned with the problem of estimating the parameters of (23) directly:

$$y_t = \mathbf{A}(\mathrm{L})\, y_{t-1} + \mathbf{B}(\mathrm{L})\, x_t + e_t, \tag{23}$$

whereas the modern trend has been to deal with reparametrisations of (23). Exactly how one would reparametrise (23) depends on the objectives of the research. For example, if attention is focused on the long-run properties of the model then, using the fact that a Taylor series expansion of any polynomial $P(\mathrm{L})$ around $\mathrm{L} = 1$ gives $P(\mathrm{L}) = P(1) + \sum_{j=1}^{\infty} P^{(j)}(1-\mathrm{L})^j = P(1) + \sum_{j=1}^{\infty} Q(\mathrm{L})\,(1-\mathrm{L})$, where $P^{(j)}$ is $\partial^j P(\mathrm{L})/\partial^j \mathrm{L}\,|_{\mathrm{L}=1}$, (23) could be re-written in the form

$$y_t = \theta x_t + C(\mathrm{L})\,\Delta y_t + D(\mathrm{L})\,\Delta x_t + \lambda e_t, \tag{24}$$

where $\lambda = 1/[1-A(1)]$ and $\theta = \lambda B(1)$ is the long-run multiplier. Equation (24) is one of several reformulations of (23) proposed by Wickens and Breusch (1988) which may be useful in studying various characteristics and follows up the idea of Bewley (1979). For example the first difference terms could be replaced by a sequence of increasingly higher order differences as in the original expansion of the polynomial above. This would permit the direct estimation of θ and at the same time preserve the distributed lag coefficients in (23). Due to the presence of Δy_t on the right-hand side of (24) the OLS estimator may not be consistent, but the instrumental variables estimator of θ obtained using all of the explanatory variables in (23) as instruments is identical to the estimator obtained by solving θ from the least squares estimator of (23). Moreover, the estimate of θ is likely to be robust to over-parametrisation of the lag structure or the neglect of restrictions on the lag structure.

Another reformulation of (23) is the error correction model (ECM), whose rationale was set out in Davidson *et al.* (1978) and which has been extensively employed in applied work since then, e.g. Hendry and Mizon (1978). The ideas underlying this model are drawn from the classical control literature, and their importation into econometrics seems to trace to A. W. Phillips (1954). Classical control theory considered the design of a controller and recommended that the control rule express the relation between a control variable y_t and a target y_t^*

as the sum of three components. These components were derivative (Δy_t^*), proportional ($y_{t-1}^* - y_{t-1}$) and integral [$\sum_{j=1}^{\infty}(y_{t-j}^* - y_{t-j})$] control actions. Embedding these in a linear control rule produces

$$\Delta y_t = \beta \Delta y_t^* + \gamma(y_{t-1}^* - y_{t-1}) + \delta \sum (y_{t-j}^* - y_{t-j}) + e_t, \tag{25}$$

and the first two terms of this summarise what is termed the Error Correction Model (ECM). The third term represents a cumulative sum and, for a flow variable y_t, is the deviation between a stock S_{t-1} and its target value, while the error e_t has been added for modelling. Most ECM models ignore the third component. After assuming that y_t^* is a linear function of x_t, it is clear that (25) could be written as (23). However, the reparametrisation yielded by the ECM seems more useful. In particular, the model is designed so that the long run response of y_t to y_t^* is always unity. When $y_t^* = x_t \theta$ the long run response of y_t to x_t is θ. In many applications $\theta = 1$ since x_t and y_t are logs of variables and the ratio of the levels is regarded as being constant. For later reference it is important to note that if $\mathbf{z}_t' = (y_t \; x_t) \boldsymbol{\alpha}$ with $\boldsymbol{\alpha}' = (-1 \; \theta)$, the ECM could also be written as

$$\Delta y_t = \gamma \mathbf{z}_{t-1} + u_t, \tag{26}$$

where $u_t = \beta\theta \, \Delta x_t + e_t$.

If θ is thought to be a value θ^* the ECM (without the integral control term) has the format

$$\Delta y_t = \beta\theta^* \, \Delta x_t + \gamma(\theta^* x_{t-1} - y_{t-1}) + \gamma(\theta - \theta^*) \, x_{t-1} + e_t, \tag{27}$$

and we can test whether the long-run response is θ^* by testing if the coefficient on x_{t-1} in (27) is zero. An interesting application of this model is Edison and Klovland (1987) in which y_t^* is the log of the Norwegian price level and $\mathbf{x}_t$ is a vector containing the log of the U.K. price level and the log of the nominal exchange rate. They test purchasing power parity by making $\boldsymbol{\theta}^*$ the vector $(1 \; -1)$ and the second term in (27) the log of the real exchange rate lagged once. A test of PPP is then a test of whether the coefficients of $\mathbf{x}_{t-1}$ are zero or not. Of course in this application, as well as in others, more than one lag in Δy_t^* is used and extra variables are added to represent additional influences on Δy_t.

It is also possible to derive ECM models as the optimal adjustment path by an economic agent seeking to minimise a discounted cost function over time, where the costs are the sum of those incurred by any deviation of y_t^* from y_t and by rapid adjustment. Nickell (1985) does this; the number of lagged values of Δy_t^* that enter the model is then found to depend upon the form of the process generating y_t^*.

V.3. *Integrated Variables and Cointegration*

V.3.1. *Dynamic specification*

So far our discussion of model building and virtually all of the literature cited was based on the assumption that both the variables and the models are 'stationary'. We shall now take account of the fact that many – some might say most – of the variables that appear in time series econometric models are nonstationary or, more specifically, are integrated variables. This has important implications both for the formulation of time series models and for the distribution of their estimators.

Granger and Newbold (1974) were among the first to be aware of possible problems. They warned econometricians that the use of trending or integrated variables could lead to spuriously high correlations and hence to misleadingly strong results. To guard against this they recommended the use of Box-Jenkins techniques and in particular that time series data be first differenced. A number of U.K. empirical studies took this advice, e.g. Wall *et al.* (1975) and Haache (1974). However, it was pointed out by Davidson *et al.* (1978) and Hendry and Mizon (1978) that there is a drawback to expressing models in first difference form because it is then impossible to infer the long-run steady state solution from the estimated model. Hendry's solution to this problem led to the adoption of the error correction model in which the long-run solution is introduced into the model as an additional variable in the form of an error correction term – in (25) it is $y^*_{t-1} - y_{t-1}$ which defines the missing long-run solution. In retrospect the wrong inference was drawn from Granger and Newbold's simulations. As shown by Phillips (1986), the difficulty is that the estimator of the correlation coefficient between independent I(1) variables tends not to zero but to a random variable.

In constructing an econometric model one of the objectives is to explain variations in the dependent variable leaving little unexplained variation in the disturbance term. Achieving a stationary, or I(0), error is usually a minimum criterion to meet. Hence if the dependent variable in an equation is I(1) then there must be at least one I(1) variable among the explanatory variables. If all of the explanatory variables are I(0) then the equation will be mis-specified and this will be reflected in the disturbance term which will be I(1) and not I(0) as required. The disturbance will also be I(1) if the dependent variable is I(0) and there is only one I(1) regressor; to achieve an I(0) disturbance there must be at least two I(1) regressors. The reason for all of these claims is straightforward and is a matter of 'integration or growth accounting', i.e. the left- and right-hand sides of the equation must be of the same order of integration or trend. To explain a series which is growing, at least one of the explanatory variables must also be growing otherwise the growth will be unexplained and will show up in the disturbance term; the remaining variables are simply explaining deviations about the growth path. If the dependent variable is stationary, there must be either zero or at least two trending explanatory variables; one is required to remove the growth of the other and leave their combined explanation stationary. The lag of a non-stationary variable may suffice, thereby creating a generalised difference in the non-stationary variable of which the first difference is a special case. Sometimes an informal application of the strictures of integration accounting can point out an inadequate specification, but for a deeper understanding some formal analysis is required, and this was supplied by Engle and Granger (1987) in their concept of cointegration.

Let $\mathbf{x}_t$ now denote a vector of variables. This vector is said to be cointegrated if (*a*) each element is $I(d)\ d > 0$, and (*b*) there exists a vector $\boldsymbol{\alpha}$, called the cointegrating vector, such that $\boldsymbol{\alpha}'\mathbf{x}_t$ is $I(d-b)$, where $\boldsymbol{\alpha} \neq \mathbf{0}$ and $d \geqslant b > 0$. In practice the most important case, and the one we shall confine our attention to hereafter, is $d = b = 1$, when $\boldsymbol{\alpha}'\mathbf{x}_t$ is $I(0)$. Care must be taken in giving an economic interpretation of $\boldsymbol{\alpha}'\mathbf{x}_t$. One interpretation is that $\boldsymbol{\alpha}'\mathbf{x}_t = 0$ defines the long-run relationship connecting these variables, but this is to define long-run in a different way from the conventional economic usage. In particular, $I(0)$ variables which are not present in $\mathbf{x}_t$ may also enter a long-run relationship. For example, suppose that money, prices and income are all $I(1)$ and are cointegrated, but the interest rate is $I(0)$, then the former interpretation would exclude the interest rate from the long-run money demand function which, at best, must be deemed unconventional. The usual approach in economics is to exclude from the long-run solution all variables whose long-run multipliers are zero, whatever their order of integrability. It should also be noted that $\boldsymbol{\alpha}$ is not necessarily unique for any given $\mathbf{x}_t$, as the definition does not exclude zero elements in the cointegrating vector. Moreover, as there is no unique normalisation of $\boldsymbol{\alpha}$, it is not possible to identify a dependent variable for $\boldsymbol{\alpha}'\mathbf{x}_t = 0$.

Building on the work of Granger (1981, 1983), Engle and Granger (1987) argue that there is a close connection between cointegration and error correction models which they formulate in the Granger Representation Theorem. The main reason why this connection is of interest is that in the ECM of (25) all of the variables can be transformed to be $I(0)$. Being able to rewrite models which contain $I(1)$ variables as an ECM may, therefore, be very helpful. A simple example due to Phillips (1989*a*) will illustrate the connection. Suppose that x_{1t} and x_{2t} are $I(1)$ variables with $\mathbf{x}_t = (x_{1t}, x_{2t})'$ and they are related by the two equation system

$$x_{1t} = \theta x_{2t} + u_{1t} \tag{28}$$

$$\Delta x_{2t} = u_{2t}, \tag{29}$$

where $\mathbf{u}_t = (u_{1t}, u_{2t})'$ is $I(0)$. Equation (28) can be written

$$\begin{aligned} \Delta x_{1t} &= \theta \Delta x_{2t} + \Delta u_{1t} \\ &= \theta u_{2t} + \Delta u_{1t} \\ &= \delta(\theta x_{2,t-1} - x_{1,t-1}) + v_{1t}, \end{aligned} \tag{30}$$

where $\delta = 1$ and $v_{1t} = (1 \quad \theta)\, \mathbf{u}_t$ is $I(0)$. Equation (30) is thus a transformation of (23) that has only $I(0)$ variables. Defining $\mathbf{z}_t = \boldsymbol{\alpha}'\mathbf{x}_t$, $\boldsymbol{\alpha}' = (-1 \quad \theta)$, we have

$$\Delta \mathbf{x}_t = \boldsymbol{\gamma} \mathbf{z}_{t-1} + \mathbf{v}_t, \tag{31}$$

where $\boldsymbol{\gamma} = (1, 0)'$ and $\mathbf{v}_t = (v_{1t}, u_{2t})'$ is $I(0)$. Comparing (31) with (26) we see that it is in ECM form. In fact the error term of ECM's in most applied work is reduced to white noise by adding in lags of Δx_{1t} and Δx_{2t}, and Phillips argues that this makes sense given the fact that $\mathbf{v}_t$ is a linear combination of the errors of each of (28) and (29). However, he also observes that it is impossible for such variables to compensate fully for the serial correlation.

More generally, if each component of a vector $\mathbf{x}_t$ is I(1) there will always exist a multivariate representation

$$(1-L)\,\mathbf{x}_t = \mathbf{C}(L)\,\mathbf{e}_t, \tag{32}$$

where $\mathbf{e}_t$ is white noise and $\mathbf{C}(L)$ can be written $\mathbf{C}(L) = \mathbf{C}(1)+(1-L)\,\mathbf{C}^*(L)$. If there are n variables and r cointegrating vectors $\boldsymbol{\alpha}$ (i.e. $\boldsymbol{\alpha}$ is now an $n\times r$ matrix) then $\mathbf{C}(1)$ has rank $n-r$, $\boldsymbol{\alpha}'\mathbf{C}(1) = \mathbf{0}$, and there exists an $n\times r$ matrix $\boldsymbol{\gamma}$ that satisfies $\mathbf{C}(1)\,\boldsymbol{\gamma} = \mathbf{0}$. Since $\mathbf{C}(L)$ is invertible we can also express $\mathbf{x}_t$ as the VAR model $\mathbf{A}(L)\,\mathbf{x}_t = \mathbf{e}_t$, or, following (26), as the error correction model

$$\mathbf{A}^*(L)\,\Delta\mathbf{x}_t = \boldsymbol{\gamma}\boldsymbol{\alpha}'\mathbf{x}_{t-1}+\mathbf{u}_t, \tag{33}$$

$$= \boldsymbol{\gamma}\mathbf{z}_{t-1}+\mathbf{u}_t, \tag{34}$$

where $\mathbf{z}_t = \boldsymbol{\alpha}'\mathbf{x}_t$. Notice that although there are n variables in $\mathbf{x}_t$, and hence n equations in (34), the rank of $\boldsymbol{\gamma}$ is $r \leqslant n$, for there are only r independent cointegrating relationships $\mathbf{z}_t$. Consequently, the first difference of a set of I(1) variables has been expressed as a linear combination of r cointegrating vectors. Just as in (30), all of the variables in (34) are I(0).

A complementary idea to cointegration is that of common stochastic trends, see for example Stock and Watson (1988) and Phillips and Ouliaris (1986). It can be shown that, if the n I(1) variables $\mathbf{x}_t$ have r cointegrating vectors, they will also possess $n-r$ common stochastic trends. To illustrate for the case of a single I(1) variable, first we recall the result due to Beveridge and Nelson (1981) that an I(1) variable can always be written as the sum of a random walk and an I(0) process, see (1)–(5). Thus if a_t is a scalar such that $\Delta a_t = \psi(L)\,e_t$, with e_t a white noise process, $a_t = \tau_t+\mathbf{D}(L)\,e_t$ and $\tau_t = \tau_{t-1}+e_t$ can be interpreted as a stochastic trend while $\mathbf{D}(L)\,e_t$ is I(0). For the vector process $\mathbf{x}_t$ which has r cointegrating vectors, the rank of $\mathbf{C}(1)$ is $n-r$ and hence $\mathbf{C}(1)\,\boldsymbol{\gamma} = \mathbf{0}$. If $\boldsymbol{\phi}$ is an $n\times(n-r)$ matrix with columns orthogonal to $\boldsymbol{\gamma}$ then $\mathbf{W} = [\boldsymbol{\gamma}\ \boldsymbol{\phi}]$ is non-singular and

$$\begin{aligned}(1-L)\,\mathbf{x}_t &= \mathbf{C}(L)\,\mathbf{e}_t = [\mathbf{C}(1)+(1-L)\,\mathbf{C}(L)]\,\mathbf{W}\mathbf{W}^{-1}\mathbf{e}_t\\ &= [\mathbf{C}(1)\,\boldsymbol{\gamma}:\mathbf{C}(1)\,\boldsymbol{\phi}]\,\mathbf{v}_t+(1-L)\,\mathbf{C}^*(L)\,\mathbf{v}_t\\ &= \mathbf{C}(1)\,\boldsymbol{\phi}\mathbf{v}_{2t}+(1-L)\,\mathbf{C}^*(L)\,\mathbf{v}_t,\end{aligned} \tag{35}$$

where $\mathbf{v}_t' = (\mathbf{v}_{1t}', \mathbf{v}_{2t}') = \mathbf{W}^{-1}\mathbf{e}_t$ partitioned conformably with $\mathbf{W}$. Integrating (35) ('multiplying by $(1-L)^{-1}$') gives

$$\mathbf{x}_t = \mathbf{C}(1)\,\boldsymbol{\phi}\boldsymbol{\tau}_t+\mathbf{C}^*(L)\,\mathbf{e}_t \tag{36}$$

with $\boldsymbol{\tau}_t = \sum_0^\infty \mathbf{e}_{2,t-i} = \tau_{t-1}+\mathbf{v}_{2t}$ an $n-r$ vector random walk. In other words, $\mathbf{x}_t$ can be written as the sum of $n-r$ common trends and an I(0) component.

One further point about the formulation of models which have I(1) variables concerns drift. It is important to include an intercept term. Often, especially in ECM's, this is omitted. The intercept may be left out if there is no drift, or if the variables are I(0). A simple example will illustrate the nature of the problem. Consider the partial adjustment model $\Delta y_t = \alpha(y_t^* - y_{t-1})$ with long-run desired value $y_t^* = \theta x_t + e_t$ which gives $y_t = (1-\alpha)y_{t-1} + \alpha\theta x_t + \alpha e_t$. If $\Delta x_t = \mu + \epsilon_t$, then $E(\Delta y_t^*) = \theta\mu$ and the model can be expressed as $y_t = y_t^* - [(1-\alpha)/\alpha]\Delta y_t$. Hence $E(y_t) = E(y_t^*)$ if $E(\Delta y_t) = 0$. In other words, for this model of y_t^*, following any departure from equilibrium y_t will only return to its long-run desired level y_t^* if $E(\Delta y_t) = 0$. But $E(\Delta y_t) = E(\Delta y_t^*) = \theta\mu$ here, making the model inconsistent with the process driving it whenever $\mu \neq 0$. Salmon (1982) pointed out this phenomenon. A solution ensuring consistency is to include an intercept in the partial adjustment model and so formulate it as $\Delta y_t = \lambda + \alpha(y_t^* - y_{t-1})$. Now $y_t = \lambda/\alpha + y_t^* - [(1-\alpha)/\alpha]\Delta y_t$, and hence $E(y_t) = E(y_t^*)$ if $E(\Delta y_t) = \lambda/(1-\alpha)$. But $E(\Delta y_t) = E(\Delta y_t^*) = \theta\mu$ and this implies that $\lambda = \theta\mu(1-\alpha)$. Thus, in general, by including an intercept in the estimating equation, when the variables are I(1) with drift a consistent long-run solution is obtained, see also Nickell (1985) and Pagan (1989).

V.3.2. *Estimation and inference*

There are a number of ways to estimate the coefficients of models which have integrated variables. What route is followed depends on the particular parameters of interest and on whether or not the integrated variables have a drift term. One of the first things to establish in an empirical study of time series is the order of integrability of each variable and, if a variable is integrated, whether or not it has a drift term. The methods described in Section I.2 can be used for this. If there are no I(1) variables then the standard methods of estimation and inference apply.

If a pre-specified model is to be estimated – assume as a minimum that the dependent variable and a list of potential explanatory variables have been proposed – then the next thing to determine is whether or not the set of integrated explanatory variable is complete. This check is made on the set of variables with the highest order of integrability. Let us assume that this involves only I(1) series, although it could concern, for example, I(2) variables instead. As noted earlier, if one or more integrated explanatory variables is omitted from the model then the disturbance term will also be integrated. Hence we require a test to establish that there are no omitted integrated explanatory variables. Such a test is known as a cointegration test because it also determines whether or not a cointegrating vector exists for these integrated series. A linear model formed from the I(1) variables is called the cointegrating regression.

A number of cointegration tests exist that are based on the OLS residuals of the cointegrating regression. In principle, any one of the I(1) variables can be chosen as the dependent variable. In practice it is natural to select the dependent variable of the model we are ultimately interested in estimating, provided it is I(1). Because it is standard computer output, the simplest test to carry out is the Cointegrating Regression Durbin–Watson (CRDW) test of Sargan and Bhargava (1983). If there is a unit root in the disturbance of the cointegrating regression then the Durbin–Watson statistic will be close to zero. Exact critical bounds for CRDW can be obtained – under a normality assumption for errors – and these are reported in Sargan and Bhargava. The usual problem of what inference to draw when a DW statistic falls within these bounds remains. Another class of tests consists of performing the tests for a unit root discussed in Section I.2.3 on the residuals. As the residuals are estimated series and not directly observed, strictly, the critical values for the DF and ADF tests used before will no longer be appropriate. However, in a set of Monte-Carlo experiments, Engle and Granger (1987) found that the residual based ADF test performed well, and much better than the CRDW which tended to over-reject. Engle and Yoo (1986) have tabulated critical values for ADF and ADF tests that are appropriate for regression residuals. They are found to depend on the number of regressors; the greater the number of regressors, the less powerful the test.

It was observed earlier that, if the vector $\mathbf{x}_t$ possesses r cointegrating vectors, the rank of $\mathbf{C}(1)$, defined by equation (32), will be $n-r$. This suggests formulating a cointegration test by checking whether $\mathbf{C}(1)$ is less than full rank. If it is then this would indicate the existence of at least one cointegrating vector, and hence an I(0) error term in the cointegrating regression. This is the basis of the test proposed by Phillips and Ouliaris (1986) who suggest testing the null hypothesis that the smallest eigenvalue of $\mathrm{E}(\Delta\mathbf{x}_t\,\Delta\mathbf{x}_t')$ is zero. Their test statistic is the smallest eigenvalue of $T^{-1}\sum_{t=1}^{T}(\Delta\mathbf{x}_t\,\Delta\mathbf{x}_t')$. Phillips and Ouliaris also suggest a bounds test which is the matrix equivalent of the bounds test for a unit root mentioned in Section I.2.3.

Stock and Watson (1988) ask how many co-integrating vectors or stochastic trends appear among the n variables. If there are none there will be n unit roots, whereas if there are r there will be $(n-r)$ unit roots. Consequently, they base a test on whether the r smallest eigenvalues of the matrix of first order serial correlation coefficients from the residuals of a principal component analysis are unity. Principal components are used to avoid the normalisation problem, that is which is the regressor and which the regressand. If $n = 2, r = 1$ this would just be the DF test applied to residuals. Analogues of the ADF test are also given as well as tabulations of critical values. Johansen (1988) and Johansen and Juselius (1988) have proposed a likelihood ratio test for the number of cointegrating vectors possessed by $\mathbf{x}_t$ based on a rearrangement of (33)[4]

$$\Delta\mathbf{x}_t = -\bar{\mathbf{A}}(\mathrm{L})\,\Delta\mathbf{x}_{t-1} - \mathbf{A}(1)\,\mathbf{x}_{t-1} + \mathbf{e}_t \qquad (37)$$

by checking how many of the eigenvalues of $\mathbf{A}(1) = \boldsymbol{\gamma\alpha}'$ are zero. On the null hypothesis of r cointegrating vectors ($n-r$ common trends) $\mathbf{A}(1)$ has rank r, and on the alternative hypothesis of zero cointegrating vectors (n common trends) $\mathbf{A}(1)$ has rank zero. The likelihood ratio test is formed by estimating (37) with the restriction $\mathbf{A}(1) = \boldsymbol{\gamma\alpha}'$ imposed and with it removed.

Having established that no integrated variables have been omitted the modelling process can proceed to the next stage, which is the estimation of the model. Suppose the equation to be estimated is (25), that is there are only two variables involved. For the moment let us assume that y_t and x_t are both I(1) without drift. Equation (25) can be expressed as (24). Since y_t and x_t are I(1) variables Δy_t and Δx_t are I(0) and, from Section III.2, the long-run multiplier

[4] Johansen actually proposes using x_{t-k} where k is the maximum lag, but x_{t-1} is more convenient.

θ in (24) can be consistently estimated even if Δy_t and Δx_t are omitted; the model that results from these omissions is in fact the cointegrating regression and θ is the cointegrating vector – ignoring the normalised coefficient. As the short-run dynamics can be written as additional differenced variables, they can therefore be omitted if the objective is solely to obtain consistent estimates of θ. Further, there is no need to take into account any distinction between endogenous and exogenous variables because any correlation with the error term will be negligible asymptotically and no asymptotic bias will ensue. Thus any of the variables can be selected as the dependent variable of the cointegrating regression. Stock (1987) and Engle and Granger (1987) drew attention to this super-consistency property of OLS for estimating the cointegrating vector and Engle and Granger used it as the basis of the first stage of a two-stage strategy for estimating the parameters of (25). In their second stage they regressed Δy_t against Δx_t and $\hat{z}_{t-1} = (x_{t-1}\hat{\theta} - y_{t-1})$ to get estimators of β and γ. Because both of these are attached to I(0) variables the limiting distribution of the OLS estimator is normal, as mentioned in Section III.2.

Areas where the idea of transforming I(1) variables so that the model estimated has only I(0) variables has proved useful includes tests for market efficiency (see Baillie, 1989, for a survey), tests of present value models (see Campbell and Shiller, 1987) and tests of life-cycle models (see for example Campbell, 1987). One of the puzzles in performing these tests that has been discussed in the literature is how to model the joint process generating the variables, given that they tend to be I(1) variables. The main issue is whether one should formulate the model in levels or in first differences? The implication of the above results seems to be that the answer is neither. A simple example will illustrate the issues. Consider the bivariate process generating (y_t, x_t) where both are I(1) and there is a single cointegrating vector. The results above suggest that if there is no drift term the model should be formulated as an error correction in the vector $(y_t - \alpha x_t, \Delta x_t)$ as both elements are stationary after this transformation. More generally, for the n-vector $\mathbf{x}_t$ one can use the error correction model for the stationary transformed vector $(\boldsymbol{\alpha}'\mathbf{x}_t, \boldsymbol{\xi}'\Delta\mathbf{x}_t)$ where $\boldsymbol{\xi}$ is an $n \times (n-r)$ matrix with columns orthogonal to $\boldsymbol{\alpha}$ thereby guaranteeing that $\boldsymbol{\xi}'\mathbf{C}(1)\boldsymbol{\phi}$ has rank $n-r$. Thus the transformed variables are the cointegrating error $\boldsymbol{\alpha}'\mathbf{x}_t$ together with any mapping of the $\mathbf{x}_t$ variables into $n-r$ variables that have $n-r$ common stochastic trends or, equivalently, no cointegrating vectors. We shall pursue these tests in more detail in Section V.5.1, which concerns expectations models.

Instead of concentrating upon a single equation estimator, Phillips (1988, 1990) has suggested that the cointegrating vector be estimated by applying FIML to (28) and (29) jointly, either in the time or frequency domain. He shows that for $\hat{\theta}_F$, the F denoting FIML, $T(\hat{\theta}_F - \theta)$ has a limiting distribution which is a certain mixture of normally distributed random variables with the implication that the t-statistic of $\hat{\theta}_F$ is asymptotically N(0, 1). However, this result is only true if the unit root in (29) is *imposed* and no attempt is made to estimate it. If the unit root is estimated the distribution of $\hat{\theta}_F$ will be non-standard unless x_{2t} is exogenous. Because of the special structure of the system

(28) and (29) it is possible to give a simplified estimator of θ which is equivalent to FIML but is closer to OLS in computational cost as it involves using single equation methods after making adjustments to the variables for simultaneity and short-run dynamics. Suppose u_t is n.i.d. $(0, \mathbf{\Sigma})$ and $\mathbf{\Sigma} = \{\sigma_{ij}\}$, then from the properties of the bivariate normal, $u_{1t} = \delta u_{2t} + u_{1\cdot 2t}$, where $\delta = \sigma_{22}^{-1}\sigma_{12}$. This result is true whenever the u_{jt} follow a jointly stationary process, although the definition of δ is more complex. Hence (28) becomes

$$x_{1t} = \theta x_{2t} + \delta \Delta x_{2t} + u_{1\cdot 2t}. \tag{38}$$

Because $E(u_{1\cdot 2t}\, u_{2t}) = 0$ by design, OLS can be applied to (38), and the regression of $x_{1t} - \delta \Delta x_{2t}$ against x_{2t} gives Phillips and Hansen's (1990) modified estimator of θ, $\hat{\theta}^{+}$. This estimator is also a mixture of normals and so the t-statistic of $\hat{\theta}^{+}$ will be N(0, 1) as well. It remains therefore only to estimate δ in order to make the estimator operational. Since the u_{1t} could be estimated using the super-consistent estimator $\hat{\theta}_{\text{OLS}}$, and $u_{2t} = \Delta x_{2t}$ is available, δ can be formed from the sample covariance matrix of the residuals $\hat{u}_t$. The variance of $u_{1\cdot 2t} = \sigma_{11} - \sigma_{12}\sigma_{22}^{-1}\sigma_{21}$, needed in the construction of the t-statistic, is determined in the same way. Obviously, x_{2t} cannot be lagged values of x_{1t}, since a special case of (38) would be (6) with $\alpha = 1$, and the distribution of $T(\hat{\alpha} - 1)$ is not asymptotically normal. Park (1988*a*) refers to this as a 'singular' case and proposes a method of estimation which produces test statistics for $\hat{\theta}$ that are asymptotically non-normal but which are free of nuisance parameters. It is similar to the Phillips–Hansen method in that it involves an OLS regression on transformed x_{1t} and x_{2t}. A by-product of his approach is a variable addition test with the *null of cointegration* rather than of no cointegration. Perhaps it is worth noting that, if $H_0 : \theta = \theta^*$ was being tested, it is unlikely that any lagged values of x_{1t} would appear in (38), since (38) could be rewritten, following (27), with all variables as I(0) except for the determinants of the long-run equilibrium position. In this instance the Phillips–Hansen modified estimator would provide a direct test of the values of the cointegrating vector by augmenting (38) with the equations for those variables featuring in the equilibrium relationship. Of course, things are more complex once u_{1t} and u_{2t} are allowed to be just stationary I(0) processes rather than independent ones, and suitable expressions for $E(u_{1t} \mid u_{2t})$ need to be found. Hansen and Phillips (1988) supply formulae for this. Using Monte-Carlo experiments, they show that in small samples the t-statistics for individual regression coefficients that are based on this fully modified estimator are quite close to normality and much better in this respect than the uncorrected t-statistics.

The previous discussion has assumed that the I(1) variables had no drift term. With drift the corresponding results of Section III.2 need to be invoked. Thus all of the super-consistency results carry over to this case, whilst the distribution and rate of convergence of the estimators depends upon whether there is a trend in the model and the number of regressors with drift.

In our discussion of estimation in the presence of I(1) variables we have considered only asymptotic properties. There must, however, be a large question mark over the small sample properties of the estimators, especially where the I(0) variables have been relegated to the error term. It is important to realise that one cannot just determine estimator properties solely by comparing the order of integration of variables. The property of super-consistency relies upon the fact that the 'variance' of an I(1) variable dominates that of any I(0) variable. For large samples this must be true, but one needs to know the *size of the variances of the innovations* in each process before one could be confident of such an outcome generally. If, for example, we had an I(0) variable that was an AR(1) with autoregressive parameter 0·7, and innovation variance σ_z^2, its variance will be $3{\cdot}33\sigma_z^2$, while that of an integrated process with innovation variance σ_x^2 is $T\sigma_x^2$. It need not be the case that $T\sigma_x^2$ dominates $3{\cdot}33\sigma_z^2$, even for quite large T. Indeed, it is not hard to find instances where I(1) series have a variance smaller than that of an I(0) series. Banerjee *et al.* (1986) observe that, in the case of a bivariate cointegrating regression $\hat{\theta}$, the OLS estimator of the single cointegrating coefficient θ, satisfies the linear relationship $\hat{\theta}-\theta \cong \theta^2(1-R^2)$, implying that the bias will decline as the R^2 for the cointegrating regression increases. Since $1-R^2$ is effectively the ratio of the variance of a supposedly I(0) variable to that of an I(1) one their conclusion is a formalisation of the general point. In view of this, and given the use of the cointegrating residuals, doubt must be cast on the small sample properties of Engle and Granger's two-step estimator. In fact there seems little to be gained in omitting the short-run dynamics, especially as in both reformulations of equation (23), namely, (24) and (25), there is no need to restrict the order of the distributed lags, see Wickens and Breusch (1988).

Our discussion has been confined to non-explosive roots ($|\alpha| \leqslant 1$). It is well known that when $\alpha > 1$ in the AR(1) model the OLS estimator of α has a limiting Cauchy distribution. Domowitz and Muus (1988) have shown that the maximum likelihood estimator in regression models with an explosive dynamic structure is a variance mixture of normal distributions, with the implication that standard Wald tests will have limiting χ^2 distributions. Gourieroux and Monfort (1987) have shown that if in static models the regressors themselves are explosive, then a norming function based on the moment matrix of the regressors of the OLS estimator such as $|\mathbf{X}'\mathbf{X}|^{-\frac{1}{2}}(\mathbf{b}_{\mathrm{OLS}}-\boldsymbol{\beta})$ will have an asymptotic normal distribution.

V.4. *Conditional Expectations Models*

Econometric models often contain variables that are conditional expectations of either the first or the second moment. Examples of the former are rational expectations models and of the latter are models with risk premia, the ARCH models. Models of this sort are especially common in the fast growing area of financial econometrics, though any model based on intertemporal optimisation is likely to possess conditional expectations variables. There was a time, not too long ago, when the dynamics in econometric models were invariably backward looking and interpreted as reflecting either adjustment lags or possibly adaptive expectations, see the surveys by Griliches (1967), Dhrymes (1971) and Hendry *et al.* (1984). It has since been realised that such dynamics may, either in part or entirely, reflect forward looking behaviour in which the significance of the lagged variables is due to their presence in the information set on which the expectations of future variables are conditioned. Further, it has been suggested by Lucas (1976) in his well known critique of econometric models that they are inherently prone to structural instability due to ignoring expectational variables and changes in the information (or conditioning) set which might be brought about by the introduction of new policies. This criticism applies especially to the dynamic structure of backward looking econometric models. It should be remarked, however, that while the theoretical implications of the Lucas critique are clear and potentially devastating, its practical importance is less so. More than a decade after the debut of the critique there is little evidence that failures in econometric models have their origin in it, a point made forcefully by Sims (1982) and lately by Hendry (1988). In the next section we shall briefly review the estimation of models with forward looking variables, of which rational expectations is a special case. As much of the literature on rational expectations has been surveyed recently by Pesaran (1987), we shall focus more on future expectations as this is where the newest results may be found.

V.5.1. *Expectations about the mean*

It is useful to draw a distinction between conditional expectations and rational expectations. Following Muth's (1961) original definition, rational expectations are the predictions of the relevant economic theory. Strictly defined, therefore, rational expectations are concerned with the conditional expectations of endogenous variables as formed from a complete economic model. A conditional expectation of an endogenous variable that is not formed from a complete economic model is, therefore, not necessarily a rational expectation. For many purposes it is sufficient to use conditional expectations that are based on a model of some sort, and not necessarily the 'true' model as required by rational expectations. This has the merit of skirting the thorny issue of the exacting information requirements of rational expectations. Our discussion will, therefore, focus on the more general concept of conditional expectations, though the terms rational expectations and conditional expectations will be used interchangeably when there is no likelihood of confusion. By definition, there is no economic model for exogenous variables, though there may be a stochastic generating process which can be used to form conditional expectations.

The expectation of x_t conditional on information available at date $t-1$ may be written $E(x_t \mid \boldsymbol{\Omega}_{t-1})$ or $E_{t-1} x_t$. If the information set contains only past values of x_t then the conditional expectation is sometimes said to be weakly rational. The expectational error, or innovation in x_t, $\epsilon_t = x_t - E_{t-1} x_t$ satisfies $E_{t-1} \epsilon_t = 0$, i.e. it is orthogonal to the information set, and implies that there is no information in it concerning ϵ_t. Technically, ϵ_t is a martingale difference sequence. More generally, the conditional expectations variable may be $E_{t-s} x_{t+i}$ $\{i \geqslant -s;\ s = 0, 1, 2, \ldots\}$.

Three methods are commonly used for the estimation of rational expectations models: the substitution method (SM), GMM of which the instrumental variables method (IV) and the errors in variables method are special cases, and FIML. First we examine the problem of estimating a single equation in which the expectation is of the current value of an exogenous variable. To illustrate, consider the equation

$$y_t = \alpha \mathrm{E}_{t-1} x_t + \beta z_t + e_t, \tag{39}$$

where e_t is i.i.d. $(0, \sigma^2)$ and z_t is exogenous and known at time $t-1$. The variable x_t is exogenous being generated by

$$x_t = \gamma' \mathbf{w}_{t-1} + \epsilon_t, \tag{40}$$

where $\mathbf{w}_{t-1}$ is a vector of variables forming the information set and $\mathrm{E}(\epsilon_t | \mathbf{w}_{t-1}) = 0$. The SM is a sequential procedure: first $\mathrm{E}_{t-1} x_t$ is replaced by $\hat{x}_t$, the prediction of x_t obtained from the regression of x_t on $\mathbf{w}_{t-1}$, then

$$y_t = \alpha \hat{x}_t + \beta z_t + e_t^*, \tag{41}$$

with $e_t^* = e_t - \alpha(\hat{x}_t - \mathrm{E}_{t-1} x_t) = e_t - \alpha(\epsilon_t - \hat{\epsilon}_t)$, is estimated by OLS to give consistent estimates of α and β.

In the IV method proposed by McCallum (1976) and Wickens (1982), and the GMM estimator proposed by Hansen (1982), $\mathrm{E}_{t-1} x_t$ is replaced by the realisation x_t and

$$y_t = \alpha x_t + \beta z_t + e_t^+, \tag{42}$$

where $e_t^+ = e_t - \alpha \epsilon_t$, is estimated consistently with $\mathbf{w}_{t-1}$ and z_t – if it is not already in $\mathbf{w}_{t-1}$ – as instruments. Interestingly, using the results established in Section III.2, if x_t is I(1) and ϵ_t is I(0) (the latter would be consistent with the notion of rationality), OLS applied to (42) gives a consistent estimate of α even if x_t and the error e_t^+ are correlated. In these circumstances (40) is irrelevant for getting a consistent estimator of α. FIML estimation involves the joint estimation of equations (40) and (42). If $\mathrm{E}(e_t \epsilon_t) \neq 0$ then GMM is asymptotically equivalent to FIML and hence is efficient, and if $\mathbf{w}_{t-1}$ contains z_t, SM and IV will be numerically identical. The relationship between the three estimators will be exactly equivalent to that between 2SLS, LIML and FIML: the two-step estimator SM is equivalent to 2SLS which is also an IV estimator; FIML reduces to LIML when the single structural equation is exactly identified; and 2SLS and LIML are asymptotically equivalent. If, however, $\mathrm{E}(e_t \epsilon_t) = 0$ then FIML will be more efficient because the IV estimator takes no account of this. There is another difference between the estimators relating to the estimation of the covariance matrix of the estimators. Due to the presence in e_t^* of the innovation in x_t, SM will produce a consistent estimator of var (e_t^*) but an inconsistent estimator of var (e_t). To correct for this it is necessary to use (42) to estimate e_t with the coefficients estimated by the SM estimator, (see Pagan, 1984*a* and Pesaran, 1987, p. 167). This problem arises in GMM estimation. These results can be extended readily to the case where the expectation is of a current endogenous variable, (see Wallis, 1980, Wickens, 1982 and Pesaran, 1987).

The estimation of models with future expected exogenous variables can be accomplished using the methods just described as it is usually possible to redefine the variable so that it is dated at time t. In contrast, there are many new problems when the expectations are of future endogenous variables. Such equations are often obtained as the first order conditions (or Euler equations) for intertemporal optimisation problems and they describe the transition path. Asset arbitrage equations often have this expectations structure. For example, consider the dynamic optimisation problem:

$$\max_{y_{t+s}} \mathrm{E}_t \sum_{s=0}^{\infty} (1+\alpha)^{-s}[(\Delta y_{t+s})^2 + \psi(y_{t+s} - y^*_{t+s})^2], \alpha, \psi > 0,$$

where y^*_t is the target. The Euler equation is the orthogonality condition for $s = 0, 1, 2, \ldots$.

$$\mathrm{E}_t\{[(1+\alpha)(1+\psi)+1]\, y_{t+s} - y_{t+s+1} - (1+\alpha)\, y_{t+s-1} - (1+\alpha)\,\psi y^*_{t+s}\} = 0, \quad (43)$$

which for $s = 0$ leads to the estimating equation

$$y_t = \lambda \mathrm{E}_t\, y_{t+1} + (1+\alpha)\,\lambda y_{t-1} + \psi\lambda y^*_t, \quad (44)$$

where $\lambda = [(1+\alpha)(1+\psi)+1]^{-1} < 1$.

A systematic treatment of single equation estimation of (44) may be found in Wickens (1986), see also Pesaran (1987). To illustrate the issues consider the estimation of

$$y_t = \lambda \mathrm{E}_t\, y_{t+1} + \beta x_t + e_t, \quad (45)$$

where e_t is i.i.d. $(0, \sigma^2)$, and

$$x_t = \sum_0^n \psi_i \epsilon_{t-i}, \psi_0 = 1 \quad (46)$$

is strongly exogenous with ϵ_t being i.i.d. $(0, \omega^2)$. It is assumed that with respect to the information set, (45) satisfies the orthogonality or conditional moment restriction

$$\mathrm{E}_t(y_t - \lambda y_{t+1} - \beta x_t - e_t) = 0. \quad (47)$$

For $|\lambda| < 1$ the solution is

$$y_t = \beta \sum_0^{\infty} \lambda^s \mathrm{E}_t\, x_{t+s} + e_t. \quad (48)$$

FIML can be implemented by substituting for $\mathrm{E}_t\, x_{t+s}$ in (48) using (46). This gives $\mathrm{E}_t\, x_{t+s} = \sum_s^n \psi_i \epsilon_{t+s-i}$ and hence

$$y_t = \beta \sum_0^n \phi_i \epsilon_{t-i} + e_t, \quad (49)$$

where $\phi_i = \sum_s^n \lambda^{s-i}\psi_i$. Equations (46) and (49) are estimated jointly with the cross equation restrictions imposed, e.g. see Sargent (1978).

In using GMM $\mathrm{E}_t\, y_{t+1}$ is replaced in (45) by $y_{t+1} - \xi_{t+1}$ where, from (49), $\xi_{t+1} = y_{t+1} - \mathrm{E}_t\, y_{t+1} = \beta\phi_0 \epsilon_{t+1} + e_{t+1}$. This gives the estimating equation

$$y_t = \lambda y_{t+1} + \beta x_t + u_t, \quad (50)$$

with $u_t = e_t - \lambda\xi_{t+1} = e_t - \lambda e_{t+1} - \lambda\beta\phi_0 \epsilon_{t+1}$, which can also be written as $u_t = v_t - \delta v_{t+1}$, i.e. a leading, instead of the usual lagged, MA(1). Because y_{t+1} is correlated with u_t instrumental variables are required for y_{t+1}. There are many potential candidates, including current and lagged values of x_t and lagged values of y_t. Taking into account that u_t is a leading MA(1), the 2S2SLS estimator of Cumby *et al.* (1983) is the appropriate GMM estimator to use.

Restricting attention to a finite number of instruments results in an efficiency loss, since the number of candidates as instruments is infinite. Hansen *et al.* (1988) characterise the variance of the most efficient GMM estimator in this context. Hansen and Singleton (1988) take the potential instruments as $(y_{t-j-1}, x_{t-j})_{j=1}^{\tau}$ and show that, as $\tau \to \infty$, the GMM estimator attains this bound. In their examples convergence was achieved for τ around 4. One important point to note is that one *cannot purge the equation of the MA term*, a feature emphasised by many authors, notably Hansen and Hodrick (1980). Attempts to do so by 'GLS-type' transformations will generally lead to inconsistent estimators of λ and β. These results can be readily generalised to models that have different expectations and dynamic structures. Thus the model might have lags in y_t, terms like $E_t y_{t+s}$ or $E_{t-1} y_{t+s}$, or expectations in x_t. For details see Wickens (1986) and Pesaran (1987).

A few additional remarks should be made. First, if x_t is generated by an AR process instead of an MA then lack of identifiability is a possibility. For example, if $x_t = \psi x_{t-1} + \epsilon_t$ then $E_t x_{t+s} = \psi^s x_t$ and the solution to (45) is $y_t = [\beta/(1-\lambda\psi)]\, x_t + e_t$. Thus λ and β are not identified. In general, if x_t is generated by an AR(p) and the greatest lag in x_t in the model is q, then a necessary condition for identification is $p > q+1$. Broze *et al.* (1985) and Pesaran (1987) provide further discussion of identification. Second, if x_t is an AR(1), the condition for the existence of a solution of y_t is that $|\lambda\psi| < 1$. This is satisfied if x_t has a unit root, and may also be met even if x_t is explosive. Third, if $|\lambda| > 1$ in (45) then, although a solution exists, it is not unique. Usually this problem does not arise if the model is derived from a well defined optimisation problem as in (44), see also Wickens (1986).

A test of the orthogonality condition – of which (43) is an example – is also a test for rationality, and has been used as a test for asset market efficiency, see Baillie (1989), Mattey and Meese (1986) and Campbell (1987). A general discussion of such tests was made earlier in Section II.1 in the context of GMM estimation. To illustrate, we shall now examine the issue in more detail for the commonly tested hypothesis $E_t(y_t - x_{t+1}) = 0$. Clearly the simplest test involves regressing $y_t - x_{t+1}$ on a set of variables dated time t which are thought to be in the information set and then carrying out a test for the significance of any one variable. Rejection for one variable is sufficient to reject rationality, see Mishkin (1983). The potential weakness of this test is that it lacks power. More precise estimates of the coefficients of the variables in the information set can be obtained by modelling the time series process generating y_t and x_t. Suppose that y_t and x_t are I(0) and that $\mathbf{z}_t = (y_t, x_t)'$ is generated by the VAR(1)

$$\mathbf{z}_t = \mathbf{A}\mathbf{z}_{t-1} + \mathbf{e}_t, \tag{51}$$

allowing the hypothesis to be expressed in terms of the coefficients of the VAR. Thus $E_t(y_t - x_{t+1}) = E_t(\mathbf{h}_1' - \mathbf{h}_2'\mathbf{A})\,\mathbf{z}_t = \mathbf{0}'$ where $\mathbf{h}_1' = (1, 0)$ and $\mathbf{h}_2' = (0, 1)$. Consequently, the hypothesis can be written $\mathbf{h}_1' - \mathbf{h}_2'\mathbf{A} = (1 - a_{21}, -a_{22}) = \mathbf{0}$. It can be tested using a Wald test of $a_{21} = 1$ and $a_{22} = 0$, implying that the generating process for x_t is $x_{t+1} = y_t + e_{2t}$. If, however, y_t and x_t are both I(1) then we would check whether or not they are cointegrated. If not then the hypothesis can be rejected immediately. Suppose they are cointegrated and that $\mathbf{w}_t = (y_t - x_t, \Delta x_t) = \mathbf{C}\mathbf{z}_t + \mathbf{D}\mathbf{z}_{t-1}$ with $\mathbf{C} = \left[\begin{smallmatrix} 1 & -1 \\ 0 & 1 \end{smallmatrix}\right]$ and $\mathbf{D} = \left[\begin{smallmatrix} 0 & 0 \\ 0 & -1 \end{smallmatrix}\right]$, is generated by the VAR(1), $\mathbf{w}_t = \mathbf{A}\mathbf{w}_{t-1} + \mathbf{e}_t$. Then the hypothesis becomes $\mathrm{E}_t(y_t - x_{t+1}) = \mathrm{E}_t[(1-a_{21})\,y_t + (1+a_{22}-a_{12})\,x_t - a_{22}\,x_{t-1}] = 0$. Again we can use a Wald test of $a_{21} = 1$ and $a_{22} = 0$, implying now that $\Delta x_t = y_{t-1} - x_{t-1} + e_{2t}$. When y_t and x_t have drift terms an intercept should be included in the VAR.

If the hypothesis were $\mathrm{E}_t(y_t - \lambda x_{t+1}) = 0$ and y_t and x_t are I(0), the VAR in $\mathbf{z}_t$ could be used once more. The null hypothesis becomes $\mathrm{E}_t(y_t - \lambda x_{t+1}) = \mathrm{E}_t(\mathbf{h}_1' - \lambda \mathbf{h}_2' \mathbf{A})\,\mathbf{z}_t = \mathbf{0}$, or $\mathbf{h}_1' - \lambda \mathbf{h}_2' \mathbf{A} = (1 - \lambda a_{21}, -a_{22}) = \mathbf{0}$. The problem now is that as λ is unknown and the first restriction cannot be used to carry out the test – it is required to estimate λ ($\hat{\lambda} = 1/a_{21}$); we are therefore reduced to a t test of $a_{22} = 0$. When y_t and x_t are I(1) we define $\mathbf{w}_t = (y_t - \hat{\lambda} x_t, \Delta x_t)$, where $\hat{\lambda}$ is a consistent estimator of λ which can be obtained from the cointegrating regression of y_t on x_t, and this makes $\mathbf{C} = \left[\begin{smallmatrix} 1 & -\hat{\lambda} \\ 0 & 1 \end{smallmatrix}\right]$. The outcome is a Wald test of $\hat{\lambda} a_{21} = 1$ and $a_{22} = 0$. A more detailed discussion of many of these issues may be found in Baillie (1989) and Campbell (1987).

V.5.2. *Expectations about the variance*

In (10) it is not always the parameters $\boldsymbol{\beta}$ that are of interest. Sometimes, the description of a relationship between the conditional variance of u_t, σ_t^2, and the past history of variables such as y_t and $\mathbf{x}_t$ may be of greater concern. Nowhere is this more evident than in financial econometrics, where σ_t^2 is commonly regarded as a major determinant of the risk premium. Some optimising models would also have agents' decisions determined as a function of the degree of uncertainty about variables such as inflation or exchange rates, and the variance of the latter, conditional on information available to the agents, may proxy the uncertainty. Pagan and Ullah (1988) and Pesaran (1987) mention a number of ways such models can arise. Consequently, it is not surprising that there has been substantial research into parametric models for σ_t^2, and these have been extensively applied to financial data.

The leading parametric specification is Engle's (1982) ARCH model, mentioned earlier in Section II.1. This sets

$$\sigma_t^2 = \alpha_0 + \sum_{j=1}^{q} \alpha_j u_{t-j}^2 \tag{52}$$

and, as described in Section II.1, the parameters α_j ($j = 0, \ldots, q$) can be estimated by maximum likelihood. Alternatively, a GMM estimator could be constructed by exploiting the orthogonality conditions $\mathrm{E}[(\partial\sigma_t^2/\partial\alpha_j)\,(u_t^2 - \sigma_t^2)] = 0$, $j = 0, \ldots, q$ (along with $\mathrm{E}(\mathbf{x}_t' \mathbf{u}_t) = 0$ for $\boldsymbol{\beta}$). It is important to realise that the conditional variance σ_t^2 is a random variable, while the unconditional variance $\mathrm{E}(\sigma_t^2)$ is a constant $\alpha_0/(1 - \sum_{j=1}^{q} \alpha_j)$. Large shocks will cause the conditional variance to exceed the unconditional variance. If u_t is conditionally normal then the fourth unconditional moment of u_t will exceed three times the second moment squared, implying that the marginal density of u_t has fatter tails than the normal. This is a common finding with asset price data.

Most work in this area has been concerned not with estimation but specification. By and large this has meant extensions of the ARCH model to give a better representation of the data. Bollerslev (1986) proposed the Generalised ARCH (GARCH) model by adding lagged values of σ_t^2 to (52); a GARCH(p, q) model was then defined as

$$\sigma_t^2 = \alpha_0 + \sum_{j=1}^{p} \beta_j \sigma_{t-j}^2 + \sum_{j=1}^{q} \alpha_j u_{t-j}^2. \tag{53}$$

Engle and Bollerslev (1986) extended this to the class of integrated GARCH (IGARCH) models by requiring that $\sum \beta_j + \sum \alpha_j = 1$. There are some problems with this identification. Writing $u_{t-1} = \sigma_{t-1} \epsilon_{t-1}$, where ϵ_{t-1} is N(0, 1), and putting $q = 1$ for expository purposes, (53) implies $\sigma_t^2 = \alpha_0 + (\beta_1 + \alpha_1)\sigma_{t-1}^2 + \alpha_1 \epsilon_{t-1}^2$, which shows that shocks to ϵ_{t-1}^2 are persistent in σ_t^2. Consequently it possesses one of the characteristics of an integrated process. It does not however possess others. Nelson (1988*b*) shows that σ_t^2 will either be a strictly stationary process (if $\alpha_0 \neq 0$) or degenerate (if $\alpha_0 = 0$), which could never be true for x_t in (6) when $\alpha = 1$. It is important to distinguish the IGARCH process from Hansen's (1988) suggestion, discussed in Section I.2.2, that u_t be modelled as the product of an I(1) and an I(0) process; shocks to σ_t^2 in this context are persistent and the process is not stationary.

As mentioned in the introduction to this section the biggest use of parametric models for σ_t^2 has been in the modelling of risk. Engle *et al.* (1987) added $\delta \sigma_t^2$ to (1) and identified σ_t^2 with an ARCH process to get their ARCH in mean (ARCH-M) model. Many extensions of this idea to GARCH etc. and to handle systems of equations have been made, most of which are reviewed in Diebold and Nerlove (1989). Nevertheless, there are some special features of certain data sets that demand a departure from the ARCH format for σ_t^2, for example it is well known that stock price volatility is greater when shocks are negative than when they are positive. This led Nelson (1988*a*) to introduce the exponential GARCH model in which $\log \sigma_t^2$ is related to $\log \sigma_{t-j}^2$, u_{t-j} and $|u_{t-j}|$. Pagan and Hong (1990) tackle the same issue by adopting non-parametric methods.

VI. CONCLUSION

Surveys are meant to be read rather than summarised, and that maxim has special force when it comes to an area such as econometrics. Gone are the days when a single individual could have a detailed knowledge of all divisions of the subject. Just twenty years ago this might have been possible. Then a good knowledge of linear algebra, multivariate statistics and time series methods was a sufficient foundation for absorbing the standard econometrics texts of the time and for performing routine applied work. But the years since then have witnessed a fragmentation of econometrics. The biggest division has been between micro and macro econometrics. To do 'state of the art' applied work in the former now demands a strong knowledge of maximum likelihood estimation and, lately, non-parametric estimation methods. For the latter, an appreciation of method of moments estimation, problems of statistical theory when regressors are trending, and the construction of dynamic models are all necessary items of knowledge for any applied researcher. Our paper has tried to give a sampling of themes from both of these literatures. Space constraints have meant that a summary of either field is impossible, and we have therefore opted to try to explain what we believe are the more important developments. Sometimes, our explanations may turn out to be too simplified, in other cases they may be too abbreviated. Consultation of the original articles is recommended therefore, the more so as the qualifications spelt out in those sources should be clearly understood by users of the methods. Despite this we hope that our description of available methods for doing 'state of the art' data analysis will encourage applied workers to use these methods on their particular problems and to record which procedures turn out to be useful and which do not.

We have addressed this survey mainly to applied workers but we hope that there is much in it that will be of interest to econometricians, and especially to graduate students seeking to learn econometrics. As the subject grows in complexity and diversity it becomes increasingly difficult even for the specialist econometrician to keep abreast of new developments. There is therefore the danger that new results designed to deal with one problem will be overlooked by those working on another problem; cross fertilisation is a powerful source of new ideas. It will be evident from this survey that there are enough unresolved problems to keep generations of econometricians busy for the foreseeable future. We hope that in selecting which of these to work on the needs of the applied worker will be kept in mind.

References

Amemiya, T. (1984). 'Tobit models: a survey.' *Journal of Econometrics*, vol. 24, pp. 3–61.

—— (1985). *Advanced Econometrics*. Cambridge, Mass: Harvard University Press.

Andrews, D. (1988*a*). 'Asymptotic normality of series estimators for various nonparametric and semiparametric models.' *Cowles Foundation Discussion Paper* No. 874, Yale University.

—— (1988*b*). 'Heteroskedasticity and autocorrelation consistent covariance matrix estimation,' Discussion Paper No. 877. *Cowles Foundation for Economic Research*, Yale University.

Baillie, R. T. (1989). 'Econometric tests of rationality and market efficiency.' *Econometric Reviews*, vol. 8, pp. 151–86.

Banerjee, A., Dolado, J., Hendry, D. F. and Smith, G. W. (1986). 'Exploring equilibrium relationships in econometrics through static models: some Monte Carlo evidence.' *Oxford Economic Papers*, vol. 48, pp. 253–77.

Bera, A. K., Jarque, C. M. and Lee, L. F. (1984). 'Testing the normality assumption in limited dependent variable models.' *International Economic Review*, vol. 25, pp. 563–78.

Beran, R. (1977). 'Adaptive estimates for autoregressive processes.' *Annals of the Institute of Statistical Mathematics*, vol. 28, pp. 77–89.

Berenblut, I. I. and Webb, G. I. (1973). 'A new test for autocorrelated errors in the linear regression model.' *Journal of the Royal Statistical Society Series B*, vol. 35, pp. 33–50.

Berger, J. O. and Selke, T. (1987). 'Testing a point null hypothesis: the irreconcilability of p values and evidence.' *Journal of the American Statistical Association*, vol. 82, pp. 113–39.

Beveridge, S. and Nelson, C. R. (1981). 'A new approach to decomposition of economic time series into permanent and transitory components with particular attention to measurement of the business cycle.' *Journal of Monetary Economics*, vol. 7, pp. 151–74.

Bewley, R. A. (1979). 'The direct estimation of the equilibrium response in a linear dynamic model.' *Economics Letters*, vol. 3, pp. 357–62.

—— and Theil, H. (1987). 'Monte Carlo testing for heteroskedasticity in equation systems.' In *Advances in Econometrics*, vol. 6 (ed. T. B. Fomby and G. F. Rhodes). Greenwich: JAI Press, pp. 1–15.

Bhagava, A. (1986). 'On the theory of testing for unit roots in observed time series.' *Review of Economic Studies*, vol. 53, pp. 369–84.

Bickel, P. J. (1978). 'Using residuals robustly I: tests for heteroscedasticity and nonlinearity.' *Annals of Statistics*, vol. 6, pp. 266–91.

Bierens, H. (1987). 'Kernel estimators of regression functions.' Ch. 3 in *Advances in Econometrics, Fifth World Congress*, vol. 1 (ed. T. Bewley), pp. 99–144.

Bollerslev, T. P. (1986). 'Generalized autoregressive conditional heteroscedasticity.' *Journal of Econometrics*, vol. 31, pp. 307–27.

Breusch, T. S. and Pagan, A. R. (1979). 'A simple test for heteroscedasticity and random coefficient variation.' *Econometrica*, vol. 47, pp. 1287–94.

—— and Schmidt, P. (1988). 'Alternative forms of the Wald statistic: how long is a piece of string?' *Communications in Statistics*, vol. 17, pp. 2789–95.

Brock, W. A., Dechert, W. D. and Scheinkman, J. A. (1987). 'A test for independence based on the correlation dimension.' *SSRI Working Paper* No. 8702, University of Wisconsin.

—— and Sayers, C. L. (1987). 'Is the business cycle characterized by deterministic chaos?' *Working Paper* No. 87-15, University of North Carolina, Chapel Hill.

Brown, B. W. and Mariano, R. S. (1984). 'Residual-based stochastic prediction and estimation in a nonlinear simultaneous system.' *Econometrica*, vol. 52, pp. 321–43.

Broze, L., Gourieroux, C. and Szarfaz, A. (1985). 'Solutions of linear rational expectations models.' *Econometric Theory*, vol. 1, pp. 341–68.

Campbell, J. Y. (1987). 'Does saving anticipate declining labor income? An alternative test of the permanent income hypothesis.' *Econometrica*, vol. 55, pp. 1249–73.

—— and Mankiw, N. C. (1987). 'Are output fluctuations transitory.' *Quarterly Journal of Economics*, vol. 102, pp. 857–80.

Campbell, J. and Shiller, R. (1987). 'Cointegration and tests of present value models.' *Journal of Political Economy*, vol. 95, pp. 1062–88.

Chamberlain, G. (1986). 'Asymptotic efficiency in semiparametric models with censoring.' *Journal of Econometrics*, vol. 32, pp. 189–218.

—— (1987). 'Asymptotic efficiency in estimation with conditional moment restrictions.' *Journal of Econometrics*, vol. 34, pp. 305–34.

Chesher, A. and Spady, R. (1988). 'Asymptotic expansions of the information matrix test statistic' (mimeo, Bristol University).

Chow, G. C. (1983). *Econometrics*. New York: McGraw-Hill.

Christiano, L. (1988). 'Searching for a break in GNP.' *Working Paper* No. 416, *Federal Reserve Bank of Minneapolis*.

—— and Eichenbaum, M. (1988). 'Is theory ahead of measurement? Current real business cycle theories and aggregate labor market fluctuations' (mimeo, Northwestern University).

—— and —— (1989). 'Unit roots in real GNP – Do we know and do we care?' (paper presented to Carnegie–Rochester Conference, April).

Cleveland, W. P. and Tiao, G. C. (1976). 'Decomposition of seasonal time series: a model for the census X-11 program.' *Journal of the American Statistical Association*, vol. 71, pp. 581–7.

Cochrane, J. H. (1988). 'How big is the random walk in GNP?' *Journal of Political Economy*, vol. 96, pp. 893–920.

Cooley, T. F. and LeRoy, S. F. (1986). 'Atheoretical macroeconomics: a critique.' *Journal of Monetary Economics*, vol. 16, pp. 283–308.

Coslett, S. (1983). 'Distribution-free maximum likelihood estimator of the binary choice model.' *Econometrica*, vol. 51, pp. 765–82.

—— (1987). 'Efficiency bounds for distribution-free estimators of the binary choice and censored regression models.' *Econometrica*, vol. 55, pp. 559–85.

Cox, D. R. (1961). 'Tests of separate families of hypotheses.' *Proceedings of the Fourth Berkeley Symposium on Mathematical Statistics and Probability*, vol. 1, pp. 105–23.

—— (1962). 'Further results on tests of separate families of hypotheses.' *Journal of the Royal Statistical Society*, Series B, vol. 24, pp. 406–24.

—— and Snell, E. J. (1968). 'A general definition of residuals.' *Journal of the Royal Statistical Society*, Series B, vol. 39, pp. 248–75.

Cumby, R. E., Huizinga, J. and Obstfeld, M. (1983). 'Two-step, two-stage least squares estimation in models with rational expectations.' *Journal of Econometrics*, vol. 21, pp. 333–55.

Dagenais, M. G. and Dufour, J. M. (1986). 'Invariance, nonlinear models and asymptotic tests.' *Discussion Paper* No. 3287, C.R.D.E., University of Montreal.

Dastoor, N. K. and Fisher, G. (1988). 'Point optimal Cox tests.' *Econometric Theory*, vol. 4, pp. 86–107.

Davidson, J. E. H., Hendry, D. F., Srba, F. and Yeo, J. S. (1978). 'Econometric modelling of the aggregate time series relationships between consumers expenditure and income in the United Kingdom.' ECONOMIC JOURNAL, vol. 88, pp. 661–92.

Davidson, R. and MacKinnon, J. G. (1981). 'Several tests for model specification in the presence of alternative hypotheses.' *Econometrica*, vol. 49, pp. 781–93.

—— and —— (1983). 'Small sample properties of alternative forms of the Lagrange multiplier test.' *Economics Letters*, vol. 12, pp. 269–75.

Deaton, A. S. (1987). 'Life cycle models of consumption: is the evidence consistent with the theory?' In *Advances in Econometrics, Fifth World Congress*, Vol. 2 (ed. T. F. Bewley). Cambridge: Cambridge University Press.

—— (1989). 'Rice prices and income distribution in Thailand: a non-parametric analysis.' ECONOMIC JOURNAL, vol. 99, pp. 1–37.

Dhrymes, P. (1971). *Distributed Lags: Problems of Estimation and Formulation*. San Francisco: Holden-Day.

Diaconis, P. and Freedman, D. (1986). 'On the consistency of Bayes estimates.' *Annals of Statistics*, vol. 14, pp. 1–26.

Dickey, D. A. (1976). 'Estimation and testing of nonstationary time series models.' Unpublished doctoral dissertation, Iowa State University.

—— and Fuller, W. A. (1979). 'Distribution of the estimators for autoregressive time series with a unit root.' *Journal of the American Statistical Association*, vol. 74, pp. 427–31.

—— and —— (1981). 'Likelihood ratio tests for autoregressive time series with a unit root.' *Econometrica*, vol. 49, pp. 1057–72.

Diebold, F. X. and Nerlove, M. (1988). 'Unit roots in economic time series: a selective survey.' In *Advances in Econometrics: Co-integration, Spurious Regressions and Unit Roots* (eds T. B. Fomby and G. F. Rhodes). Greenwich: JAI Press.

—— and —— (1989). 'The dynamics of exchange rate volatility: a multivariate latent-factor ARCH model.' *Journal of Applied Econometrics*, vol. 4, pp. 1–22.

Domowitz, I. and Muus, L. (1988). 'Likelihood inference in the nonlinear regression model with explosive linear dynamics.' In *Dynamic Econometric Modeling* (eds. W. A. Barnett, E. R. Berndt and H. White). Cambridge: Cambridge University Press.

—— and White, H. (1982). 'Mis-specified models with dependent observations.' *Journal of Econometrics*, vol. 20, pp. 35–50.

Duncan, G. M. (1986). 'A semi-parametric censored regression estimator.' *Journal of Econometrics*, vol. 31, pp. 5–34.

Durbin, J. (1970). 'Testing for serial correlation in least squares regression when some of the regressors are lagged dependent variables.' *Econometrica*, vol. 38, pp. 410–21.

—— and Watson, G. S. (1971). 'Testing for serial correlation in least squares regression, III.' *Biometrika*, vol. 58, pp. 1–19.

Durlauf, S. N. and Phillips, P. C. B. (1988). 'Trends versus random walks in time series analysis.' *Econometrica*, vol. 56, pp. 1333–54.

Edison, H. J. and Klovland, J. T. (1987). 'A quantitative re-assessment of the purchasing power parity hypothesis: evidence from Norway and the United Kingdom.' *Journal of Applied Econometrics*, vol. 2, pp. 309–33.

Effron, B. (1982). *The Jacknife, the Bootstrap and Other Re-sampling Plans*. Society for Industrial and Applied Mathematics, Philadelphia.

Eichenbaum, M. S., Hansen, L. P. and Singleton, K. J. (1988). 'A time series analysis of representative agent models of consumption and leisure choice under uncertainty.' *Quarterly Journal of Economics*, vol. 103, pp. 51–78.

Engle, R. F. (1982). 'Autoregressive conditional heteroscedasticity with estimates of the variance of United Kingdom inflation.' *Econometrica*, vol. 50, pp. 987–1007.

—— and Bollerslev, T. (1986). 'Modeling the persistence of conditional variances.' *Econometric Reviews*, vol. 5, pp. 1–50.

—— and Granger, C. W. J. (1987). 'Co-integration and error correction: representation, estimation and testing.' *Econometrica*, vol. 55, pp. 251–76.

——, ——, Rice, J. and Weiss, A. (1986). 'Semi-parametric estimates of the relation between weather and electricity sales.' *Journal of the American Statistical Association*, vol. 81, pp. 310–9.

——, Hendry, D. F. and Richard, J. F. (1983). 'Exogeneity.' *Econometrica*, vol. 51, pp. 277–304.

——, Lillien, D. M. and Robins, R. P. (1987). 'Estimating time varying risk premia in the term structure: the ARCH-M model.' *Econometrica*, vol. 55, pp. 391–407.

—— and Watson, M. (1981). 'A one factor multivariate time series model of metropolitan wage rates.' *Journal of the American Statistical Association*, vol. 76, pp. 774–81.

—— and Yoo, B. S. (1987). 'Forecasting and testing in co-integrated systems.' *Journal of Econometrics*, vol. 35, pp. 143–59.

Evans, G. B. A. and Savin, N. E. (1981). 'Testing for unit roots I.' *Econometrica*, vol. 49, pp. 753–79.
—— and —— (1984). 'Testing for unit roots II.' *Econometrica*, vol. 52, pp. 1241–70.
Evans, M. and King, M. L. (1985). 'A point optimal test for heteroskedastic disturbances.' *Journal of Econometrics*, vol. 27, pp. 163–78.
Fernandez, L. (1986). 'Non-parametric maximum likelihood estimation of censored regression models.' *Journal of Econometrics*, vol. 32, pp. 35–57.
Fisher, G. R. and McAleer, M. (1981). 'Alternative procedures and associated tests of significance for non-nested hypotheses.' *Journal of Econometrics*, vol. 16, pp. 103–19.
Fuller, W. A. (1976). *Introduction to Statistical Time Series*. New York: John Wiley.
Gallant, A. R. (1981). 'On the bias in flexible functional forms and an essentially unbiased form: the Fourier flexible form.' *Journal of Econometrics*, vol. 15, pp. 211–44.
—— (1982). 'Unbiased determination of production technologies.' *Journal of Econometrics*, vol. 20, pp. 285–323.
—— and Golub, G. H. (1984). 'Imposing curvature restrictions on flexible functional forms.' *Journal of Econometrics*, vol. 26, pp. 295–321.
——, Hsieh, D. and Tauchen, G. (1988). 'On fitting a recalcitrant series: the pound/dollar exchange rate, 1974–83.' In *Non-parametric and Semiparametric Methods in Econometrics and Statistics* (eds. W. Barnett, J. Powell and G. Tauchen). Cambridge: Cambridge University Press.
—— and Nychka, D. W. (1987). 'Semi-nonparametric maximum likelihood estimation.' *Econometrica*, vol. 55, pp. 363–90.
—— and Tauchen, G. (1989). 'Semi-nonparametric estimation of conditionally constrained heterogeneous processes: asset pricing applications.' *Econometrica*, vol. 57, pp. 1091–120.
Gasser, T. and Muller, H. G. (1984). 'Estimating regression functions and their derivatives by the kernel method.' *Scandinavian Journal of Statistics*, vol. 11, pp. 171–85.
Geweke, J. (1984). 'Inference and causality in economic time series models.' In *Handbook of Econometrics*, vol. 2 (ed. Z. Griliches and M. D. Intriligator). Amsterdam: North-Holland.
—— (1986). 'Exact inference in the inequality constrained normal linear regression model.' *Journal of Applied Econometrics*, vol. 1, pp. 127–41.
—— and Porter-Hudak, S. (1983). 'The estimation and application of long memory time series models.' *Journal of Time Series Analysis*, vol. 4, pp. 221–38.
Ghysels, E. and Karangwa, E. (1988). '"Nominal" versus "real" seasonal adjustment.' *Discussion Paper* No. 2188, C.R.D.E., University of Montreal.
Godfrey, L. G. (1978). 'Testing for multiplicative heteroscedasticity.' *Journal of Econometrics*, vol. 8, pp. 227–36.
—— (1984). 'On the uses of misspecification checks and tests of non-nested hypotheses in empirical econometrics.' ECONOMIC JOURNAL, vol. 94, pp. 69–81.
—— (1988). *Misspecification Tests in Econometrics*. Cambridge: Cambridge University Press.
Goldberger, A. S. (1964). *Econometric Theory*. New York: John Wiley.
Gordon, R. J. and King, S. R. (1982). 'The output costs of disinflation in traditional and vector autoregressive models.' *Brookings Papers in Economic Activity*, vol. 16, pp. 205–42.
Gourieroux, C., Monfort, A. and Trognon, A. (1984). 'Pseudo maximum likelihood methods: theory.' *Econometrica*, vol. 42, pp. 681–700.
—— and —— (1987). 'Regression and non-stationarity.' *INSEE Document de Travail* No. 8708.
Granger, C. W. J. (1981). 'Some properties of time series data and their use in econometric model specification.' *Journal of Econometrics*, vol. 16, pp. 121–30.
—— (1983). 'Co-integrated variables and error correcting models.' *Working Paper* No. 83-13, University of California at San Diego.
—— and Joyeux, R. (1980). 'An introduction to long memory time series models and fractional differencing.' *Journal of Time Series Analysis*, vol. 1, pp. 15–39.
—— and Newbold, P. (1974). 'Spurious regressions in econometrics.' *Journal of Econometrics*, vol. 2, pp. 111–20.
Gregory, A. W. and Veall, M. R. (1985). 'Formulating Wald tests of nonlinear restrictions.' *Econometrica*, vol. 53, pp. 1465–8.
Grether, D. and Nerlove, M. (1970). 'Some properties of "optimal" seasonal adjustment.' *Econometrica*, vol. 38, pp. 682–704.
Griliches, Z. (1967). 'Distributed lags: a survey.' *Econometrica*, vol. 35, pp. 16–49.
—— (1986). 'Economic data issues.' In *Handbook of Econometrics*, vol. 3 (ed. Z. Griliches and M. D. Intriligator). Amsterdam: North-Holland.
Haavelmo, T. (1944). 'The probability approach in econometrics.' *Econometrica*, vol. 12, pp. 1–118.
Haache, G. (1974). 'The demand for money in the United Kingdom: experience since 1971.' *Bank of England Quarterly Bulletin*, vol. 14, pp. 284–305.
Hajivassiliou, V. and McFadden, D. (1988). 'The debt repayment crises of LDC's: estimation by the method of simulated moments.' Mimeo, Yale University.

Hall, A. (1987). 'The information matrix test for the linear model.' *Review of Economic Studies*, vol. 54, pp. 257–63.
—— (1989). 'Testing for unit roots in the presence of moving average errors.' *Biometrika*, vol. 76, pp. 49–56.
Hall, P. (1988). 'Theoretical comparison of bootstrap confidence intervals (with Discussion).' *Annals of Statistics*, vol. 16, pp. 927–85.
—— and Horowitz, J. L. (1988). 'Bandwidth selection in semiparametric estimation of censored linear regression models.' *Working Paper* No. 88-18, University of Iowa.
Hamilton, J. (1987). 'A new approach to the economic analysis of nonstationary time series and the business cycle.' *Econometrica* (forthcoming).
—— (1989). 'Analysis of time series subject to changes in regime.' Paper presented to NBER Conference on New Empirical Methods in Finance, March.
Hansen, B. E. (1988). 'A model of heteroskedastic cointegration.' Mimeo, Yale University.
—— and Phillips, P. C. B. (1988). 'Estimation and inference in models of cointegration: a simulation study.' *Cowles Foundation Discussion Paper* No. 881, Yale University.
Hansen, L. P. (1982). 'Large sample properties of generalized method of moments estimators.' *Econometrica*, vol. 50, pp. 1029–54.
——, Heaton, J. C. and Ogaki, M. (1988). 'Efficiency bounds implied by multiperiod conditional moment restrictions.' *Journal of the American Statistical Association*, vol. 83, pp. 863–71.
—— and Hodrick, R. J. (1980). 'Forward exchange rates as optimal predictors of future spot rates: an econometric investigation.' *Journal of Political Economy*, vol. 88, pp. 829–53.
—— and Singleton, K. J. (1988). 'Efficient estimation of asset pricing models with moving average errors' (mimeo).
Harris, P. (1985). 'An asymptotic expansion for the null distribution of the efficient score statistic.' *Biometrika*, vol. 72, pp. 653–9.
Harvey, A. C. and Pierse, R. G. (1984). 'Estimating missing observations in economic time series.' *Journal of the American Statistical Association*, vol. 79, pp. 125–31.
—— and Todd, P. H. J. (1983). 'Forecasting economic time series with structural and Box-Jenkins models: a case study.' *Journal of Business and Economic Statistics*, vol. 1, pp. 299–307.
Haubrich, J. G. and Lo, A. W. (1988). 'The sources and nature of long-term memory in the business cycle.' Mimeo, University of Pennsylvania.
Hausman, J. J. (1978). 'Specification tests in econometrics.' *Econometrica*, vol. 46, pp. 1251–72.
Hayashi, F. and Sims, C. A. (1983). 'Nearly efficient estimation of time series models with predetermined, but not exogenous instruments.' *Econometrica*, vol. 51, pp. 783–98.
Heckman, J. J. (1979). 'Sample selection bias as a specification error.' *Econometrica*, vol. 47, pp. 153–61.
—— and Hotz, V. J. (1987). 'Choosing among alternative nonexperimental methods for estimating the impact of social programs: the case of manpower training.' Mimeo, University of Chicago.
Hendry, D. F. (1976). 'The structure of simultaneous equations estimators.' *Journal of Econometrics*, vol. 4, pp. 51–88.
—— (1988). 'Testing the Lucas critique.' Mimeo, Nuffield College, University of Oxford.
—— and Mizon, G. M. (1978). 'Serial correlation as a convenient simplification not a nuisance: a comment on a study of the demand for money by the Bank of England.' ECONOMIC JOURNAL, vol. 88, pp. 549–63.
—— and —— (1987). 'Procrustean econometrics.' Mimeo, University of Southampton.
——, Pagan, A. R. and Sargan, J. D. (1984). 'Dynamic specification.' In *Handbook of Econometrics*, vol. 3 (ed. Z. Griliches and M. Intriligator), pp. 1689–763. Amsterdam: North-Holland.
—— and Richard J. F. (1983). 'The econometric analysis of economic time series.' *International Statistical Review*, vol. 51, pp. 111–63.
—— and —— (1987). 'Recent developments in the theory of encompassing' (mimeo). In *Contributions to Operations Research and Econometrics: The XXth Anniversary of CORE* (ed. B. Cornet and H. Tulkens). Cambridge, Mass: MIT Press.
Hodrick, R. and Prescott, E. (1980). 'Post-war U.S. business cycles: an empirical investigation.' Mimeo, Carnegie–Mellon University.
Hoffman, D. and Rasche, R. (1989). 'Long run income and interest elasticities of money demand in the United States.' Mimeo, Arizona State University.
Honda, Y. (1988). 'A size correction to the Lagrange multiplier test for heteroskedasticity.' *Journal of Econometrics*, vol. 38, pp. 375–86.
Horowitz, J. L. (1986). 'A distribution-free least squares estimator for censored linear regression models.' *Journal of Econometrics*, vol. 32, pp. 59–84.
—— (1988). 'Semiparametric M estimation of censored linear regression models.' In *Advances in Econometrics: Nonparametric and Robust Inference*, vol. 7 (ed. T. B. Fomby and G. F. Rhodes). Greenwich: JAI Press.
—— and McAleer, M. (1988). 'A simple method for testing a general parametric model against a non-nested alternative.' Mimeo, University of Iowa.
—— and Neumann, G. R. (1987). 'Semiparametric estimation of employment duration models.' *Econometric Reviews*, vol. 6, pp. 5–40.

Huber, P. J. (1964). 'Robust estimates of a location parameter.' *Annals of Mathematical Statistics*, vol. 35, pp. 73–101.

—— (1967). 'The behavior of maximum likelihood estimates under nonstandard conditions.' *Proceedings of the 5th Berkeley Symposium*, vol. 1, pp. 221–33, University of California Press.

—— (1981). *Robust Statistics*. New York: John Wiley.

Hylleberg, S. and Mizon, G. M. (1989). 'A note on the distribution of the least squares estimator of a random walk with drift.' *Economics Letters* (forthcoming).

Ichimura, H. (1987). 'Consistent estimation of index model coefficients.' Mimeo, M.I.T.

Imhof, P. I. (1961). 'Computing the distribution of quadratic forms in normal variables.' *Biometrika*, vol. 48, pp. 419–26.

Jarque, C. M. and Bera, A. K. (1980). 'Efficient tests for normality, homoskedasticity, and serial independence of regression residuals.' *Economics Letters*, vol. 6, pp. 255–9.

Jaynes, E. T. (1968). 'Prior probabilities.' IEEE, *Transactions on System Science and Cybernetics*, SSC-4, pp. 227–41.

Johansen, S. (1988). 'Statistical analysis of cointegration vectors.' *Journal of Economic Dynamics and Control*, vol. 12, pp. 231–54.

—— and Juselius, K. (1988). 'Hypothesis testing for co-integration vectors with an application to the demand for money in Denmark and Finland.' *Working Paper* No. 88-05, Institute of Economics, University of Copenhagen.

Johnston, J. (1984). *Econometric Methods*. New York: McGraw-Hill, 3rd ed.

Kaplan, E. L. and Meier, P. (1958). 'Nonparametric estimation from incomplete observations.' *Journal of the American Statistical Association*, vol. 53, pp. 457–81.

Keane, M. P. (1988). 'A computationally practical simulation estimator for panel data.' Mimeo, University of Minnesota.

Kennan, J. (1985). 'The duration of contract strikes in U.S. manufacturing.' *Journal of Econometrics*, vol. 28, pp. 5–28.

—— and Neumann, G. R. (1988). 'Why does the information matrix test reject too often?' *Working Paper* No. 88-4, University of Iowa.

King, M. L. (1985). 'A point optimal test for autoregressive disturbances.' *Journal of Econometrics*, vol. 27, pp. 21–37.

—— (1988). 'Towards a theory of point optimal testing.' *Econometric Reviews* (forthcoming).

King, R. G. and Rebelo, S. T. (1988). 'Low frequency filtering and real business cycles.' Mimeo, University of Rochester.

Klein, R. W. and Spady, R. S. (1988). 'An efficient semiparametric estimator of the binary response model.' Mimeo, Bell Communications Research.

Kloek, T. and Van Dijk, H. K. (1978). 'Bayesian estimates of equation system parameters: an application of integration by Monte Carlo.' *Econometrica*, vol. 46, pp. 1–19.

Koenker, R. (1982). 'Robust methods in econometrics.' *Econometric Reviews*, vol. 1, pp. 213–55.

—— and Bassett, G. S. (1978). 'Regression quantiles.' *Econometrica*, vol. 46, pp. 33–50.

—— and —— (1982). 'Robust tests for heteroscedasticity based on regression quantiles.' *Econometrica*, vol. 50, pp. 43–61.

Koopmans, T. C. (1937). *Linear Regression Analysis of Economic Time Series*, Netherlands Economic Institution.

—— (1947). 'Measurement without theory.' *Review of Economics and Statistics*, vol. 29, pp. 161–72.

—— (1949). 'Identification problems in economic model construction.' *Econometrica*, vol. 17, pp. 125–44.

Kramer, W. (1984). 'On the consequences of trend for simultaneous equation estimation.' *Economics Letters*, vol. 14, pp. 23–30.

Kunsch, H. (1986). 'Discrimination between monotonic trends and long-range dependence.' *Journal of Applied Probability*, vol. 23 (86), pp. 1025–30.

Lafontaine, F. and White, K. J. (1986). 'Obtaining any Wald statistic you want.' *Economics Letters*, vol. 21, pp. 35–40.

Laitinen, K. (1978). 'Why is demand homogeneity so often rejected?' *Economics Letters*, vol. 1, pp. 187–91.

Lalonde, R. (1986). 'Evaluating the econometric evaluations of training programs with experimental data.' *American Economic Review*, vol. 76, pp. 604–20.

Lau, L. J. (1986). 'Functional forms in econometric model building.' In *Handbook of Econometrics*, vol. 3 (ed. Z. Griliches and M. D. Intriligator). Amsterdam: North-Holland.

Leamer, E. (1978). *Specification Searches: Ad Hoc Inference with Nonexperimental Data*. New York: Wiley and Sons.

—— (1983). 'Let's take the con out of econometrics.' *American Economic Review*, vol. 73, pp. 31–44.

Lee, B. S. and Ingram, B. F. (1988). 'Estimation by simulation.' *Working Paper* No. 88-21, University of Iowa.

Lo, A. W. and MacKinlay, A. C. (1988). 'The size and power of the variance ratio test in finite samples: a Monte Carlo investigation.' *Journal of Econometrics*, vol. 40, pp. 203–38.

Lucas, R. E. (1976). 'Econometric policy evaluation: a critique.' In *The Phillips Curve and Labor Markets*, Carnegie–Rochester Series on Public Policy No. 1. Amsterdam: North-Holland.

McAleer, M. and Pesaran, M. H. (1986). 'Statistical inference in non-nested econometric models.' *Applied Mathematics and Computation*, pp. 271–311.

MacKinnon, J. G. (1983). 'Model specification tests against non-nested alternatives.' *Econometric Reviews*, vol. 2, pp. 85–158.

Mann, H. B. and Wald, A. (1943). 'On the statistical treatment of linear stochastic difference equations.' *Econometrica*, vol. 11, pp. 173–220.

Manski, C. F. (1975). 'The maximum score estimation of the stochastic utility model of choice.' *Journal of Econometrics*, vol. 3, pp. 205–28.

Manski, C. F. (1984). 'Adaptive estimation of non-linear regression models.' *Econometric Reviews*, vol. 3, pp. 145–94.

—— (1988). *Analog Estimation Methods in Econometrics*. New York: Chapman and Hall.

—— and Thompson, S. (1986). 'Operational characteristics of the maximum score estimator.' *Journal of Econometrics*, vol. 32, pp. 85–108.

McCallum, B. (1976). 'Rational expectations and the natural rate hypothesis: some consistent estimates.' *Econometrica*, vol. 44, pp. 43–52.

McFadden, D. (1989). 'A method of simulated moments for estimation of discrete response models without numerical integration.' *Econometrica*, vol. 57, pp. 995–1026.

Mattey, J. and Meese, R. (1986). 'Empirical assessment of present value relations.' *Econometric Reviews*, vol. 5, pp. 171–234.

Mishkin, F. S. (1983). *The Rational Expectations Approach to Macroeconomics – Testing Policy Ineffectiveness and Efficient-Markets Models*, NBER Monograph. Chicago: University of Chicago Press.

Mizon, G. E. (1984). 'The encompassing approach in econometrics.' In *Econometrics and Quantitative Economics* (ed. D. F. Hendry and K. F. Wallis). Oxford: Blackwell.

—— and Richard, J. F. (1986). 'The encompassing principle and its application to testing non-nested hypotheses.' *Econometrica*, vol. 54, pp. 657–78.

Muth, J. F. (1961). 'Rational expectations and the theory of price movements.' *Econometrica*, vol. 29, pp. 315–35.

Nadaraya, E. A. (1964). 'On estimating regression.' *Theory of Probability and Its Applications*, vol. 9, pp. 141–2.

Neftci, S. N. (1984). 'Are economic time series asymmetric over the business cycle?' *Journal of Political Economy*, vol. 92, pp. 307–28.

Nelson, C. R. (1988). 'Spurious trend and cycle in the state space decomposition of a time series with a unit root.' *Journal of Economics Dynamics and Control*, vol. 12, pp. 475–88.

—— and Plosser, C. I. (1982). 'Trends and random walks in macroeconomic time series: some evidence and implications.' *Journal of Monetary Economics*, vol. 10, pp. 139–62.

Nelson, D. B. (1988*a*). 'Conditional heteroskedasticity in asset returns: a new approach.' Mimeo, University of Chicago.

—— (1988*b*). 'Stationarity and persistence in the GARCH(1, 1) model.' *Working Paper* No. 88-68, Graduate School of Business, University of Chicago.

Nelson, F. D. and Savin, N. E. (1988*a*). 'On the invariance properties of the Wald, likelihood ratio and Lagrange multiplier tests.' Mimeo, University of Iowa.

—— and —— (1988*b*). 'The nonmonotonicity of the power function of the Wald test in nonlinear models.' Mimeo, University of Iowa.

Nerlove, M. (1967). 'Distributed lags and unobserved components.' In *Ten Economic Studies in the Tradition of Irving Fisher* (ed. W. Feller). New York: John Wiley.

Newey, W. K. (1984). 'A method of moments interpretation of sequential estimators.' *Economics Letters*, vol. 14, pp. 201–6.

—— (1985*a*). 'Maximum likelihood specification testing and conditional moment tests.' *Econometrica*, vol. 53, pp. 1047–70.

—— (1985*b*). 'Generalized method of moments specification testing.' *Journal of Econometrics*, vol. 29, pp. 229–56.

—— (1988*a*). 'Semi-parametric efficiency bounds.' *Journal of Applied Econometrics* (forthcoming).

—— (1988*b*). 'Efficient estimation of semi-parametric models via moment restrictions.' Mimeo, Princeton University.

—— (1988*c*). 'Efficient estimation of Tobit models under symmetry.' In *Non-parametric and Semiparametric Methods in Econometrics and Statistics* (ed. W. Barnett, J. Powell and G. Tauchen). Cambridge: Cambridge University Press.

—— (1988*d*). 'Two step series estimation of sample selection models.' Mimeo, Princeton University.

—— (1988*e*). 'Adaptive estimation of regression models via moment restrictions.' *Journal of Econometrics*, vol. 38, pp. 301–39.

—— and Powell, J. L. (1987). 'Asymmetric least squares estimation and testing.' *Econometrica*, vol. 55, pp. 819–47.

—— and West, K. D. (1987). 'A simple, positive semi-definite heteroskedasticity and autocorrelation consistent covariance matrix.' *Econometrica*, vol. 55, pp. 703–8.

Nickell, S. (1985). 'Error correction, partial adjustment and all that: an expository note.' *Oxford Bulletin of Economics and Statistics*, vol. 47, pp. 119–30.

Ouliaris, S., Park, J. Y. and Phillips, P. C. B. (1988). 'Testing for a unit root in the presence of a maintained trend.' Forthcoming in *Advances in Econometrics and Modeling* (ed. B. Raj). Needham, Mass.: Kluwer Academic Publishers.

Pagan, A. R. (1975). 'A note on the extraction of components from time series.' *Econometrica*, vol. 43, pp. 163–8.

—— (1978). 'Some simple tests for nonlinear time series models.' *CORE Discussion Paper* 7812, Université Catholique de Louvain.

—— (1984*a*). 'Econometric issues in the analysis of regressions with generated regressors.' *International Economic Review*, vol. 25, pp. 221–47.

—— (1984*b*). 'Model evaluation by variable addition.' In *Econometrics and Quantitative Economics* (ed. D. F. Hendry and K. F. Wallis). Oxford: Blackwell.

—— (1986). 'Two stage and related estimators and their applications.' *Review of Economic Studies*, vol. 53, pp. 517–38.

—— (1987). 'Three econometric methodologies: a critical appraisal.' *Journal of Economic Surveys*, vol. 1, pp. 3–24.

—— (1989). 'Twenty years after: econometrics 1966–1986.' In *Contributions to Operations Research and Econometrics: The XXth Anniversary of CORE* (ed. B. Cornet and H. Tulkens). Cambridge, Mass.: MIT Press.

—— and Hong, Y. (1990). 'Non-parametric estimation and the risk premium.' In *Non-parametric and Semiparametric Methods in Econometrics and Statistics* (ed. W. Barnett, J. Powell and G. Tauchen). Cambridge: Cambridge University Press.

—— and Ullah, A. (1988). 'The econometric analysis of models with risk terms.' *Journal of Applied Econometrics*, vol. 3, pp. 87–105.

—— and Vella, F. (1988). 'Diagnostic tests for models based on individual data: a survey.' *Journal of Applied Econometrics* (forthcoming).

Pakes, A. and Pollard, D. (1989). 'The asymptotics of optimization estimators with applications to simulated objective functions.' *Econometrica*, vol. 57, pp. 1027–57.

Park, J. Y. (1988*a*). 'Canonical co-integrating regressions.' *Center for Analytic Economics, Working Paper* No. 88-29, Cornell University.

—— (1988*b*). 'Testing for unit roots and cointegration by variable addition.' *Center for Analytic Economics Working Paper* 88-30, Cornell University.

——, Ouliaris, S. and Choi, B. (1988). 'Spurious regressions and tests for cointegration.' *Center for Analytic Economics Working Paper* 88-07, Cornell University.

—— and Phillips, P. C. B. (1988). 'Statistical inference in regressions with integrated processes: part 1.' *Econometric Theory*, vol. 4, pp. 468–97.

—— and —— (1989). 'Statistical inference in regressions with integrated processes: part 2.' *Econometric Theory*, vol. 5, pp. 95–131.

Perron, P. (1986). 'Trends and random walks in macroeconomic time series: further evidence from a new approach.' University of Montreal, mimeo.

—— (1989). 'The great crash, the oil price shock, and the unit root hypothesis.' *Econometrica*, vol. 57, pp. 1361–401.

Pesaran, H. M. (1974). 'On the general problem of model selection.' *Review of Economic Studies*, vol. 41, pp. 153–71.

—— (1987). *The Limits to Rational Expectations*. Oxford: Basil Blackwell.

Phillips, A. W. (1954). 'Stabilisation policy in a closed economy.' Economic Journal, vol. 64, pp. 290–323.

Phillips, P. C. B. (1983). 'ERA's: a new approach to small sample theory.' *Econometrica*, vol. 51, pp. 1505–27.

—— (1986). 'Understanding spurious regressions in econometrics.' *Journal of Econometrics*, vol. 33, pp. 311–40.

—— (1987). 'Time series regression with a unit root.' *Econometrica*, vol. 55, pp. 277–301.

—— (1988). 'Optimal inference in co-integrated systems.' *Cowles Foundation Discussion Paper* No. 866, Yale University.

—— (1989*a*). 'Reflections on econometric methodology.' *Economic Record*, vol. 164, pp. 344–59.

—— (1989*b*). 'Partially identified econometric models.' *Econometric Theory*, vol. 5, pp. 181–240.

—— (1990). 'Spectral regression for cointegrated time series.' In *Non-parametric and Semiparametric Methods in Econometrics and Statistics* (ed. W. Barnett, J. Powell and G. Tauchen). Cambridge: Cambridge University Press.

—— and Hansen, B. (1990). 'Statistical inference in instrumental variables regression with I(1) processes.' *Review of Economic Studies*, vol. 57, pp. 99–125.

—— and Ouliaris, S. (1986). 'Testing for cointegration.' *Cowles Foundation Discussion Paper* No. 890, Yale University.

—— and Park, J. Y. (1988). 'On the formulation of Wald tests of nonlinear restrictions.' *Econometrica*, vol. 56, pp. 1065–83.

Poirier, D. J. (1975). *The Econometrics of Structural Change*. Amsterdam: North-Holland.

—— (1988). 'Frequentist and subjectivist perspectives on the problems of model building in economics' (with discussion). *Journal of Economic Perspectives*, vol. 2, pp. 121–44.

Potscher, B. M. and Prucha, I. R. (1986). 'A class of partially adaptive one-step M-estimators for the non-linear regression model with dependent observations.' *Journal of Econometrics*, vol. 32, pp. 219–51.

Powell, J. L. (1984). 'Least absolute deviations estimation for the censored regression model.' *Journal of Econometrics*, vol. 25, pp. 303–25.

—— (1986). 'Censored regression quantiles.' *Journal of Econometrics*, vol. 32, pp. 143–55.

—— (1989). 'Semiparametric estimation of bivariate latent variable models.' *Econometrica*, vol. 57, pp. 1403–30.

——, Stock, J. M. and Stoker, T. M. (1986). 'Semiparametric estimation of weighted average derivatives.' Mimeo, M.I.T.

Raj, B. and Taylor, T. G. (1989). 'Do "bootstrap tests" provide significance levels equivalent to the exact test? Empirical evidence from testing linear within equation restrictions in large demand system.' *Journal of Quantitative Economics* (forthcoming).

Ramsey, J. B., Sayers, C. L. and Rothman, P. (1988). 'The statistical properties of dimension calculations using small data sets: some economic applications.' Mimeo, New York University.

Rilstone, P. (1988). 'Semi-parametric instrumental variables estimation.' Mimeo, Laval University.

—— and Ullah, A. (1986). 'Nonparametric estimation of response coefficients.' Mimeo, University of Western Ontario.

Robinson, P. M. (1987). 'Asymptotically efficient estimation in the presence of heteroskedasticity of unknown form.' *Econometrica*, vol. 55, pp. 875–91.

—— (1988*a*). 'Root-N consistent semiparametric regression.' *Econometrica*, vol. 56, pp. 931–54.

—— (1988*b*). 'Using Gaussian estimators robustly.' *Oxford Bulletin of Economics and Statistics*, vol. 50, pp. 97–106.

——, Bera, A. and Jarque, C. (1985). 'Tests for serial dependence in limited dependent variable models.' *International Economic Review*, vol. 26, pp. 629–38.

Rosenberg, B. (1973). 'The analysis of a cross-section of time series by stochastically convergent parameter regression.' *Annals of Economic and Social Measurement*, vol. 2, pp. 399–428.

Rothenberg, T. J. and Leenders, C. T. (1964). 'Efficient estimation of simultaneous equation systems.' *Econometrica*, vol. 32, pp. 57–76.

Ruppert, D and Carroll, R. J. (1980). 'Trimmed least squares estimation in the linear model.' *Journal of the American Statistical Association*, vol. 75, pp. 828–38.

Ruud, P. (1984). 'Tests of specification in econometrics.' *Econometric Reviews*, vol. 3, pp. 211–42.

Said, S. E. and Dickey, D. A. (1984). 'Testing for unit roots in ARMA models of unknown order.' *Biometrika*, vol. 71, pp. 599–607.

Salmon, M. (1982). 'Error correction mechanisms.' ECONOMIC JOURNAL, vol. 92, pp. 615–29.

Sargan, J. D. (1958). 'The estimation of economic relationships using instrumental variables.' *Econometrica*, vol. 26, pp. 393–415.

—— and Bhagava, A. (1983). 'Testing the residuals from least squares regression for being generated by the Gaussian random walk.' *Econometrica*, vol. 51, pp. 153–74.

Sargent, T. J. (1978). 'Estimation of dynamic labor schedules under rational expectations.' *Journal of Political Economy*, vol. 86, pp. 1009–44.

Schwert, G. W. (1987). 'Effects of model misspecification on tests for unit roots in macroeconomic data.' *Journal of Monetary Economics*, vol. 20, pp. 73–103.

Schweppe, F. C. (1965). 'Evaluation of likelihood functions for Gaussian signals.' *I.E.E.E. Transactions on Information Theory*, vol. 11, pp. 61–70.

Silverman, B. M. (1986). *Density Estimation for Statistics and Data Analysis*. London: Chapman and Hall.

Sims, C. A. (1972). 'Money, income and causality.' *American Economic Review*, vol. 62, pp. 540–52.

—— (1974). 'Seasonality in regression.' *Journal of the American Statistical Association*, vol. 69, pp. 618–26.

—— (1980). 'Macroeconomics and reality.' *Econometrica*, vol. 48, pp. 1–47.

—— (1982). 'Policy analysis with econometric models.' *Brookings Papers in Economic Activity*, vol. 1, pp. 107–64.

—— (1988). Bayesian scepticism on unit-root econometrics.' *Journal of Economic Dynamics and Control*, vol. 12, pp. 463–74.

——, Stock, J. and Watson, M. (1986). 'Inference in linear time series models with some unit roots.' Economics Working Paper, No. E-87-1, Hoover Institution, Stanford University.

Singleton, K. (1988). 'Econometric issues in the analysis of equilibrium business cycle models.' *Journal of Monetary Economics*, vol. 21, pp. 361–86.

Sowell, F. B. (1987). 'Maximum likelihood estimation of fractionally-integrated time series models.' Research Paper No. 87-07, Institute of Statistics and Decision Sciences, Duke University.

Spanos, A. (1986). *Statistical Foundations of Econometric Modelling*. Cambridge: Cambridge University Press.

Stock, J. H. (1985). 'Nonparametric policy analysis; an application to estimating hazardous waste cleanup benefits.' *Journal of the American Statistical Association* (forthcoming).

—— (1987). 'Asymptotic properties of least squares estimators of cointegrating vectors.' *Econometrica*, vol. 55, pp. 1035–56.

—— and Watson, M. W. (1988). 'Testing for common trends.' *Journal of the American Statistical Association*, vol. 83, pp. 1097–107.

—— and —— (1988). 'Variable trends in economic time series.' *Journal of Economic Perspectives*, vol. 2, pp. 147–74.

Stone, C. J. (1975). 'Adaptive maximum likelihood estimation of a location parameter.' *Annals of Statistics*, vol. 3, pp. 267–84.

Tauchen, G. (1985). 'Diagnostic testing and evaluation of maximum likelihood models.' *Journal of Econometrics*, vol. 30, pp. 415–43.

Taylor, L. W. (1987). 'The size bias of White's information matrix test.' *Economics Letters*, vol. 24, pp. 63–87.

Ullah, A. (1988*a*). 'Non-parametric estimation of econometric functionals.' *Canadian Journal of Economics*, vol. 21, pp. 625–58.

—— (1988*b*). 'Nonparametric estimation and hypothesis testing in econometric models.' *Empirical Economics*, vol. 13, pp. 223–49.

Vinod, H. D. and Ullah, A. (1986). 'Flexible production estimation by nonparametric kernel estimators.' Mimeo, University of Western Ontario.

Wall, K. D., Preston, A. J., Bray, J. W. and Peston, M. H. (1975). 'Estimates of a simple control model of the UK economy.' In *Modelling the Economy* (ed. G. A. Renton). London: Heinemann Education Books.

Wallis, K. F. (1974). 'Seasonal adjustment and relations between variables.' *Journal of the American Statistical Association*, vol. 69, pp. 18–31.

—— (1980). 'Econometric implications of the rational expectations hypothesis.' *Econometrica*, vol. 48, pp. 49–73.

—— (1989). 'Forecasting models: a survey.' ECONOMIC JOURNAL (forthcoming).

Watson, G. S. (1964). 'Smooth regression analysis.' *Sankhya*, Series A, vol. 26, pp. 359–72.

Watson, M. W. (1986). 'Univariate detrending methods with stochastic trends.' *Journal of Monetary Economics*, vol. 18, pp. 49–75.

West, K. D. (1988). 'Asymptotic normality when regressors have a unit root.' *Econometrica*, vol. 56, pp. 1397–417.

White, H. (1980). 'A heteroskedasticity-consistent covariance matrix estimator and a direct test for heteroskedasticity.' *Econometrica*, vol. 48, pp. 817–38.

—— (1982). 'Maximum likelihood estimation of misspecified models.' *Econometrica*, vol. 50, pp. 1–26.

Wickens, M. R. (1982). 'The efficient estimation of econometric models with rational expectations.' *Review of Economic Studies*, vol. 49, pp. 817–38.

—— (1986). 'The estimation of rational expectations models with future rational expectations by efficient and instrumental variable estimation methods.' *Centre for Economic Policy Research Discussion Paper* No. 111.

—— and Breusch, T. S. (1988). 'Dynamic specification, the long-run and the estimation of transformed regression models.' ECONOMIC JOURNAL, vol. 98, pp. 189–205.

Wooldridge, J. M. (1987). 'A unified approach to robust, regression-based specification tests.' Mimeo, M.I.T.

—— and White, H. (1988). 'Some invariance principles and central limit theorems for dependent heterogeneous processes.' *Econometric Theory*, vol. 4, pp. 210–30.

Zellner, A. and Highfield, R. A. (1969). 'Calculation of maximum entropy distributions and approximation of marginal posterior distributions.' *Journal of Econometrics*, vol. 37, pp. 195–210.

INDEX